INSTRUCTOR'S MANUAL
with
TEST ITEMS
for

SOCIOLOGY

Sixth Edition
by Rodney Stark

Instructor's Manual
Lawrence Mencotti
Edinboro University

Test Items
Peter M. Lehman
University of Southern Maine

Wadsworth Publishing Company

I(T)P™ An International Thomson Publishing Company

Belmont • Albany • Bonn • Boston • Cincinnati • Detroit • London • Madrid • Melbourne
Mexico City • New York • Paris • San Francisco • Singapore • Tokyo • Toronto • Washington

Printed in the United States of America
1 2 3 4 5 6 7 8 9 10—01 00 99 98 97 96

For more information, contact Wadsworth Publishing Company.

Wadsworth Publishing Company
10 Davis Drive
Belmont, California 94002, USA

International Thomson Publishing
Europe
Berkshire House 168-173
High Holborn
London, WC1V 7AA, England

Thomas Nelson Australia
102 Dodds Street
South Melbourne 3205
Victoria, Australia

Nelson Canada
1120 Birchmount Road
Scarborough, Ontario
Canada M1K 5G4

International Thomson Editores
Campos Eliseos 385, Piso 7
Col. Polanco
11560 México D.F. México

International Thomson Publishing
GmbH
Königswinterer Strasse 418
53227 Bonn, Germany

International Thomson Publishing Asia
221 Henderson Road
#05-10 Henderson Building
Singapore 0315

International Thomson Publishing Japan
Hirakawacho Kyowa Building, 3F
2-2-1 Hirakawacho
Chiyoda-ku, Tokyo 102, Japan

ISBN 0-534-25713-5

Table of Contents

Test Items

WHY STARK? I adopted Stark in its first edition (1985). What appealed to me then appeals to me now: his uniquely integrated presentation of the basic concepts and tools of sociology (see Chapters 1-4); his "over the shoulder approach" allowing students to see how a sociological problem is developed and researched; and his extensive investigation of only a few key sociological lines of research per chapter. (It doesn't hurt that it is also the best-written sociology text on the market.)

WHY THESE SUPPLEMENTS? Taken together, the "Showcase Demonstrations," the "Test Bank," and these "Suggestions" comprise a complete package for the sociology instructor using Sociology (6th edition).

ASSUMPTIONS ABOUT STUDENTS. Since 1966 I've taught introductory sociology courses in a variety of settings: private liberal arts colleges as well as private and public universities. In general (as a sociologist how can I resist the occasional sweeping generality?), today's college students are bright, polite, and career-oriented. They often find society interesting but are, just as often, fountains of misinformation. So if we are to earn our pay we must do our most effective teaching in the introductory course (the only sociology course most students will take). With that in mind, the following are several suggestions that have worked for me and, I hope, some of them will prove useful for you.

   Weekly Quizzes. One obstacle to overcome is the stubborn fact that students (once again, in general) don't like to read. Few of them ever write in their texts for fear of lowering its resale value. So although I recommend the Study Guide, and it does seem to correlate with doing well, I think that getting them to read the assigned chapters can be an accomplishment. Using the Stark text as the foundation for the course, I have found that the most effective means of getting the students to read and understand what they are supposed to (as opposed to cramming the night before an exam) is to give weekly quizzes. We usually cover one chapter per week with an occasional week also containing a Special Topic. (I make no attempt to cover the entire text; there is simply too much material for a one-semester course.) The quiz (15 true-false and multiple-choice questions) is given at the beginning of the first class for the week. I then go over the questions and supply the students with the correct answer (and commentary

if appropriate). If I give twelve quizzes, I count the best
eleven scores. One additional hint: To remove the
temptation to cheat, I give two versions of the same quiz.
It's extremely easy to do with the Test Bank. I print one
version on yellow paper and the other on blue. The versions
are alternated so that if a student were to look to either
side he/she would see another version with questions in a
scrambled order.

Grading. I mark on a scale (total points) and not a
curve. It's a philosophical point on which we need not
dwell. The quizzes are worth 40% of the grade with the
midterm and final (comprising mostly/exclusively of in-class
material) another 40%. Finally, the remaining 20% of the
grade is allocated to class attendance and participation.
On nonquiz days I circulate an attendance sheet. I give a
minimum number of unexcused absences and then the course
grade may be lowered (this is spelled out in the course
syllabus). Admittedly, this is an old-fashioned approach to
higher education but it works: Course attendance is quite
good. I have found that by switching to the weekly quiz
format in combination with a mandatory attendance policy I
am forced to give very few Ds and Fs--10% maximum. Cs
typically run anywhere between 50% and 65% with Bs somewhere
between 25% and 35%. Usually no more than 4% are As.

Student Research at the Introductory Level. I have
wrestled with this one for many years. Generally, I reserve
it for small honors sections (please see the Addendum for
some ideas on writing and research topics). In large
introductory sections (35 or more students), the "return on
investment" has been disappointing. I know my limits and I
am most effective when I work within the imposed constraints
(class size, abilities and interests of students, etc.).

INSIDE THE CLASSROOM. I like to lecture. I've developed
some very effective ones. However, I've found that the more
refined the lecture the less the student involvement. When
I solicit reaction from some of the better students as to
why this is so, the most typical response is along the lines
of, "So what's to say?" At this point the lecture becomes,
in effect, a prepackaged experience with little need for
student interaction. I have found that demonstrations
and/or discussions are essential for significant student
involvement. It provides the greatest challenge for the
professor not to enter the class armed with sheaves of
notes. This is the time of the unexpected insight, the
unanticipated digression. The best class periods I've ever
had were in this format when everything went swimmingly:
lots of spirited participation and exchange. Interestingly,
some of my best lectures first started as unanswered

questions from extended discussions.

When lecturing, it is most effective to give concrete examples, some facts, and the occasional figure to illustrate our concepts, which are necessarily abstract. It is just flat out difficult for even the most talented and interested people to follow an oral argument without the help of relevant, understandable examples. One technique I learned early on: If a student asks a question that shows you are not getting the point across, don't take it personally. You're there for them, so try another example, this time zeroing in on them as students or their prospective careers in college and afterward. That's one of the great things about introductory sociology: You have a whole world to draw upon. One last point: Humor and anecdote go a long way in moderate amounts. I do like to use both but too much of either can be counterproductive.

Breaking Down the Barriers. Every semester I get the "butterflies." I take teaching seriously and I want to be effective, so right from the beginning I try to break down barriers. For example, on the first day I circulate an attendance sheet. Try to deliberately forget to bring a blank piece of paper. Ask a student for one and use it to get their signatures the first day. Ask two others to help pass out copies of the course syllabus. After you've gone through the course bureaucracy, including the correct pronunciation of your name (early opportunity for a joke for yours truly, I tell them not to confuse me with the pasta dish), ask them to turn to the people around them and introduce themselves. The pretext is that we are all going to spend a long semester together, so let's get to know one another. After they see you're serious, they do. Let this go on for 15-20 seconds and then (a loud voice is usually required) tell them to stop. Ask them why they were so disruptive. "You told us to." Ask them if they would have done the same if another student had told them to. With this they get their first introduction to such concepts as role and status. You may even extend this a bit and tell them what would happen if they didn't listen to you and events escalated to the point of calling the campus police (thus illustrating the movement from informal to formal social control). Other barrier-breakers include asking a different student each week to pass out the quiz answer sheets. Later in the course when the inevitable student comes in with the inevitable snack, casually walk over and, while feigning hunger, ask for a sample. Every once in a while, ask a student (make sure it's an attentive one), "Where did we leave off last time?" But whatever you do, don't hide behind the lectern! Get out and circulate! Show them that a real human being lurks behind the professorial persona.

USING STARK. Which chapters to cover? The first four comprise the core of the text. After that, selection becomes difficult. I find it hard not to cover deviance, stratification, intergroup conflict, gender inequality, the family, population, and biology and culture. In addition, some chapters have a natural link with others (e.g., 5 and 6, 7 and 8, 12 and 13, 9, 10, and 11, and 17 and 18 and 19). I do prefer not to cover the same chapters every semester and not to cover them quite the same way each semester. It keeps me honest and thus benefits the students. When making your selection, be aware of the excellent Special Topics (e.g., "Correlation and Sampling" "Aspects of Income Inequalities," and "The Life Cycle of the Baby Boom") that supplement the chapters immediately preceding them. If you include one of these with the chapter itself, to cover the assignments well you may want to allocate relatively more time to the discussions or demonstrations and somewhat less to straight lecture. The first day of class I recommend the Study Guide. I tell them that its conscientious use correlates with doing well. I think it does although I have no evidence. I also tell them to study with others. This is congruent with my grading via a scale and not on a curve: You should help one another (just don't try it while taking a test). I further recommend seeing the department tutor. Ideally, this is an upper-division or graduate student who has been through the course before (with apologies to G. H. Mead, professors are not as adept at figuring themselves out to students as are other students who have actually taken the course). Finally, I draw their attention to the Review Glossary at the end of each chapter (especially useful if they won't be using the Study Guide), and the Subject Index/ Glossary found at the end of the text, which repeats definitions found in the individual chapter glossaries. This is especially useful if one wants a quick definition of a term and has forgotten in which chapter it was first introduced.

TEACHING OBJECTIVES. We all want to impart what Mills calls the "sociological imagination." The question is, How to operationalize it? Overall, this is what I set out to accomplish in the basic course. From the functionalist perspective, I try to make students aware of the hidden patterns and consequences in society: making latent (dys)functions manifest. From the conflict perspective, an analysis of the disharmonies, especially structural, among and between groups is my major goal. Finally, from the perspective of symbolic interactionism, I attempt to give my classes an appreciation of the social forces and contexts that shape and constrain various and sundry definitions of situations.

ASSUMPTIONS REGARDING INSTRUCTORS. I assume that professors
using Stark will vary widely in teaching experience. The
suggestions contained herein are geared more for the rookie
instructor, although grizzled veterans might also find some
of them useful. I further assume that there are plenty of
professional pressures on one's time and energy: other
courses, research, writing, committee work, etc. Therefore,
I've tried to include suggestions that are reasonably do-
able. That is, they assume access to duplicating services,
film-rental monies (many of the recommended films can be
rented from video stores), and a good library and/or
interlibrary loan consortium. My most important assumption
is that we, as instructors, do more than just operate on the
principle of least effort. For the student to learn, we
must actively teach and teach effectively, and this requires
motivation and commitment on our part. One other point.
These materials are geared to smaller classes (under 45).
If you get stuck with a mass lecture I can vouch for neither
the applicability nor the effectiveness of most of what
follows.

USING THIS SUPPLEMENT. Each chapter in the supplement
corresponds to its partner in the text. Each begins with a
brief outline, proceeds to a summary, and then lists some
major learning objectives along with suggestions as to how
to get the objectives across. I have tried to tailor-make
these suggestions specifically for use with the Stark text.
In addition, each chapter also contains suggested student
readings that are interesting and yet do not presuppose
much sociological background. For this edition of the
Instructor's Manual, I have made various revisions
concerning the teaching suggestions as well as the suggested
readings. More importantly, each chapter now leads off with
an outline that provides the instructor with a snapshot
overview. At the end of all the chapters are two short
addenda. One gives some suggestions on teaching honors
sections and also contains some ideas on assigning research
projects for introductory students. The other gives a list
of films or tapes appropriate for each chapter. I sincerely
hope some of these ideas are useful. I would appreciate
your comments (positive or otherwise).

Lawrence Mencotti, Ph.D.
Department of Sociology
Edinboro University of
     Pennsylvania
Edinboro, PA 16444

Chapter 1

GROUPS AND RELATIONSHIPS:
A SOCIOLOGICAL SAMPLER

CHAPTER OUTLINE

Origins of Sociology.
  Moral Statistics.
    Quetelet: stability of suicide and crime
                     rates.

    Morselli: suicide rates vary but overall
                     are up.

    Durkheim: Le Suicide focuses on interper-
                     sonal relationships as crucial.

What is Sociology?
  Units of analysis: individuals, small groups,
                       large organizations, nations,
                       etc.

    Micro Sociology.   Close-up look at social life:
                       e.g., small groups of soldiers.

    Macro Sociology.   Much larger scale: e.g., the
                       army as a social institution.

Groups.
  Group.   People interacting over time
                     united by social relationships:
                     e.g. a family.

  Aggregate.   People with trait(s) in common
                     but interaction is incidental:
                     e.g., suicides.

  Dyads and Triads.
    Coalitions.   Tendency of a three person
                       group to turn into a *de facto*
                       dyad by coalition formation.

    Transitivity.   Relations of group members tend
                       toward balance.

    Networks.   Patterns of relationships
                       between group members. Socio-
                       grams often used to chart
                       relationships.

    Primary Groups.   Groups of great intimacy and
                       mutual identification.

    Secondary Groups. Pursue collective goals without
                       much emotional bonding.

Can Sociology Be
  Scientific?
    Scientific Method. Systematic pursuit of
                        falsifiable predictions.

Theories.	General statements regarding some part of the social world.
Research.	Systematic observation of social reality.
Studying Self-Aware Subjects.	
Unobtrusive Measures.	Attempts to overcome subjects' awareness that they are being studied.
Validation.	Testing data against an independent standard of accuracy: e.g. Hirschi checking youth's self-reports with police records.
Studying Networks.	
Mass Society Theories.	Designed to explain modern social ills.
Milgram's Small World.	Shows mass society theories as needing serious revision.
Canadian Callers.	Canada has parallel social networks based on language.
Bias.	The most effective preventative of personal bias is to emphasize disproving theories.
Origins of Social Science and Sociology.	Sociology in Europe and America dates to the last quarter of the nineteenth century.
Free Will and Social choice.	Sociologists assume rationality in Social science. Maximization of rewards and minimization of costs.

SUMMARY

Origins of Sociology. Ironically, the birth of our discipline begins with the investigation of suicide as Stark traces the invention of sociology to governments collecting systematic statistics on death. Nineteenth-century Europe revealed three patterns. From year to year the suicide rates were extremely _stable_. Spatially, they _varied_ dramatically from one country to another. However, the overall direction of the rates was moving slowly _upward_. Soon, other rates were being examined and they too showed the same three traits. From this early concern with "moral statistics," sociology emerged as the study of the social causes of individual behavior.

What is Sociology? As one of the social sciences, sociology ultimately recognizes social forces as the key independent variables in explaining and predicting human behavior. However, unlike psychologists, we are interested less in intraindividual phenomena and much more in inter-human contact--the <u>patterns and processes of human social relations.</u> Some sociologists concentrate on micro-level behavior. Their approach is that of a proud parent with a camcorder videotaping a child's graduation party. Other sociologists are more interested in large-scale macro-level phenomena, and so they need to see the social world as a meteorologist might analyze photographs taken by a reconnaissance satellite. As such, the units of analysis may vary from individuals and small groups to large organizations and whole societies.

Groups. At whatever the level sociologists choose to study, their focus will be some form of group behavior. Sometimes, what might appear to be a group is actually an aggregate: people who have some trait in common (e.g., riders in an elevator, all suicides in a given year) but who are <u>not united by social relations</u>. In its most basic form a group is a dyad. Add a third person and not only is a triad created but a host of interesting complications are introduced. For example, *transitivity* refers to the social fact that relations between members of a group will tend toward balance/consistency. Since trying to be friends with two people who hate each other causes too much tension, the triad might terminate with the member who is friendly with the others segregating his/her relations with each of them and, in effect, creating two dyads. However, triads also possess a structural trait: one that exists independently of particular people. They tend toward *coalition formation* especially when two lesser members of the group join forces to dominate a nominally superior third (e.g., mother + child > father). *Networks*, or the patterns of relations among group members, often consist of factions (cliques). If the group is large enough and possesses contending cliques, then coalitions form not around persons per se but around the cliques themselves. Finally, groups can be classified by the members' degree of loyalty to and personal satisfaction derived from the membership. *Primary groups* are ones characterized by intimacy and mutual identification between group members such as, ideally, the family. *Secondary groups* are less intimate and more given to collective endeavors. Occupational groups are usually secondary ones.

Can Sociology Be Scientific? When judged by the standards of the natural sciences, sociology does not possess the encompassing theories of, say, physics. But to downgrade sociology in comparison with physics would be to mistake scientific achievement for *scientific method*. And it is the scientific method--procedures of systematic inquiry--that legitimizes sociology's claim as a social science. The inquiry begins with <u>curiosity</u> about the social world. Then we try to explain why this phenomenon is the way that it is (i.e. we propose a <u>theory</u>). However, we must go beyond tentative explanations to more explicit statements that generate <u>predictions</u> that can be falsified. It is the systematic observation and analysis of data that we call research. Ultimately, the best theories are the ones that withstand attempts to disprove them via research. So, as with all science, sociology progresses to the extent that we attempt to disprove and fail.

Studying Self-Aware Subjects. Unlike the physical scientists, social scientists have a problem: Their subjects often act differently when they know they are being observed. So sociologists have developed techniques to try to overcome this problem. These techniques, known as *unobtrusive measures*, allow us to obtain information without disturbing the objects of research. Whatever the specific technique for gathering the information, care must be taken to ensure that the information is accurate. That is, we want to make sure that the data are genuine. To do this we engage in *validation research*--test data against some independent standard of accuracy. One way to do this is by comparing results using different measures.

Studying Networks. Modernization is the hallmark of the twentieth century. With increased modernization there was increased concern among many, including sociologists, that urban life was degrading the quantity and quality of interpersonal attachments (especially primary groups). Various *mass society theories* were developed to explain a variety of modern social ills. However, systematic research was giving us a much different picture: Cities were simply not sweeping away attachments. Mass society theorists then revised their initial claims to read that cities were composed of large numbers of small, isolated groups. Although the groups may be islands of intimacy they were, at bottom, nonconnected islands. Milgram had a different idea. His hunch was that the groups were not isolated islands but formed an interconnected network. His "small world" research addressed this issue. His method was to select two complete strangers: one a sender and the other a receiver. Then he had the sender get a letter to the receiver and monitor how many different links there were in the total chain. The overwhelming majority of the letters were received, and it took on average only five links on the friendship chain for a letter to get from sender to receiver. Similar research on Canada by MacKay and later by Simmons showed that Canada tends to have parallel social networks based on language boundaries and that Canadians and Americans tend to constitute separate national networks.

Bias. Another reason for conducting sociological research in such a way so as to try to disprove our preconceptions is that, to a degree far greater than in the natural sciences, social scientists' personal biases are much more potent obstacles to valid research. Thus, the emphasis on disproving our theories is a needed safeguard in containing the tainting of research by our biases.

The Origins of Social Science and Sociology. Perhaps the greater challenge to the development of sociology as a science is the relative youth of the discipline. Although we often date sociology to the middle of the past century and Comte, in any modern sense sociology actually begins with Spencer, Toennies, and Durkheim in the last quarter of the nineteenth century. In North America the first Department of Sociology (at The University of Chicago) was founded about 100 years ago. So we are a young discipline especially when compared with the natural sciences.

Free Will and Social Science. A religious, and at times philosophical, notion of free will argues that we cannot (should not try to?) predict and explain human behavior. The sociological retort is simple. The mistake that these outmoded thinkers make is to counterpoise free will with a version of predestination. Rather, we know that human behavior is not random but very often is quite predictable. It is so because humans possess free will and thus act in a rational matter so as to maximize rewards and minimize costs. Within limits human behavior is both explainable and predictable, but is not predestined.

TEACHING SUGGESTIONS

The objective of Chapter 1 is to introduce students to the major theme of this text and the entire sociology course: how human behavior is socially constrained, shaped, and patterned.

1. Demonstration: "Monads, Dyads, and Triads." With an object that all can inspect (I have used song lyrics in poem format and neo-realism paintings--anything that requires some interpretative work) ask each student to write in some detail his/her impressions as to the object's meaning(s). After that, randomly divide the class into dyads and ask them to discuss their musings with each other. Then ask them to write (either as individuals or as a team) an interpretation of the object. If you want to emphasize constructed meanings then ask them to write it as a team; if

you want to illustrate the social impact on individual opinions then have the students write individual opinions. Do not discuss the exercise at this point. Finally, reconstitute the dyads as triads and repeat as above with whichever variation(s) you prefer. Now discuss the project with them showing how reality can be largely a social construction.

There are several uses for this exercise:
   a) It's a great ice-breaker.
   b) It will show firsthand Simmel's insight on how a group changes qualitatively when it moves from two members to three.
   c) When the interpretations start to flow in the triadic setting, coalitions may form.
   d) By following your requests (usually automatically albeit at times half-heartedly), you can begin to talk about authority in general and that of the professor in particular.

Source: Simmel, G. _The Sociology of Georg Simmel_, (Kurt Wolff, ed.) New York: The Free Press, 1950.

[Instructor's note: the concepts of dyad and triad can be reinforced in a more comprehensive context with the following lecture.]

2. **Lecture:** "Groups and Networks: An Introduction to Sociology." This prosaic title need not be pedestrian in its impact on students. In many ways, this section of Chapter 1 is the foundation for the rest of the text and the course. I like to start by distinguishing between an aggregate and a group. Examples of **aggregates** the students find relevant include they and their roommate the first day of dorm living and they and their classmates the first day of the semester. In both instances, they have come together by accident and initially they are strangers. However, unlike elevator riders in a department store there is a great likelihood that these encounters will turn from aggregate to group. That is, with roommates and to a lesser extent with classmates, the students will eventually be united by social relations and thus constitute a group. To concentrate on the dorm example a bit, the roommates will come to see that they share a common fate: What happens to one, in large or small measure, impacts the other. If the common fate develops extensively then Cooley's "we-feeling" is inevitable: the fact that "we" constitute an in-group to be distinguished from all others (the out-group). If the friendship that begins in the freshman dorm blossoms further, the students may decide to pledge the same fraternity or sorority. If accepted, they take their dyad into a much larger group. This larger group actually functions much like a **secondary group** promising **primary group** rewards that can be very appealing to anomic 18-year-olds. Further, pledging and hazing are part of the

rite de passage that one must successfully complete to be
worthy of wearing the Greek letters on the member's jacket.

   Once accepted as members of this organization, they will
become increasingly aware that most groups (excluding dyads)
have at least the potential to <u>transcend</u> in time the members
who compose it. That is, this Greek chapter existed before
the current members were members and it will continue to
exist with new members years after the current ones have
graduated. During their first year our dynamic duo learns
quickly that, as with all quasi-tribes, there is a <u>double-
standard of morality</u>. There are obligations and rights that
are routinely expected of other group members that simply do
not apply to outsiders. This usually proves to be not much
of a problem for our friends since they have been immersed
in that morality before, first with their families and then
with their grade and high school peers.

   Toward the end of their first year, our friends decide
that dorm life is too confining and will, as sophomores,
rent an apartment in town. They find that it is very
expensive and so they decide to take in a third person (also
a chapter member) to share expenses. Immediately problems
arise, initially over household duties. But there are other
concerns, too. The newcomer has transformed the dyad into a
triad. The newcomer (known as C) likes A quite a bit but
does not get along at all with B. B becomes jealous of the
A-C friendship; after all, B has "seniority" with A. Further
complicating matters, C envies B's close ties with A.

   [Instructor's note: I find this contrivance an especially
useful way of distinguishing between envy and jealousy and
showing how both can be structurally induced in triadic
situations.]

   Of course, we have a classic instance of <u>intransitivity</u>.
A likes C as well as B and so is upset by the bickering.
Increasingly, A spends more time outside the apartment with
other chapter members and finds much to his/her dismay that
there is feuding within the chapter over a policy governing
partying. The feuding is dividing the chapter around
preexisting cliques: three to be exact and one of which
seems to be caught in the middle. A finds that the cliques
are somewhat parallel (macrolevel) to the situation at the
apartment (microlevel). To try to keep the peace, A
alternates between siding with B and with C. However, these
shifting coalitions only serve to make matters worse.

   For Thanksgiving break (which arrives none too soon) A
puts a notice up on several of the campus bulletin boards
for a ride home. A hopes that the bulletin board network
will prove fruitful and it does. During the ride home, A
discovers that one of the other passengers is a former
classmate from the freshman year. They got along well
inside (and occasionally outside) of class and this person
is looking for a roommate for the winter term. "Hmmm,"
thinks A, "there may be some possibilities here."

3. Discussion: "Homelessness and Unobtrusive Measures."
Who are the homeless? After getting past the usual
stereotypes of psychotic street ladies digress a bit by
asking the class, In what ways might students be homeless?
Does homelessness mean (a) being without a single permanent
residence to call home or does it mean (b) one has no
shelter or does it mean (c) not having an official mailing
address? If it is (a), then many students would qualify
since they may shift residences several times a year
between their parents and dorms and apartments. If it means
(b), then many of the homeless aren't technically homeless
since they do have shelter however mean it may be. If it is
(c), then hobos certainly would qualify though not having a
permanent shelter doesn't exactly traumatize them. We often
think of the homeless as the discards of **mass society**. Yet
is this always so?

Sociologist James Henslin decided to find out and came up
with a dozen types of people who might qualify as homeless.
Not all of them were homeless involuntarily. He studied
them as unobtrusively as possible by hanging out and
sleeping with them in the course of visiting over a dozen
skid rows across the country. He also interviewed them and
the portrait that emerges illustrates how sociology can
clarify "folk" definitions of reality as it calls attention
to the plight of countless victims of a dynamic and at times
uncaring society.

Source: Henslin, J. "America's Homeless" In Henslin, J.,
Social Problems, 2nd ed. Englewood Cliff, N.J.: Prentice
Hall, 1990, pp. 265-266.

4. Lecture: "Violence, Groups, and Free Will." This
lecture relates two classic experiments in modern social
psychology: Milgram's obedience to authority study and
Zimbardo's experiment with college students in a mock
prison. This lecture can introduce (by anticipating Chapter
6) the idea of role which, of course, is the essential
building block of interaction and group life. At the same
time it will serve as a supplement to Stark's treatment of
free will in this chapter as well as anticipating his
discussion of choice in Chapter 3. A spin-off discussion
from this lecture could be, How much choice within roles?
Of course, the studies selected emphasize the quasi-
determinative nature of groups, situations, and roles. The
most interesting discussions that have ensued from this
lecture revolve around the issue of rational choice and free
will: To what extent did people really choose to inflict
violence on others?

Sources: Milgram, S. Obedience to Authority: An
Experimental View. New York: Harper and Row, 1975. When
nice people thought they did some not-nice things to others.

Zimbardo, P. "Pathology of Imprisonment" Society
April, 1972: 4-8. In this experiment (gone awry), people

(in this case, college undergraduates) really did do some nasty things to each other while roleplaying as guards and prisoners.

ADDITIONAL STUDENT READINGS

All of the following are interesting, highly readable works that introductory students can easily handle.

Kotlowitz, A. There Are No Children Here: The Story of Two Boys Growing Up in the Other America. New York: Doubleday, 1991. Lafayette and Pharoah, two boys mired in poverty and surviving in a Chicago ghetto housing project, try escaping from the violence and drugs all around them. Journalistic sociology at its best.

Levin, J. Sociological Snapshots: Seeing Social Structure and Change in Everyday Life. Thousand Oaks, California: Pine Forge Press, 1993. For the beginning student who wants a fast "tour" of the field, Levin's series of short takes is lively, engaging, topical, and very well written. Nice reading for the instructor too who will surely walk away with a few nuggets for class.

Whyte, W. Streetcorner Society. Chicago: University of Chicago Press, 1945. An urban ethnography of Italian-American males in Boston just before World War II.

ESSAY QUESTIONS

1. Why are dyads and triads examples of groups and not aggregates? Why are suicides examples of aggregates and not groups?

2. Explain why the natural tendency of a group containing three people is to form coalitions and not remain a three- person group. In what kinds of groups is this tendency most pronounced? In what kinds of groups is it least pronounced? Why?

3. Give two examples of networks on campus. Are they more grouplike or are they closer to the text's definition of an aggregate? Why?

4. Draw some implications of Milgram's small world research for AIDS research and prevention.

CHAPTER OUTLINE

Society and Culture.
   Society.   Self-contained and self-
                                         sufficient group.
   Culture.   The complex pattern of living
                                         that directs social life.

Concepts for Social
   Analysis.
   Stratification.   The unequal distribution of
                                         rewards.
   Social Class.   Comprising those who share
                                         similar status.
   Caste.   Totally closed class system
                                         based on ascribed statuses (as
                                         opposed to an an open system
                                         based upon achieved statuses).
   Mobility.   Can be upward or downward and
                                         experienced by either groups
                                         or individuals.
   Prejudice.   Negative attitudes toward
                                         individuals or groups.
   Discrimination.   Negative actions against those
                                         same others.

Concepts for Cultural
   Analysis.
    Values.   General standards of a culture.
    Norms.   Specific rules governing
                                         behavior.
    Assimilation.   Exchange of the culture of
                                         one's ancestors for that of
                                         one's contemporaries.
    Accommodation   Reciprocal ignoring of cultural
                                         differences by ethnic groups.
   Cultural Pluralism.   The result of continued
                                         accommodation.
    Subculture.   Minority culture existing
                                         within the larger culture.

Jews and Italians in   Contrasting case studies in
   North America.   cultural assimilation.

The Cultural Theory.   Re-created shtetl life and
   Zborowski and Herzog.   found that reverence for
                                         learning served Jewish
                                         immigrants very well.

Covello.	Found that Italian peasant culture saw little practical use for education; transplanted in their New World experience.
The Social Theory. Steinberg.	Argued that the Jews were not peculiarly upwardly mobile since their Old World skilled occupations gave them a head start.
Perlmann's Synthesis.	Both cultural and social theories are necessary to explain Jewish success in North America.
Reference Group and Italian Traditionalism.	Having primary reference group back in Italy impeded progress both educationally and occupationally and thus assimilation.
The Persistence of Italian Culture.	Comparing Italians with other Europeans and Italian-Americans with other Americans, Greeley found that family solidarity is much stronger with Italians and Italian-Americans and no longer impedes educational and occupational achievement.

SUMMARY

Society and Culture. Chapter 1 was devoted to introducing the field of sociology and the concepts of groups and relationships. Chapter 2 extends this introduction with a more macro emphasis. The terms society and nation are often used interchangeably but not all nations are societies (examples include the former Soviet Union and Yugoslavia) and not all societies are nations (preunified Germany). A more formal definition of society would emphasize relatively self-contained and self-sufficient human groups united by social relationships that tend to occupy a definite physical location. However, the notion of society is rather static and morphological. The distinctiveness, indeed vibrancy, of people is the contribution of culture: the complex pattern of living that humans have developed and pass on from one generation to the next and to which they might add. Although culture and civilization are sometimes used interchangeably, sociologists prefer the term culture just as they prefer the concept of society (to that of nation). Finally, the terms society and culture should never be used interchangeably.

Concepts for Social Analysis. There are many concepts subsumable under societal analysis that will be examined in some depth in later chapters. However, Chapter 2 serves to introduce students to some of them. *Stratification* refers to the unequal distribution of rewards among members in a society. Groups of people who share a status (similar position) comprise a social class. When individuals or entire groups move up or down in a stratification system we can speak of *upward or downward mobility.* At any moment in time, ones status in the stratification system is determined either by inheritance (ascribed status) or by individual merit (achieved status). A totally open class system is characterized by the latter while the former may be illustrated by India's caste system. For a group to be assigned and kept in an inferior status points to two other concepts useful in stratification analysis: prejudice, negative or hostile attitudes toward the group; and discrimination--actions taken against a group to deny members, collectively, rights and privileges enjoyed freely by others.

Concepts for Cultural Analysis. The ultimate ideals and most general standards contained within a culture are known as its values. The specific rules governing behavior are known as norms. The reciprocal relationship of these two concepts can be seen as **values** justifying (make legitimate) norms while **norms** specify (make concrete) values. A role is a collection of norms associated with a particular position in a society. These norms describe how we expect someone in a particular position to act. In almost every social situation we encounter there is a clearly defined role to fulfill. One fulfills the role by conforming to preexisting codified expectations (an alternative definition of norms). In fact, we might say that the more importantly society defines a situation the more likely the situation will be normatively structured. Now, different cultures may evaluate the same role differently--so much so that different cultures may have radically different ideas about how such basic roles as parent and child should be scripted. When immigrant children grow up and have children of their own, they are often in the process of helping a family exchange one culture for another. We refer to this exchange as **assimilation.** However, not all ethnic groups become fully assimilated. When differing cultures ignore differences but rather relate to each other in terms of common interests we call this **accommodation.** In twentieth-century North America, Catholics and Protestants can hardly be said to be fully assimilated to each other but they have accommodated their religious differences by playing down putative Vatican allegiances while emphasizing their common Christianity. Continued accommodation results in **cultural pluralism:** the existence of distinctive cultures within a society. When a minority culture exists within a larger context sociologists call this a **subculture.** There are remnants of Jewish and Italian subcultures, but better examples can be found with African-American subcultures and various Asiatic and Hispanic subcultures.

Jews and Italians in North America. From the 1880s until the outbreak of World War I, millions of European immigrants came to North America. Jews and Italians were among the most numerous of these immigrants. Almost from the beginning, the "alien" cultures of so many of these immigrants were feared and often despised (e.g., at times, the virulent anti-Semitism of the day). Even "sympathetic" accounts of Italians, Jews, and others were highly prejudicial and often functioned to reinforce the popular stereotypes of these groups. Caving into the fears that the immigrants from eastern and southern Europe would defile a purer America by dragging down its moral, racial, and social standards, Congress passed a highly restrictive immigration quota policy that favored northern and western Europeans. These policies remained in effect until the mid-1960s.

In spite of initial prejudice and discrimination there has been much assimilation of Jews and Italians (and all other descendants of immigrants). One indicator of this assimilation is the degree to which the children and grandchildren of immigrants married outside their ethnic group. By the third generation a clear majority of Italian descendants in the United States and Canada had inter-married with non-Italians. The Jewish rate has been lower since Italians are able to marry people of many other ancestries and still marry within their religion. For Jews, the boundaries of ethnicity and religion coincide, thus making intermarriage of greater significance. What remains of Italian and Jewish subculture can best be described as being in an accommodative mode vis-à-vis mainstream America.

The Cultural Theory. There is a rich scholarly literature on how and why ethnic groups in general and Italians and Jews in particular have become upwardly mobile in North America. The first phase of this literature emphasized cultural factors; the second phase, social factors. Recently, there has been a synthesis of the two. Sociologists proposed that Jewish values of learning, their norms of educational achievement, and the immense respect given to the role of scholar paved the Jewish road to success. Conversely, they suggested that Italians valued not learning but family loyalty; their norms led them to drop out of school and the immense importance placed on the role of father made their original culture slow to change.

Zborowski and Herzog: Jewish Culture. These two anthropologists re-created shtetl life in Poland and western Russia. They discovered that the norms governing schooling, even in the early 1800s, were strict and demanding by modern standards and males who showed the greatest academic aptitude were expected to adopt the role of scholar and devote their lives to study and learning. When Jews migrated to North America they brought with them this cult of scholarship. By the 1920s children of immigrant Jews had higher rates of high school graduation than did native white Americans (and three times the rate of children of Italian immigrants). In fact, this generation did so well that they were soon extraordinarily overrepresented in Ivy League universities. (The attendant fear brought about direct and indirect quotas of Jews at Columbia and Harvard.) Finally, as early as 1913, the proportions of Jewish doctors, lawyers, and college professors were substantially greater than the proportion of Jews in the general population.

Leonard Covello: Italian Culture. If the culture the Jews brought with them admirably suited American values of education and success, the same could not be said of the culture that Italians (especially southern Italians) brought with them. Covello argued that, in addition to the traditional patriarchal culture, southern Italians had good reason to distrust the school system in Italy and imported that distrust with them to the New World. They felt that schooling threatened family values and that, at best, it was marginal to making a living. The role of scholar was viewed with skepticism and, at any rate, was irrelevant to family values. In addition, their values in general did not help immigrant Italians adapt to the new demands of urban society.

However, there were two problems with the cultural theory. First, there was nothing particularly unusual about the time the Italians had taken to achieve economic parity, so the supposed barriers put up by Italian culture were not particularly debilitating. Second, while Jews might have been overrepresented in schools most did not even graduate high school; yet, as a whole, they still were ahead in income. So the Jewish value of education was not sufficient to explain Jewish success.

The Social Theory. Steinberg's revision of the cultural theory said, in effect, that the rapid upward mobility of Jews hadn't really occurred. Specifically, Steinberg attributed the superior economic position of Jewish immigrants in America to their superior economic and social positions in eastern Europe. Put another way, the status of first-generation immigrants was a direct function of their status in the old country.

Stephen Steinberg: The Jewish Head Start. What Steinberg found was that Jews arriving in America during the first decade of this century were poor in money but rich in occupational skills: 73 per cent of them came to this country with higher-status skills (the average for all immigrants being 21 per cent). The immigrant Jews rapidly reentered their old occupations as printers, jewelers, cigar makers, tailors, watchmakers, tinsmiths, furriers, etc. More recently, other immigrant groups have repeated this experience, specifically, the initial wave of refugees from Castro's regime and those from the fall of South Vietnam.

Joel Perlmann: A New Synthesis. Perlmann, in a close examination of schooling and occupational achievement among ethnic groups in Providence between 1880 and 1935, found that in 1915 sons of immigrant Jews were nearly twice as likely as Yankees and nearly four times as likely as sons of Italians to graduate from high school. Further, three-fourths of the Jewish sons ended up in white-collar occupations, compared with only a third of the Italians. Using statistical analyses, he found that when Jewish and Italian children were given a hypo-thetical even start Jewish children were still much more likely to enter high school, graduate, and take good jobs. Thus, Perlmann concluded that both theories (cultural and social) are needed to account for what actually took place.

Reference Groups and Italian Traditionalism. In 1911 two-thirds of the Jews who had been in the United States less than five years could speak English whereas the figure for Italians was only one-fourth. Covello blamed many school problems experienced by Italian-Americans in the 1930s on their poor English skills. The reason the Italians were slow to learn English was a reason for many of their economic problems as well.
   A large part of this differential in language and occupational adaptability was the simple fact that a great many Italians viewed their stay in America as temporary whereas almost all Jews saw themselves as staying and never returning to face another pogrom. In fact, that is exactly what happened. Immigrants from Italy continued to regard the folks back home as their reference group. Thus, why learn English and American urban job skills when you are only here to save enough money to rejoin your *famiglia* and *paesani* in Italy? Put another way, the reference groups for practically all Jews were their family and neighbors in their American neighborhood, whereas the reference group for large numbers of Italian-Americans was the inhabitants of rural villages in southern Italy.

The Persistence of Italian Culture. Recently, Greeley examined the persistence of Italian culture in contemporary

settings. Greeley hypothesized that a strategic element of
Italian culture had not been modernized through subsequent
generations: the family. Indeed, compared with other
Americans, Greeley found that Italian-Americans were much
more likely to visit family members, nurse ill family
members, financially help family members, and share a home
with their their parents. The same results were obtained
when Greeley compared Italians with other Europeans. Thus,
the Italian family values no longer harm occupational
achievement even though the values haven't changed.
However, the norms to fulfill those values have changed by
adaptation to modernity. Eductional achievement now helps
fulfill many familial obligations (especially financial
ones) and, concommitantly, facilitates occupational
achievement.

TEACHING SUGGESTIONS

The objective of Chapter 2 is to continue the student's
introduction to sociology by concentrating on various
concepts relating to culture and society. The chapter also
shows students how a single research theme unfolds and is
revised as tentative answers bring more questions.

1. Discussion: "The Components of Culture." One way of
illustrating the idea of culture is to break it down into
its major components: symbols, artifacts, and behavior.
The objective of this discussion is to show that elements
of culture do not randomly exist contiguous to one other. A
simple example for students is something with which they are
all familiar: note-taking in the college classroom. It is a
learned behavior involving rich symbolization using specific
artifacts such as pens and notebooks. A discussion might
lead to envisioning customs as analogous to group habits--
learned, vital to maintaining a group's way of life, and
performed unconsciously. Finally, a discussion might lead
to addressing the question, If we can meaningfully talk
about behavior, symbols, and artifacts, do we really need
the concept of culture? Put another way, Is culture
reducible to its component parts or does it have its own
emergent reality?
   [Instructor's note: This idea of culture as an emergent
reality may be beyond the students' interests and
capabilities at this stage of the course. I find that this
is often, but not always, the case.]

2. Discussion: "Key Sociological Variables as illustrated
by Ascribed vs. Achieved Status." Here is a way I introduce
students to thinking about the profound impact status has on
their lives while previewing the text and the course for
them. I first try to engage them by listing what they think

are key sociological variables. When the list is complete
(according to them), I try to partial out from and/or add to
the list so that it includes the following: age, gender,
race or ethnicity, citizenship, composition and size of
family, any special physical traits (i.e., completely
healthy vs. being physically challenged), religion, social
class, education, language spoken, geographic area, and
rural-urban residence. (I have omitted occupation and
sexual orientation for reasons that I hope will be clear
momentarily.) Next, I tell them how each of the above can
profoundly impact their lives. I then show them that each of
the above can be linked to various chapters in the text.

Variable	Chapter(s)
age	5,6
gender	5,6,13
family	12
religion	14
class	9
citizenship	10,15,17
education	16
language	2,6,11
geographic area	11,18
rural/urban	18,19
physically challenged	5,6

   Up to this point, it is pretty cut and dry. Now let's
spice it up. Point out to your students that they are all,
in a sense, "born into" each of the above variables. That
is, relative to each variable they are assigned at birth, by
their society, an ascribed status inherited, directly or
indirectly, from their parents. If they are skeptical, then
ask them: "When you are born and for your formative years,
did you have any choice regarding these variables?" Now ask
them when they began to feel that they could do something
about any of these variables. In other words, which
variables stay ascribed and which are achievable?
   [Instructor's note: You may want to frame this in terms
of a hypothesis: to the extent that one can change any
ascribed status, then to that extent the status is of less
societal significance than one that cannot be altered or one
is not allowed to alter. This is fun since you can sneak in
an otherwise dry concept (hypothesis) in such a way as to
almost guarantee discussion.]

3. Discussion: "Sloganeering: Value or Norm?" If the
previous discussions bog down, a sure-fire way of getting at
least some of the students going is to introduce the notion
of "Buy American" and then apply it to that All-American
love object: the automobile. You may start by discussing
whether or not to "Buy American" is a value (an ideal to
strive for) or a norm (a prescriptive rule of behavior).

After you get much of the class to agree that buying American is a good thing, then ask how you might define American when it comes to car buying. To illustrate:

1. Does it mean buying an American nameplate to be sure of an American-made car? Then steer clear of the Ford Apsire (made in Canada), the Mercury Tracer (made in Mexico), and the Dodge Colt (made in Japan).

2. Or does it mean buy an American-designed car? Then don't buy a Geo Prizm from Chevrolet; it is actually a Toyota Corolla with an American nameplate.

3. Or does it mean buy American cars only made with American parts (do any exist)?

4. Or does "Buy American" mean putting American workers to work? Then buy a Honda (among others) that is made in Ohio.

5. But you say that profits then go back to Japan and you want to make sure that the corporate profits stay in America for reinvestment? Then don't buy from GM, Ford, or Chrysler since they are all multinational corporations. I find that this a neat way of overcoming some rank ethnocentrism.

4. Lecture: "The Amish." This is a lecture on the Old Order Amish in North America emphasizing their ways of making a living as well as their customs. Lecturing on the Amish is a good way of illustrating how definitions of culture, society, and subculture can blur. More specifically, do the Amish comprise a distinct society within the larger North American one? Given their ecological distribution, the practice of meidung, and their mode of subsistence, rather than simply defining them as an North American subculture, we might more accurately define them as a "subsociety" (given that they are (a) dispersed geographically, (b) clan based, and (c) preindustrial agrarian capitalists).

Sources: Hostetler, J. Amish Society. Baltimore: Johns Hopkins University Press, 1980. Probably the single best piece on the Amish.

Kraybill, D. The Riddle of Amish Culture. Baltimore: Johns Hopkins University Press, 1989. This most interesting work shows how the Amish have struck a bargain with modernity.

ADDITIONAL STUDENT READINGS

Kephart, W., and W. Zellner. Extraordinary Groups, 4th edition. New York: St. Martin's Press, 1991. An extraordinarily well-written and engaging collection of essays on the Old Order Amish, the Oneida Community, the Hasidim, the Father Divine Movement, the Shakers, the Mormons, the Gypsies, and the Jehovah's Witnesses.

Malcolm, A. The Canadians. Toronto: Paperbacks Ltd., 1985. An affectionate but balanced and perceptive look at Canada and Canadians. Comprehensive, informative, and highly recommended.

Miner, H. "Body Ritual Among the Nacirema." American Anthropologist (1955): 57: 503-507. Yes, Virginia, social scientists do have a sense of humor but often at the expense of the foibles of American culture.

Weatherford, J. Indian Givers: How the Indians of the Americas Transformed the World. New York: Fawcett Columbine, 1988. Important cultural, political, and economic contributions of Native Americans to advanced societies. Absolutely engrossing and highly readable.

Weatherford, J. Native Roots: How the Indians Enriched America. New York: Fawcett Columbine, 1991. An extension of the approach of Indian Givers. Also very well done.

ESSAY QUESTIONS

1. Distinguish between society and culture. Show why it is important not to use the two concepts interchangeably.

2. How would you describe the stratification system of this campus? Be sure to include the following concepts: achieved and ascribed status, prejudice, discrimination, mobility, and caste.

3. Distinguish between values and norms in the college classroom. In what ways are classroom norms negotiated and how do students enforce these norms?

4. Compare and contrast the immigrant experiences of Jews and Italians in light of cultural theory and social theory.

Chapter 3

MICRO SOCIOLOGY: TESTING
INTERACTION THEORIES

CHAPTER OUTLINE

Rational Choice.	All micro-level theories in the social sciences that are rational choice theories assume people maximize benefits while minimizing costs. Rational choice assumes self-interest but altruism is possible if one identifies with others, and incurs sacrifices on their behalf.
Interaction Theories.	May be presented more formally as exchange theories or less formally as symbolic inter-action theories.
Symbolic Interaction.	Both Cooley (the looking glass self) and Mead (mind, self, and taking the role of the other) stressed the crucial contribution of significant others in the successful socialization of children.
Interaction Patterns. Attachments. Norms.	Mutually beneficial exchange partnerships constrained by norms that govern the attachments. People exercise free will but what is chosen is greatly influenced by attachments.
Criteria of Causation. Correlation.	The statistical association of independent and dependent variables.
Time Order.	Independent variable occurs before dependent variable.
Nonspuriousness.	That the relationship between two variables is not accounted for by a hidden third variable.
Experimental Research.	Often a way of researching hypotheses. (e.g. research by Dion, and Ofshe). Two major advantages of the experiment:

	ability to manipulate the independent variable and random assignment of subjects.
Field Observation Research.	Stark and Lofland's study of the early days of the Moonies led to a theory of attachments to explain conversion to the sect. As with much field research, they were *not* able to prove nonspuriousness.
Replication.	Since their initial research, more than two dozen studies have reinforced the crucial role of attachments in the conversion process.

SUMMARY

Rational Choice. All micro theories in the social sciences assert that choice is the most basic aspect of human behavior. At bottom, these choices are rational choices in which people will try to select the option that will benefit them the most--that people will seek to gain rewards and try to avoid costs. (Another term for rational choice theory is the self-interest proposition). Depending upon the discipline, the idea of rational choice will vary in its emphasis. A narrow view of self-interest seems to falter when confronted with the fact of altruism (unselfish behavior done to benefit others). Yet if we see altruism as the product of a person identifying with the well-being of the other who is in need, then altruism becomes part of the self-interest of the helper.

Interaction Theories. Altruism becomes explainable to sociologists when they greatly expand the concepts of rewards and costs to include such intangibles as affection and self-esteem. Further, sociologists also recognize that much of what we want can only be gotten from other people. Finally, because humans seek rewards from one another, they are inevitably forced into exchange relations. In one sense then, altruism is an exchange of help for gratitude. Again, depending on the emphasis of the sociologist, interaction theories may be either formally presented as exchange theories or less formally presented as symbolic interaction theories. In the latter case, the emphasis is on common meaning as essential for interaction, while with the former, the emphasis is on equitable outcomes of interaction.

Symbolic Interaction: Cooley and Mead. Cooley, an early sociologist, carefully observed how infants developed into normal human beings (i.e., the socialization process). His central idea was one's sense of self must develop apace in order for socialization to succeed. The social nature of the development of human beings is illustrated by the concept of the <u>looking glass self</u> in that who we become is to a large extent a function of what others think of us--or, more precisely, what we think others think of us. Mead extends Cooley by emphasizing the behavioral dimension to our social nature. Mind is the active process of under-standing symbols and self is our learned understanding of the response of others to our conduct. As such, both concepts are verbs rather than nouns. As the capability of mind develops, so does the sense of self. They are linked by the child's increasing ability to <u>take the role of the other:</u> to understand interaction from the viewpoint of the other interactant(s). Out of the process of interacting and exchange with one another, we settle into a pattern of frequent interactions with certain people. We also discover and develop rules governing our interactions.

Interaction Patterns: Attachments and Norms. One of the most important propositions of micro sociology is: over time people tend to establish stable exchange partnerships that are mutually beneficial. When relationships move beyond simple utilitarian exchanges of goods and services and involve commonly shared sentiments, we now talk of attachments. We find ourselves conforming to certain expectations that our attachments have as to how we ought to behave. We have already referred to these expectations as norms, and all of Chapter 3 to this point can be summarized as follows: *Human behavior is based on choice, but what we choose to do is greatly influenced by what our attachments want us to do.*

Criteria of Causation. Most scientific hypotheses predict causal relationships. To demonstrate causation, we must show that a relationship meets three tests, or criteria, of causation. In order to think about causation we must grasp the idea of <u>variable:</u> any factor that can have two or more values. An independent variable is the cause, and a dependent variable is the effect. That being the case, the two variables must be associated, that is vary, with one another. This we call <u>correlation.</u> When two variables: x and y either rise or fall together, we can say that there is a positive correlation. When one rises and the other falls, we can say that the correlation is negative. However, to demonstrate causality we must go beyond correlation; we must demonstrate <u>time order</u>. One variable must clearly occur before the other, which is a fancier way of stating that the cause must occur before the effect. Finally, the one variable must actually cause the other; that is, their relationship must not be accounted for by some other hidden third factor. If that is the case, then the original relationship is <u>spurious</u>.

One way of researching hypotheses is the experiment whose distinguishing traits include a random assignment of subjects to either an experimental group or a control group. The behavior to be observed and explained takes place in a relatively artificial social setting with the capacity for controlling the causal variable--being able to make it vary, rise or fall, appear or disappear at will.

Once all of the observations have been recorded and analyzed, one must make sure that the results were not the product of chance. A test of significance is then conducted. Two crucial aspects of this test are the number of subjects on which the results are based and the size of the correlation.

Experimental Research. Ofshe's experiment strongly confirmed Stark's theory of loyalty: whenever people must choose between rewarding someone to whom they are attached or rewarding someone to whom they are not attached, they will reward the person to whom they are attached. In so doing, Ofshe's research illustrates the successful application of the ctiteria of causation.

Field Observation Research. Much of what sociologists want to know is simply not accessible by experiments. Thus, nonexperimental research techniques have been refined as alternative methods of gathering data. One such experimental methodology, field observation research, entails going out into the world and directly observing the phenomenon of interest. Lofland and Stark did just that with their study of the development of the Moonies cult in the San Francisco Bay Area. Their initial theory of conversion stated that conversion to a new religious group occurs when people have or develop stronger attachments to members of this group than they have to nonmembers (of other groups). After detailed observation, interviews, and analysis, Stark and Lofland concluded that while elements of the Moonie doctrine did play a role in who joined, the primary basis of conversion was attachment. In other words, rather than being drawn to the group primarily because of the appeal of its doctrines, people were drawn to the doctrines because of their ties to the group. Technically, Lofland and Stark did not meet all the criteria of causation. For example, they could not strictly demonstrate nonspuriousness. However, they were able to meet the criteria of time order and correlation between the variables of attachment and conversion.

Replication. What is absolutely crucial for the progress of science is to repeat important research. Replication takes place when subsequent researchers use different subjects but employ the same methods studying the same variables as did the original researchers. Since Stark and Lofland first published their research on the Moonies, there have been more than twenty replications involving a great variety of religious groupps of the dynamics of conversion. Attachments have consistently been found to play *the* major role in explaining who converts to a new religious group.

TEACHING SUGGESTIONS

The objective of Chapter 3 is to introduce various micro approaches in sociology. It is hoped that students will gain a much greater appreciation for how social forces shape the everyday interactions in their lives.

1. **Lecture:** "Student (Non)Participation in the Classroom." I find that lecturing on the Karp and Yoels paper is an excellent way of introducing the idea of rational choice theory. Karp and Yoels systematically studied student (non)participation in various liberal arts classes. Most students, of course, did not participate except if called upon; classroom size wasn't that great a factor. Further, professors' perceptions of why students did not participate were mostly congruent with the students' perceptions. But I think the most interesting finding was the discovery of an emergent norm that was found in class after class. The norm pretty much established that a few students would carry most of the "work" of talking but not talk so much as to be "rate-busters." I find going through this study early in the term is very helpful since it gives students a new perspective on a phenomenon with which they are intimately familiar.

   [Instructor's note: Before I go over these findings with the students I have them take the miniquestionnaire as provided in the paper and then compare the class's answers with those of Karp and Yoels. From this one can launch into a discussion of the criteria of causality.]

   Source: Karp, D., and W. Yoels. "The College Classroom: Some Observations on the Meanings of Student Participation." Sociology and Social Research 60 (1976): 421-439.

2. **Discussion:** "What Is Altruism Anyway?" In this exercise ask the students for definitions of altruism. Usually, definitions (both lay and professional) imply some notion of the altruist deriving some benefit from the altruistic act. Try two variations of this theme. First, define altruism for the class as the deliberate doing good

for another that involves mostly/all sacrifice for the altruist. Someone in the class should respond that under those circumstances the altruist is either a martyr or a masochist, or else is deriving some other psychic income from the act. That being the case, then define pure altruism as anonymous sacrifice; that is, the altruist does good for its own sake while never letting the recipient (or anyone else) know who did what for whom. Now, complicate matters by introducing Robert Park's definition of self-interest (anything for which a person takes responsibility) and link it with Lenski's idea that people/groups will do for others to the extent that they find these others useful or necessary for their own well-being. Next, ask the students if they would like to learn that someone with whom they have a deep attachment goes around doing anonymously altruistic acts for strangers. (Ask them if the parable of the Good Samaritan would apply here. Better yet, go over the research on the Good Samaritan by Darley and Batson as to when seminary students will hurriedly pass by a slumped-over man while on their way to deliver a talk on the parable of the Good Samaritan.) In any case, ask them: "Would altruistic acts done by your significant other to strangers cheapen any acts the beloved would do for you?" Can society exist on altruism? Put another way, If reciprocity is essential for society, might pure altruism be corrosive to reciprocity and, ultimately, society? Finally, if it hasn't come up yet, bring in the crucial notion of consequence: While one may mean well, does the recipient really want/need to be helped (in that particular way or at all) and what of acts of altruism that backfire? Shake well and apply to the discussion.

Sources. Darley, J. and C. Batson. "From Jerusalem to Jericho: A Study of Situational and Dispositional Variables in Helping Behavior." Journal of Personality and Social Psychology 27 (1973): 100-108.

Lenski, G. Power and Privilege. New York: McGraw-Hill, 1966.

Park, R. The Crowd and the Public. Chicago: University of Chicago Press, 1972.

Rosen, S. "Some Paradoxical Status Implications of Helping and Being Helped." In Development and Maintenance of Prosocial Behavior: International Perspectives on Positive Morality, Staub et al. eds. New York: Plenum, 1984. An insightful account of why good intentions are not enough.

3. **Demonstration:** "The Many Meanings of Friendship." I have used this exercise with some success to illustrate the idea of attachments. It requires some homework on the part of the instructor, but it is well worth it. Ask the class to identify various characteristics of friendship. Write them on the board. Usually, the list contains eight to ten items. Then ask the students to rank them (from most

characteristic to least characteristic of friendship).
This, along with gender, major, year in college, is usually
enough for a "proto" study of friendship (for in-class
consumption). I have found several uses for this
demonstration. First, it neatly shows students how the
same object--friendship--can have some radically differing
meanings for people even those who are superficially
homogeneous. Second, it can introduce them to some of the
vagaries of constructing a mini-research project. Third,
an interesting discussion can be pursued on the strengths
and weaknesses of fixed-choice versus open-ended surveys.
   [Instructor's note: This demonstration takes part
of one and all of another 50-minute period.]
   Source: Blau, P. Exchange and Power in Social Life.
New York: Wiley, 1964. Is friendship "mere" exchange and
reciprocity? Although this great work is over thirty years
young it is still worth reading.

4. Lecture: "Domestic Violence." A major upsurge in
interest in this topic coincides with the recent "discovery"
(during the past two decades) of domestic violence as a
social problem. Domestic violence is perhaps the ugliest
counterpoint to the ideal of living "happily ever after" and
a major reason for, as well as symptom of, marital
unhappiness, separation, and divorce. The literature is
growing, but the dimensions of the problem remain vague.
Still, I recommend the following sources. They emphasize
the battered woman, but material on other forms of family
violence are included. The subject matter is depressing but
of vital importance. I find it particularly stimulating to
engage the class in this question: When is spousal abuse a
rational act on the part of the perpetrator? My tack is
that whenever violence is rewarded by spousal complicity and
not punished by either spouse or outside authorities then
spousal abuse is the product of rational choice: the rewards
of control via violence significantly outweigh likely costs
that may/may not be incurred. I further point out that
techniques of neutralization (excuses and justifications)
such as "alcohol/stress made him do it" become primary
means whereby both offender and victim deny the inherent
rationality to much domestic violence. In so doing, I
anticipate the intentional vs. impulsive deviance
distinction made in Chapter 7. Finally, I include
Renzetti's excellent analysis of lesbian partner abuse as an
additional complication stressing that partner abuse is not
just a male phenomenon.
   Sources: Ferraro, K., and J. Johnson. "How Women
Experience Battering: The Process of Victimization."
Social Problems (Febrary 1983) 325-335.
   Renzetti, C. Violent Betrayal: Partner Abuse in Lesbian
Relationships. Thousand Oaks, Ca: Sage Publications, 1992.

Straus, M., R. Gelles, and S. Steinmetz. <u>Behind Closed Doors: Violence in the American Family.</u> New York: Doubleday Books, 1980.

Sykes, G., and D. Matza. "Techniques of Neutralization: A Theory of Delinquency." <u>American Sociological Review</u> 22 (1957): 664-670.

ADDITIONAL STUDENT READINGS

Carter, G. "The Interaction Between the Staff and the Denizens of a Social Security Waiting Room." <u>Sociological Viewpoints</u> (Spring 1988): 1-16. A participant observation study that illustrates how social order is an emergent phenomenon. It also nicely shows how a public area like a waiting room provides one of the few positive links with society for some social outcasts.

Memmi, A. <u>Dependence.</u> Boston: Beacon Press, 1984. A short monograph by an eminent French philosopher, this clearly written exposition of a fundamental (and inevitable) social phenomenon is sure to reward the thoughtful reader.

Williams, T. <u>The Cocaine Kids: The Inside Story of a Teenage Drug Ring.</u> Reading, Mass.: Addison-Wesley, 1989. Williams spent several years studying teen drug dealers in Spanish Harlem. Fascinating.

ESSAY QUESTIONS

1. Regarding the criteria of causation, compare the research of Ofshe with that of Lofland and Stark.

2. Apply the theory of attachments as developed by Lofland and Stark to any two voluntary groups on campus.

3. Show how rational choice theory can be used to explain and predict altruistic behavior.

4. Draw some implications from Dion's study on the development of primary grade children. How does the looking glass self apply to these implications?

CHAPTER OUTLINE

Social Structures.	Traits of groups rather than of individuals.
Survey Research.	Allows sociologists to collect data via interviews or questionnaires.
Sample.	A carefully drawn representation that enables generalization of findings to a larger population.
From Micro to Macro: Adjusting the Theory.	Stark reformulates the relationship between religiosity and delinquency arguing that religious individuals will be less likely to run afoul of the law *only* when a majority of community members are actively religious.
Social Structures and Social Systems.	Systems have interdependent elements that tend toward a state of equilibrium.
Institution and Classes.	Two examples of social structural traits.
Macro Sociological Theories. Functionalist Theories.	Illustrated by the idea of the extended family, especially as found in primitive societies where, as an adaptation to high death rates, such families help preserve the larger society.
Functional Alternatives.	To the extended family in modern societies: welfare programs, day care centers, insurance policies, etc.
Social Evolutionary Theories.	Stress that social change is not necessarily progressive. Societies with adaptive structures stand a better chance of surviving.

Conflict Theories.   Competing groups struggling for
                              power and privilege produces
                              conflict which in turn shapes
                              social structures.

Comparative Research.   Paige showed how matrilocality
                              structures males to interact
                              with nonmale kin, thus mostly
                              precluding opportunities to
                              factionalize and dampening
                              potential for violence.

SUMMARY

Social Structures. Social structures are the traits of
groups as opposed to the traits of the individual members
themselves. In an extreme sense, a social structural
perspective treats people as interchangeable and assumes
that traits of individuals are overridden by the structure
of the group to which they belong.

Survey Research. In Chapter 3 we saw that experimental
and field observation are two methodologies sociologists use
to discover what interests them in the social world. In
Chapter 4, other research approaches will be examined. With
survey research, data are collected by having each subject
fill out a questionnaire or by means of personal interviews.
Of all the major sociological methodologies, survey research
is the most concerned with drawing a proper sample. A
representative sample of adequate size allows us to
generalize our findings to a much larger population and
makes survey research a powerful tool.
The use of survey research is well illustrated in the
text by Stark and Hirschi's study on delinquency in the
Richmond, California, area. On first blush, the data
seemed to indicate that frequent church attendance
prevented delinquency. However, this simple relationship
proved spurious when controlling for gender. This non-
relationship between religiosity and delinquency proved
troublesome when others tried to replicate the original
research. Some studies (conducted on populations in the
Pacific Northwest) reinforced the Stark-Hirschi findings,
while other studies did find a strong negative correlation
between church attendance and delinquency. The resolution
of this came when the context of religiosity was examined
(i.e., moving toward a more macro focus). What counts is
not only whether a person is religious but also the proportion of religious people in their environment. Thus,
religious individuals will be less likely than others to
break the norms, but *only in communities where the majority
of people are actively religious.*
In western North America, there is an unchurched belt

(c.f. Chapter 14). Thus, with a majority of people in the West not being terribly religious, religion _per se_ is not a delinquency preventative. However, just about everywhere else where a majority of people in the community are religious, religion acts as a reinforcer of religiosity and as a delinquency preventative.

From Micro to Macro: Adjusting the Theory. Recently, using data from the High School and Beyond Study, Stark tested his interpretation and found that in the East, Midwest, and South, where church attendance rates are around 60 percent, the correlations between church attendance and delinquent behavior are strongly negative. The correlation weakens in the less religious Mountain states and disappears in the Pacific region.

Social Structures and Social Systems. Macro sociologists assume that societies are not chance collections of people, culture, and social structures--they assume instead that societies are systems. A system has several elements that are interdependent and that tend toward a state of equilibrium. (All macro theorists include micro assumptions; that is, that individuals are motivated by self-interest.) Social structures are well represented in societies. Institutions and social classes are two of the more important ones for macro sociologists.

Institutions and Classes. Social institutions contain relatively permanent patterns or clusters of specialized roles, groups, organizations, customs, and activities that function to meet important social needs. Examples include the family, economy, religion, political order, and education. Classes, or groups of people who are ranked together in a society's stratification system, are another important structural concept. For example, conflict theory emphasizes how classes interact with one another.
Therefore, outside of global systems, most macro-sociologists would view any individual society as an interrelated system of components (major examples being institutions and social classes) that tend toward a state of equilibrium.

Macro Sociological Theories. There are three major macro theories: functionalism, conflict, and social evolution. _Functionalist theories_ have three components. First, there is the part of the system to be explained. Second, we explain this part by showing how it preserves some other part of the system from disruption or overload. Third, the theory also must identify the source of this potential disruption or overload. An example is the extended family, which contains many adults in a single household and is common among primitive societies. The function of this extended family arrangement is to preserve the larger societal structure by being the main (often only) source of support for a variety of dependents: youth, elderly, sick, or disabled.   The potential source of disruption is the high death rates in these societies.   Thus, the extended family substitutes for welfare programs, retirement plans, and insurance policies. Alternatively, modern societies have released the family from having sole responsibility for supporting dependents by creating welfare programs. Modern society's welfare programs can be seen as functional alternatives to extended kin.

Social Evolutionary Theories. Functionalist theories imply social evolution. Social evolutionary theories argue that societies with structures enabling them to adapt to their physical and social environments have a better chance of survival than do societies that fail to develop such structures. These theories were very popular in the mid to late nineteenth century. In the past generation or so they have made a comeback in sociology. However, contemporary sociologists scrupulously try to avoid three errors commonly made by their predecessors. First, they avoid the indis-criminate use of biological analogies. Second, they view change as not inevitably progressive. Third, evolutionary theorists do not assume that societies necessarily grow larger and more complex.

Conflict Theories. These theories ask how social structure serves the interests of various competing groups in society. Marx is the great conflict theorist of the nineteenth century and his writings (in collaboration with Engels) comprise the core of the hard-core conflict school of thought. To this day, Marxists consider class conflict the major, if not the only source, of conflict in society. Weber derived his interests in conflict from Marx but of course went well beyond a narrow class base for conflict (see Chapter 9).

Comparative Research. Perhaps the most fully macro of all methodologies is that of comparative research which always involves aggregate units--the things it compares always include more than one person. An excellent piece of comparative research is that of Jeffery Paige who studied kinship sources of peace and violence in primitive societies. Paige argued that in primitive societies factions will form along divisions based on kinship and also along divisions based on residence. The tendency in primitive societies is for a patrilocal rule of residence where the bride leaves home after marriage and lives with or near the husband's family while his male kin live in close proximity. The reverse is sometimes true. A matrilocal rule of residence is where the groom lives with or near the bride's family. After comparing ten patrilocal societies

with ten matrilocal societies Paige found the data
overwhelming. Factionalism and violence were strongly
correlated with patrilocal societies, and communalism and
diplomacy were strongly correlated with matrilocality. The
reason given is that matrilocality males interact mostly
with males who are not their relatives. Therefore, their
tendencies to form factions with their kinsmen would bring
them into conflict with those with whom they live, while
residential factions would force men to oppose their closest
relatives. Thus, patrilocal societies are free to
factionalize and pursue violent means of resolving disputes.
Martrilocal societies provide no such easy opportunity but
rather reinforce diplomatic resolutions to conflict.
    Finally, in a broader sense, Paige, by showing how
social structure shapes internal conflict, reverses the
usual conflict approaches that stress explanations arguing
for internal conflict shaping social structure.

TEACHING SUGGESTIONS

The objective of Chapter 4 is to introduce students to the
fundamental ideas of macro sociology, especially structure,
function, conflict, and comparative research. It is
anticipated that students will discover that social
structures are crucial to understanding life and its
unavoidable constraints.

1. Discussion: "Differing Notions of Social Structure:
Connecting Micro and Macro Sociology." The instructor asks
if anyone knows the age of the college. From there the
instructor then asks what constitutes the college: just
buildings or people too? The former idea illustrates the
notion of social structure as containerlike, professors,
students, and even administrators come and go but the
college has an essential continuity of identity. Moreover,
the specific people are pretty interchangeable (within
limits of motivation and talent). What happens to them at
college is mostly a function of the container (social
structure) in which they find themselves. With this
conception, social time and space (usually on a large scale)
become the major parameters of the idea of social structure.
    Alternatively, social structure can also be seen as the
ongoing accomplishment of participants playing out their
roles-- that is, structure as patterned recurring
interaction. While the container idea sees humans as
essentially passive objects manipulated by master
institutions and processes (a traditional macro approach),
the latter interactionist approach is much more likely to
emphasize the potential for change that emerges from
interaction and, thus, it is much more a micro-sociological
interpretation of social structure in which specific types

of acts and interactions are crucial.

In sum, social structure as container focuses on the material aspects of culture: architecture, social space, boundaries, etc. It sees social structure as imposing constraints from the outside onto the participants, who are passive. The interactionist view sees structure as an emergent phenomenon more focused on behavior and social objects and therefore, more susceptible to change depending on how the interactants behave. Put another way, social structure as container emphasizes the more macro intergenerational aspects of social life while the interactionists would see structure as more temporally immediate--that is, *intragenerational*. This is one way of showing students that different ways of approaching social life (macro vs. micro) require differing conceptions of social structure. Just as importantly, it shows students that both perspectives are needed to render an adequate interpretation of social life. Moreover, it can be argued that the micro notion of social structure functions as foundation for the macro notion.

Source: Collins, R. "On the Microfoundations of Macrosociology." American Journal of Sociology 86 (1981): 984-1014. Collins states that macro sociological concepts and phenomena, while not strictly reducible to micro acts, nevertheless ultimately rely upon them as building blocks. Essentially, Collins argues for a micro to macro continuum that is mappable in terms of social time and space.

2. Discussion: "Solidarity and Attachment: Bridging the Micro-Macro Gap." Another way of bridging the gap between Chapters 3 and 4 while illustrating the idea of social structure is to engage the class in the following question: Can one choose to be attached with others? Introduce a variety of commonplace examples: parental love, romantic love, friendship. Then you may ease the students into more macro concerns such as Durkheim's classic statement on solidarity and perhaps Hechter's recent foray on the subject. To many, solidarity has been superseded by the concept of attachments. Is this so? If we can make choices that end with attachments, then is the same true for the classic concept of solidarity? Thus, is attachment a micro level version of the more macro idea of solidarity?

Sources: Durkheim, E. The Division of Labor in Society. Translated by G. Simpson. New York: Macmillan, 1933. The original sociological statement on solidarity.

Hechter, M. Principles of Group Solidarity. Berkeley: University of California Press, 1987. A very interesting approach to solidarity utilizing rational choice theory.

3. Lecture: "Utopian Groups in Historical and Contemporary America." This lecture surveys the major sociological writings on utopian groups--societies and communes--from

the perspective of comparative research. These attempts at
"heaven on earth" could be seen as natural field experiments
even though the actual structuring of the groups was/is
accomplished by the participants themselves (rather than by
sociologists). These societies truly were experimental in
their avowed self-consciousness as to what they were all
about. One of the many interesting findings of Kanter's
marvelous research is that of the societies in her study the
successful ones were successful at constraining personal
freedoms as well as structuring inequality into their group.
From here it is a short step to discussing such all-American
values as freedom and equality as perhaps being, beyond a
certain point, mutually exclusive. Another use of such a
lecture would be to clear up the misunderstanding that
communes are dead and buried and that the few that remain
are populated by burned-out hippies. (For example, Zablocki
found, in his contemporary survey, several major types of
communes: including eastern, Christian, rehabilitational,
cooperative, political, as well as counter-cultural.)

Further, it would show students that there are
alternative ways of living that have and still do make
sense to many reasonable Americans. In addition, from a
sociological point of view this would be an excellent way
of underscoring the fact that although individuals are
indeed the building blocks of groups the latter have their
own reality (and of course, level of analysis). This point
can be neatly illustrated by Zablocki's fascinating finding
that the more "reciprocated dyadic love" (both romantic and
fraternal) that was found in communes the *greater* the
membership turnover rate and the *greater* the commune
disintegration rate. Zablocki comments on this: "It seems
reasonable to conclude then that level of cathexis is a
structural property of communes as well as being an
aggregate property of networks of dyadic relationships. We
might speculate that communes develop role structures that
sustain constant levels of cathexis [independent] of the
occupants of these roles."

Sources: Berger, B. <u>The Survival of a Counterculture:
Ideological Work and Everyday Life Among Rural Communards.</u>
Berkeley: University of California Press, 1981. An
excellent study of one group of contemporary communards.
While the author's sympathies lie with the group he is
studying, this is not a Pollyanna treatment.

<u>Intentional Communities: A Guide to Cooperative Living.
1990-1991 Directory</u>. Evansville, Ind: The Fellowship for
Intentional Community, 1991. This is a fascinating
collection of information on more than 300 North American
communities and more than 50 elsewhere. It features over 35
articles about community living. The degree of networking
among these communities will probably surprise many who
think of them as mostly isolated groups.

Kanter, R. Commitment and Community: Communes and Utopias in Sociological Perspective. Cambridge: Harvard University Press, 1973. Historical sociology at its best. An excellent framework with which to interpret the work of Nordhoff (below).

Nordhoff, C. The Communistic Societies of the United States. New York: Dover, 1966. A nineteenth-century account of most of the important American utopian experiments including treatment of the Amana society.

Zablocki, B. Alienation and Charisma: A Study of Contemporary American Communes. New York: The Free Press, 1980. A massive, first-rate survey of the contemporary commune scene circa the late 1970s.

ADDITIONAL STUDENT READINGS

Dyer, G. War. New York: Crown, 1985. What could be more macabre in macro sociology than war. Yet, Dyer manages to give a fascinating account that will surely interest even the most ardent pacifist.

Harris, M. Cows, Pigs, Wars, and Witches. New York: Random House: 1974. Why do tens of millions of cows roam India? Why won't Middle Easterners eat pork? Why did they burn all of those "witches"? Well-written, fascinating topics; controversial interpretations.

Harris, M. The Sacred Cow and the Abominable Pig: Riddles of Food and Culture. New York: Simon and Schuster, 1985. Harris is back and as good as ever. Often it is difficult to interest students in macro sociology but this book is guaranteed to keep their interest with topics such as "Hippophagy, Holy Beef USA, Lactophiles and Lactophobes," and "Dogs, Cats, Dingoes, and Other Pets." Great fun!

ESSAY QUESTIONS

1. Choose a group on campus and then give three structural traits of that group.

2. What advantages does survey research have over field research in examining the relationship between religiosity and delinquency?

3. How might higher education be seen as a social system? Be specific in your answer.

4. Compare and contrast functionalism and conflict theory regarding Paige's research. Which perspective best explains Paige's major findings. Why?

CHAPTER OUTLINE

Instincts.   "Hard-wired" behavior in a
                                    species.

Heredity.
    Genotype.   Sum total of genetic
                                    instructions from parents.
        Phenotype.   Actual product of interplay
                                    between genotype and
                                    environment.

Behavioral Genetics.   Study of genetic underpinnings
                                    of traits and behavior.
                                    Especially helpful research
                                    based upon identical twins
                                    reared separately.

The Growth Revolution.
    Environmental Suppressors.   Removal of suppressors (e.g.,
                                    poor diet, inadequate health
                                    care, and poor sanitation) has
                                    been main reason for tremendous
                                    spurt in physical growth in
                                    twentieth century.

Hormones and Behavior.   A study of Viet Nam veterans
                                    found strong evidence that
                                    elevated testosterone levels is
                                    highly correlated with many
                                    less than valued behaviors.

Humans and Other Animals.   Ambivalence of social
                                    scientists regarding humans'
                                    relationship to "lower" animals
                                    is illustrated by the belief in
                                    the intellectual superiority
                                    and moral inferiority of
                                    humans.
    Primate Studies.   Demonstrated that humans are
                                    not *that* intellectually
                                    superior (see Washoe and sign
                                    language) and we are not that
                                    morally inferior (see Goodall's
                                    observations of murderous
                                    chimps). Also, studies of
                                    chimps and macaques illustrate
                                    significant complexity in
                                    social structure.

SUMMARY

   Instincts. Earlier in this century instincts (behavior
that is "hard-wired" into a species) was a prominent idea in
explaining human behavior. By the 1930s the theoretical
pendulum had swung the other way, and the social sciences
were ruled by environmental theories. However, today the
absolute environmentalist position is judged to be as
extreme as the absolute hereditary position it was reacting
against. Few social scientists accept that humans have
instincts, but most believe that human beings are the result
of the interplay between their biology and their social and
cultural environment.

   Heredity. The sum total of the genetic instructions
that an organism receives from its parents is called the
genotype. However, the environment often prevents the
genotype's full potential from being reached. What
actually comes about as the product of the interplay
between biology and environment is the organism's
phenotype. (It should be noted that much of a person's
genetic inheritance does not show up in his or her
phenotype, but it can show up in the phenotype of that
person's children.)

   Behavioral Genetics. As a separate field behavioral
genetics is in its infancy. Still, many traits have been
said to have a genetic component--for example, intelligence,
major forms of mental disorder, and alcoholism. In order to
estimate the genetic contribution to behavior, it is
imperative to study humans in which biological and
environmental contributions can be adequately controlled.
To that end perhaps the most important resource in studying
human behavioral genetics is twins. Since most twins are
fraternal (with differing genetic material), they are not
what the Ph.D. ordered. Much more valuable (and more
scarce) are identical twins (those who possess the same
genetic content). However, to study identical twins raised
in the same household does not clarify the nature vs.
nurture argument since one can easily argue that any given
similarity is due to similar upbringing. So, what is needed
are studies of identical twins raised separately. In fact,
many such studies conducted in several countries have shown
that the IQs of identical twins raised apart are extremely
similar but not identical. (Perhaps as much as 70 percent of
the variation in intelligence is caused by genetic
variation.) Further, other twins studies indicate a
significant genetic component to schizophrenia and
depressive disorders. Finally, alcoholism also shows a
strong genetic component. None of these studies says that
genetics determines behavior. All of the above phenomena
show significant environmental variance. These studies seem

to show the nature vs. nurture debate is wrongheaded. Academic turf wars notwithstanding, it is more appropriate to try to determine exactly what is the biological and environmental contribution to the specific behavior being studied.

The Growth Revolution. Nowhere is the dynamic interplay between biology and environment better illustrated than with the changes in size and growth among humans in the twentieth century. Table 5-1 shows the dramatic changes in height in Americans over the past several generations. Cohorts of American males born between 1956 and 1962 are three times as likely to be taller than 6 feet than their grandfathers' generation (born between 1906 and 1915). For females, the results have been even more striking: The later cohort is about five times more likely to be over 5 feet 5 inches than their grandmothers' generation. The other point to note is that these increases in height are occurring earlier in the life span: We now reach almost all of our adult height by age 18. Thus, our genotypical potential is being reached more fully and faster than just two generations ago. The major reason for this is the removal of environmental suppressors such as poor diet, inadequate health care, and bad sanitation.

Hormones and Behavior. Though long suspected, it has only been very recently that hormones have been demonstrated to have direct impact on human behavior. For example, recent research by the U.S. Centers for Disease Control on Viet Nam veterans showed that the higher the testosterone level the more likely men were to get divorced, physically abuse their wives, have many sexual partners, have drug problems, be in trouble with the law (both as a juvenile and as an adult), and be unemployed. Also, higher levels of testosterone correlated with less likelhood in marrying, in acquiring advanced education, and in obtaining a high status occupation.

Humans and Other Animals. Social scientists have long held ambivalent views as to the relationship between humans and the so-called lower animals. One view has stressed the tremendous *intellectual superiority of humans;* the other has stressed the *moral inferiority of humans.* The notion of intellectual superiority drew for evidence upon the self-evident claim that only humans possessed culture and only humans had the capacity to acquire language with which to learn and share culture. The idea of moral inferiority argued that because of our mental superiority we were cursed with the capacity to lie, envy, steal, murder, etc. The lower animals, lacking our powers and relying on instinct, naively and innocently played out their lives. As is so often the case, both views were overstated.

Jane Goodall's thirty years studying the chimpanzees of Gombe saw chimps making and using tools. As Stark states, "In order to keep our ancestors within the human race, we must accept the very simple definition of tools as purposeful alterations of objects [and thus] we must acknowledge the existence of technology among nonhumans such as...chimpanzees." To her dismay, Goodall has also seen her chimps kill and eat young baboons and murder other chimps.

Other studies with monkeys outside of their natural habitats have shown other remarkable similarities with humans. For example, the pioneering work of Harlow showed that rhesus monkeys raised in total isolation from other monkeys presented very abnormal behaviors. Further, even monkeys raised in isolation with their mothers were nearly as abnormal as those raised in total isolation. Moreover, many of the effects seem irreversible.

Still other research on language use in monkeys has proven even more fascinating. After the Kelloggs' early failed attempt to teach Viki the ape to reproduce human speech, the Gardiners decided to try to teach their chimp Washoe American sign language. Washoe was a stunning success at this as evidenced by her ability to speak with and understand deaf humans with whom she had no previous contact. Moreover, she has been observed teaching her adopted son, Loulis, sign language. She has also been observed swearing. However, despite the initial excitement over primate communication, research emphasis has shifted to social structure.

A study of transplanted macaques found that the group that was moved to Oregon established their dominance hierarchies by young males fighting among themselves. This differed dramatically from their original state of nature in Japan where male-dominance hierarchies were established by the fighting ferocity and prowess of the males' mothers. Thus, we can say that culture, tool making and use, social structure, and facility with human language are not the exclusive preserve of humans. Put another way, in these most rudimentary and crucial aspects of social life humans are not alone and they differ from the "lower" animals only in degree, not in kind.

TEACHING SUGGESTIONS

The objective of Chapter 5 is twofold. First, biology is a significant factor in most human development and much human behavior. Second, without social interaction all biological potential in humans remains undeveloped.

1. Discussion: "Gender Identity and Gender Reassignment." Gender identity is so fundamental to all of us that we tend to simply assume that unless something is drastically

wrong/flawed with a person then biological males will inexorably grow up male and females female. However, to illustrate the dynamic interplay between biology and culture, research by John Money shows that at birth humans are psychosexually neuter and that one's biological sex is mainly separate from one's gender status. Specifically, Money's research has demonstrated, to his satisfaction, that the gender "option" is open at birth and remains open for upward of two years for normal infants. The discussion is very useful in showing students that they could, under certain circumstances, be their "opposite number," and thus demonstrates the real-world and conceptual difference between one's sex and one's gender.

Source: Money, J., and P. Tucker. Sexual Signatures: On Being a Man or a Woman. Boston: Little, Brown 1976. An excellent source complete with case studies.

2. Discussion-Lecture: Another way of engaging students in the biology-culture interplay is by talking about reasons for male dominance--seemingly throughout our time on Earth.

[Instructor's note: By writing the students' reasons on the board--they'll usually fall into two groups: biological and cultural you can refer to them when it is time to lecture.] I like to start with Goldberg's "inevitability of patriarchy" statement and follow with Epstein's cultural determinist argument. Finally, I close with Harris's cultural ecological speculations. Great fun on a serious subject.

Sources: Epstein, C. Deceptive Distinctions: Sex, Gender, and the Social Order. New Haven: Yale University Press, 1988.

Goldberg, S. The Inevitability of Patriarchy, rev. ed. New York: William Morrow, 1974.

Harris, M. "Why Men Dominate Women." New York Times Magazine. (November 13, 1977): 46, 115, 117, 123.

3. Lecture: "Social Isolation: Or Why Biology Is Not Enough." Another way of showing students how human development is absolutely dependent upon the interplay of culture and biology is by telling them, via case studies, what happens to young children under circumstances of extreme neglect. I describe three such cases for them: Anna, Isabell, and Genie. Over the years, I have found that this has been one of my most effective teaching resources.

Sources: Curtiss, S. Genie. New York: Academic Press, 1977.

Davis, K. Human Society. New York: Macmillan, 1949, pp. 204-208.

4. Discussion: "Monkey Business." The instructor can lead the class in a discussion that would first explore how from the 1930s into the 1960s the dominant view of the behavioral

sciences posited that humans alone possessed culture and a
learned social organization. Since that time the argument
has shifted to trying to argue a uniqueness for humans based
upon their superior mental processes. However, much recent
research has called that absolutist position into question.
This discussion can extend the foundation laid by Stark of a
topic that the students always find very interesting. By
examining animals other than humans and illustrating some of
their truly fascinating capabilities, instructors can give
students another perspective on the human species.

Sources: Lampe, D. "Give Me a Home Where the Snow
Monkeys Roam." Discovery (July 1988) 36-43. Further
adventures of transplanted Japanese macaques emphasizing
their evolving social organization and the financial
problems associated with keeping them.

Linden, E. Apes, Men, and Language. New York:
Penguin Books, 1981. An excellent account of the issues
and findings in this area. Linden, an investigative
reporter, writes extremely well and introduces such
wonderful creatures as Washoe, Lucy, and Sarah.

Meddin, J. "Chimpanzees, Symbols, and the Reflexive
Self." Social Psychological Quarterly 6 (1979). A useful
summary of many important studies that indicate (among
other things) that in any absolute sense humans are not the
only primates that possess a reflexive self.

ADDITIONAL STUDENT READINGS

Des Pres, T. The Survivor: An Anatomy of Life in the
Death Camps. New York: Oxford University, 1976. Life,
death, survival, food, excremental filth: The most basic
biological phenomena are shown to be profoundly social in
meaning with Des Pres's treatment of survivors' accounts of
their experiences in death camps. One of those rare books
through which one is forever changed.

Farb, P. Word Play. New York: Bantam Books, 1975. A
painless introduction to language and its study. So well
written that you do not realize Farb is making many
sophisticated topics in linguistics readily understandable.

Thomas, E. The Hidden Life of Dogs. New York: Simon and
Schuster, 1992. Thomas, an anthropologist and novelist
writes perceptively and engagingly on dogs and their
putative owners: humans. Wonderful.

Thomas, E. The Tribe of Tiger: Cats and Their Culture.
New York: Simon and Schuster, 1994. Different animal; same
treatment. Thomas scores again!

ESSAY QUESTIONS

1. In trying to determine the relative influence of biology and environment in making people what and whom they are, show why studying identical twins reared apart is superior to studying fraternal twins reared apart.

2. What is meant by an environmental suppressor and imagine what some future environmental suppressors might be given present-day trends in global society.

3. By using examples from communication and social structure, demonstrate why the differences between humans and chimps are differences in degree and not differences in kind.

4. Define human nature. What do you think are the **essential** differences between human and non-human animals?

Chapter 6

CHAPTER OUTLINE

Socialization.   Learning process making
                                  infants into normal humans.

Biophysical Development.   Skeels and Dye showed how
                                  apparently retarded infants
                                  could flourish by placing them
                                  with older retarded girls.
                                  Conversely, giving infants
                                  special attention *doesn't* seem
                                  to speed up normal development.

Cognitive Development.   Piaget emphasized cognitive
                                  development as an active
                                  process in which the mind
                                  develops and functions via
                                  cognitive structures.

Language Acquisition.   For language acquisition,
                                  attachments to adults aren't
  "Motherese."   crucial. Motherese isn't
                                  particularly advantageous in
                                  language acquisition though
                                  kids who are talked to more
                                  learn to talk sooner and
                                  better.

Emergence of the Self.   Though children learn "other"
                                  words early, their initial
                                  world view is egocentric.

Personality Formation.   Drawing on Kluckhohn, all
                                  humans are similar to one
                                  another, alike with some
                                  others, and unique unto
                                  themselves.

  Culture and Personality.   This approach assumes cultural
                                  determinism (see Benedict and
                                  M. Mead). Stark argues that
                                  ecological constraints sharply
                                  influence personality
                                  development.

Differential Socialization.   Not all people in a society
                                  are socialized the same way.
                                  Gender, birth order, and adult
                                  socialization are examples of

	why. Kohn's longitudinal studies illustrated how occupational conditions of parents had an impact on expectations for and the socialization of children.
Performing Social Roles.	Goffman's dramaturgical model emphasizes role performance via impression management.
Teamwork.	When more than one person is involved in a performance.
Self-Conceptions and Roles.	Juhasz found junior high boys have more favorable self-concepts than do girls.
Sex-Role Socialization.	In pre-modern societies, gender differences are much greater both in the socialization of children and in the division of labor. Significant differences in views on childbearing obtain between societies but not between genders in any given society. DeLoache et al. found mothers reading gender-neutral books to children overwhelmingly gave characters male names. Richer found that gender expectations of play are learned from older same-gender children.

SUMMARY

Socialization. Socialization is the learning process by which infants become normal human beings, possessed of culture and able to participate in social relations. Lacking adult upbringing all children would be untamed: *feral children.*

Biophysical Development. Much development of the human infant occurs seemingly automatically, but that is only because the vast majority of infants are given adequate parenting. Skeels and Dye showed the importance of attachments in their study of infants in an orphanage who were considered so retarded that they were unfit for adoption. Infants who remained in the orphanage continued to deteriorate mentally while those transferred to an institution for the retarded and put under the care of older

mildly retarded girls actually flourished. A follow-up
study of them as adults found the transferees to be mostly
self-sufficient (many had gone on to college) while most of
those who had stayed in the orphanage had remained socially
and mentally stunted.

If the lack of adequate care can produce retardation,
can special treatment speed up normal development? Not
greatly. Most infants receive adequate stimulation and
care, and, more importantly, certain basic physical and
mental development must occur before infants can acquire
certain skills.

Cognitive Development. What we do know about the
general patterns of cognitive development is that it
normally passes through a series of stages, periods of slow
progress interrupted by sudden spurts. Piaget is perhaps the
leading figure in redirecting our thoughts about cognitive
development away from the inadequate conceptions of
stimulus-response learning theory, which treated humans as
mere passive objects responding to external stimuli. Piaget
realized this model could not account for anything novel or
creative (it could not even account for the creation of
stimulus-response theory).

Alternatively, Piaget thought the human mind develops and
functions on the basis of **cognitive structures.** His
greatest contribution was to uncover the development of the
basic rules of reason. There are, he posited, four stages
of cognitive development. The <u>sensorimotor</u> stage, which
starts at birth and ends around age 2, is characterized by
the infant's major discovery of <u>object permanence</u>: things
continue to exist even when they are out of sight. The
<u>preoperational</u> stage lasts from about 2 until 7 years and is
primarily devoted to language learning. Children at this
stage are usually unable to effectively take the role of the
other. The third stage is the <u>concrete operational</u> stage
that lasts until about age 12. Children here develop many
logical principles including the <u>rule of conservation</u> (the
shape may change but the volume of the substance is
constant). The last stage is the <u>formal operational</u> one in
which people learn to think abstractly and deduce logically.
Many people evidently never reach or cannot master this
stage of cognitive development. For example, many adults
are perplexed by hypothetical assertions such as: "Let's
assume." If it is true, as Kohlberg and Gilligan have
found, that as many as half the adults do not (cannot?)
master this stage of development, then they are trapped in a
literal interpretation of the world and are increasingly
shut out by accelerating demands of the job market.

Brown and Bellugi studied language acquisition among
preschoolers and found that young children's speech is
stripped of all but the most vital words. They also found

that parents frequently echo their children and that young children experiment with speech in ways that appear to involve a search for grammatical rules.

Attachments and Language: On close examination, two commonsensical notions about language acquisition are found to be wrong. First, specific attachments to adults don't seem to matter. Within the normal range of adult-infant attachments, variations seem unimportant. Second, **motherese**, the distinctive way parents (especially mothers) speak to children, is thought to be well suited to teaching language to children. However, kids not exposed to motherese acquire language as rapidly as those who are. The amount of verbal interaction with adults does matter: Kids who are talked to more learn to talk sooner and better.
Given the importance of parenting on the cognitive development of children and given the prevalence of single motherhood, it is no surprise that much research has recently tried to assess the impact of the latter on the former. Research findings have been mixed. The current assessment seems to be that the children of young single mothers do tend to score lower on cognitive development instruments, but that seems to be mainly due to the fact that women of less cognitive attainment tend to become teenage single mothers. Problems of spuriousness notwithstanding, cross-cultural surveys show that most people in a majority of the countries surveyed thought that "a single mother can bring up her child as well as a married couple." (In the United States only 38% agreed.) In that same survey, most people in a majority of the countries thought that "a preschool child is likely to suffer if his or her mother works." Interestingly, those surveyed in the United States scored lowest in agreement with this item.

Emergence of the Self. Bain discovered that children acquire other-related words sooner than self-related words. That is, we know "they" are out there before we learn that "we" are in here. Interestingly, Flavell's research shows that 14-year-olds can successfully take the perspective of the other and adjust accordingly when giving instructions whereas 8-year-olds cannot. So although children acquire "other" words earlier, their view of the world is egocentric before it becomes other- or sociocentric.

Personality Formation. Drawing on Kluckhohn, Stark makes the distinction that all humans are alike in that they all have a common biology, are subject to natural laws, acquire language, learn a culture, etc. Further, all humans are like some others in that they share a culture that others don't and have similar emotional reactions to certain events. Finally, all humans are like no other humans; that is, everyone is unique in the sense that everyone's biography is distinctively different.

Culture and Personality. The culture and personality approach of sociology, especially cultural anthropology, derives from the view of **cultural determinism.** Thus, to exponents of this view (Boas and especially his students Benedict and Mead), everything of importance is shaped by the culture in which one lives: "Culture is personality writ large." Mead herself thought that she had found the proof that sex roles can take just about any shape with her study of the nice Arapesh and the nasty Mundugumor. With the laid-back Arapesh, men and women had a gentle (idealized?) feminine side in which both parents were equal in their child rearing. With the Mundugumor, the temperament of both men and women was brutally masculine, which was well illustrated in their harsh child rearing. Setting aside the issue as to whether Mead saw what she wanted to see and taking her data at face value, Stark gives an alternative explanation. The Mundugumor occupied the choicest land on the island. They were surrounded by jealous, aggressive neighbors. In terms of group survival it was in the group interest for the Mundugumor adults to be fierce and to raise their children accordingly. The Arapesh occupied poor land and were very isolated—thus, no necessity to be nasty. A sample of primitive societies shows that, generally speaking, societies who have other societies close by often engage in war, prefer male infants (who are needed as future warriors), often hit their kids, emphasize aggression and competitiveness in socializing males and females, and stress the virtues of inflicting violence on outsiders. In effect, the Mundugumor profile (personality?) is explainable in terms of external pressures on the society.

In sum, the major problem with the culture and personality approach (of Mead and others) is that they overargued their position. Culture does matter but other factors do too. Human nature cannot be infinitely shaped and socialization does not terminate in childhood.

Differential Socialization. Another point against a strict culture and personality approach is that not all people in any society are socialized the same way. The most obvious and perhaps most important example of this is differential socialization by gender. Another is birth order. The excellent research by Kohn addresses differential socialization: the learning process based upon differing normative expectations. Kohn began his research on child-rearing values nearly a generation ago. He found that working-class parents placed greater stress on such values as obedience, neatness, and cleanliness than did middle-class parents who valued more such traits as curiosity, happiness, and self-control. Working-class parents were more concerned about their children conforming to the expectations of others while middle-class parents were more concerned about their children being capable of self-expression and independence. These values carried over into disciplining the children. Working-class parents punished what the child did regardless of his/her motivation while middle-class parents took intentions into account. Given that the occupational conditions of working- and middle-class people vary considerably, Kohn revised his explanation by jettisoning social class *per se* and instead focused on the actual work conditions (especially <u>degree of autonomy</u> and initiative) on the job. Thus, those with high autonomy on the job stressed self-expression and autonomy in their kids while those heavily supervised on the job stressed obedience in their children. Thus, the parents stressed in their child rearing what worked for them in their occupation. Kohn has also found considerable evidence of adult socialization in that the occupational traits of the parents' jobs shape the personalities of the parents themselves.

In a longitudinal study (the same people being surveyed at different points in time), Kohn found that certain people select certain jobs based upon personality factors but also that jobs subsequently shape personality. In sum, children are differentially socialized on the basis of parental expectations with the expectations being shaped by the parents' job experiences. For adults, socialization is a lifelong experience. Cross-cultural replications of this work in Taiwan, Italy, Japan, Ireland, Germany, and Poland have confirmed the U.S. data. There are, however, variations. For example, in more traditional Poland child rearing is almost exclusively left to the mother while in the United States fathers play a much greater role in transmitting values to their kids.

Performing Social Roles: Erving Goffman. Mention should be made of Goffman's dramaturgical theory, which stresses role performance: how people actual play their role as opposed to a mindless lock-step adherence to norms. Goffman argues that role performance is best summarized by the idea of impression management: the strong tendency of most of us to manipulate impressions to ensure a favorable image. When done in concert with others, this is known as teamwork so that when a couple throws a dinner party they coordinate their efforts frontstage (living room, dining area) and backstage (closing off a bedroom to hide the dirty laundry). If one of the guests happens to come across the laundry, he/she will practice studied nonobservance by pretending not to notice.

Self-Conceptions and Roles: Sex-Role Socialization. Cross-cultural data find that pre-modern societies are very unlikely to recognize extensive political rights for women but they are very likely to both differentially socialize the genders as youngsters and to impose a segregated division of labor on adults. Modern societies vary widely between each other but not amongst themselves in attitudes toward the value of childbearing for women.

Closer up, Juhasz has measured self-concepts on junior high schoolers and found that boys see themselves more favorably than do girls. Other studies have found that girls tend to rank male traits higher than female traits. This differential valuation of sex-role traits is due to many sources, some of which are subtle; some not. For example, DeLoache, Cassidy, and Carpenter studied mothers reading books to their children (the characters within were technically gender-neutral). The mothers overwhelmingly gave the characters male names. One could speculate that mothers are among the biggest reinforcers of traditional sex-role typing.

Another source of sex-role socialization comes from games. Richer studied the conditions at summer camp where older boys and girls might play together nonsexually. He found only one circumstance when they formed a single team: to compete with defined "outsiders." Younger children (ages 3 to 4) did not display these gender preferences; thus, Richer concluded that the gender preference play of the older children was learned primarily from still older children than they. And so it goes.

TEACHING SUGGESTIONS

The objective of Chapter 6 is to give students an appreciation for the enormous role that learning plays in our development as humans. Further, it must be emphasized that this socialization is a lifelong process.

1. **Lecture:** "Abolishing Television." This lecture would be based unabashedly upon Mander's neglected classic: Four Arguments for the Elimination of Television. In brief, Mander's case is that television is not a neutral technology but is inherently "mind-dimming," the ultimate effects of which are antihuman and certainly damaging to proper **cognitive development.** Many instructors will remember growing up in a world without television. Students will not. By presenting this lecture, students are confronted with an overwhelming fact of late twentieth century life: television is so much a part of the social environment that conceiving of its abolishment is beyond mere lunacy--it is literally inconceivable. Even if people don't watch it themselves, so much of our lives is affected by it and the profits and power of those who control it are so large that it is here to stay. This might be an interesting way to demonstrate how people can coconspire with those who would

use (exploit?) them, all the while footing the bill via paying for the commercials.

In addition to the subscriber vs. commercial television debate, a more important one would be, To what extent is using television as an escapist strategy actually making matters worse? To wit, if one argues that people watch television primarily as entertainment to escape dull, dreary, humdrum lives, then to the extent that they watch exciting escapist fare they will ingest images that are exciting, glamorous, romantic, action-packed, and so on. When they do get around to comparing (at whatever level) these images with their own gray lives, their own lives will appear--guess what?--even more drab. Therefore, this argument might go, the more you watch to escape yourself the worse you and your life seem to be, thus leading to... addiction???

Finally, one useful exercise to demonstrate the power of television and its possible analogy with hypnosis is to ask the class to close their eyes and visualize someone to whom they feel very close. Ask them to concentrate and try to "see" as much detail as possible of the other's face. Then ask them to open their eyes and clear their heads while asking rhetorically if they got a good picture of the loved one. Now ask them to repeat the exercise but this time envisage a television personality they've seen frequently. After they are done, ask them which image was clearer.

Sources: Mander, J. Four Arguments for the Elimination of Television. New York: Quill, 1978. A bit of a Don Quixote, Mander presents absolutely cogent arguments (four of them) for the abolishment of television. If one must watch television then one ought to give Mander a reading. Postman, N. Amusing Ourselves to Death. New York: Viking Press, 1986. Postman continues the assault.

2. Discussion: "The Shy, the Obnoxious, and the Nice." The instructor mentions three types of people commonly found in the world: the shy, the obnoxious, and the nice. The instructor then elicits reasons from the class why people act/are any of the above. Almost always a majority of responses will be of the "personality type" variety. The instructor then moves on to show that regardless of the motivation, people's behavior is not only "typed" but once typed relies on other complementary types: nice with obnoxious and shy with socially graceful/life of the party. Thus, one can argue: as you learn to be these types you are subtly subjected to differential socialization of a reciprocal sort. To a great extent, although the shy, the obnoxious, and the nice are not usually seen as social roles, these categories do seem to fulfill the definition of a role: a set of norms that defines how persons in a particular situation should behave. I find that this exercise is very helpful in moving students away from crude

psychological explanations for behavior and helping them to explore more social constructionist approaches.

Sources: Davis, M., and C. Schmidt. "The Obnoxious and the Nice." Sociometry 40 (1977): 201-213. In this wonderful little piece Davis and Schmidt show how the obnoxious and the nice not only are made for each other, they really do create each other.

Mencotti, L. "A Common Malady," a review of Shyness: Perspectives on Research and Treatment in Contemporary Psychiatry (December 1986): 268-269. This review takes a similar position to that of Davis and Schmidt.

3. Discussion: "The Sociology of Emotions." What could be more biopsychological than emotions? Well, this exercise helps sociology instructors show how social factors even influence that which most people perceive as intensely personal: emotions. I like to argue this from the symbolic interactionist perspective using concepts such as emotion work and feeling rules. I try to demonstrate the following ideas. First, not all emotions are universal: Romantic love isn't. Even those emotions that are universal are expressed in culturally structured ways: Grief may be universal but it certainly does vary in its expression. Second, since every complex emotion must be learned no one is born knowing how to grieve. Third, how to grieve is governed by feeling rules: norms that govern the intensity and appropriateness of grief. Last, when the feeling rule dictates something other than what you are feeling, then you must do emotion work to get your feelings in line with the normative expectation or perhaps fake it through impression-management.

Source: Hochschild, A. "Emotion Work, Feeling Rules, and Social Structure." American Journal of Sociology 84 (1979): 551-575. This is the original and well-argued statement of this position.

ADDITIONAL STUDENT READINGS

Ebaugh, H. Becoming an Ex: The Process of Role Exit. Chicago: University of Chicago Press, 1988. A former nun, Ebaugh has written a wonderful book on the socialization out of roles. Examples include widows, ex-nuns, divorcees, transsexuals, ex-prostitutes, mothers without custody, retirees, ex-alcoholics, and ex-convicts. Very readable and fills a gap in sociology.

Erikson, E. Childhood and Society, 2nd. ed. New York: Norton, 1963. Erikson expands Freud's stages of development to include the entire lifecycle while bringing in cross-cultural and historical materials to illustrate his ideas.

Ewen, S. All Consuming Images: The Politics of Style in Contemporary Culture. New York: Basic Books, 1988. One of our best commentators on the current scene is at his best in this analysis of the central role of style in our consumer culture and its impact on the creation of self image. Excellent but probably suited only to the more literate urbane students.

Rybczynski, W. Home: A Short History of an Idea. New York: Penguin, 1986. The author, an architect, traces 500 years of changes in Western attitudes toward the home and thus gives a fascinating glimpse at changes in self-conception.

Strauss, W. and N. Howe. Generations: A History of America's Future, 1584 to 2069. New York: William Morrow, 1991. The authors feel that they've discovered a cycle of four that characterizes generational differences. Massive, ambitious, fascinating, and surprisingly accessible.

Turnbull, C. The Human Cycle. New York: Simon and Schuster, 1983. An anthropologist's view of the lifecycle (without attempting to be comprehensive). Very humane; very literate. A welcome antidote to seeing all of human development through Western lenses.

ESSAY QUESTIONS

1. Explain how research on language acquisition complements Piaget's theory of cognitive development.

2. Explain Stark's alternative explanation to that of Margaret Mead's study of the temperaments of the Arapesh and Mundugumor.

3. In Kohn's longitudinal research, which is the stronger predictor of how parents will socialize their children: social class or occupational condition? Why?

4. Consider a mirror. Describe how a stereotypical male would differ from a stereotypical female in using the mirror. What evidence can you give to show how these stereotypes might be misleading in this particular context.

Chapter 7

CHAPTER OUTLINE

Crime and Deviance.
   Norms.   Social rules.
   Deviance.   Breaking norms.
   Deviants.   People who break norms.
   Crime.   The most serious kinds of deviance: acts of force or fraud undertaken in pursuit of self-interest.

Ordinary Crime.
   Robbery.   Taking possessions by force.
   Burglary.   Unlawful entry (usually for theft.)
   Homicide.   Non-negligent killing of another.
   Offender Versatility.   Career offenders are multi-talented.

The Criminal Act.   Short-range choices whose rewards are small and fleeting.

Biological Theories
   of Deviance.   Traditionally stressed inborn flaws preventing self-control and/or predisposing toward deviance.

Lombroso.   Primitive attempt to link criminals to primitive types.
   Goring.   Refuted Lombroso; found that most criminals weren't bright.
   Gove.   Emphasis on youthful males' "natural" edge in strength and aggression. Can't explain why most young males aren't particularly deviant.

Mental Illness.   Discharged mentally ill are more violent-prone than the general population.

Personality Theories.   Theories have been mostly much ado about nothing. Gottfredson and Hirschi posit weak self-control as the fundamental trait of offenders.

Elements of Self-Control.	Low self-control correlates with the need for immediate gratification, thrill-seeking, and indifference toward others.
Deviant Attachment Theories.	Stresses bad significant others.
Differential association.	Those that have excessive exposure to deviant relatives and/or friends are more likely to commit crimes.
Deviant Parents.	Kids raised by parents with little self-control are more likely to commit crimes.
Deviant Friends.	Great majority of delinquent acts done with others.
Deviant Subculture.	Likeminded deviants whose norms justify deviating from those of larger society. Cannot account for deviance within own group.
Structural Strain Theory.	Frustrating the achievement of socially acceptable goals leads to deviance/crime. Cannot explain white-collar crime.
"White-Collar" Crime.	Violations of trust by private or public officials.
Control Theory.	Asks why/when don't people deviate? Answer: Stakes in conformity--various pressures to conform.
Attachments.	Stable patterns of conforming interaction.
Investments.	Time, money, energy, and self-concept invested in conforming behavior.
Involvements.	In conforming activities.
Beliefs.	Internalization of norms.
Linden and Fillmore.	Found that teens with little to lose were more likely to be deviant; more so if they had likeminded friends.
Anomie and the Integration of Society.	Durkheim, the original control theorist, thought that anomie: normlessness, would lead to increased deviance. Modern sociology has lent much support to Durkheim's thesis.

Climate and Season.	Crime rates are seasonal: Higher temperatures and/or holidays bring people together, often for the worse.
The Labeling Approach to Deviance.	
Primary Deviance.	Everyday deviance.
Secondary Deviance.	Deviance ensuing after official reaction to primary deviance.
Drugs and Crime.	A majority of those arrested have used drugs within forty-eight hours of arrest. Drug use has become part of lifestyle of typical offender. Alcohol and cocaine (especially crack) linked with aggression.

SUMMARY

Crime and Deviance. Most people, most of the time, follow most of the social rules we call *norms*. Actively breaking norms, or not fulfilling them, results in *deviance*. Even though norms may vary from society to society all societies have norms and all societies punish those who violate important norms and/or are frequent violators of norms. Those who frequently violate important norms are called *deviants*. Still, the same norm will have different rates of violation both between and within societies. (For example, Figure 7-1 shows the tremendous range of burglary rates in the United States with Florida's rate being five times that of North Dakota. Further, Scotland's rate is nearly three times that of the average of Canada and the United States). This chapter concentrates on most serious forms of deviance: *crime--acts of force or fraud undertaken in pursuit of self-interest* and presents the more prominent of the many competing (sometimes complementary) theories of crime.

Ordinary Crime. Most crime is committed by young males involving short-range choices the rewards of which are small and fleeting. For example, most robbery are unplanned and garner less than $50 as most victims are people and not banks or stores. The average burglary is opportunistic and nets little. More murders are not being cleared by arrest (fewer than 2 in 3 do.) Murderers who are arrested are very similar to their victims: same sex, race, age, and criminal background. As with robbery and burglary, few homicides involve much planning. Career offenders tend not to specialize and are versatile though not necessarily efficient "jacks-of-all-criminal-trade."

The Criminal Act. Usually involves short-range choices whose rewards are small and fleeting but whose long term risks may be great. Most crimes are easy to commit, simple in design, and, given the element of risk, exciting to "pull off." Thus, most crimes tend to be <u>directly and immediately rewarding</u> regardless of the potential costs.

Biological Theories of Deviance. Most of these theories, from phrenology to the extra Y chromosome, stress some inborn flaw that either prevents self-control or predisposes one to deviance or both. In a phrase, this is the born criminal approach. Lombroso was the first modern prominent advocate of this notion. He believed that because of their genetic makeup, born criminals could not restrain their violent and animalistic urges. Because the reasons for their criminality are beyond their control the criminals could not be held culpable; nor should they be treated harshly. The major methodological problem with Lombroso was that he drew his sample exclusively from the prison population and assumed that the physical abnormalities associated with the criminals were found in larger proportions than the general population. However, Goring demonstrated that these traits occurred in the general population at about the same rate.

More recently, Christiansen, among others, has found strong evidence for a correlation between monozygotic (identical) twins and subsequent criminal behavior. However, exactly what (if any) the genetic contribution to criminality is has yet to be determined.

The distinctively sociological contribution to this theme of how biology might contribute to crime has been cogently explored by Gove. His approach tried to explain why gender and age influence crime so much; why arrest rates decline so steeply with age; and why age and sex effects are so much more important for certain crimes. Gove's common factor was that crimes differ in the extent to which they involve aggressive and physically demanding behavior. So, cross-culturally, males are always much more "criminal" than are females, but the rates for each (again cross-culturally) decline drastically with age. Further, males are stronger and more aggressive than females, so violent crime and/or physically demanding crime is their domain. Those crimes that require physical strength and endurance have arrest rates that peak with males in their twenties and decline afterward. Gove's argument is consistent with the evidence introduced on testosterone's effect on behavior (see Chapter 5.) As the male ages, not only do strength and endurance decline but so does testosterone and thus so does the "need" for thrill-seeking. Females, with much less testosterone to begin with, are predicted to be less violent at any age than are males. The strength of Gove's argument is that he gives a plausible biological underpinning for why crime is so much a young males' activity. What is needed is to explain why most young males (or most people generally) are not particularly deviant.

Mental Illness. Another approach attempting to separate the criminals from the rest of the population is that of personality theory (of which the mental illness argument is a major subtheme.). If the biological theorist tried to make a case for criminals who were *born bad,* the personality theorist tried something similar, stressing how criminals are *made bad,* often because of mental illness.

Until relatively recently, most research had indicated that mental patients were <u>less likely</u> to be arrested than was the general public. Presently, discharged mental patients are three times as likely as others to be arrested; especially so when looking at violent crimes. Violence-prone mental patients dumped back into the community without social supports--especially if they do not follow their regimen of drug therapy--are much more likely to be violent than is the general population. However, a note of caution: The mentally ill when they are not ill are not more dangerous than the general public.

Personality Theories. Though most attempts to link personality traits/types with criminality have come to naught, Gottfredson and Hirschi have persuasively posited that *weak self-control* is the fundamental trait of offenders. They do <u>not</u> regard weak self-control as inborn but rather socially created.

Elements of Self-Control. Low self-control involves the unwillingness/inability to defer gratification. (Thrill-seeking in crime can be interpreted as a form of immediate gratification.) Lacking in self-control is also associated with self-centeredness, and indifference to the plight and needs of others.

Deviant Attachment Theories. If it is true that attachments can be an irresistible force for conformity to norms, it can be equally true that the kind of attachments one has can lead to either law-abiding or law-breaking behavior. The deviant attachments approach has two major variants: social learning and deviant subculture. The social learning idea (originally conceived by Sutherland as differential association) sought to explain delinquency by pointing to a boy's delinquent friends. We learn from and act to please significant others--in this case, delinquent friends. Burgess and Akers took the social learning implicit in Sutherland and argued that by selective reinforcement one becomes attached to others who reward his or her deviant behavior. Even stronger support for the deviant attachments approach comes from recent research, which found that twenty-five percent of incarcerated delinquents reported their fathers had served time and fifty-two percent reported that at least one immediate family member was/is in jail. The differential association-social learning approach is most helpful in explaining why most delinquent acts occur with others and why delinquents have other delinquents for friends. It does not do as well explaining why delinquent friends end up with delinquent friends in the first place (by others rejecting them) rather than the delinquent behavior initially being rewarded by the other delinquent. Another major problem of this approach is that it cannot do justice to those deviant acts that are done in private by individuals. Thus, the strength of this approach lies in explaining the reinforcement of deviant behavior once established. How/why the deviant acts and actors come to be is somewhat more problematic.

The idea of a deviant subculture provides a context in which the differential association-social learning perspective can exist. Thus, subcultural deviance may break society's rules, but to the member of the subculture it is the height of conformity. The deviant subculture approach also draws our attention to the notion of power--who can define laws--a notion that the labeling theorists also find important. The two major problems with the subcultural approach are that it does not explain individual acts of deviance or deviance within the subculture.

Structural Strain Theory. Stark now examines a related approach: Merton's structural strain theory, which emphasizes how deviance is traceable to the frustration of achieving socially approved goals. In turn, this frustration is a direct function of one's place in the social system. Simply put, poverty breeds those criminals who accept the goals of success but use extralegal means of attaining them. There are several problems associated with this theory. First, why are the majority of the poor relatively law-abiding? Second, most crime committed by the poor pays very little. Third, what of the significant volume of crime committed by those from the more privileged strata? (See below, White-Collar Crime.) Fourth, social class and crime are not terribly related. Fifth, rather than poverty breeding criminals, it can be persuasively argued that poor areas attract the criminally inclined.

"White-Collar" Crime. Shapiro's suggestion to call these crimes violations of trust notwithstanding, the concept of white-collar crime functions as an important qualification of strain theory (which works best, when it works) in explaining lower-class criminality. However, a superficial reading of white-collar crime and strain theory would seem to imply different motivations for different social class criminalities.

   Control Theory. A very different approach to explaining crime and deviance is taken by control theorists. Taking their cue from Durkheim these sociologists address the central question of conformity: With deviant acts both attractive and available, why do so many people conform? The answer: People are free to deviate to the extent that the costs of deviance to them are low. Put another way, to the extent people have significant stakes in conformity they will conform. Among others, Hirschi has pointed to four crucial elements that determine one's stakes in conformity: attachments, investments, involvements, and beliefs. Attachments, the stable patterns of interactions between individuals, show us that we will tend to conform to the wishes of those significant others with whom we are most closely bonded be they conforming or deviant. Thus, the time of moving from puberty to young adulthood is a time of rearranging attachments, and not surprisingly rates of deviance often increase in this stage of life. In addition, because the quality of parent-child bonds varies within social classes, control theory can explain both middle-class delinquency and lower-class conformity. Furthermore, attachments to other young adults increase one's stakes in conformity and thus dampen deviant tendencies. Investments refers to the time, money, energy, and self-concept that one has put into a particular line of action. The more we have sacrificed to attain a respectable life-style the more we have at stake reinforcing our need to conform. Where investments are lowest (teen years through the twenties; among the single and recently divorced or separated), deviance will be high. Involvement simply refers to the fact that the more you involve yourself in various activities (presumably straight ones), the less time and energy you have left over to deviate. Finally, control theorists refer to conforming beliefs, sometimes called the internalization of norms. In one sense, beliefs might be seen as a dependent variable that allows people to justify the stakes in conformity that they have built up. In another way, anticipating Chapter 8 just a bit, we might say that the internalization of norms makes formal and informal social control unnecessary. By internalizing norms we become self-controlling. In sum, we can say that the great strength of control theory is the straightforward predictions one can make as to who will conform/deviate from either the larger society *or* a particular subculture.

   Linden and Fillmore: A Comparative Study of Delinquency. Linden and Fillmore extended Hirschi's original work by comparing it with a sample of Canadian students in Edmonton.

They proposed that teenagers with low stakes in conformity have little to lose by associating with other delinquents, and that such association will further amplify their delinquency as they learn new criminal techniques and are reinforced for new acts of deviance. They found that in both nations their model fit the data well. Thus, teenagers with little to lose by giving in to temptations are very likely to do so. But they are even more likely to do so if, in addition, they have friends who support them.

Anomie and the Integration of Societies. The loss of attachments results in normlessness-- anomie, as Durkheim put it. He contrasted the state of anomie as found in the large city with that of the moral community of the traditional rural village. These moral communities possessed two major components: social integration and moral integration. By social integration Durkheim meant the quality and quantity of attachments. By moral integration he meant shared moral (especially religious) beliefs. Durkheim feared the corrosive quality of the large, modern city on people's attachments and beliefs. Thus, at the macro level Durkheim was an early mass society theorist while at the micro level he was the father of control theory. For the most part, Durkheim's potentially rich schema lay fallow mostly due to methodological inadequacies.

Climate and Season. Crime rates are seasonal: in general, higher rates are found in the summer months. However, the relationship is not a simple one of higher temperatures *per se*. There are at least two complications. One, the seasonal effects are much greater in the colder northern states. Two, except for rape, crime rates hit a second peak in December. Thus, it is more accurate to conclude that higher temperatures and/or holidays bring people together, with increased opportunities for crime.

The Labeling Approach to Deviance. In effect, labeling theory emphasizes the power of some people (usually social control agents) to label others as deviant. Moreover, the labels themselves are a powerful impetus to further acts of deviance. Thus, the causal flow is

> 1. primary deviance (deviance that is the stuff of ordinary life);
> 2. coming to the attention of the authorities or public opinion, who often capriciously attach a label; and
> 3. secondary deviance (subsequent behavior due to the deviant label and perhaps deviant identity).

Liska cites three ways in which a deviant label disposes people to further deviance:

1. by limiting contacts with legitimate
   opportunities;
2. by limiting one's interpersonal contacts; and
3. by shaping one's self-concept.

Labeling theory's contributions have been to sensitize rather than reframe the field of deviance. They have alerted sociologists to the arbitrary way that norms are created and applied. Thus, as with their control theory brethren, they refocus our attention on conformity by asking why we decide to prohibit certain norms. Labeling theorists also argue that the higher a person's status, the less chance he or she will be labeled deviant. Labeling theory further shows how many attempts to stop deviance may intensify it (i.e., social control as *iatrogenic*).

With all of the theoretical richness of this approach there are problems. First, much research has not confirmed the hypothesis that people labeled as delinquents as a result of arrest and conviction subsequently increase their level of illegal activity. Second, it is not necessarily true that primary deviance is usually insignificant and harmless. For example, if the primary deviance is rape, that is both significant and harmful to the victim. Third, labeling theory can't really deal with why the person committed the primary deviant act in the first place. Fourth, much of labeling theory has a "chicken-egg" quality. For example, does doing drugs cause crime or does crime encourage drug use?

Drugs and Crime. A massive survey by the Institute for National Justice found that people arrested on felony charges will have used drugs (very likely cocaine) during the preceding forty-eight hours. While most of those arrested are males, female arrestees are even more likely to have used drugs prior to arrest. It would seem that since drug-taking has become part of the typical lifestyle of the chronic offender, concepts such as primary and secondary deviance (when applied to chronic offenders) blur and lose much of their salience. The evidence is very convincing for a direct link between both alcohol and cocaine (especially "crack") and violence. There is also a strong correlation between drugs and property crime although it is obvious, upon reflection, that offenders steal/rob to buy other things besides drugs. Finally, it should be noted that most offenders were introduced to drugs *after* they had started to offend.

Conclusion. While there is no one comprehensive theory that includes all of what sociologists find of interest in this area it seems that control theory comes closest. All the other theories are able to be explicitly linked with control theory or be potentially subsumable within it.

TEACHING SUGGESTIONS

The objective of Chapter 7 is to show students how sociologists can offer unique approaches in explaining why people deviate.

1. **Discussion:** "Gay Rights and Gay-Bashing." One of the hottest of the 1990s "culture wars" is the legitimacy of homosexuality and homosexuals in society.

[Instructor's note: I assume, and it is reflected in this discussion, that homosexuals are people first with sexual orientations that are seen by many/most others as deviant. I further assume that most of class identifies themselves as straight.]

You might want to ease into this by first asking the class to write down their thoughts on their acceptance of gays and, if applicable, what is more difficult for them to accept (and why): a gay, a lesbian, or a bisexual. You might want to ask them to do this anonymously as an exercise to hand in in conjunction with participating in a quasi-social distance scale adapted to the issue of homosexuality. For example, ask them, if they had their "druthers," would it be acceptable for homosexuals to:

    1. be in the country (United States/Canada);
    2. participate in your work group (e.g., in class);
    3. live in your neighborhood (dormitory?);
    4. participate in your voluntary organization (e.g., fraternity/sorority);
    5. be a personal friend;
    6. become kin by marriage;
    7. Would you consider dating a gay person?
    8. Would you consider having sex with a gay person?
    9. Would you consider marrying a gay person?

[Instructor's notes: Remember that numbers 7,8, and 9 do not imply that the student is gay but only that the person that the student might date, have sex with, or marry is a gay person. You may or may not want to bring this up to students ahead of time. Also, you may want to make finer distinctions by applying each of these situations to gay males, lesbians, bisexual males, and bisexual females.]

If you initially define homophobia as avoidance of and/or discrimination against gays, then you might want to ask the class, At which of the above thresholds does homophobia begin for you? I would bet that for most heterosexuals the notions of dating, let alone marrying, a homosexual are out of the question. But perhaps, for dating at least, the key is "knowingly." If any of the heterosexual students are at all active socially, the chances are not remote that they have dated a person who was bisexual or gay but in the closet. Ask them how they could "tell" who was what.

You might now vary the social distance idea by asking for arguments as to why gays should/not be allowed to marry.

If allowed to marry should they be allowed to raise
children, by adoption or a previous marriage, or, in the
case of lesbians by artificial insemination?

[Instructor's note: On the issue of gays raising children
I have found the following to be a very interesting exchange
between professor and students.]

Student A:	Gays can't raise kids to be straight; they would raise them to be gay.
Professor:	But don't straight parents have gay children? Gays had to have had straight parents, no? Did these parents raise their kids to be gay?
Student B:	No, they didn't raise them that way. Gays are born that way.
Professor:	But if gays (and straights) are born "that way" then children raised by gays will be what they are meant to be not what their parents are
Student C:	But wouldn't a child born to be straight be confused if he or she is raised by gays neither of whom is a same-gender role model?
Professor:	Yes, but would those children be any more confused about their gender identity than are "born to be straight" children who are not raised with the same gender role model? Example: a boy raised by a heterosexual single mother.
Student D:	Do we have to assume that gays are always born that way?
Professor:	Of course not.

At this juncture you may want to bring up situational
homosexuality (summer camps, military barracks, prison,
dormitories) and thus make the crucial distinction between
behavior and identity. You can also point out that many
people identify themselves as gay or bisexual but for
extended periods practice heterosexuality.

Interestingly, what people do in their private lives,
especially concerning marriage and children, often meets
with more homophobia than rights/nonrights for gays in
occupations. Still, if you feel particularly venturesome,
ask the class what they feel about gays in the military;
as primary school/day care workers; as health care
professionals? Ask them to defend, on practical not
ideological/religious grounds, why they think homosexuals
should or should not be allowed to legally pursue any of
these occupations.

Now you can expand the definition of homophobia to
include hatred and/or fear of gays. If you're still game,
it might be lively to ask the class why young, stridently
heterosexual males are in the forefront of gay-bashing. You
can have some fun by challenging the notion that gay males

threaten straight males' masculinity. After all, if gay
males are *that* "devalued" as males how could they *possibly*
be a threat to secure, privileged straight males? For more
fun, you could posit that the real threats to straight
males' masculinity would be lesbians, because they don't buy
into the whole male dominance package.

   In turn, this could lead to a discussion of changing and
challenging conceptions of masculinity and scapegoating. To
show the class that stereotypes of homo- and heterosexuality
are woefully simplistic, consider discussing with them the
many key elements that go into one's sexuality. First,
there is *biology*. Is one born male or female? Second,
there is one's *gender status:* man/woman. Third, there is
the degree of *convergence* between one's gender status and
one's "comfort zone," i.e., regardless of which gender one
is assigned, does one see oneself as more masculine or more
feminine. Fourth, there is one's *sexual orientation:* heterosexual, bisexual, gay, or lesbian. Fifth, there is one's
actual *sexual behavior:* from (1) exclusively heterosexual,
                               (2) mostly heterosexual,
                               (3) approximately equally
                                   heterosexual and homosexual,
                               (4) mostly homosexual,
                   to   (5) exclusively homosexual.

   At this juncture you can show how variable the outcomes
can be once you start combining the five elements. Finally,
you could make some open-ended observations on the self-
hatred that so many gay males and lesbians experience as a
way of looking at the widespread and pernicious side of
homophobia in the larger culture and then wrap up the
discussion by asking the following question concerning
heterosexism: Does the assumption that everyone should be
heterosexual imply a latent homophobia?

2. **Lecture:** "The Data Do Not Speak For Themselves." I find
the following exercise can do double-duty. In addition to
the title showing how data do not speak for themselves, the
variables can be used as a basis for debate as to what might
be intentional and what might be impulsive factors in
behavior: deviant or conformist. Progressively, the same
set of data is presented in several different ways. I have
found that the most successful way of conducting this
exercise is to write the data on the blackboard with the
students dutifully writing the stuff down in their
notebooks. Be specific when asking them to do this since it
involves the students; don't tip them as to what the final
data look like (as would be the case if you handed out
photo-duplicates of the presentations). The data are
derived from the same study. Although the instructor can
tailor both the study and the presentation to suit his/her
needs, this demonstration requires (as will become obvious)
that the same data be used in each presentation.

The exercise that I have found useful is a study in which several university students participated in a lab experiment. Initially, they completed a learning task and the experimenter arbitrarily gave half of them a negative rating (in order to provoke them). For the next stage, two-thirds were shown slides: one-third saw slides of weapons, one-third saw furniture (the other third was not shown anything). In the last stage, all of the subjects (provoked or not; exposed to slides or not) were given fifteen chances to give a "target" electric "shocks" as "punishment" for making mistakes on a task.

I simplify matters by showing only two of the three groups: those who were shown weapons slides and those who were not shown any slides. I argue that regardless of which group of data is shown as long as you show the identical data in alternative ways you can demonstrate the intended point: how data are "packaged" is crucial to its argument.

[Instructor's note: The maximum intensity of the shock in all variations was 12, and all scores shown are means.]

First presentation of the data

| Provocation/ | Gender | | |
exposure to slides	Males	Females	Difference
Provoked--shown weapons	8.2	6.8	1.4
Provoked--shown nothing	5.7	4.8	0.9
Not provoked--shown weapons	4.2	3.5	0.7
Not provoked--shown nothing	3.4	2.5	0.9

As can be readily deduced when looking at differences by gender, the differences are slight (to say the least). This finding tends to disappoint the "inherent differences between the sexes" advocates (which I have found are fairly equally divided by gender).

Second Presentation of the Data

| Gender/ | shown | | |
provocation	slides of weapons	nothing	Difference
Males--provoked	8.2	5.7	2.5
Males--not provoked	4.2	3.4	0.8
Females--provoked	6.8	4.8	2.0
Females--not prov.	3.5	2.5	1.0

In this second presentation for the same data, there seems to be a greater magnitude of differences by exposure to the aggression stimulus than when just looking at differences between the genders. This "finding" usually excites the gun-control and/or media watchdog advocates while further depressing the "inherently aggressive males" adherents.

Third Presentation of the Data

Provocation

Gender/ exposure	Provoked	Not provoked	Difference
Males--weapons	8.2	4.2	4.0
Males--nothing	5.7	3.4	2.3
Females--weapons	6.8	3.5	3.3
Females--nothing	4.8	2.5	2.3

The first point about the third presentation is that those who were provoked were consistently more aggressive than those who were not. More importantly, this "finding" is not readily apparent until the data are presented in this fashion. Further, when inspecting the difference column, we see that the sum of the magnitudes of difference is greater in the third presentation than in either of the other two. Next, the least magnitude of difference in the third presentation (provoked vs. unprovoked for both males and females who were shown nothing = 2.3) is almost as large as the greatest magnitude of difference in the second presentation and is three times that of the least magnitude of difference in the first presentation. Finally, females who are shown nothing but who have been provoked have a mean score of aggression greater than that of males who have been shown slides of weapons but who have not been provoked. As you might expect students can find this last point provocative.

Source: Caprara, G., et al. "The Eliciting of Cue Value of Aggressive Slides Reconsidered in a Personalogical Perspective: The Weapons Effect and Irritability." European Journal of Social Psychology 14 (1984): 313-322.

ADDITIONAL STUDENT READINGS

Best J., and T. Luckenbill. "The Social Organization of Deviants." Social Problems 28 (1980): 14-28. An excellent piece, that can put a lot into perspective for the beginning student, the authors specify five types of deviant patterns: loners, colleagues, peers, mobs, and organizations.

Chambliss, W. "The Saints and the Roughnecks." _Society_ 11 (1973): 24-31. Two groups of youths (one middleclass, the other lowerclass) engage in rowdy behavior and guess which one is seen as delinquent. A vindication (partial) of labeling theory.

Kirk, S. and H. Kutchins. _The Selling of DSM: The Rhetoric of Science in Psychiatry_. Hawthorne, New York: Aldine de Gruyter, 1992. A bit of an expose of the psychiatric conceit that diagnostic categories are valid indicators of genuine diseases. Very enlightening.

Weatherford, J. _Porn Row: An Inside Look at the Sex-for-Sale District of a Major American City_. Weatherford, an anthropologist, goes into the field for some observations. Working as a clerk in an adult bookstore-peep show, he examines the denizens of this particular subculture. Interlaced with these insights are even more eye-opening observations contrasting sexual practices of primitive tribes with those of contemporary Americans.

Weinberg T., and G. Falk. "The Social Organization of Sadism and Masochism." _Deviant Behavior_ 1 (1980): 379-393. This piece gives a sociological treatment of the seemingly bizarre. Although it can be read on its own, it makes more sense to assign it as a companion piece to the Best and Luckenbill article.

ESSAY QUESTIONS

1. Choose any two of the following: biological theory of Gove, personality theory, deviant attachments, structural strain, control theory, and labeling theory. Show why one is superior to the other in explaining deviance. Show why the other is superior in explaining crime.

2. Explain why deviant subcultures imply differential association but why differential association does not necessarily imply deviant subcultures.

3. Apply the idea of deviant subculture to the perspective of control theory in explaining how one can conform and commit a crime while performing the same act.

4. How might labeling theory complement structural strain theory's analysis of how poverty can create crime?

CHAPTER OUTLINE

Informal Control.   Major source is attachments to
                                     conforming others facilitated
                                     by internalization of norms
                                     resulting in self-control.
  Group Pressure.   Can check impulses to deviate:
                                     Asch and Schachter experiments.

Formal Control.   When informal control is
                                     ineffective then official means
                                     are often invoked.

Prevention.   Denying deviants the motivation
                                     or opportunity to break norms.
                                     Cambridge-Somerville: classic
                                     experiment in which boys
                                     exposed to delinquency
                                     prevention programs were no
                                     less likely to be convicted
                                     than control group. Set the
                                     standard for the failure of
                                     delinquency prevention.
  Opportunity Theory.   Emphasizes the absence of
                                     effective guardians.

Deterrence.   Use/threat of punishment. To
                                     be effective, must be perceived
                                     as swift, certain, and severe.

Capital Punishment.   Research is mixed as to
                                     effectiveness in deterring
                                     homicide.

The Wheels of Justice.   In North America punishment is
                                     not certain, nor swift, nor
                                     severe, although the United
                                     States has the world's highest
  Incarceration Rate.   rate of imprisonment which is
                                     not overly effective as further
  Recidivism Rate.   deterrent since the rate of
                                     rearrest is so high.

Reform and Resocialization.   TARP experiment: released
                                     convicts receiving monies to
                                     tide them over until they could
                                     find legitimate employment had
                                     no lower a recidivism rate than
                                     a control group.

SUMMARY

Chapter 8 deals with all of the collective efforts to ensure conformity to group norms--that is, social control.

   Informal Social Control. Attachments to conforming significant others are the major source of informal social control (the control that results as an everyday by-product of social interaction). Exposure to a consistent set of group norms over an extended period of time usually results in the internalization of those norms that functions as the basis of informal social control. In this sense, people usually are self-controlling. However, since humans are social beasts there is also the strong tendency to conform to the expectations and reactions of others around them, which is called group pressure. Asch's experiments were classic examples of just how strong group pressure can be. In one experiment, subjects were asked to compare lengths of lines when all of the others present (confederates of Asch) gave obviously wrong answers. While practically all subjects withstood group pressure in the beginning, 75 per cent eventually went along with the confederates at least some of the time. Further, almost one-third of the subjects went along with the confederates' judgments at least half of the time and only 25 per cent refused to yield at all. Perhaps the most significant aspect of the Asch experiment is the high degree of conformity with the judgments of strangers. With variations on his experimental theme, Asch found that the influence of group pressure depended not so much on the absolute size of the group but on the unanimity of the confederates. When just one of the confederates defected to the subject, only 5 per cent of the subjects conformed half the time.
   At about the same time, Schachter conducted research that focused on a different problem. Here, however, the confederates would be in a minority while the subjects comprised a majority. The ostensible focus of the experiment was to determine attitudes toward a young male on death row. The deviants would express contrarian opinions, and when they did so they immediately became the center of attention. Then when they stuck to their position, the majority subjects subsequently gave them less attention. Finally, everyone among the subjects was liked, save the deviants. One variation of this experiment found Schachter introducing a second deviant into the proceedings except that this deviant (the slider) would at first take a strong contrary stand but would then "come around." This person was not so disliked as the steadfast deviant but not as well liked as the subjects themselves.

   Formal Social Control. Most of the time, informal social control works well enough in interactions between people who have formed attachments. For that matter, most of the time, strangers behave decently to each other. What happens when serious normative violations occur? At this point, formal social control efforts are needed. As opposed to informal control where group members exercise pressure incidental to their particular status with formal social control, those that exercise pressure are paid to do it (for example, the police, the courts, the prisons, etc.). It is their job to enforce conformity.

Prevention. One way of denying deviants their deviance is to deny them the opportunity or the motivation to break norms. Opportunity theory emphasizes the absence of effective guardians of victims whether they are people or property. For example, female employment has increased suitable targets (affluence breeds more goodies) and has also increased opportunity (empty homes) for daytime burglary. Neighborhood-watch and home security systems are two responses to the effective guardian problem. Further, these ideas have been applied to the urban structure itself, with the sweeping generalization that anything that functions as a magnet for the young (the location of a high school or a fast-food restaurant) will increase crime in the immediate area.

However, most attention has been directed to preventing crime and deviance via efforts at (re) socialization so that deviant motives are redirected along more conventional lines. An early classic attempt to do just that was the Cambridge-Somerville experiment. A decade-long delinquency prevention project, it began late in the Depression by randomly assigning 650 young boys (average age = 11) into two groups. The 325 boys in the experimental group were furnished with free health care, tutoring, vacations at summer camps, field trips, an elaborate recreational program, and individual counseling. The control group of 325 were left alone. When all of the boys had reached 18, the researchers, much to their understandable dismay, found that 40% of the control group and 40% of the experimental group had been convicted of a crime. A follow-up study by McCord and McCord of these men as young adults found no difference in criminality. Research since the Cambridge-Somerville project has been done assessing various delinquency prevention programs--all of them singularly unsuccessful. Recently, however, Patterson has had some success in his approach that starts with the premise that many delinquents never outgrow the selfish, aggressive, antisocial behavior that is normal for 2- and 3-year-olds. The reason is poor parenting. Thus, training adults to be better parents may strengthen weak attachments within a family; simply providing a kid with a counselor is not an adequate substitute for parents or close friends, and a typical delinquency program fails to give kids a stake in conformity and it may even do the reverse. Kids who mess up do not risk being kicked out of a delinquency program.

Deterrence. Deterrence is the use/threat of punishment to dissuade people from deviance. Gibbs' deterrence theory, simply stated, is: the more rapid, the more certain, and the more severe the punishment for a crime, the lower the rate at which such crime will occur. All three conditions are needed for deterrence to work, and what counts is not the objective swiftness, certainty, and severity of the punishment but rather people's perceptions of them. Thus, one might predict that different parts of the social structure will have differing perceptions of punishment and thus deterrence will vary accordingly.

Capital punishment is the ultimate form of deterrence in that it prevents the offender from ever committing the offending deviant act (or any other act) again, and it is probably the most controversial aspect of the deterrence theory debate. The history of capital punishment has been long if not glorious. In the twentieth century, Canada abandoned it while it was temporarily prohibited in the United States a generation ago. However, by the late 1980s, more than 2,000 prisoners were on death row. The opposition to capital punishment may be due to religious belief, or grounded in charges of racial discrimination; or because of fears of the brutalizing effect on the public. For years, it was stated that capital punishment had no deterrence effect. Then about fifteen years ago, Isaac Ehrlich published a study using advanced statistical techniques and claimed that each execution prevented eight additional homicides. Amid the controversy that Ehrlich's research has elicited, much subsequent research has failed to find for or against capital punishment as an effective deterrent of homicide.

The Wheels of Justice. Extending the discussion of deterrence leads us to the criminal justice system and the basic and important question: Are those North Americans who confront the system certain that they will be punished, swiftly and severely? The answer is no! The probability of being punished for any given crime is extremely low. One reason is that only about half of all crimes are reported to the police. Another reason is that of those reported most are not cleared by arrest (although this is less true for violent crimes). (Table 8-3 illustrates cross-nationally how similar are the rates of serious crime cleared by arrest. The United States seems to do a rather poor job of clearing such offenses as homicde, rape, assault, and vehicle theft. Overall, only Sweden is worse.) Even with an arrest, there are other considerations. Arrests can be dismissed because of shortcomings in the arrest procedure itself. There can also be problems with the sufficiency of evidence. In addition, if a case has made it this far in the criminal justice system, it will probably be plea bargained to a lesser offense and often the offender will be placed on probation or end up serving a fraction of the original sentence. So that for every 1,000 felonies committed in a given year, three will result in someone being sentenced to more than a year in prison. This is particularly sobering since despite this very low rate of doing "serious time" the United States has the world's highest incarceration rate. That incarceration is not working is demonstrated by the fact that the recidivism rate (three years after release) is 59.5% for violent criminals and 78.4% for property offenders.

   Reform and Resocialization. Ironically, these most brutalizing places we call prisons were seen to be humane alternatives to the historic patterns of torture and execution. The Quakers tried to experiment with offenders by putting them in places where they would become "penitent" of their sins in an almost monastic atmosphere. Early in the nineteenth century, the Auburn plan set the model for the modern prison, both architecturally and ideologically. Since the 1940s most prisons have not been able to provide meaningful jobs to inmates so they could at least help earn their own keep. Consequently, it now costs more than $40,000 to keep each prisoner per year. Attempts at resocialization within the prison context yield few positive results. Whether you argue the failure of resocialization from labeling theory (the stigma of the label of ex-con) or from control theory (the lack of conforming attachments), the result is the same: a very high recidivism rate. The major reason for the high rate is that ex-convicts often have little to lose by subsequent deviance. This being the case, the TARP experiment provided salaries for randomly selected adult male and female prisoners, and their rearrest rate (after one year of release) was compared to that of a control group. A 49% rearrest rate was found for both groups. Just as delinquency prevention programs have been notable failures, so too have been postincarceration programs for adult offenders. Ultimately, prisons do one thing well: They incapacitate inmates by isolating them temporarily from mainstream society.

TEACHING SUGGESTIONS

The objective of Chapter 8 is to demonstrate to students how the idea of social control, especially formal social control, is absolutely crucial to the full understanding of crime and deviance. As such, these learning exercises assume that Chapter 8 will be covered after Chapter 7.

1. **Lecture/Discussion:** "How Do Authorities Create Deviance and Crime?" This begins as a focused discussion in which the instructor asks the class to suggest various ways in which those in authority actually create crime and deviance--in other words, how might formal social control agents create that which will be treated as crime. This exercise will show students the distinction between how crimes are created via classification and legislation and how crimes are created by *commissions* and *omissions* of those in authority. Further, it will show them how, in a literal sense, deviance and crime are impossible without social control; that is, social control is neither merely preventative nor reactive but is actually creative of deviance and crime. This exercise can also illustrate the power of various groups, agencies, and organizations in defining who is deviant and/or criminal and who isn't. One contemporary way of organizing some of the derivative issues is by talking about the issue of legalizing drugs, especially pot, heroin, and cocaine. This is guaranteed to get and keep the students involved.

At some point you should introduce data showing how blacks suffer disproportionate to their numbers with regard to arrest for drug offenses. For example, the arrest ratio of blacks to whites is:

  2:1 in New York
  4:1 in Philadelphia
  14:1 in Pittsburgh. For the nation overall, the

ratios are 6:1 in the suburbs
  4:1 in the central cities
  3:1 in small towns. Yet estimates of illegal drug use is 1:6 and the "guesstimates" of drug selling is that at least as many whites as blacks deal. These are daunting ratios indeed.

Sources: Becker, H. Outsiders: Studies in the Sociology of Deviance. New York: Free Press, 1965. The old standard. Cohen, S. Visions of Social Control. New York: Polity Press, 1985. The new standard and more. In this area, *the* work on modern trends in formal social control.
Kleiman, M. Against Excess: Drug Policy for Results. New York: Basic Books, 1992. A very thorough and well reasoned appeal to a policy of moderation it is sure to displease libertarians as well as sero-tolerance advocates.
Marx, G. "Ironies of Social Control: Authorities as Contributors to Deviance Through Escalation, Nonenforcement, and Covert Facilitation." Social Problems (February 1981): 221-233. Excellent and thoughtful.
Pitts, J. "Social Control: The Concept." In The International Encyclopedia of the Social Sciences. David Sills, ed. New York: Macmillan, 1968, Vol. 14, 381-396. Although this is a "souped-up" Parsonian treatment of social control, Pitts writes so well and has such wonderful insights that this piece "wears" remarkably well.

For the pro and con on legalizing drugs, I recommend
Mills, C., "The War on Drugs: Is It Time to Surrender?" and
Wilson, J., and J. DiIulio, "Crackdown." Both are found in
Finsterbusch, K., and G. McKenna, <u>Taking Sides: Clashing</u>
<u>Views on Controversial Issues</u>. 6th ed. Guilford, Conn.:
Dushkin Publishing Group, 1990, pp. 270-287.

2. **Demonstration/Discussion:** "Why Conformity?" When it
comes to deviance and crime, I am an advocate of control
theory. Several semesters ago while trying to illustrate
the primacy of informal social control in our everyday
lives, I devised the following exercise. I distribute the
following narrative to students and ask them to take a few
minutes to read it carefully. Afterward, I ask them to jot
down some impressions as to what kind of person they think
"X" represents.

   1. X gets up around 6 AM and like most mornings puts on
some coffee and then takes a shower though not particularly
dirty. X drinks absent-mindedly while scanning the front
page of the paper. Two cups of coffee later (the first of
eight to be drunk that day despite the family doctor's
chiding), the day's dark wool suit nicely in place, and one
last yell upstairs for the kids and spouse to get moving X
is out the door and off to work.

   2.   Once at the office X looks over the mail and sees a
memo from the president, who has talked with counsel and
advises a particular course of action over an affirmative
action suit that has been filed regarding a recent hiring.
The search committee was chaired by X and though personally
insulted over the implication of being a party to any
"--ist" practices, X's natural wariness of such legal
entanglements leads X to agree with the president's advice.

   3.   Another memo asks for employee volunteers for
community service. X eagerly sits down at the computer and
types an e-mail acceptance, as the effort seems to deal with
helping the disadvantaged to help themselves (X believes in
this fervently since this is the route to whatever success X
has attained). It doesn't hurt that this campaign's primary
sponsor is X's church in which X is quite active.

   4.   Later that morning X meets with the department
secretary whose absenteeism is proving troublesome. The
secretary is increasingly absent because (X suspects) of an
alcohol problem. The one time X broached the topic (at
lunch) the secretary vehemently denied it. The secretary
has been in the department longer than X and has been
especially helpful over the years. Further, the secretary
is a member of a union whose local is very protective of its
members especially in cases of management harassment. After

hearing the secretary out X decides to file an informal note
to the personnel file blaming the absenteeism on "personal
problems" (in part true, since one of the sons at home seems
to be predelinquent). X also has the secretary's assurance
that "things will clear up." After all, the secretary is a
good worker and is liked a lot by X, who tactfully brings up
the organization's not inconsiderable facilities for helping
employees who have problems.

5. For lunch, X decides to venture outside. It's a
sunny, unseasonably warm March day and most of the ice and
snow from the weekend storm is melting. While sitting and
eating a hot dog, X spots an elderly woman (poorly dressed
but no bag lady) slip on some ice and go down in a heap. X
sits and stares with mouth open not quite letting go of a
little yelp. By the time X gets half up from the park bench
two young student-types are helping the woman up. The old
woman seems to be all right but does show a slight limp as
she waddles right past X's bench. Averting the gaze from
the woman, X rather furtively steals a glance at the two
altruists and is pretty sure that they don't know X.

6. On the way back to the office, X waits perhaps a
little longer than usual to hold the door open for the
canteen delivery person and the crates of candy bars. Back
at the office there is a general meeting of department heads
chaired today by X's chief nemesis who is once again
bluffing his way with his great communicator skills.
Another bravura performance; "Just once I'd like to call
his bluff," muses X but, being an instinctive diplomat,
thinks the better of it and keeps quiet. "Besides," X
thinks, "this jerk knows too many people that count."

7. Finally, X's alternative to the interminable
discussion presents itself: The Intro course must be taught.
After excusing themselves, X and two other department heads
hurry over to the bank of classrooms in the brick building
the design of which (if design is the right word) can best
be termed "neo-Bauhaus institutional cheap." The lecture
is on poverty and the underclass; with the lecture completed
and seven minutes to go in the period, the one question
forthcoming deals with what to do about the welfare cheats
who blow their food stamp money on good times. X is at
first startled and then dismayed at the question, which
seems almost a non sequitur in light of the concluding
remarks of the lecture. Nevertheless, after a deep breath
and a short stare out the window, X asks the student, half
rhetorically, if there is an analogy between his example
and that of a college student blowing birthday money or,
better yet, student grant money in the local bar. The
student doesn't think so but proffers no response when X
asks whether there should be penalties attached to those who

do drink up their grants. With four minutes to go and no signs of intelligent dialogue in sight, X decides to let everyone get beamed up early. On the way out, X overhears a rather loud but anonymous remark to the effect that the instructor is a "bleeding heart." X, more tired than angry, squelches the desire to respond and pretends not to hear.

8. Pressed for time, X decides to leave immediately. Reaching the parking lot, X feels tired and a little angry. On the commute home X dashes into a convenience store to get Mom a belated birthday card (my God, almost a week late!) and realizes upon getting back into the car that across the street several young toughs have been eyeing X, X's car, or whatever. X responds by slipping out into traffic at something more than a snail's pace.

9. Finally, at home with hugs all around, and a fast-food dinner hastily procured and consumed, X and spouse and *kinder* make Easter celebration plans that seem to have been stolen from Norman Rockwell. X cares little for Easter hoopla but it has been a long winter and the kids are really excited so X gets into the spirit (sort of) and that's what counts. And finally X and spouse go to bed themselves: worn out but not forgetting their ritual "I love you" before the lights are doused.

Commentary. After the students have jotted down their ideas, get some of the ideas on the board. Many of the comments will be of the "I think he is a conformist" variety. Sooner or later you will ask them why X is a he. You can point out that nowhere in the narrative is gender specified. Nevertheless, the major point here is to show the variety of reasons, "motives" if you are a symbolic interactionist, that people have for why they act the way they do. Many of the motives directly illustrate the notion of stakes in conformity. Sometimes I just list these motives on the board and let the students match the motive with the paragraph that I feel best illustrates it.

I have had great success arguing that the foregoing illustrates the idea of a typical person who conforms not to what idealized norms dictate we must do in various situations but rather conformity to norms as expectations that predict what most of us, with considerable stakes in conformity, will do.

3. **Discussion/Thought Experiment:** "Good Risks, Bad Risks, and Deterrence." Suppose we posit two hypothetical people: conforming citizen and career offender. The former is a good risk in terms of breaking the law while the latter is, appropriately enough, a bad risk. How might we formulate the issue of deterrence regarding these two types? We can, of course, exclude those who break the law because of impulsive acts or compulsive desires. In either case, deterrence is not really a factor. However, if the good citizen conforms, is that really due to deterrence? Could we not as easily invoke control theory's ideas of conformist attachments, stakes in conformity, and internalization of norms to explain this behavior? After all, most opportunities for deviance are not even seen as such by our good citizen. An unattended purse, if noticed, is seen to be that: an unattended purse and not an invitation for theft. Now, if you counter by saying that it is not worth it for the model citizen to take the purse, then why is it not worth it? Because of stakes in conformity? Now we are back to control theory. So for our model citizen you might argue that control theory can explain his/her nondeviance rather than having to resort to deterrence theory. If, however, our goody two-shoes does mess up then control theory didn't control but the perception of certain, rapid, and severe punishment didn't work either.

Now, turning to our career criminal, if he deviates because of peer pressure then might we not just simply invoke deviant attachments? If he does commit some misdeed on his own after thoughtful calculation, then as control theory tells us his stakes in conformity were low and his freedom to indulge the opportunity for deviance was high. In any case, deterrence did not work. Now if he did not commit a crime despite deviant peer pressure to do so, is that because of deterrence theory or because of some personality trait or an impulsive desire to be contrary? Finally, if he did not deviate because of rational calculation, we could argue deterrence. However, we can also recall Stark's discussion in Chapter 7 of the widespread use of drugs as an integral part of the contemporary criminal life-style. How can extensive drug use do anything but blur finer calculations of the possible costs of crime especially when many drugs such as alchohol and cocaine give thrill-seeking offenders a heightened sense of bravado.

As cited in Chapter 8, the perception of deterrence is

obviously not working well. As evidence we can look at our crime and recidivism rates. So I wonder: Just what is the need for deterrence theory when predicting crime and recidivism? Is it able to stand on its own theoretical feet or is it a special case of control theory?

ADDITIONAL STUDENT READINGS

Fletcher, C. What Cops Know. New York: Pocket Books, 1990. Intreviews with Chicago police officers covering such topics as violent crimes, sex crimes, organized crime, narcotics, and working the street. A fascinating read that can be finished in a single sitting.

Walker, S. Sense and Nonsense About Crime: A Policy Guide. Belmont, Calif.: Wadsworth, 1985, Chapter 2. An excellent secondary source from which any intelligent undergraduate can benefit. A very readable account of the "wedding cake" approach to the criminal justice system is given.

Wiseman, J. Stations of the Lost: The Treatment of Skid Row Alcoholics. Chicago: University of Chicago Press, 1979. An excellent ethnography of the real-world problems of social control agents, agencies, strategies, and tactics and the impact on their target/clients. Both sides of this sad story are told.

ESSAY QUESTIONS

1. Incorporating the concept of deviant attachments from Chapter 7 show how the experiments of Asch and Schachter can be used to explain conformity within a deviant subculture.

2. Is there an essential difference between prevention and deterrence? Why/why not?

3. How might control theory help explain why both the Cambridge-Somerville project and the TARP experiment failed?

4. Is control theory inapplicable if deterrence is invoked as a criminal justice policy? Why/why not?

Chapter 9

CHAPTER OUTLINE

Marx's Concept of Class.
   Means of Production.

   Class Consciousness.

   Unidimensional.

History as class struggle.
Everything that produces
wealth.
Workers recognizing their
common relationship;
essentially untestable.
All aspects of social existence
derived from relationship to
means of production.

Weber's Three Dimensions
   of Stratification.

   Class.
   Status.
   Party.

Unlike Marx, Weber can explain
managers who run companies they
do not own. Social position an
interplay of one's:
property
prestige
power.

Status Inconsistency.

Extension of Weber: Lenski
argued that status
inconsistency often leads to
actions against "tormentors."
Gary Marx's research with
African-American professionals
lent confirmation.

Social Mobility.

   Ascriptive rules.
   Achievement rules.
   Structural mobility.

   Exchange mobility.

Chances for mobility are
enhanced or blocked depending
if stratification system uses:
as with caste system or uses
as with class system.
Changing the proportion of job
types usually upward from blue
to white collar.
Some people move up at the
expense of others moving down.

Marx and the Classless
   Society.
      Utopian.
      Anarchistic.

Abolish classes.
Abolish the State.

Functionalist Theory of
   Stratification.
   Replaceability.

Adequate rewards must be given

	as enticements for fulfilling important positions: those roles or people that are most difficult to replace.
Social Evolution Theory of Stratification.	Stratification seen as inevitable and necessary adaptation to societal change.
Conflict Theory of Stratification. Exploitation.	Societies always more stratified than necessary. Those in high positions to extract surplus from those below. Also, those in key positions work to make selves less replaceable; e.g. trade unions and professional associations.

SUMMARY

Stratification is not only a key concern for sociologists, it is also a topic of great personal and moral importance. As Stark points out stratification, in a sense, is the inevitable suffering of many people.

Marx's Concept of Class. Although all of history had been marked by class struggle, the number and type of classes depended on the type of society. The stratification system of capitalism would ultimately reflect the development of capitalism itself and only two classes would dominate: **bourgeoisie** and **proletariat**. Each would be defined by the other in relation to the **means of production**: everything that goes into producing wealth save human labor. The means of production included land, capital, and technology, and the bourgeoisie owned these means. The proletariat possessed nothing except their labor, which they sold to the bourgeoisie for meager wages. Marx did allow for other classes in capitalism: an independent middle class of merchants and self-employed professionals who would eventually be absorbed into the proletariat; the **lumpenproletariat** whom today we might dub the underclass; and the peasants whom he contemptuously (and mistakenly) thought to be irrelevant to revolution. The self-proclaimed Marxist revolutions of the twentieth century have occurred in less developed nations and have found their primary support among peasants.

Even if Marx's analysis of the types and importance of classes was accurate, greater problems with his theory remain. Class consciousness renders his theory untestable since people (especially the proletariat) constitute a class only if they share a common relationship to the means of production and recognize their collective interests in relationship to their enemy (i.e., the class struggle). The logical problem with his theory of class consciousness is that class struggle is inevitable by definition since you can only have a self-conscious class that is engaged in class struggle. This is so because for the proletariat to side with the enemy (the bourgeoisie) indicated false class consciousness and thus disqualified them from the realm of real social classes.

Perhaps the greatest problem with Marx's theory of stratification is that it is unidimensional: All other aspects of one's social existence are derived from one's relationship to the means of production. It is precisely this limitation that prompted Marx's greatest critic, Max Weber, to define the contours of stratification analysis.

Weber's Three Dimensions of Stratification. To Weber social position was not reducible to property relations. Modern capitalist society was simply too diverse for such an obvious oversimplification. Any person could be classified according to three independent criteria: **property**--what Weber called class; **prestige**--what he labeled status; and **power**--what he termed party.

Property or class traits referred to people's life chances or their economic position in society. Weber avoided two of Marx's pitfalls. He did not make class consciousness necessary for similar life chances and he separated ownership of property from its control.

Prestige, or social honor, was not strictly derived from one's property relations; indeed, enterprising people could parlay prestige into property (e.g., Olympic stars doing commercials).

Finally, power--the ability to have one's way despite the resistance of others--varies independently from both property and prestige (e.g., high-level bureaucrats).

Status Inconsistency. One of the most useful extensions of Weber's work has been the area of status inconsistency-- when people vary considerably in their ranking of social criteria. Lenski argued that status-inconsistent persons who are denied the position they think should be theirs will favor actions and policies aimed at their "tormentors." Gary Marx tested Lenski's ideas with well-educated upper- status African-Americans (who are status inconsistent because of their devalued racial status). He found that African-American physicians and bankers were more politically radical than African-Americans who had "objectively" inferior jobs paying a pittance.

Social Mobility. Social mobility refers to the up or down movement of people/groups within the overall stratification system of a society. Who rises or falls and how many rise and fall are determined by two factors. One such factor is the rules governing how people gain or keep their positions-ascription and **achievement**. Both are found in all known societies. It is their mix that differs from society to society. Traditional India with its complex and imposing caste system is the classic example of a society in which status is primarily ascribed with mobility sharply curtailed. The United States and Canada are two instances in which status is primarily achieved and mobility is much more open. The other factor would be the larger, structural changes that occur in society. If you hold the population constant while decreasing the proportion of low-status positions and replace them with a like number of high-status positions then inevitably there will be upward **structural mobility**. However, if you hold the positions as well as the population constant, then the upward mobility of some people will come at the expense of the downward mobility of others; this is **exchange mobility**.

Marx and the Classless Society. Although differing sharply from the nineteenth century utopians and anarchists, Marx's idea of a classless society was, in its own way, both utopian and anarchistic: utopian in that the coming workers' revolution would abolish all class differences and anarchistic in that it would abolish the state as a major instrument of oppression. Marx's version (and vision) of a classless society was effectively de-mythologized by Dahrendorf who, drawing on Weber, showed that a classless society could only be true by definition. If the people are the state and only the state owns the means of production, then the society is classless. However, with the bureaucratic apparatus needed to administer production (and consumption), stratification remains. Actually, Dahrendorf's critique had been anticipated by Mosca, who argued that the need to coordinate a complex society required political organization. Political organization results in inequalities of power that, given the self-seeking and self-serving nature of humans, ensures inevitable material inequality benefiting those who hold political power. Former Soviet bureaucrats opposing perestroika and seeking a restoration of the Communist party's hegemony are certainly a contemporary vindication of Mosca's thesis.

Functionalist Theory of Stratification. To Davis and Moore, stratification exists in societies because it is built into important roles and into the problem of filling them adequately. Theirs is a supply-and-demand argument in which the object is for society to motivate enough people to pursue the most important positions. Thus, adequate rewards must be offered as inducement to fulfilling these roles. Functionalists can escape the initial Davis-Moore tautology regarding functional importance by concentrating on replaceability, or "the degree that either the position itself or its occupants are hard to replace." (The toy society illustration demonstrates the basic points of the functionalists.) Accusations of tautology notwithstanding, Table 9-1 shows that the principle of replaceability is generally and rather decisively accepted.

Social Evolution Theory of Stratification. When culture becomes too vast and complex for individuals to master, specialization occurs bringing with it stratification. To the evolutionists then, stratification *per se* is not something to bemoan but is an inevitable and necessary adaptation to cultural change.

Conflict Theory of Stratification. Conflict theorists might admit, albeit grudgingly, to the inevitability of stratification, but they would certainly dispute its allegedly benign nature. Since humans do tend to pursue their own narrow self-interests, conflict theorists argue that those in high economic, political, and other key positions will use their position to further their own ends. In so doing they will extract more surplus (exploitation) than is necessary for their own well-being at the sacrifice of the well-being of the more numerous and less powerful. As a result, societies are always more stratified than they need to be.

One way people try to maximize their lot in life is by making themselves less replaceable, and such attempts to monopolize some resource, good, or service are found throughout history. If groups cannot gain monopolies via coercion, then they may resort to artificial means to decrease replaceability--for example, professions and unions. In the former case, professions first attempt to establish their positions as irreplaceable and then make their members irreplaceable in the position. Put another way, they first try to increase and then stabilize the demand for the position and then try to limit entry into the position (the supply of practitioners) usually by means of credentialing. Unions (white/blue collar) attempt very much the same thing.

TEACHING SUGGESTIONS

The objective of chapter 9 is to refocus crude emphases on individualistic interpretations of achievement, prestige, power, success, and failure to more sophisticated interpretations of these phenomena.

1. **Lecture:** "From Marx to Weber and Beyond." This lecture presents to students how concepts of social stratification have moved from a unidimensional conceptualization (Marx) to a multidimensional one (Weber). This part of the lecture can be used to review what they have been assigned to read in Chapter 9. The actual extension of this lecture is to then present Bellah's ideas on how, especially among the more affluent, class is not so much an axis of social identity and consciousness as the emerging plethora of life-styles made available by widespread affluence. The lecture can close by showing how class and life-style complement one other by arguing that life-style is based on consumption and is increasingly becoming as important an element in people's social identity as is class (i.e., how people make a living by providing various goods and services).
    Sources. Bellah,: R. et al. Habits of the Heart: Individualism and Commitment in American Life. Berkeley: University of California Press, 1985. This very important book carries on the national character concerns of Riesman's The Lonely Crowd. More importantly, the authors argue that life-style is supplanting social class as a major organizing force in contemporary America.
Swift, D.: "The American Heart." Cross Currents, (Winter 1986-87): 385-393. A thoughtful review of Habits of the Heart by an historian.

2. **Discussion:** "Why Work?" In this discussion you can introduce the ethnomethodological technique of questioning tacit assumptions of everyday life. To me, this is what might have happened if Marx, Weber, and Garfinkel had had a couple of hours to kill. The students usually see no reason why an instructor would ask such a dumb question: "Why work?" But every time they give an answer--any answer-I ask them what they mean by it: "Couldn't you be a little clearer?" It's a little unfair to leave students with some of the rarified conclusions of ethnomethodology, so you can bring them back to earth by reintroducing the "why work" question in terms of social mobility. For example, you may ask them, "If work becomes a problematic issue then do concerns for social mobility, traditionally conceived, become obsolete?" (For a link with another learning objective see teaching suggestion 3 "What has happened to the middle class?" in Chapter 10 of this manual.) Finally, you may want to point out that the "why work" question impacts the genders somewhat differently: for males, it is

not an option; the expectation is for all males to work.
For many females, it is, still, more of an option.

Sources: Garfinkel, H. Studies in Ethnomethodology.
Englewood Cliffs, N.J.: Prentice Hall, 1967. The standard
collection of Garfinkel's ethnomethodological tricks with
which to question everday reality.

Rifkin, J. et al. "In Praise of Idleness." Utne Reader:
The Best of the Alternative Press (Sept./Oct. 1987): 46-65.
A series of articles showing people "the way" (not to
success but rather how to live well outside the fast lane).
Watson, G. "The Decay of Idleness." The Wilson Quarterly
(Spring 1991): 110-117. Watson, a fellow of St. John's
College, Cambridge University, traces the decline of the
idle rich segment of the upper class and its replacement:
the busy, sometimes workaholic rich. An incisive critique
of the Achievement Society.

3. Discussion: "Christian Materialism?" Often the
presentation of the conflict theory of stratification is a
straight-ahead, no-holds-barred critique of contemporary
society. This does not have to be so; one can critique
contemporary society using a conflict theory approach
without necessarily pounding the students with figures,
facts, and horror stories. Here is an example of how the
essence of the conflict approach can be transmitted with a
somewhat unorthodox, albeit controversial, discussion.

It begins by asking students why concepts such as
power, privilege, and prestige should be so dominant in the
sociological literature on stratification. As a matter of
course, some student will articulate the idea that these
concepts reflect some social reality out there. That being
the case the instructor then reinforces the importance of
these concepts by pointing out that they seem to address
some core values at the heart of American culture. At this
point the instructor states that if indeed this is the case
then all three concepts (and the values they represent)
seem to be the major incentives to motivate people to fill
the most important occupations in society. (The brighter
students might begin to detect a rodent since why would the
instructor be taking such an obviously functionalist path?)
The instructor then directs the dialogue to the fact that
each concept-value is quite "this-worldly"--one might say
materialistic--in what the values represent and, in turn,
how the values are communicated to self and others.

Now the instructor asks the class how these materialistic
concerns can be squared with the official Christian ideology
of the country. One way may be pointed out: Although greed
and envy certainly are deadly sins, they can be turned
inside out and harnessed to the greater cause of a
prosperous society by way of such euphemisms as promotions,
productivity, sales quotas, incentives, easy credit,
rebates, tax loopholes, and so on. Anything that either

delays the cost of paying for goods/services and/or shifts the payments of said goods/services to others is antithetical to the Christian virtues of charity and altruism.

I have found that at this juncture the discussion usually ceases to be a discussion; the silence is often deafening. Two routes seem usual. First, some student points out that we aren't the only society with this trait, and this usually is met with the rejoinder from others to the effect that that doesn't excuse us. Second, someone often asks whether or not as a social scientist I am overstepping my bounds by bringing religion into all of this(???). This, I have found, is a perfect opportunity to discuss Weber's distinction between sociology as (ideally) value-free while still being value-relevant.

Source: Lyman, S. _The Seven Deadly Sins: Society and Evil._ New York: St. Martin's Press, 1978. For reasons that I've never been able to fathom this excellent sociological work received a rather tepid reception from the discipline. It is a wonderful excursus in social thought; see especially the chapters on greed, envy, and sloth.

4. Lecture/Discussion: "Whither Stratification?" If the stratification systems of contemporary societies are open-ended, constantly evolving phenomena then the evolutionary theory of stratification will, by necessity, be an incomplete schema. It might be fun to get the class to conjecture on what future stratification patterns might look like and in so doing bring to their attention the distinction between projection and prediction. With the former we simply extend present trends into the future. With the latter we predict the future knowing full well that present trends never present themselves simply as the future unfolds. One such conjecture might have to do with the split in capitalist society: the contradiction between cultural expectations of citizens as producers (stoical, disciplined, team players) and as consumers (hedonistic individualists). I try to show how students' roles reflect this by asking them, in effect: "Do you party the way you attend class? God! I hope not! If so, I'd even rather party with faculty. They're more lively!" Besides being an excellent reinforcement of the notion of multiple roles, this dramatizes to them the difference between the expectations governing their work role (producers of good grades) and their leisure role (consumer of good times). I then ask them: How do people keep the different roles separate? Can this culturally induced split personality continue indefinitely?

Another possible tack would be to conjecture on the logical outcome of meritocracy. If a society should evolve to a point where there is strict equality of educational and occupational opportunity (i.e., no discrimination by class, age, gender, race, religion), then what would limit people's achievements would be a relative lack of skills, intelligence, or motivation. Besides probably leading to an even greater emphasis on all-out competition and the attendant hyperindividualism when you finally did run into some limits, you could not blame some nonexistent "-ism" for your failure. No, you'd have to accept responsibility yourself: not smart enough; not motivated enough. (This certainly would keep the psychiatrists busy. This would also begin to make liberals uneasy since they would have to contemplate a "bias-free" stratification system.) Further, given the fact that intelligence does have a biological component, could we not conjecture that after a while the best and brightest would exclusively mate (as is their desire) with the best and the brightest and give as their issue still more best and brightest? And does that mean that the dumb and/or lazy would be left only with each other? What might emerge is a new caste system (a la Young's Rise of the Meritocracy) of "gods and clods."

Sources: Bell, D. The Cultural Contradictions of Capitalism. New York: Basic Books, 1976. A first-class analysis of some of the more profound predicaments of contemporary liberal capitalism. This is a must-read.

Young, M. The Rise of the Meritocracy: 1877-2033: The New Elite of Our Social Revolution. New York: Random House, 1959. Who says that social scientists don't have a sense of humor? Social science fiction at its satirical best on a very serious subject. Could be read as a companion piece to Bell.

ADDITIONAL STUDENT READINGS

Fussell, P. Class. New York: Ballantine Books, 1983. I love this book! Without getting bogged down in technical analyses of life-style, Fussell carefully dissects the pretensions of us all. As one reviewer put it: "His aim is to offend.... He succeeds, with considerable wit and fine malice." At the end is an exercise, "Learning to Draw Class Inferences," as well as an updated version of Chapin's Living Room Scale, which could be taken as a self-administered quiz.

Lewis, M. Liar's Poker: Rising Through the Wreckage on Wall Street. New York: W.W. Norton, 1989. A former bond salesperson for Salomon Brothers tells what it was like to be in the middle of all of the action during the leveraging of America.

ESSAY QUESTIONS

1. Compare and contrast Marx and Weber on the position of the company manager who is a salaried employee.

2. Explain how white males who are status inconsistent might scapegoat minority males who are status inconsistent.

3. Using the concept of structural and exchange mobility explain how exporting blue-collar jobs impacts contemporary stratification systems.

4. Given that physician and nurse are complementary occupations show why functionalist and conflict theories of stratification are complementary or competing explanations for why physicians have more privilege and prestige than nurses.

Chapter 10   COMPARING SYSTEMS OF
                                              STRATIFICATION

CHAPTER OUTLINE

Simple Societies.   Small, nomadic, directly
                               connected to the environment.
                               Very poor. Stratified by age
                               and gender.

Agrarian Societies.   Productivity. Consistent food
                               surpluses give rise to real
                               cities, warfare, durable
                               wealth, exploitation, and
                               hereditary aristocracies.

Industrial Societies.   Harnessing of inanimate energy
                               to advanced machinery.
                               Standard of living dramatically
                               increases while workers work
                               "smarter," become more
                               productive and less replaeable.

Social Mobility in
  Industrialized Societies.   Lipset and Bendix. They find
                               much structural and exchange
                               mobility in all industrialized
                               democracies. Blau and Duncan
                               find more long distance
                               mobility in the United States.
                               Education is more critical for
                               mobility than family back-
                               ground. Their status attainment
                               model is duplicated for Canada
                               by Pineo. Recently, structural
                               mobility in the United States
                               is declining while exchange
                               mobility is increasing.

SUMMARY

Chapter 10 compares stratification and mobility in three
types of societies: simple (including hunting-gathering,
horticultural, and herding), agrarian, and industrial.
Bearing in mind that in many culture areas of the world
(much of the Mediterranean, for example) there has been a
social evolution from simple to agrarian to industrial.
The evolutionary process is neither inevitable nor uniform.

Simple Societies. This societal type has dominated most of homo sapiens' time on earth. These societies were (are) small, usually nomadic, and maintained a direct ecological relationship with the environment. In addition, population growth was slow if not negligible. Hunter-gatherers, the simplest of the simple societies, possessed no elaborate technology to aid them in their quest for survival. This, combined with their nomadism, meant that material possessions were minimal. One can illustrate this simply by showing that theft was not a problem in such a society. First, since material possessions were practically nonexistent and certainly limited to what you could carry, there wasn't much to steal. Second, if one did steal something, how would you hide it? Third, at any rate, stealing was unnecessary since everyone had more or less equal access to the same objects. With accumulating a surplus next to impossible and power differentials minimized, exploitation was nonexistent. The only (oldest?) bases of stratification were those of age and gender, and within these statuses stratification was minimal. Even herding societies as large and complex as the Masai were stratified primarily along the lines of age and gender. With hereditary considerations nonexistent, any differences in prestige and power perished when the powerful/influential person died. Thus, universal poverty was the basis of equality among the hunter-gatherers. The more sedentary of the simple societies (especially the horticultural ones) could develop rather more complex stratification systems but nothing like agrarian and industrial societies.

Agrarian Societies. Agrarian societies are the most sedentary of all societies. With improvements in food production and the consequent surplus, several things are possible: better shelter; the accumulation of possessions; and, by freeing some people from having to produce food, differentiation of roles and institutions. Productivity also creates real cities as well as warfare, hereditary aristocracies, and exploitation. Agrarian societies were chronically threatened by other societies, if not actually engaged in warfare, and this was both cause and consequence of extremes in stratification of power, property, and prestige. Consistent food surpluses allow the development of durable wealth, and thus concepts and rights relating to property begin to develop. In fact, humans as property, the person as a means of production, reaches its most complex form in agrarian societies.

All agrarian societies require some formal government, almost always dominated by an elite whose existence depended upon extracting surplus production in the form of taxes and tributes from the peasants. The continued existence of the agrarian elite depended upon its effective domination of the

military, which in turn meant soldiering as a specialized
role and weaponry as a specialized technology. Thus, the
elite exploited the peasantry by coercing them via the
military into giving up much of their production. Some of
what was extracted was used to support the military. Thus,
agrarian taxation was typically institutionalized extortion.
While the peasantry toiled, the elite "leisured" and thus
were able to develop a higher culture of speech, etiquette,
protocol, literacy, and the like, which functioned as
markers of their higher, ascriptive status. Thus, when you
look at the differences in power, prestige, and property
between the elite and the peasantry, agrarian societies
represent the apogee of stratification.

Industrial Societies. The life of the average person
under early industrialization (which would be synonymous
with early capitalism) can hardly be said to have
immediately improved. But with the harnessing of inanimate
energy to advanced machinery, the standard of living of
everyone in an industrialized society eventually far
surpassed that of agrarians and the overall degree of
stratification decreased dramatically. Generally, as
industrialization progressed, occupational positions
required greater degrees of training, skill, and education.
Thus, everyone needed to work "smarter." With more invested
in them industrial workers become less replaceable as they
become more productive. Industrial workers also become
personally and collectively more powerful than their
agrarian counterparts since it is much more difficult to
force people to work smarter. By changing the nature of
work, industrialization causes a quantum leap in the
standard of living while it narrows the gap between the rich
and poor.

Social Mobility in Industrialized Societies. The first
truly systematic study of comparative social mobility was
undertaken by Bendix and Lipset. They found a great amount
of social mobility in all of the industrialized democracies
studied, the total amount being virtually identical.
Inherent to the industrial process itself was a premium on
individual achievement. Consequently, there was a great
deal of exchange mobility. In addition, they found a good
amount of structural mobility since the development of
industrialism created a greater proportion of higher-status
occupations than was the case with agrarianism.
Somewhat later, Blau and Duncan found that where the
United States did have an edge was in its superior rates of
long-distance mobility: a huge shift in status, usually
upward. Their research focused on status attainment:
Mobility aside, how do people acquire a status? They found
that the primary mechanism linking the occupational status
of fathers and sons was education, and not family

background. The rather minimal effect of family background
was reinforced by Jencks, who found that brothers were
nearly as different in their levels of status attainment as
were randomly selected pairs of men from the general
population. This research theme has been further elaborated
by Cohen and Tyree, who found that education has greater
importance for status attainment for people from poor homes
than it does for others. But for escaping poverty and
attaining affluence, the most important factor was to be
dual-income families.

The relative frequency of long-distance mobility in
America has apparent correlates with attitudes on
stratification. Tables 10-5 and 10-6 show that when compared
with citizens of eight representative European nations, few
Americans agree that income differences are too large and
that you have to come from a wealthy family or have
political connections to get ahead. Conversely, Americans
more than any of their European counterparts believe that
hard work is vital to getting ahead.

Still, parents can and do influence their children's
status attainment. One way is that affluent parents can
send their kids to better schools thus increasing the
latter's chances for a well-paying, prestigious occupation.
Another, albeit related, way is for the parents to be older
when they have their children. As Mare and Tzeng found,
older parents are wealthier and have more education. They
also have smaller families and spend more time with their
children. As a point of contrast, all these positive
effects are relatively absent with children whose parents
started their parenting as teens.

John Porter, perhaps Canada's most famous sociologist,
examined status attainment in Canada and surmised that the
opportunities for social mobility were much diminished
compared with the situation in the United States. He cited
a lack of educational mobility as well as sharp ethnic
cleavages as the major reasons. However, Pineo, among
others, found that Canada's rate of social mobility is
almost identical to that of the United States. Moreover,
the Blau and Duncan status attainment model for the United
States is duplicated in Canada.

An interesting difference occurs when examining status
attainment and gender: Women are underrepresented in both
the highest-status, highest-paying jobs and in the lowest
paying lowest-status jobs. In the former case, sexism and
diminished aspirations can account for much of the variance.
In the latter case, low/no-skill females (especially ones
with young children) find it simply isn't worthwhile to work
outside the home.

Finally, Hout examined some recent trends in status
attainment and found, as many have predicted, that
structural mobility has indeed declined. There are simply
not enough unskilled jobs left to be transformed into

higher-status ones. This trend has been counterbalanced by the fact that the correlation between family background and occupational attainment declined by one-third between 1972 and 1985 for both men and women. Thus, with a commensurate increase in exchange mobility, especially due to the increase in holding college degrees, the United States stratification system remains an open one.

TEACHING SUGGESTIONS

The objective of chapter 10 is to illustrate through a comparative perspective the profound impact stratification has on people's lives.

1. **Discussion and Thought Experiment:** "The Importance of Reciprocity." The objectives are to demonstrate to students how one of the basic elements of primitive society (the norm of reciprocity) is highly relevant for understanding sophisticated society. More importantly, this thought experiment can dramatize the fundamental tension between group survival and individual needs/desires.

Far and away most of human time on Earth has been spent in a simple societal structure: hunting and gathering, horticulture, or herding. As Stark points out, group survival in terms of getting enough food becomes paramount. Let's extend this reasoning a bit. Concentrating on the hunter-gatherer mode, ask the class to break into small "families," the totality of which comprises a fictitious society. If the class size is about forty or fifty or so, that would be about right since hunter-gatherer societies usually did not exceed fifty. In any case, suppose you have five "families" of eight each. On a given hunt only two families come back with any appreciable catch. Arbitrarily pick two to be the lucky ones. Ask all five to confer first among themselves as to what they should do with the kill: Share it or keep it for their respective family members?

Now stage a minidebate between representatives of each of the families. If the students do not arrive at the following point on their own then introduce it at a propitious time: the norm of reciprocity, sharing with those who are needy today so that tomorrow when your family is needy and others are flush with their kill will share with you. From a functionalist standpoint if the society is to remain together the norm of reciprocity has an adaptive value. A nice way to generalize this idea is from Lenski and his proposition of self-interest: People will share with others to the extent that those others are necessary for the survival if not well-being of themselves.

From here introduce the *idea of social responsibility:* looking out for those whom you are obligated to support and care for. Ask them if the norm of social responsibility might clash with the norm of reciprocity. (Might this be another way of analyzing role conflict?). Finally, move back to the idea of simple societies. If human nature is basically self-centered at birth and if because of reciprocity simple societies (and elements of all other societies) must socialize their newborns into sharing, then might we say the quasi-communitarian simple societies must overcome the anti-social nature with which we are born? In other words, to what extent do (must) social requirements supersede natural needs/wants? If you really want to bring this line of reasoning home in another way, then remind the class that Freud made much the same point in his Civilization and Its Discontents: Given man's nature, the price of civilization is neurosis.

Sources. Gouldner, A. "The Norms of Reciprocity: A Preliminary Statement." American Sociological Review 25 1960: 161-179.
Haviland, W. Anthropology, 5th ed. New York: Holt, Rinehart, and Winston, 1989. The following passage is particularly pertinent.

> When an animal is killed by a group of hunters in Australia, the meat is divided among the families of the hunters and other relatives. Each person in the camp gets a share, the size depending on the nature of the person's kinship tie to the hunters. If there were arguments over the apportionment, it would be because the principles of distribution were not being followed properly. The hunter and his family would seem to fare badly according to this arrangement, but they have their turn when another man makes his kill. The giving and receiving are obligatory, as is the particularity of the distribution. Such sharing of food reinforces community bonds and ensures that everyone eats. It might also be viewed as a way of having perishable goods. By giving away part of his kill, the hunter gets a social IOU for a similar amount of food in the future.

2. Lecture/Discussion: "Why Poverty? Why Wealth?" This is a focused discussion in which the instructor helps students to critically analyze current trends in income distribution in the United States. In effect, the goal is to take the class from an initial (usually) position of blaming the victim (in this case the poor) for their plight to that of a more structural approach. For example, to the common response that welfare recipients cheat the taxpayers I pose a simple question: Is there any essential difference between a welfare mother buying junk food, cigarettes, booze for a boyfriend, and so on, and a college student blowing student loan money at the local pub? How about changing it to money from home? Finally, how about money from a student

government grant? Often, the discussion seems to turn around the meaning of "essential difference." Usually, at some point, I sneak in Gans's functional analysis of poverty by asking the students what would happen if the poor disappeared--instantaneously and totally. From there it is a short hop to linking patterns of privilege (and not just the wealthy) to poverty.

The following table has proven to be of great interest to my students. It documents changes from 1977 to 1988 in the average *after-tax* family income. To account for inflation, the figures are given in *constant 1987 dollars*. The income groups are arranged by deciles from the poorest to the richest 10 per cent. Additional data are presented for the richest 5 per cent and 1 per cent.

The source is the Congressional Budget Office.

Decile	% change	$ + or −
First	−10.5	−371
Second	−1.3	−94
Third	−1.2	−126
Fourth	− 0.4	−57
Fifth	+ 0.2	+33
Sixth	+ 1.1	+250
Seventh	+ 3.0	+798
Eighth	+ 5.4	+1,714
Ninth	+ 7.9	+3,087
Tenth	+27.4	+19,324

(Stated another way, the average after-tax income of the richest 10% went from $70,459 in 1977 to $89,783 in 1988.)

Further, you can break down the richest decile as follows: the average after-tax income of the richest 5 per cent went from $90,756 to $124,651, an increase of 37.3 per cent (or +$33,895). In addition, the average after-tax income of the richest 1 per cent went from $174,498 to $303,900, an increase of +74.2 per cent (or +$129,402).

Updating the data and simplifying the presentation somewhat by using quintiles, we find that average changes in after-tax income in real dollars between 1977 and 1992 were as follows:

the poorest	20%	showed a	13% decrease,
the next	20%	showed a	10% decrease,
the middle	20%	showed a	7% decrease,
the next	20%	showed a	2% increasse,
the richest	20%	showed a	32% increase.

Next, given the foregoing, the discussion can address how much incentive (differential wealth and prestige) should go to those who occupy critical positions (the definition of critical I leave for the class to deal with). This would also be a good time to discuss the Piven and

Cloward thesis on how welfare policy is a strategic mechanism for controlling the poor. The discussion usually closes with some ideas on how much wealth should pass to children of the rich.

Sources. Gans, H. "The Uses of Poverty: The Poor Pay All." Social Policy 2 (1971): 20-24. A wonderful piece that uses functional analysis to critique the continuation of poverty amid plenty. Simply put, the poor are too functional for the American affluents' way of life for the affluent to seriously attempt to eliminate poverty.

Piven F., and R. Cloward. Regulating the Poor: The Functions of Public Welfare. New York: Random House, 1971. The thesis of this award-winning book is straightforward: welfare policy as political and social control. Many of my colleagues might disagree but I feel that the message(s) of this book transcend ideology.

3. Lecture: "What has happened to the middle class?" An effective lecture can be composed to address the issue of status attainment and social mobility. The aim is to show students that education and hard work are too often not enough to guarantee the fulfillment of middle-class aspirations. In so doing, the instructor can show how intra- and supra- class dynamics shape the evolution of the middle class. I generally preface (and justify) it by telling the students that if they come from middle-class backgrounds then they are going to college, in large part, to continue a middle-class life. If their background is working/lower class, I remind them that they are not going to college to remain that; rather, they are going for upward mobility. In any case, the lecture emphasizes the aspirations of middle-class careerists and points out many of the problems associated with attaining/maintaining a middle-class life. I try to show how the title of the lecture can be taken two ways: how has the middle class changed over the past generation and has the middle class grown/shrunk during the same timespan?

Sources: Ehrenreich, B. Fear of Falling: The Inner Life of the Middle Class. New York: Harper Perennial, 1989. Everything that Ehrenreich writes is timely, readable, and important and this book is no exception. It traces the development of the professional middle class (especially its own class consciousness) from the 1960s through the 1980s. Superb!

Newman, K. Falling From Grace: The Experience of Downward Mobility in the American Middle Class. New York: Vintage Books, 1988. This can be read as a companion piece to Fear of Falling or on its own. Either way it is a poignant tale of downward mobility based on 150 in-depth interviews.

Mander, J. In the Absence of the Sacred: The Failure of Technology & the Survival of the Indian Nations.
San Francisco: Sierra Club Books, 1991. Hi-tech vs. holistic living may be an oversimplification of Mander's thesis but he does argue brilliantly on behalf of the old ways of native peoples facing the onslaught of modernization.

Moore, B. Reflections on the Causes of Human Misery.
Boston: Beacon Press, 1970. Moore argues for the unity of misery (certain conditions are bad for people regardless of time and space: war, cruelty, hunger, injustice, oppression, etc.) and the diversity of happiness (highly variable by time and place). Outside of slavery might any other stratification seem objectively oppressive to outsiders but subjectively legitimate to those who are immersed within it? This short work is important if only for the clarity it brings to fundamental issues of social life. If pushed, Moore might be able to argue a case for a social science approach to natural law.

ESSAY QUESTIONS

1. Which was the greater change: the movement from simple to agrarian society or from agrarian to industrial society? Why?

2. Why did stratification differences decrease with the advent of industrialization?

3. For attaining upward mobility in modern society, why is education more important than family background?

4. As industrialism continues to develop, why is structural mobility decreasing? Does this mean that exchange mobility decreases or increases in importance? Why?

Chapter 11

CHAPTER OUTLINE

Intergroup Conflict.

Disputes over cultural and/or racial differences.

Ethnic Groups.

Cultural groups with salient, distinguishable differences.

Cultural Pluralism.

Coexistence of different cultural groups.

Assimilation.

Adoption of dominant culture.

Accommodation.

Groups that ignore differences and emphasize similarities.

Caste System.

A closed system with position based on ascribed status.

Preoccupation with
Prejudice.

Research on prejudice that has failed to explain why people are prejudiced.

Theory of Contact.

Prejudice varies inversely with equality between interacting groups. Sherif studies created/dissipated intergroup hostility by altering type of contact: cooperation/competition.

Slavery and the American
Dilemma.

Legacy of slavery: contradiction between racism and democratic values.

Status Inequality and
Prejudice.

Prejudice not a cause but a result of inequality.

Markers.

Indicators of underlying conflicts over status.

Economic Conflict and
Prejudice.

Bonacich points out that, for many reasons, minority groups will work for substandard wages.

Exclusion.

The demand to keep some/all foreigners out.

Caste Systems.

When exclusion is not possible, majority groups try to isolate undesirable minority groups in lowly occupations.

Middleman Minorities.   Minority groups that function as links and buffers between upper and lower classes. These groups may also be the object of frustration and violence of upper and lower classes.

Identifiablility.   Cultural and/or physical traits of minority groups that facilitate hatred by majority groups.

Equality and the Decline of Prejudice.   Once a subordinate group achieves economic equality, it is no longer seen as a competitor (e.g., Japanese of North America).

Mechanisms of Ethnic and Racial Mobility.
Economic Enclave Theory.   Geographic concentration allows development of internal economic specialization.

Hispanic-Americans.   America's fastest growing ethnic group, Hispanic-Americans do not identify themselves as such but rather identify selves with any one of the particular groups that make up the larger aggregate.

Immigration Effects.   Difficult to measure since native Puerto-Ricans are not considered foreign born and many foreign born are illegal immigrants. All three major Hispanic ethnic groups have a high degree of geographic concentration, internal economic development, and, specialization.

Going North: African-American "Immigration" in the United States.   Rural southern life left behind very analogous to the white immigrant experience.

African-Americaan Progress.   If we assume that the African-American migration to the North was comparable to European

	immigration then record of African-Americans achievement compares very favorably to white immigrant experience.
Integration.	In the past generation, prejudice has declined significantly.
The Decline in Prejudice.	During the past two decades degree of prejudice toward African-Americans has been declining at an accelerated rate.
Barriers to African-American Progress.	Legacies of slavery, lack of homeland, visibility, numbers.

SUMMARY

Intergroup Conflict. While intergroup conflict can exist for numerous reasons, Chapter 11 focuses on those disputes based upon noticeable physical or cultural differences. An example of the former would be conflict between members of groups from different races while an illustration of the latter would be antagonisms between members of different religions.

Ethnic Groups. Ethnic groups are groups whose cultural heritages differ. However, not all people with a common ancestry recognize themselves as part of that ancestry. Witness the growing number of "unhyphenated" white Americans. When people believe that racial identity is associated with other traits such as character, ability, and behavior racial differences do affect human affairs. However, even within the same race members of different ethnic groups may also impute derogatory estimations of the others' character, ability, and behavior. Prejudice and discrimination are world-wide phenomena and vary widely. Table 11-2 shows that the Swedes are much more prejudiced regarding cultural differences than are their fellow Scandinavians--the Finns, Norwegians, and Danes.

Both the United States and Canada are societies in which cultural pluralism is an apt characterization. Faced with bitter ethnic antagonisms, many well-meaning souls on both sides of the cultural fence would hope for the swift, orderly, and peaceful assimilation of the various ethnics in their midst. However, much ethnic conflict has reduced or disappeared without assimilation. Rather, groups learned to accommodate themselves to one another despite the persistence of ethnicity because the differences between the groups simply became unimportant.

Sadly, less humane ways of dealing with ethnic minorities have been too often practiced. Expulsion and extermination are the two harshest measures whereby the majority seeks to rid themselves of a noxious minority. In addition, a caste system allows the minority to remain within the dominant system, but usually at the cost of being chronically exploited.

Preoccupation with Prejudice. Well into the post World War II era, social scientists tended to use prejudice as the proximate cause of intergroup conflict. In other words, such conflict was due to at least one of the groups containing sufficiently prejudiced members to antagonize and/or be antagonized by the outgroup. In turn, the prejudices were part of a larger, usually rigid personality profile (e.g., the authoritarian personality) that rejected those very different "others" who threatened the prejudiced people's world view.

Gradually, a reorientation in social science took place and prejudice increasingly was seen to be the effect of intergroup conflict rather than its cause. Leading the charge for the revisionists was Allport, armed with his *theory of contact,* which stated that prejudice will decrease if different groups approximately equal in status interact in cooperative (or at least noncompetitive) ways. Alternatively, groups of unequal status competing with one another will probably intensify their intergroup hatreds. The Sherifs' famous <u>Robbers Cave</u> research provided experimental reinforcement for Allport's propositions.

Slavery and the American Dilemma. Until recently, slavery was nearly universal (save Australia, slavery existed on all of the continents for centuries and by the late eighteenth century "Western Europe was the only region of the world where slavery {had} been abolished altogether.")

Though many Americans have held dehumanizing ideas about African-Americans, at first this prejudice was an outgrowth of and later an ideological justification for the ownership of people--that is, slavery. Later, it provided another justification for Jim Crow laws and the continued segregation of the Negro from the white. This continuing racism has been perhaps the most pernicious legacy of the slave-owning past as well as a predictable outgrowth of the slave system. Its continuance in the postslave era has functioned to reconcile democratic ideals with something less than equal opportunity and treatment, which as Myrdal pointed out, was precisely the "American Dilemma."

Status Inequality and Prejudice. The master-slave relationship is an extreme version of status inequality and, when institutionalized in slavery it becomes the prototype for status inequality. Thus, prejudice and discrimination become effects of inequality. Yet so long as structurally unequal groups interact, prejudice and discrimination will remain and perhaps increase. So the trick is to eliminate/reduce the inequality, and the diminution/elimination of prejudice and discrimination will follow. That this is difficult goes without saying, but it is possible to pull it off, as the development of Protestant-Catholic relations illustrate. When Catholics came to America in appreciable numbers they arrived poor, unskilled, and ignorant of American ways. They often competed with the Protestant majority for jobs, and this direct competition between unequals resulted in the expected interethnic conflict. After much hard work Catholics drew even and many times surpassed Protestants. As Allport and Sherif would explain it (albeit with the benefit of hindsight), the bases of the conflicts disappeared with the emergence of a rough equality. Further, Lieberson argues that cultural, religious, and even racial differences are markers that are often mistaken for the real cause of conflict between groups: direct economic competition. This competition is the *raison d'etre* for whites' racial stereotypes of African-Americans. When the underlying competition disappears, so will the importance of the markers.

Economic Conflict and Prejudice. Bonacich has conducted research on economic competition with unequal groups. She cites four points in explaining why disadvantaged groups will work for substandard wages, thereby undercutting the majority group's position. The disadvantaged group
1. comes from an area with a standard of living so low that present substandard wages are a distinct improvement;
2. lacks information that they are being exploited by their new employers;
3. lacks political power; and
4. has different economic motives (as with those temporary workers who will stay only long enough to save enough for a better life back home).

Many Hispanic workers who are illegal aliens fit these criteria. Bonacich cites two strategies that are used to combat the cheap labor of the subordinate group: exclusion (see immigration policies and border patrols) and a caste system (see relegating the subordinate group to the most menial jobs). In addition, a third structural phenomenon is often present in a society: a middleman minority whereby the minority links several of the indigenous groups in a society while often being used as convenient scapegoats for tensions between a society's indigenous groups.

Equality and the Decline in Prejudice. Once a subordinate group has achieved economic equality it does not threaten to be a source of cheap labor or to be competition for higher-status jobs. Indeed, the inroads have already been made. The Japanese in North America provide an excellent illustration of this phenomenon. Although few in numbers, from the beginning Japanese immigrants caused much consternation in North America. In spite of considerable legal discrimination, Japanese-Americans achieved early economic successes especially in farming and small businesses and they sent their children to school. In fact, education was so much emphasized that by 1930 Japanese-Americans had twice the rate of college enrollment as did native-born whites. Incredible as it may seem, the capricious dispossessing of Japanese-North Americans of their property and civil rights and their subsequent internment during World War II only delayed their continued success in the United States and Canada. Today both their educational and income attainment exceeds that of white Americans, and with status equality has come a decline in antagonism toward them, as indicated by their high rate of intermarriage. By 1989 this high intermarriage rate, in turn, had led to three babies being born having only one Japanese-American parent for every two babies born with both parents Japanese-American.

Japanese-Canadians facing the same early problems, as well as similar discriminatory policies (including internment during World War II), have achieved comparable rates of income and occupational attainment with their American counterparts. Prejudice against them has declined as well, as indicated by the high intermarriage rates to non-Japanese Canadians.

Mechanisms of Ethnic and Racial Mobility. The parade of ethnic and racial groups in North America has shown a consistent pattern: Begin at the bottom rung, work very hard, and eventually, move up the social ladder. Several mechanisms have been shown to facilitate this upward mobility. Geographic concentration, whether by choice or necessity, is functional for the subordinate group at least early in their immigration because it minimizes contact with hostile outsiders while it maximizes the building of intra-community economic and political power. The concentration of the group's population also allows the development of internal economic development and as seen especially in starting their own financial institutions and cultivating certain occupations. These forces (economic enclave theory) develop both successful businesses and employment opportunities not available in the larger world, thus reinforcing community institutions and ethnic solidarity. Ultimately, a middle class develops and with it an emphasis on education. Later generations are prepared to move beyond the community and into mainstream society.

Hispanic-Americans. More than 20 million Americans identify themselves in some way as Hispanic-Americans and their numbers are growing quickly enough so that within a generation they will be America's largest ethnic group. They are concentrated in a few states (Texas, California, New York, and Florida) and are overwhelmingly of Puerto-Rican, Mexican, or Cuban descent. (However, the various groups differ significantly from one another. Further, one should note that the vast majority of those termed Hispanic-American (usually by non-Hispanics) prefer rather to be identified by national origin: Mexican-American, Cuban-American, etc.) The median family income of Cuban-Americans is quite a bit higher than that of Mexican-Americans and Puerto Rican-Americans. This is in part explainable by the fact that many Cuban-Americans were middle class when they fled Castro's revolution. They are also older, and income tends to increase with age. Finally, as a whole, Cuban-Americans are the best educated of the three groups. However, Puerto Rican-Americans, though better educated than their Mexican-American counterparts, have a lower median family income that is depressed by their higher rate of families on welfare.

Immigration Effects. There are two major reasons why it is difficult to estimate the proportion of Hispanic-Americans who are non-native born. First, Puerto-Rican natives who emigrate to the United States are not defined as foreign-born. The other reason is that conventional survey techniques tend to substantially underestimate the number of illegal immigrants (see especially Mexican-born). Thus, comparisons with mobility and success of previous immigrant groups are most difficult. In addition, these comparisons are akin to hitting a moving target since substantial Hispanic immigration continues. Further, such analyses are complicated by the fact that the newest immigrants are not similar to the native born. For example, immigrant Mexicans drop out earlier than do native born Mexican-Americans who stay in school in California at the same rate as the statewide average. In addition, there is more than an ethnocentric suspicion that bilingualism in the home undermines sufficient fluency in English to retard economic progress. Where a person was born is the most critical factor regarding Hispanic fluency in English. Of the Hispanic groups, Mexican-Americans are the most fluent in English. Overall, the trend toward increasing English fluency compares favorably with the speed of English acquisition of European immigrants. It would seem that the concern over Hispanic bilingualism is a red herring.

To summarize, all three major Hispanic ethnic groups
have a high degree of geographic concentration, substantial
internal economic development, and specialization. For
those Hispanic-Americans who have been in the United States
for some time, the degree of assimilation has been growing
apace. In these respects the Hispanic-American experience
is mimicking that of earlier immigrants from Europe.

**Going North: African-American "Immigration" in the
United States.** World War II was the watershed for African-
American immigration to the North and a turning point in
African-American history and in African-American-white
relations. In many ways the rural southern life that so
many African-Americans left behind for their northern
destinations was analogous to the transoceanic migrations
of the earlier European immigrants. A comparison over time
(Table 11-12) of Iowa and New York with Mississippi shows
how poor and backward the latter was in contrast with the
former two.

African-American Progress. Against this backdrop, and
bearing in mind Lieberson's reminder that African-Americans
are so newly arrived from the South, then African-American
progress has been significant. We see that only in recent
years have a substantial number of African-Americans been
born in the North, and relatively few African-Americans are
the children of parents born in the North. The more
generations of African-Americans that have lived in the
North, the higher their education and the better their jobs.
With two-income families the relative affluence of middle-
class African-Americans is parallel to that of the white
middle-class. However, this is masked to a considerable
extent by the sharp rise in the proportion of African-
American families lacking an adult male (from about 10 per
cent in 1950 to 47 per cent in 1980). Still, when examining
two-income families the African-American income is 85 per
cent of that of whites (compared with 71 per cent in 1967.)
All in all, if we accept the notion of African-Americans as
immigrants, then they began to arrive in large numbers only
forty years ago, and many came much more recently. Viewed
this way, their record of achievement compares favorably
with that of most earlier ethnic and racial groups. This is
all the more impressive given the virulent racism that so
many African-Americans have encountered.

Integration. Media portrayals notwithstanding, only half
of whites and less than a third of African-Americans live in
neighborhoods without members of the other race. Support
for segregation is so low that prejudice would seem to be
declining drastically. Further, large majorities of both
African- and White Americans report that they have at least
one fairly close friend of the opposite group. In addition,

interracial marriage is increasing substantially.

The Decline of Prejudice: Firebaugh and Davis. To track prejudice these researchers used the General Social Survey to compare answers to identical questions asked during the early 70s and the mid-80s. They found not only did prejudice against African-Americans significantly decline during this period but also that the rate of decline was accelerating throughout the period. This decline was due about equally to changes in whites' attitudes and to the fact that older, more prejudiced whites were dying. Perhaps of more interest is the fact that the decline in prejudice was greatest in the South.

Barriers to African-American Progress. There are several barriers to African-American progress that their white European counterparts never had to contend with, or did so on a lesser basis.

1. The legacies of slavery. African-American ancestors did not come willingly to the New World and they and their descendants stayed in bondage for hundreds of years. Consequently, the racism and attendant discrimination caused by slavery has been the most enduring burden for African-Americans.
2. No homeland. Since they lacked a homeland, there was no place to go back to if things didn't work out in the New World.
3. Visibility. Unlike the descendants of white immigrants who, once they learn the language and acquire a modicum of education, can learn to pass as a "true" American, the differences in skin pigmentation of African-Americans set them apart. (Still, the experience of Japanese-Americans shows that racial differences *per se* do not necessarily preclude status and income equality.)
4. Numbers. Sheer numbers prevent African-Americans from adopting some of the tactics other groups used. Occupational specialization is one of these.

TEACHING SUGGESTIONS

The objective of Chapter 11 is to reorient, as necessary, students' thinking on intergroup conflict toward greater tolerance and understanding. This is particularly hard to do. I find it to be the most challenging topic to teach in an introductory course, since students often are more reluctant to discuss these topics than any other. Yet you can tell by their facial expressions and body language that they are interested. I often end up lecturing, but sometimes I can get some discussion going.

[Instructor's note: The following possibilities could be done sequentially. In fact, they are arranged for that purpose.]

1. Discussion: "What Is Racism?" With this exercise I hope to show students that how they learn of a racial incident is in large part determined by what and how the media choose to report. You might start with the wilding incident in New York City's Central Park in which nonwhite youths beat and raped a professional white female jogger. Question to class: If an African-American or Puerto Rican-American scrub woman had been beaten, would it have gotten nearly the media play? Is this racism? Now counter this with the Brooklyn incident when several white youths attacked and killed Yusef Hawkins who had ventured into the Bensonhurst neighborhood to buy a car. Here the races of victim and offender have switched. What of the incident in South Carolina where the white mother of two drowned her baby boys and then blamed the murders on a black carjacker. Sadly, for a while much of the local area (and the country) were all too willing to "buy into" that one. Finally, if the media focus on nonwhite Americans killing other nonwhite Americans, is this racism? Do the media simply report the news or reinforce cultural stereotypes? Is the deliberate darkening by a major newsweekly of O.J. Simpson's mug shot racism? A closing question: discuss what might be the net effect on the populace if there were a three month moratorium on all reporting of violence, including all instances of intergroup conflict? Are the media "only giving the people what they want," or is what they want what sells TV commercial time and newspaper ad space?

2. Discussion: "The Ultimate Attribution Error." Given the persistence of status inequality, then how do people explain it when

    1. a member of the ingroup does something nice/good/decent they are likely to credit his/her character but when members of an outgroup foul up it is their character that is blamed; and
    2. members of the ingroup don't do as well on some valued task as do members of a status-inferior outgroup?

The ultimate attribution error refers to the common tendency to cite internal reasons (e.g., individual character) when either the in-group member does something good or the out-group member does something not so good. When the pattern is reversed--the in-group member does poorly and/or the out-group member does well-- then external reasons are given (e.g., luck, special advantages such as affirmative action). The net effect is to reinforce group solidarity while maintaining a negative stereotype of the outgroup, all the while keeping intact a positive self-image of the in-group members. You might ask the class for ideas on how to deal with this phenomenon.

3. Discussion: "*Intra*group Solidarity and *Inter*group Conflict." This is a thought experiment that hopefully can explain some important real life phenomena. For the moment assume that the ultimate attribution error is functional for in-group solidarity and, liberal protestations to the contrary, this error might be an important qualifier of Allport's theory of contact. Ask the class if the reduction of intergroup conflict is a worthy goal. Next ask for some suggestions about how to achieve it. If students have read the text, they'll cite the section on Allport's theory of contact. Ask them if they know what happens to various previously solidary ethnic groups as they achieve entree into mainstream society. After discussing the loss of community in groups that have made it, you might present the following model (or some variant of it).

Step 1: Group members prefer to associate with their "own kind" (identification with each other).
Step 2: Group members engage in everyday interactions as well as important group rituals with one another.
Step 3: Group solidarity (we-feeling) is the result of steps 1 and 2.
Step 4: Group avoidance of and minimal interactions with outside groups. When there is interaction it is necessarily limited and superficial. The ultimate attribution error fits in especially with steps 3 and 4.
Step 5: Result of steps 1 through 4 is self-fulfilling interactions.
Step 6: Ethnocentrism is reinforced.
Step 7: Contact (especially competition with an outgroup that is perceived to be inferior) will lead to conflict (and back to step 1?).

This exercise introduces students to the idea that solidarity and conflict may be inevitably complementary phenomena. It also shows how social identities are not only forged by membership in solidary groups (identifying with the ingroup--i.e., who you are) but also concurrently are reinforced by having definable outgroups (to resent or look down on) with which to identify who you are not.

ADDITIONAL STUDENT READINGS

Doob, C. Racism: An American Cauldron. New York: Harper Collins, 1993. A brief, readable, informative overview of the causes and effects of racism in the United States. This would make an valuable resource for beginning students who want to prepare speeches or term papers on this topic.

Mangione J. <u>Mount Allegro</u>. New York: Harper and Row, 1989. First published in 1942, it is the memoir of the son of Sicilian immigrants who "made it" in America: Professor at an Ivy League university. Arguably the best account we have of growing up "ethnic."

Matthiessen, P. <u>In the Spirit of Crazy Horse</u>. New York: Penguin Books, 1992. A masterful job of documenting the Lakota's long struggle with the U.S. government from Little Big Horn to Wounded Knee. Infuriating.

Suttles, G. <u>The Social Order of the Slum</u>. Chicago: University of Chicago Press, 1970. One of the best accounts ever of the interactions both within and between ethnic groups that once more reminds us that to live in what the middle class calls a slum is not to live without morals and order.

ESSAY QUESTIONS

1. Regarding Allport's theory of contact that purports that prejudice and discrimination decline with contact between groups who are approximately equal, how is it possible to decrease prejudice and discrimination between groups that are currently unequal?

2. Compare the experiences of Hispanic-Americans with that of African-Americans. Are differences in bilingualism and migration history relevant to this discussion. If so, why? If not, why not?

3. Why have Japanese-Americans been so successful in overcoming initial problems of language, racial prejudice, and cultural differences to attain their present high level of achievement?

4. Show why an increase in exchange mobility and a decrease in structural mobility is relevant in explaining intergroup conflict.

CHAPTER OUTLINE

Introduction.

No known society has experienced gender equality. Premodern societies are generally very chauvinistic; modern societies generally somewhat less so. Whether premodern or modern the key question is *why* are some cultures more sexist.

Sex Ratios and Sex Roles:
A Theory.
  Sex Ratio.

Number of men per 100 women.

  Causes of Imbalance.

Female infanticide, geographic mobility, health and diet, war, differential life expectancy, sexual practices.

Ancient Athens and Sparta.

Athens (high sex ratio) was chauvinistic while Sparta (low sex ratio) was relatively liberated.

Sex Ratios and Power Dependence.
  Dyadic Power.

Whichever gender is in short supply. Interactions governed by rational choice theory.

  Structural Power.

Whichever gender controls major societal institutions. Interactions governed by conflict theory.

Gender and Social Movements.

The suffrage movement of the nineteenth century and the feminist movement of the 1970s were facilitated by women lacking dyadic power.

Changing Female Roles.

Both the work revolution and the sex revolution of the past few decades coincide with women being in oversupply.

Minority Groups and the Sex Ratio Thesis.

African-American males having been in even greater scarcity

than white males (poorer health and higher mortality) has had an especially high negative impact on African-American families. Mexican-American females (with dyadic power) are more traditional than are Puerto Rican-American females (in relative oversupply).

Conclusion.   Stark's research on early Christianity, where women far out-numbered men, confirms Guttentag's prediction of greater equality of women. Regardless of societal type there remains a link between biological reproduction and economic production.

SUMMARY

    Introduction.   No known society has experienced true gender equality. Premodern societies are generally very chauvinistic (c.f. Table 12-1) as evidenced by the vast majority of which always have males as political and kinship leaders and in the vast majority wife beating is acceptable and commonly practiced reflecting that men should and do dominate their wives. Further, in only ten per cent of these societies do women have the *right* to assume a political leadership role. In modern societies there is more variation as evidenced when comparing men and women in relation to literacy and college enrollment rates. Whether premodern or modern the key question is *why* are some cultures more sexist than others.
    Chapter 12 is concerned with gender inequalities regardless of the specific class, race, or educational level of particular people. As such, along with ranking by age, differentiation by gender is the most fundamental principle of stratification in society. Rather than examining the position of women via cross-cultural comparisons, Stark uses a simple and powerful concept to unravel gender inequality: sex ratio imbalance.

    Sex Ratios and Sex Roles.   In a single decade the study of gender relationships in general and gender inequality in particular has been revolutionized by the pioneering work of Guttentag and Secord. The idea of sex ratio (the number of men per 100 women) is not by itself of interest but only so when it is significantly imbalanced in either direction. There can be several reasons for an imbalanced sex ratio:

1. female infanticide--perhaps the major cause of
   imbalanced sex ratios throughout (pre)history;
2. geographic mobility--especially long-distance
   emigration leaves the donating area relatively
   depleted of males and the recipient area relatively
   inundated with males;
3. health and diet--female fetuses and infants are more
   robust;
4. differential life expectancy--all else being equal,
   females outlive males;
5. war--still another source of disproportionate male
   mortality; and
6. sexual practices--timing intercourse, for example,
   to maximize the production of males.

Ancient Athens and Sparta. Classical Athens had a
significant excess of males due to female infanticide. The
remaining females were married early and led restricted
lives while celebrated (in the arts) as romantic objects.
Respectable women were isolated by sexual norms;
disreputable women (mistresses and prostitutes) were highly
visible; and male homosexuality was extensively practiced.
Sparta, a most ferocious militaristic society, practiced
infanticide without gender preference. This, combined with
the high male mortality due to frequent warfare, led to an
excess of females. Spartan females were much less
restricted than were Athenian females and had substantial
educational opportunities, economic power, and legal rights.
They led open public lives and quite the opposite of their
Athenian counterparts, they were not idealized love objects.
Alternatively, there was a good deal of sexual
permissiveness and lesbianism.

Sex Ratios and Power Dependence. Athens and Sparta are
prototypical cases for understanding the sex ratio thesis.
At the micro level there is rational choice theory:
Individuals seek to maximize benefits while minimizing
costs. The gender that is in short supply possesses dyadic
power thus making the opposite gender that is in relative
oversupply less advantaged-- that is, more dependent.
However, when possessing dyadic power women should be able
to dictate terms of their lives to men. To explain why the
opposite is the case--women living restricted lives (see
Athens)--Guttentag and Secord introduce the idea of
structural power: using institutional means to a group's
advantage. Thus, at the macro level men act to keep women
subordinate, and the authors invoke conflict theory (groups
utilizing power to shape social structures to serve their
own interests). Men, therefore, create norms to counteract
women's dyadic power. These norms can include brides shall
be virgins; wives shall be chaste; women shall be relegated
to the limited roles of wife and mother; and women will be

defined as temperamentally unsuitable for roles of power and authority. When both structural and dyadic power favors men, they will exploit their advantages to the fullest (see especially the United States in the 1970s and 1980s). In addition to the cases of Athens and Sparta not disproving the theory, similarly favorable results are found when examining sex ratios in medieval Europe and more significantly in the United States, Canada, and Mexico. Given the baby boom of the 1940s and 1950s and the preferential norm of women marrying males slightly older than themselves American women faced a marriage squeeze from the late 1960s throughout the 1980s. This squeeze was especially acute in the 1970s.

Gender and Social Movements. Guttentag and Secord also predict that the gender in oversupply (i.e., lacking dyadic power) will seek to redress its disadvantage by organizing to maximize structural power. The Woman Movement of nineteenth century America shows exactly that (this movement was centered in the Northeast with its chronic undersupply of men.) Stark then traces the work of Nancy Cott showing the shift to the suffrage movement and eventually the flowering of feminism. Of special note is the upsurge in feminist issues in the 1970s: the modern decade with the most acutely imbalanced sex ratio.

Changing Female Roles. In the past three decades, faced with changing expectations in relations between the sexes, females have increasingly pursued, by choice or necessity, additional education and full-time employment. For illustration, coinciding with shifts in sex ratio imbalances, between 1950 and 1985 a _fourfold_ increase in the percent of American mothers with children under the age of 6, were employed full-time outside the home. And while women bring in significantly less money than do men, a number of reasons besides direct sexism explain this, including sex-role socialization, the younger average age of employed women, subordination of the woman's career to her husband's, and greater turnover in the workplace. In addition to a revolution in the workplace, there has been a sexual revolution of sorts predictable from the sex ratio thesis. With women in oversupply, traditional notions of feminine virginity and chastity and the double standard in sexual morality have given way to an increasingly sexually permissive standard with increased sexual exploitation of women by men.

Minority Groups and the Sex Ratio Thesis. In the case of African-Americans, undersupply of males has paralleled, to a greater degree, that of white males. In the African-American case the undersupply has been even more pronounced due to poorer nutrition and health care, higher infant mortality, and especially high mortality among young African-American males due to accidents, drugs, and violence. The impact on the African-American family is as predicted by Guttentag and Secord and has been particularly distressful for many African-American females and children. Fossett and Kiecolt found that variations in the African-American sex ratio were highly correlated with the proportion of one-parent families and South indicates that African-American males are far less likely than American men in general in their desire to marry.

Stark shows that males are in oversupply among Mexican-Americans and in undersupply among Puerto Rican-Americans. Again, as predicted from the theory the role of Mexican-American females should be more traditional than that of their Puerto-Rican counterparts and available data indicate that this prediction is borne out.

Conclusion. Stark's research on early Christianity, where women far out-numbered men, confirms Guttentag's prediction of greater equality of women. The tenet against infanticide contributed to the surplus of females.

Finally, regardless of societal type there remains a link between biological reproduction and economic production but in modern societies this is mitigated in favor of increased equality of women due to the moderating effects of feminism.

TEACHING SUGGESTIONS

The objective of Chapter 12 is to demonstrate how a single concept, the sex ratio, can be used to explain and predict a wide variety of sex role behaviors.

1. Discussion: "Linking the Micro and Macro Levels." One objective is to show students how this single concept can successfully link micro and macro levels of analysis. At the micro level, using rational choice theory you have intragender competition and inter-gender cooperation. That is, regardless of which gender possesses dyadic power men compete with men and women with women during the mate selection process (intragender competition). When mates are paired off then there is intergender cooperation in the form of marriage. However, from the macro level of analysis, conflict theory can be seen as groups also acting as individuals do in rational choice theory--that is, seeking to maximize the group's self-interest. Seen in this way, all the members of a gender cooperate with one another as they seek to gain/maintain structural advantages relative to their opposite number. Thus, at the macro level, there is intragender cooperation and intergender competition.

2.   Lecture: "Date Rape."   As we all know, however, not
all dyadic interaction between the sexes is pleasant.   This
lecture can show how one gender can use coercion to
sexually exploit the other gender. Of course, the topic
would be rape, in general, and date rape in particular.
This lecture would seek to show how power, not sexuality, is
at the heart of rape. Parenthetically, rape and especially
date rape have been major concerns of feminists throughout
the 1970s and 1980s showing how consciousness-raising
regarding rape occurred during a period of great imbalance
of the sex ratios. Further, you can show how a dyadic
phenomenon is addressed structurally in rape prevention
programs.

Sources: Brownmiller, S. Against Our Will: Men, Women,
and Rape. New York: Bantam Books, 1976. Far and away the
best treatise ever written on this topic.

Fairstein, L. Sexual Violence: Our War Against Rape. New
York: William Morrow, 1993. An Assistant District Attorney
of Manhattan writes a searing work as only an insider can.

Sanday, P. Fraternity Gang Rape: Sex Brotherhood and
Privelege on Campus. New York: New York University Press,
1990. Do men *really* gang rape for other men? Sanday's work
is mandatory reading in this area.

Warshaw, R. I Never Called It Rape: The MS. Report on
Recognizing, Fighting, and Surviving Date and Acquaintance
Rape. New York: Harper and Row, 1988. Not only is this a
well-written monograph on a most important topic, it also
contains a methodological afterword by one of the leading
figures in the field, Mary Koss. The definition of rape
used in this study illustrates how far-reaching rational
choice theory can be: "(When)...the aggressor makes a
decision to force his victim to submit to what he wants."

3.   Discussion/demonstration. "More Than Numbers." The
objective is to show students how the Guttentag-Secord
thesis is not reducible to numbers: that structural power is
equally important in understanding sex ratio theory. In the
first chapter of the Guttentag and Secord book, there is a
section dealing with two fictitious societies: Eros and
Libertinia. Eros possesses a low sex ratio while Libertinia
has a high one. However, in both these fantasy situations
the females hold structural power. I read aloud to the
class accounts of these two societies.   The men do not find
it funny at all and many of the women, appear uncomfortable
also. An open-ended discussion on the role of structural
inequalities between the sexes is then encouraged.

Males find it difficult enough to accept parity with
females but to be subordinate to them? This can also
function as an attempt at consciousness-raising in the
introductory course; to what avail...? This also answers
critics who misread Guttentag and Secord and then say that
the authors reduce everything to numbers.

4. **Lecture:** "America's Symbolic Civil War: The Great Abortion Debate." I find that this lecture works with several different chapters; as well with the one on gender inequality as any of the others. (Another possibility is with Chapter 11: intergroup conflict.) As Stark points out early in the chapter, cultural differences are also relevant. I find the respective ideological positions of rabid prolifers and prochoicers to be excellent examples of markers functioning in a reciprocal manner to be excellent examples of how *markers* need not be narrowly interpreted as only physical traits that people carry around. In agreement with Luker, the abortion debate is not just about abortion. It is also about contrasting and competing conceptions of womanhood and that of course links directly with how women (and men) deal with gender inequality. Of all the lectures I give this is one of the very best in getting and keeping students' collective attention while driving home some telling examples of sociological principles.

[Instructor's note: I go to extra lengths to present both sides fairly and to avoid any debate over the morality of abortion. I have found that by concentrating on Luker's study of abortion activists I can steer clear of dangerous waters.]

Sources: <u>Abortion: Opposing Viewpoints.</u> (no editor cited.) San Diego: Greenhaven Press, 1991. Pros and cons of all aspects of the abortion debate. Recommended.
Luker, K. <u>Abortion and the Politics of Motherhood</u>. Berkeley: University of California Press, 1984. An award-winning monograph concentrating on abortion activism. Of particular note is the idea that abortion attitudes come out of a long investment in particular lifestyles which in turn derive from earlier decisions about marriage, family, education, etc. Strongly recommended.

ADDITIONAL STUDENT READINGS

Atwood, M. <u>The Handmaid's Tale</u>. New York: Basic Books, 1986. Can the advances in women's rights and opportunities be reversed, even obliterated? This nightmarish novel chronicles the plight of one young woman during a "misogynistic" coup in the United States. Excellent.

Davis, K. "The Sociology of Prostitution." <u>American Sociological Review</u> 2 (April 1937): 744-755. Still the classic statement on the topic; still readable; still worth reading.

Ehrenreich, B. <u>The Hearts of Men: American Dreams and the Flight From Commitment</u>. New York: Doubleday, 1983. Ehrenreich argues that during the 1960s substantial numbers of American males "defected" from their traditional roles as father/breadwinner/provider. This piece is fascinating and provides essential background for (and qualification of?) the Guttentag thesis.

Ehrenreich, B., E. Hess, and G. Jacobs. <u>Re-making Love: The Feminization of Sex</u>. Garden City, N.Y.: Anchor Books, 1987. Very readable with a seemingly endless parade of great insights into changing female sexuality. Chapter titles tell it all: "Up from the Valley of the Dolls"; "The Battle for Orgasm Equity"; "The Lust Frontier"; "The Politics of Promiscuity"; and "Fundamentalist Sex: Hitting Below the Bible Belt."

French, M. <u>The War Against Women</u>. New York: Summit Books, 1992. French supports with historical and cross-cultural examples the opporession of females. For those who need reminding that misogyny has been more the rule than the exception.

Tavris, C. <u>The Mismeasure of Woman: Why Women Are Not The Better Sex, The Inferior Sex, Or The Opposite Sex</u>. New York: Simon and Schuster, 1992. Tavris' award winning book is simply the best work on this subject. When 'man is the measure of all things' woman is forever trying to measure up. Be sure you have a generous block of free time when you start this one since you won't want to put it down.

ESSAY QUESTIONS

1. How do Guttentag and Secord explain how the fertility increases of the post-World War II baby boom impacted sex roles in the 1970s and 1980s.

2. How would you answer critics who might claim that the sex ratio thesis reduces sex role behavior to changes in dyadic power?

3. In addition to females being in oversupply what are some other necessary preconditions to a women's movement?

4. Presuming lower-class status what differences could you predict in family structure given a low sex ratio situation for group X and a high sex ratio situations for group Y?

CHAPTER OUTLINE

Defining the Family.	Small kinship structured group (usually grounded in a marriage) charged with raising of newborns.
Cross-cultural Traits.	Families tend toward being sexist. Rather easy for men to divorce wives. Great majority of societies do not find couples spending much leisure time together. Nuclear family is the exception.
Family Functions.	Sexual gratification; economic and emotional support.
The Traditional European Family.	Extended family living in a single household was typical only of the wealthy. For the rest, family was not large but was crowded. Fertility and mortality high. Because of death, female-headed households were not unusual. Temporary adult members were often present and children left the household at early age. Marriages were economic arrangements and people sought emotional companionship from same-gender friends. Parent-child bonds were weak.
Modernization and Romance.	Romantic love becomes primary means of mate selection. Happiness and fulfillment expected from spouse.
Modernization and Kinship.	Quantity of relations within extended families has declined while quality of relations is quite high.
Modernization and Divorce.	Rising marital expectations has been a major reason for the high divorce rate but modernization probably explains

both. Regarding living together, the trend is up and research from Sweden indicates that those who live together prior to marriage have a significantly greater liklihood of divorcing.

The One-Parent Family and Incompetent Parenting. Divorce and increased illegitimacy have increased one-parent families. Patterson has found that poor parenting, regardless of family structure, is a primary reason for problem children.

Remarriage. Jacobs and Furstenberg found women who remarried soon after divorce tended to marry men close in status to their first husband. Booth and White found that chances of divorce increase dramatically if it is a remarriage for both and at least one brings children from a previous marriage. The "empty nest" marriage can be quite satisfying.

SUMMARY

The sociology of the family asserts, with confidence, the universality of the family as a basic social institution. This is predicated upon the ample evidence that though the family may vary in form it is still fundamental to all societies. In addition to the universality theme, much of the scholarly literature on the family has maintained that the family, at least in modern society (especially contemporary America), is in decline. As Stark points out, the recent evidence on this issue begs for a reconsideration of the claim for such a decline.

Defining the Family. Stark's definition of the family-- a small kinship-structured group with the key function of nurturant socialization of the newborn--emphasizes the function of ensuring the perpetuation of society. This function is the most universal of this universal institution. Societies have found that marriage, when a long-term relationship involving specific rights and responsibilities, is maintained facilitates nurturance.

An examination of family life in premodern societies finds that at least three-quarters of these societies are polygynous and make it rather easy for a man to divorce his wife. Most men marry women much younger but only in a handful of such societies do husband and wife spend much leisure time together. Moreover, in half of these societies men do no domestic chores. In contemporary terms, these societies are highly sexist. Finally, the nuclear family is the exception. Further, none is composed of solitary nuclear families. Rather, the basic family unit includes several nuclear families--it is an extended family.

Family Functions. In addition to the basic function of procreation and nurturance of newborns, functions include channeling sexual gratification via norms governing sexual behavior; economic support for members who cannot support themselves; and emotional support by providing a sense of belonging and security. Table 13-2 shows that a majority of couples in most countries in the World Values Survey shared the same sexual attitudes (somewhat more so in Canada than in the United States). The congruence was highest for countries in western Europe and by far the lowest in Japan. Table 13-3 reports findings as to the importance of sexual relationship in a successful marriage. Again, it is least important in Japan and most important in western Europe, Canada, and the United States. Things reverse themselves somewhat in Table 13-4, which addresses the importance of income for marital success. Here Japan places first with much of western Europe (with its welfare state protection a possible mitigating factor) bringing up the rear. The United States and Canada seem to place midway between the extremes. Finally, Tables 13-5 through 13-7 tap emotional closeness and satisfaction of family life and again the pattern prevails with selected western European nations ranking highest, Japan lowest, and the United States and Canada in between. If Japan is more traditional than its western counterparts then the notion of the traditional family as stronger and/or more satisfying than its more modern cousin needs to be revised.

The Traditional European Family. Drawing primarily on the work of Shorter, Stark points out that the extended family living in a single household was typical only of the wealthy. The size of the household was not large (five to six members) and often contained temporary adult members. Fertility was high but so was infant mortality. Children left the household at very early ages. Female-headed households were as typical then as now except that presently divorce has replaced spousal mortality as the major reason. Although the average household was not large, it was crowded (literally into a single room). Thus, the traditional family lacked privacy and a well-defined boundary. Child care was indifferent if not downright neglectful. This pushed even higher the very substantial infant and childhood death rates caused by poverty, malnutrition, and a lack of fundamental public health practices. Emotional attachments between husband and wife were the exception and not the rule. Marriages were economic arrangements between families, and neither partner expected emotional fulfillment from marriage. Rather, men and women found their closest expressions of bonding with same-sex cohorts, that is, friends. Men valued women as valuable "goods" not as beloved companions. Finally, bonds between parents and children were weak. Parents made little emotional investment in newborns, and with children leaving the house at an early age parent-child bonds were tenuous.

Modernization and Romance. Romance has replaced the economically motivated arranged marriage. In one sense then, the affluence of modern society has facilitated the institutionalization of romantic love as the basis for mate selection. People no longer hope to avoid antagonism in marriage but actively seek happiness and fulfillment in their spouse. Consequently, husband and wife now expect their relationship to take priority over relationships with their peers.

Modernization and Kinship. While families, especially extended ones, are not nearly as large as they were two or three generations ago, the family remains tightly knit and satisfying for most people. Thus, while the quantity of relations within families has declined, the quality of the relations is quite high.

Modernization and Divorce. The high divorce rate of contemporary America signifies the importance of the marital relationship rather than its alleged decline. Marital expectations have been subjected, along with much else in contemporary society, to rising expectations. For most who divorce, the particular relationship did not provide adequate emotional satisfaction. It does not mean that they've given up on marriage or family. While the divorce rate itself is very high in America, computing it and its direction is quite difficult. Still, from what is known we can "guesstimate" that both of the following assertions are probably true: Most married people will not divorce although about half of all marriages will end in divorce. The reason is that a substantial percentage of all who divorce were divorced before.

When sexuality is a primary basis for emotional attachment between husbands and wives, then marriages will tend to weaken as familiarity causes a loss of fervor. Thus, a good deal of divorce may reflect a form of swapping sexual partners. For those who move beyond the "hormonal" stage, marital satisfaction seems to be higher the longer a couple has been married. Modernization brings increased opportunities for divorce. When Trent and South analyzed divorce patterns in 66 nations, they found that as nations develop the divorce rates rise. Also, where there are a larger proportion of women are employed outside the home divorce is higher, but where men outnumber women (age 15-49), divorce is lower. Catholicism *per se* does not lower divorce. One should also note that a recent study of Swedish women found that living with their eventual husbands prior to marriage increased the likelihood of divorce.

The One-Parent Family and Incompetent Parenting. Both divorce and a climbing legitimacy rate have contributed to a much larger proportion of children living in one-parent families. Children of divorced parents have lower levels of well-being and are also more likely to have problems with academics, delinquency, self-esteem, and psychological adjustment. These problems seem to correlate with being raised in a one-parent home. Of all the consequences associated with this situation, *poverty* and a *lack of time* for proper parenting are two of the most worrisome. However, poor parenting, regardless of the structure of the family, is a primary cause of deviant behavior among children. Patterson has studied and worked with problem children and their parents. He has found that many children never are forced to outgrow antisocial behavior and will continue to act in such ways unless parents effectively use punishment to teach them not to. One major reason for a lack of effective parenting is that many of the parents that Patterson worked with didn't like their children, or didn't feel particularly obligated toward them, or didn't want to be parents in the first place.

Remarriage. Jacobs and Furstenberg studied women who remarried and found that the sooner the woman remarried the closer in social status was the second husband to the first. Those who married later did significantly "better" or "worse" than the first time around. Women with children under age 10 were not preferred by prospective second husbands. White and Booth examined the influence of step-children on subsequent marriages. They found that if there are not stepchildren in the home or if it is the first marriage for the other partner, then these couples do not have a higher divorce rate than for those marrying for the first time. However, the chances of divorce increase by 50 per cent if it is a remarriage for both partners and one or both bring with them children from a previous marriage. A subsequent study of the original White and Booth sample found quite positive effects of the "empty nest." Thus, depending on the circumstances, the presence of stepchildren can be a destabilizing force in remarriage.

Increasingly, two-income families have to deal with the issue of sharing household chores. Canada and the United States rank near the top in nations that feel that sharing chores is very important for a successful marriage (cf. Table 13-13). Indeed, regardless what the overall population of any particular country thinks about this both men and women hold very similar views on the relative importance of sharing (thus illustrating also the symmetry of gender socialization.)

TEACHING SUGGESTIONS

The objective of Chapter 13 is to sociologically analyze contemporary American patterns and trends of mate selection, marriage, and divorce.

1.   Lecture: "Marriage and Family as Property Relationships." I usually construct my lectures from several sources. However, every once in a while something comes along that is, in effect, canned and terrific. Such is the case with Randall Collins's essay "Love and Property." It is a wonderfully insightful piece on the different property relationships that govern marriage: erotic, generational, and household. (I add a brief discussion on emotional property and its rising importance in contemporary marriage.) This is especially effective in supplementing the discussion on family functions.
    Source. Collins, R. Sociological Insight: An Introduction to Non-Obvious Sociology. New York: Oxford University Press, 1992. 2nd ed. pp.119-154, though the whole volume is worth reading.

2.   Discussion: "Picking a Partner." Modern marriages tend not to be parentally arranged. One might say that, given our very high divorce rate, we refuse to have our parents tell us with whom to be miserable: We'll make that choice ourselves. In any case, I have found that the best way to lead into a sociological discussion of mate selection is to ask (once again with feigned innocence though the quicker ones are getting wise to my routine by now), What do you look for in picking a marriage partner? The usual responses almost always revolve around personal attributes (not excluding monetary situations). After these necessary preliminaries are disposed of, the instructor should announce: "I'll tell you what *all* of you look for." He/she then cites five "givens"--exogamy (not from one's nuclear family); a person of the appropriate gender; one of the same nationality; a person of the same race; and someone living close by (proximity). After some discussion as to why these are givens in 99 per cent of the cases, the instructor can then go on to discuss those areas in which some leeway can

be expected: education, religion, social class, marital
status, age, and so on. Once again however, the instructor
points out how (especially for first marriages) like tends
to marry like on these dimensions. At this point, you can
always amaze most of the class with a few historical and
anthropological examples of exotic courtship and matchmaking
behavior. Finally, you remind students that the sex ratio is
of crucial importance in terms of offering opportunities to
meet members of the opposite sex. Only now do you allow the
personality-personal attribute argument to have any
credence.

If marriages are made in heaven, then God is part
sociologist. Once again, this kind of demonstration is
quite effective in combating the rampant personalizing of
decision making in our society. Yes, people do choose
their partners in our kind of society but only after they
have ruled out considering (for sociological reasons) the
vast majority of theoretically available partners.

3. **Discussion:** "Some Sociological Dimensions to Emotions."
Given that romantic love is a culturewide myth (and some
would argue a collective neurosis) this exercise can
demonstrate some of the social interactional constraints
on emotional behavior in a context in which most students
have more than a passing interest. The instructor can
start by describing a situation that all of the students
know of if they haven't actually experienced it themselves:
a love triangle. After setting up the usual A+B with C
as the more than interested third party, a distinction is
drawn between envy and jealousy. C wants A and begrudges B
for having him/her (envy) while B knows of C's designs and
reacts possessively (jealousy). There are usually some
voices of protest (not that envy and jealousy exist but...)
that you are treating affairs of the heart as if they are
property squabbles. This is your opportunity to affirm
that you agree--they are property disputes--and that you
don't have to have dowries or exchange goats for women to
have students see the connection between property and
marriage. For proof I refer them to the use of possessive
pronouns to explain their close relationships with loved
ones--for example, *our* relationship, *his* girlfriend,
her husband, *their* marriage, *your* partner, and so on. At
this point I admit that while it is true that adults in our
society are not the property of each other in the legal
sense of ownership, that certainly does not rule out
treating each other as emotional property. Waller's
principle of least interest fits nicely to tie this
discussion with that of Guttentag's dyadic power: If your
gender enjoys dyadic power, then in any given relationship
(especially during courtship) with all else equal you have
less interest than does your partner in maintaining the
relationship and, consequently you have more power in acting

in that relationship. This can be compounded by one gender, already in excess supply (women in the 1970s and 80s), being socialized into needing a relationship more and accepting more responsibility for maintaining the relationship. So while the 1970s and 1980s were good for the careers of many women they were bad news for more women seeking good marriages.

Sources. Davis, K. Human Society New York: Macmillan, 1948. See Chapter 7, "Jealousy and Sexual Property" for a classic statement on the social conditions for sexual jealousy.

Schoeck, H. Envy: A Theory of Social Behavior. New York: Harcourt Brace Jovanovich, 1970. Sadly, a much neglected monograph. It is the most extensive treatment of envy in sociology. Schoeck argues that envy is a universal problem of social control.

Waller, W. and R. Hill. The Family. New York: Dryden, 1953, pp. 190-192. Waller's insight still holds: Those who care the least wield the most influence (if not power). The caveat, of course, is that they must be defined as essential to the relationship. So, as a cynic would put it, the trick is to care enough to keep the other interested but not so much as to lose your advantage.

4. **Discussion:** "Role-Negotiation and the Dual-Career Family." As cited in the text one of the major problems facing the single parent (in the overwhelming number of cases: female) is time. So it is with the dual-career family in which the woman who "has it all" finds that too often all is too much and exhausting to boot. One reason is that in the dual-career family males may contribute to household tasks but they still do not do anywhere near 50 per cent of the work. Consequently, a discussion based on the idea of *equity* can elicit many of the dilemmas that your students will face in their not-too-distant future.

Source: Hochschild A. The Second Shift. New York: Viking Press, 1989. Examines the allocation of household tasks from a sociologist's perspective. Very well written.

5. **Discussion.** "Second Chances." Divorce is never pleasant. Not only are our students living in a society with the world's highest divorce rate, but many of them grew up in the 1970s and 1980s when divorce reached its present levels. I have found that this topic, more than most others, is of great interest to them. They are, as a group, leery about what marriage offers/does not offer them. They are just as concerned about the long-term effects of divorce on parents, on children, on children as eventual parents. The notion that divorce (and possibly remarriage) offers some the hope of a second chance too often masks the reality that not everyone benefits from a divorce. A possible entree to discussion would be to ask

the students for candidates as to who wins/who loses in a
divorce. After getting some candidates and perhaps some
reasons why, introduce the idea of a time frame: one year
after; five years after; ten years after. If the discussion
gets too speculative, then slip in some material from the
Wallerstein and Blakeslee book (see below.)
     Source: Wallerstein, J. and S. Blakeslee. Second
Chances: Men, Women, and Children: A Decade After Divorce.
New York: Ticknor and Fields, 1989. This is, by turns, a
hopeful and heartbreaking work. Beautifully written and a
must read for anyone who has ever gone through divorce: man,
woman, child.

ADDITIONAL STUDENT READINGS

Amneus, D. The Garbage Generation: The Consequences of
the Destruction of the Two-Parent Family and the Need to
Stabilize It by Strengthening its Weakest Link, the
Father's Role. Alhambra Calif.: Primrose Press. 1990.
Whew! Quite a title and quite a book. Professor Amneus
wants a return to patriarchy to redress the familial
destruction wrought by feminism and the sexual revolution.

Berger, P., and H. Kellner. "Marriage and the Construction
of Reality." Diogenes (Feb. 1964): pp. 1-25. Marriage as an
accomplishment in more ways than one.

Blumenstein P., and P. Schwartz. American Couples: Money/
Work/Sex. New York: William Morrow, 1983. A very large
survey full of interesting data on contemporary couples.

Koontz, S. The Way We Never Were: American Families and the
Nostalgia Trap. New York: Basic Books, 1992. Koontz, a
social historian, has written a marvelous tract demolishing
myths about the American family. Especially an effective
antidote to much of the claptrap being passed off as
assumptions to public policy debates.

Mount F. The Subversive Family: An Alternative History of
Love and Family. London: Unwin, 1982. Mount takes on
(among others) some of the ideas of Edward Shorter as well
as making the persuasive argument that church and state
have been the two most adamant enemies of the sanctity of
the family. Students will like this very readable piece,
and sociologists will find it challenging.

Shoumatoff, A. The Mountain of Names: A History of the
Human Family. New York: Simon and Schuster, 1985.
Shoumatoff gives a comprehensive account of the basic
institution of society. He covers primitive, traditional,
aristocratic, and modern patterns of kinship. As befitting

a staff writer for the New Yorker, this book is lively and extremely well written.

Vaughn, D. "Uncoupling: The Social Construction of Divorce." In Social Interaction, 3rd ed. edited by Clark and Roboy, eds. New York: St. Martin's Press, 1988, pp. 384-403. This should be read with the Berger and Luckmann article. Together they are excellent representatives of the constructivist tradition in contemporary sociology.

ESSAY QUESTIONS

1. Given the kinship traits found in the Standard Cross-Cultural Sample how do you account for the pattern that families are so sexist?

2. "Romantic love is a great way of getting people together but a poor way of keeping them together." Critically evaluate this quote.

3. Do you see a link between one-parent families and poor parenting as studied by Patterson. Why or why not?

4. Why should women with children under the age of 10 not be not preferred by prospective mates. Does this mean that women with children over 10 years are preferred? Be specific.

CHAPTER SUMMARY

The Nature of Religion.   Socially organized patterns of
                                 belief and practices addressing
                                 questions of ultimate meaning
                                 and invoking the supernatural.

Religious Economies.   To what extent is religion
                                 governed by the state.
   Religious Pluralism   The state of a religious
                                 economy even if one religion is
                                 given a formal monopoly.

Church-Sect Theory.   Developed by Niebuhr to show
                                 how different types of
                                 denominations are socially
                                 patterned and appeal to
                                 different religious needs.
                                 Overall tendency is to move
                                 from sect to church.

Secularization and Revival.   With advancing secularization
                                 revival ensues: creating new
                                 sects out of old churches.

Innovation: Cult Formation.   Groups created outside
                                 the religious tradition.

Charisma.   Ability of one person to form
                                 extraordinarily strong
                                 attachments among followers.

The American Religious   Characterized by laissez-faire
   Economy.   status, an unchurched belt in
                                 the West, and churches losing
                                 members to sects.

Who Joins Cults?   Generally, those who grew up
                                 with no religious affiliation.

The Canadian Religious   Comparable to United States
   Economy.   rates of religious affiliation
                                 with far fewer groups.
                                 Catholics more concentrated
                                 geographically. Weak religious
                                 affiliation in the West.

Cult Movements in Europe.   Melton finds twice the rate as
                                 compared with North America.

The Protestant Explosion in Latin America.	So explosive that if present trends hold in 20 years Protestants will be a majority.
The Russian Revival.	With the fall of the Soviet Union, religiosity, never totally extinguished, has staged a strong comeback.
The Universal Appeal of Faith	Only religion can address effectively disappointment, suffering, and death.

SUMMARY

The Nature of Religion. Religion is one of humankind's oldest cultural possessions: our Neanderthal ancestors had religion at least 100,000 years ago. It is also a cultural universal in that some version of religion is found in all known societies. Perhaps religion's most distinctive feature, one that makes it unique, is that nothing else addresses as effectively and provides satisfactory answers to the big questions of life and death--that is, <u>questions about ultimate meaning</u>. As such, religion must assume the existence of the supernatural and thereby invoke the power, wisdom, authority, and the aid of gods, a capacity that nonreligious philosophies lack. By invoking the **supernatural** (beings/forces that account for the creation of the physical world and/or are not bound by its natural laws), humans hope to circumvent their imprisonment to those same natural laws. Religion can therefore be defined as socially organized patterns of belief and practices that concern ultimate meaning, and assume the existence of the supernatural. However, in providing these answers to questions of ultimate meaning religion also provides guidelines for how believers are to live, day to day, in their earthly existence. They do this as spokespersons for the gods, and thus the social rules that religions formulate and/or sanctify illustrate religion's function as a key legitimator of norms. Table 14-1 shows an overwhelming majority of adults in most of the world's economically advanced societies believe in God.

Religious Economies. With the evolution of societal complexity, religion differentiated itself as a separate institution while it manifested itself in a variety of forms. However, with societal complexity religion must come to grips with its relationship to the state. As with commercial economies, a key issue is the degree to which a religious economy is regulated by the state. Since the natural state of a religious economy is religious pluralism, the natural state of religion in a complex society is one of competition. Medieval Europe shows that even when one religion is granted a legal monopoly, dissent, heresies, and fissioning were always near, if not at, the surface.

Church-Sect Theory. Drawing on Weber, Niebuhr showed how a religious economy functions to appeal to the needs of different groups. Churches intellectualize religious teachings and restrain emotionalism in their services. They offer an image of the gods as somewhat remote from daily life and the individual. Sects stress emotionalism and individual mystical experiences and stress fundamentalism in their teachings. They present the gods as close at hand, taking an active interest and role in the lives of individuals. The natural clients of sects are the downtrodden, who are provided religious succorance and the hope of the next world in exchange for their forbearance with the misery in this one. However, the tendency is to move from a next-world focus to an increasing concern with the here and now. As religious groups grow and members become more prosperous, the need to reject this world lessens as does the consequent tension with mainstream society. Eventually, materially deprived lower-class constituents will become increasingly spiritually deprived as well and will translate their dissatisfaction with this formalistic remote approach to God by defecting and forming new denominations. This sect-formation process will occur any time the spiritual needs of the materially disadvantaged are neglected. (Johnson has refined Niebuhr's analysis by reframing it as a matter of deviance. Sects are deviant from mainstream society in both belief and practice and thus exist in a state of tension with it while churches reside quite peacefully within the larger societal context.)

Secularization and Revival. The next question is whether churches might become so enmeshed in mainstream society that they will become extinct because their adherents will be won completely over to science, thus making for a completely secularized society. However, secularization is self-limiting in a number of ways. Once again, as long as there is a need for answers to questions of ultimate meaning, people will turn to religion; and if the existing churches won't provide the necessary support, then new sects will develop. However, this process of creating new sects out of old churches (revival) is not the only way secularization is short-circuited. Sometimes, people in need of spiritual sustenance turn to completely new faiths (innovation).

Innovation: Cult Formation. Sects claim to have returned to a more authentic version of the traditional faith from which its parent organization has strayed. Thus, a set of churches and sects will form a single religious tradition. When religious groups are outside of the conventional religious tradition (either through importation from another society or through genuine innovation), they are usually defined as deviant and thus are at great tension with mainstream society. Thus, cults are religious movements that represent a new or different tradition. As such, all religions begin as cult movements. New religions crop up all the time, and while nearly all of them fail those that do catch on very often do so because of the excessive secularization of the indigenous religious situation. Seen this way secularization spurs religious change by precipitating revival (sect formation) where the existing religious tradition is strong and by encouraging innovation (cult formation) where the existing tradition is weak.

Charisma. One of the most crucial elements in successful cult formation is charisma, the extraordinary ability of one person to create strong attachments with others (especially in eliciting devotion and sacrifice from others). This "followership," especially in the early stages of cult formation, tends to be composed of those who already had prior attachments to the charismatic leader.

The American Religious Economy. It is not just that the American religious economy is diverse (with more than 1500 denominations at last count), but its most distinctive characteristic is that it is an exceptionally free market with little regulation from the state. Because of the prevailing laissez-faire arrangement the processes of secularization, revival, and innovation tend to rather freely play themselves out. As Table 14-5 in the text points out, during the past generation the more secularized faiths in contemporary America have been losing substantial membership generally to the benefit of the sects. In addition, the existence of an unchurched belt (the western states) predicts that in this secularized geographic area where conventional religious tradition is weak then cult formation should be greatest. Westerners do believe in the supernatural, but they are much less likely to be formally affiliated with a church. This is a major consequence of constant and rapid population movement, and as expected the West has the highest rates of cult activity in the nation.

Who Joins Cults? Stark and colleagues have found that people who say they have no religion are those most likely to express faith in unconventional supernatural beliefs (e.g., astrology, reincarnation, Eastern mysticism). They also found extraordinary representation of persons who had grown up with parents claiming no religious affiliation who were members of the Moonies, Hare Krishna, Scientology, etc.

The Canadian Religious Economy. Though Canada has comparable rates of religious affiliation (with that of the

United States) they are distributed over far fewer religious groups. Unlike the United States, Canadian Catholics are geographically and residentially much more concentrated, but,as with the United States, the more secularized denominations have been getting smaller. Further, the association between cult growth and secularization found in the United States seems to hold true in Canada. Finally, like the United States Canada's West is characterized by weak religious affiliation (due to population instability) and by relatively great cult activity.

   Cult Movements in Europe. Europe contains many countries with low church attendance rates (a good indicator of secularization); on close examination, it can be shown that cults are much more plentiful and successful in most of northern Europe and Great Britain than in the United States or Canada. Melton has studied European religion in general, and cult phenomena in particular. He has found, contrary to assuarances of European sociologists but in support of predictions made from secularization trends, that Europe has twice the rate of cult groups as does the United States. Indeed, given the high probability of significant undercounting the rate is probably higher than that.

   The Protestant Explosion in Latin America. The explosion of Protestant growth is actually in its fifth decade and shows no sign of abating. Indeed, Protestant groups of the Pentecostal variety are sweeping over most of the continent. If the present rates of conversion hold for the next 20 years, Protestants will be the majority in many Latin American nations. This extraordinary growth is possible due to a decline in government opposition to non-Catholic groups (thus creating a genuine religious economy) and inability of Catholicism to meet the religious needs of millions of Latin Americans.

   The Russian Revival. Despite 7 decades of official and unofficial discrimination belief in God is alive and well (comparable to that found in Scandinavia.) Not suprisingly, atheism is in retreat. More suprisingly, religion is gaininig many adhereents among the younger inteligentsia. (It should be noted that the revival is not limited to Russian orthodox religion but also is found with the Jewish and Moslem populations as well as with Protestantism.)

   The Universal Appeal of Faith. As Stark concludes: So long as people want to know what existence means, so long as they are prone to disappointment, suffering, and death, the religious impulse will not be stilled. Only religion, only systems of thought that include belief in the supernatural, can address problems of this magnitude.

TEACHING SUGGESTIONS

The objective of Chapter 14 is to show students how a sociological approach can delineate crucial social sources of religious behavior. In other words, the major but not only contribution of sociologists of religion is to treat religion as a dependent variable and various social structural traits as independent variables.

1. **Discussion: "Updating Durkheim's Theory of Religion."** Besides Weber, the other great founding sociologist of religion was Durkheim. Durkheim's assertion that religion is the disguised worship of the group--that is, the sacred is the group in an idealized form--is an overlooked source of theoretical inspiration for church-sect theory. If it is true that when a religious group worships the sacred it is really unconsciously worshiping an idealized version of itself then when the standard way of worship is no longer satisfying to many/most members the members, in turn, will stay away from religious services and look for alternatives. From there I have argued that one way of looking at Durkheim's insights is to use a movie production analogy. Every religion is a movie that periodically is edited and revised (sometimes drastically: see Vatican II). The movie producers, directors, and technicians tend to be the clergy while the audience tends to be the laity. What is projected onto the screen at any time is the latest version of the religion and every religion's movie of itself is itself idealized. If the audience begins to tune out--time for revisions. The tricky part is to convince the students that what the laity (audience) thinks they see on the screen is what lies behind the screen: the ultimate reality of the sacred. But they can never look behind the screen; they can see only what is on it. They are, as long as they are alive, chained to their seats (pace Plato). When members of the laity/audience die they get to leave their seats, go up on the stage, peek behind the screen, and then exit. Typically, the clergy try to convince the laity that the clergy and clergy alone know what is behind the screen (occupational self-interest? Some of them have convinced themselves that they've been allowed to peek ahead of time.) I never say that all of the movies are wrong but if there is one sacred reality then by definition at least $N-1$ of the movies are substantially incorrect. Further, you can spin off from this the idea of competing theaters (religions)-- what's showing down the block? -- and thus talk about the religious economy. What happens when movies get too old? Sect formation. When some new film genre is introduced? Cult formation. This crude updating of Durkheim tries to explain why there are such radically differing conceptions of the sacred throughout the world. Different groups with different histories make different (though homologous)

"movies" of themselves. If there is time, I try to extend the argument by showing the class that differing social structures ought to have correspondingly different religious beliefs and practices and thus try tying in this Durkheimian perspective with the previously discussed data from Swanson.

Sources: Durkheim, E. <u>The Elementary Forms of Religious Life</u>. New York: Free Press, 1965. The original structural-functionalist gives the classic statement on the connections between social structure and religious belief and practice. Eliade, M. <u>The Sacred and the Profane.</u> New York: Harcourt Brace, Jovanovich, 1959. A wonderful "read" by a noted historian of religion.

2. **Mini-lecture:** "Extending Durkheim." Stark's definition of religion as socially organized patterns of belief and practices that concern ultimate meaning and assume the existence of the supernatural can be explicated by two different though related illustrations drawn from Swanson's work. First, with regard to the existence of the supernatural the point I like to make is that conceptions of the supernatural vary with the type of social structure. To show this, I cite Swanson's data positing a strong positive association between societal complexity and belief in monotheism (the argument being that simple societies have no functional need to believe in monotheism so their religion is direct and animistic). However, as societies grow more complex, in order to prevent them from fissioning the belief in a single, all-powerful God is an idea in which all of the societal members can believe. From this perspective, monotheism becomes an adaptive form of solidarity. The other example I give the students is to show how the belief in a supernatural morality (life after death) tends to be associated with the existence of social classes in a society. Thus, from a functionalist perspective, the belief in a life after death directs potential dissent away from sources of authority and, in a sense, teaches deferred gratification: "Sure, things are lousy now but hold on! Don't kill the lord of the manor and rape his women. Be patient and God will reward you." At this point you may want to elaborate on this a bit by pointing out how the economically disadvantaged are the ones who are the most fervent believers that justice for themselves and others awaits us all in the next world. You can also show how at times seemingly disparate sociological perspectives could come close to the same conclusion. For example, while a conflict theorist would argue the opiate-of-the-masses theme, a functionalist might argue that the alternative to belief in the next life would be a demand for social change more along the lines of increased justice in this world. The divergence between the perspectives might be that the conflict theorist would emphasize how religion is may be disadvantageous for the oppressed group of believers while

the functionalist could argue that the belief in the next world payoff is functional for the system.

Source: Swanson, G. The Birth of the Gods. Ann Arbor: University of Michigan Press, 1960. A cross-cultural test of a Durkheimian perspective: social structure as the independent variable and religious beliefs and practices as the dependent variables. Most interesting.

3. Lecture: "Secularization and America's Civil Religion." I still find Bellah's thesis a fascinating blend of Durkheim's concern for solidarity in modern society and the secularization thesis. Certainly, Americans (and others) often glorify their particular way of life as the best in the world. (Interestingly, this rank ethnocentrism seems to be most intense with those who have never been abroad and have no intention of doing so.) Snide observations aside, all our civil rituals (standing for the national anthem) and myths ("liberty and justice for all") and sacred places (Lincoln Memorial) and taboos (flag burning) do have a quasi-sacred quality to them. I like to wrap up this lecture with a discussion of flag burning by asking students the following: If the flag is sacred, then who should consecrate it? If we ban the deliberate destruction of the flag because of what it represents, do we ban the deliberate destruction of representations of the flag showing them (the problem of infinite regress)? If we ban flag destruction, then what about flag desecration? Must we ban the use of all of those gigantic flags over car lots and fast-food restaurants? (After all, aren't the flags being used for purposes of crass commercialism?) Finally, might not the flag stand for freedom of expression and dissent (including its own burning)?

Sources: Bellah, R. The Broken Covenant: American Civil Religion in a Time of Trial. New York: Seabury Press, 1975. Fenn, R. "The Relevance of Bellah's 'Civil Religion' Thesis to a Theory of Secularization." Social Science History 1, No. 4 (1977): 502-517. A subtle, thoughtful essay on some of the implications of the civil religion idea.

4. Discussion: "Moral Progress: A Classical Sociological Look." This exercise is useful in discussing the future of religion especially in the context of the universal appeal of faith. After all, organized religion is still thought of by many people as a fundamental vehicle for moral progress; so let's trace this idea a bit. We'll begin with the notion that a group of believers on this earth can dedicate themselves to and indeed approach moral perfection. The first thing the instructor does is to get the class to agree that belonging to a solidary group (from marriage to a religion to anything in between) is a good idea. The next item is to have the class agree that, at least in theory, moral progress in that group is a goal worthy of pursuit.

At this point read to the class (it's short enough) Durkheim's passage on the community of saints. What is especially crucial for the students to grasp is that although progress can be made, guilt and punishment must still be present for the solidarity of the group to persist. That is, moral progress, according from a Durkheimian perspective, would indicate that guilt and punishment and thus expiation are constants in solidary groups but are increasingly called out for smaller and smaller infractions. Another way of putting it is that progress means punishing as intolerable exactly those phenomena that in the past the group would have let slide. Is the price for progress and diminished guilt a solidary-less existence? Is this possible? Is it worth it?

[Instructor's note: Freud, in his <u>Civilization and Its Discontents</u>, made much the same point when he argued that in order to achieve civilization man's aggressive drives must be stifled. That is, the price of civilization is neurosis.]

Source: Durkheim, E. <u>The Rules of Sociological Method</u>. New York: Free Press, 1982. Chapter 3.

ADDITIONAL STUDENT READINGS

Deloria, V. <u>God Is Red</u>. New York: Dell, 1973. Deloria, a distinguished Native American scholar, champions a return to Indian beliefs as a viable alternative to the failure of Christianity. Well argued and provocative.

O'Keefe, D. <u>Stolen Lightning: The Social Theory of Magic</u>. New York: Continuum, 1982. Definitely not a how-to book but rather a sophisticated exposition of the role of magic in society.

Pagels, E. <u>The Gnostic Gospels</u>. New York: Random House, 1979. Women as priests? Pagels draws a fascinating picture of an early Christian group: the Gnostics.

ESSAY QUESTIONS

1. "If disappointment, suffering, and death are constants to the human condition then so is religion." Critically comment on this quote.

2. Compare the United States and Canada vis-à-vis their respective religious economies.

3. Compare Europe and North America on cult formation.

4. Detail why churches grow from sects and vice-versa.

CHAPTER OUTLINE

The "Tragedy of the Commons."	Everyone who uses a free good maximizes their position until the utility of the good is extinguished.
In the Laboratory.	Messick and Wilke: Subjects in all experimental groups tended to increase their harvest. With overuse condition players voted to put harvesting under control of a leader: make a government. The leaders tended to regulate to optimize the harvest while also somewhat exploiting other players.
Public Goods and the State.	The state, as the organized embodiment of political processes, implements and regulates
Public Goods.	that to which all citizens need access.
Functions of the State.	To provide for public goods, especially internal order.
Rise of the Repressive State.	The fully developed and often repressive state has high agricultural development.
Taming the State.	Key question: how to control the abusive potential of the state without unduly weakening its capacity to provide public goods.
Elitist and Pluralist States.	Elitist: dominated by single or a few minorities; pluralist: governed by several minorities.
Democracy and the People.	Because of practicality and indifference, democracy rests on representative government.
George Gallup: The Rise of Opinion Polling.	During 1936 election, Gallup ushers in the age of the poll.
Female Candidates.	Studies in Canada and United States show that voters don't

keep female candidates from
winning but incumbents, largely
male, hold an enormous
advantage in elections.

Ideology and Public Opinion.   Very few voters can be termed
                                ideological.

Elites and Mass Opinion.   Political elites tend toward
                                ideological consistency; most
                                citizens do not. On most
                                issues, only a subset of
                                citizens express an interest.
                                Compared to Europe, successful
                                American (and to a lesser
                                extent Canadian) political
                                parties are not ideological.

SUMMARY

The tragedy of the commons illustrates the underlying
contradiction of the need for the state: Many things vital
to humans as social beings conflict with things vital to
humans as individuals. To provide for the common good,
people often are forced to surrender considerable control
over their lives to leaders and governments. This
surrender, unfortunately, often results in much misery when
leaders use their power and authority to repress, exploit,
and even enslave their people.

The principle of the tragedy of the commons is that for
those who use for free a collective good/resource, it is in
their self-interest to expand their use of the resource so
as to maximize their self-interest. Therefore, with the
consequent expansion the free resource in question becomes
depleted, and unless all are forced to change their ways the
resource will ultimately become extinguished.

The Tragedy of the Commons: In the Laboratory. Messick
and Wilke wanted to find out if the conditions of the
tragedy of the commons could be replicated in the laboratory
and, if so, how subjects respond to these conditions. The
goals of this laboratory game were that players should try
to accumulate as many points as possible while making the
resource last as long as possible.

[Instructor's note: What should be kept in mind is that
although the players thought they were making selections in
response to the other players, in actuality they were
responding to   selections made by a computer.]

The game began with each player in the condition of
freedom that paralleled that of the herd owners. The two
independent variables controlled by the computer were

level of harvest--overuse, underuse, optimal--and the degree of equity-- equitable or inequitable. The other condition of the game was to identify a leader who would allocate points. (Every subject was told he or she had been elected leader.) Subjects in all of the groups tended to increase their harvest over time. When players thought there was great inequity, they took larger harvests and increased their harvests more rapidly. Players increased their harvests in the underuse more than in the overuse condition. Further, the overwhelming majority of those in the overuse condition voted to put harvesting in the hands of a leader (i.e., government regulation). As leaders, they decreased the size of the harvest to the level of optimal use; they were quite equitable in assigning shares to the other players; and they gave themselves larger shares than they gave others. In effect, the players resented their perception of being exploited, but when put in the position of power they in turn exploited others.

Public Goods and the State. In its original form the tragedy of the commons is a subsistence problem, but it also exemplifies the idea of public goods: that which is vital to the survival and welfare of human societies. However specified, public goods inherently contain the "free rider" problem: The best deal for any individual is to reap the benefits without sharing the costs. Thus, as Olsen concludes, though it is always in the individual's best interest not to contribute to the public good, there will be no public goods unless means exist to force individuals to do their share. The best example of a chronic public goods issue is taxation, which is the principal instrument of coercion whereby the state--the organized embodiment of political processes--is able to implement public goods.

Functions of the State. The principal function of the state is to provide for public goods. The most basic public good is for the state to prevent the Hobbesian state of the "war of all against all." Thus, the state monopolizes coercion to prevent private coercion. Put another way, to ensure some freedom for all, the state must make sure that some do not have absolute freedom. However, this begs the question as to how to limit the state.

Rise of the Repressive State. An analysis by Stark based on the span of control of political leaders of the societies included in the Standard Cross-Cultural Sample shows that 44 per cent were stateless, 40 per cent were "semi-stated," and 16 per cent were "fully stated." The fully developed state is associated with high agricultural development. In turn, the development of the state means frequent external warfare. Finally, the state is also associated with a high degree of stratification. Thus, fully developed agriculture means a consistent surplus of food that can sustain a larger population some of whom occupy full-time positions in highly articulated political and military institutions, which allows for the development of an elaborate stratification system as well as the rise of the state and a condition of near chronic warfare.

Taming the State. Given the abuse of power inherent in the state as evidenced by exploiting the members of a society, the question becomes, How can the abuse of these coercive powers be limited without weakening the ability of the state to fulfill its necessary functions? Abandoning the quest for philosopher-kings, political thinkers by the eighteenthth century thought that the only chance of taming the state lay with specific rights guaranteed by structures in which power was dispersed among many groups: pluralism. To illustrate, English democracy evolved from a single principle, the right to private property. The English believed that the state could be tamed if taxes could not be imposed or collected without the approval of those being taxed. Whereas Marxists saw private property as the root of all evil, liberal pluralists saw the protection of property as the security of individual rights and they had the development of English democracy to point to as proof. The English king increasingly had to rely on the cooperation of Parliament, and the several factions within Parliament meant that compromise was the rule not the exception.

The American version of liberal democracy was structured to prevent two types of tyranny: of the minority (so as to prevent them from exploiting the many) and of the majority (so as not to trample over the rights of minorities). Thus, the American invention of checks and balances in which any one of the three main divisions of government might nullify actions taken by the other two was conceived. Canada evolved a similar democratic system without a written constitution until patriation in 1981.

Elitist and Pluralist States. An elitist state is one governed by a minority, and it is almost impossible for it not to be tyrannical. A pluralist state is one governed by competing minorities and, as such, it is almost impossible not to have a minimal degree of freedom. Thus, for critics like C. Wright Mills, the greatest perceived threat to democracy was a single interlocking power elite dominated by leaders from the military, the government bureaucracy, and large corporations. The pluralist critics of Mills such as Riesman countered by stating that significant conflicts of interest exist among the so-called power elite.

Democracy and the People. It is not practical for large numbers of people to try to practice direct democracy. Also, many people simply are not interested in taking part even minimally in political life. In fact, Tables 15-4 through 15-6 show that within western democracies there is tremendous variation in the degree to which citizens involve themselves. Thus, for both of these reasons, practicality and indifference, democracies rest on the principle of representative government. As a result, the politically apathetic give disproportionate political influence to those who do participate.

George Gallup: The Rise of Opinion Polling. In the 1936 presidential election two polls of significance were taken. One poll, conducted by the <u>Literary Digest</u>, used telephone books and automobile registration lists for their sample of millions (which of course was hardly representative of those who actually voted). It failed miserably in predicting the winner. The other poll, conducted by Gallup, was based on 2,000 respondents (carefully sampled) and correctly predicted the Roosevelt landslide. Later in that decade Gallup's findings revealed widespread misperception and misrepresentations of public opinion, and it was these successes by Gallup that made the opinion poll an important and indispensable part of the political landscape.

Female Candidates. For years, women have comprised a small minority of members of the Canadian Parliament. Conventional wisdom held that Canadian voters keep women out. Canadian social scientists Hunter and Denton argued otherwise. First, incumbents (overwhelmingly male) always have an advantage in an election. Second, Canadian parties are more likely to nominate women during times when the party has been less successful; that is, after they have been losing, they increase their rate of female nominations. Third, women are often nominated for lost-cause seats. What the researchers found under careful analysis is that the differences in the vote-getting abilities of male and female candidates "disappeared entirely" when the candidates were equated in terms of party, incumbency, and competitiveness. So the voters do not keep women out; but the existing male elites do. The same results have been found in the United States and similar results have been found in Australia.
Jody Newman's recent research has demonstrated that a candidate's sex does not affect chances of winning an election but that incumbents do have a great advantage. Most incumbents are male but take away incumbency and males are shown no particular preference by voters.

Ideology and Public Opinion. Ideology, a connected set of beliefs based on a few general and abstract ideas, seems to characterize few adults. Moreover, a substantial part of the population in any society ignores most of the issues, reserving attention for occasional matters of great urgency or with special personal implications. In a classic study of U.S. voters, Converse could classify only about 3 percent as basing their decisions and opinions on an ideology. Another 12 percent he classified as making some use of any underlying political ideology. Almost half of the voters took a mildly issue-oriented approach to politics, and the rest seemed to ignore all policy, issue, and ideological matters.

Elites and Mass Opinion. Studies of opinions and attitudes show that ideologies and world views typically are limited to small elites, and the reason for this is the structural positions these elites hold. McClosky demonstrated this by distributing questionnaires to more than 3,000 Democratic and Republican presidential delegates and compared them with the results of a national sample of 1500 American adults. He found that members of political party elites tend to have highly internally consistent political views. Even most college-educated persons do not experience the pressures toward ideological consistency felt by professional politicians, but because they are well educated they will be more sensitive than the less-educated to more obvious inconsistencies.

Panel studies (the same sample of respondents interviewed several times) have found that a substantial part of the population has no political opinion and/or will give a series of inconsistent responses to the same questions over time. Therefore, on any given issue, only a subset of the public will have opinions or interest. Further, people will belong to one public issue and not another, depending on how much that issue directly affects them personally. In part, the absence of an ideological nature of Americans is due to the structure of the U.S. political system. Compared with Europe, successful American political parties are not ideological. The same holds true to a lesser extent for Canadian political parties. Further, just as European political parties are more ideological than are Canadian and American political parties so too are their unions. (C.f. Tables 15-8 and 15-9.) The structure of political representation and winning office at all levels of government shapes a party system that must appeal to a wide variety of groups. Thus, American parties, to the extent that they are ideological, significantly overlap with one another in their drive to maximize votes. Therefore, American political parties are not terribly ideological and the electorate as a whole isn't, either.

TEACHING SUGGESTIONS

The overall objective of Chapter 15 is to introduce political sociology to the students by showing them that there are separate political institutions in advanced societies that always articulate with other institutions and processes. In other words, the basic premise of political sociology is that politics can never be understood independently of its social context.

1. Discussion: "A Dilemma for Liberal Capitalism." Is guaranteeing (or allocating) work a proper government function? This is not quite a free-wheeling discussion in the sense that some prefatory comments from the instructor are necessary. Specifically, if as a liberal capitalist democracy, we assume that the dominant trend toward an electronic and knowledge-based economy continues and if we further assume, as befits political liberalism, that people should be judged on their own merits and nothing else, then are we moving toward a situation in which a sizable portion of the population can neither be employed nor are employable full-time in anything remotely resembling a dignified, productive, decent paying job? If, however, we move to a managed economy so as to guarantee full(er) employment, then we risk further losses to global competitiors. We also run the risk of an unacceptable level of government intervention in our economy and our private lives. Complicating this dilemma is a further assumption: if we posit curtailing welfare benefits but *not* raising the minimum wage then even *if* minimum wage jobs are available they cannot support a single individual let alone a small family.

[Instructor's note: You do not have to agree that this dilemma exists as presented in order to present it to the class for discussion and argument.]

After exploring (tentatively) the potential of this situation for increased social unrest the instructor can show how many citizens might demand some governmental initiative in resolving some of these issues. This, of course, would run counter to the current climate of reduced deificit spending and lesser government intervention. Finally, introducing such concepts as a meritocracy and an underclass into the mix the students are confronted with the crucial concept of *structural contradiction* (in a non-Marxian way).

Sources: Auletta, K. <u>The Underclass</u>. New York: Random House, 1982. Journalistic sociology at its best. An excellent account of a growing problem whose solution defies the usual bromides and platitudes.
Morf, M. "Eight Scenarios for Work in the Future."
<u>The Futurist</u> (June 1983). Morf presents several possibilities regarding the distribution of work in the future including extreme taylorism, feudal unions, work coupons, gods and clods, and the electronic cottage. Certainly grist for the public policy mill.
Walzer, M. <u>Spheres of Justice: A Defense of Pluralism and Equality</u>. New York: Basic Books, 1983. Walzer presents a

persuasive case for equality and diversity and for justice and autonomy as worthy complements and not mutually exclusive phenomena. An important work by a noted political philosopher.

2. Discussion: "Policing the Family: *Quis custodiet ipsos custodes*?" The important concept of taming the state can be covered in another way. When people marry they exchange a set of vows (to each other and only indirectly to any potential children). One can open a discussion by making this rather obvious point and then by asking, with feigned innocence, whether children have rights too--rights so important that parents should openly make explicit and solemn vows when they marry. You can then complicate matters a bit by saying that it is one thing to acknowledge the rights of children, but how do you enforce them? How do you check to see if the parents are doing as they should? Should people be licensed before they can parent? After all, we require licenses for fishing, hunting, and driving. Isn't parenting just as important? Who devises the test for certification? Must couples be married in order to parent? What of single people? Should single parents be allowed to adopt? Can't gays be good parents (through adoption or surrogate parenting)? After the discussion has wandered far and wide, bring it back by showing that behind both cases: children's rights and parents' rights, there ultimately lies the legislative and police powers of the state. Thus, when curbing the powers of the state you must allow leeway (freedoms?) in all areas of life including the family.

Sources: de Jouvenal, B. <u>On Power: Its Nature and the History of Its Growth</u>. Boston: Beacon Press, 1962. In the debate on the taming of the state (and by implication the state's impact on society), this is an essential work of enduring value. A classic in modern political thought.

Donzelot, J. <u>The Policing of Families</u>. New York: Pantheon, 1979. Besides the state, might not other institutions and processes need "taming"? Donzelot's work breaks new ground and reformulates many family issues in challenging ways.

3. **Discussion:** "Gun Control."

[Instructor's note: I don't like guns. I am not an owner let alone an enthusiast. I do acknowledge the fact that the vast majority of gun owners are law-abiding citizens. However, I would remind others that since there are tens of millions of guns in the U.S. even a miniscule percentage of them, used for ill, produce an incredible amount of carnage. That being said, in what follows I emphasize legal argumentation and thus avoid the cheap shot of Freudian analyses in conjecturing *why* gun ownership assumes a theological status for so many Americans.]

Start with this from the 2nd Amendment: "...The right of the people to keep and bear arms shall not be infringed." Pretty straightforward, isn't it? Ask the class why gun enthusiasts emphasize this part of the Amendment but not what comes before it: "A well-regulated militia, being necessary to the security of a free state..." Hmm. It seems that a strict interpretation of the Amendment does not lend itself to unrestricted ownership and use but rather *specifically delineates* the conditions of firearms keeping and bearing: in order to protect the government (from invasion?) a militia (National Guard?) is necessary. It says nothing about protecting oneself *from* the government as so many survivalists emphasize.

See how the class responds to this: in keeping with the Constitution--if you want to *legally* keep and bear arms you must be part of a militia; and a well-regulated one to boot (camp?) How much do you love your guns? Two weeks a year active duty plus meetings every other weekend?

Finally, ask how confining weapons to a militia would help in "**taming the state.**" If you want to get particularly nightmarish (especially so as to terrorize those few who might be self-identified liberals) conjure up a vision of militia staffed by young American versions of "brownshirts" with zero tolerance for First Amendment rights.

Hopefully, the only drive-bys to which you will be exposed will be verbal broadsides and not the "street-sweeper" variety. Good luck.

Source. Fussell, P. <u>Thank God for the Atom Bomb and Other Essays.</u> New York: Ballantine Books, 1988. (c.f. pp. 118-123 especially; all of the essays are provocative.)

ADDITIONAL STUDENT READINGS

Bartlett, D. amd J. Steele: <u>America: What Went Wrong</u>. Kansas City: Andrews and McMeal, 1992. Two journalists turn in a modern muckraking *tour de force* exposing a multitude of shams and scams along the way. I'm sure that Ida Tarbell and Lincoln Steffens would approve.

O'Rourke, P.J. <u>Parliament of Whores: A Lone Humorist Attempts to Explain the Entire United States Government</u>. New York: Atlantic Monthly Press, 1991. Starting with his preface, "Why God Is a Republican and Santa Claus Is a Democrat" a former <u>National Lampoon</u> writer lampoons the federal government and everyone associated with it. Even funnier if it wasn't so accurate.

Weatherford, J. <u>Tribes on the Hill: An Investigation into the Rituals and Realities of an Endangered American Species, the Congress of the United States.</u> South Hadley Mass.: Bergin and Garvey, 1985. A cultural anthropologist looks at the folkways, rituals, myths, and taboos of Congress and uncovers one primitive culture trait after another. It's a wonder anything ever gets done. A wonderful antidote for those who take congressional politics at face value.

ESSAY QUESTIONS

1. How might a government's failure to prevent a modern "tragedy of the commons" be an example of how the state fails in its essential duty of providing public goods?

2. What is the dilemma inherent in the issue of "taming the state"?

3. Explain how practicality and indifference make representative government essential in a democracy.

4. Why is it wrong to say that American and Canadian voters are opposed to female political candidates.

Chapter 16

CHAPTER OUTLINE

Occupational Prestige.

Most people operate from a functionalist perspective: the greater the education and income, the higher the prestige of the occupation.

The Transformation of Work.

Productivity derived from working smarter; not harder.

The Transformation of the Labor Force.

Significant increases of females in the labor force is the major reason. Several reasons why modernization brings more women into labor force: more education, later marriage, reduced fertility. In general, job satisfaction is high in advanced societies.

Unemployment.

Tends to increase with prosperity since many actively seek work. African-American unemployment is due to discrimination and high drop-out rate.

The Transformation of Education.

Industrial Revolution was the impetus to great expansion of finishing high school and attending college.

"Educated" Americans.

ETS study shows that half of all Americans scored in the lower reaches of each form of literacy. Even a college degree doesn't preclude a poor showing.

Do Schools Really Matter?

Coleman found that good teachers matter. Heyns found that summer reading matters. U.S. Department of Education found that homework matters. Cross-nationally, Heyneman and Loxley found that the overall wealth of the nation matters.

High school Today.	Public high schools are over-represented with underachieving students.
Does Education Pay?	A strong correlation exists between degree of education and amount of income.
Meyer's Theory of Educational Functions.	Schools grant statuses to individuals (micro level) and the educational system creates new occupations (macro level).

SUMMARY

From the simplest of societies to the most complex, the education of members is a basic societal need since until people are sufficiently educated, they cannot fulfill their economic responsibilities.

Occupational Prestige.   This idea refers to people's general notion as to which jobs are better and which are worse. Immediately after World War II Hatt and North pioneered the study of occupational prestige. The study was replicated in 1962, and the correlation with the first one was .99. Later Porter and Pineo replicated this study for Canada, and the results yielded a correlation of .98 with the U.S. study. Additional studies have shown similar results for Germany, Great Britain, Japan, New Zealand, the Soviet Union, Ghana, Guam, India, Indonesia, the Ivory Coast, and the Philippines. Blau and Duncan have found that for a given occupation average income and average education can accurately predict the overall occupational prestige: In general, higher average income and higher average education result in greater occupational prestige. Thus, most people, it would seem, operate from a perspective that supports the functionalist approach to stratification (see Chapter 9).

The Transformation of Work.   Drucker's analysis of the dramatic increases in economic productivity that support modern living standards stressed the fact that people have not been working harder as much as they've been working smarter; and it is various technological innovations that have made this possible. However, technological innovations are not the whole story. Scientific management--(the application of scientific techniques to improve work efficiency--was also an early contribution to the movement of working smarter. Still, technological advances have changed the character of work. In 1900 fewer than 20 percent of North Americans had white-collar jobs whereas now there are more white-collar workers than blue-collar workers, and the gap between these two categories continues to increase.

The Transformation of the Labor Force. In the past 120 years the percentage of North Americans over the age of 16 in the labor force went from about 40 per cent to 66 per cent. The major reason for this is that women have been steadily increasing their participation in the labor force until today they comprise more than 40 per cent of the North American labor market. The reasons why this has occurred are many, but several stand out. First, at times, large increases of women in the labor force have coincided with sex ratios where women significantly outnumber men (see most recently the 1970s). Second, reduced fertility has meant shorter time given to childbearing and child rearing and more time available for careers. Third, advances in household appliances have meant reduced time needed to keep up a home. Fourth, with the shift from muscle to knowledge work more women can effectively compete for jobs today compared with earlier generations. Indeed, the more industrialized the nation the greater the female participation in the labor force. Fifth, many women work simply for money. Today, many households cannot get by on one paycheck. Given the above, can we determine whether women have achieved equal pay for equal work? This is almost impossible to answer since we must compare people in the same occupations, with the same number of years of experience. Such data are difficult to assemble since female entry into the better occupations in significant numbers has been a recent phenomenon.

Assuming employment, most workers in advanced econmies exhibit a high degree of job satisfaction and would work for pay even if they could afford not to (Tables 16-3 to 16-5). Another major issue involves unemployment. One must be careful here since the term unemployed does not apply to everyone who is not employed but rather only to those who are without jobs and seeking work. In fact, unemployment often rises when economic times are good and the number of jobs increase because then many who were previously not actively seeking employment begin to do so. Another caveat: At any moment in time many people are between jobs so that the unemployment rate will actually seem higher than it is. However, the unemployment that is a cause of social concern cannot be explained away. For example, the high rates of unemployment among African-Americans is due in part to racial discrimination and in part to the high drop-out rate. So, although African-Americans today are about as likely as whites to enter college, they remain more likely than whites to drop out of high school. Further, when examining the geography of dropping out of high school, we find that the upper Midwest has the lowest rates while the South has the highest rates.

The Transformation of Education. The Industrial Revolution marked the turning point in public attitudes toward children attending school. Nevertheless, not until well into the twentieth century did most people attend high school. In 1920, only 42.9 percent of all Americans age 16 or 17 were enrolled in school. This was not an even distribution in that cities from the West had much higher enrollment rates than did cities in the Northeast and South as the former had many foreign-born youths and the latter much more poverty. So, it was not until after World War II that the majority of Americans began to finish high school and, concurrently, the real explosion in higher education occurred during the past 40 years. For example, between 1950 and 1988 the number of students enrolled in college rose by a factor of 6 so that today the majority of Americans start college and nearly one-third earn degrees. In Canada today more than a quarter million students attend nearly 300 colleges and about 20 percent of all persons 18 to 24 are enrolled. These college attendee rates are far higher than those for European nations.

"Educated" Americans. While Canada and the U.S. send a far greater proportion of their young to college it is problematic to infer that in general the citizens of these nations are more literate than their counterparts in the rest of the world. A random sample of 26,000 Americans surveyed by the Educational Testing Service found that 1/2 of the sample scored in the lower two categories of each form of literacy: quantitative, documentary, and prose. To make matters worse, a majority of the sample native born and holding a four year college degree scored in the three lower categories of quantitative and prose literacy and in the lower two of document literacy thus making it impossible to avoid issues of the *quality* of American education.

Do Schools Really Matter? Coleman found, contrary to the conventional wisdom at the time, that there were few differences in the quality of schools African-Americans and whites attended in terms of expenditures per student, age and quality of the buildings, libraries, class size, and teacher training. Further, these aspects of school quality had no detectable impact on student achievement scores. Coleman did find that how well students from any background did in school was correlated with the scores that their teachers made on a vocabulary test.

However, whether the students' teachers are competent or not kids do not go to school all year, and Heyns decided to study what happens to learning during the summer. She found that children from higher-income families learned about as much during vacation as during the school year while children from the most deprived backgrounds actually lost ground during the summer. Heyns also found that attending summer school did not prevent summer learning losses. Further, she discovered reading is the single summer activity most strongly and consistently related to summer learning and that a major factor affecting reading, independent of a student's background, was the distance from the student's home to the nearest public library. In sum, school can greatly improve the situations of poor children while school seems to matter rather minimally for the more affluent students.

High School Today. A massive U.S. Department of Education survey of high school has turned up some important findings regarding (non)achievement. First, homework matters. Those who didn't do it received poor grades and often dropped out. Second, few students spend 5 hours a week on homework. (Asian students are the exceptions.) Third, Catholic and other church-related schools achieve much better results from their students even though they spend considerably less per student, and it is not just because these schools have better students to work with. When Coleman compared students from similar backgrounds, the Catholic schools still far surpassed the public schools in terms of the educational achievements of their students.

When looking at effects of school worldwide, Heyneman and Loxley in a World Bank study yielded the following four major findings:

1. Children in the wealthier, more industrialized nations learn more during the same number of school years.
2. The poorer the nation, the less that student backgrounds influence school performances.
3. The effects of school and teacher quality are comparatively greater in the poorer nations.
4. The poorer the nation, the greater the economic return for getting an education.

Does Education Pay? Despite numerous qualifications it does seem that school matters especially to those who need it most. But does it pay? When relatively few people earned college degrees, they possessed a scarce occupational qualification. Hence, the decline in the value of a college education is the result not of colleges ceasing to prepare people for careers but of colleges preparing so many people for careers. Put another way, as the need of a college degree in terms of employability increased, the value of a college degree declined. So the more a college degree is seen as a necessary ticket for a good-paying job, the more colleges and universities have accommodated themselves with a more vocational orientation.

Still, does education pay? A perusal of Table 16-11 answers that question with a resounding yes! There is a strong positive correlation between amount of education and amount of income. However, when you take into account the inflation of academic credentials of the past twenty years then just when African-Americans and Hispanics were making significant gains in college attendance the value of obtaining a college degree was declining. This credential inflation can also be seen in the context that not all who receive degrees actually need them in any objective sense for their entry-level positions. As allocation theorists would argue, the major function of credential inflation is to provide a way of allocating a limited number of valued positions to a potential oversupply of applicants.

Meyer's Theory of Educational Functions. Meyer's addition to the credentialing debate addressed both the micro and macro levels of analysis. At the micro level he argued that levels of education, in and of themselves, are social statuses and that schools can be seen as institutions empowered by society to grant statuses to individuals. Thus a major effect of education is that people learn to play the role appropriate to the status that their school confers on them. Therefore, the bigger difference in status would be that between high school graduate and college graduate and not between elite college graduate and "podunk" college graduate. This powerful socializing effect of educational status continues throughout the person's lifetime.

At the macro level Meyer argued that the educational system has the power to create new occupations, even elite occupations, and to control the placement of these in the occupational structure. According to Meyer, many of the most highly paid, highest-status occupations in contemporary society exist because universities invented them, defined their occupational worth, and determined the conditions under which people could enter these occupations.

Finally, Meyer argued that the rising level of mass education has expanded the proportion of the population regarded as having citizenship capacities, rights, and responsibilities, Rather than seeing the educational establishment as merely reproducing the class system, Meyer sees it as capable of changing the class system (by creating new statuses and occupations) while increasing the opportunity of more people to attain upward mobility.

TEACHING SUGGESTIONS

The objective fo Chapter 16 is to articulate the linkage between education and occupation. Given their career orientations students should care about the issue.

1. **Discussion:** "The Underground Economy." I have found that this discussion is a way of examining the notion of

occupational prestige since the whole notion of underground economic activities smacks of shady dealings. And yet, once you get students to think about it, underground economic activity is widespread and not always as nefarious as its label implies. Students selling textbooks to roommates, typing term papers in exchange for car repairs, buying and selling term papers, baby sitting, garage sales, selling drugs, prostitution, buying stolen merchandise-- all are examples of participating in the underground economy (here defined as the exchange of goods and services for money or other goods and services with such transactions not being officially recorded).

After establishing the definitional parameters with appropriate illustrations, the instructor can then point out that the underground economy is a kind of primitive capitalism: labor intensive and relying primarily upon large amounts of human ingenuity. More specifically, to participate, one does not need much capital nor a huge inventory. Further, participation does not depend upon educational certification and is not bound to traditional occupational constraints of time schedules or work spaces. Rather, participation in this economy is fluid, involves low overhead, and is tax-free. (Though often illegal and sometimes immoral it is rarely fattening.) Here is an opportunity to examine straight life--conventional occupations and their attendant educational requirements-- by looking at their mirror opposites. Students not only find the contrast interesting but also are surprised, upon discussion and reflection, to see how much ordinary citizens are involved in a sector of the economy that involves several billion dollars of goods and services each year.

Source: Valentine, B. <u>Hustling and Other Hard Work</u>. New York: Free Press, 1978.

2. **Lecture:** "Higher Education or Advanced Vocationalism?" This lecture explores the difference between training and education. As such it addresses the topics of "The Transformation of Education" and "'Educated' Americans." I see training as technical preparation for work. It is skill-oriented and primarily concerned with preparing students with a reasonable background for an entry-level job. Examples of such majors would include criminal justice, social work, nursing, engineering, business, and so on. The focus is narrow and at times borders on indoctrination.

Alternatively, education, *in extremis,* can be seen as the pie-in-the-sky pursuit of ideas for their own sake: the much celebrated liberal arts ideal that prepares you for life but not necessarily for a job. Just what is the place of liberal arts requirements in these vocationally oriented majors? Further, even presuming that liberal arts courses are good in and of themselves, what about the issue of politically correct thinking: should the western classics be jettisoned in favor of a nonwhite nonmale curricula?

Source. Bloom, A. The Closing of the American Mind. How Higher Education Has Failed Democracy and Impoverished the Souls of Today's Students. New York: Simon and Schuster, 1987. As indicated by the title, this is heady stuff indeed. The book hardly needs an annotation and probably few students are sufficiently versed to follow the arguments. Still, it puts an enormous number of ideas into perspective (Bloom's). Even (especially) if you don't agree with him, it is an exhilarating read.

3. Discussion: "College Students: Clients or Consumers?" This discussion is useful in pointing out the often contradictory aspects of being a modern college student while slipping into the section "Meyer's Theory of Educational Functions." The discussion presumes that there are extant two major role orientations available: the student as consumer and the student as client. Further, these two orientations are not necessarily complementary. For example, given the facts of college life that students do have some say-so in choosing (1) the college they attend as well as (2) their major field, course professors, electives, and room and board arrangements, the "student as consumer" might state that there should be no specific major field course requirements let alone general education distribution requirements. Along this same line the student as consumer may assert the absolute primacy of individual rights in being able to drop a course or selectively fulfill the assignments as the spirit moves him or her. Further, the student as consumer could argue that if the above holds true then the notion of the necessity of a college education the requirements of which are dictated to the student is rendered problematic.

An additional complication is the factor of cost: Probably no student directly pays all of the costs for his/her college education. This, of course, corrodes the student-as-consumer position. However, since most students pay for at least some of the costs as well as the fact that a college degree is increasingly seen by the larger society as a necessary (but not sufficient) condition for a person to be considered for the better jobs, then from the individual student's perspective enough is at stake so that

Alternatively, the student as client is not so much a free economic agent as a person in need of some specialized service, and as such, is due respect and fair treatment but not unlimited degrees of freedom. (From this perspective the student is more analogous to a psychiatric outpatient than a shopper at the local mall.) Consequently, from this perspective, the student as client is told what to do by professionals who know better and who have the legitimate power to certify a client as deserving (or not) to move on to the great occupational lottery.

some consumer rights are a reasonable demand.

This kind of topic can be used not only to try to discern what is the student's proper role (place?) but also to get an answer to perhaps the more interesting question, What should be that role? Ultimately is there/should there be just one all-encompassing vision of the college student?

Source: Horowitz, H. Campus Life: Undergraduate Cultures From the 18th Century to the Present. New York: Alfred Knopf, 1987.

ADDITIONAL STUDENT READINGS

Drane, J. Becoming A Good Doctor: The Place of Virtue and Character in Medical Ethics. Kansas City: Sheed and Ward, 1988. A leading medical ethicist cogently explores ethical issues inherent to the physician's occupation.

Kozol, J. Savage Inequalities: Children in America's Schools. New York: Crown Publishers, 1991. "Kids have no choice about where they're born or where they live." So says a school superintendent and so is this quote a summary of Kozol's cogent indictment as to how America funds its schools. This study shows why so many poor kids from impoverished school districts will never approximate equality of educational opportunity. Do the kids fail the schools or do the schools fail the kids? And if the latter, then does the larger society fail the schools?

ESSAY QUESTIONS

1. Explain how the transformations of work, the labor force, and of education have reinforced one another.

2. Show how one can argue that a decline in quality of education is correlated with both an increase in the availability of education and the decrease in teacher quality.

3. Why is it that as the need of a college degree has increased the value of a college degree has decreased.

4. Explain how Meyer's theory of educational functions operates at both the micro and macro levels of society.

CHAPTER OUTLINE

Modernization.   Transformaing agrarian nations
                                        into industrial ones (and
                                        beyond).

Internal Sources of
    Social Change.
    Innovations.   New technologies, culture,
                                        social structure.

    Change and Cultural Lag.   Delay before change produces a
                                        realignment in rest of culture.

External Sources of Change.   Conflict, ecological, and
    Diffusion.   the transferring of cultural
                                        items from one society to
                                        another.

The Rise of the West.   Capitalism and technological
                                        innovation were key factors.

Marx on Capitalism.   Because of worker alienation,
                                        the tremendous productive
                                        potential of industrialism
                                        must be separated from
                                        capitalism.

Capitalism and   Elites decide what work is to
    Precapitalist Command   be done and who will do it.
    Economies.

The Protestant Ethic.   Weber argued that rise of
                                        Protestantism coincided with
                                        rise of capitalism and that the
                                        development of the latter was
                                        facilitated by the imperatives
                                        of the former.

The State Theory of   Taming of the state necessary
    Modernization.   for both the rise of
                                        Protestantism (cf. religious
                                        pluralism) and development of
                                        capitalism (undermining command
                                        economies).

Dependency and World   Stresses interrelationships
    System Theory.   among world economies.
    Core Nations   Advanced, diversified economies
                                        that dominate

Peripheral Nations	underdeveloped and highly specialized ones.
Dominance and Mechanisms of Dependency.	Core nations exploit peripheral nations, the former become absolutely richer and the latter become at least relatively poorer.
Delacroix: Testing Dependency Theory.	Modernization is influenced primarily by internal processes. Firebuagh and Beck demonstrate that economic development for 3rd world nations increases the quality of life for everyone.

SUMMARY

To many people, everything seems up for grabs--that is, changeable. However, as previous chapters have indicated some things endure. We probably will never have societies without stratification or deviance or religion or some form of family. Although the particulars may vary across time and space, these phenomena seem to be social universals.

Modernization. The process of transforming agrarian societies into industrial ones and beyond is what sociologists term modernization.

Internal Sources of Social Change. One major change internal to a social system is that of innovations. In turn, there are various subtypes of innovation: new technology--the automobile; new culture--the ideal of progress; and new social structure--formal organizations. (A caveat: Many citizens of some of the most advanced nations believe that in the long run scientific advances will harm more than help humankind: Table 17-1.) Besides innovation there are other endogenous sources of change. Prominent among the others are religious, racial, ethnic, and class conflicts as well as population growth.

Change and Cultural Lag. If society is indeed a system, then change will often produce cultural lags: the delay before a change in one part of a society produces necessary realignment of other parts. A chronic example of cultural lag has been society's inability to prepare for the large influx of baby boomers throughout their life-cycle (see Special Topic 6). Another example, to be discussed in greater detail in Chapter 18, is that of the introduction of pesticides to tropical nations after World War II.

External Sources of Change. One major source of change exogenous to the society would be culture borrowing, or diffusion, which transfers a cultural item from one society to another. Examples include bringing the horse from Spain to the New World and in turn diffusing corn, tomatoes, turkeys, and peppers from the New World to the Old. In contemporary society, perhaps television illustrates just how rapidly and widely a communications invention may be diffused (cf. Table 17-2).

Conflict, often in the guise of warfare, occurs when one society threatens to invade another. Finally, another prominent form of external change would be ecological factors, or changes in the physical environment. One potential example of this that would affect all societies is the greenhouse effect.

The Rise of the West. For a long period dating from the fall of Rome, Europe was hardly competitive let alone preeminent among the major areas of the world. However, from the sixteenth century on, technological innovation grew rapidly and Europe pulled away from its Asiatic neighbors. One way of phrasing this is, Why had China not kept pace? Most western scholarship has addressed another question: why had social change been so rapid in Europe? There are four major "schools" that have addressed this latter question: Marxian, Weberian, state theory, and dependency theory. On one point all can agree: A key phenomenon to be explained in this puzzle is capitalism.

Marx on Capitalism. Marx marveled at the tremendous increase in productivity emanating from the Industrial Revolution in Europe. He felt that societies were finally capable of providing everyone with a good life. The potential was there; it had only to be shared. It was Marx's studied opinion that the new technology ushering in this era of plenty was in turn a product of something more fundamental: capitalism, a new economic system that would constantly revolutionize the instruments of production while it institutionalized naked economic self-interest. As incredibly productive as it was, Marx thought that it exacted too great a human cost (alienating humans from themselves, from others, and from the products of their labor). Marx felt that the productive potential of industrialism could be harnessed for the general good, but it must be separated (alienated if you will) from its capitalistic moorings. Capitalism must be destroyed and replaced by a communist utopia.

Capitalism and Precapitalist Command Economies. The unique feature of capitalism is its reliance on a free market where the various choices of individuals, all seeking to maximize personal gain, set prices and wages. In turn, prices and wages are set by supply and demand. The positive differentials (profits) between prices and wages and costs and income can be then accumulated without fear of arbitrary seizure by government.

Contrast the above situation with that of precapitalist societies, command economies in which the elite decided what work is to be done and commanded others to do it. The weakness of command economies is that those doing the work have nothing to gain by doing it well. The irony of self-styled Marxist governments is that they have sought to modernize via highly centralized command economies—in effect, trying to seek the productive benefits of capitalism with precapitalist techniques. What escapes the Marxist societies is that they preclude realizing the productivity of capitalism by refusing to reward surplus production. Hence the stagnation or outright failure of Marxist economies is assured.

The Protestant Ethic. If capitalism caused the rise of the West, what caused capitalism? For a clue to the answer to this question we turn to Weber. It was Weber's argument that the rise of capitalism coincided with the Protestant Reformation in which the uncertainty of one's salvation drove Calvinists to look for temporal signs of their salvation. They reasoned that if you were industrious, abstemious, and successful in this life, you were pretty sure that God had predestined you for eternal salvation in the next one. Thus, capitalism rose in those countries that were most severely Protestant. While a strict interpretation of predestination did not last for long, the spirit of capitalism (hard work, saving and reinvestment, etc.) certainly did. Hence the old adage: Catholics worked to live while Protestants lived to work.

Contemporary reappraisals of Weber's arguemnt are severe in their implications. For example, historical economic research suggest that Protestatiism had little or nothing to do with the rise of the modern world. Other scholarship seems to indicate that Weber misread (or didn't read at all) Calvin and that Christianity rather than calvinism *per se* may have been a precondition for the rise of capitalism.

The State Theory of Modernization. While admitting that Marx and Weber made interesting points, state theorists argue that those interpretations are limited. They argue that the development of capitalism and its interplay with Protestantism was only possible by limiting the powers of government— that is, the taming of the state. As Chirot would put it, "An untamed state is incapable of not stifling economic development because it is incapable of not overtaxing.... However, if the powers of the state are limited so that private property is secure from seizure and people are free to pursue their economic self-interest, capitalism becomes attractive and possible." Further, it was the tamed state that allowed religious pluralism (i.e., the Protestant Reformation) to take root thus reversing Weber's argument to read that the taming of the state allowed for the rise of capitalism, which in turn elicited certain Protestant doctrines that in turn legitimated capitalist behavior.

Dependency and World System Theory. The preceding explanations have focused on internal rationales for the cause of the Industrial Revolution. Dependency theory's time of departure (the sixteenth century) is about that of the other theories but instead concentrates on the interrelationships between economies as the critical factors in explaining the rise of the West. The initial statement of this perspective was by Wallerstein, who felt that the crucial development in the sixteenth century was the growth of an international economy that was not politically united. What emerged was the ability of certain nations to extract wealth from other nations without taking on the burdensome costs of warfare or the administration of empire.

Wallerstein applied a Marxist schema to the relations between nations. Thus, within this world system a few nations form an upper class, some a lower class, and a few a middle class. The dominant nations are the **core nations** with diversified economies that are the most industrialized and modernized. They have stable governments and little class conflict. At the bottom of the world systems are the **peripheral nations** with weak internal political structures and a low standard of living for workers. They are ruled by repressive governments and have highly specialized economies, typically relying on the sales of a narrow range of raw materials. In between core and periphery are those nations with economies that have characteristics of the other two: **semiperipheral nations.**

Dominance and Mechanisms of Dependency. The crucial issues to dependency theorists are: (1) Why is there so little modernization among so many countries despite extensive contacts with advanced economies and (2) can these backward countries ever become fully modernized? Dependency theorists point to what they feel is a fundamental fact: The less developed nations are dominated by foreign firms and investors that control their economies. Major consequences flow from this fact. First, profits go back to the investor nations rather than being reinvested in the local economy. Second, foreign firms and investors control what economic activities take place in underdeveloped nations. Third, nations that specialize in exporting raw materials must remain poor (since demand remains constant due to the small population growth of the developed nations). The result is a dual economy that is modernized in the export sector but is undeveloped due to exploitation in all other areas.

Delacroix: Testing the Dependency Theory. Delacroix wanted to test the dependency portion of world system theory: that specialization in the export of raw materials prevents modernization. His two indices of modernization were per capita gross national product and high school enrollment rates. He did not find that per capita GNP increases more slowly in nations to the extent that they specialize in exporting raw materials. Neither did he find that dependent nations--those specializing in exporting raw materials--lack the resources to expand their educational systems. He did find that secondary school enrollments and increases in per capita GNP were strongly correlated. This led Delacroix to suggest that modernization is influenced primarily by internal processes rather than external processes of the world system.

Firebaugh and Beck's research reinforced Delacroix's position finding in that economic growth in 3rd world countries not only benefits the society as a whole but also improves the quality of life for individual citizens.

TEACHING SUGGESTIONS

If indeed change is both ubiquitous and fast-paced, then students need to have some basic conceptual tools with which to cognitively cope with this fact of modernity.

1. Lecture: "Anomie, Imitative Violence, and Media Censorship." This lecture never fails to arouse a lively (at times heated) discussion upon its conclusion. The first part of the lecture is devoted to an explanation of Durkheim's concept of anomie especially as it relates to his critique of the rise of capitalism. The next part of the lecture involves presenting the findings of a series of fascinating studies by David Phillips on a neglected aspect of Durkheim: imitative behavior.

[Instructor's note: I've long wondered if Durkheim de-emphasized imitative suicide because of his feud with Tarde who of course gave imitative behavior a major "play" in his own work.]

When you reach the findings regarding imitative homicide and the losers of prizefights as well as the findings correlating airplane crashes with highly publicized suicides, many of the students are at the point of disbelief. Besides covering some important methodological ground while explaining Phillips's procedures, the more obvious benefit of this lecture is that you can keep the students' absolute (more or less) attention while engaging them in a important issue: How responsible is/should be the

mass media for what they disseminate? To be more specific,
is the claim of freedom of the press an obsolete cultural
lag if it can be demonstrated that giving prime attention to
suicides leads to many other additional suicides in the
general population?

Of equal scholarly importance is making the distinction
between the presentation of scientifically derived findings
and the lack of a detailed explanation as to why the
findings are as they are. In other words, students can be
made to realize that often coherent explanations for valid
research do not necessarily follow. Such are the vagaries
of science.

Sources: Phillips, D. "The Influence of Suggestion on
Suicide: Substantive and Theoretical Implications of the
Werther Effect." American Sociological Review 39 (1974):
340-354.

Phillips, D. "Suicide, Motor Vehicle Fatalities, and
the Mass Media: Evidence Toward a Theory of Suggestion."
American Journal of Sociology 85 (1979): 1150-1174.

Phillips, D. "Airplane Crashes, Murder, and the Mass
Media: Towards a Theory of Imitation and Suggestion."
Social Forces 59 (1980): 1001-1024.

Phillips, D. "The Impact of Fictional Television Stories
on U.S. Adult Fatalities: New Evidence on the Effect of the
Mass Media on Violence." American Journal of Sociology 88
(1982): 1340-1359.

Phillips, D., and K. Bollen. "Suicidal Motor Vehicle
Fatalities in Detroit: A Replication." American Journal of
Sociology 87 (1981): 404-412.

Phillips, D., and K. Bollen: "Imitative Suicides: A
National Study of the Effects of Television News Stories."
American Sociological Review 47 (1982): 802-809.

2. Lecture; "Cyclical Theories of Social Change." When I
taught classical sociological theory I liked to do this one,
and with some modification it can be readily intelligible to
the beginning student. I like to compare Vico's three
stages of history (the age of the gods, the age of the
heroes, and the age of men) with Sorokin's alternating
stages of sensate and ideational culture. It might be
interesting to then move on to the latest in the rise-and-
fall school: David Kennedy's idea of imperial overreach.
Any or all of these can be useful correctives to the
straight-line forever progressive enthusiasts of the rise of
the West. Finally, comparing Kennedy's thesis with
Schlesinger's is an interesting exercise in "futurism" based
on the past.

Sources: Kennedy, D. The Rise and Fall of the Great
Powers: Economic Change and Military Conflict from 1500 to
2000. New York: Random House, 1987. Can the United States
really beat the odds and retain its dominant position, or is
a managed accommodation to a new distribution of global

power the best that it can do? This well-written book
addresses a truly crucial issue of our times.
   Schlesinger, A. The Cycles of American History. Boston:
Houghton Mifflin. 1986. Do cycles really represent
change? Schlesinger's book is well worth the time if only
because he writes so eruditely on topics of such importance.
   Sorokin, P. Social and Cultural Mobility. 4 vols. New
York: American Book Company, 1937-1941. Who now reads
Sorokin, especially all four volumes? I have to admit that
my discussion of Sorokin comes not from the original volumes
but from graduate school lecture notes. Oh well, the notes
are still valid (I hope).
   Vico, G. The New Science. Ithaca, N.Y.: Cornell
University Press, 1948. Originally published in 1725, Vico
was a scholar way ahead of his time.

3. Discussion: "Should the United States Qualify for
(someone's) Foreign Aid?" Suppose a country exports an
enormous amount of its wealth such as technological designs,
money, timber, and raw foodstuffs in exchange for finished
goods and in the process becomes the greatest debtor nation
in the world all the while following the dictates of neo-
laissez-faire capitalism as well as consumer preferences.
Does all of this taken together make this country a
dependent nation within the core of advanced powers? How do
you explain this within the perspective of dependency
theory? How dependent is America's affluence upon foreign
investors continuing to float our Federal debt? This kind
of discussion could be particularly useful in presenting
some of the ideas of Paul Kennedy while setting up
dependency theory as a conceptual straw person.
   Sources: See Kennedy D., above, plus relevant newspapers
and periodicals such as The New York Times, The Wall Street
Journal, The Economist, The Christian Science Monitor,
The Nation, and so on.
   Figgie, H. Bankruptcy 1995: The Coming Collapse of
America and How to Stop it. Boston: Little, Brown and
Company, 1993. Talk about nightmare scenarios: this is the
monetary equivalent of a nuclear meltdown.

ADDITIIONAL STUDENT READINGS

Caplow, T. American Social Trends. Orlando, Fla.: Harcourt
Brace Jovanovich. 1991. A readable and comprehensive
treatment of social trends in contemporary America. A good
source for updating some of your lectures.

Lamm, R. "Post-Crash Institutions." The Futurist. (August
1988.) The former governor of Colorado predicts, as
befitting a secularized Old Testament prophet, that our
profligate ways beg for a societal crash. That being

assumed, Lamm argues that we ought to start thinking now about what we want our postcrash society to look like. Could be read in conjunction with Figgie.

Naisbitt, J. and P. Aburdene, Megatrends: Ten New Directions For the 1990's. New York: William Morrow, 1990. If Figgie is too alarmist and Kennedy too melancholic try Naisbitt. All of the gusto of unflagging optimism and fewer the calories of pessmism.

Toffler, A. Powershift: Knowledge, Wealth, and Violence at the Edge of the 21st Century. New York: Bantam Books, 1990. Toffler argues that knowledge is rapidly becoming the new currency of power and hence a concommitant shift in basis of stratification both within and between societies is developing. As with his other works, it is often glib but just as often stimulating.

Turkle, S. The Second Self: Computers and the Human Spirit. New York: Simon and Schuster, 1984. A controversial work since Turkle argues that the human-computer interface can fundamentally change self-concepts (of humans, that is; not computers, at least not yet).

ESSAY QUESTIONS

1. Compare innovation and diffusion. Give an example of each and show how cultural lag may result from each.

2. Compare internal and external sources of change. When might an internal source of change simultaneously be/give rise to an external source of change?

3. Compare Marx and Weber on the development of capitalism. How do modern state theorists qualify both Marx and Weber?

4. What is dependency theory? In what ways is dependency theory an application of Marxist theory to the international economy?

CHAPTER OUTLINE

Demographic Techniques.	
Growth Rate.	Net population gain (or loss) divided by size of population.
Crude Rates.	Number of births (or deaths) divided by total population for year.
Fertility Rate.	Total number of births divided by total number of women within an age bracket.
Age-specific Death Rate.	Number of deaths per 1,000 members of a particular age group.
Infant Mortality Rate	Important example of an age-specific death rate.
Birth Cohort	All people born in a specific time period.
Age and Sex Structures.	The distribution of a given population by age/sex.
Population Structures.	
Expansive.	Population is young and growing rapidly.
Stationary.	Population is not growing.
Constricted.	Population is old and shrinking.
Preindustrial Population Trends.	Hunter-gatherer populations grow slowly if at all. Agrarianism was first great population shift. Populations held in check by famine, disease, war.
Malthusian Theory.	Populations will follow cycles of growth and decline. Food supply ultimately determines mortality (and thus population size).
Modernization and Population.	Europe's population shift caused by revolutions in food and industrial production.
The Demographic Transition.	Shift from high birth and death rates to low birth and death rates. Europe first to undergo.

Kingsley Davis: Demographic Transition Theory.	With modernization, children shift from being economic assets to being economic liabilities. People choose to have fewer children.
The Second Population Esplosion.	Occurs in Third World countries with diminishing death rates but very high birth rates.
The Population Explosion Wanes.	In most of Asia and Latin America and much of Africa, fertility is declining as predicted by transition theory.
"Depopulation."	Notestein predicted that the baby boom would be a momentary aberration to the long term decline in fertility. Over two dozen nations have fertility rates that are below replacement level. It is possible that in advanced nations fertility could drop to near absolute zero and if not offset by immigration then depopulation is not just a moot point. Combining modern medical technology with depressed fertility and gender bias we find sex ratios significantly askew in parts of China and India.

SUMMARY

Demography is the numerical description of people based on three major variables: births, deaths, and migration. As such, demography is one of the most important subfields of macro sociology. It can also be seen as a critical extension of the idea of social change.

Demographic Techniques. Perhaps the most basic of all demographic techniques is the growth rate, which is computed as the net population gain (or loss) divided by the size of the population. The total gain (or loss) is a function of the increase (or decrease) in a year of births, deaths, and migration. As Stark points out, if you increase a population by a constant amount over time the growth rate becomes smaller over time because the base population size continues to increase.

Crude rates--birth and death--are simply computed as the number of births (or deaths) divided by the total population for the year. However, these crude rates are just that-- crude. So demographers prefer more refined techniques that are, nevertheless, easily computed. One such measure is the fertility rate: the total number of births, divided by the total number of women within an age bracket (usually 15 through 44). In lieu of the crude death rate, the age-specific death rate is preferred. This is computed by determining the number of deaths per 1,000 members of the particular age group. The infant mortality rate is one such very important age-specific death rate.

Often demographers wish to predict the impact of population size and/or change at some future date. A useful concept that allows them to do this is the birth cohort--all the people born in a particular time period. Although the time period is usually one year, it may be longer (e.g., many demographers treat the baby boom as an entire cohort-- all those born between 1946 and 1964). Stark points out that from 1870 through World War II France was at a constant disadvantage with Germany as the latter always had larger cohorts of young males than did the former with predictable and significant military repercussions.

Age and Sex Structures. Two other useful concepts for demographers are the age structure (the distribution of a given population by age) and the sex structure (the gender distribution of a population).

[Instructor's note: The consequences of a dramatic shift in age structure are covered in Special Topic 6 and the idea of an unbalanced sex structure is treated by the notion of sex ratio. The two together were covered in Chapter 12 with Guttentag and Secord's sex ratio thesis.]

Now, a population shaped like a pyramid is an expansive population structure like those found in many underdeveloped nations. Each younger cohort is progressively larger and such a population grows rapidly. At any given moment, there are many more people who have not yet begun to reproduce. Even if couples suddenly limit their families to only enough children to replace themselves, the populations will continue to grow until each of the increasingly larger, younger cohorts has gone through the reproductive period.

When reproduction passes from the baby boomers to the "birth dearth" cohort of the 1970s, the age and sex structure of the United States may resemble a stationary population structure where the base of this structure is in proportion to the other cohorts. Factoring out in-migration the population would not be expected to grow. A constricted population structure (characteristic of much of Europe) finds the bottom smaller than the top, and if not supplemented by in-migration such a population would be expected to shrink.

Preindustrial Population Trends. For several million years the world's population grew slowly and as of 10,000 years ago there were only about 5 million people. Today there are 5 billion. To get from then to now there have been four (and possibly five) great population shifts. The first began more than 10,000 years ago with the development of agriculture. As humans ceased being nomadic hunter-gatherers and settled in one place to grow crops, life became more secure. More food and better diets meant a decrease in childhood mortality with a consequent rise in population. However, there were periodic and significant increases in the death rate--so much so that the world's population certainly did not always increase. One major reason for the periodic decline in population (at least in certain areas) was famine. There was famine in Europe (the last great one was caused by the potato blight in Ireland in 1845); famine in India (in the 1890s with perhaps as many as 19 million perishing); and famine in China (in the 1870s leaving 9 to 13 million dead and in the late 1950s as many as 30 million dying). Disease came in the form of the Black Death (which may have decimated more than of 40 per cent of Europe and Asia), smallpox, and influenza (after World War I); these are major examples of the virulent nature of pandemic diseases. Finally, war has been a most severe way of checking population growth. The Thirty Years War destroyed 80 per cent of German villages. Another ghastly example is the Taiping Rebellion that killed at least 30 million Chinese.

Malthusian Theory. Using Adam Smith's idea that human populations grow or decline according to the availability of the necessities of life, especially food, Malthus argued that populations tend to grow geometrically (2-4-8-16) while foodstuffs can increase only arithmetically (1-2-3-4). Thus, Malthus figured that populations were prevented from realizing their natural propensity for doubling every generation by the so-called positive checks--famine, war, and disease. Nevertheless, he felt that populations will always rise to the level of subsistence; that is, fertility will always be high and the rise and fall of mortality are what ultimately determines population size. The Malthusian theory of population predicts that populations will follow cycles of growth and decline and what ultimately determines mortality (and thus population size) is the food supply.

Modernization and Population. Although Malthusian theory seemed to explain early agrarian societies quite well, a second great population shift was occurring while he was writing that would seriously qualify if not disprove his overall theory. This tremendous growth in Europe's population seemed to occur without triggering the Malthusian positive checks. The Industrial Revolution facilitated the growth of the factory and the city by freeing surplus farm labor to migrate. It did so with machines that replaced draft animals and hand labor, better plant and animal varieties, new techniques of crop rotation and field design, and the use of chemical fertilizers. Thus, more food grown by fewer people allowed for a better diet and indirectly improved public health so as to decrease mortality. And so the population increased significantly (e.g., between 1700 and 1841 the population of England tripled).

The Demographic Transition. Malthus assumed that fertility would always remain high. By the 1860s fertility joined mortality in a downward spiral, and by the 1930s growth in Europe pretty much ceased because fertility no longer exceeded mortality. This was true for North America as well. What had been accomplished was the world's third great population shift: that is, the demographic transition or the change from the age-old pattern of high fertility and high but variable mortality to a new pattern of low mortality and fertility. If this trend in North America had continued, then replacement-level fertility would have been reached theoretically producing zero population growth.

Kingsley Davis: Demographic Transition Theory. Davis argued that modernization naturally leads to conditions encouraging low fertility. People in modern societies had fewer children because they no longer wanted large families. The reason they no longer wanted large families is, given the assumption of choice theory, in a modern urban setting children are no longer the economic assets they were on the farm. Rather, they have become costly economic liabilities. People thus gravitate to contraception (something that primitive peoples know and practice). Therefore, to Davis, modernization leads to reduced fertility especially (as clarified by Berelson) when certain thresholds are crossed:
1. less than half of labor force are in agriculture;
2. less than half of young are enrolled in school;
3. average life expectancy is 60;
4. infant mortality is less than 65 per 1,000;
5. 80 per cent of females age 15-19 are not married;
6. per capita GNP is $450; and
7. adult literacy rate is 70 per cent.

The Second Population Explosion. Just as Davis was publishing his theory, the fourth great population shift began (in Third World countries). Mortality fell in the less developed countries thus initiating the greatest population explosion in history. Throughout most of the 1950s and 1960s population in most of the less developed nations grew by a rate of from 2 to 3.5 percent a year. Such rates mean that populations double in size every twenty to thirty-five years. If that were to hold for only

200 years, there would be 157 billion people. The dramatic lowering of mortality came from the importation from industrialized countries of public health technologies (e.g., liquid pesticides) and advanced agricultural technologies (e.g., new plant strains, farm machinery, modern irrigation techniques). These introductions left Third World countries with high fertility and much lowered mortality. Thus, the key question posed is whether they will have time to pass through the demographic transition before their populations become so huge that mass starvation results.

The Population Explosion Wanes. By the 1970s, fertility declines were becoming apparent in some of the larger, less developed nations. For example, in 1965 the average Chinese woman gave birth to 6.4 children. By 1991 this had declined to 2.4. A similar decline has been detected in India. Other Asian nations (excepting Pakistan and Bangladesh) have also experienced significant drops in fertility. For the larger Latin American nations, the same holds true, as it does in Africa north of the Sahara.

Looking more closely at China, it is obvious that extraordinary economic growth (more than 9 per cent per annum for the entire decade of the 1980s) has led to significant advances in China's economic development. This, in turn, has facilitated declines in fertility. Further, China has accomplished these declines without fully reaching all of Berelson's thresholds (e.g. more than half of the Chinese are still in agriculture and per capita income is still less than $450). Still, coercion has in part compensated for this although fertility rates in other Third world countries declined significantly without comparable coercion.

Finally, numeracy about children and contraception and wanted fertility must be reckoned with as factors contributing to declining fertility. Numeracy about children refers to the self-consciousness of parents regarding preferred family size. However, without available contraception the actual number of children will still be much greater than the ideal size family (wanted fertility.) Demographers have noted that much of sub-Saharan Africa shows a significant discrepancy between ideal fertility and actual fertility and that a major reason for this is difficulty in obtaining contraceptions.

"Depopulation." Notestein predicted that the baby boom would be a momentary aberration to the long term decline in fertility. Table 18-6 details 30 countries (includeing Canada and the United States) with below replacement level fertility rates. It is possible, though not necessarily probable, that in modernized nations fertility could drop to near absolute zero and if not offset by immigration then depopulation would ensue.

Combining modern medical technology with depressed fertility and gender bias sex ratios are significantly imbalanced in parts of China and India.

TEACHING SUGGESTIONS

The objective of Chapter 18 is to introduce students to the basic concepts, theories, and techniques of demographic analysis. In so doing, the instructor will provide students with an appreciation for the enormous impact of population on society (and vice-versa).

1. **Discussion.** "A Personal Inventory of Affluence and Effluence." Demographic transition theory assumes a rational choice model to human action regarding population issues. To the extent that it explicitly addresses issues of material consumption and what to do with the by-products therefrom, it would presumably follow that once populations make the transition to low birth rates and low death rates (with or without actually achieving zero population growth) people will address a variety of other concerns. Included among these would be quality of life issues. Now, quality of life can be defined in a variety of ways. It could mean increasing levels of material consumption. It could also mean clean air and water, better health, and so on. Ask students to fill out (in an open-ended fashion a la the Twenty Statements Test) a personal inventory of what they value in terms of quality of life. Next ask them to list all possible items that they own and how they acquired them. You might also ask them how often they use these items and if they are really essential to their lives. Next ask the students to link their possessions with their quality of life values. Finally, ask them to note next to their items: Were they used or obtained new? Are they repairable and/or replenishable? Are they recyclable or disposable? You might close this with a discussion on what to do with people who value a cleaner, pollution-free world but are up to their necks in stuff. What is really necessary to enhance the "quality of life"? More specifically, What are the costs to the literal quality of life (effluence) with the exaggerated emphasis on a figurative interpretation of quality of life (affluence)?
  Source. Bookchin, M. Remaking Society: Pathways to a Green Future. Boston: South End Press, 1990. Bookchin lucidly points out the trap of capitalism: its addiction to growth and the inevitable environmental degradation that ensues.

2. **Discussion.** "Can a *Stable* Population Size Be Ecologically Destabilizing?" This discussion can serve as a vehicle for leading into a variety of related issues such as

population, standard of living, technology, and so on. It
is especially relevant for extending some of the
implications of Third World nations attaining demographic
transition (see "The Population Explosion Wanes").   It is
useful in helping students to think in global terms. Begin
the discussion by presuming (optimistically perhaps) that
the world's population stabilizes by the end of the first
quarter of the twenty-first century at around 9 billion.
Then further posit that the resource usage rate per capita
will remain about what it is today. Now we will have to
make enormous efforts merely to maintain current consumption
patterns of various goods and services (let alone improve
standards of living for Third World peoples). This is
further complicated by the fact that given North American
patterns of consumption there are significant problems with
pollutants as by-products. (Seen another way, the United
States is several times larger than its actual population
size if we look at the ecological load that our collective
way of life imposes on the earth's carrying capacity.) Thus
we will have to (as citizens of the world and not just one
particular country) be able to develop incredibly efficient
technologies that are almost pollution-free or redistribute
goods and services to the lesser nations or scale back
expectations regarding consumption levels or...?

  Source. Hirsch, F. The Social Limits to Growth.
Cambridge: Harvard University Press, 1976. A short
readable account that, among other points, reminds us that
increases in population and affluence do not necessarily
bring automatic access to the vast multitudes of many of
the finer things in life since certain highly valued
objects/experiences are by their nature limited to just a
few: beautiful vistas, Old Master paintings, etc. Highly
recommended.

3. Discussion. "How is illegal immigration rational?" This
discussion does not take long to describe and it might
function as a preliminary to the film El Norte (see the
appendix.) If you initially pose this question a good many
students will view it from the perspective of the typical
United States citizen and thus repsond with something like:
illegal immigrants are a burden and we ought to kick them
out and so on and so forth. But then you shift the frame
and say: No, when is it rational to immigrate even if it is
illegal thus presenting the case of the immigrant. An
obvious link is possible with rational choice theory and
the hardships that the illegal immigrants endure can help
refocus the idea of rational choice as dependent upon a
particular perspective.

  Source. Chavez, L. Shadowed Lives: Undocumented
Immigrants in American Society. Ft. Worth: Harcourt Brace
Jovanovich College Publishers, 1992. A sympathetic portrait
of illegal Mexican workers and their families.

ADDITIONAL STUDENT READINGS

Elgin, D. <u>Voluntary Simplicity: An Ecological Lifestyle That Promotes Personal and Social Renewal</u>. New York: William Morrow, 1981. Elgin simply but cogently argues for a "soup-to-nuts" agenda for personal and civilizational renewal in an era of resource constriction. Often students ask what can they do to make this a better world. Elgin's book provides a challenging start.

Erikson, K. <u>Everything in Its Path</u> New York: Touchstone Books, 1978. A heart-breaking book on the destruction (literally) of a West Virginia community. This hybrid of investigative journalism and sociological analysis is award-winning social science at its best. Among other things this is a case study of the devastating consequences that came from a sudden and drastic disruption of the ecological underpinnings of a population.

Hobhouse, H. <u>Seeds of Change: Five Plants That Transformed Mankind</u>. New York: Harper and Row, 1985. A fascinating and nontechnical social history of the impact of quinine, sugar, tea, cotton, and the potato on the ecology and population of the societies that grew and imported them.

ESSAY QUESTIONS

1. Explain the effects of net in-migration or net out-migration on each of the following:
   a. an expansionary population
   b. a stationary population
   c. a constricting population

2. Compare the population transitions of Europe with that of the Third World.

3. Is demographic transition theory an extension of the Malthusian population theory or is it refutation of Malthusian population theory? Be specific.

4. To what extent does China's remarkable decline in fertility coincide with demographic transition theory. Please pay particular attention to the thresholds developed by Berelson.

CHAPTER OUTLINE

Preindustrial Cities.	Dirty, disease-ridden, dense, dark, and dangerous.
Industrialization and Urbanization.	Reciprocal cause and effect.
Agricultural Revolution.	Industrial Revolution allows unprecedented agricultural productivity.
Specialization and Urban Growth.	Inseparable processes since industrialism requires concentration of workers.
Metropolis.	Central city and its suburbs.
Fixed-rail Metropolis.	Preindustrial in origin; characterized by high density and mass transit.
Freeway Metropolis	Almost wholly automobile-oriented; less dense; suburbs more dominant.
Urban Neighborhoods.	Historically, characterized by racial/ethnic immigrant groups and descendents.
Theory of Ethnic Succession	Park and Burgess' idea that the history of neighborhoods is the history of ethnic groups who move as they become more successful only to be replaced by newer, lower-status groups.
Index of Dissimilarity.	Measures extent a given racial or ethnic group lives in integrated or segregated neighborhoods compared with the ethnic makeup of the city as a whole. Guest and Weed support Park and Burgess's position that as ethnic groups increase their status the more likely they were to live in integrated neighborhoods. Taeuber showed that integration was occurring because African-Americans were moving to the suburbs or into white neighborhoods in cities. Little reverse integration was occurring.

Farley and Frey: Metropolitan Integration and Segregation.	Working with all metropolitan areas and using the Index of Dissimilarity, they found that increases in integration were greatest in the South and West and that integration also increased as African-Americnas' incomes approximated those of whites.
Theories of Urban Impact. Anomie	As people lose attachments, they lose their moral compass.
Social Disorganization.	High rates of social disorganization lead to high rates of social pathologies. The social drift hypothesis counterargues that people (see especially unattached males) develop problems and then drift into poor neighborhoods for lack of any alternative.

SUMMARY

Chapter 19 examines the urbanization of industrialized societies, the structure of cities, and the impact of urban life of groups and individuals.

Preindustrial Cities. Preindustrial cities rarely contained more than 10,000 inhabitants. In large part, this was due to the poor transportation available to bring food from the countryside to the city. In addition, disease also checked the size of cities. As recently as 1900, the death rate in English cities was 33 percent higher than·that in the countryside. Historically, the much higher density of cities facilitated the spread of infectious diseases that until the twentieth century were the leading sources of mortality. In turn, some cities were dense because of the walled fortress nature of many of the ancient cities. More importantly, the density was due to the slow means of transportation thus limiting the preindustrial city to about 3 miles from its center.

It was the unsanitary living conditions of pre-twentieth century cities that caused much of the disease. Sewage treatment was unknown and even sewers were uncommon. Garbage was not collected but was strewn everywhere.

Stark concludes that the preindustrial city was dirty, disease-ridden, dense, dark, and dangerous. This begs the question as to why people lived there at all. A major reason was economics: cities offered many people a chance to increase their incomes. Further, cities offered an interesting and stimulating alternative to the mind-numbing peasant village. To many, cities also offered an opportunity to pursue extranormative desires (i.e., vices) that would not be readily available in a village. Whatever the motive(s), it was primarily adventuresome, single, young adults who constantly replenished city populations.

Industrialization and Urbanization. These processes are inseparable. Technically cities can exist without industrialization; however, industrialization made it feasible for most people to live in cities. It also made it necessary: Industrialization requires the concentration of highly specialized workers who must perform their tasks in a few central locations. If people must gather in large numbers to work, then they will also concentrate in the same area to live: urbanization and industrialization are inseparable.

What allowed these twin processes to emerge and then dominate global development? The answer is simple but often overlooked: the Agricultural Revolution. More specifically, the Industrial Revolution allowed an unprecedented increase in agricutural productivity. With the introduction of new machines, new animal breeds, new varieties of plants, weed sprays, fertilizers, drainage, crop rotation, and irrigation systems--in short, the application of science and engineering to farming--farm productivity increased enormously. For example, the average American farm worker could feed ten times as many people in 1970 as in 1820. So, in the most fundamental way possible, industrialization and urbanization derived from the revolution in agriculture while the ongoing revolution in agriculture allowed for increased industrialization and urbanization.

Metropolis. American demographers classify a locale as an urban place if it has a population of more than 2,500 people. Yet to most people a place of 2,500 inhabitants hardly would qualify as a city. Suburbs, variably smaller communities in the immediate areas outside of a city, are definitely urban areas and often are cities in their own right. So, demographers began to lump suburbs with their central city as a single unit: the metropolis. To further refine the study of the city, the U.S. Census created the **Standard Metropolitan Statistical Area (SMSA)** centered around cities of at least 50,000 and including certain nearby counties. In Canada, there is the Census Metropolitan Area (CMA) with an urban core of at least 100,000 people. However defined, the shape of the metropolis tends toward one of two types: fixed-rail or freeway. As a generalization we can say that form follows and is a function of transportation. The older form is the fixed-rail metropolis, which usually was preindustrial in origin. Most major European and eastern North American cities have at least at their core a dense center, which originally had a rail transportation system that shuttled people back and forth between residence and work. The evolution of the fixed-rail system started with horse-drawn trolleys and now has sleek computerized subways. (Buses, in part, perform the function of fixed-rail transport but are, of course, much more flexible in terms of routes.) Fixed-rail systems reinforced the central area as the focal point of the city. North American cities that more or less are still classifiable as fixed-rail in shape are Montreal, Toronto, New York, Chicago, Philadelphia, Pittsburgh, Boston, and San Francisco. Although each of these is now a sprawling metropolis, each retains a vibrant downtown. It remains to be seen to what extent the downtowns of these cities can retain their traditional dominance in the overall metropolitan structure.

There are other (freeway) metropolises that have more or less given themselves wholly over to the automobile and the truck. Some of them never really had a downtown in any traditional sense (Los Angeles), or they did but it has been superseded in influence by suburban satellite centers (Detroit). One major cause of the freeway metropolis was a shift in manufacturing technique. As assembly-line methods of manufacturing required long, low buildings and therefore considerable space, plants have shifted to outlying areas where land is plentiful and cheap. To a considerable extent the debate over what constitutes a real city has been undercut by the fact that most people want cities to be decentralized.

The evidence seems overwhelming that most people prefer a low-density decentralized way of life. When given the chance, most opt to move out of and perhaps away from central cities. Also, people running large industrial and business firms have joined in the move to less dense areas, taking their plants and offices with them. (An interesting debate is to what extent manufacturing followed suburban development or people followed jobs that relocated.) Large numbers of people have been migrating from the old, high-density cities to the new decentralized metropolitan areas of the South and West. Finally, people avoid public transportation and are just as likely to walk to work as use public transit. More importantly, the overwhelming percentage of North Americans prefer to drive their own cars to work. When asked where they want to live, the overwhelming majority of Americans prefer a suburb or a place that qualifies as a far suburb. (Even those who said they wanted to live on a farm or a small town wanted to be within 30 miles of a city.)

Urban Neighborhoods. The character of North American cities, especially those that have been magnets of considerable overseas immigration, has been that of a mosaic distributed along class, ethnic, and racial lines. Historically, minority ethnic and racial groups concentrate in particular neighborhoods for several reasons. Members of a group are lured to the same neighborhoods in which their relatives and friends live--a place where their native language, customs, food, and religion predominate. They are also pulled toward these neighborhoods because they can afford to live there. Higher housing costs in other neighborhoods and discrimination keep members of ethnic groups out of these other neighborhoods. The Park and Burgess **theory of ethnic succession** was an early attempt to deal with the urban mosaic and how and why neighborhoods would change their ethnic composition. Paralleling the economic explanation of prejudice and discrimination (see Chapter 11) they argued that as new groups succeed in America they move out of ethnic neighborhoods because they can afford to live in better ones; they are not so tied to their traditional culture; and they no longer bear the stigma of low status.

However, Darroch and Marston and Kantrowitz argued for continued racial and ethnic segregation with prejudice as the primary barrier to integration. Given the decline in prejudice these findings were hard to square. A potential resolution was found in the work of Guest and Weed. While Darroch and Marston focused on individual members of various groups, Guest and Weed instead concentrated on the entire group. Using the **index of dissimilarity** (which measures to what extent a given racial or ethnic group lives in integrated or segregated neighborhoods when compared with the ethnic makeup of the city as a whole), Guest and Weed's findings basically supported the Park and Burgess position. In general, the higher the status of the ethnic group the more likely it was to live in integrated neighborhoods (especially in the eastern cities studied: Boston and Cleveland; less so in Seattle). Status inequality between groups seems to be the primary neighborhood barrier. As status inequalities disappear, so do racial and ethnic neighborhoods because western cities are newer, ethnic enclaves were never as firmly rooted so that western cities tend to be more integrated no matter what the racial or ethnic group. In perhaps the most unremittingly ethnic of all U.S. cities, Chicago, it stands to reason that it is also the most racially segregated U.S. city. Nevertheless, as Taeuber showed, in most American cities African-American segregation has been decreasing as their status has been increasing. Taeuber showed that integration was occurring because African-Amemicans were moving to the suburbs or into white neighborhoods in cities but that little reverse integration was occurring. Farley and Frey, using the Index of Dissimilarity while working with all 232 metropolitan areas, found that increases in integration were greatest in the South and West and that integration also increased as African-Americans' incomes approximate those of whites (thus supporting Guest and Weed.) They also found that the highest levels of integration were in areas dominated by military bases and university communities with very low levels in retirement communities.

Finally, Denton and Massey have found that neither Hispanics nor Asians are as segregated from non-Hispanic whites as are African-Americans. Moreover, the degree to which Hispanics and Asians are segregated declines markedly with income: The more they earn, the less likely they are to live in segregated neighborhoods. Table 19-7 shows that citizens from twenty-one countries are generally unconcerned with living near others of a different race. No country, not even South Africa, indicated that living near members of another race was nearly as undesirable as living near neighbors who were either heavy drinkers or who had a criminal past.

Theories of Urban Impact. As the dual processes of industrialization and urbanization grew apace, early sociologists such as Tönnies and Durkheim fretted as to the corrosive effect the urbanization of society would have on its inhabitants. Wirth, in his classic paper, "Urbanism as a Way of Life," drew on Simmel for inspiration but Wirth's students Faris and Dunham were more in line with the Durkheimian tradition of anomie whereby people, when they lose their attachments, also lose their moral compass. Substituting social disorganization for anomie, Faris and Dunham argued that high rates of social disorganization led to high rates of various social pathologies (alcoholism, mental illness, etc.). A more plausible alternative to the social disorganization idea is the social drift hypothesis that counterargued that people develop their problems and then drift into poor neighborhoods for lack of any alternative. This is especially true of unattached male drifters in the most socially disorganized neighborhoods. So while it is true that a lack of attachments results in deviance and anomie (see Chapter 7), it is not necessarily true that anomie is a distinctive trait of urbanites.

We can examine another line of research on the impact of urbanism on people: the effects of crowding. At the macro level it was not found that people in dense neighborhoods were more prone to alcoholism, mental illness, suicide, and so on. However, at the micro level Gove and others have found that excessive crowding of a person's immediate environment has some negative effects although, for example, in the United States fewer than 10 per cent of households contain more than one person per room.

TEACHING SUGGESTIONS

The objective of Chapter 19 is to show how modern society in general and North America in particular have become urbanized societies. In so doing, students are to acquire a greater appreciation for some important macro forces that shape their lives.

1. **Discussion-debate:** "The 'Superiority' of Urban Living." By the time this chapter is covered (usually late in the course) the instructor should know who are his/her more articulate students. From among these, select at least two students who hail from each of the following areas: cities (if possible having a core population of at least one-quarter million), suburbs, small cities, small towns, and farms. After each pair has consulted with one another, have each residence-type present the best possible case for life in that type of ecological environment paying particular attention to recreation, housing, shopping, commuting to and from work, crime, pollution, community activities-- that is, all the important nonemployment activities that fill a day. Then have the other student from each pair present some of the problems associated with that type of living. This exercise can be used either to sharpen the focus on the section preferring a decentralized metropolis or to illustrate a variation on the urbanism as a way of life theme. I've used it for each.

Everyone knows that urban areas offer superior employment opportunities. But what do people do and how do people live after work? Just how much of a difference does residence-type make? For example, if after work and sleep, television is the major activity of the average American, then given the prevalence of satellite dishes, cable television, VCRs, and video stores the nonemployment differences between the various residence-types must diminish appreciably. (Another leveling factor is mail-order shopping with the UPS truck supplanting the Wells Fargo wagon.) One of the interesting points that usually emerges from such a debate is that most/each residence-type will have a vociferous defender whose arguments tend to be "logic-proof" from criticism.

2. **Discussion:** "College Towns: A Stable Ecology?" If your college is in a college town, then this discussion could be useful in explaining, by contrast, ethnic succession. In a college town both on- and off-campus housing are reasonably stable in location and in the buildings themselves. What I find interesting is that the same "ethnic" group--students-- succeed each other year after year and generation after generation for that matter. This can lead to a loyalty among certain alumni for the alma mater that is rarely approached by ethnics returning to the old neighborhood. This succession cum continuity as opposed to the usual

ethnic discontinuity of succession can also occur in
company towns. In any case, I have found, once again, that
an effective way of broaching and explaining a topic often
begins with that which the students are familiar.
    Source: None needed. Just a thorough understanding of
the ecology of the campus and surrounding area.

3. Discussion: "Do Cities Have a Future?" If Americans
prefer to live near their work and at the same time live
outside of a city but near one, then two questions are
begged. First, if businesses continue to move offices and
plants from the city to the suburbs and beyond, then the
old traditional city is no longer necessary for economic
purposes. Second, if leisure opportunities continue to
follow population trends, then what is left for the city to
do except to house those leisure activities that must be
attended in person: sports, concerts, museums, and so on.
And if cities then come to be seen mostly as repositories
of disreputable people, might these in-person leisure
activities suffer also? This discussion might be seen as
bringing the chapter back full circle to discussion of
pre-industrial cities: "Why live in such cities?" We might
re-phrase this as, "Why even go near cities if everything I
think I need is found outside of them?"

ADDITIONAL STUDENT READINGS

Chafets, Z. Devil's Night: And Other True Tales of Detroit.
New York: Random House, 1990. An up-close survey of the
decline and fall of one of America's biggest cities.
Sobering.

Jacobs, J. Cities and the Wealth of Nations. New York:
Random House, 1984. Jacobs argues for the primacy of cities
over nations as generators of wealth. A compact, cogently
argued treatise from which any intelligent undergraduate
will benefit.

Mumford, L: The City in History. New York: Harcourt Brace
Jovanovich, 1961. Another magisterial effort by Mumford
containing all kinds of goodies. Well worth the time for
the motivated undergraduate (and sociology professor for
that matter).

Yergin, D. The Prize: The Epic Quest for Oil, Money and
Power. New York: Simon and Schuster, 1991. If Jacobs
argues for cities as generators of wealth then Yergin argues
that in the twentieth century control of oil is the
lifeblood of modern urban civilization. A fascinating read.

ESSAY QUESTIONS

1. Discuss how you can have urbanism without industrialism but not industrialization without urbanization.

2. Explain why fixed-rail metropolises and vibrant downtowns go together while traffic and residential patterns of freeway metropolises undermine the downtown.

3. What is the theory of ethnic succession? Show how the index of dissimilarity is relevant for testing the idea of ethnic succession.

4. Show how the following three ideas (*anomie, social disorganization*, and *social drift*) can be integrated to explain the existence of crime-ridden neighborhoods.

CHAPTER OUTLINE

Formal Organizations.	Socially adaptive response to size-induced complexity. Major traits: (1) official goals, (2) principles and procedures, (3) leaders selected and trained, (4) clear lines of communication and authority, (5) written records.
The Crisis of Growth.	To cope with complexity variations on divisional system are introduced.
Geographical Divisions.	Divides the organization into separate entities by area.
Functional Division.	Controls each step of the production process.
Weber's Rational Bureaucracy.	An attempt to subdue human affairs to rule of reason.
Rational Versus Natural Systems.	Natural system theorists emphasize overriding goal of any organization: survival.
Goal Displacement.	When formal goals threaten the organization's existence, the goals will be changed.
Goal Conflict.	Different groups pursuing different goals.
Informal Relations.	*De facto* lines of cooperation that ignore or circumvent the formal lines of authority.
The Crisis of Diversification.	When functional divisions become dysfunctional.
Span of Control.	With managers's expertise and effective authority inherently limited one solution is to create:
Autonomous Divisions.	(independent firms) within the larger corporation; the net result being the
Decentralization	of power and authority.
Blau's Theory of Administrative Growth.	Growth causes differentiation; and, consequently, the administrative component grows relative to others.

Rational and Natural Factors in Decentralization.	To maximize performance create the smallest possible operating units and delegate maximum flexibility.
Management by objective.	The doctrine that emphasizes discretion.
Bureaucracy and the Bottom Line.	Inherent accountability of business demands adopting the principle of decentralization. Governments can "afford" not to.

SUMMARY

Formal Organizations. Beginning with the nineteenth century and continuing to the present formal organizations (often termed bureaucracies) have become a major and inevitable response to the growing size and complexity of modern life. In fact, we can go further and state that formal organizations are a socially adaptive response to complexity that is size-induced. The major characteristics of a formal organization distinguish it from older forms of organization: (1) it has a statement of official goals;

  (2) principles and procedures for achieving these goals are established;

  (3) leaders are selected and trained in congruence with these principles and procedures;

  (4) clear lines of authority and communication; and

  (5) written records are kept.

The evolution of bureaucracy has been greatly influenced by academic theories and research. Therefore, as befitting this situation Chapter 20 will trace the development of both organizations and theories of organizations at the same time.

The Crisis of Growth. Perhaps the first great applied practitioner of bureaucracy was von Moltke who upon taking command of the Prussian army built a new principle of organizing it: Develop an interchangeable but highly trained staff officers thus forsaking the obsolete reliance upon the brilliance of a charismatic leader (such as Napoleon) for the reliability of competent military managers. The point of all this training was to overcome the inability of a single commander to direct a war fought with mass armies. Because the supreme commander could not be everywhere at once, the Prussians tried to create many duplicates trained to act as he would act.

Not only did von Moltke take care to properly socialize promising military talent, he also did not neglect matters at the macro level of the Prussian army. There he also perfected another military system that gave these managers standardized units to work with: the divisional system each similar to the others in makeup, training, size, and structure. Since von Moltke, the principle of delegating command to officers on the spot, who are highly trained in a common military theory and in the command of standardized military units, has remained the only workable solution to the problem that overwhelmed Napoleon.

At about the same time that von Moltke was reorganizing the Prussian army, problems with size and complexity were beginning to plague U.S. businesses, and in many landmark instances these problems were resolved in similar fashion. McCallum reorganized the Erie Railroad since the larger it became the more money it lost. In response, he broke his railroad into geographical divisions of manageable size. Each was headed by a superintendent responsible for the operations within his division. Each divisional superintendent was required to submit detailed reports to central headquarters. As other railroads adopted McCallum's reforms, there were major effects on American business. The railroads made it possible for other firms to grow by using rail shipments to reach national rather than just local markets, and the railroads provided the first crude organizational model for operating large firms. As they grew, new industrial firms created functional divisions that controlled each step in production through a process called vertical integration.

A giant of the meat-packing industry, Swift and Co., was one such firm that adopted the idea of vertical integration. In so doing, Swift controlled each step in the process of bringing meat products to the consumer. But rather than creating geographic divisions, as the giant railroads had done, Swift based its divisions on different functions such as a marketing division, a meat-packing division, and so on.

Still another example of organizational evolution came from civil service. As long as governments did little save tax the peasantry and conduct war, kings could afford to appoint by nepotism and cronyism. Even in the early stages of American democracy the spoils system, cronyism, and patronage were the rule. However, as government became more complex and the abuses more flagrant, civil service reform in which professional bureaucrats administered government agencies became more and more the rule.

Weber's Rational Bureaucracy. Max Weber first systemized the development of formal organization in his analysis of bureaucracy (which he applied to business as well as government). He emphasized that bureaucratic organizations were an attempt to subdue human affairs to the rule of

reason. As such bureaucracy was inseparable from
rationality. Several features made bureaucracies rational
and included:

1. functional specialization;
2. clear lines of authority;
3. expert training of staff;
4. appointment and promotion based on
   merit;
5. decisions based on rules; and
6. business conducted via written rules,
   records, and communications.

Weber's approach dominated this field for quite some time.
However, after World War II criticism of Weber began in
earnest, and focused on his neglect of the human side of
bureaucracy.

Rational Versus Natural Systems. Weber stressed the
rationality of bureaucratic organizations that are created
to pursue clearly defined goals, and the structure and
operation of organizations are the result of reasoned,
conscious efforts to attain these goals. However, the
natural system approach to formal organizations stresses
that the rarely stated but overriding goal of organizations
is simply to survive mainly because the human beings who
staff an organization develop a personal stake in the life
of that organization, regardless of its stated goals. Goal
displacement illustrates this by declaring that when the
formal goals of an organization threaten its existence, the
goals will be changed.

One such example was the March of Dimes changing its
goal to a much more open-ended one: eliminating birth
defects, after its original goal of defeating polio was met.
Further, the natural system theorists emphasize goal
conflict where different groups within an organization tend
to pursue different goals, which often have nothing to do
with, if not conflict with, the goals of the larger
organization. Finally, formal organizations are often
riddled with *de facto* lines of cooperation that ignore or
circumvent the formal lines of authority. These informal
relations belie the organization chart and are, according to
the natural system theorists, the real stuff of any
organization.

But if the rational system approach over-emphasized the
organizational blueprint, the natural system approach tends
to forget that there is one. Consequently, neither the
rational nor the natural system approach can fully explain
formal organizational activities.

The Crisis of Diversification. The case of Du Pont shows
how an adaptation to one set of problems contributes to
other problems once goals and/or activities change. More
specifically, when Du Pont reorganized itself along

functional divisions that was fine as long as Du Pont confined itself to arms manufacturing. As Du Pont moved into chemical products (i.e., diversified) functional divisions that were effective for a business narrow in scope became dysfunctional when diversification entered the picture. Because the span of control (and of expertise) of any manager is inherently limited, Du Pont's solution was to create several autonomous divisions (in effect, independent firms) within the larger corporation for each of its separate activities. These autonomous divisions transformed single firms that had become too big and too complex to manage into a cluster of smaller, coordinated firms. This was the second step taken in a new approach to managing big organizations: decentralization. The problem of managing large corporations has been perhaps most succinctly addressed by Blau's theory of administrative growth. Blau argued that growth caused differentiation and therefore the size of the administrative component increases relative to the size of other components so much so that the larger the organization, the greater the proportion of total resources that must be devoted to management functions. Blau's theory again leads to the principle of decentralization as organizations exceed an optimal size.

Rational and Natural Factors in Decentralization. To theorists such as Drucker it follows that companies ought to create the smallest possible operating units in order to give maximum flexibility to the person on the spot. As long as the overall performance of a department is satisfactory, leave it alone. If performance fails, then appoint new people, but never try to run it from upstairs. This doctrine is often called management by objective, which emphasizes discretion--giving the manager responsibility as well as the authority for decision making.

However, as Thompson has pointed out, when people believe they cannot adequately control conditions affecting decisions, they will try to evade discretion by passing responsibility for decision making on to others. Thus, "discretion-evasion" will occur when people must rely on others to achieve their goals and when the negative consequences of poor decision making would be great. Alternatively, it can be argued that the more discretion assigned to a position in an organization, the more a person holding that position will seek power over those affected by his or her decisions ("discretion-absorption"?) The point to remember then is that the attempts to evade or absorb discretion run counter to prevailing tendencies toward decentralization. Further, whenever an individual given discretion has insufficient power to control conditions governing his or her decision, that individual will seek added power by forming a coalition with other decision makers often with people outside the organization.

Bureaucracy and the Bottom line. In business the general trend has been toward decentralization while in government, if anything, the dominant trend has been the opposite. Businesses have a clear standard by which to judge their performance: profit and loss (and possible bankruptcy). So businesses have adopted the principle of decentralization to cope with growing size and complexity. Governments, in the sense of not having to fear bankruptcy, have less accountability and, therefore, much less incentive to decentralize.

TEACHING SUGGESTIONS

The objective of Chapter 20 is to sensitize students to the all-pervasive social invention of the past 100 years: large-scale formal organizations through a close examination of case studies as well as the major theories designed to explain bureaucratic phenomena.

1. Discussion: "The Documentation of Social Identities." A discussion that explores the various salient identities that contemporary Americans may claim. In one sense, it is a vindication of Weber's gloomy prediction that the future of modernity is the inexorable encroachment of rational bureaucracy. The discussion may begin with a simple list of important status passages such as birth, death, marriage, and so on, common to a variety of societal types. In each instance, the professor can show how the American version of these changes involves some outside agency that must validate the event before it is officially recognized. The students often claim, of course, that birth (including gender), death, and marriage have some objective existence, but according to the respective agencies nothing has happened unless it has been officially verified-- that is, documented. With this point students can see the difference between the existential quality of the status/fact/event that is lived and the bureaucratic quality of the status or fact or event as recorded. Further, various other statuses are either bureaucratically generated or, at the least, monitored: college student, religious/ethnic group affiliation, driver's licensing, social security and credit cards, and so on. Interestingly, a key variable that sociologists love to use to differentiate various aggregates of people and their behavior--social class--seems neither to be recorded systematically in an official manner nor do Americans find it to be a highly salient social identity. The closest we come is occupation, but of course, that is not quite the same thing. In sum, this discussion can show students not only the social nature of modern identities but also that organizations, in addition to monitoring status identity-passages, may actually generate them.

2. **Lecture-Discussion:** "College Students: Clients or Inmates?" is an exercise that initially specifies the impersonal life of inmates in total institutions and then shifts the focus to college students (ostensibly to contrast their lot with those of prisoners, mental patients, etc.). The class eventually begins to see some parallels. The depersonalization of human beings is, as has been sadly noted time and again, a sine qua non for the organization of dehumanization. This discussion can be an effective means to remind students that while their lot as college students is certainly less than the propaganda painted by the recruitment brochures it could be much worse.

It is interesting and challenging if the instructor reinterprets the usual interpretation of a college education in terms of goal displacement and goal conflict. For example, how many policies are designed to ensure staff and faculty a raison d'etre to continue working at the college? One example would be the notorious turf battles waged whenever general education requirements are to be revised. (I have found that, more than any other group, humanities professors are masters at rhetorical justifications for their defending their respective disciplines.)

More importantly, the discussion can point to many important continuities waiting for them after they graduate: careers in large organizations. You may also extend this discussion by showing students that in modern society there is perhaps only one time in which their primary status is not on file and being processed by some formal organization: as a very young child, before starting to school. (Even after one retires there are still the matters of pension and social security benefits, medicare, nursing homes, hospital stays, etc.)

Sources: Downs, A. _Inside Bureaucracy._ Boston: Little, Brown, 1967. A much neglected work that has especially interesting discussions on level-of-analysis distinctions between bureaucracies and bureaucrats, types and motives of bureaucrats, and interactions between bureaucracies.

Goffman, E. _Asylums._ New York: Doubleday, 1961. See especially the chapter on the characteristics of _total institutions_. This is another one of those pieces that we've all read and bears no further mention save for the fact that it is probably easier to lecture on than to have beginning students read in its entirety.

Perrow, C. _Complex Organizations_. rev. ed. Glenview, Ill: Scott Foresman, 1979. Overall, I think that this is the best modern piece on bureaucracy. Especially well done is a critical analysis of official goals of organizations.

3. **Lecture:** "Parkinson's Law and the Peter Principle." Frankly, I used to have a devil of a time trying to explain in any viable way Blau's theory of administrative growth. However, while rummaging through a section of my books that

I hardly ever use, I came across Parkinson and his famous law: "Work expands so as to fill the time available for its completion." If this is true, then how much administrative growth is due to the increasing complexity of tending to a growing concern, and how much administration is due to the make work of other bureaucrats? (Personally, I do not think that Blau and Parkinson are incompatible.)

After you have gotten through that, you might try the Peter Principle, which states that people rise to their level of competence and then are promoted to a level beyond their competence for which they are ill-suited and perform poorly and in which they become stuck indefinitely. To the extent that this is true, then bureaucracies are run by people in positions in which they should not be. Students can't believe that Peter or you are serious so you reassure them that it is all a sendup. Still....

Sources: Parkinson, C. Parkinson's Law. Boston: Houghton Mifflin, 1962.

Peter, L. and R. Hull: The Peter Principle: Why Things Always Go Wrong. New York: William Morrow, 1969.

ADDITIONAL STUDENT READINGS

Ferraro, B. and P. Hussey, with J. O'Reilly. No Turning Back: Two Nuns' Battle with the Vatican over Women's Right to Choose. New York: Poseidon Press, 1990. A case study in taking on one of the world's most formidatble bureaucracies Ferraro and Hussey document ideolgoical clashes within the context of organziational imperatives. Fascinating.

Hummel, R. The Bureaucratic Experience. 2nd ed. New York: St. Martin's, 1982. Perhaps the best of the modern critiques of bureaucracy since it delineates not only how bureaucracy expands into various and sundry corners of social life (Weber's message) but more especially how it implodes upon itself (Kafka's message).

Rosenhan, D. "On Being Sane in Insane Places." Science, (January 1973): 250-258. Protestations by psychiatrists notwithstanding this experiment involving normal people faking symptoms to get themselves into mental hospitals and the bizarre world they found there was largely a product of the rational-bureaucratic strategies of the hospital staffs. A social science classic.

Shilts, R. And the Band Played On: Politics, People, and the AIDS Epidemic. New York: St. Martin's Press, 1987. Shilts investigates how political, medical, and mass media organzations actually facilitated the spread of AIDS. Shilts was an excellent investigative reporter who himself died from complications of AIDS.

Yates, B. _The Decline and Fall of the American Automobile Industry_. New York: Empire Books, 1983. A readable account by perhaps America's foremost automotive writer on how arrogance, complacency, and isolation led the domestic car manufacturers to a position of where they now must copy the foreign competition and not just each other. A case study of how huge organizations lose touch with their markets and ultimately with themselves and what they must do to reassert their dominance. [Detroit did end up copying the Japanese and regaining a bit of lost market share.]

ESSAY QUESTIONS

1. Define formal organization and then show why this university qualifies as a formal organization.

2. Compare and contrast the rational vs. the natural systems approach to organizations.

3. Explain how with the crisis of diversification functional divsions can become dysfunctional.

4. Show why businesses can't afford not to decentralize while governments can afford not to.

CHAPTER 21

CHAPTER OUTLINE

Social Movement.

People oranized to cause or prevent social change.

Sociological Approaches to Social Movements.

Collective Behavior.

The older approach which identifies social movements as part of outbursts of group activity in response to grievances.

Resource Mobilization.

The newer approach to social movements that argues that grievances aren't important but available resources and rational planning are.

Stark's Synthesis.

Emphasizes that some people must share a grievance they want to resolve by changing some condition. A precipitating event must trigger the release and channel the grievances. For the movement to succeed it must effectively mobilize people and resources while withstanding external opposition for which they will need external allies.

Application to the Civil Rights Movement:

Shared Grievances

Economic, political, personal. Yet hope had led to a revolution of rising expectations that was galvanized by Rosa Park's refusal to give up her bus seat (precipitating event). The bus boycott mobilized the participants while outside help in the form of contributions and overturning local segregation laws was critical.

Freedom Summer: Mississippi 1964.

SNCC leaders enlisted aid of hundreds of students from northern elite schools to help with voter registration and focused country's attention.

Freedom Summer Study:
  Doug McAdam.

McAdam finds that participants
were "biographically
available": didn't need to work
or go to school. Ninety per
cent were previously involved
in activism; 20-year follow up
finds the participants still
politically active (left-wing)
as well as alienated and
isolated from 1980s America.

SUMMARY

Social Movement. Chapter 21 addresses the ways in which
individuals can get together to cause or to prevent social
change. More specifically, whenever people organize to
cause or prevent social change, we identify them as part of
a social movement. To illustrate the notion of social
movement this chapter focuses on the Civil Rights Movement
of the 1950s and 1960s. In so doing, Stark addresses the
issue: Does history make people or do people make history?

Sociological Approaches to Social Movements. The older
approach has typically been to identify social movements as
an important instance of a larger phenomenon dubbed
collective behavior. Here social movements are seen as
outbursts of group activity in response to deeply felt
grievances. The collective behavior approach also places
great significance on the role of ideology in fixing the
goals and tactics of a social movement and stresses the
importance of emotions and feelings, as opposed to rational
decision making by participants. The key question is Why do
these people want social change so badly and believe that it
is possible?
    The newer approach to social movements is that of
resource mobilization. Grievances are of little import
since, as McCarthy and Zald claim, "There is always enough
discontent in any society to supply the grass-roots support
for a social movement." Rather, as its name implies, this
perspective stresses the importance of resources, both human
and material, and rational planning as the source of social
movements and as the basis for their success. It places its
greatest stress on the crucial role of leadership. So, the
key question to be asked is How can these people organize,
pool resources and wield them effectively?
    Stark feels that each perspective is strongest precisely
where the other is deficient: Collective behaviorists pay
more attention to grievances and less to resources and

resource mobilization theorists reverse the priorities. Stark continues by stating that elements of each are needed for a full account of any social movement and proposes several propositions for a social movement to occur and succeed.

For a movement to occur some people must share a grievance that they want to resolve by changing (or preventing the change of) some condition. Further, the people must have hope that they can be successful in resolving their grievance(s). Finally, some precipitating event must trigger the release and channel the grievances. Now, for a movement to succeed, Stark feels that it must effectively mobilize people and resources while withstanding external opposition for which they will need external allies. In addition, the movement will be embodied in several separate organizations.

Application to the Civil Rights Movement. Shared grievances can be summarized by African-Americans' ideas that whites unfairly and inequitably controlled them economically (in the form of income and job discrimination), politically (whites controlling the disposition of tax revenues as well as making African-Americans in the South take a literacy test to vote that they always failed), and personally (in America's less virulent form of apartheid: segregation). Hope was manifested by the fact that within the lifetimes of many of the African-Americans their situation had become better, and with these changes came the ability to hope--to think that something could be done to make things much better. These hopes received a big boost in 1954 when the Supreme Court ruled against segregated schools. The result was a revolution of rising expectations in which people act to change their situation when their hopes for change far outstrip the actual progress taking place. The precipitating event that galvanized African-Americans was Rosa Park's refusal to give up her bus seat.

Successful mobilization of a movement depends on the existence of certain internal and external factors. The primary internal factor is to overcome the free rider problem by enlisting the support and sacrifice of sufficient numbers of people (the bus boycott). What seems to be necessary to accomplish this is for there to pre-exist an effective social network of contacts (spearheaded by Ann Robinson and the political action committee of the Dexter Avenue Baptist Church) as well as sufficient material resources (cars for carpooling). However, this can all come together only if there are highly competent leaders (Martin Luther King Jr. among others).

Social movements involve external factors, which means overcoming opponents while enlisting the aid of helpful allies. The boycott ran into significant opposition with the issuance of numerous traffic violations, arbitrary arrests, and even house bombings. At the same time, help was forthcoming from the outside from church groups (North and South; white and African-American); donations (e.g., $30,000 from the UAW); and the U.S. Supreme Court ruling that Alabama's state and local laws requiring segregated buses were unconstitutional.

Freedom Summer: Mississippi, 1964. For several years African-American student volunteers from SNCC had been trying to organize African-Americans in Mississippi to overcome perhaps the most virulent forms of racism in the country. Fundamental to ending the oppression manifested by a separate and unequal segregation of the races was white control of political power; and as long as fewer than 7 per cent of the African-Americans were registered to vote that would not change. A breakthrough occurred when SNCC leaders were able to enlist hundreds of white students from elite northern colleges. The strategy worked as daily reports on idealistic, white students from good families risking death on behalf of African-Americans in Mississippi dominated the national news media. And while few Mississippi African-Americans did register to vote, public opinion was mobilized nationally and culminated in landmark civil rights legislation being passed and enacted.

Doug McAdam and the Freedom Summer Study. McAdam began his study of the white student volunteers (and what became of them) by first locating the original applications. From these he contacted the volunteers via their alma maters. He sent questionnaires to those he could locate and then interviewed samples of forty of those who did participate and of those who had applied but did not participate in Freedom Summer (no-shows).

Perhaps the most important factor McAdam found was that those who did participate were "biographically available." Going down to Mississippi in the summer did not interfere with classes, and since so many of the volunteers were from affluent families they did not have to worry about working at summer jobs for college money. Further, few were married. As importantly, the volunteers strongly believed in racial equality and were optimistic that their collective efforts could change conditions for the better. They also, overwhelmingly, had parental approval for their sojourn. As seen earlier in the text, social networks were also crucial. The volunteers were not individuals acting on their own, each seeking to fulfill his or her ideas. People volunteered on the basis of personal ties to others, and their opportunity to volunteer typically arose through their previous activity in civil rights organizations. In fact, 90 percent of the volunteers "had already participated in various forms of activism." McAdam found it impossible to distinguish participant from no-show on the basis of

195 /Chapter 21

attitudes and values. All were optimistic idealists. What did distinguish between the groups was their availability and their network ties. No-shows tended to be younger and female (see parental nonapproval) while participants were three times as likely as no-shows to have friends who also went to Mississippi.

Twenty years later the participants tended to tell McAdam that the Freedom Summer was a watershed experience in their lives. Participation had made them politically radical (see their leadership roles in the New Left), and their liberalism and involvement in various social movements have in no way been diminished. (For example, see their protesting against the draft, the Vietnam war, nuclear power and their protest on behalf of feminism, abortion rights, gay rights, and disarmament). Personally, they are far less likely than their general cohorts to be married (see their high divorce rate and their greater likelihood never to have been married). They are also alienated and socially isolated from the America of the 1980s and are found to be disproportionately over-represented among the ranks of college professors.

TEACHING SUGGESTIONS

The objective of Chapter 21 is to examine social change from the perspective of social movements, thus demonstrating how history is shaped by people as well as how it shapes people's lives. This is accomplished by an in-depth analysis of the Civil Rights Movement of the 1950s and 1960s.

1. **Discussion.** "College Students: A Movement Waiting to Happen?" Might college students of the 1990s stage movements of their own as their older sixties brethren did? Might it start with the emerging issue of political correctness in thought, word, and deed? This discussion can be organized around Stark's synthesis of the collective behavior and resource mobilization models of social movements detailing the conditions that need to be met for movements to occur and succeed.

2. **Lecture.** "Social Problems, Social Movements, and the Mass Media." If you have not broached the idea of social problems yet, this is certainly a now-or-never juncture. I find it impossible to conceptualize social problems apart from social movements. One of my favorite ways of doing so is by lecturing from Hilgartner and Bosk's public arenas model of social problems. Treating public attention as a scarce resource, the model emphasizes competition and selection in the media and other arenas of public discourse to analyze why some phenomena grow to be social problems

and what happens to them afterward. It is a provocative piece with some interesting implications. The students have to stay focused for this one.

Source: Hilgartner, S., and C. Bosk. "The Rise and Fall of Social Problems: A Public Arenas Model." <u>American Journal of Sociology</u> 94 (1988): 53-78.

3. Lecture: "Hysterias as Mass Movements." If the revolution of rising expectations is an important factor in the development of social movements, then what you might call the revolution of rising fears is a sine qua non of hysterias. Now, if we define a hysteria as a type of dispersed pattern of emotional (irrational?) behavior to some real or imagined threat, then it seems to me that many kinds of collective phenomena qualify: stock market meltdowns, the "War of the Worlds" broadcast, gay-bashing in response to the AIDS epidemic.

[Instructor's note: A panic can be defined as a type of localized outburst to some stimulus (real or imagined) causing seemingly irrational and emotional collective behavior. So defined, are hysterias nothing more than an aggregate of similar localized panics?]

You might conclude this lecture by hypothesizing under what circumstances a social movement might evolve from hysterias. Perhaps the organized counter-reaction to gay rights in the light of the AIDS epidemic qualifies.

Sources. There are several available. For example, Rose, J._<u>Outbreaks: The Sociology of Collective Behavior</u>. New York: Free Press, 1982. A good text of this field, it is suitable for beginning students.

See also McPhail, C. <u>The Myth of the Madding Crowd</u>. New York: Walter de Gruyter, 1991. McPhail gives a new interpretation of crowd behavior. Presupposes some familiarity with the area.

ADDITIONAL STUDENT READINGS

Gamson, W. <u>The Strategy of Social Protest</u>. 2nd ed. Belmont, Calif: Wadsworth, 1990. Gamson studies numerous historical protest groups and finds that the successful ones tended not to be nice and docile and patient. America tends not to reward the meek, especially in this rough and tumble arena.

Gitlin, T. <u>The Sixties: Years of Hope, Days of Rage</u>. New York: Bantam Books, 1987. Gitlin, a sociologist, writes a retrospective of the era as one who not only lived through it but was smack in the middle of it. This book has many admirers and several detractors. Fascinating indeed.

Hall, J. Gone from the Promised Land: Jonestown in American Cultural History. New Brunswick, N.J.: Transaction Books, 1987. Was the mass homicide-suicide of Jonestown followers in 1978 collective outburst or social mobilization?

Malcom X with Alex Haley. The Autobiography of Malcolm X. New York: Grove Press, 1964. A modern classic and as fresh today as when I read it as an undergraduate. Spike Lee's cinematic rendering is excellent.

Taylor, J. Paved With Good Intentions: The Failure of Race Relations in Contemporary America. New York: Carroll and Graf, 1992. Taylor contends that outmoded social policies (e.g. affirmative action) have many perverse latent dysfunctions regarding race relations; the brunt of them borne by African-Americans. Not at all politically correct but very effectively argued.

ESSAY QUESTIONS

1. Compare and contrast the collective behavior and the resource mobilization models of social movements. What does Stark think is strength of each? The weakness of each?

2. Apply Stark's synthesis of social movements to Freedom Summer 1964.

3. What does McAdam mean by "biographical availability" and how is it affected by social class standing?

4. How does Freedom Summer 1964 and McAdam's follow-up study illustrate the idea that people make history as history shapes people?

I have found the following projects useful when I teach an honors section of Principles of Sociology. I find that honors sections (usually 15-20 students) "need" and can benefit from something like the following. The projects are do-able within the framework of a semester-long course.

Honors Project 1: "Different Slants on the News."

1.   Have each student choose some ongoing news story.
          [Instructor's note: The O.J. Simpson murder
          trial would have been one obvious choice.]
       Then have each write a short paper on it analyzing
       it from the perspective of two different news
       media: either radio and a newsweekly (preferably
       Time or Newsweek) or television and a newspaper.
       The reasons for fixed choices are as follows:
          a.   Each fixed choice has one nonprint news
               source (radio/TV).
          b.   Each choice has only one image-rich
               possibility (TV/newsweekly).
       [Instructor's note: I warn the students that I
       don't consider Rush Limbaugh as anything
       approaching a reliable objective news source for
       radio or television.]

2.   Have them write a short paper detailing how each
       medium treated the story paying particular
       attention to how the format of the medium affects
       how the story is presented and thus any possible
       effects on how the audience might perceive the news
       event.

3.   Ask them to turn in two copies of their paper to
       the instructor.

4.   The instructor keeps one copy and distributes the
       other randomly to another student in the class
       making sure that there are no instances in which
       any two students simply are exchanging papers. It
       is also better if papers from students on one side
       of the room are exchanged with those on the other
       side so as to minimize friendships from having an
       impact on the project.

5.   Each student then critiques the other paper for
       content and style.

6. Each student hands back two copies of his/her critique of the paper plus the paper to the instructor.

7. Each student will eventually receive the original two copies of his or her paper (one critiqued by the professor and one by a peer) plus one copy of the critique he or she did of a peer (graded by the professor).

8. Ultimately, the instructor will have two grades for each student: that of their original paper and that of the critique of a peer's paper.

I have found several uses for this project.
   a. It exposes students to a most important truism of contemporary society: the "news" does not come unvarnished.
   b. It gets them used to writing for the course early on.
   c. It gives them valuable experience in editing and critiquing.
   d. It shows them that people's products (such as college papers) can be presented and certainly viewed in more than one way, thus making an analogy between their papers and the news stories about which they originally wrote.

Honors Project 2: "Advertising, the Mass Media, and Sociology." Each group of students is responsible for a class presentation as well as a written version of it to be handed in toward the end of the term. The project goal is to analyze representative ads from a variety of media sources that address some concept or theme found in one of the chapters of the text. Obvious ones would include Chapter 6 on socialization, Chapter 7 on deviance, Chapter 9 on stratification. In their presentations I let the students use posters, VCRs—whatever is helpful to get their points across. I have found that the students really get into it and develop a critical awareness of the impact of advertising on their lives.

1. Randomly assign the students into three- or four-member groups.

2. Conduct a draft in which chapters to be covered in the course are selected by the groups for class presentations.

3.   Have each group work out its own division of labor. Make sure that the person who delivers the class presentation is not the one who will be fielding the questions from the other students and the course instructor. This increases communication within the group so that the presenter and press secretary have to be on the same page.

4.   Have each group present their topic and answer questions within a 45-minutes to 1-hour block of time during the week that their chapter will be covered in class.
    [Instructor's note: I've found that on presentation days it is better to let the group go first. If you carry over something from the last unit or are beginning the current unit, some of the class will be very nervous and of little help while waiting to give their presentation. Further, as you proceed with the unit you may refer to the presentation as an in-common experience to which the entire class can relate.]

5.   After feedback from the class and the instructor, each group hands in a written version of their presentation toward the end of the semester.

6.   I give each group an overall grade, and each student in the group receives that grade for his or her participation in the project. I explain to them the free-rider possibilities here and point out that Chapter 8 addresses the issue of group pressure.
    [Instructor's note: In addition to all the above considerations, I find that this project gives students a valuable opportunity to develop their teamwork skills.]

Resource. A Guide to Writing Sociology Papers, 2nd ed. Sociology Writing Group. New York: St. Martin's Press, 1991. A helpful how-to manual for both the beginning and the advanced undergraduate student.

   To be candid, I am not academia's leading advocate of
films/videos in the classroom. As with most pedagogic
supplements I feel that they should be used sparingly.
After all, our responsibility as instructors of basic
sociology is to impart basic sociology, and I feel that
this is most effectively accomplished by the traditional
instructor-student relationship.

   That being said, there are times when a (motion) picture
accomplishes more than a thousand words of lecturing. For
example, you could lecture for hours on hunter-gathering
societies, but the two reels of the nomadic desert people of
Western Australia (see below under Chapter 10) are an
incredibly effective teaching aid. Moreover, we all miss
the occasional class. Whether it is sickness, a personal
emergency, a professional meeting, whatever, there are times
when you can't make class. Rather than put the onus on a
colleague to cover it as you want it covered, perhaps it is
best for all concerned to show a film.

   To that end I have culled many of the better films/videos
for a principles class and arranged them by chapter. As far
as I can tell, all are currently available for rental, and
most could be purchased as well. For this edition I have
included one "popular" movie per chapter. My reasoning is
that often a Hollywood production, though more lengthy, will
accomplish as much if not more and in a much more
entertaining way, than the conventional "educational" piece.
So, for those days when nothing but something visual will
do, here goes.

Chapter 1

Title:	Eye of the Storm
Length:	29 minutes
Medium:	film
Description:	A classic way of teaching about group dynamics and discrimination. Rural white third graders are taught firsthand about discrimination (based on eye color).
Producer/Distributor:	Yale University

Title:	Lord of the Flies
Length:	90 minutes
Medium:	video
Description:	Adapted from the novel a chilling, none too charitable view of group dynamics of stranded schoolboys.

Chapter 2

Title: My Town
Length: 26 minutes
Medium: video
Description: Italian immigrants settle in
                             the United States and many of
                             them still see their *paesani* in
                             Calabria as their primary
                             reference group.

Producer/Distributor: UMEMC

Title: This is Spinal Tap
Length: 82 minutes
Medium: video
Description: This wonderful sendup of a
                             downwardly mobile hard rock
                             group also has some acerbic
                             asides on mass rock culture.

Chapter 3

Title: The Wave
Length: 46 minutes
Medium: video
Description: The re-creation of a chilling
                             experiment in which high school
                             students willingly choose to
                             embrace fascism.

Producer/Distributor: FI

Title: Glengarry Glen Ross
Length: 2 hours
Medium: video
Description: 24 hours in the life of real
                             estate salesmen where greed is
                             ubiquitous rational choice.
                             Great performances by Al Pacino
                             and Jack Lemmon.

Chapter 4

Title: Yanomamo: A MultiDisciplinary
                             Study
Length: 48 minutes
Medium: film
Description: Here is the perfect visual
                             supplement to Chagnon's study
                             of this fascinating people.

Producer/Distributor: USNAC

Chapter 4 (continued)
    Title: Network
    Length: 121 minutes
    Medium: video
    Description: Mass society, mass media, mass
                                    madness. Television as a
                                    metaphor of the American way of
                                    life. Faye Dunaway has never
                                    been better. By turns,
                                    howlingly funny and caustically
                                    incisive.

Chapter 5
    Title: Jane Goodall and the Baboon
                                    Troop
    Length: 23 minutes
    Medium: film
    Description: Focuses on intratroop
                                    aggressiveness and submission.
    Producer/Distributor: FI

    Title: Awakenings
    Length: 121 minutes
    Medium: video
    Description: Medication given to catatonic
                                    patients has miraculous (albeit
                                    temporary) effects. DeNiro's
                                    performance is astonishing.

Chapter 6
    Title: Faces of Culture 7--Culture and
                                    Personality
    Length: 30 minutes
    Medium: film
    Description: The development of the concept
                                    of culture and personality
                                    especially through the works of
                                    Margaret Mead.
    Producer/Distributor: CDTEL

    Title: Educating Rita
    Length: 110 minutes
    Medium: video
    Description: A working class English girl
                                    goes to college and becomes the
                                    star pupil of a besotted
                                    professor. Socialization as a
                                    life-long experience is the
                                    topic of this delightful
                                    comedy.

Chapter 7
    Title: Why Men Rape
    Length: 40 minutes
    Medium: video
    Description: Interviews with convicted
                        rapists and with experts on
                        sexual violence.
    Producer/Distributor: National Film Board of Canada

    Title: The Crying Game
    Length: 113 minutes
    Medium: video
    Description: Ostensibly a story about IRA
                        terrorism but that ain't the
                        half of it! Absolutely first-
                        rate movie-making.

Chapter 8
    Title: The World's Safest City: Public
                        Security in Tokyo
    Length: 28 minutes
    Medium: film
    Description: A good case study of informal
                        and formal social control.
    Producer/Distributor: The Japan Foundation

    Title: One Flew Over the Cuckoo's
                        Nest
    Length: 133 minutes
    Medium: video
    Description: Formal social control a la a
                        mental institution. Award-
                        winning performances by Jack
                        Nicholson and Louise Fletcher.

Chapter 9
    Title: New Harvest, Old Shame
    Length: 60 minutes
    Medium: video
    Description: An updating of Edward R.
                        Murrow's "Harvest of Shame."
                        Not much has changed.
    Producer/Distributor: PBS Frontline

    Title: Metropolis
    Length: 120 minutes
    Medium: video
    Description: Fritz Lang's silent film
                        masterpiece about a futuristic
                        society with class
                        polarization. Should be seen
                        for the cinematography alone.

Chapter 10

Title: The Desert People
Length: 51 minutes
Medium: film
Description: A typical day in the life of a
                         now extinct Paleolithic people
                         from Australia's Western
                         Desert.
Producer/Distributor: CRMP

Title: The Gods Must Be Crazy
Length: 109 minutes
Medium: video
Description: A wonderful comedy about
                         culture clashes in South
                         Africa. A must-see.

Chapter 11

Title: A Class Divided
Length: 60 minutes
Medium: video
Description: An excellent updating of "The
                         Eye of the Storm."
Producer/Distributor: PBS Frontline

Title: Jungle Fever
Length: 135 minutes
Medium: video
Description: Spike Lee's take on interracial
                         romance; poignant and powerful.

Chapter 12

Title: No Longer Silent
Length: 57 minutes
Medium: video
Description: The film examines several
                         serious forms of sexism
                         (many of which have an impact
                         on the sex ratio) as faced by
                         women in India.
Producer/Distributor: IFB

Title: The Color Purple
Length: 130 minutes
Medium: video
Description: A movie about women but for
                         everyone. Whoopi Goldberg is
                         superb.

Chapter 13

Title: Stepdancing: Portrait of a Remarried Family

Length: 28 minutes

Medium: film

Description: A fictionalized case study of a young boy confronting the new relationships as well as the dynamics that result from divorce and remarriage.

Producer/Distributor: PYR

Title: Who Are The Debolts and Where Did They Get 19 Kids?

Length: 73 minutes

Medium: video

Description: That's right: 19! A great documentary and for once, one with a positive message.

Chapter 14

Title: The Holy Ghost People

Length: 55 minutes

Medium: film

Description: A fascinating account of Appalachian fundamentalists who happen to incorporate (rattle)snakehandling into their religious services.

Producer/Distributor: MGHT

Title: Elmer Gantry

Length: 145 minutes

Medium: video

Description: Sinclair Lewis' novel on phony evangelism gives Burt Lancaster a chance to strut his award-winning stuff.

Chapter 15

Title: The Search for the Disappeared

Length: 60 minutes

Medium: video

Description: Many states still need taming. In this case, more than 10,000 Argentineans disappeared in six years during the military junta's crackdown on so called leftist subversives.

Producer/Distributor: PBS Nova

Chapter 15 (continued)
    Title: Missing
    Length: 122 minutes
    Medium: video
    Description: Another superb Costa-Gavras political thriller (see Z) with Jack Lemmon and Sissy Spacek as the father and wife of an American journalist who vanishes during a coup.

Chapter 16
    Title: Success Stories: Winners
    Length: 29 minutes
    Medium: video
    Description: Examines three adults who attained their GEDs and overcame earlier obstacles of pregnancy, drug abuse, illiteracy, etc.
    Producer/Distributor: Penn State Television

    Title: The Conversation
    Length: 113 minutes
    Medium: video
    Description: Francis Ford Coppola's fascinating yarn (and tight character study) of a surveillance expert. You'll need a private detective to follow the plot twists. One of my favorites.

Chapter 17
    Title: Change, Change
    Length: 58 minutes
    Medium: video
    Description: A Bill Moyers retrospective on the 1960s and how that decade changed America.
    Producer/Distributor: PBS

    Title: Inherit the Wind
    Length: 127 minutes
    Medium: video
    Description: The Scopes monkey trial with Frederic March and Spencer Tracy representing fundamentalism and secularism respectively. Superb drama.

Chapter 18
    Title: The Business of Hunger
    Length: 28 minutes
    Medium: film
    Description: Argues that the earth could feed everyone with present capabilities and that hunger is largely the product of public policy.
    Producer/Distributor: MAYRK

    Title: El Norte
    Length: 139 minutes
    Medium: video
    Description: To what extent is illegal immigration a function of foreign policy? Before reaching for some knee-jerk proposition to close the borders one ought to see this heart-breaking movie.

Chapter 19
    Title: Habitat 2000: Human-Scale Cities
    Length: 22 minutes
    Medium: film
    Description: Some radical alternatives to high-rises and suburbia.
    Producer/Distributor: CINGLD

    Title: Roger & Me
    Length: 106 minutes
    Medium: video
    Description: What happens to a city (Flint, Michigan) when the major employer (General Motors) lays off tens of thousands of workers. Michael Moore's acerbic documentary explores these issues.

Chapter 20
    Title: Leadership: Style or Circumstance?
    Length: 30 minutes
    Medium: video
    Description: Examines task-oriented vs. relationship-oriented leadership styles.
    Producer/Distributor: CRM

Chapter 20 (continued)

Title: Afterburn
Length: 103 minutes
Medium: video
Description: Air Force widow takes on
                                General Dynamics for design
                                defects that caused her
                                husband's death. Infuriating.

Chapter 21

[Instructor's note: Because of the very concentrated
focus of this chapter, any of the episodes in the Eyes on
the Prize series could be used. The series chronicles
the Black Civil Rights Movement from the mid-1950s to the
mid-1980s. Each video is 60 minutes long and was
produced by PBS.]

Title: Malcolm X
Length: 193 minutes
Medium: video
Description: Spike Lee's masterpiece (so
                                far) is the cinematic
                                adaptation of Malcolm X's
                                life. Movie-making doesn't get
                                any better than this.

Test Items

Test Items

Teaching With Testing:
Some Notes on Evaluation of Students

So you want to test your students. You whip out your trusty pencil or word processor and write:

>Where was Albion Small born and raised?
>a. Chicago, Illinois
>b. Whitfield, Kansas
>c. Muncie, Indiana
>d. Buckfield, Maine
>e. Des Moines, Iowa

So much for testing. No mystery. This is a legitimate and important examination question on Albion Small. C. Wright Mills (1942) thought that where Albion Small was born and raised had enormous consequences for several generations (at least) of sociology.

But consider this question again. It provides us with an excellent example of how we might think through questions before they reach our students. Every question should be examined closely by asking ourselves "*Why* am I asking this question and what do I hope to accomplish?" First, are we really concerned about where Small was born? (It's Buckfield, Maine—I had to look it up.) The important point for Mills is that it was small-town rural America, not whether it was Iowa or Maine. So, second, are we really concerned with Small at all? How about:

>According to Mills, where were most of the early American sociologists born?
>a. Western Europe
>b. New York City
>c. small rural towns in the United States
>d. urban areas in the Northern United States
>e. none of these

The difference between the first and the second question transcends issues of whether they are fair, too detailed, etc. The two questions ask for different things. And the difference will profoundly affect the way our students read and study *every single future word* in our course. If we ask the first question, we can't complain that they can't see the forest for the trees—we are evaluating them on the trees. The second version at least has the virtue of being a major point rather than a minor piece of evidence.

But even the second version merely tests a bit of knowledge extracted from its context of meaning. It is still a memory question, clearly and directly answered in Mills's article. We can further improve the question by asking for comprehension of Mills's point:

Mills argues that an important source of anti-urbanism in American sociology is
    a. neglect of the importance of demographic changes.
    b. the racism of early sociologists.
    c. that most early sociologists were white.
    <u>d.</u> the small-town rural backgrounds of many early sociologists.
    e. all of these.

This version addresses both knowledge and understanding of the logic of Mills's argument. It *teaches* students to look for *why* the author is discussing a particular point and *how* it connects to the overall argument being developed. Now we are testing for *higher level cognitive skills* rather than scattered bits of knowledge. In the process of testing for these skills, we are rewarding and encouraging their mastery. In addition, when we test this way we are creating an opportunity, when we carefully review the examination in class, to discuss how to reach this sort of understanding—foreign territory for most of our introductory students. *Tests should* not only evaluate but *instruct and motivate* as well (Sanders, 1966:1).

Testing is one of the most important things that we do. Just ask your students! And they are right, although not necessarily for the right reasons.

For students, evaluations of their performance are crucial because they determine the bottom line—their grade for the course, which in turn can have a substantial effect on their future life chances. No matter what we may say, and even believe, about substantive learning, the joy of knowledge, personal growth, etc., the grade is a tangible and consequential outcome for students. We need to be careful about how we arrive at it.

For faculty, evaluation is equally crucial because it is where the goals and objectives of a course are put into concrete practice—operationalized. The more important students think tests are, the more important tests are in shaping the learning experience. If we want students to think for themselves, then that's what we need to concretely assign and assess. Tests and other forms of evaluation tell students *how they should learn* as well as *what* they should learn.

Yet we spend relatively little time on designing our evaluations of students—on deciding about appropriate forms of evaluation and their content. Most of the faculty I know frequently spend less time writing an examination than they spend developing a single class lecture.[1]

---

[1] The same neglect is evident in our professional discourse about evaluation, and especially traditional testing. Years go by without any articles in *Teaching Sociology* on evaluating students. Most of these address "different" or "innovative" approaches to teaching and evaluating students—the use of journals or observation assignments, for example. These are sometimes valuable but almost all of the teachers I know, including the authors of some of those articles on alternative approaches, also rely heavily on traditional examinations (tests).

"Traditional examinations" come in three main flavors: out-of-class essays (take-home exams), in-class essays, and in-class "objective" tests. You can look a long time for articles on these—the literature by sociologists for sociologists is extremely sparse. Even the ASA Teaching Resource Center booklet on "Methods of Evaluating Student Performance" (Turk, 1982)

The most important thing I have learned is that *testing teaches*—however we test and whatever we do—and that the challenge is to consciously integrate and *use* this fact.

It helps to think of testing as a form of research[2]—we are trying to find out something. It is evaluation research—we are attempting to find out how well goals and objectives have been met. And one of the most difficult and productive parts of evaluation research is clarifying the goals and objectives of the research—the goals and objectives that will be evaluated (Glaser, 1988). It seems to me that the most important implication of viewing testing as research is that it reminds us to carefully and systematically conceptualize what we are doing, how, and why.

But it goes beyond this; testing is clearly connected to what we do as sociologists. This is, after all, a large part of what we are trying to teach students. Goldsmid and Wilson stress the goal and the means of achieving that goal in each course.

> The goal is reliable knowledge about the social world, sought by the best methods available. The stress, that is to say, is on the seeking, not the absorbing. We seek answers, however tentative. Answers imply questions. Questions are what testing is about. (1980:326)

Testing is not only evaluation research, it is *formative evaluation* research —research aimed at improving or changing the extent to which goals and objectives are met. Tests do not stand alone, they are part of an ongoing course and courses are part of an ongoing process of trying (sometimes desperately) to educate. All evaluation has an effect on the activities being evaluated—it influences the way things are done, the way people feel, and what they value. Evaluation reinforces some activities and accomplishments at the expense of others.[3] Formative evaluation makes this effect a conscious goal. So should testing.

I have already suggested that our tests—regardless of how they are written or constructed—convey messages and teach students. Therefore, make this conscious. Integrate testing into the course. Use it as a teaching tool in as many ways as possible.

---

generally ignores the traditional examination. An exception is a very helpful and thoughtful chapter on "Evaluating Student Achievement" in Goldsmid and Wilson (1980)—a book that I highly recommend.

[2] Unfortunately, this insight is often followed by discussions of how to make testing instruments valid and reliable, scaling, and other such technical considerations. These issues are probably important but often miss the point. As Hedley (1978) puts it, these considerations are to ensure that "we will be measuring what we intended to measure." *First* we need to figure out what we are intending to measure—or even whether measurement is our primary objective. "Traditional approaches to disciplined inquiry in test design have tended to focus on optimizing the measurement efficiency of tests rather than on optimizing their instructional efficacy" (Nitko, 1989:448).

[3] Glaser (1988:15) makes this point in terms of "people-changing institutions" in general. Natriello and Dornbusch (1984), in their sociological study of teacher evaluation, consider the "evaluation of students by teachers" as a "primary mechanism" for encouraging and shaping student effort.

How? The first question is "What do we hope to accomplish?" A look at a typology of cognitive goals and objectives can help.

Cognitive Goals and Objectives

In 1956, as part of a larger project by the College and University Examiners, Benjamin Bloom and others developed a taxonomy of the cognitive domain—"the cognitive area of remembering, thinking and problem solving" (1956:2). They classified educational outcomes in order to assist teachers in clarifying objectives as well as thinking about how to evaluate or measure them. Bloom's, et al. original work came complete with sample test questions illustrating the various cognitive levels. The scheme has remained extraordinarily useful in discussions of goals (e.g. Vaughan, 1980; Wagenaar, et al., 1982) and even in helping to organize study guides for students (Mosher, 1989). A summary is presented in Table 1.

Table 1: The Cognitive Domain: Bloom et al.

Level	Description
1. Knowledge	recalling specifics and ways of dealing with specifics, remembering universals, abstractions, generalizations, and theories.
2. Comprehension	understanding material so that one can translate it, interpret it, or extrapolate from it.
3. Application	applying abstractions (ideas, rules principles, theories) in particular situations.
4. Analysis	identifying elements and parts, relationships, and organizational principles.
5. Synthesis	forming wholes from elements and parts, assembling them into a new pattern.
6. Evaluation	judging the value of material and methods in relation to a given purpose.

Source: Bloom et al., 1956, with descriptions
as summarized by Vaughan, 1980: 270.

The hierarchical nature of the schema is quite important in designing teaching strategies. The model builds from the "simple" to the "complex." The abilities and skills of one stage "make use of and [are] built on the behaviors found in preceding" stages (1956:18). Thus, comprehension requires knowledge, application requires knowledge and comprehension, and so on. This hierarchical nature provides us with clues about how to develop higher-level skills. It also warns us against unrealistic expectations.

The hierarchical nature of the schema doesn't imply a positivist epistemology—fact then interpretation. "Knowledge" here refers to recall of information presented in the text, in class or elsewhere. Sanders (1966) renames this category "memory" to clearly denote that the category refers to material the student remembers, or finds, rather than creates. For example, in the treatment of crime rates students may be presented with information about how they are constructed and their problematic nature. This information about the social construction of crime rates then becomes "knowledge" in the sense that you want them to be able to remember and recite it.

In the case of the crime rates, *comprehension* means the ability to translate the knowledge into their own words and/or interpret the knowledge. More concretely, a comprehension question might be:

> The Uniform Crime Report produced by the FBI is titled "Crime in the United States." Write a better (more descriptive) title.

Or, in a multiple choice format:

> The Uniform Crime Report produced by the FBI is titled "Crime in the United States." A better (more descriptive) title would be:
> a. "Criminal Behavior in the United States."
> b. "Reported Crimes in the United States."
> c. "Estimates of Crime in the United States."
> <u>d.</u> "Police Recorded Crime in the United States."
> e. all of these

Both these questions build on *knowledge* but, in addition, require *comprehension*. *Application* is another step—taking understanding of the ideas and using them in a concrete instance. For example, consider the following question:

> In August 1990, the Portland, Maine, police released their UCR statistics for the first half of 1990. According to the news report, rapes decreased 30 percent compared to 1989—they decreased from 23 in the first half of 1989 to 16 in the first half of 1990.
> a. There were fewer rapes in Portland in the first half of 1990 compared to the first half of 1989.
> b. This shows that the risk of rape in Portland has declined.
> c. This helps demonstrate the effectiveness of rape avoidance education programs for women in Portland.
> d. This probably reflects efforts by the police department to increase responsiveness to rape victims.
> e. All of these
> <u>f.</u> None of these

Many of the questions we ask, and the objectives we *actually* implement and teach in the introductory course stay at the first level, knowledge. Only at the next level do Bloom et al. consider the objectives "intellectual" and I assume that most of us agree. Certainly, our course objectives tend to go past the simple conveyance of a body of knowledge (Vaughan, 1980:268). We want students to develop critical thinking, reflective thinking, or problem-solving skills. Certainly this is true of teachers who adopt the

Stark textbook with its emphasis on process and discovery—on questions—rather than a passive "body of knowledge."[4] But our tests often do not get that far.

We need to make sure that the questions we ask, and other assignments we may give, include the "intellectual abilities and skills" described in the Bloom typology. While remembering that knowledge is a necessary basis, questions and other assignments should emphasize higher levels in the typology—levels that require a student to make active *use* of knowledge. "This begins with a consideration of the forms of thinking which are appropriate for the course and a decision to place new emphasis on certain kinds of questions." (Sanders, 1966: 155)

This does NOT mean that all our questions or assignments should focus on these higher levels. We can create synthesis and evaluation assignments that call for a knowledge base and skills not possessed by many of our students, especially at the introductory level. Remember that we are generally starting with students who need to *learn* to accomplish these higher level skills. We need to encourage and nurture their development, not crush them.

It is easy to make assignments that are more difficult than they appear—that call for skills beyond what our students possess. In this case we set ourselves up to be disappointed and set our students up to fail. Consider an assignment to

> Critically evaluate Weber's model of bureaucracy in understanding the operation of the local Burger King restaurant as you observed it.

This assignment actually calls for all six of the cognitive levels. The student is being asked to form and present a reasoned judgment about a set of ideas in relation to a standard or value developed by the student.[5] The student is being asked to take observations and not only identify elements and parts but to discern patterns and essences—to answer the question "What's going on here?" at Burger King. Answering this question calls for analysis and synthesis. It also requires that the student deal with values in deciding what is *important* in what's going on.

In addition, the student is being asked to understand Weber's model and analyze how its elements apply. Finally, the student is being asked to judge how well Weber's model gets at what's going on and give reasons for her or his judgment. Overall, the assignment is probably out of the reach of most of our students and certainly out of the

---

[4] "Textbooks create a major problem for teachers concerned with composing good questions. ...*the textbook is weak in that it offers little opportunity for any mental activity except remembering.* If there is an inference to be drawn, the author draws it, and if there is a significant relationship to be noted, the author points it out. ... The result is that the creative process and the controversy of competing ideas are hidden from the student." (Sanders, 1966: 158) The Stark textbook is notable in avoiding much of this.

[5] The student must both develop the standards and apply them—decide how well they are met—for a question or assignment to be considered "evaluation." If the standard is given, then the exercise is really interpretation or application, not evaluation. "If no standards are offered in the question or if the standards are only suggestive and require refinement in order to [apply them], then the question is classified as evaluation." (Sanders, 1966: 142)

reach of our introductory students. Again, students need to *learn* to accomplish these higher-level skills. We need to encourage and nurture their development.

The Bloom typology can help us to structure questions or assignments to help this development process. "Teachers can lead students into all kinds of learning through careful use of questions, problems and projects." (Sanders, 1966:2) For instance, have students do an assignment in steps—knowledge, comprehension, etc. An elementary example:

> Identify a group that you belong to or have belonged to recently. Give reasons why this should be considered a "group" in the sociological sense. Give an example of a norm distinctive to this group. Give reasons why you think this should be considered a "norm" in the sociological sense.

Various types of questions can be structured. Here is an example from the student "Study Guide" (Mosher, 1989):

> Name some assumptions of mass society theorists. [knowledge] Explain Milgram's research [comprehension]. Show how Milgram's results did or did not support mass society theory. [analysis]

One of my favorite techniques is a series of true-false questions.[6] The following series moves from knowledge of a concept to various dimensions of comprehension of the concept, including its implications.

> The concept of a role:
>
> T F   refers to a collection of norms specific to a status in society.
> T F   refers to a collection of values.
> T F   refers to a script that says how a particular person is supposed to act at all times.
> T F   is illustrated by a statement such as "Police officers must not drink on duty."
> T F   helps explain why the same person may act very differently at different times of day.

This same sort of technique can be extended to *illustrate as well as test* the reasoning process by using a concrete statement of information followed by a set of questions. This can become quite complex and sophisticated.[7]

> In class, we examined the relationship between getting drunk and where people live (urban, rural, etc.). We found that it didn't make a significant difference where they lived—the proportion reporting getting drunk is very similar.
>
> T F   The dependent variable here is getting drunk.
> T F   The thing we are trying to explain here is where people live.

---

[6] A technique that I first encountered in Rod Stark's introduction to the test bank in the first edition (1985). The following example is taken from Stark's original test bank.

[7] These are taken from the current test bank, Chapter 1, and refer to ShowCase Exercise 1.3, although the questions are comprehensible without the ShowCase.

T **F** A sociologist would suggest that whether a person lives in a small town or a city determines their drinking behavior.

T F Our results are not consistent with what mass society theorists would expect.

T **F** This research tends to support Durkheim and Morselli's contention that modernization and urbanization lead to increased social isolation and deviance.

T **F** We might be able to explain these results by suggesting that people who have drinking problems tend to become poor and homeless and move to urban areas.

Enhancing the Process

The questions we ask, then, are part of what we are teaching. But the initial asking is only one part of the process. Whatever we do, we must go over it carefully and thoroughly in class afterwards. "It is desirable to follow through on a test, using it as a means of review, as a diagnostic instrument, and as a tool for filling lacunae and remedying deficiencies" (Goldsmid and Wilson, 1980:326). The more carefully we have conceptualized what skills we are asking for, the more clearly we will be able to help students understand how to get there. Don't be afraid to spend time. "If we are to raise questions, as we do in examinations, they had better be worthwhile ones. And if they are, in fact, worthwhile ones, then they merit dwelling on" (Goldsmid and Wilson, 1980:326).

On closed-ended questions (no one who has ever discussed an exam with a class could ever call them "objective") I make overheads of the test and spend at least a whole class period reviewing them. This allows me to clear up confusions, explain things a different way, and coach students in needed skills. I also try to emphasize how questions—or rather the issues and ideas *in* the questions—relate to one another.

Be responsive (rather than defensive) in discussing test items. Listening to how students thought about issues helps us correct them—or correct ourselves if the question is invalid or ambiguous. Neither answering questions nor asking them is an easy task; *this is a lesson well worth teaching*. David Heise includes a form, attached to the exam, for students to vote to drop ambiguous or especially difficult questions; he then drops items voted against by 25 percent of the class (in Goldsmid and Wilson, 1980:324). I prefer the chaos of doing this in class, in part because it pushes students (and me) to clarify and articulate the issues—a teaching/learning experience.

This process of review does more than just extend the cognitive learning process. It should, if well done, impart a sense of reliability and validity to students, as well as a sense of comparative evaluation of their own performance. There is good evidence that students' perceptions of evenhanded evaluation are related to enhanced student effort and that how results are communicated has a strong bearing on how students perceive the evaluations (Natriello and Dornbusch, 1984).

Along these lines, don't ambush students. The clearer idea students have about what they will be asked to do, the better their preparation. Remember that their review and preparation—their trying to pull things together and make sense of them—is one of *our* teaching goals. Moreover, their sense of fairness—evenhandedness and validity—

affects how students perceive the evaluations and increases their effort. When students feel they are being dealt with fairly, they respond. Students know respect when they encounter it.

This does not mean that evaluations need to be easy or rare. Studying student performance and motivation, Natriello and Dornbusch found that "frequent and challenging" teacher evaluations of student work increases student effort (1980: 144). This applies to *all* students; "even students with low levels of skills seem to benefit from more frequent and challenging evaluations" (*Ibid.*). This research finding is consistent with the only good advice I got as a novice teacher: evaluate early and evaluate often. The earlier we test, the earlier we communicate our expectations to students and the earlier we begin the process of teaching through testing and feedback. The more often we test the more review we give students and the more feedback everyone gets. In addition, frequent evaluation lowers anxiety.[8]

Along with frequent evaluation, consider open book and open note tests. Why not? This is the most articulate way to say, "Understand what's going on rather than memorize it." It allows us to more effectively test for understanding and application. It enhances students' perceptions of fairness. And, finally, it's nice to eliminate at least one form of cheating simply by making it legal (a good lesson for studying deviance).

Choosing the Format

With all of these things in mind, what are the best formats for evaluating? It depends, of course, upon our objectives.

Closed-ended questions (multiple choice, true-false, completion or matching questions) are excellent in assessing knowledge, comprehension, and application, and can be very good at assessing analysis. They have the advantages of being able to more fully sample different areas of the course as well as isolating subject specific skills from general language skills. Closed-ended questions are not really effective in assessing synthesis and evaluation (including organization and creativity).

Interestingly, closed-ended questions have been shown to be extremely effective in assessing the ability to work with novel problems (Chase, 1978; Thorndike and Hagen, 1969). The multiple choice question about local rape rates, discussed earlier, is an example of this potential—it presents new information and asks students to work with it using their knowledge and understanding of the materials studied.

Unfortunately, good closed-ended questions are difficult and time-consuming to write and it is easy to fall into the trap of simply testing bits and pieces of knowledge (as we saw in our example). "It requires much thought and time to construct a battery of [multiple choice] test items that adequately sample a sector of sociology" (Goldsmid and Wilson, 1980:322). However, they are much more reliable, create more sense of evenhandedness among students, are a clearer focus for review and class discussion,

---

[8] Probably, this can be overdone. The weekly quiz tends to focus on knowledge alone and, unless brilliantly done, tends to detract from discussion of "what's going on here?"

and they allow prompt return—all of which contribute to the learning/teaching enterprise.

Essay questions are most effective in assessing analysis, synthesis and evaluation. They have the advantage of being open-ended and thus allow students to explore territory on their own and integrate diverse materials. Open-ended questions permit creativity and self-direction.

This makes responses to open-ended questions difficult to consistently evaluate, in part because "students may not tackle the same problem—or the same aspects of a given problem" (Goldsmid and Wilson, 1980:324). They are not very effective for assessing basic knowledge, and weak in assessing comprehension and application (Chase, 1978; Thorndike and Hagen, 1969).

The earlier assignment concerning the Uniform Crime Reports exemplifies some of these problems.

The Uniform Crime Report produced by the FBI is titled "Crime in the United States." Write a better (more descriptive) title.

Responses to this open-ended question will be extremely difficult to evaluate. The multiple choice version of this question explicitly polled various misunderstandings. For instance, the title "Estimates of Crime in the U.S." is an inferior *choice* in the closed-ended question but how would you evaluate it in an open-ended context? And what about the student who writes: "The FBI Does It By the Numbers"? This is a wonderful title but does the student know and understand the material?

The weakness of open-ended questions is especially acute because it is impossible to isolate subject specific skills from general skills, particularly in language. Students who write well and are facile with language will generally do well on essays even though their mastery of the material might not be superior.

Finally, essay questions can encourage bluffing. In part this is because general facility with language can mask lack of mastery of the specific subject. More generally, however, since essay assignments are not very good at systematically assessing knowledge and comprehension, it is very difficult for the teacher to call the bluff. It is often unclear how much the student really knows and understands.

Despite all these problems with essay exams, there are still good reasons to use them, at least to supplement other types of evaluation. The Bloom typology and the discussion thus far has only addressed cognitive goals. There are other goals, such as improving writing skills. Writing practice is an important foundation for further courses; it is also an important tool in developing higher-level cognitive skills.

One approach is to use essays in conjunction with closed-ended questions—probably with less weight placed on the essays. This approach allows evaluation of higher-level skills while separately assessing the student's knowledge and comprehension base.

Unfortunately, many essay questions used in introductory courses aren't very appropriate to meeting these goals. First, an effective essay question, particularly at this level, should be fairly concrete and help the student structure her/his discussion. For instance, the question might begin by asking the student to summarize or relate something ("Summarize Ofshe's research") before asking for the higher-level analytic task ("and explain how this research tells us something about the importance of attachments.").

Second, in order to meet these language and thinking goals, essays should not be hastily written. Good writing requires drafting, and redrafting, clarifying ideas and thinking through issues, as well as clarity of style. This is not done on the spur of the moment in class. "Trial by ambush" essays—the traditional model for in-class exams— teach all the wrong things about writing, including a tendency towards fluff.

One way around this dilemma without assigning take-home essays (which are simply too large and unwieldy for introductory students), is to give them the essay questions ahead of time. I do this in a number of courses. Typically, I give students two or three essay questions to prepare ahead of time. At the exam, I will choose one of these for them to write on (or actually transfer into a bluebook if they have prepared a full draft). This approach keeps the exam manageable (they still have to write the essay down in a limited time) while allowing ample opportunity not only for drafting and thinking, but for class discussion of ideas and strategies before the exam.[9]

Another approach is simply to "test" using closed-ended questions and use out-of-class assignments to promote writing and foster higher-level intellectual skills. These assignments can ask students to actively connect concepts from the course with their own observations or experiences. We need to be careful not to overwhelm the student—as in the Burger King assignment—as well as to provide structure.

In my judgment, this is the overall implication of this discussion: closed-ended questions are the appropriate primary evaluation tool at the introductory level but other formats are important to supplement and expand this primary evaluation. Carefully done, closed-ended questions are the best tool for assessing knowledge, comprehension, and application. They are not as good a vehicle for developing skills in analysis, synthesis, and evaluation. They do not really assess or reflect capacity for imagination or creativity and, obviously, they do little to promote or develop language skills.

To address these objectives, other tools need to be used. The traditional examination essay is one possibility but, given clearly defined objectives and the clearly defined role of closed-ended questions, other approaches may be even more appealing. Ironically, there is much more written about these "other approaches"—alternative, creative, or innovative techniques such as student journals (e.g. Wagenaar, et al., 1982). Some textbooks provide supplementary exercises and assignments. Instruc-

---

[9] When I do this in an introductory level course, the essay is only a portion (typically 30%) of the exam. The rest is close-ended. This strategy allows me to be demanding of the essays without demolishing the students. The two parts also allow me to check for consistency of result and, in part, distinguish between serious writing problems and problems of basic knowledge and application.

tors' manuals or guides and student study guides tend to be full of ideas. The most successful of these are exercises that ask students to *do* sociology.

The mix of methods each of us chooses to evaluate and teach will differ. But however we do it, we need to carefully define what we are trying to accomplish and carefully evaluate whether we are choosing the right tools.

References

Bloom, Benjamin S., M. Engelhart, E. Furst, W. Hill and D. Krathwohl. 1956. *Taxonomy of Educational Objectives, Handbook I: Cognitive Domain.* New York: David McKay.

Bloom, Benjamin S., Thomas J. Hastings and George Madeaus. 1971. *Handbook on Formative and Summative Evaluation of Student Learning.* New York: McGraw-Hill.

Canglelosi, James. 1990. *Designing Tests for Evaluation Student Achievement.* New York: Longman.

Chase, Clinton. 1978. *Measurement for Educational Evaluation.* Beverly Hills, CA: Sage.

Glaser, Daniel. 1988. *Evaluation Research and Decision Guidance for Corrections, Addiction-Treatment, Mental Health, and Other People-Changing Agencies.* New Brunswick, NJ: Transaction.

Goldsmid, Charles and Everett K. Wilson. 1980. *Passing On Sociology: The Teaching of a Discipline.* Washington, DC: American Sociological Association.

Hedley, R. Alan. 1978. "Measurement: Social Research Strategies and Their Relevance to Grading." *Teaching Sociology.* 6:21-29.

Mills, C. Wright. 1942. "The Professional Ideology of Social Pathologists." *American Journal of Sociology.* 49:165-180.

Mosher, Carol. 1989. *Study Guide for Sociology, Third Edition, by Rodney Stark.* Belmont, CA: Wadsworth.

Natriello, Gary and Sanford Dornbusch. 1980 *Teacher Evaluative Standards and Student Effort.* New York: Longman.

Nitko, Anthony J. 1989. "Designing Tests that are Integrated with Instruction." Pp. 447-474 in Robert Lin, ed. *Educational Measurement*, Third Edition. New York: American Council on Education, MacMillan.

Sanders, Norris. 1966. *Classroom Questions: What Kinds?* New York: Harper and Row.

Thorndike, Robert and Elizabeth Hagen. 1970. *Measurement and Evaluation in Psychology and Education.* New York: Wiley.

Turk, Theresa G., ed. 1982. *Methods of Evaluating Student Performance.* Washington, DC: American Sociological Association Teaching Resources Center.

Vaughan, Charlotte. 1980. "Identifying Course Goals: Domains and Levels of Learning." *Teaching Sociology.* 7:265-279.

Wagenaar, Theodore, Judy Corder-Bolz and Ingeborg Knol. 1982. "Student Journals in Sociology." pp. 1-15 in Turk, ed., 1982.

Introduction to the Test Bank

The test bank for the sixth edition further expands some of the new features introduced in the fourth edition. Most notable is the expansion of "vignette questions" — multiple true-false series — and the expansion of cumulative questions that reflect the cumulative nature of the Stark text.

Cumulative questions are clearly identified in this printed volume, and in the electronic test bank.

"Vignette questions" consist of a brief story or statement followed by a series of true-false questions similar to the examples in the "Teaching With Testing" essay. This type of question is especially useful in testing **application** of concepts, both from a current chapter and cumulatively. For instance, there are a number of vignettes that tell about a piece of research; they are followed **both** by questions related to the research process (e.g. independent variable, theory, concepts) **and** by questions related to the substantive issues in a particular chapter (e.g. religion, family, and stratification) as well as previous chapters as appropriate.

These vignette questions are also useful as a source of ideas. Many of the vignettes could form the basis for multiple choice questions—a multiple choice question is really a series of true-false choices which give credit only for the identification of the correct answer and not the rejection of the incorrect ones. Likewise, many of the multiple choice questions in the test bank could become the basis for a vignette series. A test bank is not just a collection of ready-made questions; it can be a source of ideas for more questions and even examples for teaching.

The test bank includes a variety of *types* of questions: questions about detailed information, questions about more general knowledge, and questions focused on comprehension and application. Not all questions are appropriate for all uses—some will be more appropriate for quizzes and some will be more appropriate for comprehensive final examinations. The testing software allows you to randomly select questions from the bank; I don't recommend that you use this feature. *Select carefully* from the wide range of options available.

A conscious effort has been made to represent the topics and items stressed in the Student Study Guide. Again, you need to select carefully if you are confining your questions to information specifically mentioned in the Guide.

Users of any test bank (or student study guide or similar materials) must be acutely aware that preparation of such materials is an actively interpretive enterprise. Test items reflect a conceptualization of the materials in the text as well as the field of sociology. For instance, what *is* the most important implication of the functionalist theory of stratification? Or the "tragedy of the commons" in Chapter 15? In this sense, the questions, and the test bank, are not neutral.

This is one of the reasons a test bank should be extensive, and is one of the advantages of a test bank such as this one, which has been worked on by various people through various editions of the text. Of course I have tried to represent various interpretive possibilities. But, again, the user needs to carefully define her or his own conceptualization of the materials and choose appropriate questions from the bank.

The *Diploma* software is a pleasure to use. It provides a range of options, information and flexibility that can meet a variety of needs. I have used it to develop the bank itself and recommend it highly.

One nice thing about *Diploma* is that it uses words rather than arcane computer designations to describe section of the test bank.

In this printed volume, information about each item is printed with the item, including the correct answer and the page reference. A brief reference name ("Refer to:") is printed if the item refers to a vignette or other common "stimulus" for a set of questions.

Multiple choice items show a "scramble range." This refers to the answers that may be scrambled—their order changed. You can use this feature to produce multiple versions of the same exam, but with the answer order changed in all the questions. This is an excellent weapon against cheating in a packed classroom.

The questions in the test bank come from a variety of people. Some questions are mine, of course. The rest come from an array of people who have contributed to the test bank over the years. These include Rod Stark, Mary Beth Collins, Joan Krenzin, David Treybig, and probably others. The test bank benefits from this diversity of perspective and style and their contribution is gratefully acknowledged.

Finally, if you use the test bank please drop me a note and tell me what you like and dislike, what you want more of, and what changes should be made. Suggestions are invited and encouraged. Write to me at University of Southern Maine, Department of Sociology, 96 Falmouth St., Portland, Maine 04103. Or, my Internet address is: Peter@usm.maine.edu.

Chapter 1: Groups and Relationships

True/False

Correct: F   Page: 1
1. Sociology was invented in the middle ages.

Correct: F   Page: 1
2. Suicide rates vary a great deal from year to year.

Correct: F   Page: 1
3. Suicide rates are similar in most places.

Correct: T   Page: 3
4. Quetelet first used the concept of the "average man."

Correct: T   Page: 4
5. Guerry, writing in 1833, was the first to notice that crimes of violence and property crimes seem to be unrelated.

Correct: F   Page: 4
6. When the violent crime rate is high we can expect that the property crime rate will also be high.

Correct: F   Page: 4
7. Durkheim argued that suicide reflects weaknesses in character or personality.

Correct: T   Page: 6
8. The main topic of sociology is social relations.

Correct: F   Page: 6
9. "Unit of analysis" refers to whether a sociologist uses metric measures such as centimeter.

Correct: T   Page: 6
10. "Unit of analysis" refers to the things being observed by a researcher.

Correct: T   Page: 6
11. "Aggregate units of analysis" are created by summing information on individuals.

Correct: F   Page: 11
12. Most cowboys were Afro-American.

Correct: F   Page: 11
13. Almost all cowboys in the United States were white.

Correct: F   Page: 12
14. People make up a group only if they feel strong emotions toward one another.

Correct: T   Page: 12
15. Sociologists apply the term "group" to all collections of people who are united by social relationships.

Correct: T   Page: 12
16. Dyads are any two people united by social relations.

Correct: F   Page: 12
17. An aggregate is any set of persons who gather less often than once a month.

Correct: T   Page: 13
18. According to the transitivity rule, if A likes B and hates C, and B likes C, A may come to hate B, too.

Correct: T   Page: 13
19. According to the transitivity rule, if A likes B, and B likes C, A will probably like C.

Correct: F   Page: 13
20. In forming coalitions among players of unequal power, weak players will usually seek to combine forces with the most powerful player.

Correct: T   Page: 13
21. In forming coalitions among players of unequal power, weak players will ordinarily seek to combine forces with other weak players.

Correct: T   Page: 13
22. In forming coalitions among players of unequal power, it often is a disadvantage for a player to be too powerful.

Correct: F   Page: 15
23. A second-grade class of 32 students is a good example of what sociologists mean by a primary group.

Correct: F   Page: 17
24. The more theories a field has discovered, the more scientific it is.

Correct: T   Page: 17
25. The primary purpose of research is to test theories.

Correct: F   Page: 17
26. The scientific method begins with a theory.

Correct: F   Page: 17
27. Science is a set of discoveries and facts.

Correct: T   Page: 17
28. Science is the process of trying systematically to explain things.

Correct: F   Page: 18
29. The primary purpose of research is to reveal and describe social problems.

Correct: T   Page: 18
30.   Research is the process of making systematic observations, and it is used primarily to test predictions from theories.

Correct: T   Page: 18
31.   The text argues that social sciences have a more difficult subject matter than do natural sciences such as chemistry.

Correct: T   Page: 20
32.   The amount of validity in social science can be determined by comparing the results of several independent measurements.

Correct: F   Page: 21
33.   People generally lie a lot when asked about things like their own delinquency.

Correct: F   Page: 22
34.   "Attachment" is a type of unobtrusive measure.

Correct: T   Page: 23
35.   Mass society theories predicted that the development of large cities would cause city people to lose their attachments.

Correct: T   Page: 23
36.   People in big cities are as likely as those living in suburbs, small towns, or rural areas to have frequent visits with relatives, neighbors, and siblings.

Correct: F   Page: 24
37.   Milgram's "small world" research is an example of validation research.

Correct: T   Page: 24
38.   Milgram's "small world" research found that the average letter took five friendship links to go from sender to receiver.

Correct: T   Page: 24
39.   Milgram's "small world" research failed to support mass society theories.

Correct: F   Page: 27
40.   Sociology is the oldest of the social sciences.

Correct: F   Page: 28
41.   By "free will" we mean that people can do anything they want.

Correct: F   Page: 28
42.   "Free will" is another way of saying that someone has extreme or radical ideas.

Correct: F   Page: 28
43.   The idea that humans have free will implies that social scientists can't predict behavior.

Correct: T   Page: 28
44.   Virtually all social science theories assume that people make choices and in making them seek choices that maximize their gains and minimize their losses.

Reference Key: STORY1.1
Jane, Martha, and Fred are close friends who have grown up together and gone to school together. They care a great deal about each other and rely on each other for support even though all three of them have other friends, particularly in their high school.

Correct: F   Page: 12   Refer to: STORY1.1 Topic: groups
45.   This is an example of a dyad.

Correct: T   Page: 15   Refer to: STORY1.1 Topic: groups
46.   This is an example of a primary group.

Correct: F   Page: 13   Refer to: STORY1.1 Topic: groups
47.   Within their high school, these three should be considered a clique.

Correct: F   Page: 23   Refer to: STORY1.1 Topic: networks
48.   Mass society theorists would expect that situations like this would be more likely in cities than in rural areas.

Correct: F   Page: 24   Refer to: STORY1.1 Topic: networks
49.   Milgram's research on social networks confirms that situations like this are less likely in urban areas.

Correct: F   Page: 29   Refer to: STORY1.1 Topic: Free will
50.   Sociologists would argue that where Jane goes to college will be determined by where Martha and Fred go to college.

Reference Key: STORY1.2
A sociologist came up with the following table using the 1991 General Social Survey,
a survey of adults in the United States.

	Place of Residence		
	City	Suburb	Small Town or rural
Percent who:			
Spend evening with a relative once a week	37%	33%	37%
Spend evening with a neighbor once a week	34%	24%	23%
Have ever been divorced	20%	21%	21%
Report that their marriage is "very happy"	60%	67%	63%
Know someone who has committed suicide in the last year	10%	11%	13%

Correct: T   Page: 23   Refer to: STORY1.2
51.   The 33% means that thirty-three percent of those living in suburbs spend an
      evening once a week with relatives.

Correct: F   Page: 23   Refer to: STORY1.2
52.   The 33% means that thirty-three percent of those who spend an evening once
      a week with their relatives live in suburban areas.

Correct: F   Page: 23   Refer to: STORY1.2
53.   This shows that people in cities are less likely to spend time with relatives
      and neighbors than those in small towns or rural areas.

Correct: T   Page: 23   Refer to: STORY1.2
54.   This shows that people in small towns or rural areas are less likely to spend
      social evenings with their neighbors than are people in cities.

Correct: F   Page: 6   Refer to: STORY1.2
55.   The unit of analysis here is individuals.

Correct: T   Page: 6   Refer to: STORY1.2
56.   The unit of analysis here is aggregate.

Correct: T   Page: 23   Refer to: STORY1.2
57.   The findings in this table are not what we would expect if mass society theory
      is correct.

Correct: T   Page: 23 Refer to: STORY1.2
58.   Mass society theory would predict that there would be much less contact with
      relatives and neighbors than shown in this table.

Correct: F   Page: 21
59.   These findings appear to support mass society theory.

Correct: F   Page: 4   Refer to: STORY1.2
60.   This research tends to support Durkheim and Morselli's contention that modernization and urbanization lead to increased social isolation and deviance.

Reference Key: SHOW1.3
In class, we examined the relationship between getting drunk and where people lived. We found that it didn't make a significant difference where they lived--the proportion reporting that they get drunk is very similar.

Correct: T   Page: Show1.3   Refer to: SHOW1.3 Topic: show1.3
61.   The dependent variable here is getting drunk.
NOTE: ShowCase question

Correct: T   Page: 6   Refer to: SHOW1.3
62.   The unit of analysis in this research is individuals.
NOTE: ShowCase question

Correct: F   Page: 6   Refer to: SHOW1.3
63.   The unit of analysis in this research is towns.
NOTE: ShowCase question

Correct: F   Page: Show1.3   Refer to: SHOW1.3
64.   The thing we are trying to explain here is where people live.
NOTE: ShowCase question

Correct: F   Page: 29   Refer to: SHOW1.3
65.   A sociologist would suggest that whether a person lives in a city or a small town determines their drinking behavior.
NOTE: ShowCase question

Correct: F   Page: 4   Refer to: SHOW1.3
66.   This research tends to support Durkheim and Morselli's contention that modernization and urbanization lead to increased social isolation and deviance.
NOTE: ShowCase question

Correct: T   Page: 23   Refer to: SHOW1.3
67.   Our results are not consistent with what mass society theorists would expect.
NOTE: ShowCase question

Correct: F   Page: na   Refer to: SHOW1.3 Topic: Logic
68.   We might be able to explain these results by suggesting that people who have drinking problems tend to become poor and homeless and move to urban areas.
NOTE: ShowCase question

Multiple Choice

Correct: D   Page: 1 Scramble Range: A-E

69. Sociology was invented by scholars who wanted to know why _____ were so stable, yet differed so much from place to place.
    A) personalities
    B) economic systems
    C) frequency of wars
    D) suicide rates
    E) birth rates
    F) none of these

Correct: F   Page: 2 Scramble Range: A-E

70. Sociology came into existence as a field of study as scholars in Europe and England became interested in stabilities and variations in
    A) the maternal mortality rate.
    B) the rate of executions.
    C) alcoholism rates.
    D) the percent of populations in the poverty category.
    E) homicide rates.
    F) none of these

Correct: B   Page: 2 Scramble Range: ALL

71. Nineteenth-century scholars whose work led to what we recognize as the beginning of sociology were fascinated by a type of behavior that most people considered individualistic, "motivated by personal considerations." They began to collect and analyze national statistics on this behavior, which was
    A) romantic love as the basis for marriage.
    B) suicide.
    C) emigration as the result of feeling disgraced in one's community.
    D) treason.
    E) conscientious objectorship.

Correct: E   Page: 2 Scramble Range: A-D

72. Early scholars found that suicide rates
    A) varied greatly from place to place.
    B) were extremely consistent from year to year.
    C) were slowly rising.
    D) were consistent in their variations from place to place.
    E) all of these
    F) none of these

Correct: A   Page: 2 Scramble Range: ALL

73. Sociology was "invented" during the _____ century when a few scholars in Europe and England created and studied maps and statistics about some types of human behavior.
    A) nineteenth
    B) eighteenth
    C) seventeenth
    D) third
    E) second

Correct: D   Page: 3 Scramble Range: ALL
74. Research about such things as crime rates and homicide rates in various nations led to the development of what researchers in those days called
A) demography.
B) criminality mapping.
C) public correlations.
D) moral statistics.
E) sociopath data.

Correct: B   Page: 3 Scramble Range: ALL
75. Quetelet was among the first to suggest that the _____ of suicide rates force(s) us to look at this phenomenon not primarily in individual, psychological terms but instead as the result of social causes outside the individual.
A) unusual causes
B) stability
C) cyclical patterns
D) governmental agencies' views
E) fadlike nature

Correct: C   Page: 4 Scramble Range: ALL
76. Henry Morselli studied the historical shift from small towns and rural life to modern, industrialized, impersonalized cities. Among Morselli's conclusions was the view that suicide reflects the "universal and complex influence to which we give the name of_____."
A) social statics
B) moral decay
C) civilization
D) Decline and Fall
E) motivation

Correct: F   Page: 4 Scramble Range: A-D
77. Durkheim argued that suicide rates
A) vary rapidly from year to year.
B) are better explained by psychologists than sociologists.
C) are the consequence of widespread personality disorders.
D) are higher in less modernized society.
E) all of these
F) none of these

Correct: A   Page: 5 Scramble Range: ALL
78. The author of your text thinks the best way you could learn sociology would be by helping sociologists conduct research. But since that is not too practical for many students to do, the approach taken by your text is to
A) let you learn sociology by reading how sociologists raise sociological questions and conduct research necessary to answer those questions.
B) go through the findings of the various sociologists and give you a detailed summary of those research findings.
C) give you researchers' names, definitions of the terms and concepts they invented, and a summary of the things they discovered.
D) give you a set of procedures to conduct research and let you conduct your own research using classmates, friends, and family members.
E) use the comparative approach to see how different nations and cultures cope with universal human problems.

79. What we call "sociology" is one of several related fields known as _____. They share the same subject matter: human behavior.
    A) the humanities
    B) the social sciences
    C) the social humanities
    D) the physical sciences
    E) the arts and sciences

80. Sociologists differ from psychologists because they are not concerned so exclusively with the individual, with what goes on inside the individual's head. Sociologists are more interested in:
    A) the relationship between the individual and the government
    B) how the individual creates and responds to the social issues and/or problems in everyday life
    C) relationships between and among people.
    D) how to bring about a better, more fair, more humane world
    E) how to improve the world along the lines of what some people call "socialist" principles

81. Sociology differs from psychology in that
    A) sociology is more scientific.
    B) sociology is more theoretical.
    C) sociology focuses on group relationships more than it does on individuals.
    D) sociology is less scientific.
    E) psychology is theoretical, and sociology is research-based.

82. Sociologists
    A) study human social relationships.
    B) examine patterns of individual behavior.
    C) focus on preliterate societies.
    D) try to change society to conform to socialist principles.
    E) try to make people realize that free will doesn't exist and that people are mainly controlled by the environment.

83. Which of the following is sociologists' main topic of study?
    A) The patterns and processes of human social relations
    B) Methods or techniques to reduce the major social problems
    C) The ways in which individuals acquire normal personality
    D) The discovery of practical ways to improve social conditions in the world
    E) Methods and techniques to improve relations between people in everyday social life

Correct: B   Page: 7 Scramble Range: A-C
84. When a sociologist compares "pro-life" and "pro-choice" groups, the unit of analysis is
   A) individuals.
   B) groups.
   C) attitudes about abortion.
   D) none of these

Correct: A   Page: 7 Scramble Range: A-C
85. When a sociologist compared "pro-life" and "pro-choice" groups, groups were her
   A) unit of analysis.
   B) mass society hypothesis.
   C) theory.
   D) all of these

Correct: C   Page: 7 Scramble Range: A-c
86. A sociologist found that 73 percent of adults who live in cities drink alcohol and 63 percent of adults who live in small towns or rural areas drink alcohol. The unit of analysis in this research
   A) is drinking alcohol.
   B) are individuals.
   C) are aggregates.
   D) is all of these

Correct: D   Page: 6 Scramble Range: ALL
87. Because _____ are so central to sociology, _____ is the primary sociological subject of attention and investigation.
   A) cultures; comparison
   B) people's ideas; the case study
   C) scientific laws; research method
   D) relationships; the human group
   E) individual human behaviors; individual mental functioning

Correct: C   Page: 6 Scramble Range: A-D
88. A sociologist studying drug use in American society is most likely to be interested in
   A) what medication is prescribed for "cocaine babies."
   B) the insecurity of young teens in the society.
   C) why Afro-Americans in the United States are less likely to use alcohol than whites.
   D) the causes of substance dependence.
   E) all of these
   F) none of these

Correct: E   Page: 6 Scramble Range: ALL
89. QUESTION: What do sociologists study?   ANSWER: Sociologists study
   A) social facts.
   B) how to bring about social change.
   C) the logistics of solving social problems.
   D) the various methods of helping people to live more productive lives and of helping the world's nations to live in peace.
   E) the patterns and processes of human social relations.

Correct: C   Page: 9 Scramble Range: ALL

90. A sociologist who is intensely interested in the relationship between dentists and dental assistants obtained permission to observe 150 pairs of dentists and dental assistants as each pair went about the daily work of dentistry. This sociologist
    A)   studied something for which validity can never be strongly established.
    B)   studied the dysfunctional aspects of dentistry.
    C)   studied this topic from the micro structure perspective.
    D)   used the "experimental model" to guide her research.
    E)   had a perfect sample because the practitioners of dentistry had been certified previously as graduates of accredited medical programs.

Correct: B   Page: 12 Scramble Range: ALL

91. Which of the following is an aggregate?
    A)   A PTA meeting
    B)   People shopping at a mall
    C)   General Motors executives
    D)   A couple kissing
    E)   A dentist and her patient

Correct: D   Page: 12 Scramble Range: ALL

92. From the point of view of the general American culture, weddings in American society today should consist of _____ who approach a member of the clergy or other official to ask that they be legally married.
    A)   synchronous couples
    B)   need-linked pairs
    C)   triads
    D)   dyads
    E)   kinship constellations

Correct: B   Page: 12 Scramble Range: ALL

93. A carnival ride that offers "thrills and chills" can take customers only in twos. One can't ride alone, and more than two can't ride in a compartment, either. Clearly, this carnival ride could make good use of a sign that says
    A)   "NO CLIQUES"
    B)   "DYADS ONLY, PLEASE"
    C)   "AGGREGATE FORMATION PROHIBITED"
    D)   "WARNING: MACRO SOCIOLOGY STUDIES IN PROGRESS ON THIS RIDE"
    E)   "SECONDARY GROUPS ONLY ARE ALLOWED ON THIS RIDE"

Correct: E   Page: 12 Scramble Range: A-E

94. A(n) _____ consists of two or more persons who maintain a stable pattern of relations over a significant period of time. Some are tiny; others are large.
    A)   institution
    B)   social arrangement
    C)   club
    D)   subculture
    E)   group
    F)   none of these

Correct: A   Page: 12 Scramble Range: ALL
95.   Which of the following is an example of a "dyad"?
A)   Shelley and Joel
B)   Carol, Norma, and John
C)   Linda, Joy, Paula, and Jack
D)   Margaret, David, Lou, Diane, and Mike
E)   Mike alone, with no friends or acquaintances

Correct: C   Page: 12 Scramble Range: ALL
96.   According to sociologists, people can be called a "group" only when
A)   there is some practical goal or purpose that the people are trying to achieve.
B)   there are no intransitive aspects to the group.
C)   the people are united by a social relationship.
D)   they are recognized as a group by people outside the group.
E)   there is a formal, written document about the structure of the group.
F)   all of these

Correct: B   Page: 13 Scramble Range: ALL
97.   Your text states that "intransitive" triads are _____ and usually _____.
A)   transitional; become stabilized
B)   unstable; break up
C)   temporary; seek institutionalization
D)   relatively "unfeeling"; become passive
E)   conflict filled; stabilize as time goes by

Correct: D   Page: 13 Scramble Range: ALL
98.   Intransitivity arises in a group when:
A)   there are too few people to carry out group tasks
B)   the group attracts too few new members to balance members who leave the group
C)   sociometric attractions and repulsions are neutralized
D)   two sociometric "stars" dislike one another
E)   interaction falls below a level detectable by the interaction recorder

Correct: C   Page: 13 Scramble Range: ALL
99.   One of the things that you can expect to result from intransitive groups is
A)   racial and cultural prejudice.
B)   networking.
C)   coalitions.
D)   stable groups that do not move but instead remain the same.
E)   the group breaking up.

Correct: D   Page: 13 Scramble Range: A-E
100.   Intransitive triads are
A)   likelier to happen in formal situations than in informal situations.
B)   among the most productive of work groups.
C)   groups with low levels of "social power."
D)   unstable and usually break up.
E)   likelier to stay in one location than to move around geographically.
F)   all of these

Correct: D   Page: 13 Scramble Range: ALL
101.   It is very common for intransitive groups to
       A)   rotate leadership democratically among group members.
       B)   have little or no conflict between group members.
       C)   resist studies using sociograms.
       D)   produce coalitions among group members.
       E)   be especially prone to high levels of creativity in pursuit of group goals.

Correct: A   Page: 13 Scramble Range: ALL
102.   When a larger intransitive group breaks up into "cliques," one of the things
       that ordinarily happens is that
       A)   transitivity is restored.
       B)   the social network of the larger group becomes simplified.
       C)   it is less possible to study the group scientifically.
       D)   relationships between the cliques strongly tend toward harmony.
       E)   the political structure of the larger group becomes simplified.

Correct: B   Page: 13 Scramble Range: ALL
103.   A "sociogram" might reasonably be used to study
       A)   the relationship between coming to class and getting higher or lower
            grades.
       B)   friendship choices among graduate students who are all in the same
            course.
       C)   the extent to which environment can affect students' IQ scores.
       D)   individual student attitudes about their college or university.
       E)   the extent to which students are sure or unsure about their choices of a
            major field of study.

Correct: A   Page: 15 Scramble Range: ALL
104.   A primary group is characterized by
       A)   great intimacy among its members.
       B)   people who want to be first at almost everything they do.
       C)   being in an early grade at school, such as the second or fourth grade,
            and having a number of acquaintances.
       D)   people who feel that they have to meet that group's obligations first, and
            then they will meet the demands of others.
       E)   being the first group of professional problem-solvers to whom one turns
            when trouble rears its ugly head.

Correct: E   Page: 15 Scramble Range: A-E
105.   Primary group relationships
       A)   are typical of business and work situations.
       B)   involve brief interactions.
       C)   involve only positive feelings of love and concern.
       D)   are less intimate than secondary groups.
       E)   invoke a strong sense of belonging.
       F)   all of these

106. Which of these would be a good example of a primary group?
   A) A small number of policemen who have retired but still see each other socially and who moan and groan about not being back on the force together
   B) A small number of first graders who complain about not being taken seriously enough by adult employees of the school
   C) People who do not know one another, but who do have some characteristic in common
   D) People who do not know one another yet, but who will come to know one another in the future
   E) A young man and young woman who do not know each other yet, but who have the potential to get along together very well when they finally do meet

107. Groups in which people know one another well, have strong emotional ties, and gain much of their self-esteem and sense of identity are
   A) less important today than in previous times.
   B) termed "socio-emotional groups" by sociologists.
   C) examples of "primary groups."
   D) likelier to form later in life rather than earlier in life.
   E) likelier to be larger groups seeking practical, specific goals.

108. What makes a field of study scientific?
   A) The level of education achieved by the researchers
   B) The fact that technologically complex instruments are ordinarily used
   C) Studying only those topics traditionally recognized as science
   D) The methods used to study that which is being investigated
   E) The extent to which the research results are accepted by educated people

109. Your text considers "mass society theory" a "theory" because it
   A) has been supported by empirical observations.
   B) was developed after extensive research.
   C) is possible to describe observations that can prove it false.
   D) all of these
   E) none of these

110. An excellent example of an "unobtrusive measure" would be which of the following?
   A) Making phone calls or visiting the homes of people during the hours of 9 A.M.-5 P.M., when most people are least likely to be disturbed
   B) Using a set of interview questions that consist of "plain English"
   C) Conducting interviews with BOTH a psychiatrist AND his/her patient, to try to understand how well the therapy is proceeding
   D) Making an exhaustive library study of a topic to make sure that all previous research is known about before gathering data
   E) Examining hospital computer files to determine, for deceased patients, who was with them when they died

111.   The whole point of what the text calls "unobtrusive measures" is that
A)   the researcher is direct and straightforward with the people he/she is interviewing.
B)   the people being interviewed have no reason to distrust the researcher.
C)   the group being experimented with gets some actual benefit out of participating in the research.
D)   the researcher's project has been approved by a group of his/her peers who feel that the research is appropriate.
E)   the people being studied are never aware that the research is being conducted.

112.   Your text discusses something called "unobtrusive measures." Which of the following illustrates the meaning of unobtrusive measures?
A)   Measuring students' problem-solving ability by observing their ability to solve the researcher's puzzles in a laboratory
B)   Using college parking ticket files as an indicator of nonconformity
C)   Sending new students questionnaires to find out about their leisure activities
D)   Using statistics to find out whether or not a researcher's prediction is supported by his or her research results
E)   Asking people on the street to answer a few questions

113.   A sociologist asks 200 students what their grade point average (GPA) is. The sociologist then selects 25 of these students and compares their self-reported GPA with their actual GPA according to records in the Registrar's Office. This is
A)   an admission that some research topics cannot be studied "scientifically."
B)   evidence that common sense and everyday experience are often sufficient to answer sociological questions.
C)   an illustration of investigator bias in sociological research.
D)   proof that asking students about their grades probably will not yield helpful research results.
E)   an example of what sociologists call "validation research."

114.   A researcher wants to know whether or not students consult with their faculty advisor before adding or dropping courses. The registrar has the add/drop forms completed by students indicating whether or not this consultation has occurred. Thinking that this information given by students might not be accurate, the researcher gets the same information from other sources and compares it with the information on the students' add/drop forms. The researcher is
A)   breaking one of the foremost ethical rules in conducting sociological research.
B)   conducting an almost pure type of research procedure known as a "double blind" research design.
C)   engaged in validation research.
D)   being anti-theoretical.
E)   a psychologist rather than a sociologist.

115. Travis Hirschi asked boys if they had ever been picked up by the police. Then he checked police records to see if the boys were telling the truth. This kind of research is called
    A) network analysis.
    B) transitivity research.
    C) sociograms.
    D) validation research.
    E) small world validation.

116. Mass society theorists
    A) believe that city life doesn't allow people to form and maintain close ties.
    B) believe that city life greatly enhances the quality of people's lives.
    C) have proven that cities are made up of small, isolated cliques.
    D) believe that people living in cities have close, stable, intimate ties with family and friends.
    E) have been proven correct by researchers like Stanley Milgram.

117. According to mass society theorists, the cause of the breakdown of social relationships among urban dwellers was
    A) integration.
    B) modernization.
    C) assimilation.
    D) acculturation.
    E) none of these

118. Compared to people who live in small towns and rural areas, people who live in urban areas
    A) are not as likely to spend social evenings with relatives and other family.
    B) tend to be more socially isolated.
    C) tend to belong to small isolated groups with few attachments to other groups.
    D) are more vulnerable to propoganda because of their lack of networks of social support.
    E) all of these
    F) none of these

119. Which of the following is currently thought by sociologists to be FALSE about life in cities?
    A) Human relationships in cities involve "chains of attachments."
    B) Cities are mainly collections of small, closed networks of intimacy.
    C) There are a few people in cities who seem adrift in an ocean of strangers, but the great majority of people are not.
    D) Complete strangers often discover that they have mutual friends and acquaintances.
    E) Networks of acquaintances have been found that stretch across state boundaries.

Correct: E   Page: 24 Scramble Range: ALL
120. Which of the following was used to explain a great many social problems but has since come under severe criticism by many, including Stanley Milgram and his "small world" research?
A) Biosociology, or sociobiology
B) Ginottian theory
C) Diminished capacity theory
D) Anomie theory
E) Mass society theory

Correct: C   Page: 24 Scramble Range: ALL
121. According to your text, Stanley Milgram conducted some research in which people were asked to mail letters to the persons to whom the letters were addressed or to send the letters to acquaintances who might know the addressee. Milgram found that
A) most of the letters never reached the persons to whom they were addressed.
B) most letters changed hands about 15 times before getting to the right person.
C) the study did not support "mass society" theories.
D) letters reached the right person locally or regionally, but not nationally.
E) many people purposely did not deliver letters because of personal dislike for the intended receivers.

Correct: C   Page: 24 Scramble Range: A-D
122. Mass society theories
A) were supported by Milgram's "small world" research.
B) suggest that networks are common in modern society.
C) stress the social causes of individual behavior.
D) are more supported by McKay's research in Canada than by research in the United States.
E) all of these
F) none of these

Correct: B   Page: 24 Scramble Range: ALL
123. When Milgram used an innovative approach to deliver letters from one person to another, the idea that ended up being rejected or disproved was that
A) North Americans are loosely connected to one another by chains of attachment.
B) the forces of mass society have created a situation in which people are isolated from one another.
C) large-scale bureaucracies are more efficient at some tasks than are more informal social arrangements.
D) most people are willing to take part in efforts that benefit others, but at the same time they tend to be too busy to do so.
E) there is a strong, distinct system of social classes in North American society.

Correct: E   Page: 24 Scramble Range: ALL
124. With a randomly selected group of senders and receivers, Milgram asked people to mail letters to personal acquaintances who might know the addressees or intended receivers. His study of chains of friendship disproves the idea that
A) people are likelier to carry out a task to completion when they are paid for it.
B) many people have a chain of acquaintances that stretches across the country.
C) people cannot follow instructions well enough to complete a project of this type.
D) chain letters are a type of fraudulent crime and should be discouraged.
E) city life has left most people without enough social relations.

Correct: D   Page: 25 Scramble Range: ALL
125. Canadians and Americans tend to
A) "network" occupationally when searching for work, but less frequently for other reasons.
B) constitute one large binational network of social relationships.
C) have a binational social network that is parallel to that of South America.
D) have separate national social networks.
E) network occupationally in terms of tourism, but not so much in terms of occupational activities.

Correct: A   Page: 25 Scramble Range: ALL
126. There are probably several nationally extended social networks. There may be a national social network of accountants, for example, and there may be a national social network of migrant laborers. Sociologists refer to this as
A) parallel networks.
B) network redundancy.
C) a social backup system.
D) galaxies of influence.
E) acquaintance "streams."

Correct: B   Page: 25 Scramble Range: ALL
127. Your text explored the existence of several nationally extended social networks. One example used was based on _____ and another was based on _____.
A) race; leisure
B) race; language
C) language; level of education
D) level of education; participation in sports
E) sports activity; belief in the supernatural

Correct: C   Page: 25 Scramble Range: ALL
128. Which of the following is TRUE regarding Canadian social networks?
A) Canadians tend to have social networks based on education and occupation more than for other reasons.
B) Canada tends to ignore the reality of social networks, with resulting inefficiency in many areas of life.
C) Canada tends to have parallel social networks based on language boundaries.
D) More than other nations, Canada has been able to keep parallel social networks out of its critical occupations such as air traffic controllers.
E) Parallel social networks spread to Canada from the United States, but they tend not to "flow" in the opposite direction.

Correct: D   Page: 25 Scramble Range: ALL
129. When MacKay studied telephone traffic between French- and English-speaking Canadian cities and cities in the United States, he found that
A) the international border had almost no effect on phoning, and it was the distance phoned that mattered most.
B) Canadians phoned Americans more than Americans phoned Canadians.
C) Canadians phoned Americans less because American phone company. operators have difficulty understanding them, to the Canadians' annoyance.
D) language barriers within Canada are much less powerful than are national boundaries.
E) language barriers within Canada are much less powerful than are language barriers in the United States.

Correct: B   Page: 25 Scramble Range: ALL
130. In a follow-up study to MacKay's research on Canadian telephone calling patterns, Simmons found that
A) old people's phone calls are much more influenced by distance than are the phone calls of the young.
B) residential phone calls are much more influenced by distance than are business phone calls.
C) students' phone calls are much more influenced by distance than are the phone calls of nonstudents.
D) phone calls by Afro-Americans are much more influenced by distance than are the phone calls of whites.
E) phone calls by married people are much more influenced by distance than are the phone calls of those who are single.

Correct: E   Page: 26 Scramble Range: ALL
131. Which of the following provides some protection against scientists' biases distorting their work and/or against cheating in the production of research results, according to your text?
A) The levels of education achieved by scientists
B) The relatively precise instrumentation used by scientists
C) The fact that excellent scientific training eliminates biases
D) The strong religious codes of most scientists
E) The public nature of science

Correct: A   Page: 26 Scramble Range: A-D
132. One purpose of the scientific method is
A) to minimize the possibility of bias in doing research.
B) to make it more difficult for untrained people to do research.
C) to ensure that sociologists uncover the truth.
D) to make sociologists more like the natural sciences.
E) none of these

Correct: A   Page: 26 Scramble Range: ALL
133. In discussing research and theory in sociology, the author of your text states that "the proper approach to research" is to
A) try to DISPROVE those things that the researcher actually believes to be true.
B) formally state research expectations as HYPOTHESES, since without formally stated hypotheses there is nothing to test.
C) try to state as hypotheses only those predictions which the researcher feels will be proved TRUE.
D) try to avoid confronting the theory with EMPIRICAL data for as long as possible, making every attempt to test the theory in a mentalistic way.
E) refrain from involvement with THEORY, since the use of theory tends to distort the data that is uncovered in research.

Correct: D   Page: 27 Scramble Range: ALL
134. The author of your text believes that _____ was the first sociologist.
A) Ibn Kaldhun
B) Aristotle
C) St. Erasmus
D) Adam Smith
E) Cesare Lombroso

Correct: D   Page: 27 Scramble Range: ALL
135. The first initial base for sociology in North America was _____, and the second initial base was created by _____.
A) Harvard University; Parsons
B) Duke University; Ratzenhofer
C) Baylor University; Lundquist
D) University of Chicago; Du Bois
E) Peedee Academy; John Shaunessey

Correct: C   Page: 28 Scramble Range: ALL
136. An early sociologist who created a sociological laboratory at Atlanta in 1897 and later shifted his efforts from sociology to direct social action said that "sociology is the science of
A) awareness of possibilities"
B) studying the infrastructure of society"
C) free will"
D) effort"
E) social history"

137. Free will
A) means that people can do anything they want.
B) refers to the tendency of some people to make irresponsible choices.
C) is inconsistent with predicting behavior.
D) reflects wild and even deviant ideas.
E) all of these
F) none of these

138. The idea that humans have free will
A) means that sociologists cannot predict behavior.
B) assumes that people make choices about their behavior.
C) is inconsistent with mass society theory.
D) puts sociology in direct conflict with psychology.
E) is rejected by most sociologists.

139. On the subject of whether or not human beings have "free will," your text concludes that
A) humans do have free will, and their choices can be studied scientifically.
B) humans do not have free will, because human behavior is patterned and predictable.
C) humans had free will in the past but do not have it now, making science easier.
D) free will as an idea is only wishful thinking on the part of insecure individuals.
E) because humans have free will, they can disrupt any pattern social scientists find.

140. In class, we examined suicide rates and homicide rates for the states of the United States.
A) We found that there is great variation in the rates among states.
B) We found that the pattern of rates for states is quite consistent over time.
C) Our findings were consistent with those of the 19th century moral statisticians.
D) We found that there are forces outside the individual that play an immense role in governing individual behavior.
E) All of these

NOTE: ShowCase question

141. In class, we found that drinking behavior and where people live are not significantly related. This finding
A) is consistent with mass society theory.
B) might be interpreted as a good example of coalition formation in groups.
C) is consistent with Durkheim and Morselli's ideas about the effects of modernization and urbanization.
D) is consistent with Milgram's "small world" research.
E) all of these

NOTE: ShowCase question

142.   Jane, Martha and Fred are close friends who have grown up together and gone to school together. They care a great deal about each other and rely on each other for support even though all three of them have other friends, especially in their high school.
A)   This is an example of a dyad.
B)   Mass society theorists would expect that situations like this would be more likely in cities than in rural areas.
C)   Milgram's research on social networks confirms that situations like this are less common in urban areas.
D)   Sociologists would argue that where Jane goes to college will be determined by where Martha and Fred go to college.
E)   All of these
F)   None of these

True/False

Correct: T   Page: 34
1. All sciences exist to explain WHY.

Correct: T   Page: 36
2. A scientific theory must be testable.

Correct: F   Page: 36
3. Decades of research--not merely hours, months, or years--are required to PROVE that a theory is true.

Correct: F   Page: 36
4. Years of research ordinarily are required to PROVE that a theory is true.

Correct: T   Page: 36
5. No amount of research can ever PROVE that a theory is true.

Correct: F   Page: 36
6. A researcher who constructs a theory should exhaust all possibilities to prove that the theory is true.

Correct: F   Page: 36
7. It is impossible to PROVE that a theory is false.

Reference Key: RESEARCH1.1
Your text makes the following statement: "People living in large American cities will be less likely to spend social evenings with relatives and friends than people living in suburbs, small towns or on farms will be."

Correct: F   Page: 34   Refer to: RESEARCH1.1
8. This is an example of a theory.

Correct: T   Page: 35   Refer to: RESEARCH1.1
9. This is an example of a hypothesis.

Correct: T   Page: 34   Refer to: RESEARCH1.1
10. "Relatives" and "friends" are examples of concepts.

Correct: T   Page: 35   Refer to: RESEARCH1.1
11. This statement is a prediction.

Correct: F   Page: 35   Refer to: RESEARCH1.1
12. If this statement is true then it will show that mass society theory is wrong.
NOTE: Cumulative question.

Correct: T   Page: Ch1   Refer to: RESEARCH1.1
13. Based on Stanley Milgram's "small world" research, we would expect that this statement would turn out to be incorrect.
NOTE: Cumulative question

Reference Key: RESEARCH2
Early sociologists associated growing cities with deviance of all sorts. They suggested that cities are impersonal and destroy attachments among people. People without attachments are less likely to behave -- they are more likely to become deviant.

Later sociologists thought, "if that's true, then we will find more deviance and fewer attachments in cities than in less urban areas." Using the 1991 General Social Survey, a survey of adults in the United States, one sociologist came up with the following table:

| | Place of Residence | | |
	City	Suburb	Small Town or rural
Percent who:			
Spend evening with a relative once a week	37%	33%	37%
Spend evening with a neighbor once a week	34%	24%	23%
Have ever been divorced	20%	21%	21%
Report that their marriage is "very happy"	60%	67%	63%
Know someone who has committed suicide in the last year	10%	11%	13%

Correct: T   Page: 34   Refer to: RESEARCH2
14.   In this research, attachment is a concept.

Correct: T   Page: 34   Refer to: RESEARCH2
15.   In this research, suicide is a concept.

Correct: F   Page: Ch1   Refer to: RESEARCH2
16.   The unit of analysis in this research is individual.
NOTE: Cumulative question

Correct: T   Page: Ch1   Refer to: RESEARCH2
17.   The unit of analysis in this research is aggregate.
NOTE: Cumulative question

Correct: F   Page: 34   Refer to: RESEARCH2
18.   The statement: "if that's true, then we will find more deviance and fewer attachments in cities than in less urban areas" is a theory.

Correct: T   Page: 35   Refer to: RESEARCH2
19.   The statement: "if that's true, then we will find more deviance and fewer attachments in cities than in less urban areas" is an hypothesis.

Correct: F   Page: 35   Refer to: RESEARCH2
20.   The statement that cities are impersonal and destroy attachments among
people and that people without attachments are less likely to behave -- they
are more likely to become deviant is an example of an hypothesis.

Correct: T   Page: 35   Refer to: RESEARCH2
21.   The statement that cities are impersonal and destroy attachments among
people and that people without attachments are less likely to behave -- they
are more likely to become deviant is an example of a theory.

Correct: T   Page: Ch1   Refer to: RESEARCH2
22.   The statement that cities are impersonal and destroy attachments among
people and that people without attachments are less likely to behave -- they
are more likely to become deviant is a summary of mass society theory.
NOTE: Cumulative question

Correct: T   Page: 34   Refer to: RESEARCH2
23.   In this research, spending an evening with relatives or neighbors is the way
this sociologist operationalized the idea of attachments.

Correct: F   Page: 34   Refer to: RESEARCH2
24.   In this research, knowing someone who has committed suicide in the last year
is the way this sociologist operationalized the idea of attachments.

Correct: F   Page: Ch1   Refer to: RESEARCH2
25.   This research lends support to mass society theory.
NOTE: Cumulative question

Correct: F   Page: Ch1   Refer to: RESEARCH2
26.   This research lends support to the idea that cities destroy attachments among
people.
NOTE: Cumulative question

Correct: F   Page: Ch1   Refer to: RESEARCH2
27.   This research lends does not support the idea that cities destroy attachments
among people.
NOTE: Cumulative question

Multiple Choice

Correct: E   Page: 34 Scramble Range: ALL
28. To _____ a concept is to make it measurable.
   A) hypothesize
   B) computerize
   C) theorize
   D) linearize
   E) operationalize

Correct: B   Page: 34 Scramble Range: ALL
29. A criminologist studies crime in grocery stores and discovers an interesting type of behavior. Some people eat a few grapes before buying the bunch. Others take advantage of the store's offer to taste a new sausage, and eat six or seven pieces before buying a ring of sausage. The criminologist decides to call these customers "browsers" because all of them eat things for which they haven't paid. In this example, "browsers" illustrates a(n):
   A) theory
   B) concept
   C) hypothesis
   D) thesis
   E) assessment

Correct: C   Page: 34 Scramble Range: ALL
30. _____ identify some set or class of things that are said to be alike.
   A) Theories
   B) Hypotheses
   C) Concepts
   D) Statistical tests
   E) Predictions

Correct: D   Page: 34 Scramble Range: A-D
31. A name for a group or catagory of things is a(n)
   A) variable.
   B) theory.
   C) hypothesis.
   D) concept.
   E) none of these

Correct: D   Page: 35 Scramble Range: A-E
32. A scientific theory of group behavior should try to _____ group behavior.
   A) change
   B) support
   C) increase
   D) explain
   E) concretize
   F) all of these

Correct: B   Page: 35 Scramble Range: A-E
33. To operationalize a concept is to make it:
     A) scientific
     B) measurable
     C) abstract
     D) explanatory
     E) segmentalized
     F) none of these

Correct: E   Page: 34 Scramble Range: ALL
34. "Scientific concepts" are
     A) constructed after experimental research, not before it.
     B) not part of the research process, but are part of theorizing.
     C) part of theory-building, but not part of the interpretation of research.
     D) empirical items.
     E) ideas, not things.

Correct: C   Page: 34 Scramble Range: A-E
35. Theories
     A) once constructed can never be proven false.
     B) must not be constructed using more than one concept.
     C) must be stated so that they run the risk of being proven false.
     D) are roughly the same as "guesses," except that the terminology is more precise.
     E) consist of several hypotheses connected in a logical, testable manner.
     F) none of these.

Correct: E   Page: 34-36 Scramble Range: A-D
36. Your text makes the following statement: "People living in large American cities will be less likely to spend social evenings with relatives and friends than people living in suburbs, small towns or on farms will be."
     A) This is an example of an hypothesis.
     B) "Relatives" and "friends" are examples of concepts.
     C) Based on Stanley Milgram's "small world" research, we would expect that this statement would turn out to be incorrect.
     D) If this statement is true then it will support mass society theory.
     E) All of these.
     F) None of these.

Chapter 2: Concepts

True/False

Correct: F   Page: 41
1. All nations are societies even though not all societies are nations.

Correct: T   Page: 43
2. The term "culture" helps explain why some groups of Americans think some other groups are weird.

Correct: T   Page: 43
3. The term "culture" can be applied to everything you will learn in this course.

Correct: T   Page: 43
4. The term "culture" refers to the complex pattern of living that people have developed and that they pass from one generation to the next.

Correct: F   Page: 43
5. To say that one goal of this school is to make the students "cultured" is not a correct sociological use of the term "culture."

Correct: T   Page: 44
6. Discrimination against a particular group within a society often involves ascribed status.

Correct: T   Page: 44
7. A society's stratification system includes the distribution of wealth among its population.

Correct: T   Page: 44
8. A "class" (or "social class") is a group of people at about the same level in a stratification system.

Correct: T   Page: 45
9. The West Point motto "Duty, Honor, Country" illustrates the concept of values.

Correct: F   Page: 45
10. Refusing to rent an apartment to people because of their race or religion is an example of prejudice.

Correct: F   Page: 45
11. The concept of a role refers to expectations about how a particular category of person is supposed to act in various circumstances.

Correct: T   Page: 45
12. The concept of a role is illustrated by a statement such as "police officers must not drink while on duty."

Correct: T   Page: 45
13. A sign at the yacht club's new-member section saying "Do NOT throw trash into the water!!" is an example of what sociologists mean by "norm."

Correct: T   Page: 45 Topic: Role
14.   "Friend" is a particular position in society.

Correct: F   Page: 45 Topic: Role
15.   People only fill one role at a time.

Correct: F   Page: 45 Topic: Roles
16.   Values are rules governing behavior.

Correct: T   Page: 48
17.   When Catholics no longer were discriminated against by Protestant-owned hotels and resorts, it was an example of successful accommodation.

Correct: F   Page: 48
18.   The Irish are an example of a group that met with little antagonism and rapidly became assimilated in the United States.

Correct: F   Page: 48
19.   The term "subculture" implies that some cultures are not as advanced as others.

Correct: F   Page: 49
20.   Although Jewish immigrants were subjected to much anti-Semitism, Italians were welcomed because they were Christian.

Correct: F   Page: 55
21.   The term "ghetto" was first applied to sections of medieval cities where Italians were required to live.

Correct: T   Page: 55
22.   In a Jewish shtetl, children spent much more time in school than children in the United States do today.

Correct: F   Page: 56
23.   In the 1920s, a higher proportion of Italians than Jews were graduating from high school in the United States.

Correct: T   Page: 56
24.   In the 1920s, many famous eastern universities adopted quotas to limit enrollment by Jewish students.

Correct: T   Page: 58
25.   There were valid reasons why peasants in southern Italy distrusted the local schools.

Correct: T   Page: 60
26.   Most male Jewish immigrants to the United States had been merchants or skilled craftsmen in the old country.

Correct: T   Page: 60
27.   The average status of immigrant groups in their new society will reflect their average status in the society from which they came.

Correct: T   Page: 60
28. Steinberg's research suggests that, unlike the Italians, Jews already were essentially middle class when they arrived in the United States.

Correct: F   Page: 65
29. Recent research suggests that when the status of immigrants is similar, cultural variations will have little effect.

Correct: F   Page: 66
30. Most dentists probably regard their patients as their reference group.

Correct: T   Page: 66
31. The majority of Italians who came to America before World War I returned to Italy.

Reference Key: STORY2.1
Rachael and Belinda both try out for the high school softball team for the first time. Rachael has been on another team before and has also played in the "pick-up" games in her neighborhood. Belinda hasn't played much before and there aren't any "pick-up" games in her neighborhood. They both make the team. Rachael is in the starting lineup for the first game while Belinda is sitting on the bench. However, by their senior year they are both starters.

Correct: F   Page: Ch1   Refer to: STORY2.1
32. Belinda joins a new group but Rachael doesn't.
NOTE: Cumulative question.

Correct: T   Page: ResProc   Refer to: STORY2.1
33. "Team" is an example of a concept.
NOTE: Cumulative question.

Correct: T   Page: 45   Refer to: STORY2.1
34. Both Rachael and Belinda will have to learn new norms.

Correct: T   Page: 60   Refer to: STORY2.1
35. Compared to Belinda, Rachael's situation is similar to that of Jewish immigrants to the United States.

Correct: F   Page: 54   Refer to: STORY2.1
36. The reasons for Rachael's quick success are similar to those suggested by a cultural theory of assimilation.

Correct: T   Page: 54   Refer to: STORY2.1
37. The reasons for Rachael's quick success are similar to those suggested by a social theory of assimilation.

Correct: T   Page: 44   Refer to: STORY2.1
38. Making the starting team, in this story, is an example of an achieved status.

Reference Key: STORY2.2

One theory about the rapid economic success of Jewish immigrants is that "Jewish values of learning, their norms of education, their norms of educational achievement, and the immense respect given to the role of scholar paved the Jewish road to success. Conversely, Italians valued not learning but family loyalty; their norms led them to drop out of school, and the immense importance placed on the role of father made their original culture slow to change."

Correct: T   Page: ResProc   Refer to: STORY2.2 Topic: concept

39.   "Success" here is a concept.

NOTE: Cumulative question.

Correct: F   Page: 53   Refer to: STORY2.2

40.   The thing we are trying to explain here is variation in immigrants' backgrounds.

Correct: F   Page: 54   Refer to: STORY2.2

41.   This theory looks at social causes.

Correct: T   Page: 54   Refer to: STORY2.2

42.   This theory looks at cultural causes.

Correct: T   Page: 55   Refer to: STORY2.2

43.   Examination of shtetl life supports this theory.

Correct: F   Page: 59   Refer to: STORY2.2

44.   The fact that the rate of Italian assimilation was similar to that of other groups of immigrants is consistent with this theory.

Correct: F   Page: 63   Refer to: STORY2.2

45.   Steinberg's finding that Italians held higher status jobs before immigrating tends to support this theory.

Correct: F   Page: 63   Refer to: STORY2.2

46.   Steinberg's findings about the social status of immigrants before they came to the United States tends to support this theory.

Correct: F   Page: 65   Refer to: STORY2.2

47.   Perlmann's research on Jewish and Italian children in Providence falsified this theory.

Correct: T   Page: 65   Refer to: STORY2.2

48.   Your text concludes that this theory must be combined with social theories to understand differential rates of assimilation.

Correct: F   Page: 66   Refer to: STORY2.2

49.   The tendency of Italian immigrants to not bring families and return home provides further confirmation of the power of this theory.

Reference Key: STORY2.3
The following table shows the proportion of various immigrant groups who had skilled labor and farm positions before they immigrated to the United States between 1899 and 1910.

	Jews	Southern Italians	Irish
Skilled labor	67%	15%	13%
Farming	2%	35%	7%

Correct: F Page: Ch1 Refer to: STORY2.3
50. This shows that 15 percent of the skilled laborers were from Southern Italy.
NOTE: Cumulative question

Correct: T Page: Ch1 Refer to: STORY2.3
51. This shows that 67 percent of the immigrant Jews were skilled laborers.
NOTE: Cumulative question

Correct: T Page: Ch1 Refer to: STORY2.3
52. The unit of analysis here is an aggregate.
NOTE: Cumulative question

Correct: T Page: ResProc Refer to: STORY2.3
53. "Southern Italians" is a concept.
NOTE: Cumulative question

Correct: F Page: 61 Refer to: STORY2.3
54. This shows that Jews were as likely as Southern Italians to have farming backgrounds.

Correct: F Page: 54 Refer to: STORY2.3
55. This table gives better support to the cultural theory than the social theory of assimilation.

Correct: T Page: 54 Refer to: STORY2.3
56. This table gives better support to the social theory than the cultural theory of assimilation.

Correct: T Page: 63 Refer to: STORY2.3
57. From these data, we might infer that the assimilation rate for the Irish would be more like that of the Southern Italians than that of the Jewish immigrants.

Reference Key: SHOW2.1
In class we looked at the ratio between the circulation rates of two women's magazines (Ms. and Ladies Home Journal). We looked at the correlations between this ratio and various other variables, including National Organization of Women ratings for the states.

Correct: T Page: ResProc Refer to: SHOW2.1
58. The ratio we used is an example of an "indicator."
NOTE: ShowCase question

Correct: F   Page: Show2.1   Refer to: SHOW2.1

59.   The concept we were trying to measure was assimilation.
      NOTE: ShowCase question

Correct: T   Page: Show2.1   Refer to: SHOW2.1

60.   In this research, we were trying to measure "traditional women's roles."
      NOTE: ShowCase question

Correct: T   Page: Res Proc   Refer to: SHOW2.1 Topic: concepts

61.   "Traditional women's roles" is a concept.
      NOTE: Cumulative question.

Correct: T   Page: Ch1   Refer to: SHOW2.1

62.   When we examined the correlation between the circulation ratio and the NOW
      rating we were engaged in validation research.
      NOTE: Cumulative question.

Correct: F   Page: Show2.1   Refer to: SHOW2.1

63.   Examining the map of the circulation ratio, we found that the North and West of
      the United States are much more traditional.
      NOTE: ShowCase question.

Multiple Choice

Correct: D   Page: 40 Scramble Range: ALL

64.   According to Table 2-1, Income of Employed Males 18 and Over in the United
      States, 1908 (nonfarm only), which of the foreign-born had the largest average
      weekly income?
      A)   Canadian (French)
      B)   Canadian (English)
      C)   Jewish (Russian)
      D)   Jewish (other)
      E)   English

Correct: C   Page: 40 Scramble Range: A-D

65.   Both Italians and Jews had arrived in the United States during the same
      period, had brought little money, and faced considerable hostility from the
      native-born. So what's the sociological issue discussed in the text?
      A)   The difference between anti-Catholicism and anti-Semitism
      B)   Why both groups, from quite different cultural backgrounds, progressed
           similarly
      C)   Why Jews achieved such rapid economic success compared to the
           Italians
      D)   Why both groups had such difficulty assimilating into United States society
      E)   None of these

Correct: D   Page: 41 Scramble Range: ALL
66. According to sociologists, the concept of society refers to:
A) the wealthy people of a community
B) the highest standards of behavior a culture has to offer
C) nontechnological culture
D) patterns of relationships among people in a geographic location who share a common culture
E) patterns of intergroup relationships in urban areas

Correct: E   Page: 42 Scramble Range: ALL
67. "A relatively self-sufficient and independent group of people who are united by social relationships" is what sociologists mean when they use which of the following concepts?
A) Culture
B) Primary group
C) Secondary group
D) Reference group
E) Society

Correct: D   Page: 42 Scramble Range: ALL
68. If the concept "society" refers to certain kinds of groups, then its most basic features have to do with
A) those who are acknowledged as being leaders in the community.
B) the top positions in the social class system of a particular town or city.
C) physical differences among subpopulations.
D) relationships among people.
E) dysfunctions within a society.

Correct: E   Page: 42 Scramble Range: ALL
69. "A group of people who are united by social relations, who are relatively self-sufficient and independent, and who have a distinct geographical boundary" is what sociologists refer to when they use which of these terms?
A) Culture
B) Infrastructure
C) Nation
D) Metaculture
E) Society

Correct: C   Page: 43 Scramble Range: ALL
70. "The complex pattern of living (technology, values, beliefs, norms) that is created by humans and that is passed on from one generation to the next" is what sociologists mean by which of the following concepts?
A) Material reality
B) Society
C) Culture
D) Intergroup relations
E) Transitional statuses

71. Culture
    A) is based on a group's genetic predisposition to certain behaviors
    B) refers to learned patterns of feeling, thinking, and behaving
    C) is a feature of societies that have written languages but is not found in preliterate groups
    D) is an attribute of people rather than of groups
    E) refers to nontechnological areas of life--music, literature, and art
    F) all of these

72. As a human creation, _____ is strictly a product of human society, and it would not exist as a part of the "natural" world if it were not for the fact that it is created by human activity.
    A) ecology
    B) a metanorm
    C) megactivity
    D) culture
    E) predation

73. The term _____ is often synonymous with the term "civilization," and the two terms are sometimes used interchangeably.
    A) culture
    B) society
    C) metanorm
    D) megactivity
    E) collectivity

74. What sociologists call _____ is the way of life that characterizes the people in a society.
    A) culture
    B) normative attitude
    C) pluralism
    D) social attitude
    E) metabehavior

75. The fact that the many independent German states merged so easily during the middle of the last century suggests that:
    A) the individual states had relatively little national identity to merge so readily
    B) the states' cultures were in an early stage of development and for that reason were relatively flexible
    C) the states may have been one society before they were made into one nation
    D) the states could not have been merged so easily without socioemotional authority
    E) the Darwinian struggle for survival applies as much to states as it does to biological organisms

Correct: A   Page: 44 Scramble Range: ALL
76.   Stratification:
A)   refers to a system of social inequality in which some groups get more rewards than others
B)   refers to a system of ranking individuals based on their ability to assimilate a new culture
C)   characterizes urban industrial societies rather than agricultural and hunting and gathering societies
D)   characterizes capitalist rather than socialist societies
E)   is a way of categorizing minority groups into two distinct classes

Correct: C   Page: 44 Scramble Range: A-C
77.   The idea that some people in society get more rewards and others get less is called
A)   prejudice.
B)   status.
C)   stratification.
D)   none of these

Correct: B   Page: 44 Scramble Range: ALL
78.   According to your text, two words or concepts that are used interchangeably (or that can substitute for one another) are
A)   "status" and "role."
B)   "status" and "position."
C)   "society" and "culture."
D)   "accommodation" and "assimilation."
E)   "prejudice" and "discrimination."

Correct: B   Page: 44 Scramble Range: ALL
79.   "Which musicians get paid the most? The ones who play instruments that are so exposed that when they make a mistake, EVERYBODY knows. The trumpets, the oboes, the harps, the French horns--they all get paid more. The less obvious a musician's instrument is, the less they get paid. And of course, the longer musicians have been with the orchestra, the more they get paid." This is an example of what your text calls
A)   ascribed status.
B)   stratification.
C)   assimilation.
D)   cultural pluralism.
E)   reference group pluralism.

Correct: B   Page: 44 Scramble Range: ALL
80.   Statuses based on inheritance are termed
A)   achieved statuses.
B)   ascribed statuses.
C)   secondary statuses.
D)   achieved roles.
E)   norms.

Correct: C   Page: 44 Scramble Range: ALL

81.   _____ are rules governing behavior, and _____ justify them.
    A)   Statuses; roles
    B)   Values; norms
    C)   Norms; values
    D)   Cultures; subcultures
    E)   Statuses; values

Correct: E   Page: 44 Scramble Range: A-E

82.   If a bank manager's daughter is hired as assistant bank manager because she
    IS the bank manager's daughter (even though the daughter's knowledge of
    banking is minimal), a sociological concept that applies to the situation would
    be
    A)   cultural pluralism making upward mobility possible.
    B)   assimilation.
    C)   pro-Semitism.
    D)   intransitivity.
    E)   ascribed status.
    F)   none of these

Correct: A   Page: 44 Scramble Range: ALL

83.   In society Z, women cannot obtain higher education, hold lucrative jobs, or run
    for political office because they are women. This is an example of:
    A)   ascribed low status
    B)   downward mobility
    C)   anti-Semitism
    D)   altruism
    E)   shtetl culture

Correct: E   Page: 44 Scramble Range: ALL

84.   Francine is FEMALE, she is 44 YEARS OLD, and she is HISPANIC.
    Sociologically, you have just been told about three of Francine's:
    A)   social roles
    B)   cultural roles
    C)   mobility aspirations
    D)   mobility nexuses
    E)   ascribed statuses

Correct: B   Page: 44 Scramble Range: ALL

85.   When the daughter of a financially poor family goes to college/university,
    studies hard, gets a good job, and obtains a desired life-style and high
    income, sociologists would say that which of the following has occurred?
    A)   Ascribed status
    B)   Social mobility
    C)   Caste-based activity
    D)   Caste-based stability
    E)   Consciousness of kind

Correct: A   Page: 45 Scramble Range: ALL
86. _____ refers to negative attitudes toward a group, while _____ refers to
     negative actions against a group.
     A) prejudice; discrimination
     B) discrimination; prejudice
     C) prejudice; accommodation
     D) subordination; discrimination
     E) prejudice; assimilation

Correct: E   Page: 45 Scramble Range: A-E
87. "What do you think about that new freshman over in the Alpha Phi Sigma
     fraternity house?" "Can't stand him. Can't stand any of those people who
     came over after the war. They make me uncomfortable just to be in the same
     room with them when they look so odd and have weird names like Kwok
     Chong Kle or whatever." What does this response illustrate?
     A) Accommodation
     B) Discrimination
     C) Semitic assimilation
     D) Cultural pluralism
     E) Prejudice
     F) All of these

Correct: E   Page: 44 Scramble Range: ALL
88. "I now find myself in the unusual position of having to discourage people of
     my own Vietnamese background from coming to my restaurant. None of my
     white customers have said anything about it, but I just want to play it safe. So I
     vigorously persuade my people to find someplace else to eat when they dine
     out." On the basis of the quoted information, which of the following does the
     quoted material illustrate?
     A) Self-hatred among the Semites
     B) Accommodative abstraction
     C) Assimilative abstraction
     D) Prejudice
     E) Discrimination

Correct: A   Page: 45 Scramble Range: ALL
89. Prejudice
     A) refers to an attitude, whereas discrimination refers to behavior.
     B) leading to discrimination inevitably results from intergroup contact.
     C) refers to unequal treatment of a group based on its race, religion, or
         national origin.
     D) was eliminated by the Civil Rights Act of 1964 and no longer occurs.
     E) is directed toward individuals because of bad experiences with them.

Correct: B   Page: 45 Scramble Range: ALL
90. When members of a group are refused consideration for employment,
     promotion, residence in a neighborhood, and the like, such actions are called
     A) prejudice.
     B) discrimination.
     C) egalitarianism.
     D) static achievement.
     E) hostility values.

91. Sociologically speaking, "values" do what to norms?
     A) Test them
     B) Justify them
     C) Prompt them to change
     D) Elevate them to higher levels
     E) Separate the functional ones from the dysfunctional ones

92. _____ is a type of attitude, while _____ is a type of behavior.
     A) Norm; value
     B) Role; norm
     C) Accommodation; assimilation
     D) Prejudice; discrimination
     E) Mobility; urbanization

93. Sociologists understand "norms" to be:
     A) published standards that are made into law by legislatures
     B) a part of the material culture of a community
     C) the feelings people have about certain topics
     D) people's attitudinal "heritage" handed down from previous generations
     E) rules governing behavior
     F) all of these

94. The expectations that tell men how they should interact with others AS MEN
     are called:
     A) their reference group
     B) their values
     C) their abstractions
     D) their role
     E) their status

95. Which is a good example of a norm?
     A) Rachael plays basketball with her friends.
     B) John is expected to not eat until his mother begins eating.
     C) Frank decides to take a summer course this year instead of working full
         time.
     D) Keisha is elected president of her student organization.

Correct: E   Page: 45 Scramble Range: ALL
96. An experienced orchestral musician tells the newly hired trumpet player "In this orchestra we tune up our instruments BEFORE we go out onto the stage and sit quietly until the maestro comes onto the stage. And we all stand up the moment the maestro sets foot onto the stage area.   So it amounts to this-- no tuning up while on the stage, and stand up when the maestro comes onstage to conduct." This illustrates which of the following?
A) Prejudice
B) Cultural pluralism
C) Values
D) Ascribed status
E) Norm

Correct: C   Page: 45 Scramble Range: A-D   Topic: role
97. The concept of "role"
A) refers to a collection of values.
B) only refers to specific requirements of an organization.
C) helps explain why the same person may act very differently at different times of day.
D) is illustrated by Guerry's work on suicide rates.
E) none of these

Correct: A   Page: 45 Scramble Range: A-E
98. "To behave as a college student should behave," "to do those things that professors are ordinarily expected to do," and "to do the tasks most people expect of a bank teller" are examples of which of the following?
A) Social roles
B) Social values
C) Ascribed statuses
D) Cultural pluralism
E) Transitivity
F) none of these

Correct: B   Page: 48 Scramble Range: ALL
99. In a suburb of London, England, there are several distinctive groups living adjacent to one another. The Hindus, people from Barbados, and previous residents of the Bahamas all live together in peace and quiet, have a community "council," and still maintain their distinctive ethnic identities. Clearly, this is an example of
A) assimilation.
B) accommodation.
C) classes.
D) achieved status.
E) plutocracy.

Correct: A   Page: 48 Scramble Range: ALL
100. Alicia Mendoza, from Panama, moved from that Central American nation to England, where she has studied piano for 15 years. She is almost completely British now. No one can tell she's not British unless they look in her kitchen cabinets, where she has a few Panamanian canned foods. This illustrates
A) assimilation.
B) cultural pluralism.
C) anti-Semitism.
D) subordinate group membership.
E) viable subculture.

Correct: D   Page: 48 Scramble Range: ALL
101. During the 1950s, German refugees came to the United States, learned English, and adopted American ways. This process is called
A) cultural pluralism.
B) mobility.
C) accommodation.
D) assimilation.
E) anti-Semitism.

Correct: B   Page: 48 Scramble Range: ALL
102. The fact that people of many different religions live and work together in the United States with relatively low levels of conflict is an example of
A) anti-Semitism.
B) cultural pluralism.
C) assimilation.
D) reference group socialization.
E) shtetl culture.

Correct: A   Page: 48 Scramble Range: A-E
103. The existence of different religions side by side in the United States today is an example of
A) cultural pluralism
B) assimilation.
C) subordinate groups.
D) discrimination.
E) cultural lag.
F) all of these

Correct: D   Page: 48 Scramble Range: ALL
104. Subcultures
A) are undesirable features in a society.
B) usually conflict with the dominant culture but not with each other.
C) disappear when groups achieve economic success.
D) may or may not exist in harmony with the dominant culture
E) are more prevalent in downwardly mobile groups.

Correct: C   Page: 48 Scramble Range: ALL
105.   Along the Texas coast, there are small communities composed almost
        entirely of "shrimpers," whose families have been in the shrimping industry
        for several generations. They are definitely a part of the general American
        society. At the same time, they have some ways of thinking and doing that
        are significantly different when compared to American society in general.
        Being a "shrimper" is important to these people. Many hope that their
        children will grow up to be "shrimpers" and continue to live the shrimper life-
        style. Clearly, what we have here is an example of
        A)   an emerging society.
        B)   caste system.
        C)   a subculture.
        D)   cultural "skidding."
        E)   occupational subordinance.

Correct: D   Page: 48 Scramble Range: ALL
106.   When several distinctive cultures continue to exist within a society, are able
        to ignore some important cultural differences among themselves, and
        emphasize common interests, sociologists refer to such a situation as
        A)   urbanization.
        B)   stratification.
        C)   normalization.
        D)   cultural pluralism.
        E)   assimilation.

Correct: A   Page: 49 Scramble Range: ALL
107.   Your text contains a map indicating where Italian immigrants to the United
        States settled in 1920. Mainly, the Italian immigrants had settled in
        A)   the West Coast and the East Coast.
        B)   the north central and south central states.
        C)   the Great Lakes area.
        D)   the Great Lakes area and the central states.
        E)   the northwestern states and the Great Lakes states.

Correct: D   Page: 49 Scramble Range: ALL
108.   Your text contains a map indicating the residence of Jews in the United
        States in 1926. According to this map, the Jews at this time were settled in
        all of the states but seemed to be concentrated mainly in which of these
        areas?
        A)   The Pacific Northwest
        B)   The area just to the east of the Pacific Northwest
        C)   Minnesota and Wisconsin, and the states just below these two states
        D)   Indiana, Ohio, and eastward to New York
        E)   Along the East Coast from Florida to Maine

109. Your text mentioned a book published in Canada in 1909 by the Methodist Church, a book intended to improve people's attitudes toward immigrants. In the chapter devoted to "Hebrew" immigrants, the reader is told that Jews "may be miserly along some lines" and that they have "keen business instincts." The book, then, contains some elements of
A) discrimination.
B) cultural abstraction.
C) undisguised equalitarianism.
D) anti-Semitism.
E) hyper-accommodative assertions.

110. When the United States Congress imposed strict quotas on immigration in 1921, which of the following groups was excluded?
A) Africans
B) Italians
C) Egyptians
D) South Americans
E) Iranians

111. Jewish intermarriage rates have risen steadily in Canada and in the United States, and the rates are especially higher when
A) the Jewish population is relatively small.
B) the Jewish population does not have its own school system.
C) the Jewish population consists mainly of Jews of non-European background.
D) the community consists of many new residents to the community.
E) the educational level of the Jews is either very high or very low.

112. Your text notes that _____ intermarriage rates are lower than those of _____, both in Canada and in the United States.
A) Irish; Hispanics
B) Hispanic; Central Americans
C) Hispanic; Mormons
D) Irish; Jews
E) Jewish; Italians

113. The idea that values about education accounted for the different assimilation rates for Italians and Jews is
A) a cultural theory.
B) a theory of discrimination.
C) a social theory.
D) a reference group theory.
E) a hypothesis.

114. The idea that knowing about a person or group's norms and values will help us understand and predict how they will act is a _____ theory.
    A) cultural
    B) social
    C) mass society
    D) none of these

115. According to Zborowski and Herzog, Jewish immigrants to the United States
    A) placed little value on formal education.
    B) had subcultural values that emphasized learning at a time when educational opportunities were expanding in the United States.
    C) came to the United States at a time when agricultural skills were more highly prized than professional skills.
    D) should have been restricted in college admissions in order to give members of other ethnic groups a chance.
    E) were downwardly mobile due to anti-Semitism.

116. Zborowski and Herzog studied Jewish immigration to the United States and concluded that
    A) the Jews' lack of upward mobility in the United States was due largely to anti-Semitism.
    B) the Jews' downward mobility in the United States was due to a desire to someday live in Israel rather than to put down "roots" in the United States.
    C) the Jews' upward mobility in the United States was due to the fit between their education-oriented culture and opportunities in America.
    D) the Jews' own anti-Semitic ideas turned most Americans against them, thus greatly inhibiting their chances to get ahead in America.
    E) the reasons for the Jews' "mixed" mobility experience were too numerous and too obscure to allow for any firm conclusions.

117. In exploring why Jews made such a rapid advancement in upward mobility, the text suggests that one reason is that when most Jewish immigrants arrived
    A) the federal government was encouraging new immigrants to become better educated.
    B) the colleges and universities were making room for more students and were actively seeking larger enrollments.
    C) the Jewish currency was devalued very little when brought into the United States, while other currencies retained as little as 20 percent of their value.
    D) the Jewish bankers and university financial aid officers tended to give the Jewish students more financial aid than they gave to most other students.
    E) other Americans who were already citizens were recruited to fight in the war, leaving a "vacuum" of jobs into which the Jews could move.

118. Leonard Covello's research on Italian immigrant culture
    A) showed that Italians valued education very highly.
    B) found that anti-Semitism was a major factor in the slow assimilation of Italians.
    C) was consistent with the cultural theory of assimilation.
    D) found that Italians value family loyalty and social importance of the father.
    E) all of these

119. According to Stephen Steinberg
    A) American culture was extremely tolerant of the Jewish religion.
    B) Jewish immigrants were more likely than Italian immigrants to have been skilled craftsmen in Europe.
    C) Jewish immigrants have been one of the few groups to be upwardly mobile in the United States.
    D) Italian immigrants lacked values and became personally disorganized in a new country.
    E) Jewish immigrants were not subjected to the prejudice and discrimination that Italians were.

120. Rachael and Belinda both try out for the high school softball team for the first time. Rachael has been on another team before and has also played in the "pick-up" games in her neighborhood. Belinda hasn't played much before and there aren't any "pick-up" games in her neighborhood. They both make the team. Rachael is in the starting lineup for the first game while Belinda is sitting on the bench. However, by their senior year they are both starters.
    A) Belinda will have to learn new norms but Rachael won't.
    B) Compared to Belinda, Rachael's situation is similar to that of Jewish immigrants to the United States.
    C) Making the team, in this story, is an example of ascribed status.
    D) The reasons for Rachael's quick success are similar to those suggested by the cultural theory of assimilation.
    E) All of these
    F) None of these

121. First-generation immigrants' status in their new society will be determined in large measure by
    A) the manner in which they are perceived by other members in their new society.
    B) their status assignment or allocation by immigration authorities.
    C) the extent to which the legal system protects them from discrimination.
    D) their status in their former society.
    E) the level of agreement between their desire to succeed and their efforts to succeed.

Correct: B   Page: 63 Scramble Range: A-D
122. The idea that knowing about a person or group's experience, skills, and social status will help us understand or predict how they will act is a _____ theory.
A) cultural
B) social
C) mass society
D) none of these

Correct: E   Page: 65 Scramble Range: A-D
123. The results of Perlmann's research on Jewish and Italian children in Providence
A) showed that middle class Italian children were less likely than Jewish children to continue their education.
B) found that social status had a great deal to do with educational attainment.
C) demonstrates that neither the social nor cultural theories are adequate alone.
D) illustrates how norms and values can affect achieved status.
E) all of these

Correct: D   Page: 66 Scramble Range: ALL
124. According to your text, whom did early Italian immigrants use as their reference group?
A) Successful Italian-American businessmen like Amadeo Giannini, the founder of the Bank of America
B) Jewish immigrants
C) Irish Americans
D) Family and friends in southern Italy
E) White Anglo-Saxon Protestants

Correct: D   Page: 66 Scramble Range: ALL
125. Which of the following is given by your text as a specific reason for Italian immigrants' failure to achieve rapid upward mobility in the United States at the beginning of this century?
A) Discrimination against Italian children was present in American schools.
B) Many, if not most, were Roman Catholic, which was a serious handicap at the time.
C) Almost all of the Italian immigrants had lived in cities before coming to the United States.
D) Many of the Italian immigrants never intended to learn English.
E) The Italian immigrants tended to cut off all ties with the old country, and thus did not have help from kin when they needed it.

126.   Which of the following statements regarding the Jewish and the Italian immigration experience is FALSE?
A)   The Jews tended to come with marketable skills, making possible rapid mobility
B)   The Jews rose in the American class system more rapidly than did the Italians
C)   In some colleges and universities, there were so many Jews that quotas were imposed to limit Jewish enrollment
D)   Most of the Italians coming to the United States were entire families--mothers, fathers, and children--while most of the Jews who came were unmarried males
E)   Most of the Italians coming to the United States came from rural areas of Italy

127.   A concept that helps explain why Italians had low mobility in the United States is
A)   reference group.
B)   anti-Semitism.
C)   accommodation.
D)   gentrification.
E)   secondary group affiliation.

128.   Which of the following situations is similar to a main reason why Italian upward social mobility was so relatively slow in the United States?
A)   A male registered nurse finds he can make more money in trucking, and so becomes a truck driver.
B)   Pauline feels that she has been the victim of sexual discrimination at work but is reluctant to use the legal system to right the wrong.
C)   An Afro-American female decides that ethnicity is relatively unimportant to her, so she begins to enter "the white world" in every possible way.
D)   A Native American goes to the state's major city to earn money, and when she has earned what she thinks is enough, she returns to the reservation.
E)   A migrant laborer works at migrant laboring tasks during the summer, because he and his wife both enjoy having the family working together in the fields.

129.   A professor of computer science is successful at his profession as a researcher and teacher at a major university. At the same time, he makes sure that he names his children in a way that will be acceptable to his kin in the old country, takes his children to the old country every summer, and makes sure that they have a good knowledge of their kin's expectations. Which concept is illustrated?
A)   Assimilation
B)   Incomplete socialization
C)   Incomplete referencing
D)   Reference group
E)   Cross-national mobility

Correct: D   Page: 66 Scramble Range: A-E
130.   Groups with which individuals identify are termed
       A)   roles.
       B)   normative groups.
       C)   status groups.
       D)   reference groups.
       E)   assimilated groups.
       F)   none of these

Correct: B   Page: 70 Scramble Range: A-D
131.   Andrew Greeley, in his research on the persistence of the Italian family, said
       that if he was correct then "Italian-Americans will closely resemble people in
       Italy in terms of family culture."
       A)   Greeley studied novels to examine this idea.
       B)   This statement is an hypothesis.
       C)   His research showed that Italian-Americans are assimilated so
            completely that their families are indistinguishable from other American
            families.
       D)   Greeley concluded that values of family solidarity continue to impede the
            success of Italian-Americans.
       E)   All of these
       F)   None of these

Correct: A   Page: 70 Scramble Range: A-C
132.   Italian-Americans
       A)   tend to turn to their families for support and aid more than other
            Americans.
       B)   continue to have slow upward mobility because of their family values.
       C)   continue to be less educated than other Americans due to their cultural
            emphasis on family solidarity.
       D)   all of these
       E)   none of these

Correct: F   Page: 71 Scramble Range: A-D
133.   Greeley's research on Italian-American families
       A)   found that Italian-Americans continue to be les educated than other
            Americans.
       B)   found that Italian-American emphasis on family solidarity continues to
            block upward mobility.
       C)   shows that the cultural theory of ethnic mobility is false.
       D)   illustrates the use of unobtrusive measures.
       E)   all of these
       F)   none of these

Chapter 3: Micro Sociology

True/False

Correct: F   Page: 76
1. There is only a very loose connection between theories and research methods in sociology. Sociology's different sorts of theories require basically the same specific research methods.

Correct: T   Page: 76
2. There is a very close correspondence between theories and research methods. Different sorts of theories require different sorts of research methods.

Correct: T   Page: 76
3. The distinction between micro and macro sociology has profound implications for WHAT sociologists study and HOW they study it.

Correct: T   Page: 76
4. Micro theories in sociology focus on person-to-person interaction among individuals.

Correct: F   Page: 77
5. Figure 3-1, Marriages per 1,000 Population, is a map of variations in the marriage rate across Europe, and it indicates that there are proportionately many more marriages in Western Europe than in Eastern Europe.

Correct: F   Page: 77
6. Figure 3-1, Marriages per 1,000 Population, is a map of variations in the marriage rate across Europe. Micro sociologists would be especially interested in accounting for the differences in rates between Eastern Europe and Western Europe.

Correct: T   Page: 78
7. Micro theories in sociology are also called rational choice theories.

Correct: T   Page: 78
8. The text states that humans operate on the basis of rational choices. This "rational choice" assumption is referred to by some as the "self-interest" proposition.

Correct: F   Page: 78
9. Micro theories in sociology reject the idea that people act only on the basis of self-interest.

Correct: T   Page: 79
10. A basic idea in micro theories in sociology is that people seek rewards.

Correct: T   Page: 80
11. A grunt or a shrug by a human could be a symbol.

Correct: F   Page: 80
12. Symbols are not abstractions.

Correct: F   Page: 81
13.   Micro theories in sociology conflict with symbolic interaction theories.

Correct: T   Page: 83
14.   Micro theories in sociology lead to the conclusion that attachments influence conformity.

Correct: T   Page: 84
15.   Applying a general sociological principle, we should expect that basketball team members with stronger attachments to the team will break team member-established rules less often than will team members with weaker attachments to the team.

Correct: T   Page: 835
16.   Causation cannot exist unless the cause and effect are correlated.

Correct: F   Page: 86
17.   Causation cannot exist unless an exception to the rule can be found.

Correct: F   Page: 86
18.   Causation cannot exist when the independent variable occurs before the dependent variable.

Correct: F   Page: 86
19.   Causation cannot exist when two variables are negatively correlated.

Correct: F   Page: Res Proc
20.   Hypotheses are very abstract statements about why and how certain concepts are related.
NOTE: Cumulative question.

Correct: F   Page: 87
21.   It is much harder to demonstrate nonspuriousness in an experiment than in observational research.

Correct: T   Page: 88
22.   In Lofland and Stark's study of religious recruitment, conversion is an example of a variable.

Correct: T   Page: 88
23.   Income is an example of a variable.

Correct: T   Page: 88
24.   Sex (gender) is an example of a variable.

Correct: F   Page: 88
25.   A variable is any factor to which researchers cannot assign values.

Correct: F   Page: 89
26.   In an experiment, it is not possible to manipulate the independent variable.

Correct: T   Page: 89
27.   In an experiment, the larger the number of subjects used, the lower the probability of random errors.

Correct: F   Page: 89
28.   In an experiment, it is often difficult to establish the time order of the independent and dependent variables.

Correct: T   Page: 91
29.   Field observation studies are more appropriate than experiments for studying religious conversion.

Correct: T   Page: 92
30.   In their study of religious conversion, Lofland and Stark found that attachments were more important than beliefs.

Correct: F   Page: 92
31.   In their study of religious conversion, Lofland and Stark found that the group had formed on the basis of shared religious anxieties.

Correct: F   Page: 92
32.   In their study of religious conversion, Lofland and Stark found evidence of brainwashing.

Correct: T   Page: 93
33.   Field observation studies have more difficulty demonstrating nonspuriousness than do experiments.

Correct: F   Page: 93
34.   In their study of religious conversion, Lofland and Stark could prove that their findings were not spurious.

Reference Key: STORY3.1
Phillip, a sociology student, loves to watch people at parties. He goes to a party that a friend of his, Manuel, had helped to organize. He notices that Manuel, who is usually quite shy, is introducing new students to some of the upperclassmen. Manuel explained, "Otherwise they'll be lonely."

Correct: T   Page: 91   Refer to: STORY3.1
35.   Phillip is conducting a field observation.

Correct: F   Page: 89   Refer to: STORY3.1
36.   Phillip is conducting an experiment.

Correct: T   Page: Ch2   Refer to: STORY3.1
37.   This story illustrates the concept of "role."
NOTE: Cumulative question.

Correct: T   Page: 82   Refer to: STORY3.1
38.   Manuel is "taking the role of the other."

Correct: F   Page: 78   Refer to: STORY3.1
39. Sociologists would argue that Manuel's altruistic behavior violates rational choice theory.

Correct: F   Page: 78   Refer to: STORY3.1
40. Manuel's behavior is determined by his role as host.

Correct: F   Page: 78   Refer to: STORY3.1
41. Manuel's behavior is determined by the norms of his group.

Reference Key: STORY3.2
To determine whether special tutoring could improve student scores in college entrance tests, researchers randomly assigned some high school students to receive this tutoring while withholding tutoring from the other half of the seniors. When the tests were given, those who had been tutored scored substantially higher than those who had not been tutored. The odds were found to be 30 to 1 against the results being caused by chance.

Correct: T   Page: 89   Refer to: STORY3.2
42. This study is an example of an experiment.

Correct: F   Page: 89   Refer to: STORY3.2
43. This is an example of field observation research.

Correct: T   Page: 88
44. In this research, special tutoring is variable.

Correct: F   Page: Ch1
45. The unit of analysis in this research is individual.
NOTE: Cumulative question.

Correct: F   Page: 88   Refer to: STORY3.2
46. The independent variable in this research is college test scores.

Correct: T   Page: 89   Refer to: STORY3.2
47. There is little reason to believe this result is spurious.

Correct: F   Page: 89   Refer to: STORY3.2
48. There is a time order problem with this research.

Correct: T   Page: 88   Refer to: STORY3.2
49. The dependent variable in this study is test scores.

Correct: F   Page: 88   Refer to: STORY3.2
50. We would have greater confidence in the findings if the researcher had interviewed the students about their test anxiety.

Reference Key: STORY3.3
A sociologist wanted to know whether women liked algebra better than men liked it.
He chose a random sample of incoming students and enrolled them in algebra. At
the end of the semester, 15 percent of the men and 35 percent of the women had
dropped the class. From this he concluded that men liked algebra more than
women did.

Correct: F   Page: 88   Refer to: STORY3.3
51.   The dependent variable in this research is gender.

Correct: F   Page: 89   Refer to: STORY3.3
52.   This study is an example of an experiment.

Correct: F   Page: 88   Refer to: STORY3.3
53.   The independent variable in this research is dropping the class.

Correct: F   Page: 88   Refer to: STORY3.3
54.   There is a time order problem with this research.

Correct: F   Page: 86   Refer to: STORY3.3
55.   No correlation between gender (sex) and dropping algebra was found in this
      study.

Correct: F   Page: 86   Refer to: STORY3.3
56.   Using randomization in this way, the sociologist prevented spuriousness.

Multiple Choice

Correct: D   Page: 76,89 Scramble Range: A-D
57.   Karen Dion's research on whether teachers excuse cute kids
      A)   observed student-teacher interactions at a large number of playgrounds.
      B)   showed that mass society theory is incorrect in ignoring the relationships
           in schools.
      C)   is an example of macro-sociology.
      D)   is an example of an experiment.
      E)   all of these
      F)   none of these

Correct: E   Page: 76 Scramble Range: ALL
58.   Dion conducted research about student teachers' suggested disciplinary action
      for instances of children's misdeeds at school. The research found that the
      student teachers suggested discipline that was less severe for _____ children
      and more severe for _____ children.
      A)   athletic; nonathletic
      B)   white; nonwhite
      C)   neighborhood; transferred or bussed
      D)   noisy; quiet
      E)   cute; homely

59.   Figure 3-1, Marriages per 1,000 Population, is a map of the marriage rates
      across Europe. It is accompanied by a photograph of a wedding ceremony.
      A)   A micro sociologist would be more likely to focus on the photograph than
           the map.
      B)   Both the map and the photograph might tell us something about culture.
      C)   Some sociologists would be more interested in the map, others in the
           photograph.
      D)   Both the map and the photograph can tell us something about norms.
      E)   All of these
      F)   None of these

60.   When the author of your textbook says that "bacteria don't blush," he is
      referring to
      A)   the interplay between instinct and behavior.
      B)   the embarrassment that some Moonies feel about their faith.
      C)   the problems of experimental research.
      D)   the human capacity to find rewards in hope, dreams, love and ideals.
      E)   all of these
      F)   none of these

61.   When the author of your textbook says that "bacteria don't blush," he is
      referring to
      A)   the tendency for biologists to anthropomorphize their subjects -- to think
           of them as if they were human.
      B)   the embarrassment that some Moonies feel about their faith.
      C)   the problems of experimental research.
      D)   one of the difficulties of doing sociology which distinguishes the practice
           of sociology from the natural sciences.
      E)   all of these
      F)   none of these

62.   Your text sees a clear, direct connection between which of the following?
      A)   Functional theories and hypotheses that are difficult to test
      B)   Micro sociology and testing hypotheses about national economic
           productivity
      C)   Micro sociology and choice theory
      D)   Choice theory and macro sociology
      E)   Individual psychological functioning and the functioning of society as a
           whole

63.   According to choice theory
      A)   people act in order to maximize their rewards and minimize their costs.
      B)   transitive triads are inherently unstable.
      C)   humans are rather programmed.
      D)   human behavior is essentially random.
      E)   most human behavior is altruistic.

64. According to the text, the "rational choice" or "self-interest" proposition is connected to which of these ideas?
   A) Guilt
   B) Free will
   C) Altruism
   D) The life of the mind
   E) Cynicism

65. Sociologists believe that
   A) much human behavior is completely irrational.
   B) people find rewards only in their narrow self-interests.
   C) people are basically materialistic and don't do anything unless it is economically profitable.
   D) human behavior is random and unpredictable and therefore exciting.
   E) people who behave altruistically are not necessarily acting against their own self-interests.
   F) all of these

66. Sociologists believe that
   A) much human behavior is completely irrational.
   B) people act so as to maximize their rewards and minimize their costs.
   C) people are basically materialistic and don't do anything unless it is economically profitable.
   D) human behavior is random and unpredictable and therefore exciting.
   E) all of these

67. Altruism is
   A) behavior that occurs because it is consistent with tradition.
   B) unselfish behavior done to benefit others.
   C) actions taken by a person mainly for financial gain.
   D) behavior that is ethically neutral.
   E) acts undertaken by a group rather than by an individual.

68. Which of the following is an example of altruistic behavior?
   A) A brother gives his lunch money to his sister, who has forgotten hers.
   B) A husband gives his wages to his wife, who by tradition pays the family bills.
   C) A large electric utility company sells its electricity to the public for as much money as is allowed by the public utilities commission
   D) A violinist doesn't feel like playing Mozart's Fortieth Symphony one evening but is willing to play it because he has nothing else in particular to do.
   E) A supermarket cashier exchanges work shifts with another supermarket cashier who needs the exchange, but only for a $5 "inconvenience fee."

69. "Human relationships in which the people involved attempt to influence each other, with the result that they are forced into exchange relations," is what sociologists mean when they use this concept:
    A) coercion
    B) variable analysis
    C) social interaction
    D) altruism
    E) spuriousness

70. Micro sociology consists primarily of the study of
    A) interaction.
    B) institutions.
    C) functions.
    D) dysfunctions.
    E) societies.

71. Theories of _____ have long dominated micro sociology.
    A) conflict
    B) exchange
    C) structural functionalism
    D) functionalism
    E) symbolic interactionism

72. On a sheet of music, a printed musical note such as E-flat, G, or F-sharp can be seen as an example of:
    A) a variable
    B) a correlation
    C) time order
    D) a significance level
    E) a symbol

73. More formal interaction theories are referred to as _____ theories.
    A) functional
    B) exchange
    C) structural
    D) relationship
    E) conflict

74. Less formal, older interaction theories are referred to as _____ theories.
    A) choice
    B) relationship
    C) symbolic interaction
    D) exchange
    E) system

75. Sociologists use the term _____ to describe the process by which student teachers become teachers, youngsters learn to be professional musicians, and coaches teach their athletes to be successful.
    A) institutionalization
    B) socialization
    C) objectification
    D) assimilation
    E) effective acculturation

76. Both G. H. Mead and C. H. Cooley agree that the self or self-concept arises as a result of
    A) biological instincts.
    B) social instincts.
    C) the gradual emergence of germinal aspects of culture.
    D) the technical aspects of culture.
    E) social interaction.

77. G. H. Mead, who discussed mind and self, also discussed something called "taking the role of the other," which meant
    A) trying to see other people's point of view in a situation or in an event.
    B) entering into a conflict about who will get whose way in a situation or event.
    C) being able to take for ourselves a role that previously belonged to another.
    D) having a group persuade us to take a role previously occupied by another.
    E) making it impossible for another person to play a specific role in a group, organization, or society.

78. G. H. Mead, who carried Cooley's concept of the looking-glass self even further and who analyzed the development of mind and self, came to the conclusion that the "mind"
    A) develops as a matter of instinct.
    B) is present even in human fetuses after 6-8 months of fetal development.
    C) is the one thing individuals have that is NOT the product of culture.
    D) is present in nonhuman animals such as horses and dogs.
    E) arises wholly out of our repeated interaction with others.

79. C. H. Cooley's concept of the "looking-glass self" refers mainly to the idea that
    A) we come to have a self-concept by observing others' responses to us.
    B) the self-concept is a relatively fragile part of the personality structure.
    C) mental health requires that we have an undistorted idea of who we are.
    D) "mirrors don't lie" when it comes to developing a self-concept.
    E) individuals have a better idea of who and what they are than any other person can have; we know ourselves best.

80.   Cooley believed that the self-conceptions humans develop come from
   A)   family tradition.
   B)   a "genetic tide" of impulses from within that cannot be resisted.
   C)   feedback from others.
   D)   the human phenotype.
   E)   interaction with the ecosphere or ecostructure.

81.   Which of the following illustrates what G. H. Mead called "taking the role of the other"?
   A)   An accountant dies in an accident, and other accountants apply for the job
   B)   A person is condemned to death, and the spouse asks to be allowed to die in his/her place
   C)   A bored student tries to appear interested in class, for fear of being graded down on the next exam
   D)   A college athlete is sorry to hear that his teammate can't play because of illness but agrees to swim in his slot in the swimming competition
   E)   An actor conspires to get his competitor a job requiring relocation to another state so that he can take the now-vacant part in the play

82.   Every person's sense of self is
   A)   socially and psychologically connected to his/her biological kin line.
   B)   socially created.
   C)   the result of the development of natural instincts.
   D)   the unfolding of possibilities that were present in the individual from the moment of conception.
   E)   totally determined by the biological aspects of the brain.

83.   Both Charles H. Cooley and George H. Mead were interested in mind and self. We now understand that mind and self cannot emerge unless
   A)   people are able to understand symbols.
   B)   the feral self is replaced by the social self.
   C)   the individualistic self is replaced by the social self.
   D)   the person's instincts can be uncovered and allowed to manifest themselves.
   E)   individuals are able to overcome the oppression of the group and the "true self" emerges in its natural form.

84.   Peggy Ann can't decide whether she is "pretty" or not. She thinks she may be, but she isn't sure. She decides to ask her friends to tell her in a very frank way whether they think she is pretty. They all tell her that she IS pretty. She then notices that they all behave toward her as one would toward a person who is "pretty." This illustrates
   A)   ferality.
   B)   the importance of secondary groups.
   C)   feral attachments.
   D)   social psychological insecurity.
   E)   the looking-glass self.

85. Phillip, a sociology student, loves to watch people at parties. He goes to a party that a friend of his, Manuel, had helped to organize. He notices that Manuel, who is usually quite shy, is introducing new students to some of the upperclassmen. Manuel explained, "Otherwise they'll be lonely."
   A) Sociologists would argue that Manuel's altruistic behavior violates rational choice theory.
   B) Manuel's behavior is determined by his role as host.
   C) Phillip is conducting an experiment.
   D) Manuel is "taking the role of the other."
   E) All of these
   F) None of these

86. According to G. H. Mead
   A) Babies are born with a self-concept.
   B) Interaction with others is necessary in order for a human to develop a sense of self.
   C) Children can develop healthy self-concepts if they do not learn to manipulate symbols.
   D) Children will develop better self-concepts if they do not learn to "take the role of the other."
   E) The generalized other stifles the process of becoming fully human.

87. Sociologists use which of the following terms to identify a stable and persistent pattern of interaction between two people?
   A) Triads
   B) Norms
   C) Attachment
   D) Reference group
   E) Superordinate group

88. Which of the following statements is FALSE?
   A) An exchange will not take place unless both persons believe they will benefit from it.
   B) Older people shift their attachments more often and with less reluctance than do younger people.
   C) To interact involves understanding and abiding by socially constructed roles.
   D) If we violate norms, we risk losing our attachments.
   E) College students' self-perceptions have been found to be remarkably similar to ratings made of them by their fellow students.

89. Over time, people tend to establish
   A) stable exchange partnerships.
   B) symbiotic biological relationships.
   C) dysfunctional personal social arrangements.
   D) interaction patterns that benefit themselves more than others.
   E) altruistic interaction patterns to a larger degree than patterns that are not altruistic.

90. Theories
   A) once constructed properly, can never be proven false.
   B) must not be constructed using more than one concept.
   C) are roughly the same as "guesses," except that the terminology is more precise.
   D) must be stated so that they run the risk of being proved false.
   E) consist of several hypotheses connected in a logical, testable way.
   F) all of these

91. We are attached to other people because
   A) they fail to exchange with us.
   B) we like their looking-glass selves.
   C) they are spurious.
   D) shared norms make their behavior predictable.
   E) they act against their own self-interest.

92. Within any human group, those having _____ will tend to conform to the norms.
   A) knowledge of the group's goals
   B) higher group status
   C) status stability
   D) recently joined the group
   E) attachments to others in the group

93. Explanations are provided by _____.
   A) hypotheses
   B) tests of significance
   C) statistical tests
   D) concepts
   E) theories

94. The term "hypothesis" is similar in meaning to which of the following?
   A) Guess
   B) Theory
   C) Cause-and-effect sequence
   D) Prediction
   E) Experiment

95. Hypotheses
   A) are conclusions that have been proven by research.
   B) are specific predictions about how two variables are related to each other.
   C) try to prove theories.
   D) are unrelated to theories and research.
   E) are unnecessary if the researcher has a control group.

Correct: D   Page: 86 Scramble Range: A-E
96.   Correlations can be
       A)   causative or relational.
       B)   relational only.
       C)   connected to nonempirical reality only.
       D)   positive or negative.
       E)   uncertain or nonexistent.
       F)   all of these

Correct: C   Page: 86 Scramble Range: A-E
97.   When we say that two variables are "correlated," we are saying that
       A)   one variable stems from or "flows out of" the other variable.
       B)   the independent variable is the cause of the dependent variable.
       C)   change in one variable is associated with change in the other variable.
       D)   change in both variables is the result of change in some third, unknown
            variable.
       E)   the two variables are in the same variable "family."
       F)   all of these

Correct: C   Page: 86 Scramble Range: ALL
98.   When a sociologist discovers a "correlation" between two factors, it means
       that
       A)   one of the factors is the cause of observed changes in the other factor.
       B)   changes in the two factors are basically unrelated to each other.
       C)   change in one factor is related to change in the other factor.
       D)   change in both factors is due to change in some third factor.
       E)   one of the factors is the "core" factor and the other is less important.

Correct: A   Page: 86 Scramble Range: A-D
99.   To argue that one factor causes another we need to show
       A)   a correlation between the two.
       B)   that the two factors are similar.
       C)   that the two factors are not related.
       D)   a negative time order between the two factors.
       E)   all of these
       F)   none of these

Correct: B   Page: 86 Scramble Range: A-D
100.   In order to show that peer pressure from friends causes delinquent behavior
       we need to show
       A)   that the delinquent is younger than his or her friends.
       B)   that the delinquent chose the friends before she or he became
            delinquent.
       C)   that the immigrant status of the peers is similar to that of the delinquent.
       D)   that the group size is consistent with Ofshe's theory.
       E)   all of these
       F)   none of these

101. Let's pretend that a sociologist found a correlation between coming from a
      family of divorced parents and being divorced oneself. However, this
      correlation disappeared when people of the same educational background
      were compared. What could you conclude?
      A) People should not get divorced.
      B) The correlation between family background and divorce is spurious.
      C) Coming from a broken home causes people to have less stable
          marriages.
      D) There is a negative correlation between family background and divorce
          rates.
      E) People whose parents are divorced should seek higher education in
          order to avoid divorce themselves.

102. Your text cites recent newspaper reports that elderly men can prolong their
      lives by marrying younger women. The ones who married young women had
      death rates 13 percent lower than the others. But the report did not take into
      account the kind of elderly men who would be apt to seek and marry a young
      wife. Such elderly men, we might conjecture, would probably be healthier
      elderly men anyway! Which of the following problems is built into the
      reported research?
      A) Time order
      B) Nonexperimental attachment
      C) Spuriousness
      D) Lack of tests of significance
      E) Insufficient field observation

103. The text reported Richard Ofshe's study in which students were asked to
      agree or disagree with the judgments of the other persons about the
      attractiveness of visual patterns. In this experiment, Ofshe was able to
      provide strong support for the idea that
      A) attractiveness or unattractiveness is a matter of individual taste.
      B) sustained disagreement can lead to a breakup, even among friends.
      C) people tend to support their friends' judgments, even when they do not
          personally agree with their friends' judgments.
      D) in a conflict situation, when two people find that they strongly disagree
          with a third person, friendship between the two in agreement is
          sometimes created.
      E) the lower the social class of the two friends, the likelier it is that there
          will be no disagreement about the attractiveness of the visual patterns.

104. In Ofshe's study, friendship was the independent variable and _____ was the
      dependent variable.
      A) length of friendship
      B) intensity of friendship
      C) unwillingness to "use" friendship
      D) bias in favor of friends
      E) level of social class prejudice

Correct: A   Page: 88 Scramble Range: A-E
105. Morselli, who studied suicide, suggested that modernization caused suicide. That is to say, Morselli saw modernization as being
A) the independent variable.
B) the long-term result of suicide.
C) caused by some third variable, just as suicide was.
D) the intervening variable.
E) negatively correlated with suicide.
F) none of these
NOTE: Somewhat cumulative.

Correct: B   Page: 88 Scramble Range: ALL
106. What is a "variable" in the scientific sense of the term?
A) Anything that is by its very nature unstable
B) Anything that can take on two or more values
C) Anything that can remain unchanging or constant
D) Anything that is known very well, very firmly, very clearly
E) Anything that the researcher is unsure of but is going to investigate scientifically

Correct: A   Page: 88 Scramble Range: ALL
107. To say "independent variable" and "dependent variable" is to say
A) "cause" and "effect."
B) "trial" and "error."
C) "known" and "unknown."
D) "self-sufficient" and "insecure."
E) "stated" and "unstated."

Correct: A   Page: 88 Scramble Range: ALL
108. In 1980, the Department of Education found that male students were more likely to drop out of high school than female students. What is the dependent variable in the Department of Education study?
A) Dropout rates
B) High school students
C) Gender or sex
D) Discrimination against male students by female teachers
E) High school education

Correct: E   Page: 88 Scramble Range: ALL
109. Paul wants to have an experimental group and a control group in his research project. He could match people in each group if only he knew all of the variables he ought to match them on, but he doesn't know all of the variables involved. Nevertheless, he can assume that the two groups are alike if he uses the procedure called
A) experimental intake process.
B) group self-selection.
C) convenience assignment.
D) statistical replication.
E) random assignment.

Correct: C   Page: 89 Scramble Range: ALL
110. If you wanted to do a study and needed a random sample of twenty people in your sociology class, you would
   A) ask for twenty people to volunteer for your study.
   B) ask the twenty people who sit near you if they would be your subjects.
   C) put all the students' names in a hat and draw twenty names.
   D) choose twenty people who seem most friendly to you.
   E) choose twenty people of your race, sex, and age group.

Correct: B   Page: 89 Scramble Range: ALL
111. Experiments
   A) do not need control groups if the subjects are chosen at random.
   B) try to show that a change in the independent variable causes a change in the dependent variable.
   C) are easily conducted on human subjects.
   D) are not subject to ethical concerns at most universities.
   E) can show only that two variables are correlated.

Correct: B   Page: 89 Scramble Range: ALL
112. A technique used by social scientists to make two experimental groups alike or similar for the purpose of the experiment is
   A) to correlate the people in the two groups.
   B) to randomly assign people to each of the two groups.
   C) to use field observation and then to put people in the appropriate group.
   D) to allow the research participants to "self-select" the group they prefer.
   E) to make sure that each group has the same number of people.

Correct: B   Page: 90 Scramble Range: ALL
113. Richard Ofshe conducted research in which he made some people BELIEVE that they were participating in an experiment with one of their friends when in fact no one else was present (so that he could randomly expose some people to pressure to support their friends). According to your text, Ofshe's research
   A) was unethical.
   B) was not unethical.
   C) should have been conducted, even though it used unethical research.
   D) should not have been conducted because it used unethical research methods, even though it did discover important information
   E) produced severe, long-lasting anxieties in the research subjects when they discovered the deception.

Correct: D   Page: 91 Scramble Range: ALL
114. Stark and Lofland hypothesized that friendship was more influential than ideology in explaining why some people converted to the Unification church (the Moonies). What is the independent variable in their hypothesis?
   A) Unification church converts
   B) Reverend Moon
   C) Conversion to the Unification church
   D) Friendship
   E) Ideological beliefs

Correct: E   Page: 91 Scramble Range: A-E
115.   Field observations
A)   are more scientific than experiments.
B)   necessitate the random assignment of subjects to different groups.
C)   usually include a control group.
D)   are able to prove causal relationships between variables.
E)   are a form of non-experimental research.
F)   all of these

Correct: E   Page: 92 Scramble Range: ALL
116.   According to your text's narrative regarding the research about the
"Moonies," once the Moonie movement got started in Eugene, Oregon,
people who became members tended to be recruited
A)   after they had failed at a significant occupational task.
B)   when they had tidied up their family and business affairs, and not before.
C)   only when their family was not significantly opposed to their intention.
D)   only when they did not already know (but liked anyway) their "recruiter."
E)   by their friends who were already in the Moonie movement.

Correct: D   Page: 92 Scramble Range: ALL
117.   In their study of conversions to the Moonie movement, Lofland and Stark
found that conversion to the movement seemed to require that the new
recruit
A)   be an academic "failure" and an occupational "failure" as well.
B)   not have strong negative attitudes about the use of hallucinogens.
C)   have very strong negative attitudes about drugs and very weak negative
attitudes about authority figures.
D)   have strong attachments to Moonies and weak attachments to non-
Moonies.
E)   have attachments to the importance of self-examination and lack
attachments to the everyday world of employment and economic gain.

Correct: A   Page: 92 Scramble Range: ALL
118.   When Lofland and Stark studied the beginnings of the Moonie religious
movement in the San Francisco Bay Area, they found that people who were
recruited into the Moonies tended to
A)   have a friend who was already a Moonie.
B)   have a nonshareable personal problem that the Moonie movement
seemed able to solve.
C)   come from lower-middle-class and working-class backgrounds almost
exclusively.
D)   have high levels of intelligence but low levels of practical skills.
E)   be mildly neurotic or have slight health problems that the Unification
Church seemed to be able to "cure."

Correct: A   Page: 94 Scramble Range: ALL

119.   Widespread acceptance of scientific research ordinarily
A)   requires getting the same results in several "replications."
B)   occurs after one research effort IF the scientists are persuasive because their research methods have been technically correct.
C)   occurs in about 2-5 years.
D)   occurs only after the death of the scientists who originally conducted the research.
E)   does not involve research using people or groups from cultures other than our own.

Correct: C   Page: ResProc Scramble Range: A-D

120.   "Attachment" is
A)   an example of lack of conformity.
B)   another term for correlation.
C)   an example of a concept.
D)   a way of describing the relationship of experimental and control groups.
E)   all of these

NOTE: Cumulative question.

Chapter 4: Macro Sociology

True/False

Correct: T   Page: 98
1. The sex ratio of groups is a "social structure."

Correct: T   Page: 98
2. When groups differ from one another in terms of the proportion in each group who are children, it can be said that they have different social structures.

Correct: T   Page: 99
3. When groups differ in terms of the percent who are males and the percent who are females, they can be said to have different social structures.

Correct: T   Page: 98
4. Social structure is the primary focus of macro sociology.

Correct: F   Page: 100
5. Survey research is the research method best able to prevent spurious findings.

Correct: T   Page: 100
6. Survey research is based on samples.

Correct: T   Page: 104
7. Studies done today in most parts of the United States would find that teenagers who attend church are less likely to be delinquents.

Correct: T   Page: 104
8. Religious individuals will be less likely than others to break norms, but only in communities where the majority of people are actively religious.

Correct: F   Page: 105
9. The idea of a system is consistent with the claim that all parts are independent of one another.

Correct: F   Page: 106
10. The idea of a system implies that societies can change only very slowly.

Correct: T   Page: 108
11. Functional theories in sociology try to explain something on the basis of its effects on other parts of the system.

Correct: F   Page: 108
12. The idea of a system is rejected by functional theories.

Correct: T   Page: 108
13. Functional theories in sociology assume that societies are systems.

Correct: T   Page: 108
14. The idea of a system assumes that what goes on in one part will influence what goes on in other parts.

Correct: F   Page: 108
15.   Functional theories in sociology need not assume that societies are systems.

Correct: F   Page: 108
16.   Functional theories in sociology are used primarily by micro sociologists.

Correct: T   Page: 108
17.   Functional theories in sociology can analyze dysfunctions as well as functions.

Correct: F   Page: 110
18.   Modern social evolutionary theories explain differences between societies as being caused by biological differences among their members.

Correct: F   Page: 110
19.   Modern social evolutionary theories reject the assumption that societies are systems.

Correct: F   Page: 110
20.   Modern social evolutionary theories contradict functional theories.

Correct: T   Page: 111
21.   Conflict theories include Marxist theories.

Correct: T   Page: 111
22.   Conflict theories try to explain social structure by asking who benefits from it.

Correct: F   Page: 111
23.   Conflict theories are primarily micro sociological theories.

Correct: F   Page: 111
24.   Conflict theories argue that social structures arise because of the survival benefits they offer societies.

Correct: T   Page: 111
25.   Conflict theories tend to emphasize how power is used to rig social arrangements in favor of one group or another.

Correct: T   Page: 112
26.   Comparative research usually means research using units larger than the individual.

Correct: F   Page: 116
27.   Paige found that primitive societies had less internal conflict when men lived near their brothers and sons.

Correct: T   Page: 116
28.   The third step in Paige's theory of internal conflicts in primitive societies identifies males as the primary participants in violence.

Correct: T   Page: 116
29.   Paige stated that primitive societies will tend to have little violence when men who are kin do not share common residence.

Correct: F   Page: 116
30.   Patrilocal societies have relatively low levels of internal conflict.

Reference Key: STORY4.1A
A sociologist wanted to know if tall people were more likely than short people to be basketball fans. She drew a random sample of residents of Texas and had them interviewed. After the data had been put into the computer, she obtained the following results:

	Tall	Short
Likes Basketball	65%	45%
Doesn't like Basketball	35%	55%
	------	------
	100%	100%

Correct: F   Page: Ch3   Refer to: STORY4.1A
31.   This study is an example of an experiment.
                    NOTE: Cumulative question.

Correct: T   Page: Ch1   Refer to: STORY4.1A
32.   The unit of analysis in this research is individual.
                    NOTE: Cumulative question.

Correct: T   Page: 100   Refer to: STORY4.1A
33.   This study is an example of survey research.

Correct: T   Page: Ch3   Refer to: STORY4.1A
34.   The independent variable in this study is height.
                    NOTE: Cumulative question.

Correct: T   Page: 100   Refer to: STORY4.1A
35.   The data show that there is a correlation between height and liking basketball.

Correct: F   Page: Ch3   Refer to: STORY4.1A
36.   In this study it might make sense to reverse the independent and dependent variables.
                    NOTE: Cumulative question.

Correct: F   Page: 100   Refer to: STORY4.1A
37.   The data show that 65 percent of the basketball fans are tall.

Correct: T   Page: 100   Refer to: STORY4.1A
38.   The 55% means that 55 percent of the short people don't like basketball.

Correct: F   Page: Ch3   Refer to: STORY4.1A
39.   There is a problem with time order in this research.
                    NOTE: Cumulative question.

Correct: T   Page: ResProc   Refer to: STORY4.1A
40.   In this research, basketball fan is a concept.
                    NOTE: Cumulative question.

Correct: T   Page: ResProc   Refer to: STORY4.1A
41.   In this research, tall people is a concept.
NOTE: Cumulative question.

Reference Key: STORY4.1B
However, the sociologist was worried about spuriousness. So she imposed controls
for sex (gender). The results looked like this:

| | Males | | Females | |
	Tall	Short	Tall	Short
Likes Basketball	85%	55%	55%	25%
Doesn't like Basketball	15%	45%	45%	75%
	-----	----- -----	-----	
	100%	100%	100%	100%

Correct: F   Page: 101   Refer to: STORY4.1B
42.   These results show that the relationship between height and liking basketball
      is spurious.

Correct: T   Page: 100   Refer to: STORY4.1B
43.   These results show that men are more likely than women to be basketball
      fans.

Correct: T   Page: 100   Refer to: STORY4.1B
44.   These results show that tall women are as likely as short men to be basketball
      fans.

Correct: T   Page: 100   Refer to: STORY4.1B
45.   Most of the men in Texas are basketball fans.

Correct: T   Page: 100   Refer to: STORY4.1B
46.   Three out of four short women in Texas do not like basketball.

Correct: F   Page: 100   Refer to: STORY4.1B
47.   Because men are taller than women and also are more likely to like
      basketball, there only seemed to be a correlation between height and being a
      basketball fan.

Reference Key: STORY4.2
A sociologist argued that norms limiting sexual relations (such as a two-year ban on
sex following the birth of a child) were common among people living on isolated
islands because they kept the population size within the limits of their food supply.

Correct: T   Page: 108   Refer to: STORY4.2
48.   This is an example of a functionalist theory.

Correct: F   Page: 111   Refer to: STORY4.2
49.   This is an example of a conflict theory.

Correct: T   Page: 103   Refer to: STORY4.2
50.   This is an example of a macro theory.

Correct: F   Page: Ch3   Refer to: STORY4.2
51.   The part of society that this theory tried to explain is overpopulation.
NOTE: Cumulative question.

Correct: F   Page: Ch3   Refer to: STORY4.2
52.   The source of disruption examined in this theory is sexual tension.
NOTE: Cumulative question.

Correct: T   Page: Ch3   Refer to: STORY4.2
53.   The purpose of this theory is to explain norms limiting sexual relations.
NOTE: Cumulative question.

Correct: T   Page: 105   Refer to: STORY4.2
54.   This theory would make no sense unless we assume societies are systems.

Correct: T   Page: Ch2   Refer to: STORY4.2
55.   A two-year ban on sex following the birth of a child is part of culture.
NOTE: Cumulative question.

Correct: F   Page: ResProc   Refer to: STORY4.2
56.   This is an example of a hypothesis.
NOTE: Cumulative question.

Reference Key: STORY4.3A
A sociologist noticed that students who sat in the front of the class seemed to get better grades. She tested this impression by looking at her gradebook and noting where students sat in the classroom. This is what she found:

	Seating	
Grade	Front	Back
A	25%	5%
B or below	75%	95%
	------	------
	100%	100%

Correct: F   Page: 100   Refer to: STORY4.3A
57.   Twenty-five percent of the A students sat in the front.

Correct: F   Page: Ch3   Refer to: STORY4.3A
58.   This is an experiment.
NOTE: Cumulative question.

Correct: F   Page: 100   Refer to: STORY4.3A
59.   This is an example of survey research.

Correct: F   Page: ResProc   Refer to: STORY4.3A
60.   This sociologist has stated a theory.
NOTE: Cumulative question.

Correct: F   Page: 98   Refer to: STORY4.3A
61.   In this research, seating is a social structure.

Correct: F   Page: 101   Refer to: STORY4.3A
62.   This research demonstrates that changing your seat would probably change your grade.

Correct: F   Page: 101   Refer to: STORY4.3A
63.   There is little reason to suspect that this relationship is spurious.

Reference Key: STORY4.3B
The sociologist suspected spuriousness so she divided students into two groups, those who studied an hour or more a day and those who studied less than an hour. This is what she found:

	Study Time per Day			
	One hour or more		Less than one hour	
Grade	Front	Rear	Front	Rear
A	30%	30%	2%	2%
B or below	70%	70%	100%	100%
	------	------	------	------
	100%	100%	100%	100%

Correct: F   Page: 100 Refer to: STORY4.3B
64.   This result suggests that seating influences your grade regardless of how much you study.

Correct: T   Page: 100 Refer to: STORY4.3B
65.   Although there appeared to be a relationship between grade and seating, it turns out that this is because study time is related to both seating preference and grade.

Correct: T   Page: 100 Refer to: STORY4.3B
66.   The relationship between seating and grade is spurious.

Reference Key: STORY4.4
Jeffrey Paige examined the idea that matrilocal societies will be low in factions and violence while patrilocal societies will be high on measures of each.

Correct: T   Page: ResProc   Refer to: STORY4.4
67.   Paige's idea is a hypothesis.
NOTE: Cumulative question.

Correct: T   Page: Ch1 Refer to: STORY4.4
68.   The unit of analysis in this research is societies.
NOTE: Cumulative question.

Correct: F   Page: ResProc   Refer to: STORY4.4
69.   Paige's idea is a theory.
NOTE: Cumulative question.

Correct: F   Page: Ch3   Refer to: STORY4.4
70.   The dependent variable here was location of residence.
NOTE: Cumulative question.

Correct: F   Page: 112   Refer to: STORY4.4
71. This is a good example of micro sociology.

Correct: T   Page: 98   Refer to: STORY4.4
72. Matrilocality is a social structure.

Correct: T   Page: Ch3   Refer to: STORY4.4
73. There is a problem with time order in this research.
NOTE: Cumulative question.

Correct: T   Page: Ch2   Refer to: STORY4.4
74. Rules of residence are part of a society's culture.
NOTE: Cumulative question.

Correct: T   Page: ResProc   Refer to: STORY4.4
75. In this research, violence is a concept.
NOTE: Cumulative question.

Reference Key: STORY4.5
In class, we examined the relationship between proportion "not moved" and suicide rates for the United States. We found a correlation coefficient (Pearson's r) of -.79

Correct: F   Page: Show4.1   Refer to: STORY4.5
76. This finding showed that the two variables are not related at all.
NOTE: ShowCase question.

Correct: T   Page: Ch3   Refer to: STORY4.5
77. The dependent variable in this examination was suicide rates.
NOTE: Cumulative question.

Correct: F   Page: Show4.1   Refer to: STORY4.5
78. This finding showed that moving causes suicidal depression.
NOTE: ShowCase question.

Correct: F   Page: Ch2   Refer to: STORY4.5
79. This finding helps us understand the differential rates of assimilation for various groups.
NOTE: Cumulative question.

Correct: T   Page: Ch1   Refer to: STORY4.5
80. This finding can be seen as support for Durkheim's theory of anomic suicide.
NOTE: Cumulative and ShowCase question.

Correct: F   Page: Ch3   Refer to: STORY4.5
81. This was an experiment.
NOTE: Cumulative question.

Multiple Choice

Correct: E   Page: 98 Scramble Range: A-E
82. A social structure is
    A) an aspect of culture that is intentionally created by humans.
    B) an aspect of culture that is relatively unchanging, especially in modern times.
    C) something that occurs at the macro level, but not at the micro level.
    D) something that occurs at the micro level, but not at the macro level.
    E) a characteristic of a group or society rather than of an individual.
    F) none of these

Correct: A   Page: 98 Scramble Range: ALL
83. Darley and Latane conducted research in which the participants were led to believe that they were in a discussion group. Suddenly one of the participants apparently had a seizure, gasped "Help!" and fell down. Given what happened next, Darley and Latane concluded that which of the following had a big impact on how the research participants responded?
    A) Group size
    B) Personal appearance and/or manner
    C) Power structure of the group
    D) Presence/absence of group norms
    E) Social class of the participants

Correct: C   Page: 98 Scramble Range: ALL
84. Which of the following statements is FALSE?
    A) People are more willing to go to the aid of strangers when they don't think it is too risky to intervene.
    B) People in small towns are more often helpful in such situations than people in large cities.
    C) When they confront an emergency, people will more often help when others are also present than when they are alone.
    D) The bystander-intervention experiment found that people are likelier to help in a three-person group than in a six-person group.
    E) The bystander-intervention experiment found that perceptions of group size must have been the cause of the likelihood of people going for help.

Correct: C   Page: 98 Scramble Range: ALL
85. According to Darley and Latane's research, who are more likely to react to an emergency?
    A) People in a three-person group
    B) People in a six-person group
    C) People in a two-person group
    D) People in a large crowd (fifty or more people)
    E) There is no difference among groups of different sizes in how fast a group's members react to an emergency

86. Darley and Latane demonstrated that if there are two people in a room, as opposed to three or six people, the two people will be
A) slower to respond in an emergency.
B) likely to make an emergency worse rather than better when they act.
C) less likely to panic in an emergency.
D) more likely to respond in an emergency.
E) less likely to feel personal responsibility in an emergency situation.

87. Darley and Latane studied people's likelihood of coming to the assistance of strangers apparently in need of help. Given what these researchers found, in which of the following situations would people be LEAST likely to come forward to offer assistance?
A) In a science class
B) In a class on Accounting II
C) In a class taught by a male rather than by a female
D) In a "large" lecture class of 120 students
E) In a professor's office where several students are waiting for an appointment

88. When Darley and Latane were conducting research on the likelihood of people giving assistance to strangers apparently in need of help, they found that the likelihood of people giving such aid is strongly related to
A) the purpose of the group: utilitarian vs. expressive.
B) the size of the group as an aspect of social structure.
C) the structure of the group in terms of formality: bureaucratic vs. nonbureaucratic.
D) the individual personality of the various group members.
E) socio-political considerations that developed as group members went about their tasks in the previous group meetings.

89. When Darley and Latane were studying people's willingness to go to the assistance of strangers who were apparently in need of help, they found that 100 percent began to assist the stranger in which of the following situations?
A) When the stranger was well-dressed and appeared to be "nice"
B) When the stranger was the same age and sex as the person rendering aid
C) When the researchers were studying a pair of individuals
D) When the researchers were allegedly paying people to participate in the research
E) When the researchers were not paying people to participate in the research

90. Which of the following played a critical role in the bystander-intervention experiment?
A) Analysis using multiple regression statistics
B) The absence of deception
C) A correlation that was strong enough to be designated as spurious
D) The use of survey questionnaires
E) Random assignment

91. In survey research, if the researcher cannot interview everyone who should be interviewed, then the desirable alternative is to interview
A) as many as possible who will agree to be interviewed.
B) a sample of the total population who should be interviewed.
C) as many people as possible, given the amount of money available for the project.
D) the people who are the most convenient to interview.
E) the people whose interviews would be pleasant, threat-free, and brief.

92. The use of personal interviews or questionnaires and the use of samples are
A) features of survey research.
B) among the basic procedures in an experiment.
C) increasingly considered old-fashioned in sociological research.
D) likely to lead to reliable results but rarely lead to valid results.
E) likelier to be used in studies of conflict than in other types of research.

93. If you are going to conduct survey research that will lead to useful information about a population in which you have an interest but that is too large to allow you to survey everyone, then you will need to
A) cut down on the size of the questionnaire.
B) survey only those persons who are in closest proximity to the research coordinator's office.
C) survey only those persons who are in closest proximity to the individual interviewers.
D) use a properly selected sample.
E) redefine the research question so that research funds are adequate to the research task.

94. Which of the following is NOT one of the criteria used to test the presence of a cause-and-effect relationship?
A) Agreement with previously accepted ideas
B) Time order between the factors studied
C) Nonspuriousness
D) Existence of a correlation
E) All of the above are required to support a cause-and-effect relationship

95. If a correlation between two variables disappears when some third variable is controlled, the correlation is probably
A) dependent.
B) independent.
C) causal.
D) spurious.
E) significant.
F) all of these

Correct: C   Page: 101 Scramble Range: A-D
96. We say that a relationship between two variables is "spurious" when
     A) it disappears when we control for gender.
     B) a third variable is found to cause both of them.
     C) the causal order of the variables must be reversed.
     D) the sample size is insufficient to gain statistical significance.
     E) all of these

Correct: E   Page: 101 Scramble Range: A-E
97. A strong correlation between the volume of popcorn sales in the city of New
     Orleans and the volume of water flowing down the Mississippi River is almost
     certain to be
     A) a "causal" relationship.
     B) based on inaccurate facts.
     C) an example of what your text means by "comparative research."
     D) a finding that cannot be the result of statistical analysis.
     E) a spurious relationship.
     F) none of these

Correct: E   Page: 102 Scramble Range: ALL
98. Stark and Hirschi found that
     A) boys who attend church are less likely to be delinquent than boys who
         don't attend church.
     B) girls who attend church are more likely than girls who don't attend church
         eventually to have a "career" of delinquency.
     C) the more people in a room, the faster they will react to an emergency.
     D) not going to church causes boys to be delinquent.
     E) there was no significant correlation on the West Coast between frequency
         of church attendance and delinquency.

Correct: B   Page: 104 Scramble Range: ALL
99. Stark and Hirschi's research on delinquency shows that
     A) religion has a strong influence on the individual's behavior.
     B) it is important to consider social structure as well as individual
         characteristics in explaining delinquency.
     C) it is important to consider whether or not students were lying about their
         church attendance.
     D) scientific findings are the same no matter what part of the country is
         studied.
     E) micro sociology leads to more valid results than macro sociology.

Correct: D   Page: 104   Scramble Range: ALL
100. An implication of the Hirschi and Stark study on the topic of adolescent
      delinquency and religious participation would seem to be that we could
      expect to find low rates of delinquency among which of the following?
      A) Teens whose family members go to "fundamentalist" churches
      B) Teens whose religious leaders have a strong interest in ministry to the
          entire family unit, not just to individuals
      C) Adolescents who have a wide circle of friends from a variety of social
          situations
      D) Adolescents in communities with higher rates of religious participation
      E) Teenagers who do not take an intellectual approach toward religious
          ideas

Correct: B   Page: 104   Scramble Range: ALL
101. The research on delinquency mentioned in your text showed that
   A) communities with high church involvement had higher rates of delinquency.
   B) the religious involvement of one's friends and associates seems to influence the likelihood of committing a delinquent act.
   C) in all parts of the country there is a correlation between church attendance and delinquency.
   D) the correlation between church attendance and delinquency is due to the fact that girls have higher rates of church attendance and lower rates of delinquency than boys.
   E) boys who attend church more frequently actually have higher rates of delinquency.

Correct: E   Page: 104   Scramble Range: A-D
102. The conclusion Stark draws about the relationship between juvenile delinquency and religion illustrates
   A) the range of variation in human behavior.
   B) the inability of sociologists to answer questions definitively.
   C) the importance of structural factors, like the religiousness of a group, on human behavior.
   D) the relevance of free will, since some juveniles choose to be delinquent.
   E) all of these

Correct: D   Page: 104   Scramble Range: A-E
103. The relationship between delinquency and religious participation is related to the extent of religious participation in an area. Which of the regions of the United States has the lowest extent of religious participation?
   A) East
   B) Midwest
   C) South
   D) Pacific
   E) Northeast

Correct: D   Page: 104   Scramble Range: ALL
104. The author of your text reports research findings about the impact that the general level of teen religiosity in an area has in reducing juvenile delinquency.   This type of research is basically
   A) from a conflict theory orientation.
   B) an essay on ethnomethodology.
   C) from the symbolic functionalism perspective.
   D) an example of macro sociology.
   E) research on forces of change occurring within a religious institution.

Correct: E   Page: 104   Scramble Range: ALL
105. Does religion reduce juvenile delinquency or doesn't it? Your text says that
   A) it does, but only when the teens' parents are themselves religious.
   B) it does not, even when the teen's entire family is religious.
   C) it does, when the religion involved is not a "fringe" religion.
   D) it does, but only when the religion is a "fundamentalist" religion.
   E) it does, but only when the teen's community is also religious.
   F) it does, but only for boys.

Chapter 4: Macro Sociology -- Page 308

106. When Hirschi and Stark reaffirmed a relationship between religion and delinquency, they did it by realizing that religion gains its power and impact on the individual
   A)   as an aspect of social structure.
   B)   only through the individual personality processing religious ideas.
   C)   as one social institution has multiple effects on other social institutions.
   D)   only through the formal church exercising control over the individual.
   E)   only when religion is experiencing a renaissance of influence, after a period of lessened influence.

107. The text reports research by Hirschi and Stark on the topic of adolescent delinquency and religious participation. The main conclusion of this research is that for the adolescents studied religion was found to
   A)   have a minimal effect on delinquency when the other variables were controlled.
   B)   strongly deter delinquency, even when no other variables were controlled.
   C)   inhibit delinquency only among the major denominations.
   D)   deter delinquency when teenagers and their parents were involved in religion.
   E)   inhibit delinquency only when the teenager's community was also religious.

108. When a sociologist examines the relation between Protestant ideas and the development of capitalism she is
   A)   engaged in micro sociological research.
   B)   overlooking the problem of spuriousness.
   C)   examining the distribution of ascribed status.
   D)   examining social institutions.
   E)   none of these

109. The family system of the San Blas Indians, the economic system of Tanzania, the Lutheran religion, socialism in Yugoslavia, and the college/university system in North America are all examples of
   A)   relatively independent social systems.
   B)   social categories.
   C)   social institutions.
   D)   extended status systems.
   E)   insular status systems.

110. To speak of the rich people, the white-collar workers, the unskilled laborers, and the poor who are unemployed is to speak of
   A)   status dissimilars.
   B)   social classes.
   C)   social aggregates.
   D)   the functional exploiters and the functionally exploited.
   E)   evidence of nonstratification.

111. When sociologists speak of societies as being "open systems," they are referring to the fact that
    A) the societies that survive are those that do not have closed minds in terms of social change.
    B) societies are continuously reacting to outside forces.
    C) normal societies SHOULD be open to suggestions from individual members of the society or from groups within the society.
    D) various things are more or less constantly "falling out" of societies and are available to other societies.
    E) societies are always capable of changing in an infinite number of ways.

112. Groups of people with a similar position within a society's stratification system are called
    A) institutional residents.
    B) classes.
    C) functional residents.
    D) equilibrium stabilizers.
    E) nonmobiles.

113. Relatively permanent patterns or clusters of specialized roles, groups, organizations, customs, and activities devoted to meeting fundamental social needs are called
    A) social models.
    B) social statuses.
    C) social institutions.
    D) extended units.
    E) practical roles.

114. Viewing society as existing in equilibrium and as being composed of a number of different parts, with interdependence among those parts, is to see society as
    A) part of an evolutionary historical process.
    B) a system in terms of its social structure.
    C) highly unstable.
    D) more tolerant of nonconformity than other types of society.
    E) highly vulnerable to attack from forces outside the society.

115. Which of the following is NOT a major social institution found in all societies?
    A) Economic system
    B) Family
    C) Political system
    D) Social science
    E) Education

Correct: E   Page: 105 Scramble Range: ALL
116.   Social institutions
A)   are found in modern urban societies but not in primitive cultures.
B)   refer to the organizations that are set up to help people with economic and family problems.
C)   are relatively unrelated to each other.
D)   stifle individual growth and learning by demanding conformity to traditional cultural patterns.
E)   are social arrangemtns which satisfy important group needs.

Correct: A   Page: 105 Scramble Range: ALL
117.   The assumption that the social structures found in a society are connected is the assumption that all societies are
A)   systems.
B)   evolving slowly.
C)   too complex to ever be fully understood.
D)   relatively simple microcosms that can be largely understood.
E)   informally bureaucratic.

Correct: D   Page: 107 Scramble Range: ALL
118.   Paul, Dave, and Denise are air traffic controllers who work together. Imagine now that regulations change and they find themselves working with a fourth air traffic controller, Shelley. All four vow that things are going to continue as before and that nothing will change because they were doing so well before. However, according to the text, which of the following should happen?
A)   They should be members of what sociologists call a quadratic group.
B)   The productivity of the group should decrease.
C)   The efficiency of the group should decrease.
D)   The group structure should change.
E)   The visibility of the group to supervisors should increase by a factor of six.

Correct: A   Page: 107 Scramble Range: ALL
119.   Macro sociologists assume that
A)   social institutions are interdependent.
B)   social institutions disrupt the equilibrium of society.
C)   functionalists do not understand interrelationships among institutions.
D)   each part of society is related to every other part.
E)   the society reacts more to internal forces for change than it does to external forces.

Correct: B   Page: 107 Scramble Range: ALL
120.   The college/university Board of Trustees or Regents ordinarily can be expected to think long and hard before making a significant change in one part of the college/university, because its members usually are aware that a change in one part of the school will affect other parts of the school. That is, the Board of Regents or Trustees is sensitive to what sociologists call
A)   system dysfunctions.
B)   system interdependence.
C)   a bureaucracy.
D)   an "open" system.
E)   intuitive management.

Correct: D   Page: 107 Scramble Range: ALL
121.   The legislature of a state sharply decreases the money available to help pay
for the costs of running the state university. The university increases the
individual student's tuition and fails to replace 78 faculty members who
retire, thus bringing about a balanced university budget once again. This
brief example illustrates what aspect of system theory?
A)   Latent functions
B)   Static structure
C)   The anti-Marxian nature of system theory
D)   Equilibrium
E)   Its emphasis on economics as the fundamental cause of social change

Correct: E   Page: 108 Scramble Range: ALL
122.   Macro sociology consists of several schools of thought. The school of
thought that sees society as made up of various social elements or parts,
each of which "does something" to help the society to survive, especially
when those parts come under pressure from the environment, is called
A)   interactionism.
B)   evolutionism.
C)   environmentalism.
D)   mechanistic theory.
E)   functionalism.

Correct: A   Page: 108 Scramble Range: ALL
123.   An African society near Lake Victoria has sexual practices that include
considerable freedom to engage in sex with multiple partners. But with the
appearance of the AIDS epidemic, having more than one sex partner turns
out to greatly increase the spread of AIDS among both men and women.
Among these people, then, having multiple sexual partners
A)   is dysfunctional for the people involved.
B)   provides a functional alternative for the society in which this occurs.
C)   is a good example of what the text means by system equilibrium.
D)   gives a sociological argument to prove that having multiple sex partners
is immoral.
E)   is functional for extended families but not for nuclear families.

Correct: B   Page: 110 Scramble Range: ALL
124.   Which macro sociology point of view maintains that societies have tended to
accumulate more effective technology and to become more efficient at
producing food, more complex, larger, more urban, and more powerful?
A)   Interactionism
B)   Evolutionism
C)   Mechanistic theory
D)   Functionalism
E)   Determinism

Correct: B   Page: 110 Scramble Range: ALL
125. Evolutionary theory says that
   A) society remains constant although individuals may change.
   B) societies tend to become more complex, more urban, and more powerful.
   C) societies with genetically superior people evolve into superior societies.
   D) each society becomes more complex and progressive.
   E) religious influences tend to become less important as societies modernize and become more scientific.

Correct: D   Page: 110 Scramble Range: ALL
126. The idea that societies have tended to become larger, to accumulate more effective technology, to become more efficient at producing food, to have more specialized occupations, to become more urban and to become more powerful is
   A) an argument that is vigorously attacked by Marxist theorists.
   B) something that has not yet been persuasively supported by evidence.
   C) a phenomenon that is in the micro sociology sphere of analysis.
   D) the basic idea of social evolutionary theory.
   E) not consistent with what functionalist theories tell us about human history and evolution.

Correct: D   Page: 110 Scramble Range: ALL
127. According to modern evolutionary theory
   A) societies differ because of biological differences within their population.
   B) each society will go through a set of evolutionary steps.
   C) change is always progress.
   D) societies tend to become more specialized.
   E) societies tend to become less complex.

Correct: B   Page: 111 Scramble Range: A-E
128. Conflict theorists
   A) believe we should all live in patrilocal societies.
   B) emphasize the distribution of power in a society.
   C) believe that conflict is bad for a society.
   D) focus on conflicts between different economic groups.
   E) focus on interpersonal conflicts.
   F) all of these

Correct: C   Page: 111 Scramble Range: A-D
129. The conflict perspective
   A) assumes that conflict is beneficial for society.
   B) focuses on economic conflict.
   C) emphasizes the distribution of power in society.
   D) focuses on the evolution of human groups.
   E) none of these

Correct: D   Page: 111   Scramble Range: ALL

130. Your text says that _____ theory asks how social structure serves the interests of various competing groups within a society.
    A) resource
    B) strategic planning
    C) symbolic functionalist
    D) conflict
    E) systems

Correct: B   Page: 113   Scramble Range: ALL

131. Chagnon studied killings among the Yanomamo Indians. He found that nearly 70 percent of Yanomamo adults over the age of 40 have had at least one close relative killed by other Yanomamo. Initial events starting a series of revenge killings were almost always
    A) quarrels over food-producing territory.
    B) conflicts about women.
    C) insults about kinship and lineage history.
    D) started by non-Yanomamo "outlanders."
    E) started by quarreling Yanomamo children, whose quarrels spread to adults.

Correct: A   Page: 113   Scramble Range: ALL

132. In _____ societies such as the Yanomamo Indians studied by Chagnon, groups within the society pursue their own interests at the expense of other groups.
    A) factional
    B) proto-social
    C) competitive
    D) egoistic
    E) polarized

Correct: D   Page: 113   Scramble Range: ALL

133. Chagnon connected the Yanomamo Indians' high rate of revenge killings to which of the following aspects of their social structure?
    A) Conflict between their two major religions
    B) Conflict between the Yanomamo Indians and their rivals, the Ignacci
    C) Their fertility rate
    D) The sex ratio
    E) Rate of population increase

Correct: A   Page: 115   Scramble Range: ALL

134. The two primary bases of factionalism in primitive societies are
    A) kinship and residence.
    B) race and ethnicity.
    C) race and social class.
    D) ethnicity and age.
    E) age and religion.

135. Which basis for group formation came to play an important part in Paige's study of conflict in "primitive" societies?
A) Shared authority
B) Avuncular authority
C) Level of voluntariness
D) Patrilocality
E) Point of effectivity

136. When Jeffery Paige conducted research that eventually supported the idea that conflict can shape social structure AND that social structure can shape conflict, he was analyzing the effects of
A) kinship and residence.
B) kinship and religion.
C) religion and economics.
D) economics and literacy.
E) literacy and mobility aspirations.

137. Which of the following political systems seems to produce much conflict?
A) Insider-outsider politics
B) Instrumental politics
C) Suppressive politics
D) Factional politics
E) Expressive politics

138. Paige's theory of internal conflict in primitive societies states that primitive societies will tend to lack factions and to have little violence when
A) the society has an economic system based on farming.
B) tribal decision making is shared rather than autocratic.
C) the political institution is tied to economics rather than to kinship.
D) kinsmen do not share common residence.
E) they are isolated from other societies.

139. When Paige studied social structure and conflict in primitive societies, he found that matrilocal societies
A) were structured so as to increase the amount of conflict among males.
B) had lower levels of conflict than patrilocal societies.
C) did not differ from patrilocal societies in their level of conflict.
D) were competitive and conflict-oriented for both males and females.
E) were less evolved than patrilocal societies.

140. Paige studied social structure and conflict in primitive societies. According to Paige, what type of society has the least internal political conflict?
A) Matriarchal societies
B) Patrilocal societies
C) Matrilocal societies
D) Neolocal societies
E) Patriarchal societies

141. When Paige studied social structure and conflict in primitive societies, he found that factional politics and conflict were LOWEST in which of the following?
A) Matrilocal societies
B) Patrilocal societies
C) Societies characterized by abundance rather than by scarcity
D) Societies practicing avuncular politics
E) Societies experiencing threat from a nearby military society

142. In the conclusion section of Chapter 4, the author of your text states that _____ often determine what rewards are available and how they can be gained.
A) the interstices of human behavior
B) quasi-material cultures
C) human instincts
D) social instincts
E) social structures

143. Jeffery Paige, in his research on violence in simple societies, .
A) found that matrilocal societies have more factions and more conflict.
B) argued that matrilocal residence creates crosscutting attachments.
C) found that almost all simple societies have a very low level of conflict and violence.
D) theorized that residence would have little impact on factionalism and residence.
E) all of these

NOTE: ShowCase question.

Topic 1: Correlation

True/False

Correct: F   Page: 123
1. A correlation of -.83 is a very weak correlation.

Correct: F   Page: 123
2. A positive correlation is a strong correlation; a negative correlation is a weak correlation.

Correct: T   Page: 123
3. Correlations can be either positive or negative.

Correct: F   Page: Ch3
4. If two variables are correlated it means that one causes the other.
   NOTE: Cumulative question.

Reference Key: CORR1
The correlation between the percentage of the population of a state that is Afro-American and the male life expectancy in the state is -.77 for the United States.

Correct: F   Page: Ch3   Refer to: CORR1
5. The dependent variable here is race.
   Note: Cumulative question.

Correct: T   Page: Ch4   Refer to: CORR1
6. In this research, percent Afro-American is a social structure.
   Note: Cumulative question.

Correct: F   Page: 123   Refer to: CORR1
7. This means that states with a higher proportion of Afro-Americans also have higher proportion of people who live longer.

Correct: F   Page: 123   Refer to: CORR1
8. This means that percent Afro-American and life expectancy are not related.

Correct: T   Page: 123   Refer to: CORR1
9. This means that people who live in states with a higher proportion of Afro-Americans have a lower life expectancy.

Multiple Choice

Correct: C   Page: 123 Scramble Range: A-E
10. Your text compares maps of the percent voting for Franklin Roosevelt in 1940 and the percent of urban homes with a radio the same year
    A) to illustrate changing entertainment trends in the United States
    B) as evidence that people with radios listened to Roosevelt.
    C) to see if there is a correlation between these two variables.
    D) to illustrate historical changes in the United States
    E) as an example of validation research.
    F) all of these

Correct: A   Page: 123 Scramble Range: ALL
11. A correlation of -.85 is a _____ correlation.
    A) strong
    B) weak
    C) spurious
    D) nonspurious
    E) minimal

Correct: A   Page: 123 Scramble Range: ALL
12. Which of the following correlations supports the conclusion that the more people use public transportation, the less likely they are to be hospitalized for traffic injuries?
    A) -.78
    B) 0.0
    C) +.89
    D) 52
    E) 1.13

Correct: B   Page: 123 Scramble Range: ALL
13. Which of the following is the weakest correlation?
    A) +.74
    B) +.17
    C) -.25
    D) -.58
    E) -.92

Correct: D   Page: 123 Scramble Range: ALL
14. Which of the following is a correlation that would indicate strongly that the more frequently students attend class, the higher their exam scores are?
    A) -92
    B) +87.4
    C) -78
    D) +.76
    E) 91/56

Correct: C   Page: 124 Scramble Range: ALL
15. When we select relatively few members of a population, find out about them, and assume that the results apply to the entire population, the procedure is called
A) conjecturing.
B) randomizing.
C) sampling.
D) subdividing.
E) hypothesizing.

Correct: A   Page: 125 Scramble Range: ALL
16. A sample based on 1,500 cases is more accurate than one based on 1,000 cases but
A) is less accurate than one based on 2,000 cases.
B) is more reliable than one based on 2,000 cases.
C) is likelier to contain deviant cases that will introduce error.
D) such large samples are almost impossible to use for testing hypotheses.
E) there are more severe ethical problems in using such large samples.

Correct: C   Page: 125 Scramble Range: ALL
17. Which of the following is needed in order to select a simple random sample?
A) A population that is literate and can answer written questions
B) A research design that approximates an experiment
C) A complete list of the population
D) A very small sample size
E) A questionnaire of no more than 1-3 pages

Correct: E   Page: 125 Scramble Range: ALL
18. Sociologists can be sure of getting information about specific groups (Italians, Irish, Puerto Ricans; urbanites, suburbanites, etc.) by using which of the following research methods?
A) Quasi-experimental research methods
B) Experimental research methods
C) Objective discrimination
D) Sample trait analysis
E) Stratified random samples

Correct: D   Page: 125 Scramble Range: ALL
19. Which of the following represents a technique frequently used by sociologists to draw samples?
A) Holographic selection
B) Automatic selection
C) Erasure of dwelling units
D) Use of census tracts
E) Imaging samples with each other

20. According to the text, which of the following have been of great research value to sociologists?
   A) Average citizens who spontaneously come forward to offer their views
   B) Tertiary analysis of exotic sources of data, such as sampling short-wave radio broadcasts
   C) Large commercial polling companies, such as the Gallup Poll
   D) Sociological studies of abnormal psychological functioning
   E) Asking governmental agencies to initiate, conduct, and draw conclusions about human behavior

Chapter 5: Biology, Culture, and Society

True/False

Correct: T   Page: 131
1.   Human infants are born with the ability to imitate facial expressions.

Correct: F   Page: 131
2.   At about 8 to 10 months of age, human infants acquire the ability to imitate facial expressions.

Correct: T   Page: 132
3.   Humans receive the same number of chromosomes from their mothers and from their fathers.

Correct: T   Page: 132
4.   When you look at the person sitting next to you, you see his or her phenotype.

Correct: F   Page: 134
5.   Identical twins are caused when two ova are fertilized by the same sperm.

Correct: F   Page: 134
6.   Despite the name, identical twins have subtle genetic physical differences.

Correct: F   Page: 137
7.   People today are bigger than people were 100 years ago and therefore take longer to finish growing.

Correct: T   Page: 136
8.   Football and basketball players are bigger today than they were 50 years ago because more people take part in athletics than before, so there are more people from which to select players.

Correct: T   Page: 136
9.   Football and basketball players are bigger today than they were 50 years ago because the average person is much bigger today than 50 years ago.

Correct: T   Page: 138
10.   Recent changes in growth and maturation show that for most of history the human phenotype did not fulfill its genotype.

Correct: T   Page: 138
11.   Football and basketball players are bigger today than they were 50 years ago because of better diets.

Correct: F   Page: 138
12.   Hormones never influence human behavior.

Correct: T   Page: 138
13.   Hormones transmit information to various parts of the body.

Correct: T   Page: 138
14. A major problem in early studies of the behavioral effects of hormones was the small number of people studied.

Correct: T   Page: 138
15. Testosterone is a hormone.

Correct: F   Page: 138
16. Testosterone is produced by the female ovaries.

Correct: T   Page: 139
17. The higher the level of testosterone, the less likely men are to become highly educated.

Correct: F   Page: 139
18. The higher the level of testosterone, the more likely men are to obtain high status occupations.

Correct: F   Page: 140
19. The famous anthropologist and paleontologist Louis Leakey made it possible for Jane Goodall to begin her excellent research about chimpanzees. Leakey facilitated Goodall's work because he was impressed with her Ph.D. credentials and with her renown as an expert researcher.

Correct: F   Page: 143
20. Only humans have culture.

Correct: T   Page: 143
21. Goodall reported that chimpanzees kill and eat bushbucks, bushpigs, monkeys, and young baboons.

Correct: T   Page: 143
22. Humans are not unique in toolmaking or in teaching our young how to behave.

Correct: F   Page: 143
23. Goodall confirmed that chimpanzees are vegetarians and do not eat meat.

Correct: F   Page: 143
24. Goodall confirmed that only human animals commit murder.

Correct: T   Page: 143
25. Goodall saw chimpanzees make and use tools.

Correct: F   Page: 144
26. Among apes, sexual behavior is instinctual.

Correct: T   Page: 144
27. Toolmaking has been observed among animals other than humans.

Correct: F   Page: 144
28. Only humans have technology.

Correct: T   Page: 144
29.   In their study of monkeys, the Harlows found that monkeys must grow up in a monkey society or they will always be abnormal.

Correct: F   Page: 145
30.   One reason nonhuman animals have no culture is their lack of efficient communication.

Correct: T   Page: 145
31.   One reason why nonhuman animals cannot develop more elaborate cultures is the lack of efficient communication.

Correct: T   Page: 145
32.   In their study of monkeys, the Harlows found that the effects of infant isolation are permanent.

Correct: F   Page: 145
33.   Only humans can learn a language.

Correct: T   Page: 146
34.   Chimps are physically incapable of "speech" as we ordinarily use the term "speech."

Correct: F   Page: 146
35.   Although chimps have been taught sign language, they do not teach their children to use sign language.

Correct: T   Page: 147
36.   In Japan, dominance among male macaques is based on how mean and successfully aggressive their mothers are.

Reference Key: STORY5.1
Here are the world records in the 100-meter freestyle swim from 1905 to 1993 for men and women:

	Men	Women
1905	65.8	95.0
1924	57.4	72.2
1956	55.4	64.0
1976	49.44	55.65
1993	48.42	54.48

Correct: T   Page: Ch3   Refer to: STORY5.1
37.   The dependent variable here is the world records.
                        NOTE: Cumulative question.

Correct: F   Page: Ch3   Refer to: STORY5.1
38.   The dependent variable here is sex.
                        NOTE: Cumulative question

Correct: F   Page: 133   Refer to: STORY5.1
39.   This shows a change in genotype since 1905.

Correct: F   Page: 133   Refer to: STORY5.1
40.   This shows there has been a dramatic change in genotype, especially among women.

Correct: T   Page: 133   Refer to: STORY5.1
41.   This shows a change in phenotype since 1905.

Correct: T   Page: 136   Refer to: STORY5.1
42.   These changes are partly due to both men and women becoming larger and stronger.

Correct: T   Page: 136   Refer to: STORY5.1
43.   These changes are partly due to the increase in public education--the increase in the number of people going to high school and college.

Correct: F   Page: 133   Refer to: STORY5.1
44.   These changes reflect a genetic shift in the population created by intermarriage.

Correct: T   Page: 136   Refer to: STORY5.1
45.   In large part, these records have changed because of changes in nutrition.

Correct: F   Page: 136   Refer to: STORY5.1
46.   These improved records have been linked to changes in testosterone, particularly in the male population.

Reference Key: SHOW5.1
The percentage of Afro-American infants born with a low birth weight is much higher (12.4% in 1984) than the percentage of white infants with a low birth weight (5.6%).

Correct: F   Page: 133   Refer to: SHOW5.1
47.   This difference reflects differences in genotype.

Correct: T   Page: Ch3   Refer to: SHOW5.1
48.   In this research, life expectancy is a variable.
NOTE: Cumulative question.

Correct: T   Page: Show5.1   Refer to: SHOW5.1
49.   This difference reflects differences in nutrition of both mothers and THEIR mothers.
NOTE: ShowCase question.

Correct: T   Page: Show5.1   Refer to: SHOW5.1
50.   This difference illustrates how nutrition can be a mechanism in reproducing poverty across generations.
NOTE: ShowCase question.

Correct: T   Page: Show5.1   Refer to: SHOW5.1
51.   This difference illustrates the importance of examining both genetic and environmental influences on biology.
NOTE: ShowCase question.

Correct: T   Page: Show5.1   Refer to: SHOW5.1
52.   This difference may be seen as a consequence of the culture of the United States--a culture of racial prejudice.
NOTE: ShowCase question.

Reference Key: SHOW5.2
In class we found that a correlation of -.77 between the percentage of the population of a state that is Afro-American and the male life expectancy in the state.

Correct: F   Page: Ch3   Refer to: SHOW5.2
53.   The dependent variable here is race.
NOTE: Cumulative question.

Correct: T   Page: Ch4   Refer to: SHOW5.2
54.   In this research, percent Afro-American is a social structure.
NOTE: Cumulative question.

Correct: F   Page: Topic1   Refer to: SHOW5.2
55.   This means that percent Afro-American and male life expectancy are not related.
NOTE: Cumulative question.

Correct: F   Page: Topic1   Refer to: SHOW5.2
56.   This means that states with a higher proportion of Afro-Americans also have a higher proportion of people who live longer.
NOTE: Cumulative question.

Correct: F   Page: 133   Refer to: SHOW5.2
57.   This shows the influence of genotype on life expectancy.

Multiple Choice

Correct: B   Page: 129 Scramble Range: A-E
58.   Complex behavior that occurs in all members of a species and is not learned is called
   A)   a drive.
   B)   an instinct.
   C)   a biological determinant.
   D)   a phenotype.
   E)   a genotype.
   F)   all of these

Correct: C   Page: 129 Scramble Range: ALL
59. Pelicans in a California bay were fed by tourists for several generations of pelicans. When the area was turned into a wildlife preserve, the tourists no longer came to the bay. But the pelicans no longer were able to obtain fish by their own efforts. It was as if they had "forgotten" how to do it. Pelicans from other bays were introduced, and diving/catching once again became part of the pelicans' repertoire of behavior. This illustrates
A) that human beings are the only animals with culture.
B) that animals such as pelicans have sophisticated brains, but their brains are not very retentive.
C) that catching fish was not instinctive among these pelicans.
D) that catching fish was not as functional as being hand-fed by tourists, so the dysfunctional instincts disappeared from the pelicans' repertoire of behavior.
E) that proper natural diet is crucial to the development and behavior of pelicans as well as that of people.

Correct: B   Page: 129 Scramble Range: ALL
60. Max, a full-bred boxer, was the only puppy born to a dog that died during the pup's birth. Raised with humans and without any contact with any other boxer dogs, the pup grew to maturity and was a satisfactory family pet. The owner of a female boxer wanted to mate his dog with Max, but there was concern about Max's response. When the two were introduced, Max did what was necessary to impregnate the female dog, even though he had never seen another dog in his life. This can be used to illustrate
A) the importance of "drives" in determining behavior.
B) the importance of "instincts" in determining behavior.
C) the ability of some female canines to teach complex behaviors in a short period of time.
D) the necessity of having excellent vets to facilitate reproductive behavior.
E) that Max must have come into contact with some other dogs at some other time, or he would not have known what to do.

Correct: D   Page: 129-32 Scramble Range: ALL
61. An examination of the history of the social scientific explanation of the relationship among biology, culture, and society indicates that at the beginning of this century, _____ explanations were dominant and then, beginning around 1930, _____ explanations were most accepted for differences in human behavior.
A) sociological; psychological
B) biochemical; instinctual
C) environmental; instinctual
D) instinctual; environmental
E) nurture; nature

62.   Most sociologists believe that
A)   humans have eighteen instincts.
B)   all human behavior is determined by environmental, not biological, factors.
C)   humans have three instincts: motherhood, sex, and survival.
D)   human behavior in preliterate societies is instinctual.
E)   humans don't have instincts, with the possible exceptions of sucking and imitation of facial expressions.

63.   Current sociological thinking asserts that
A)   almost all complex human behavior is influenced by learning.
B)   it is useless to consider biological influences on human behavior.
C)   people have eighteen instincts at birth, but society teaches us to control them.
D)   everything people do is entirely the product of cultural and social influences.
E)   human nature is essentially plastic and can be molded by culture into any form.

64.   Current sociological thinking asserts that
A)   human behavior results from the interplay of heredity and culture.
B)   it is useless to consider biological influences on human behavior.
C)   people have eighteen instincts at birth, but society teaches us to control them.
D)   everything people do is entirely the product of cultural and social influences.
E)   society works because it "fits" the instincts humans naturally have.

65.   Of the following, the best description of phenotype is
A)   the type of genetic coding that produces similarities in twins.
B)   the organism that we see after genetic inheritance has been acted on by environment.
C)   the nongenetic environment.
D)   a "test" to determine whether or not the genetic inheritance is normal or abnormal.
E)   that which is found in monozygotic twins after the zygote splits.

66.   Human behavior is based on choice, but what we choose to do is influenced by
A)   what our friends want us to do.
B)   what instincts compel us to do.
C)   what nonempirical factors indicate we should do.
D)   what our phenotype indicates we should do.
E)   all of these
NOTE: cumulative question.

Correct: D   Page: 133 Scramble Range: ALL
67.   The _____ can be seen as the genetically inherited potential a person has to develop or to become.
A) genetic stream
B) phenotype
C) archetype
D) genotype
E) genoteric

Correct: D   Page: 133 Scramble Range: ALL
68.   When a human infant is undernourished and deprived of social interaction, that person grows up to be something less than the existing inherited genetic potential. Another way of putting it is to say that in such a case
A) the individual did not live up to the racial phenotype.
B) the genes were altered because of adverse circumstances.
C) the chromosomes were altered because of adverse circumstances.
D) the phenotype did not fulfill the genotype's potential.
E) the genotype and phenotype are both relatively latent, awaiting further "instructions" from the environment.

Correct: C   Page: 134 Scramble Range: A-E
69.   Behavioral geneticists
A) have proven that mental illness is entirely due to environmental factors.
B) think that genotypes play no important role in explaining human behavior.
C) believe that tendencies toward schizophrenia and alcoholism have a biological base.
D) have abandoned twin studies in their attempts to measure the relative strength of biological and social factors.
E) have shown that culture is an insignificant influence on personality.
F) all of these

Correct: A   Page: 134 Scramble Range: ALL
70.   Mental illness and alcoholism show that human characteristics and behavior
A) are influenced to a substantial degree by genetic inheritance.
B) are still almost completely a mystery in terms of understanding the "causes" underlying these behaviors.
C) have as much impact on the genotype as the phenotype has on these behaviors.
D) are more subject to the mentalistic control by the individual than to the so-called forces of nature.
E) are all influenced more by personality characteristics than by either biology or the biochemistry of the brain.

Correct: B   Page: 133 Scramble Range: ALL
71. Let us imagine for purposes of this question that some people can recognize a musical note for what it is and name it without ever having been taught the scale or music theory. That is, some people have what is called "perfect pitch." They know it without having to be taught. Now, if identical twins are born and one has perfect pitch and becomes a concert musician while the other doesn't even LIKE music, this would be persuasive evidence of
A) the influence of heredity on producing results in human beings.
B) the impact of the environment on hereditary characteristics.
C) the impact of heredity on the environment of musical economics.
D) the imperfect ability of music critics to distinguish musical talent from the lack of musical talent.
E) the fact that even the cases of identical twins are not sufficient proof that identical twins are GENETICALLY identical.

Correct: A   Page: 134 Scramble Range: ALL
72. Identical twins
A) ARE genetic duplicates.
B) are ALMOST genetic duplicates.
C) have the POTENTIAL to be genetic duplicates.
D) WERE genetic duplicates before being acted on by groups and society, but now are no longer genetic duplicates.
E) can be monoclonal duplicates but can NEVER be biclonal duplicates, as normal infants can be.

Correct: D   Page: 135 Scramble Range: ALL
73. The currently accepted point of view in social science regarding the "nature vs. nurture" (or heredity vs. environment) controversy is that human behavior is
A) almost entirely determined by biological/genetic inheritance.
B) almost entirely determined by social or cultural conditioning.
C) best explained by the environmental suppressor perspective.
D) best explained on the basis of interplay between heredity and environment.
E) largely the result of society being made to "fit" the instincts humans have.

Correct: C   Page: 135 Scramble Range: ALL
74. Researchers recently have discovered that a gene located on chromosome 11 seems to cause depressive disorders among the Old Order Amish of Pennsylvania. The text cites this research to affirm that
A) most mental illnesses have biological--not developmental--origins.
B) some courtship and marriage institutions have negative consequences.
C) biological as well as social factors have developmental consequences.
D) intense involvement in religion can have negative biological consequences.
E) religion is not an antidote to depressive illness.

75. Which of the following has NOT been found and is NOT supported by evidence in your text?
    A) Sports stars have become bigger as the years have gone by.
    B) People in the general public are growing larger than before.
    C) People in the general public are growing faster than before.
    D) People mature at an earlier age and finish growing earlier.
    E) People are becoming intellectually brighter at earlier and earlier ages.

Correct: D   Page: 136 Scramble Range: ALL
76. Which of the following is a FALSE explanation of why football and basketball players are bigger today than they were 50 years ago?
    A) There are more people playing these sports to select from.
    B) A larger percentage of the population plays these sports than before.
    C) The average person is much bigger today than 50 years ago.
    D) There have been changes in human genotypes.
    E) Players today have better diets and/or nutrition.

Correct: E   Page: 136 Scramble Range: ALL
77. The text includes a picture of the University of Washington basketball team of 1929. The reason for including the photograph was to show that this particular basketball team
    A) was composed without exception of players who were Caucasians.
    B) included several women, but it went unnoticed because women's liberation was not a well-known social movement at the time.
    C) included not a single Caucasian, since two-thirds of the team claimed Native American ancestry, and the remainder were Afro-Americans.
    D) was very relaxed about playing basketball, considering it more of a gentleman's/gentlewoman's sport than a competitive, dog-eat-dog event.
    E) was composed of very short men who probably would not be able to hold their own in basketball competitions today.

Correct: A   Page: 137 Scramble Range: A-E
78. People today are larger than their ancestors
    A) and are reaching their full size at younger ages.
    B) because our ancestors did not eat as many starches.
    C) because of changes in the human genotype.
    D) because the age at puberty has risen.
    E) because they have different genetic potential.
    F) none of these

Correct: C   Page: 137 Scramble Range: ALL
79. Which of the following is the best explanation of "environmental suppressor"?
    A) Something in the environment changes forever the genetic pool of a species
    B) The presence of a species eventually has a negative effect on the environment
    C) The genetic potential to develop is lessened by something in the environment
    D) The environment changes the genetic code of one individual animal but not that of the animal's entire species
    E) An animal (usually man) keeps the environment from being in its natural state

Correct: E   Page: 137 Scramble Range: ALL

80. In the last several hundred years, there have been rapid changes in human physiology: height and speed, for example. Which of the following areas explains the occurrence of rapid changes in height and speed?
A) Changing quality of the land mass to support human populations
B) Improved medical advances in terms of improving human fertility
C) Changes in the geostructure of the earth itself
D) Later and later maturation, so that performance necessarily increased
E) The reduction and/or elimination of environmental suppressors on the human genotype

Correct: C   Page: 137 Scramble Range: ALL

81. During the fifteenth through the nineteenth century (and probably earlier), it was hardly surprising that human development was
A) spurred mainly by cross-national or cross-cultural conflicts.
B) spurred mainly by genetically acquired differences in ability levels.
C) stunted and that maturation was delayed for a long time.
D) accelerated, with maturation occurring earlier than it does in modern times.
E) accelerated, with maturation occurring earlier among those who had the most difficult, dirtiest, and hardest work to do.

Correct: E   Page: 137 Scramble Range: ALL

82. The larger picture seems clear: there has been a dramatic shift in _____ in modern times, according to your text's discussion of biology, culture, and society.
A) the remarriage rate
B) the middle-aged mortality rate
C) the impact that biology has on culture
D) the independence ratio
E) the human phenotype

Correct: B   Page: 138 Scramble Range: A-D

83. Testosterone is
A) produced by the female ovaries.
B) found in both men and women.
C) only found in men.
D) only found in women.

Correct: C   Page: 139 Scramble Range: A-D

84. Testosterone
A) levels tend to be higher in men who obtain higher status occupations.
B) is found only in men.
C) is a hormone.
D) level appears to be positively related to increased likelihood of higher education.
E) all of these

85.   Recent research on hormones and behavior suggests that
      A)   biology rarely, if ever, affects behavior.
      B)   the relationship is spurious when controlled for family background.
      C)   men with high testosterone levels are less likely to be employed in high
           status occupations.
      D)   women with high testosterone levels are more likely to be unemployed.

86.   Recent research on the relation between hormones and behavior
      A)   was based on a study of Viet Nam veterans.
      B)   has found little or no relation between biological processes and behavior.
      C)   reveals that testosterone is found only in men.
      D)   none of these

87.   According to the text, a tool is an object that is
      A)   used to achieve group, not individual, goals.
      B)   found in the natural world, suits a particular purpose, and is used toward
           that end.
      C)   modified to suit a particular purpose.
      D)   constructed by a group, not by an individual, to achieve social goals.
      E)   none of these

88.   According to your text,
      A)   a great deal of monkey behavior is learned.
      B)   mating is instinctual in monkeys and apes, but not in people.
      C)   monkeys do not have culturally patterned ways of doing things.
      D)   mating is instinctual in all primates--monkeys, apes, and humans.
      E)   all monkey behavior is instinctual.

89.   Goodall saw chimpanzees throw rocks and use sticks as clubbing weapons.
      The significance of this is that it affirms the existence of _____ among
      chimpanzees.
      A)   the protective instinct
      B)   the aggressive instinct
      C)   stable territoriality
      D)   tool use
      E)   treaty breaking

90.   Chimps
      A)   do not have culture because they do not manufacture tools.
      B)   do not have culture because they do not use tools.
      C)   make tools but do not pass them on from generation to generation.
      D)   make, use, and share crude tools.
      E)   share objects found in nature but do not make tools.

91. Which of the following can be given as evidence that some nonhuman animals do have some "culture" (as culture is defined in the text)?
    A) Toolmaking
    B) Child-rearing behaviors
    C) A built-in desire to please others
    D) The ability to invent drawn symbols on their own initiative
    E) The ability to become "normal" animals even when raised in isolation

92. Sexual behavior
    A) is mostly learned in Biology 101.
    B) is instinctual only in apes.
    C) is instinctual only in human beings.
    D) is mostly learned in Introduction to Sociology.
    E) none of these

93. The behavioral deficits of young monkeys studied by the Harlows
    A) were capable of being transmitted to "normal" monkeys in monkey troops.
    B) could, without exception, be reversed if the monkeys were raised by humans.
    C) could be reversed with almost constant human companionship, except for sex.
    D) include some deficits that seem irreversible.
    E) apparently seeped into the gene pool, since they were transmitted to the young of these monkeys when they reproduced.

94. According to the Harlows' studies of monkeys, monkeys must _____ or they will fail to become normal monkeys.
    A) have a diet that is picked for them by their biological mothers
    B) also have contact with animals other than monkeys
    C) have a diet containing "natural" L-dopa from fruits and vegetables
    D) experience the political structure of monkey society, even if they experience it at the hands of humans
    E) be exposed to monkey society from an early age

95. The Harlows' experiments
    A) studied children in orphanages as compared to children who received a lot of personal attention.
    B) found that monkeys raised in isolation with their mothers were more normal than those raised in total isolation or those raised with peers but without adults.
    C) showed that monkeys must be raised in monkey society if they are to be fully normal.
    D) demonstrated that the effects of early isolation on monkeys are completely reversible.
    E) proved that the primary tie between infants and their mothers is connected with nursing rather than cuddling.

Correct: C   Page: 145 Scramble Range: ALL
96.   According to your text, _____ is without doubt the human trait most responsible for our great "superiority" when compared with other animals.
A) a complex political structure
B) human pair-bonding
C) language
D) prolonged infant dependency
E) toolmaking

Correct: A   Page: 145 Scramble Range: ALL
97.   There have been several attempts to teach chimpanzees to speak human words. The text summarizes two such efforts. The result of the efforts was that
A) the chimps learned from 0-4 sounds approximating English words.
B) the chimps learned about 23-25 words from math and none from other areas.
C) the chimps found English impossible to learn but did learn 25-30 Spanish words beginning with the letters "M" and "B."
D) the chimps could not learn any English words but were able to learn 10-15 words in the African language called Mabibwalese.
E) the chimps were able to learn only those words requiring very little intelligence, and even these dozen or so words were food- or comfort-related.

Correct: D   Page: 145 Scramble Range: ALL
98.   Speaking is _____ for chimpanzees because _____.
A) impossible; they lack a sufficiently complex brain
B) difficult; their neurological structure is mainly "visual"
C) relatively easy; they are like humans in so many ways
D) impossible; they lack the necessary vocal apparatus
E) unnecessary; they are "intuitive," not "instrumental"

Correct: B   Page: 145 Scramble Range: ALL
99.   Which of the following is TRUE?
A) Only humans are intelligent enough to learn language.
B) Speaking is nearly impossible for chimps because their vocal chords are not complex enough to produce speech.
C) Chimps are unable to use sign language because their hands are not able to form the necessary shapes.
D) Chimps do not pass on their language skills to their young.
E) Chimps imitate sign language but do not seem to attach any meaning to the signs.

Correct: A   Page: 146 Scramble Range: ALL

100.   Which of the following regarding the text's discussion of the chimpanzee Washoe is FALSE?
   A) Washoe could use sign language to communicate, but she could not transmit the use of these signs to other chimps.
   B) Washoe was able to use 160 signs by the time she was 5 years old.
   C) Washoe was able to teach some sign language to her "adopted" infant, Loulis.
   D) Washoe invented an appropriate "bad word" to use for what she didn't like.
   E) Washoe and several other chimpanzees apparently were able to make use of a relatively simple kind of culture.

Correct: E   Page: 147 Scramble Range: ALL

101.   A comparison of macaques in Japan and in Oregon produced some stimulating ideas about the possibility of macaque culture based on the fact that, unlike macaques in Oregon, the Japanese male macaques proved their dominance on the basis of
   A) sheer ability to put on a show of ferocity, even when they were not ferocious.
   B) ability to win battles of ferocious strength, with no bluffing attempted.
   C) the volume of peanuts and popcorn they were able to beg from passersby.
   D) ability to thrust up their hindquarters higher than the other macaques.
   E) the size and ferocity of their mothers.

Chapter 6: Socialization and Social Roles

True/False

Correct: F   Page: 151
1. There have been some authenticated cases of human children who have been raised in the wild by animals.

Correct: F   Page: 154
2. The stimulus-response (S-R) theory of learning recognizes that much behavior is based on general rules learned by the individual.

Correct: T   Page: 154
3. The stimulus-response (S-R) theory of learning treats all behavior as a response to external stimuli.

Correct: T   Page: 156
4. During the preoperational stage, children cannot take the role of the other.

Correct: T   Page: 156
5. Many adults fail to reach the formal operational stage of development.

Correct: T   Page: 157
6. Young children use a stripped-down version of language.

Correct: T   Page: 157
7. Children often speak sentences that they are very unlikely to have learned from someone else.

Correct: T   Page: 162
8. According to the cultural determinists, human nature is so flexible that culture can shape it into unlimited forms.

Correct: F   Page: 162
9. According to the cultural determinists, only a limited number of cultural forms are possible.

Correct: F   Page: 162
10. According to the cultural determinists, culture is determined primarily by the interaction of human biology with the physical environment.

Correct: F   Page: 164
11. Despite being headhunters and cannibals, the Mundugumor were very gentle with their children.

Correct: T   Page: 165
12. Your text concludes that the cultural determinists are excessive in saying that culture is the only thing that matters.

Correct: F   Page: 165
13. Your text strongly embraces a cultural determinist view.

Correct: F   Page: 165
14. Examination of the effects of external forces, such as external threats, tends to confirm the views of the cultural determinists.

Correct: F   Page: 168
15. In his research on differential socialization, Melvin Kohn found that middle-class parents stressed obedience more than self-expression.

Correct: F   Page: 168
16. In his research on differential socialization, Kohn found that working-class parents stressed happiness.

Correct: T   Page: 168
17. In his research on differential socialization, Kohn found that working-class parents made discipline the father's responsibility.

Correct: T   Page: 168
18. In his research on differential socialization, Kohn found that working-class mothers tended to be the supportive parent.

Correct: F   Page: 169
19. In his research on differential socialization, Kohn found that.class, not working conditions, was the real cause of differential socialization.

Correct: T   Page: 169
20. In his research on differential socialization, Kohn found that parents in either class raised their children on the basis of their own work experiences.

Correct: F   Page: 169
21. In his research on differential socialization, Kohn found that men's personalities no longer changed in response to occupational changes after the age of 50.

Correct: T   Page: 170
22. Role performance is how people in a role actually behave.

Correct: F   Page: 170
23. Role performance refers to how people in a role are supposed to behave.

Correct: T   Page: 173
24. Differential socialization refers to teaching different children to act differently when parents (and others) expect they will need to act differently as adults.

Correct: T   Page: 173
25. If women are responsible for the hunting in a society and men are responsible for child care, we expect that women and men will be differentially socialized.

Correct: T   Page: 173
26. It is rare for women to have equal political rights in small, non-technological societies.

Correct: F   Page: 173
27.   There is little variation among small, non-technological societies in the political rights they accord to women.

Correct: T   Page: 173
28.   Differences in gender roles among small, non-technological societies reveals that most differences between the sexes in most societies are cultural rather than biological.

Correct: F   Page: 173
29.   Most people in modern societies believe that women need to have children in order to be fulfilled.

Correct: T   Page: 173
30.   In most modern societies the majority of men believe that women do NOT need to have children in order to be fulfilled.

Correct: F   Page: 175
31.   DeLoache, Cassidy, and Carpenter's work confirms that gender-neutral books significantly reduce perceptions that gender-neutral characters are males.

Correct: F   Page: 175
32.   DeLoache, Cassidy, and Carpenter found that gender-neutral teacher characters in children's books were likelier to be identified as male teachers.

Reference Key: STORY6.1
As discussed in the text, DeLoache, Cassidy, and Carpenter observed mothers reading to small children. They found that the mothers referred to gender-neutral characters as male.

Correct: F   Page: Ch2   Refer to: STORY6.1
33.   The dependent variable in this research was the gender of the child.
                    NOTE: Cumulative question.

Correct: F   Page: 175   Refer to: STORY6.1
34.   "Gender-neutral," in this research, only meant that the characters didn't have obviously male or female names.

Correct: T   Page: ResProc   Refer to: STORY6.1
35.   "Gender-neutral," in the research, is a concept.
                    NOTE: Cumulative question.

Correct: T   Page: 175   Refer to: STORY6.1
36.   The researchers found that the characters were generally referred to as male even when they were engaged in stereotypical female activities.

Correct: T   Page: Ch3   Refer to: STORY6.1
37.   This is a good example of micro sociology.
                    NOTE: Cumulative question.

Correct: F   Page: Ch4   Refer to: STORY6.1
38.   This is a good example of macro sociology.
                    NOTE: Cumulative question.

Correct: T   Page: 175   Refer to: STORY6.1
39.   One implication of this research is that the world as generally presented to children by their parents is dominated by men.

Correct: T   Page: 175   Refer to: STORY6.1
40.   It is reasonable to suggest that this research shows us some of the mechanisms that lead to boys seeing themselves more favorably than girls, as found by Juhasz.

Correct: F   Page: 169   Refer to: STORY6.1
41.   This research illustrates what Kohn found regarding differential socialization and occupational roles.

Reference Key: STORY6.2
Margaret Mead argued that stressing toughness in boy children causes a higher incidence of war. The following table uses cross-cultural data from more than 300 small, premodern, non-technilogical societies to test Mead's ideas. Those societies which did not stress toughness are coded as "low" and those which stress toughness are coded as "high." We find:

	Tough Boys	
Extent of War:	Low	High
Less often	68%	31%
More often	32%	69%
	----	----
	100%	100%

Correct: T   Page: Ch3   Refer to: STORY6.2
42.   For Mead, the dependent variable here is war.
NOTE: Cumulative question.

Correct: F   Page: Ch4   Refer to: STORY6.2
43.   This shows that tough boys and war are not related.
NOTE: Cumulative question.

Correct: T   Page: ResProc   Refer to: STORY6.2
44.   Mead's argument is a theory.
NOTE: Cumulative question.

Correct: T   Page: Ch3   Refer to: STORY6.2
45.   In this research, there is good reason to doubt causal order.
NOTE: Cumulative question.

Correct: T   Page: ResProc   Refer to: STORY6.2
46.   In this research, war is a concept.
NOTE: Cumulative question.

Correct: F   Page: Ch4   Refer to: STORY6.2
47.   This proves that raising tough boys causes more wars.
NOTE: Cumulative question.

Correct: F   Page: Ch4   Refer to: STORY6.2
48.   This is an example of micro sociology.
                    NOTE: Cumulative question.

Correct: F   Page: Ch1
49.   The unit of analysis in this research is individual.
                    NOTE: Cumulative question.

Correct: T   Page: 162   Refer to: STORY6.2
50.   This finding is consistent with the ideas of cultural determinism.

Correct: T   Page: Ch3   Refer to: STORY6.2
51.   In this research, it could make sense to reverse the independent and
      dependent variables.
                    NOTE: Cumulative question.

Correct: F   Page: 168   Refer to: STORY6.2
52.   Applying Kohn's research on differential socialization to these data lends
      support to Mead's argument.

Correct: T   Page: 168   Refer to: STORY6.2
53.   Kohn's research on differential socialization would lead us to suggest that war,
      or the threat of war, is the independent variable.

Correct: T   Page: 161   Refer to: STORY6.2
54.   Harris and other critics of cultural determinism argue that the threat of
      external wars pushes societies to emphasize toughness in raising boys.

Reference Key: STORY6.3
Stark and Hirschi (Chapter 4 of your text) found that boys who are very religious still
sometimes engage in delinquent behavior.

Correct: F   Page: Ch1   Refer to: STORY6.3
55.   This suggests that people don't have free will.
                    Note: Cumulative question.

Correct: T   Page: 170   Refer to: STORY6.3
56.   This illustrates the difference between learning roles and role performance.

Correct: F   Page: 168   Refer to: STORY6.3
57.   This illustrates Kohn's findings about differential socialization.

Correct: F   Page: 162   Refer to: STORY6.3
58.   This suggests that Mead and the cultural determinists should have paid more
      attention to religion.

Correct: T   Page: ResProc   Refer to: STORY6.3
59.   In this study, "deliquent behavior" is a concept.
                    Note: Cumulative question.

Reference Key: STORY6.4
Here are the world records in the 100-meter freestyle swim from 1905 to 1993 for men and women and the percent difference between the men's and women's records:

	Men	Women	Difference
1905	65.8	95.0	44.4%
1924	57.4	72.2	25.8%
1956	55.4	64.0	15.5%
1976	49.44	55.65	12.6%
1993	48.42	54.48	12.5%

Correct: T   Page: Ch3   Refer to: STORY6.4
60.   The dependent variable here is the world records.
NOTE: Cumulative question.

Correct: F   Page: Ch3   Refer to: STORY6.4
61.   The dependent variable here is sex.
NOTE: Cumulative question

Correct: F   Page: Ch5   Refer to: STORY6.4
62.   This shows there has been a dramatic change in genotype, especially among women.
NOTE: Cumulative question

Correct: F   Page: Ch5   Refer to: STORY6.4
63.   This shows that genotype is more important than phenotype.
NOTE: Cumulative question

Correct: T   Page: Ch5   Refer to: STORY6.4
64.   This table demonstrates the importance of both genotype and phenotype.
NOTE: Cumulative question

Correct: F   Refer to: STORY6.4
65.   The difference between the men's and women's scores has remained fairly constant.

Correct: F   Page: Ch5   Refer to: STORY6.4
66.   The difference between men's and women's scores is a result of changes in the phenotype -- removal of environmental suppressors on human development.
NOTE: Cumulative question

Correct: T   Refer to: STORY6.4
67.   It is reasonable to suggest than changes in roles, such as changes in acceptable swimwear, have affected these records.

Correct: T   Refer to: STORY6.4
68.   It is reasonable to suggest an increased proportion of women who are enrolled in high school and college has affected the differences between men's and women's records.

Correct: T   Page: 168   Refer to: STORY6.4
69. Research on differential socialization might help understand the changing relationship between men's and women's roles.

Correct: T   Page: Ch5   Refer to: STORY6.4
70. This research illustrates the difficulty in discerning the effects of genotype on human behavior.

NOTE: Cumulative question

Multiple Choice

Correct: B   Page: 151 Scramble Range: ALL
71. Feral children
   A) are successfully raised by mother foxes and dogs.
   B) have often been severely neglected.
   C) are children whose instincts have never been socialized out of them.
   D) are raised successfully by chimpanzees and gorillas.
   E) are children who have been raised by retarded parents.

Correct: D   Page: 152 Scramble Range: ALL
72. According to sociologists, socialization
   A) means going out with friends.
   B) is the biological process of growing up.
   C) begins at birth and ends in the early twenties, when personality becomes stabilized.
   D) involves learning and internalizing one's culture.
   E) will occur without the presence of other humans.

Correct: D   Page: 152 Scramble Range: ALL
73. The learning process by which infants become normal human beings who possess culture and who are able to participate in social relations is
   A) acculturation.
   B) operationalization.
   C) differential association.
   D) socialization.
   E) group process.

Correct: A   Page: 152 Scramble Range: ALL
74. The text discusses the issue of feral children to make the point that
   A) our biological heritage by itself cannot make us into adequate persons.
   B) there are only a few instances of children being raised from infancy by animals or surviving from infancy in the wild.
   C) most of us have the potential to survive in the wild from infancy, but few of us get the chance to demonstrate the ability.
   D) the feral children who have been observed after rescue have not proved to be the object of parental neglect or mistreatment.
   E) the word "feral" means self-educated or self-cultured.

Correct: A   Page: 151 Scramble Range: A-E
75. Your text suggests that feral children have experienced which of the following?
A) Extreme parental neglect
B) Extreme self-sufficiency in the wild
C) Low levels of the instinct for culture
D) Low levels of the instinct of proneness to socialization
E) High levels of instinct for survival
F) All of the above

Correct: D   Page: 151 Scramble Range: ALL
76. A feral child is one who
A) has only average or fair scores of mental and physical ability.
B) always acts as if he/she is in a private little world that resembles nothing so much as it does a carnival with the child center stage.
C) engages in behavior that emphasizes etiquette so much that s/he makes other people uncomfortable.
D) seems wild or untamed.
E) was born prematurely.

Correct: D   Page: 152 Scramble Range: ALL
77. Feral children who have a normal capacity for development teach us the lesson that
A) children who are allowed to continue to live in a fantasy world without consequences often turn into adults who behave similarly.
B) children who are only average in terms of measured performance scores can end up being far above "fair" when they become adults.
C) TAG (Talented and Gifted) and similar programs do the community little service when they set some children apart from others in tracking programs.
D) biological inheritance cannot by itself ensure normal human biosocial development.
E) people who want to get ahead in this world can, regardless of family social background, if they want to badly enough.

Correct: A   Page: 152 Scramble Range: A-E
78. Feral children who had the capacity to become adequate human beings did not do so, according to the text, because they lacked _____.
A) socialization
B) institutionalization
C) peer group pressures
D) a world outside their fantasy world
E) any idea of the importance of the long-term significance of the tests they were taking
F) all of these

Correct: D   Page: 152 Scramble Range: A-D
79. The process of immigrants assimilating into the culture of the United States, discussed in Chapter 2, is a good example of
A) ascribed status.
B) the importance of genotype in differential rates of assimilation.
C) studied nonobservance.
D) socialization.
E) all of these

Correct: C   Page: 152 Scramble Range: A-D
80. The process of learning norms is referred to as
A) phenotype.
B) gender.
C) socialization.
D) role performance.
E) none of these

Correct: E   Page: 152 Scramble Range: ALL
81. The infant daughter of a shrimp-boat family grows up wanting to be a shrimper and does become one. A Carib Indian infant grows up to be a member of the Carib society. A family in which both the mother and father are symphonic violinists has three daughters, all of whom have grown up to become symphonic violinists. What social process has been at work to help move these malleable, plastic infants who were "bundles of potential" to fit in very well with the groups of which they are members?
A) Institutionalization
B) Personalization
C) Operationalization
D) Cognitive structuring
E) Socialization

Correct: D   Page: 153 Scramble Range: ALL
82. Studies such as those by the Harlows (of infant monkeys) and by Skeels and Dye (of orphans) seem to address the question of whether or not earlier deprivation can be followed by normal development if "special treatment" is given. The study of deprived human orphans (by Skeels and Dye) suggests that the effects of early deprivation
A) can be made up for almost entirely if the special treatment is special enough.
B) cannot be made up for at all, even when the special treatment is very special.
C) are likelier to be made up in females than in males, given special treatment.
D) can be made up for, given special treatment, but not by very much.
E) can be compensated for only by parental stimulation.

Correct: B   Page: 153 Scramble Range: ALL
83. The Skeels and Dye study, which took place in an orphanage, seemed to lead to the conclusion that orphans
A) who have been deprived of BIOLOGICAL parental care and affection do not do as well when raised by ADOPTIVE parents.
B) who get some attention--even if it is from a somewhat retarded girl rather than from a parent--thrive more than do orphans without ANY such care.
C) are likelier to repay caregivers for their care than are BIOLOGICAL children by caring for their caregivers later in life when the tables are turned.
D) are never fully accepted by adoptive parents because of the fear that the orphans have some genetic fault that will eventually result in "disaster."
E) instinctively know that the adoptive parents are not the biological parents, and eventually this comes out in the form of aggression.

Correct: C   Page: 152 Scramble Range: ALL
84.   Skeels and Dye placed retarded infants from an orphanage under the personal care of mildly retarded girls. What happened?
A)   Most of the children were returned to the orphanage within the first year so they could develop more normally.
B)   Most never became self-supporting adults.
C)   Most graduated from high school, and a substantial number went on to college.
D)   The children in the control group who stayed at the orphanage improved their IQ scores. The children reared by the retarded girls showed no IQ gains.
E)   The infants reared by the retarded girls turned into feral children.

Correct: B   Page: 153 Scramble Range: A-E
85.   Since the Harlows' earlier studies of infant monkeys, there have been more recent studies of human orphans, as conducted by Skeels and Dye. These studies of orphans provide strong support for the view that
A)   orphans thrive better when raised with their own age-mates, even in an institutional setting, as long as it is a clean, healthy environment.
B)   orphans at age one-and-a-half who were deprived and understimulated seemed to improve a lot when personally cared for by an older, mildly retarded girl.
C)   human orphans can provide their own stimulation and social environment when they are neglected, unlike the infant monkeys studied by the Harlows.
D)   a human orphan at age three is much further along developmentally than is a monkey infant of the same age.
E)   social and emotional deprivation, once it has occurred, is something that is almost entirely irreversible.
F)   all of these

Correct: C   Page: 154 Scramble Range: ALL
86.   In the case of infants, the answer to whether normal development can be accelerated by special treatment seems to be
A)   that it can be considerably accelerated in girls, but not in boys.
B)   that it can with boy infants, but not with girl infants.
C)   yes, but only a little bit.
D)   that it can be accelerated a great deal, but only with very high levels of individual attention given to the infant by parents and several specialists.
E)   no, it cannot be, even when parents and specialists use a team approach to speed development in this way.

Correct: A   Page: 154 Scramble Range: A-C
87.   To stop her child from munching on the dog's food, Professor Laz punished her child with a loud "No" and praised him when he left the food alone. This is an example of
A)   stimulus-response theory.
B)   the theory of cognitive development.
C)   symbolic interactionism.
D)   all of these

Correct: D   Page: 154 Scramble Range: ALL
88. Piaget developed the theory of cognitive stages, which was in part a criticism of strict application of stimulus-response learning theory. Piaget reasoned that stimulus-response theory is inadequate to explain
    A) how human behavior can so closely copy the social environment it inhabits.
    B) the connection between biological process and psychological functioning.
    C) the connection between biological process and biochemical process.
    D) how people behave in new ways or behave in a creative manner.
    E) how people can do things like learn to drive a car and do so strictly in accordance with the motor vehicle code.

Correct: D   Page: 156 Scramble Range: ALL
89. Piaget perceived four specific developmental stages. The final or last stage was the _____ stage.
    A) concrete operational
    B) sensorimotor
    C) latent orientational
    D) formal operational
    E) objectification

Correct: D   Page: 155 Scramble Range: ALL
90. According to your text
    A) in the next twenty years, we should expect average children to be able to read at between three and four years of age.
    B) normal development can be greatly accelerated by special treatment, because human development is entirely dependent on environmental stimulation.
    C) children learn through stimulus-response reinforcement and are basically passive in the learning process.
    D) children learn rules for reasoning and approach problems in different ways according to their age and intellectual development.
    E) Piaget was important for discounting biological and psychological factors in explaining human development.

Correct: B   Page: 156 Scramble Range: ALL
91. According to Piaget
    A) children learn by repeating behaviors that are reinforced by rewards.
    B) children actively construct rules for thinking about their environment.
    C) learning occurs in two stages.
    D) stimulus-response learning theory fully explains human learning.
    E) children will develop normally if they never learn to conserve space.

Correct: B   Page: 156 Scramble Range: ALL
92. Piaget's theory of cognitive stages sees people going through various stages of cognitive development. Which of the following is NOT one of those stages?
    A) Sensorimotor
    B) Social mediation
    C) Formal operational
    D) Concrete operational

Correct: D   Page: 156 Scramble Range: ALL

93. Piaget's "rule of object permanence" is illustrated by which of the following?
    A) A soldier thinks that he won't be killed in battle and will be here tomorrow.
    B) Felicia's mother has died, but Felicia knows that her mother has gone to heaven and Felicia must now turn her attention to her children.
    C) Anita says that she will NEVER forgive her boyfriend for not letting her watch yesterday's episode of "As the World Turns."
    D) David sees his ball roll under the bushes and out of sight, but he's not concerned because he knows where it is if he wants it.
    E) Andy thinks that the characters in comic strips are real people rather than fictional characters.

Correct: D   Page: 156 Scramble Range: ALL

94. Which of Piaget's stages of cognitive development never ends?
    A) Sensorimotor
    B) Preoperational
    C) Formal operational
    D) Concrete operational

Correct: C   Page: 156 Scramble Range: A-D

95. According to Piaget's theory of cognitive development, if you can think about a sociological theory you have learned and produce a hypothesis about the relationship between two variables that follows from the theory, then you are in which of the following stages of cognitive development?
    A) Concrete operational
    B) Sensorimotor
    C) Formal operational
    D) Preoperational
    E) None of these

Correct: C   Page: 156 Scramble Range: ALL

96. Evaluating examinations in a sociology course, a student writes: "I think it should be cut and dry. Right or wrong." Which of Piaget's stages does this evaluation reflect?
    A) Sensorimotor
    B) Preoperational
    C) Concrete operational
    D) Formal operational

Correct: D   Page: 156 Scramble Range: ALL

97. In Piaget's theory of cognitive stages, which of the stages is the most "advanced" and signifies the highest stage of development?
    A) Sensorimotor
    B) Preoperational
    C) Concrete operational
    D) Formal operational

Correct: A   Page: 157 Scramble Range: ALL
98.   Brown and Bellugi conducted a case study of two children whom they called
Adam and Eve. Perhaps the most important finding of this study was that
A)   children experiment in trying to discover rules of language.
B)   children have an attraction to the use of words they don't understand.
C)   when male and female parents have different language rules, children
become seriously confused, with medical side-effects.
D)   children tend to echo parents' speech; parents do not echo children's
speech.
E)   children of Adam's and Eve's age mimic sentences they have heard, but
they do not know enough to "experiment" by making their own sentences.

Correct: A   Page: 157 Scramble Range: ALL
99.   If learning is the key to socialization, _____ is the key to learning.
A)   language
B)   vision
C)   homeostasis
D)   passive memory
E)   institutionalization

Correct: E   Page: 157 Scramble Range: ALL
100.   Perhaps the most important of Brown and Bellugi's research results was the
clear evidence that
A)   the subculture of children has a language all its own.
B)   the grammatical structure of adolescent language is unique to
adolescents.
C)   children's language reflects the many changes they are going through.
D)   children's language is more highly inferential than the language of
adults.
E)   children experiment with speech in an apparent search for grammatical
rules.

Correct: A   Page: 157 Scramble Range: ALL
101.   When Brown and Bellugi studied language acquisition, one of the things they
found was that young children's speech is
A)   stripped of all but the most vital words.
B)   frequently logically contradictory regarding adjectives.
C)   ineffective in the ability to communicate, even to those who know them
well.
D)   more elaborate when talking to brothers and sisters than when talking to
parents.
E)   more elaborated in form when the topic is relationships than when the
topic is things.

102.   Brown and Bellugi studied language acquisition. Among other things, they found that
    A)   children learn more language from children than they do from adults.
    B)   not only do children repeat what parents say, but parents also frequently echo their children.
    C)   contrary to what most thought, children do not learn language from watching television or from listening to the radio, except for educational programs.
    D)   male children have higher verbal levels than do female children.
    E)   female children learn more words than male children but cannot make sentences that are as complex as male children can make using fewer words.

103.   Brown and Bellugi found that
    A)   children repeat shortened versions of what their parents say to them.
    B)   children are not capable of inventing sentences they have never heard.
    C)   language is acquired in a period of about six months
    D)   language is acquired in seven stages.
    E)   parents who repeat and correct what their children say are less effective models than parents who merely listen to their children.

104.   In the 1970s, a number of child development theorists, such as Jerome Brunner, stressed the importance of _____ as being fundamental to children's language acquisition, but recent research has not supported this idea.
    A)   adequate restful sleep
    B)   religious assurance
    C)   attachments
    D)   privacy
    E)   a strong adult culture

105.   Over the past several years, an immense amount of research has been done to assess the importance of attachments for cognitive development and language acquisition. Social scientists have been amazed by the results. It appears that in order to develop cognitively and in terms of language, children need
    A)   intense attachments for many hours every day.
    B)   only the normal range of adult-infant attachments.
    C)   very few--almost no--adult-infant attachments to develop, as long as there are other children the same age available for interaction.
    D)   attachments and language communication from any source, and even sources such as television and radio seem sufficient.
    E)   intentional developmental efforts from adults, and informal efforts alone are not sufficient.

106. In a number of cultures, adults use a simplified and exaggerated version of their language to communicate with young children. Research on this topic reveals that if children are NOT exposed to this type of simplified language, then
   A) they seem to have difficulty learning compound, complex sentence structure.
   B) they acquire very limited ability to manage verbs, especially active verbs.
   C) they acquire language much more rapidly because of the linguistic richness.
   D) they acquire language just as rapidly as those who are exposed to it.
   E) they acquire language fairly rapidly, but they suffer a deficit in being able to do mental manipulations.

107. According to your text, which of the following makes a difference in children learning to talk sooner and better?
   A) The amount of verbal interaction with adults
   B) The style with which adults communicate to children
   C) The amount of verbal interaction with other children and/or adolescents
   D) The style with which other children and/or adolescents communicate with children
   E) Whether or not "spoken" mass media are available in the home: TV, tape cassettes of fairy tales, radio, and so on

108. It has been found that when parents speak to their young children they use a simplified, repetitive form of language that often exaggerates the aspects of a given language that children find most difficult to learn. What has this modified language been named?
   A) Motherese
   B) Proto-talk
   C) Parentobabble
   D) Meta-speech
   E) Outline communication

109. When the sociologist Reed Bain (1936) studied children's vocabulary development, he found that they
   A) specialized in action-oriented words.
   B) specialized in descriptive-oriented words.
   C) learned other-related words sooner than self-related words.
   D) learned self-related words sooner than other-related words.
   E) acquired more words and acquired them more efficiently if they had visual as well as verbal linguistic input.

Correct: C   Page: 160 Scramble Range: ALL
110.   The sociologist Reed Bain was not alone in his interest in when children acquired words to indicate others and when they acquired words to indicate self. G. H. Mead and Jean Piaget also looked into this issue. They all found evidence to support the idea that the language patterns of very young children are
A)   relatively unpatterned.
B)   matricentric.
C)   egocentric.
D)   filled with extemporality.
E)   future-oriented.

Correct: E   Page: 161 Scramble Range: ALL
111.   Favel and associates (1965) conducted research that involved having children give instructions to other children, one of whom the researchers had blindfolded. The researchers were able to demonstrate that 8-year-olds
A)   are likely to practice avoidance of those who have some handicap.
B)   form peer groups based on normality as compared to deviance.
C)   form peer groups based on ability to perform, not on the basis of worth
D)   are likely to take advantage of a handicapped person because of immaturity
E)   have difficulty understanding other people's point of view or perspective

Correct: C   Page: 161 Scramble Range: ALL
112.   No two people--even adolescents who are identical twins--have precisely the same personality, because
A)   even parents are smart enough to learn from their child-rearing mistakes.
B)   though the phenotype may respond identically to similar experiences, the genotype does not.
C)   no two people have identical biographies or personal histories.
D)   the expression of personality creates an element of distortion in terms of the difference between personality and behavior.
E)   all people have a wish to be different from other people.

Correct: C   Page: 161 Scramble Range: A-D
113.   A person's personality
A)   is completely unique.
B)   almost completely reflects their genotype.
C)   is a consistent pattern of thoughts, feelings and actions.
D)   is located in the thalamus.
E)   all of these

Correct: A   Page: 162 Scramble Range: ALL

114. Franz Boas was an early supporter of the principle of cultural determinism.
      Margaret Mead, his student, also took this point of view. Which of the
      following is NOT one of the basic ideas of cultural determinism, according to
      Franz Boas?
      A) There are clear limits to the personalities and behaviors that can be
          created by culture.
      B) Culture has its effects on people during early childhood.
      C) There is a strong link between child rearing and personality.
      D) The individual personalities of the members of a society are tiny replicas
          of their overall culture.
      E) The variety of cultural and social forms is almost infinite.

Correct: C   Page: 162 Scramble Range: ALL

115. Cultural determinism
      A) deemphasizes the influences of early childhood socialization.
      B) asserts that culture influences people most when they are adults.
      C) asserts that human personality is easily molded by the environment.
      D) is increasingly supported by social and psychological research.
      E) asserts that much learning takes place through reinforcement by peers.

Correct: B   Page: 162 Scramble Range: ALL

116. Cultural determinism
      A) asserts that human nature is rather rigid.
      B) is no longer totally supported by modern social scientists.
      C) claims that personality is a biological product and behavior is a social
          product.
      D) asserts that childhood learning is not crucial in shaping personality.
      E) says that culture and personality are in conflict with each other.

Correct: D   Page: 162 Scramble Range: ALL

117. A basic idea in the perspective called "cultural determinism" is that
      A) those cultures that survive are those with the most will to do so.
      B) the fine arts--ballet, opera, and theater--must compete with the other
          social institutions if they wish to have financial support.
      C) cultures have personalities, just as individuals do, so it is possible to
          analyze culture using Freud's ideas of id, ego, and superego.
      D) people's individual personalities are just tiny replicas of the overall
          culture in which they live.
      E) it is the personality of strong-willed individuals that decides in which
          direction culture is to change or evolve.

Correct: E   Page: 164 Scramble Range: A-D

118. Mead's examination of the Arapesh tribe in New Guinea
      A) emphasized the gentle child-rearing in which both parents played a role.
      B) tended to ignore the isolation of the tribe.
      C) seemed to assume that socialization is something that happens only to
          young children.
      D) argued that gender roles have no biological basis.
      E) all of these

Correct: B   Page: 164 Scramble Range: ALL

119. Margaret Mead's conclusions about the Arapesh and the Mundugumor are incorrect, according to your text, primarily because
   A) Mead's publisher edited some of her writings without consulting her first.
   B) she ignored the physical context of the two tribes.
   C) much of her data against her hypothesis was lost and thus was unanalyzed.
   D) there was a conspiracy of cultural determinists to feed her erroneous information and thus discredit her criticisms of them.
   E) being so fully "nativized," she could see only the Arapesh point of view.

Correct: C   Page: 164 Scramble Range: A-D

120. Societies somewhat isolated from other societies
   A) tend to emphasize warlike traits in their children--especially males.
   B) tend to prefer male infants.
   C) are less likely to be rough in raising their children.
   D) are less likely to raise women to engage in external wars.
   E) all of these

Correct: C   Page: 164 Scramble Range: ALL

121. When we examine thoughtfully the pros and cons of Boas's and Mead's views of cultural determinism, we find that most social scientists conclude that Boas and Mead were correct in coming to which of the following conclusions?
   A) In determining the nature of personality, childhood is almost the only period that matters.
   B) It is possible for people to develop virtually any cultural and personality pattern.
   C) Culture is extremely important in shaping humans' personalities
   D) Inborn personality facts seem to outweigh social influences in terms of producing personality and behavior.
   E) There are important racial differences that can never be erased or significantly influenced, such as differences in creativity and IQ.

Correct: A   Page: 164 Scramble Range: A-D

122. Your text's criticism of cultural determinism emphasizes
   A) that socialization is a lifelong process.
   B) that Margaret Mead's observations were confined to a single island.
   C) that there is little evidence of differential socialization in Samoa.
   D) that warlike personalities reflect genetic differences among groups.
   E) all of these

Correct: C   Page: 166 Scramble Range: ALL
123. Which of the following is an example of "differential socialization"?
   A) Two sections of the same course use a different text for the course, even though both sections of the course are taught by the same professor.
   B) A professor is not willing to go out to dinner with other professors but does go out to dinner frequently with her family.
   C) A professor treats his male students differently from his female students when it comes to encouraging them to consider a career in sociology.
   D) Two students spend a lot of time having fun, but one gets good grades while the other one gets poor grades.
   E) A student majoring in psychology learns how to use special tests to distinguish between different levels of spatial visualization.

Correct: E   Page: 166 Scramble Range: ALL
124. Which of the following would be a good example of differential socialization?
   A) Each of ten mothers wishes to raise her daughter differently from the others.
   B) Various races tend to have different ideas about what makes for a good child.
   C) Helping children with homework makes a difference in how good their grades are.
   D) An Amish family teaches world peace to its children; a Kuwaiti family teaches military preparedness to its children.
   E) A husband and wife raise their daughter differently from the way they raise their son.

Correct: D   Page: 166 Scramble Range: ALL
125. The expectations that tell men how they should interact with others AS MEN are called their _____.
   A) reference group.
   B) values.
   C) abstractions.
   D) role.
   E) status.

Correct: C   Page: 166 Scramble Range: A-D
126. The concept "role"
   A) refers to a collection of values.
   B) only refers to specific requirements of an organization.
   C) helps explain why the same person may act very differently at different times of day.
   D) is illustrated by Guerry's work on suicide rates.
   E) none of these

Correct: A   Page: 166 Scramble Range: ALL
127. "To behave as a college student should behave," "to do those things that professors are ordinarily expected to do," and "to do the tasks most people expect of a bank teller" refer to which of the following?
   A) Social roles
   B) Social values
   C) Ascribed statuses
   D) Cultural pluralism
   E) Transitivity

128. According to Melvin Kohn
  A) parents' occupations have little influence on how they rear their children.
  B) unlike working-class parents, middle-class parents place a high value on honesty.
  C) working-class parents place little value on cleanliness.
  D) middle-class parents place a high value on self-expression and independence.
  E) middle-class parents place a high value on cleanliness and obedience.

129. According to Melvin Kohn
  A) the father is the main disciplinarian in middle-class homes and the mother is the main disciplinarian in working-class homes.
  B) middle-class parents are too busy to try to understand why their children behave as they do.
  C) working-class parents emphasize self-control and self-expression.
  D) middle-class parents are more likely to believe that both the mother and the father should support and discipline the children.
  E) middle-class parents are primarily interested in obedience and conformity.

130. Socialization is
  A) something that happens to infants and then stops.
  B) something that happens to infants and children and then stops.
  C) a lifelong process.
  D) unknown in Samoa, where people behave more naturally.
  E) an Arapesh preoccupation.

131. A longitudinal study is one in which the research studies
  A) a larger group rather than a smaller one.
  B) several different groups, all at the same time.
  C) several different individuals, all at the same time.
  D) one group at one time, a second group at another time, and a third group at an even later date.
  E) the same group over an extended period of time.

132. Which of the following is one of the two major findings of Melvin Kohn's study of occupational roles and socialization?
  A) Working-class parents had less interest in socializing their children than did middle-class parents.
  B) Parental socialization of children varied greatly on the basis of the number of children in the family.
  C) Socialization is a lifelong process, showing up even in older workers.
  D) Workers 50 and older did not seem to show personality changes in response to job changes.
  E) Working mothers were less interested in socializing their children than were mothers who were not working, regardless of social class.

Correct: D   Page: 169 Scramble Range: ALL
133.   Melvin Kohn, in his study of occupational roles and socialization, found which
of the following to have an influence on workers' personalities and the way
they raised their children?
A)   The size of the work group in which the individual performed a job
B)   Whether the worker chose the job or had to settle for it
C)   The amount of job security the worker had
D)   The degree to which people worked under the supervision of others
E)   Whether or not day-care facilities were available in the work setting

Correct: D   Page: 168 Scramble Range: ALL
134.   Melvin Kohn studied socialization of children by middle-class parents and by
working-class parents. On the basis of the research results, Kohn concluded
that the kind of socialization that children get depends on
A)   the way the parent was socialized as a child.
B)   family economic resources, which set the direction and amount of
socialization.
C)   the child's willingness and readiness to accept parental authority.
D)   parents' expectations about the kinds of roles the children will assume
as adults.
E)   the amount of status anxiety parents hold about their own current social
status.

Correct: E   Page: 168 Scramble Range: ALL
135.   Modern sociologists think that
A)   personality is fixed in childhood.
B)   cultural determinism places too much emphasis on biological factors.
C)   culture is the only thing that matters in shaping personality and behavior.
D)   human nature is really very rigid and inflexible.
E)   socialization is a lifelong process.

Correct: B   Page: 169 Scramble Range: ALL
136.   People who are flexible and self-directed
A)   will become less self-directed in time--especially if they have children.
B)   probably were brought up by parents whose jobs rewarded individual
initiative.
C)   will probably choose jobs that are structured and highly supervised.
D)   were probably brought up in a working-class environment.
E)   will gravitate toward working-class jobs.

Correct: B   Page: 169 Scramble Range: A-D
137.   Recent international studies of childhood socialization have found
A)   that parental values reflect the husband's experience more than the
wife's.
B)   that parental values are very effectively transmitted to their children.
C)   that the relationship between occupational experience and child rearing
is much stronger in the United States than in other countries such as
Poland.
D)   that the fathers play a smaller role in child rearing in the United States
compared to other countries.
E)   all of these

Correct: B   Page: 170 Scramble Range: A-D
138. Stark and Hirschi (Chapter 4 of your text) found that boys who are very religious still sometimes engage in delinquent behavior.
   A) This suggests that people don't have free will.
   B) This illustrates the difference between learning roles and role performance.
   C) This illustrates Kohn's findings about differential socialization.
   D) This suggests that Mead and the cultural determinists should have paid more attention to religion.
   E) All of these

Correct: C   Page: 170 Scramble Range: A-E
139. Lisa puts on lipstick before she goes off to work. This illustrates which of the following concepts?
   A) Values
   B) Norms
   C) Role performance
   D) Gender roles
   E) Object permanence
   F) All of these

Correct: A   Page: 170 Scramble Range: ALL
140. A young newspaper reporter gains access to the medical files of a mass murderer by putting on a white coat and hanging a stethoscope around his neck. This would be an excellent illustration of
   A) impression management.
   B) studied nonobservance.
   C) studied observance.
   D) reportorial craftsmanship.
   E) teamwork.

Correct: B   Page: 170 Scramble Range: ALL
141. Erving Goffman's important insights involving such concepts as studied nonobservance and impression management point to the basic conclusion that we all
   A) are deviant because we try to project false images of ourselves to others.
   B) consciously manipulate things to influence other people's view of us.
   C) are confused regarding who and what we are and thus act out inconsistent roles.
   D) are basically honest and straightforward and seldom appear to be what we know we are not.
   E) are so frequently engaged in pretending to be what we are not that perhaps a majority no longer know who or what they are.

Correct: C   Page: 170 Scramble Range: ALL
142. Your father-in-law belches after a big meal. You pretend not to notice. This is an example of
   A) culture shock.
   B) laissez-faire leadership.
   C) studied nonobservance.
   D) differential socialization.
   E) front stage/back stage behavior.

Correct: D   Page: 173 Scramble Range: A-C
143. Examination of gender roles in small, non-technological societies reveals that
A) women have equal political rights in some of these societies.
B) these societies differentially socialize their children by sex.
C) training for adult roles generally begins at the same age for boys and
girls.
D) all of these
E) none of these

Correct: B   Page: 173 Scramble Range: A-C
144. Looking at responses to the question "Do you think that a woman has to
have children in order to be fulfilled or is this not necessary?" in modern
countries we find that
A) most men in most of the countries believe it is necessary.
B) a majority of people in most countries do not believe it is necessary.
C) there is a great difference between the responses of men and women in
these countries.
D) all of these
E) none of these

Correct: A   Page: 173 Scramble Range: A-C
145. Examination of gender roles in small, non-technological societies reveals that
A) women have equal political rights in some of these societies.
B) there is little division of labor.
C) that socialization for girls almost never stresses toughness and
aggression.
D) none of these

Correct: A   Page: 175 Scramble Range: ALL
146. DeLoache, Cassidy, and Carpenter found that mothers referred to gender-
neutral characters in children's books as
A) males.
B) females.
C) mothers.
D) animals.
E) "it" characters.

Correct: B   Page: 175 Scramble Range: ALL
147. DeLoache, Cassidy, and Carpenter conducted research about gender-neutral
characters in children's books. Their research results led them to conclude
that the only strategy that is likely to result in more egalitarian sex roles in
young children's picture books is to
A) completely and consistently reverse the traditional sex roles in such
books.
B) portray more overtly female characters in a wider variety of
nonstereotyped roles.
C) portray more gender-neutral characters in a wide variety of
nonstereotyped roles.
D) write storylines in which gay characters are portrayed positively.
E) write storylines in which characters' gender is left to the readers'
imagination.

Correct: A   Page: 171 Scramble Range: ALL
148.   Richer's research findings suggest that the strong gender preferences of slightly older children are learned, and that they are learned primarily from
A)   older children.
B)   camp counselors.
C)   formal educational efforts in the camp setting.
D)   informal educational efforts by young adult camp counselors.
E)   informal educational efforts by older adult camp counselors.

Correct: C   Page: 176 Scramble Range: ALL
149.   When Stephen Richer studied games and gender, he found only one circumstance under which boys and girls would play together without manifesting strong gender preferences. That circumstance was when
A)   the task of the group was mental rather than physical.
B)   the task of the group was political rather than psychological.
C)   they formed a single team to compete either against the staff or against outsiders.
D)   the reward was immediate rather than in the distant future.
E)   they all thought that fate was crucial for success in the activity.

Chapter 7: Crime and Deviance

True/False

Correct: T   Page: 181
1. Most of us play by the rules most of the time.

Correct: F   Page: 181
2. Like police investigators, criminologists ask "who did it?"

Correct: T   Page: 181
3. Criminologists ask why people commit crimes.

Correct: T   Page: 182
4. A major problem in defining crime as a violation of law is that it suggests that all illegal acts are morally equivalent.

Correct: F   Page: 182
5. Your text defines crime as acts which are violations of law.

Correct: T   Page: 182
6. Crime, as defined by your text, are acts of force or fraud undertaken in pursuit of self-interest.

Correct: F   Page: 184
7. The majority of crimes are committed with advance preparation and planning.

Correct: T   Page: 184
8. Most crime is unplanned and not very profitable.

Correct: F   Page: 184
9. "Ordinary crime" is trivial crime.

Correct: F   Page: 184
10. When a person breaks into a house while no one is home and steals a stereo system, it is called "robbery."

Correct: F   Page: 184
11. Boston, New York, Miami, and Pittsburgh all have approximately the same robbery rate.

Correct: T   Page: 184
12. Fewer than 10 percent of robberies target service stations or convenience stores.

Correct: T   Page: 185
13. Burglaries and robberies are generally committed near to the criminal's home.

Correct: F   Page: 185
14. Juvenile gang killings accounted for nearly a quarter of all homicides in 1992.

Correct: T Page: 185

15. Homicide victims and their killers are generally the same sex, race, age, and have the similar previous criminal involvements.

Correct: F Page: 185

16. Most homicides are carefully planned, even when incompetently carried out.

Correct: F Page: 185

17. Most homicide victims are killed by a relative or friend.

Correct: F Page: 186

18. "Offender versitility" refrs to the tendency of both robbers and burglars to vary their targets.

Correct: T Page: 186

19. Most criminal acts are not well planned.

Correct: T Page: 186

20. Most criminal acts involve short-range choices.

Correct: F Page: 186

21. Most crimes are well planned--crime is an occupation for most criminals.

Correct: F Page: 189

22. There is little evidence that criminals are different from non-criminals in terms of their intelligence.

Correct: F Page: 189

23. Lombroso's theory of born criminals remains a major criminological theory.

Correct: T Page: 192

24. Your text suggests that biological factors, and especially levels of testosterone, may be linked to rates of criminal behavior.

Correct: F Page: 192

25. People who have lower testosterone levels are more likely to commit crimes.

Correct: T Page: 194

26. Self-control is a major variable in predicting who will be a criminal.

Correct: T Page: 194

27. Your text suggests that the major task of criminology is to account for the development of weak self-control.

Correct: F Page: 195

28. Parenting seems to play a surprisingly small role in the development of self-control.

Correct: F Page: 197

29. Criminals generally "march to a different drummer"--they do not share the general societal notions about "right" and "wrong."

Correct: T   Page: 198
30. A major problem with subcultural theory is its failure to explain crime within the subcultural group.

Correct: T   Page: 198
31. One of the problems with differential association theories is time order--which came first, the peers or the delinquency?

Correct: T   Page: 196
32. The differential association theory of crime is inadequate to explain many criminal acts done alone, in secret.

Correct: T   Page: 197
33. Subcultural theories of crime argue that much that is called crime is actually conformity.

Correct: T   Page: 198
34. Structural strain theories of crime argue that people choose crime because they are deprived.

Correct: T   Page: 198
35. Structural strain theories of crime trace crime to frustrated desires.

Correct: T   Page: 198
36. Structural strain theories of crime assume that the great majority of people prefer to conform to the norms.

Correct: F   Page: 199
37. Poor, lower-class kids are more likely to commit delinquent acts than their more wealthy peers.

Correct: F   Page: 199
38. Social class is highly correlated with delinquency.

Correct: F   Page: 199
39. As unemployment goes up, the crime rate goes up.

Correct: T   Page: 199
40. According to the text, poor neighborhoods tend to attract--not produce--people who engage in crime.

Correct: F   Page: 199
41. According to the text, poor neighborhoods tend to produce people who soon learn to engage in crime.

Correct: F   Page: 200
42. White-collar crime is completely different from other types of crime.

Correct: T   Page: 202
43. The control theory of crime emphasizes the question: "Why don't people break norms?"

Correct: F Page: 202
44. The control theory of crime assumes that people will tend to conform unless they have more to gain by deviating.

Correct: T Page: 202
45. Your text suggests that it's really rather easy to understand why Ivan Boesky stole millions of dollars.

Correct: T Page: 204
46. The control theory of crime argues that we deviate to the extent that we are free to do so.

Correct: T Page: 204
47. The control theory of crime predicts that married adults will be less likely to commit crimes than those who are unmarried or divorced.

Correct: F Page: 204
48. The control theory of crime is particularly good for explaining impulsive acts of crime.

Correct: T Page: 204
49. The control theory of crime focuses on the bonds between the individual and society.

Correct: T Page: 205
50. The control theory of crime suggests that busy people deviate less than people who are not very busy.

Correct: T Page: 206
51. People who attend church less than once a year are more likely than weekly attenders to have been picked up by the police.

Correct: F Page: 208
52. Durkheim's anomie theory of crime rejects the existence of moral communities.

Correct: F Page: 208
53. Durkheim's anomie theory of crime has been rejected by modern sociologists.

Correct: T Page: 211
54. The labeling theory of crime suggests that once people are identified as criminals, their crime increases.

Correct: T Page: 212
55. The labeling theory of crime fails to explain why people committed the criminal act that earned them a label.

Correct: T Page: 214
56. Biological, psychological, and sociological theories of criminal behavior tend to complement one another.

Reference Key: STORY7.1
Once upon a time, not too long ago, in a town not too far from here, Stanley broke into a neighbor's house and stole some stuff, including a stereo system and some cash.

Correct: T   Page: 184   Refer to: STORY7.1
57.   This is an ordinary crime.

Correct: F   Page: 184   Refer to: STORY7.1
58.   This crime is called "robbery."

Correct: T   Page: 185   Refer to: STORY7.1
59.   This crime is called "burglary."

Correct: F   Page: 184   Refer to: STORY7.1
60.   Most likely, Stanley carefully planned this crime.

Correct: T   Page: 186   Refer to: STORY7.1
61.   Most likely, Stanley decided to do this crime on the spur of the moment.

Correct: T   Page: 185   Refer to: STORY7.1
62.   Most likely, this crime took place near Stanley's home.

Correct: F   Page: 197   Refer to: STORY7.1
63.   Subcultural theorists would ask about Stanley's economic circumstances.

Correct: T   Page: 198   Refer to: STORY7.1
64.   Structural strain theorists would ask about Stanley's economic circumstances.

Correct: T   Page: 198   Refer to: STORY7.1
65.   Structural strain theorists would ask about Stanley's bonds to his family and school.

Correct: F   Page: 196   Refer to: STORY7.1
66.   Differential association theorists would ask about Stanley's height and weight.

Correct: T   Page: 192   Refer to: STORY7.1
67.   Walter Gove would ask about Stanley's height and weight.

Correct: T   Page: 197   Refer to: STORY7.1
68.   Subcultural theorists would ask whether Stanley's burglary is criminal for Stanley.

Correct: T   Page: 202   Refer to: STORY7.1
69.   Control theorists would ask about Stanley's age and marital status.

Correct: F   Page: 193   Refer to: STORY7.1
70.   Psychological theorists would ask about the moral integration of Stanley's community.

Correct: T   Page: 211   Refer to: STORY7.1
71.   Labeling theorists would ask about social responses to Stanley's previous behaviors.

Correct: T   Page: 202   Refer to: STORY7.1
72. Control theorists would ask about the beliefs of Stanley's community.

Correct: T   Page: 193   Refer to: STORY7.1
73. Psychological theories are not very effective in dealing with this type of crime.

Correct: F   Page: 198   Refer to: STORY7.1
74. If we were to find that Stanley was broke and unemployed, this would lead us to conclude that strain theory was more applicable than control theory.

Correct: T   Page: 202   Refer to: STORY7.1
75. Control theorists would be less interested in Stanley than in why Stanley's friend Richard DIDN'T join Stanley in the burglary.

Correct: F   Page: 193   Refer to: STORY7.1
76. If we found that Stanley had weak self-control we would have demonstrated support for psychological theories of crime and delinquency.

Multiple Choice

Correct: A   Page: 181 Scramble Range: ALL
77. Deviant behavior is essentially
   A) behavior that doesn't conform to society's norms.
   B) illegal behavior.
   C) behavior that is severely punished by society.
   D) behavior that causes major disruptions in society.
   E) immoral behavior.

Correct: E   Page: 182 Scramble Range: A-C
78. Your text accepts a definition of crime that includes
   A) all acts that are illegal.
   B) all acts that harm others.
   C) drug offenses and prostitution.
   D) all of these
   E) none of these

Correct: A   Page: 182 Scramble Range: A-C
79. The definition of crime adopted by your text
   A) includes acts of force or fraud only when they are committed in pursuit of self interest.
   B) excludes non-ordinary crimes such as the slaying of a celebrity or political leader.
   C) includes all acts that are violations of criminal law.
   D) all of these

Correct: D   Page: 182 Scramble Range: A-C
80. Why do sociologists need a clear definition of crime independent of legality?
   A) Because laws vary over time and from place to place.
   B) Because illegal acts are so diverse.
   C) Because criminal acts should be morally equivalent.
   D) all of these
   E) none of these

Correct: C   Page: 182 Scramble Range: A-C
81.   Your text sees the primary task of sociologists interested in crime as
      A)   describing the patterns of crime in the society.
      B)   understanding how some acts become defined as crimes and others do
           not.
      C)   explaining why people commit crimes.
      D)   all of these
      E)   none of these

Correct: B   Page: 182 Scramble Range: A-C
82.   Jake gives Jane $100 to have sex with him.
      A)   Your text would consider this an ordinary crime.
      B)   Your text would not consider this a crime.
      C)   Strain theory would be particularly useful in understanding Jake's
           behavior.
      D)   all of these
      E)   none of these

Correct: A   Page: 182 Scramble Range: A-C
83.   A landlord fails to return the security deposit after her tenants move out even
      though they have not done any damage and have paid all their rent.
      A)   Your text would consider this an ordinary crime.
      B)   Your text would consider this a non-ordinary crime.
      C)   Your text would not consider this a crime.

Correct: C   Page: 182 Scramble Range: A-C
84.   A person comes upon a couple arguing loudly. The man is threatening the
      woman and saying nasty things about her. The person pulls out a gun and
      shoots the man, killing him.
      A)   Your text would consider this an ordinary crime.
      B)   Your text would consider this a non-ordinary crime.
      C)   Your text would not consider this a crime.

Correct: A   Page: 182 Scramble Range: A-C
85.   Amy cheats on her algebra test.
      A)   Your text would consider this an ordinary crime.
      B)   Your text would consider this a non-ordinary crime.
      C)   Your text would not consider this a crime.

Correct: C   Page: 183 Scramble Range: ALL
86.   According to Figure 7-1 in your text, the highest burglary rates are found in
      A)   the northeastern states.
      B)   the Great Lakes states.
      C)   the "Sun Belt" states.
      D)   the western states.
      E)   the north central states.

Correct: D   Page: 183 Scramble Range: A-D
87.   According to your text (Figure 7.1)
A)   the United States has one of the highest burglary rates in the world and
England has one of the lowest.
B)   burglaries are most likely to occur in the Northeastern United States and
least likely in the South.
C)   Canada has a much lower burglary rate than the United States.
D)   both Scotland and the Netherlands have burglary rates more than twice
the rate of the United States.
E)   all of these

Correct: A   Page: 183 Scramble Range: ALL
88.   According to the text, you are likeliest to find that your home has been broken
into while you were elsewhere in which of the following states?
A)   Florida
B)   Mississippi
C)   New York
D)   Ohio
E)   Louisiana

Correct: E   Page: 184 Scramble Range: A-C
89.   Ordinary crime includes
A)   all burglaries, robberies, and homicides.
B)   all acts which are violations of law.
C)   most drug offenses.
D)   all of these
E)   none of these

Correct: B   Page: 184 Scramble Range: A-C
90.   Marcia and Betty are driving home from a bar at one in the morning. They
stop at a small store to get a pack of cigarettes. There are no other customers
in the store. Marcia pulls out a knife and threatens the clerk. She calls Betty
to come over and empty the cash register. They take their cigarettes and the
money and leave.
A)   This is a burglary.
B)   This is an ordinary crime.
C)   This event does not fit into your text's defintion of crime.
D)   None of these

Correct: A   Page: 186 Scramble Range: A-C
91.   Offender versitility
A)   refers to the wide range of different criminal activities engaged in by
ordinary criminals.
B)   refers to the careful way in which most criminals change the area of their
crimes and the way they commit them.
C)   demonstrates that the intelligence of most criminals is at least as great as
that of the average non-criminal.
D)   all of these
E)   none of these

Correct: D   Page: 186 Scramble Range: A-C
92. The typical criminal act
     A) is impulsive.
     B) does not involve any special skills.
     C) involves short-term choices.
     D) all of these
     E) none of these

Correct: B   Page: 186 Scramble Range: A-D
93. Most crimes
     A) require special skills and experience.
     B) are easy to commit and simple in design.
     C) involve some planning.
     D) produce fairly large and tempting rewards.
     E) all of these

Correct: E   Page: 185 Scramble Range: A-E
94. Most burglars burglarize homes and stores
     A) when the victims exhibit obvious signs of affluence.
     B) located in the social class immediately below their own.
     C) located in the social class immediately above their own.
     D) during the daylight hours, not during the nighttime.
     E) located within a few blocks of their own home.
     F) all of these

Correct: E   Page: 188 Scramble Range: ALL
95. Lombroso's theory of "born criminals"
     A) led him to support capital punishment.
     B) compared the physical traits of criminals with those of the general
         population.
     C) was substantiated by further research.
     D) examined the effects of the XYY chromosome pattern on behavior.
     E) was based on his study of the body size and shape of prisoners.

Correct: C   Page: 189 Scramble Range: ALL
96. Which of the following is SPECIFICALLY SINGLED OUT by your text as being
     false?
     A) It is possible that by being careless one can make it possible for others to
         be criminal.
     B) There is no fool like an old fool.
     C) Some people are just born "bad."
     D) You can't cheat an honest man.
     E) There's a sucker born every minute.

Correct: A   Page: 188 Scramble Range: ALL
97. According to Lombroso's theory, violent criminals
     A) differ biologically from noncriminals.
     B) have low self-esteem.
     C) have an extra Y chromosome.
     D) learn crime in association with other criminals.
     E) were harshly punished as children.

98.   A recent study done in Denmark examined 3,586 pairs of twins to see what effect the twin phenomenon had on the likelihood of criminality among pairs of twins. Christensen found that
A)   twins were no more or less likely to commit criminal acts than were others of the same socioeconomic status who were not twins.
B)   recorded criminality was almost completely nonexistent among twins.
C)   in the case of monozygotic (identical) twins, if one twin had a criminal record, the odds were 50 percent higher that the other twin did also.
D)   fraternal twins--dizygotic--were likelier to both have criminal records than were monozygotic twins.
E)   female twins were likelier to both have criminal records than were male twins.

99.   According to your text, Gove's new approach for exploring the relationships among age, gender, biology, and crime has a hard time accounting for which of the following phenomena?
A)   The high level of criminality committed by preadolescents
B)   The increasing level of criminality committed by those past age 65
C)   The increasing level of violent, dangerous crime committed by women
D)   The fact that it is middle-aged and older persons who fire-bomb insured office and apartment buildings
E)   The fact that most people never commit risky, physical crimes at any age

100.   Table 7-1 in your text provides data to show that the nation with the HIGHEST percent of females among all people arrested for crimes is
A)   China.
B)   Finland.
C)   Israel.
D)   England.
E)   West Germany.

101.   According to your text's data about the United States, the lowest percent of women is arrested for committing the crime of
A)   robbery.
B)   shoplifting.
C)   embezzlement.
D)   forgery.
E)   aggravated assault.

102.   Table 7-5 in your text provides information to support the observation that the offense with the highest percent of female arrests in the United States is
A)   homicide.
B)   running away.
C)   robbery.
D)   fraud.
E)   aggravated assault.

Correct: A   Page: 192 Scramble Range: ALL
103. Walter Gove realized that physically demanding crime is
A) overwhelmingly committed by males.
B) committed as much by females as by males.
C) overwhelmingly committed by minority-group members.
D) concentrated in the southern and southwestern states.
E) concentrated primarily in the months of May through October.

Correct: C   Page: 192 Scramble Range: ALL
104. Walter Gove noted that aggressive and physically demanding behaviors
A) are likelier to occur among military personnel than among other populations.
B) are likelier to occur among the uneducated than among other populations.
C) occur mainly among young persons.
D) have been declining since 1965 in terms of frequency of occurrence.
E) are increasing at the highest rate among the functionally illiterate sections of the population.

Correct: C   Page: 193 Scramble Range: A-C
105. Your text argues that a major characteristic of most criminals
A) is low esteem.
B) are abnormal personality traits.
C) is weak self-control.
D) all of these
E) none of these

Correct: B   Page: 193 Scramble Range: A-C
106. Weak self-control
A) is apparently not related to most criminal activity.
B) often leads to a lack of skills.
C) usually makes people more cautious in their actions.
D) all of these
E) none of these

Correct: A   Page: 193 Scramble Range: A-D
107. The word which might best describe people who have poor self-control is
A) impulsive.
B) creative.
C) energetic.
D) uncertain.

Correct: C   Page: 193 Scramble Range: ALL
108. Psychological theories of crime
A) are quite successful in predicting criminality on the basis of self-esteem.
B) are least effective in accounting for crimes of passion, such as the typical homicide.
C) don't distinguish between criminals and noncriminals very well.
D) focus on the social bonds between the individual and the community.
E) are most effective in predicting minor crime.

109. Popular ideas such as "he fell into bad company" and "it's the kids she hangs out with" remind you of what kind of theory?
A) Differential association
B) Strain
C) Control
D) Labeling
E) Psychological

110. Differential association theory identifies the source of crime as
A) association with one's own class position in society.
B) uncontrollable impulses.
C) attachment with people who support the crime.
D) lack of moral integration into the community.
E) all of these

111. In terms of causal inference, a major difficulty with the idea that peers cause a person to become criminal can be summarized as a problem of
A) spuriousness.
B) lack of correlation.
C) lack of randomization.
D) lack of control groups.
E) time order.

112. Differential association theories of criminal behavior are not able to deal effectively with which of the following, according to your text?
A) Some forms of crime are directly rewarding.
B) Some forms of crime are the result of mental illness.
C) Some types of crime are legislated against by legal processes.
D) Some types of crime are not recognized as such by criminologists.
E) Perhaps as much as 40 percent of crime is the result of abnormal psychological functioning, not social processes.

113. A serious criticism of (or flaw in) differential association theory is that not all boys with delinquent friends engage in delinquency. Travis Hirschi found that boys with delinquent friends who did NOT themselves become delinquent were boys who
A) did not have histories of delinquency during their preteen years.
B) saw themselves as "loners" and as "motivated," and could make up their own minds.
C) did well in school and were attached to their parents.
D) had their first contact with the police in a positive way.
E) were involved in social relationships with nondelinquent girls.

Correct: E   Page: 194 Scramble Range: ALL
114. According to Edwin Sutherland's differential association theory of criminal behavior, teens become delinquent because
      A) their parents associate with parents whose delinquent kids spread crime.
      B) teens associate delinquency with being cool or with being atop the pack.
      C) some teens belong to formal organizations that actually promote delinquency.
      D) teens who are TOO attached to their parents have weak resistance to peers.
      E) too many of their attachments are to others who engage in and approve of delinquent act.

Correct: D   Page: 194 Scramble Range: ALL
115. The theory that traces criminal behavior to hanging around with others who engage in the criminal behavior and to eventually giving these people's views more importance than those of society in general, is called the _____ theory of crime.
      A) structural strain
      B) anomie
      C) control
      D) differential association
      E) social integration

Correct: A   Page: 195 Scramble Range: ALL
116. The differential association theory
      A) is supported by research that shows that most delinquent behavior is carried out with other people.
      B) is supported by research that shows that boys who are attached to their parents do not commit criminal acts even if their friends are delinquent.
      C) attributes most crime to poverty.
      D) attributes crime to personality disorders.
      E) argues that people do not usually acquire criminal friends until after they begin to deviate themselves.

Correct: E   Page: 194 Scramble Range: ALL
117. The view that people commit criminal acts because their attachments to those encouraging crime outweigh their attachments to those discouraging crime is called the _____ theory of crime.
      A) structural strain
      B) control
      C) moral integration
      D) anomie
      E) differential association

Correct: E   Page: 197 Scramble Range: ALL
118. Which of the following would be best explained by the concept of subcultural crime?
      A) Child abuse
      B) Incest
      C) A navy officer selling military secrets to a foreign government
      D) shoplifting
      E) Illegal handling of poisonous snakes by members of a church that believes the Bible says it is to be done

Correct: D Page: 197 Scramble Range: ALL
119. Sometimes we can observe an entire group of people who have some ways of thinking and behaving that are considered criminal by people in the rest of society. That this behavior exists, is learned through socialization, and may be perceived and punished by the wider society is a central idea of
A) structural strain theory of crime.
B) control theory of crime.
C) anomie theory of crime.
D) subcultural crime.
E) moral disintegration crime.

Correct: C Page: 197 Scramble Range: ALL
120. Sally's grandparents were proud members of the Ku Klux Klan. The grandparents raised their son--now Sally's father--to be a member of this organization. Sally's father married the woman who was to become Sally's mother and recruited his wife into the organization. Sally herself does what she can to support the Klan's activities these days, preparing picnic lunches for Klan outings, laundering white clothing for Klan meetings, and so on. Sally and her parents have a hard time understanding why some people are so against the Klan. What theory of criminal behavior fits this example?
A) Structural strain theory of crime
B) Anomie theory of crime
C) Subcultural theory of crime
D) Lombrosian theory of crime
E) Labeling theory of crime

Correct: B Page: 197 Scramble Range: ALL
121. The Oedulis oyster of Europe mates with both males and females during its lifetime. Some people who are bisexual wear a small piece of jewelry depicting the Oedulis oyster as a sign of their bisexuality. Most people are probably unaware of the significance of such jewelry, but many people who are bisexual are aware of its significance and behave accordingly. Which theory of criminal behavior is illustrated by this example?
A) Structural strain theory of crime
B) Subcultural theory of crime
C) Control theory of crime
D) Anomie theory of crime
E) Primary crime theory

Correct: B Page: 198 Scramble Range: ALL
122. Which of these, according to your text, is the major omission of the subcultural theory of crime (that is, the main thing it has difficulty explaining)?
A) Deviance in the main culture of the society
B) Deviance within any subcultural group
C) Deviance occurring with the blessings of the larger society
D) Deviance that happens as the result of an accident
E) Deviance that occurs across international borders

123. A radio reporter interviewed a drug pusher who was selling cocaine and crack on a New York street. When asked WHY he was selling it, the seller said that he had to buy clothes, had car payments, had an apartment to pay for, had to buy groceries, and needed money to take his girl out. He said, "You gotta get the money from somewhere and this is the only way I know how to get it." Based only on this information, what theory of criminal behavior fits this example?
A) Subcultural theory of crime
B) Structural strain theory of crime
C) Impulsive crime theory
D) Control theory of crime
E) Lombrosian theory of crime

124. According to your text, which of the following is the greatest weakness of structural strain theory of crime (that is, the thing it is least able to explain)?
A) The crime rate is going up while the poverty rate is going down.
B) Most crimes are committed by people who are feeling no stresses at all.
C) The structure of most criminals' brains is in every way biologically normal.
D) Many social structures can stand great strain and still function very well.
E) Committing crimes is very weakly, if at all, related to social class.

125. What theory of crime emphasizes the importance of frustration or discontent caused by a person's being in a disadvantaged position in the social structure?
A) Subcultural crime theory
B) Differential association theory
C) Social bonds theory
D) Structural strain theory
E) Status anxiety theory

126. A key idea in the structural strain theory of crime is that people who want "the good things of life"
A) may be less open to the usual methods of social control than most people.
B) may use illegitimate means to obtain them if they don't have access to the legitimate means.
C) can ordinarily be expected to give up these goals if they realize that they haven't much hope of getting them, though a few persist and become criminal.
D) almost always have to resort to illegal, criminal, or abnormal behaviors in order to get them.
E) ordinarily end up being unhappy and dissatisfied, which causes them to turn to criminal behavior to try to find some degree of happiness.

127. Which of the following would be a type of crime that could be best explained by the structural strain theory of crime?
    A) Involvement with the Mafia
    B) Homosexuality
    C) Marijuana and/or cocaine use
    D) Rape
    E) Vandalism resulting in destruction of public property

128. According to Robert Merton,
    A) most people enjoy breaking rules.
    B) crime results from poverty.
    C) the poor are no more likely to deviate than are the middle class.
    D) working-class child-rearing practices promote crime in later life.
    E) poverty is really an excuse to explain why people steal and turn to alcohol and drugs and is not a legitimate explanation of these behaviors.

129. When people engage in criminal behavior because they feel they have to use criminal or illegitimate ways of attaining socially approved goals, the _____ theory of crime is illustrated.
    A) structural strain
    B) control
    C) labeling
    D) subcultural
    E) Lombrosian

130. Structural strain theory (or strain theory) has difficulty explaining
    A) sexual differences in type of crime committed.
    B) year-to-year stability in crime rates.
    C) cyclical changes in the cause of criminal behavior.
    D) different crime rates among racial and cultural minorities.
    E) crime committed by high-status people.

131. Where homes, apartments, retail stores, and light industries are located in the same area
    A) types of crime are more diverse.
    B) criminals tend to be older rather than teenaged.
    C) police tend to respond more quickly to appeals for help.
    D) opportunities for crime and delinquency are higher.
    E) crime rates are lower, but the probability of arrest, trial, and serving time is also lower.

132. Crime rates are higher in
    A) peripheral census tracts.
    B) economies in a forward-motion spiral.
    C) areas in which residents have higher-than-average levels of education.
    D) election years.
    E) mixed-use neighborhoods.

Correct: E   Page: 202   Scramble Range: ALL
133.   The theory stressing that weak bonds between the individual and society make people feel free to deviate, while strong bonds make crime seem more costly, is called
A)   differential association theory.
B)   subcultural crime theory.
C)   structural strain theory.
D)   labeling theory.
E)   control theory.

Correct: A   Page: 202   Scramble Range: ALL
134.   One who feels that the crime or noncrime of teenagers can be explained mainly by whether or not the teens have a stake in conformity because of what they risk losing if they deviate, is in basic agreement with which theory of crime?
A)   Control theory
B)   Differential association theory
C)   Labeling theory
D)   Secondary crime theory
E)   Tertiary crime theory

Correct: D   Page: 202   Scramble Range: ALL
135.   Annie is not doing well academically at high school. She has no friends there. In fact, she has no friends at all. She doesn't like herself very well. Her family is very busy, and family members pretty much operate on their own separate schedules. Family members' relationships with each other can best be described as "stranger-roommates." One day, Annie meets a man she doesn't exactly like, but who says she has a lot of potential to make money by engaging in sex for cash if she will let him be her "manager." She thinks for a while and says, "Why not? I can't think of any reason not to." The theory of criminal behavior illustrated here is
A)   differential association theory.
B)   labeling theory of crime.
C)   secondary theory of crime.
D)   control theory of crime.

Correct: D   Page: 202   Scramble Range: ALL
136.   For the ____ theory of crime, the causes of conformity are the social bonds between an individual and the group. When these bonds are strong, the individual conforms. When these bonds are weak, the individual deviates.
A)   functionalist
B)   differential association
C)   labeling
D)   control
E)   subcultural

Correct: D   Page: 202 Scramble Range: ALL
137.   Which of the following examples is best explained by social bond theory?
A)   A poor child shoplifts some candy from a neighborhood convenience store.
B)   A happily married man has a brief affair with his secretary.
C)   Ruthie nearly fails a test because she was late getting to class.
D)   John resists his friends' desires to drink and drive because he knows it would upset his parents.
E)   A teenage prostitute seeks friends who are also prostitutes.

Correct: E   Page: 202-206 Scramble Range: ALL
138.   The text discusses the control theory of crime and conformity. Which of the following does NOT belong among the concepts/ideas in the control theory?
A)   Attachments
B)   Investments
C)   Involvements
D)   Beliefs
E)   Containment

Correct: C   Page: 207 Scramble Range: ALL
139.   Linden and Fillmore constructed a theoretical model of delinquency saying that teenagers with low stakes in conformity have little to lose by hanging around with other delinquents and that such association will further amplify their delinquency as they learn new criminal techniques and are reinforced for new acts of crime. Basically, then, Linden and Fillmore constructed a mode of delinquency that combined
A)   labeling theory with differential association theory.
B)   control theory with labeling theory.
C)   differential association theory with control theory.
D)   structural strain theory with enforcement theory.
E)   enforcement theory with control theory.

Correct: A   Page: 207 Scramble Range: ALL
140.   When Linden and Fillmore measured stakes in conformity of Canadian and American teenagers, they measured them on the basis of attachments to parents and
A)   liking school.
B)   level of religiosity.
C)   participation or membership in local community organizations.
D)   number of hours spent watching television.
E)   attachments to others.

Correct: B   Page: 208 Scramble Range: ALL
141.   Anomie
A)   refers to the strengthening of people's commitment to important norms after they have been violated.
B)   refers to a group's confusion over norms or widespread lack of belief in them.
C)   refers to the process of labeling primary criminals.
D)   is most prevalent in communities with low rates of geographic mobility.
E)   is a major influence on all types of crime.

142. Durkheim's anomie theory predicts that crime rates will vary as ____ varies.
    A) social integration
    B) population pressure
    C) economic pressure
    D) educational preparation
    E) adequacy of surveillance

143. Emile Durkheim was interested in the role that anomie played in affecting rates of criminal behavior. Durkheim was, therefore, interested in the role that _____ and _____ had in affecting rates of criminal behavior.
    A) parents; neighbors
    B) community leaders; educators
    C) racial integration; educational integration
    D) social integration; moral integration
    E) informal norms; bureaucratic regulations

144. Durkheim answered the question of why more people don't commit criminal acts by saying that "we are _____ to the extent that we are _____."
    A) moral beings; convinced that we are moral
    B) moral beings; social beings
    C) criminal beings; in no fear of being apprehended
    D) criminal beings; capable of criminal thoughts
    E) members of the community; not members of a subculture

145. When the sociologist Emile Durkheim spoke of moral integration in society, what he had in mind was the extent to which
    A) people of various moral beliefs are able to get along together.
    B) people are in agreement about what the norms are and why they are correct.
    C) actions such as racial busing are planned to meet social goals.
    D) religion is connected to practical outcomes in everyday life.
    E) people are integrated morally but not necessarily in other ways.

146. Which of the following would be good questions by which to measure "social integration" as that concept was used in the chapter on criminal behavior?
    A) How long have you been in school and what kind of grades are you getting?
    B) What is your job, how long have you had it, and how much money do you make?
    C) How many good friends do you have and how often do you see them?
    D) How far do you live from work and what transportation do you use to get there?
    E) Do you have minority-group people in your community? at work? at church?

147. The subject of anomie brought one sociologist to analyze what he called social integration. If a community had a high level of social integration, then that community
    A) had people with high levels of relationships with others and high levels of intimacy between people.
    B) had been able to minimize the stratification system's effects on daily life in the community.
    C) had been able to bring members of all ethnic, racial, and religious groups into a common sense of fellowship.
    D) had been brought into social, economic, and political contact with other communities in the society.
    E) had been able to achieve racial, ethnic, and religious integration at dinner dances, museum parties, and similar occasions.

148. Which of the following is part of the labeling approach (or labeling theory of crime)?
    A) Primary and secondary crime
    B) Structured and nonstructured crime
    C) Conformist and nonconformist crime
    D) Informal and bureaucratic crime
    E) Short-term (rather than long-term) consequences of crime

149. Which of the following theories of crime sees the essence of crime in the reaction to criminal behavior rather than in the criminal act itself?
    A) Social bond theory
    B) Structural strain theory
    C) Moral integration theory
    D) Labeling theory
    E) Differential association theory

150. Which of the following is the major shortcoming of the labeling theory of crime?
    A) It has a hard time explaining what happens to people after they have committed a criminal act.
    B) It has a difficult time explaining what happens in cultures different from our own.
    C) It has a hard time explaining why a criminal act is committed in the first place.
    D) It can explain structured crime rather well but has a difficult time explaining nonstructured crime.
    E) It can explain people who can be put into neat categories but has a difficult time explaining more individualistic crime.

Correct: B   Page: 212   Scramble Range: ALL
151.   Labeling theory is most useful in explaining
   A)   why criminals do criminal things initially.
   B)   why many criminals have a hard time going straight.
   C)   why criminal subcultures exist.
   D)   why arrest and punishment seem to inhibit further incidence of crimes
        such as wifebeating.
   E)   why most people agree on what behavior is criminal and what is
        acceptable.

Correct: C   Page: 212   Scramble Range: A-C
152.   There is a relationship between drugs and crime.
   A)   This is primarily cuased by the physical effects of drugs.
   B)   This is primarily a result of users committing crimes to get money to buy
        their drugs.
   C)   This is primarily a spurious relationship.
   D)   none of these

Correct: B   Page: 212   Scramble Range: A-D
153.   The correlation between illegal drug use and crime appears to be
   A)   positive.
   B)   spurious.
   C)   negative.
   D)   non-existent.

Correct: E   Page: 212   Scramble Range: A-C
154.   According to your text, illegal drug use
   A)   is a major cause of crime.
   B)   is an ordinary crime.
   C)   is a form of burglary.
   D)   all of these
   E)   none of these

Chapter 8: Social Control

True/False

Correct: T   Page: 217
1. Most social control is informal.

Correct: T   Page: 218
2. Interactions and attachments are important sources of social control.

Correct: T   Page: 218
3. Social control is concerned with why people DON'T deviate from the norms.

Correct: T   Page: 218
4. Ofshe's experiment in Chapter 3 examined social control.
    NOTE: Cumulative question.

Correct: T   Page: 219
5. The Asch experiment showed that people dislike disagreeing with a group.

Correct: T   Page: 219
6. The Asch experiment showed that people were much more willing to resist group pressure if at least one other member agreed with them.

Correct: T   Page: 221
7. Schachter's research showed that the first result of being deviant is to become the center of attention.

Correct: F   Page: 221
8. Both Asch and Schachter's experiments demonstrate the importance of group pressure in creating deviance.

Correct: T   Page: 222
9. Condominiums provide much better security against crime than do single-family dwellings.

Correct: T   Page: 222
10. Shopping malls have lower crime rates than retail areas laid out along regular streets.

Correct: T   Page: 223
11. The Cambridge-Somerville study of delinquency prevention found no difference in the delinquency records of boys in the program and a control group of boys omitted from the program.

Correct: T   Page: 225
12. The latest research suggests that "bad" kids are in large part the result of poor parenting practices.

Correct: T   Page: 228
13. Gibbs's theory of deterrence asserts that to reduce crimes, authorities must increase the probability of criminals being caught and punished.

Correct: F   Page: 228
14. Gibbs's theory of deterrence suggests that if punishment is too severe, it loses its effect.

Correct: F   Page: 228
15. Gibbs's theory of deterrence is inconsistent with control theories of crime and deviance.

Correct: F   Page: 228
16. Gibbs's theory of deterrence suggests that as long as punishment is certain and swift, it need not be very severe.

Correct: F   Page: 231
17. Your text points out that the question of whether capital punishment deters homicide is fundamental to the moral debate about whether the death penalty should be used.

Correct: T   Page: 231
18. The key element in deterrence theory is PERCEPTION of risk.

Correct: T   Page: 231
19. For those who commit crimes in the United States, punishment is far from certain or swift, and often not severe.

Correct: F   Page: 231
20. Although capital punishment doesn't deter many crimes, it clearly deters homicide.

Correct: T   Page: 233
21. One out of four people whose cars are stolen don't bother to report it to the police.

Correct: F   Page: 233
22. For the police, homicide is one of the crimes that is least often solved.

Correct: T   Page: 234
23. Most people arrested by the police for crimes for which they could be sent to prison do not end up actually spending time in prison.

Correct: F   Page: 238
24. A recent experiment showed that people are better able to stay out of trouble after leaving prison if they receive financial aid until they can get a job.

Correct: F   Page: 238
25. The TARP experiment showed that ex-convicts were much less likely to commit new crimes if they had financial support for a while after they got out.

Correct: T   Page: 238
26. The TARP experiment found that about half of those released had been rearrested within a year of their release.

Reference Key: STORY8.1
Many states have attempted to reduce drunk driving by requiring stiff jail sentences for people convicted of operating under the influence.

Correct: F   Page: 218   Refer to: STORY8.1
27.   This is an example of informal social control.

Correct: F   Page: 232   Refer to: STORY8.1
28.   This is an example of a prevention strategy.

Correct: T   Page: 226   Refer to: STORY8.1
29.   This is an example of a deterrence strategy.

Correct: F   Page: Ch7   Refer to: STORY8.1
30.   This policy is consistent with psychological theories of crime and deviance.
      NOTE: Cumulative question.

Correct: F   Page: Ch7   Refer to: STORY8.1
31.   This policy is inconsistent with the control theory of crime and deviance.
      NOTE: Cumulative question.

Correct: F   Page: 237   Refer to: STORY8.1
32.   Control theorists would suggest that the time in jail will likely be effective in reducing further deviance.

Reference Key: STORY8.2
Deterrence theory, as conceptualized by Jack Gibbs,

Correct: F   Page: 228   Refer to: STORY8.2
33.   emphasizes that severity of punishment is the primary factor in deterrence.

Correct: F   Page: Ch1   Refer to: STORY8.2
34.   rejects the concept of free will.
      NOTE: Cumulative question.

Correct: T   Page: Ch3&6   Refer to: STORY8.2
35.   builds on the proposition that people act to gain rewards.
      NOTE: Cumulative question.

Correct: F   Page: Ch7   Refer to: STORY8.2
36.   is consistent with psychological theories of crime and deviance.
      NOTE: Cumulative question.

Correct: F   Page: 231   Refer to: STORY8.2
37.   really only refers to the issue of capital punishment.

Correct: T   Page: Ch7   Refer to: STORY8.2
38.   is consistent with control theory.
      NOTE: Cumulative question.

39.   is very sociological in the sense of emphasizing choice, the individual, and
social structures.

NOTE: Cumulative question.

Multiple Choice

Correct: A   Page: 218 Scramble Range: ALL
40.   In a small group of people who have come together for no particular purpose
but who meet from time to time for the sheer pleasure of being together, the
type of social control that is most likely to occur is
A)   informal.
B)   short-term.
C)   long-term.
D)   individual-centered.
E)   moral orientation.

Correct: A   Page: 218 Scramble Range: ALL
41.   The chapter on social control begins by distinguishing between the following
two types of social control
A)   informal and formal.
B)   long-term and short-term.
C)   individual-centered and group-centered.
D)   practical orientation and moral orientation.
E)   political orientation and psychological orientation.

Correct: A   Page: 218 Scramble Range: ALL
42.   What do sociologists call the various efforts made by society and social
groups to ensure that people conform to the norms?
A)   Social control
B)   Normative surveillance
C)   Behavioral modification
D)   Societal parensis
E)   Social delimitation

Correct: C   Page: 218 Scramble Range: A-D
43.   Most social control
A)   is formal.
B)   is concerned with deterrence.
C)   is informal.
D)   is clear and public.
E)   all of these

Correct: A   Page: 218 Scramble Range: ALL
44.   According to your text, the major factor in preventing crime and deviance is
A)   socialization.
B)   improving criminal rehabilitation programs.
C)   improving and increasing victim compensation programs.
D)   increasing the swiftness and severity of criminal penalties.
E)   detection of criminality.

45.   Research shows that we won't conform to norms
  A)   unless our reference group is present.
  B)   if we are alone.
  C)   if we have been socialized.
  D)   if we think we can escape detection by the police.
  E)   if we don't value the social approval of those around us.

46.   Which of the following is an example of informal social control?
  A)   A boy is expelled from school for carrying a pocket knife.
  B)   Paul starts to dress better because his girlfriend called him a nerd.
  C)   A collection agency calls on Sarah because she has failed to make her car payment for two months in a row.
  D)   Nancy's husband has her admitted to a psychiatric ward because she has become increasingly depressed and violent.
  E)   Harry has a head-on collision with another car, and a witness calls the police.

47.   The Asch research in which people were asked to make judgments about the length of lines leads us to which of the following conclusions?
  A)   Training in perceptual tasks leads to little improvement in perceptual ability.
  B)   There is a strong tendency for people to conform to group pressure.
  C)   People with an insecure personality are likely to be very uncomfortable when asked to make measured perceptual judgments.
  D)   Groups tended to break up into cliques based on type of judgment about line length when disagreement occurred.
  E)   Dogmatic people make poor arbitrators.

48.   The Asch experiment that involved judging the length of lines found that
  A)   only 25 percent of naive subjects never yielded to group pressure.
  B)   naive subjects were emotionally comfortable with their nonconforming responses.
  C)   group size strongly influenced conformity.
  D)   most naive subjects never yielded to group pressure.
  E)   most people had a hard time distinguishing which line matched the standard line.

49.   The Asch research in which people were asked to judge the length of lines has interesting implications. Which of the following comments has a direct relationship to the implications of the Asch research?
  A)   "I never try to do two things at one time. One at a time, please."
  B)   "I may be the first graduate in my family history, but I WILL graduate."
  C)   "Practice makes perfect. But if I can't be perfect . . . then I quit."
  D)   "Well, the rest of them did it and wanted me to do it, so I did it."
  E)   "I have been out with a lot of women in my time, but Susan is special. I'll be seeing her Thursday night for dinner, and then again on Friday."

50. When Stanley Schachter paid someone to express deviant opinions in a group, he discovered that
   A)   the paid deviants were usually ignored by the group.
   B)   the group eventually abandoned interest in the deviant.
   C)   group members disliked deviants more if they shifted their original positions to be closer to group norms.
   D)   the deviants were some of the best-liked members of the group.
   E)   group members continued to reward the deviants by giving them more attention than the "sliders."

51. Cohesive groups
   A)   are likely to have high rates of deviance.
   B)   exert more pressure to conform to group norms.
   C)   have about as much deviance as groups that aren't so cohesive.
   D)   exert influence on behavior but not on belief.
   E)   exert influence on members' beliefs but not on their behavior.

52. Research has found that the influence of groups on individual conformity is greatest when
   A)   the group codifies its expectations in written form.
   B)   there is evidence that group expectations have been communicated to all group members.
   C)   the group members have long-standing ties of friendship and intimacy.
   D)   the group members are relatively unanalytical in their personality style.
   E)   there is a mixture of the two sexes among group membership.

53. According to your text, research results have found that
   A)   the more children there are in a family, the greater the cohesiveness between husband and wife.
   B)   the younger the students in a dormitory, the greater the ability of the administration to impose behavioral rules.
   C)   the more members of city councils agree with one another, the greater the amount of cohesiveness and the greater the number voting Independent.
   D)   the more members of congregations are united by ties of friendship, the more they agree about religious doctrine.
   E)   the less the staff in local television newsrooms associate with one another off the job, informally, the less the conversational tone of TV broadcasts.

54. Schachter has studied group response to deviants. One of Schachter's findings is that when the group discerns that one of its members is responding in a deviant manner, it
   A) experiences a momentary loss of social cohesion, but then an expansion of cohesion.
   B) concentrates for a time on trying to make the deviant conform, but if the deviance persists, ignores the deviant.
   C) first tries to ignore that deviance is in fact occurring, but then when it has to be dealt with, slowly tries to "bring the deviant around."
   D) informally sends a delegation to work on the deviant while other members of the group go about the main group task.
   E) splits into two groups about 40 percent of the time, with one group going over to the side of the deviant and the other group consisting of "purists."

55. Schachter's experiments on group response to deviance support the generalization that the deviant is more strongly disliked when
   A) the group is a formal one than when it is informal .
   B) the deviant possesses some stigmatizing personal characteristics.
   C) the deviant selects religious or political topics to be deviant about.
   D) the group feels that the deviant is being "playfully or intentionally" deviant as opposed to being seriously so.
   E) the group members have high scores on the extent to which they like one another.

56. In Schachter's research on the topic of group response to deviance, the term "slider" referred to
   A) a person who was originally a conforming group member, but slid away into deviance in spite of group pressures to conform.
   B) a message that the experimenter gave to group members slowly, one by one.
   C) a person who slowly left the group as his/her disagreements continued.
   D) a very tricky experimental manipulation of the dependent variable
   E) a person who originally was deviant, but slowly returned to conformity.

57. Both the Asch and the Schachter experiments demonstrate
   A) the unreliability of deterence theory.
   B) the difficulty of getting people to report crimes.
   C) the problems of rehabilitation.
   D) the unpredictability of response to deviant, and especially criminal, labeling.
   E) the importance of group pressure in social control.
   F) all of these

Correct: A   Page: 222 Scramble Range: ALL
58. Which of the following would be an example of crime prevention?
A) Neighborhood block watch programs, and state-of-the-art antitheft devices
B) Court referral systems in juvenile justice
C) Experimental programs that try to make sure that juvenile or adult offenders are rehabilitated in prison
D) The existence of a prison system
E) Inmate-to-inmate programs

Correct: B   Page: 222 Scramble Range: A-E
59. Making alcohol totally unavailable, producing automobiles with mechanisms that make it impossible to steal them, and having delivery vans that do not carry cash (and so cannot be robbed of it) are all examples of
A) deterrence.
B) prevention.
C) social hysteria.
D) deviance defeatism.
E) contrasocialization.
F) none of these

Correct: A   Page: 222 Scramble Range: ALL
60. Anything that draws ____ to a neighborhood increases the ____.
A) teenagers and young adults; crime rate
B) older people; assault rate
C) racial minorities; assault rate
D) middle-aged people; spouse-abuse rate
E) homosexuals; child molestation rate

Correct: D   Page: 222 Scramble Range: ALL
61. Crime rates fall as one gets farther away from
A) areas with unequal sex ratios.
B) areas with high divorce rates.
C) traditional family relationships.
D) fast-food restaurants.
E) areas undergoing economic development.

Correct: E   Page: 222 Scramble Range: ALL
62. Which of the following neighborhoods have higher than average crime rates?
A) Neighborhoods adjoining public parks
B) Neighborhoods near major transportation routes
C) Suburban fringe neighborhoods
D) Neighborhoods with large numbers of old people
E) Neighborhoods near public high schools

Correct: C   Page: 224 Scramble Range: ALL
63. In the Cambridge-Somerville project of the 1930s-1940s, about what percent of the boys had records of delinquency by age 18?
A) 10 percent
B) 20 percent
C) 40 percent
D) 65 percent
E) 85 percent

64. The Cambridge-Somerville project results were reanalyzed by McCord and McCord. These researchers examined the data to see whether or not the expected effects of the project had made a difference in adult criminality of those who had been given the enrichment experience. The McCords discovered
A) no difference between the groups.
B) a difference for the religiously involved but not for those inactive in religion.
C) that the enrichment group had higher rates of criminality than the control group.
D) that the control group had such a high mortality rate that further analysis was meaningless.
E) that the experimental group had such high rates of geographical mobility (because of success in life) that individuals were hard to locate.

65. In the late 1930s, Dr. Cabot started the Cambridge-Somerville project to see the extent to which an "enrichment" program for young boys would reduce their involvement with delinquency before they became 18 years old. An "enriched" group of boys was compared with a group that was not given the enrichment experience. Comparison of the two groups yielded which of the following results?
A) No difference between the two groups
B) A difference, but only during the preteen years
C) A difference, but only after age 12
D) A difference in the type of delinquency, but not in amount of delinquency
E) An increase in the delinquency rates of the "enriched" boys

66. Your text states that the directors of the Cambridge-Somerville project got the following reply by one of the participants: "He told me what to do--what's right and wrong--not to fool around with girls. It gives a boy a good feeling to have an older person outside the family to tell you what's right and wrong--someone to take an interest in you." The text goes on to point out that this particular person
A) eventually served a 5-year sentence for a serious sex offense.
B) eventually went on to become a federal judge.
C) ceased all delinquent activity and had a complete "turn-around" behaviorally.
D) was eventually "graduated" from the program because of his utter conformity to all societal expectations, and was no longer appropriate for the program.
E) began to do well academically and socially and eventually became an employee of the project.

Correct: D Page: 224 Scramble Range: ALL
67. The Cambridge-Somerville experiment showed that
A) many children are probably delinquent because of personality disorders.
B) juvenile crime can be deterred by exposing boys to counseling and recreational activities.
C) children from wealthy families are less likely to be delinquent.
D) counseling, health care, and summer camp did not lower rates of juvenile delinquency.
E) researchers can be totally objective in analyzing research results and evaluating programs.

Correct: A Page: 224 Scramble Range: ALL
68. The Cambridge-Somerville experiment conducted in two economically distressed industrial communities tried to see whether or not an experiment to prevent delinquency could work. The researchers found that
A) the enriched-environment boys committed as many crimes as the other boys.
B) the boys with economic incentive to conform had a lower rate of deviance.
C) the boys had a lower rate of deviant behavior than the girls.
D) properly conceptualized, such projects have a significant effect.
E) the experiment worked in the short term (six to twelve months) but not in the long term (one to six years).

Correct: A Page: 225 Scramble Range: ALL
69. The Oregon project
A) tries to prevent delinquency by teaching parenting skills.
B) tries to deter delinquency by scare tactics.
C) tries to deter delinquency by counseling high-risk youths.
D) takes delinquents out of institutions and puts them into group counseling.
E) focuses on female delinquency rather than crimes committed by teenage boys.

Correct: D Page: 225 Scramble Range: ALL
70. Considerable interest, time, and money have been and continue to be invested in various therapeutic techniques aimed at correcting patterns of deviant behavior or preventing its recurrence. Evaluation of these techniques now suggests that
A) they work better with whites than with minority-group persons.
B) they work better with adults than with adolescents.
C) they work better with adolescents than with adults.
D) there is nothing to indicate that such therapy succeeds in achieving these goals.
E) the people who receive these therapies actually have higher crime and deviance rates than the untreated criminal and deviant population.

71. Your text includes a photograph of a group of young people who are taking part in an encounter group led by an adult therapist. The text notes that
A) such groups succeed in delinquency prevention when an aura of trust exists.
B) in such groups, success is heightened when the therapist is "streetwise."
C) in such groups, success occurs only when the predelinquents are preteens.
D) evidence suggests that a combination of therapy and drug therapy succeeds better than encounter group therapy alone.
E) there is no research evidence to suggest that such therapy succeeds.

72. Your text suggests that programs aimed at reducing delinquency have been unsuccessful because
A) they have selected, perhaps unknowingly, teens who were already motivated to change.
B) there has been inadequate funding of such programs, so it follows that better-funded programs would have a higher likelihood of success.
C) the programs did not really change the life circumstances of people.
D) the people running the programs were mainly social workers, and if they were typical, they probably were well-intentioned but lacked knowledge/skill.
E) the teens the programs were aimed at were quite happy and few or none had any interest in changing.

73. Which of the following areas of delinquency prevention does your text mention as having had some modest success?
A) Programs bringing inner-city kids into the suburbs for the summer
B) Programs to teach parents how to be more effective in their parenting behavior
C) The area of abusing controlled substances
D) Alcoholism prevention
E) Teen pregnancy programs

74. What generalization is warranted or justified on the basis of the various programs that have been tried and evaluated regarding delinquency prevention?
A) Programs using individual psychotherapy seem to have been most successful.
B) Participant, in-neighborhood programs by social workers have been the most successful.
C) It is difficult to give an assessment of success because there are no valid instruments to determine program outcomes.
D) Almost without exception, these programs have made no difference in delinquency rates, and the rare successful ones have had very modest success.
E) Almost without exception, the programs that have worked are those that have addressed the problems of neighborhoods rather than individuals' problems.

75. When sociologists study efforts that make would-be delinquents or would-be criminals fail to commit crimes because they are afraid of being caught and of the consequences once they ARE caught, it is proper to speak of which of the following?
A) Prevention
B) Deterrence
C) Misapprehension
D) Pre-apprehension avoidance
E) Psychological controls

76. In England during the eighteenth century, how many crimes carried the death penalty?
A) None
B) Only one
C) Three
D) Forty-four, approximately, depending on what gets counted as crime
E) More than two hundred

77. When was the last time an execution was carried out in Canada?
A) 1550
B) 1790
C) 1910
D) 1962
E) 1990

78. As Plato put it 2,300 years ago, "Punishment brings wisdom; it is the healing act of wickedness." Plato goes on to say that this happens because the point of punishment is not to "retaliate for a past wrong," but to make sure that "the man who is punished AND HE WHO SEES HIM PUNISHED will be kept from doing wrong." The part of the preceding sentence that is capitalized refers to that which sociologists call
A) crime prevention.
B) visualization technique.
C) deterrence.
D) psychological crime prevention.
E) punitive awareness.

79. Deterrence is
A) making the punishment fit the crime.
B) using the threat of punishment to get people to obey the rules.
C) relying on treatment rather than punishment to change people's behavior.
D) all of these.

80.   Which of these statements is an implication of Gibbs's deterrence theory?
A)   Perception is as important as reality.
B)   What is sauce for the goose should be sauce for the gander.
C)   Know thyself? If I knew myself, I would run away!
D)   Confusing the ideal with the real never goes unpunished.
E)   You can't cheat an honest man.

81.   Psychological theories of crime and deviance imply that
A)   more serious punishments will reduce crime.
B)   deterrence theory should work.
C)   preventive measures, such as street lighting, will reduce crime.
D)   increased patrol measures, particularly if visible, will reduce crime.
E)   none of these
NOTE: Cumulative question.

82.   Jack Gibbs's deterrence theory suggests that the crime rate will be lower when the punishment for a crime is all of the following EXCEPT
A)   swift.
B)   certain.
C)   severe.
D)   consistent.
E)   both c and d.

83.   According to Jack Gibbs, deterrence
A)   works if one is likely to get caught.
B)   works even if punishment is not swift.
C)   is not effective at all.
D)   works as long as it does not include capital punishment.
E)   works for women but not for men.

84.   Jack Gibbs's deterrence theory suggests that when three conditions are met, deviant acts will be reduced. Some social scientists have noted, however, that it is not so important that these conditions actually be met, but that
A)   people in the general public perceive that the conditions exist.
B)   there be a plan that will create the three conditions in the definite future.
C)   parents, aware of the three conditions, socialize their children better now than in the past.
D)   the very suggestion and planning of the three conditions get the attention of the criminal element of the population, thus reducing crime.
E)   the court system be ready to put the conditions into effect, should the need arise, thus producing greater willingness to deal with the problem.

85.   Which of the following best illustrates Gibbs's deterrence theory?
   A)   A group of teens refrains from shoplifting because their church teaches
        that they will be punished for it eventually in the afterlife.
   B)   A group of high school girls considers painting the school roof but decides
        there is a 30 percent chance of getting caught, so they do not do it.
   C)   A group of 200 junior high schoolers attends a course of five 30-minute
        lectures on the hazards of drinking.
   D)   A person who is found guilty of drinking WHILE driving ("open container"
        violation) has his driver's license taken away for five years minimum.
   E)   A university parking lot has five-inch spikes that automatically puncture
        each of your tires in four places if you try to go into the lot without a
        proper card.

86.   According to your text, whether capital punishment deters homicides and
      whether it is morally justified are
   A)   basically the same question.
   B)   both answered "No."
   C)   both answered "Yes."
   D)   wholly distinct questions.
   E)   questions that must await more research.

87.   Which of the following is true?
   A)   Only about half of serious crimes are ever reported to the police.
   B)   Most criminals are caught and go to prison.
   C)   Larceny, burglary, and auto theft have high arrest rates.
   D)   Most murders are never solved.
   E)   Most criminals are caught but less than half of these are sent to prison.

88.   Which of the following statements is FALSE, according to the text?
   A)   Most murders are solved in the United States, resulting in an arrest.
   B)   About 75 percent of known crimes are at least reported to the police.
   C)   Less than one in nine reported burglaries are cleared by an arrest.
   D)   Reported assaults and rapes result in arrests about half the time.
   E)   More than a quarter of auto thefts go unreported.

89.   Your text cites the F.B.I. 1990 information about reported crimes that are
      cleared by arrest. According to this information, the reported crime most often
      cleared by arrest is _____ and the crime least often cleared is _____.
   A)   murder; robbery
   B)   larceny; robbery
   C)   murder; burglary
   D)   larceny; auto theft
   E)   assault; rape

90. According to research by Zeisel, of every 1,000 felonies committed in the United States, _____ result in sentences to serve more than one year in prison.
   A) 3
   B) 79
   C) 176
   D) 240
   E) 558

91. People who have been punished by the criminal justice system
   A) are more likely than other people to believe that crime doesn't pay.
   B) perceive lower risks in crime.
   C) tend to believe that they have a good chance of getting caught and punished.
   D) are less likely to return to prison if they have committed a crime for which the police have low arrest rate.
   E) are as likely to return to prison for rape as they are for burglary.

92. Up until the end of the seventeenth century, imprisonment was very rarely used as a punishment for the guilty and convicted because
   A) there were no effective prisons in those days, since the materials did not then exist.
   B) people were allowed to buy their way out of imprisonment.
   C) imprisonment was considered too expensive, so the usual punishment was death or physical punishment such as flogging or mutilation.
   D) the church had institutionalized the taking of the guilty and putting them into monasteries or cloisters, but the effect of "removal" was the same.
   E) the prisons were so unsanitary and dangerous that being sentenced to one meant death almost without exception.

93. For centuries, jails and prisons were places where people who were arrested awaited trial or sentencing. Once sentenced, punishment was usually
   A) decided upon by the victim of the crime.
   B) carried out by a community member whose reputation was itself damaged.
   C) expulsion from the community (which usually meant death anyway).
   D) swift and painful, if not fatal.
   E) probation for members of the community who had been law-abiding until their offense.

94.   The idea of prisons in the sense that we know them today in the United States as a place where people are sent to serve out a sentence appeared for the first time in
A)   Japan during the 1500s and was brought to Europe around 1600 by Jesuit priests.
B)   Italy and Sicily, because of a need to have a holding area for political prisoners.
C)   the upper-class circles of Europe, who chose not to execute upper-class offenders.
D)   Pennsylvania at the direction of the Quaker William Penn.
E)   the area that is now Turkey and Afghanistan, for religious reasons.

95.   The recidivism rate
A)   is lower in modern therapeutic prisons than in traditional punitive ones.
B)   is about 60 percent.
C)   is the percent of crimes reported to the police.
D)   is about the same no matter what the crime.
E)   shows that our attempts to resocialize prisoners have been successful.
F)   all of these

96.   The recidivism rate refers to which of the following?
A)   The rate of persons found guilty vs. those actually spending time in prison
B)   The ratio of homosexuals to heterosexuals in prison populations
C)   The ratio of heterosexuals who are recruited into the prison homosexual subculture, as compared to those who are not recruited in this way
D)   The proportion of those arrested who are never brought to trial because of legal maneuvering and the inability of the courts to process so many offenses
E)   The proportion of those released from prison who eventually end up there again

97.   At present, it costs more than _____ a year to keep a person in prison in the United States.
A) $15,000
B) $40,000
C) $35,000
D) $20,000
E) $25,000

98.   In what sense are prisons functional?
A)   They deter crime
B)   They rehabilitate criminals
C)   They discourage deviant attachments
D)   They provide prisoners an opportunity to learn valuable skills and do important work for the state
E)   None of these

Correct: D   Page: 238 Scramble Range: ALL
99.   The TARP experiment
A)   was successful in reducing juvenile delinquency.
B)   paid ex-convicts while they were in prison.
C)   found that monetary payment reduced recidivism.
D)   showed that monetary payments had no effect on re-arrest rates.
E)   supported Lombroso's theory of the born criminal.

Correct: B   Page: Ch7 Scramble Range: A-D
100.   The control theory of crime and deviance implies that which of the following control measures will be most effective?
A)   Counseling
B)   Publicizing arrests
C)   Capital punishment
D)   Longer jail terms
E)   None of these

NOTE: Cumulative question

Correct: D   Page: Ch7 Scramble Range: A-D
101.   The strain theory of crime and deviance implies that which of the following control measures will be most effective?
A)   Counseling
B)   Capital punishment
C)   Longer jail terms
D)   Reducing inequality
E)   None of these

NOTE: Cumulative question.

Chapter 9: Concepts and Theories of Stratification

True/False

Correct: T   Page: Ch4
1. Stratification is a social structure.
    NOTE: Cumulative question.

Correct: T   Page: 246
2. Plato saw only two classes in Greek society--the rich and the poor-- and he saw them involved in eternal conflict.

Correct: F   Page: 247
3. Karl Marx concluded that all societies, at whatever historical period, have three social classes.

Correct: F   Page: 247
4. Karl Marx believed that as the capitalist system evolved the middle class would thrive and eventually dominate the proletariat class.

Correct: F   Page: 247
5. By "means of production," Marx meant the masses of people who did the real work in society.

Correct: T   Page: 247
6. Karl Marx's conception of social class in capitalist societies divides the classes on the basis of ownership or nonownership of the means of production.

Correct: F   Page: 247
7. Karl Marx's conception of social class in capitalist societies divides society into four major classes.

Correct: F   Page: 247
8. Karl Marx's conception of social class in capitalist societies incorporates the insight that control of property, not just ownership, is an important basis for stratification.

Correct: T   Page: 247
9. Karl Marx's conception of social class in capitalist societies includes a "psychological" element.

Correct: F   Page: 249
10. Karl Marx's conception of social class in capitalist societies is multidimensional.

Correct: F   Page: 249
11. Max Weber's concept of social class defines classes on the basis of ownership of the means of production.

Correct: T   Page: 249
12. Max Weber's concept of social class is able (unlike Marx's concept) to deal with managers who control companies they do not own.

Correct: T   Page: 249
13. Max Weber's concept of social class defines control of property, not simply its ownership, as crucial for stratification.

Correct: F   Page: 251
14. Max Weber's concept of social class does not have enough categories to analyze status inconsistency.

Correct: F   Page: 251
15. People who have status inconsistency tend to support conservative political movements.

Correct: T   Page: 251
16. Most people don't have status inconsistency.

Correct: F   Page: 252
17. The caste system in India is a good example of an achieved status system.

Correct: F   Page: 252
18. In a society with an ascribed status system, people tend to rise or fall according to their individual merit.

Correct: F   Page: 252
19. Social mobility is when people move from one place to another to find work.

Correct: F   Page: 252
20. Frequently changing jobs is an example of social mobility.

Correct: T   Page: 252
21. There is more social mobility in societies with achieved status systems.

Correct: T   Page: 257
22. Marx's claim that communist societies would be classless was based on the elimination of private ownership of the means of production.

Correct: F   Page: 258
23. Mosca argued that only democratic societies could be unstratified.

Correct: T   Page: 258
24. Mosca argued that it is impossible for societies to exist without social stratification.

Correct: F   Page: 259
25. The functionalist theory of stratification denies that some positions in society are more important than others.

Correct: F   Page: 259
26. The functionalist theory of stratification predicts that the less replaceable a position, the lower its level of rewards.

Correct: F   Page: 262
27. The evolutionary theory of stratification explains how unstratified societies have developed.

Correct: F   Page: 262
28. The evolutionary theory of stratification contradicts the functionalist theory.

Correct: T   Page: 262
29. The conflict theory of stratification incorporates Mosca's proposition that people will use their power to exploit others.

Correct: T   Page: 262
30. The conflict theory of stratification sees stratification systems as the result of competition among groups for rewards.

Correct: T   Page: 262
31. The conflict theory of stratification argues that political power can be used to increase or decrease replaceability.

Correct: F   Page: 262
32. The conflict theory of stratification takes the position that unstratified societies are possible.

Correct: T   Page: 264
33. Unions try to use power to decrease position replaceability.

Reference Key: STORY9.1
Looking at the United States, we find that some occupations rank higher on income and others rank lower. In other words, we see inequality in economic rewards among occupations in our society.

Correct: F   Page: 251   Refer to: STORY9.1
34. This is called status inconsistency.

Correct: T   Page: 245   Refer to: STORY9.1
35. This is called stratification.

Correct: T   Page: Ch4   Refer to: STORY9.1
36. This is an example of social structure.
                    NOTE: Cumulative question.

Correct: F   Page: 259   Refer to: STORY9.1
37. This inequality depends on the individual characteristics of those people in those occupations.

Correct: F   Page: 259   Refer to: STORY9.1
38. To understand this inequality, functionalists would ask about how much the occupation controls itself.

Correct: T   Page: 260   Refer to: STORY9.1
39. To understand this inequality, functionalists would ask about the education and training period for the occupations.

Correct: T   Page: 263   Refer to: STORY9.1
40. To understand this inequality, conflict theorists would ask how much control members of the occupation have over the occupation.

Correct: T   Page: 249   Refer to: STORY9.1
41.   Weber would ask about other than economic rewards from the occupations.

Correct: F   Page: 247   Refer to: STORY9.1
42.   Marx would ask about the relative prestige of the occupations.

Reference Key: STORY9.2
The occupation of medical doctor (MD) in the United States is economically well rewarded and very prestigious. The occupation of nurse, in contrast, is comparatively poorly rewarded and much less prestigious.

Correct: T   Page: Ch4   Refer to: STORY9.2
43.   This is an example of social structure.
NOTE: Cumulative question.

Correct: F   Page: 252   Refer to: STORY9.2
44.   In our society, medical doctor is an ascribed status.

Correct: T   Page: 259   Refer to: STORY9.2
45.   Functionalists would point to the longer education of doctors to explain this.

Correct: T   Page: 260   Refer to: STORY9.2
46.   Davis and Moore would argue that doctors are more important for the society than nurses.

Correct: T   Page: 260   Refer to: STORY9.2
47.   Functionalists would argue that nurses are more replaceable than doctors.

Correct: F   Page: 263   Refer to: STORY9.2
48.   Conflict theorists would argue that nurses are more important than doctors.

Correct: T   Page: 263   Refer to: STORY9.2
49.   Conflict theorists would point out that doctors control their own occupation while nurses don't.

Correct: T   Page: 263   Refer to: STORY9.2
50.   Conflict theorists would point out that the difference between doctors and nurses is greater than the functionalists would predict.

Correct: F   Page: 249   Refer to: STORY9.2
51.   Functionalists would point out that power has a great effect on replaceability.

Reference Key: STORY9.3

A sociologist looked at information from the 1990 and 1991 General Social Survey (a national survey of adults in the United States). He examined responses to the question "If you were to get enough money to live as comfortably as you would like for the rest of your life, would you continue to work or would you stop working?" in relation to the respondent's income. This is the cross-tabulation he produced:

	Less than $10K	$10-25K	$25-40K	$40-60K	Over $60K
Work	71%	68%	68%	76%	79%
Stop	29%	32%	32%	24%	21%
	------	------	------	------	------
	100%	100%	100%	100%	100%

Correct: F   Page: Ch3   Refer to: STORY9.3
52.   This sociologist performed an experiment.
Note: Cumulative question.

Correct: F   Page: Ch4   Refer to: STORY9.3
53.   The 29% in the table shows that 29 percent of those who would stop working earn under $10,000 per year.
Note: Cumulative question.

Correct: T   Page: Ch4   Refer to: STORY9.3
54.   The 79% in the table shows that 79 out of every 100 respondents with incomes of over $60,000 a year would keep working.
Note: Cumulative question.

Correct: F   Page: Ch4   Refer to: STORY9.3
55.   This table shows that the lower your income the greater your desire to keep working.
Note: Cumulative question.

Correct: F   Page: 259   Refer to: STORY9.3
56.   These findings give strong support for the functionalist theory of stratification.

Correct: T   Page: 259   Refer to: STORY9.3
57.   These findings suggest that the functional theory of stratification may overstate financial rewards as an incentive for work.

Correct: T   Page: 260   Refer to: STORY9.3
58.   In terms of the toy society discussed in Chapter 9, these findings suggest that Ay might well continue to produce air even if he were not well rewarded for it.

Correct: F   Page: 259   Refer to: STORY9.3
59.   This finding seems consistent with the wide agreement with the statement, "No one would be expected to study for years to learn to be a doctor or a lawyer unless they expected to earn a lot more than ordinary workers."

60. Given differential socialization, we would expect that there would be a difference between men and women's responses to the "would you stop working" question.
Note: Cumulative question.

61. This finding suggests that wanting to work is instinctual in human beings.
Note: Cumulative question.

Multiple Choice

62. The Roman stratification system included the "proletarii" (a term that played a part in the writings of another social scientist). What is a literal translation of the term "proletarii?"
A) Having many children
B) Possessing abundant courage
C) Having an abundance of property
D) One who has much spare time
E) To be in favor of gradual social reform

63. In a general way, the concept of stratification comes closest to which of these?
A) Justification
B) Differentiation
C) Ranking
D) Exploitation
E) Equality

64. The word "class" comes to us from the Romans, who used the term "classis" to divide the population into a number of groups for the purpose of
A) taxation.
B) military conscription.
C) assigning people to "the games" as spectators or as participants.
D) economic exploitation.
E) carefully planned economic expansionism.

65. One of the classes in the Roman stratification were the "assidui" (from which the word "assiduous" comes). The assidui were
A) the hard-working laboring class.
B) the hard-working class that today would be called "white-collar."
C) the class that today would be called "blue-collar."
D) the richest Romans.
E) the slave caste, not even included in the census.

Correct: C Page: 247 Scramble Range: ALL
66. When Karl Marx talked about "everything besides human labor that goes into producing wealth," he called it
A) the interstices of the economy.
B) the nonmaterial economy.
C) the means of production.
D) the instruments of oppression.
E) the People's Cultural Possibilities.

Correct: D Page: 247 Scramble Range: ALL
67. Which of the following would be examples of what Marx called "lumpenproletariat"?
A) A cashier and a currently unemployed waitress
B) Farmers and commercial fishermen
C) Two banker's kids who have been temporarily suspended from school
D) A long-time wino and a "bag lady"
E) A corporate biochemist and a state senator

Correct: A Page: 247 Scramble Range: ALL
68. Marx felt that the main determinant of a person's social class position was which one of these?
A) One's position in the economic system
B) One's intelligence, but more importantly, one's level of formal education
C) The view a person had about the nature of reality, especially political reality
D) The view a person had about the nature of reality, especially as regards religion
E) The reputation that a person's family has in a community in which the family is known

Correct: C Page: 247 Scramble Range: ALL
69. In the Marxian view, which of the following owns the means of production in a capitalist society?
A) Presidium
B) Grosse fugue
C) Bourgeoisie
D) White-collar workers
E) Proletariat

Correct: C Page: 249 Scramble Range: ALL
70. Perhaps the most serious flaw in Marx's theory of stratification was failure to include _____ in his classes.
A) owners
B) workers
C) peasants
D) people who were marginal to the economy
E) self-employed professionals

71. Marx termed those who own the means of production the
    A) proletariat.
    B) bourgeoisie.
    C) blue-collar workers.
    D) lower class.
    E) lumpenproletariat.

72. Marx termed those who do not own the means of production and therefore must sell their labor to those owners
    A) the bourgeoisie.
    B) the proletariat.
    C) the lumpenproletariat.
    D) the middle class.
    E) none of the above.

73. According to Marxian theory, one dimension of class serves as the independent variable. All other dimensions are dependent on it. What is the independent variable?
    A) Economics
    B) Education
    C) Family
    D) Government
    E) Religion
    F) None of the above

74. Marx termed working class people as
    A) poor.
    B) white-collar.
    C) proletariat.
    D) bourgeoisie.
    E) unfortunate.
    F) all of these

75. Possession of which of the following is LEAST significant in Marx's theory of social class?
    A) Capital
    B) Education
    C) Land
    D) Machines
    E) Tools

76. Marx saw that there is no single answer to the question of how many classes to identify in societies. Instead, he thought the answer depends on which society and when. But Marx expected modern capitalist societies to consist of which two classes?
    A) Working class and the parasitic class
    B) Proletariat and the bourgeoisie classes
    C) Proletariat and the managerial classes
    D) Lumpenschaft class and the wissenschaft class
    E) Intelligentsia and the bourgeoisie

77. According to Karl Marx, _____ has been the main driving force of history, propelling societies through various stages of development.
    A) discovery of new capital
    B) competition between nations for natural resources
    C) competition between nations for strategic advantage
    D) mankind's instinct to be as advanced as possible
    E) class conflict

78. Which of the following would be a good example of what Karl Marx meant by "false consciousness"?
    A) A waitress at a fast-food restaurant who thinks she is upper middle-class
    B) A man who thinks that males should be the heads of households
    C) A teenager who feels that the current culture is evil and ought to be abolished or run by young people
    D) A person who has completely unrealistic ideas about economic reality and completely unworkable ideas about how to renew the world
    E) A lower-class person who thinks that lower-class people ought to rise up and overthrow the classes above them

79. Karl Marx implied that all differences in position among people in society are wholly the result of
    A) kinship.
    B) long-term consequences of inherited intelligence and its consequences.
    C) the unknowable twists and turns taken by evolutionary history.
    D) conflict between the life-styles of the various social classes.
    E) property ownership.

80. Max Weber (1864-1920) was a sociologist who was stimulated in part by Marxist ideas. According to Weber, a person's position in the stratification system has the three dimensions of
    A) education, occupation, and income.
    B) class, status, and party.
    C) influence, authority, and force.
    D) personal, familial, and social position.
    E) other-perception, self-perception, and objective reality.

Correct: A   Page: 249 Scramble Range: A-D
81. When Weber said that stratification in society has three dimensions he meant
A) that there are three important types of inequality in societies.
B) that we must look at the historical dimension as well as current structures.
C) that physical context is as important as phenotype and genotype.
D) that age, sex and race must be included in any discussion of stratification.
E) all of these

Correct: E   Page: 249 Scramble Range: ALL
82. Max Weber's chief criticism of Karl Marx's theory of stratification was that
A) Marx failed to see the power in the hands of the peasants.
B) Marx failed to anticipate unions.
C) Marx did not anticipate the rise of a middle class.
D) Marx's theory applied only to Germany.
E) Marx's theory was unidimensional.

Correct: A   Page: 249 Scramble Range: ALL
83. According to your text's discussion of the work of Max Weber, Junkers were
A) aristocrats.
B) cheap pulp magazines with overly romanticized stories, read by clerks and cashiers in their spare time.
C) lower-class people who live on the leavings of other social classes.
D) working-class people's most common form of automotive transportation.
E) illiterates.

Correct: C   Page: 249 Scramble Range: ALL
84. To Weber, the term "class"
A) defines the ability to get one's way despite resistance of others.
B) denotes any particular position in the stratification system.
C) defines economic advantage.
D) has no relevance for social scientists.
E) was not significant.

Correct: B   Page: 249 Scramble Range: A-D
85. Weber termed groups of people with similar life chances as determined by the economic position in society
A) prestige groups.
B) classes.
C) statuses.
D) replaceability groups.
E) none of these

Correct: D   Page: 250 Scramble Range: ALL
86. Weber's term "status" is interchangeable with
A) structural mobility.
B) utopia.
C) production.
D) prestige.
E) power.

Correct: A   Page: 250 Scramble Range: ALL

87.   Paulette has a personal net worth of $6 million. Her parents were penniless and out of work before Paulette won the lottery. Paulette acts, speaks, and engages in activities that people in her community associate with the bottom of the stratification system. In the three-part system proposed by Weber, it is clear that Paulette has a lot of
A)   class.
B)   political power.
C)   status.
D)   prestige.
E)   caste.

Correct: D   Page: 250 Scramble Range: ALL

88.   Pierre is the relatively poor son of a previously wealthy but still "distinguished" family in France. Pierre and his family no longer have any impact on the political facts of life in their area, but they are still looked up to by "the very best people" as living the kind of life that "the very best people" ought to live. According to Weber's three-fold conceptualization, it seems clear that Pierre has a lot of
A)   class.
B)   party.
C)   power.
D)   prestige.
E)   nouveau flaire.

Correct: E   Page: 249 Scramble Range: ALL

89.   Who proposed that stratification is based on the factors of class, status, and power?
A)   Dahrendorf
B)   Lenski
C)   Marx
D)   Mosca
E)   Weber

Correct: D   Page: 250 Scramble Range: ALL

90.   Weber's concept of prestige would be best illustrated by
A)   the manager of a fast-food restaurant demanding that all employees wear red socks.
B)   the son of a wealthy man paying his playmates to let him be the team pitcher.
C)   a famous football player speaking to a group on the immorality of the Dallas Cowboy cheerleaders.
D)   a respected artist influencing the other members of the university's board of regents to allocate more of the university's budget to the fine arts.
E)   a professor refusing to admit students to class after the bell has rung.

91. The chief controller of the Panama Canal does not have an enormous amount of money. And he does not have an elaborate, "jazzy," or admired life-style. But he is listened to and is given a great deal of attention by businessmen and politicians in the Panama Canal Zone because the chief controller has a lot of
A) power.
B) prestige.
C) class.
D) infrastructure.
E) dysfunctional "punch."

92. The ability to get one's way despite the resistance of others is termed
A) property.
B) class
C) prestige.
D) status.
E) none of these

93. A high school teacher may not be able to afford a house on the same block with some of his former college classmates. This is an example of
A) class consciousness.
B) false class consciousness.
C) status inconsistency.
D) false status inconsistency.
E) structural mobility.

94. The capacity to prevail even though others don't want you to is called
A) class.
B) status.
C) chutzpa.
D) power.

95. Which person would MOST likely experience status inconsistency?
A) A white male doctor
B) A female nurse
C) A white male college professor
D) A Afro-American female college president
E) A female telephone operator

96. The status inconsistency theory of Gerhard Lenski
A) explains why Republicans are conservative.
B) has not been tested empirically.
C) applies primarily to people who have a mixture of lower-class and middle-class statuses.
D) can be used with Max Weber's stratification theory but not with that of Karl Marx.
E) is a direct outgrowth of Karl Marx's ideas on stratification

Correct: A   Page: 251 Scramble Range: ALL
97. Gary Marx's study of radical attitudes of Afro-American bankers and physicians was done in relation to the theory of
A)   status inconsistency.
B)   class consciousness.
C)   social mobility.
D)   conflict.
E)   functionalism.

Correct: C   Page: 251 Scramble Range: ALL
98. A pilot for a major airline who also happened to be female, Cherokee, and a political leader in her Buddhist community would bring to mind which of the following sociological concepts?
A)   Proletarianism
B)   Dysfunctional complexity
C)   Status inconsistency
D)   The "Brahman problem"
E)   The dilemma of achieved status

Correct: D   Page: 251 Scramble Range: ALL
99. Which of the following is the BEST example of status inconsistency?
A)   Paul gets an A on one exam, a C on the second exam, and a B on the third exam.
B)   Paul goes out with Shimatsu Wanatabe, with Immugamba Mukasa, with Ginela Vasquez, and with Elizabeth Beckwith.
C)   Andy is angry with his father, but his father is not angry with Andy.
D)   Bobby, a Afro-American, works hard and becomes a certified public accountant and joins the Episcopal church.
E)   Carol doesn't know whether or not to leave her secretarial job to marry a man who is an insurance agent, but she eventually does so.

Correct: D   Page: 252 Scramble Range: ALL
100. Age 21; male; Japanese; born illegitimate--these characteristics are all examples of which of the following?
A)   Middle class
B)   Negative life-chances
C)   Mixed life-chances
D)   Ascribed statuses
E)   Flexible roles

Correct: B   Page: 252 Scramble Range: A-D
101. In a caste system
A)   status is based entirely on ascription.
B)   ascription is the overwhelming basis for status.
C)   status is based solely on achievement.
D)   achievement is the overwhelming basis for status.
E)   none of these

102. A stratification system that is overwhelmingly castelike is one in which
    A) tradition is approximately as important as achievement.
    B) education counts for nothing or almost nothing in determining position.
    C) kinship is inconsequential for the allocation of statuses.
    D) there are high rates of individual vertical mobility.
    E) ascription plays an important role.

103. The status gained on the basis of merit is
    A) ascribed status.
    B) achieved status.
    C) deserved status.
    D) mobilized status.
    E) distinguished status.

104. In a caste system
    A) exchange mobility is the only type of mobility possible.
    B) there is absolutely no mobility.
    C) one maintains one's caste position through achievement.
    D) one's occupation is determined by one's caste position.
    E) one is guaranteed one's position in society regardless of performance level.

105. If you MUST inherit your parents' position in the stratification system and if there is NOTHING you can do about it, then
    A) you have the problem of the pariah.
    B) your situation is very castelike.
    C) you can experience only vertical mobility.
    D) you have no statuses, strictly speaking.
    E) you are not functionally integrated with adjacent statuses.

106. For the purposes of this question, let's imagine the following situation: Carol is born to a lowly ranked minority group in southeastern Louisiana. She is economically disadvantaged because no one in her family qualifies for a job that earns much money. She is illiterate and can't improve her education. She meets only boys from a situation similar to her own. People from the "better classes" of the area know by her clothing, food, and manner that they want nothing to do with her. She avoids them, too. Sociologically, Carol's situation is
    A) primed for high levels of vertical mobility.
    B) a good example of achieved status.
    C) castelike.
    D) an excellent example of what it is like to be in the bourgoise.
    E) similar to that found in times of rapid social change.

Correct: C   Page: 252 Scramble Range: A-D
107.   Social mobility refers to
A)   the tendency of people to change jobs as they seek better conditions.
B)   people moving from place to place to find work.
C)   the relationship of a person's status to the status of their parents.
D)   changes in status that people experience during their careers.
E)   all of the above.

Correct: E   Page: 254 Scramble Range: ALL
108.   Edmund, son of a cotton-picker, studies hard and eventually becomes a bank vice-president. Josephine, daughter of a banker, messes around in college, flunks out, and finds herself picking cotton and depositing her meager earnings with bank tellers supervised by Edmund. What we have here is an example of
A)   intensive castelike situations.
B)   an "estate system" at work.
C)   status inconsistency.
D)   Aristotelian mobility justice.
E)   exchange mobility.

Correct: E   Page: 254 Scramble Range: ALL
109.   One can expect the most mobility in a society in which
A)   a caste system predominates.
B)   ascribed status is more important than achieved status.
C)   achieved mobility is minimal.
D)   exchange mobility is the chief form of mobility in operation.
E)   industrialization necessitates structural mobility.

Correct: C   Page: 254 Scramble Range: ALL
110.   There is very little _____ when the ascriptive status rule operates in a society, but if status is through achievement, there is a fair amount of such mobility.
A)   class conflict-based mobility
B)   status inconsistency-based mobility
C)   exchange mobility
D)   individual horizontal mobility
E)   group horizontal mobility

Correct: A   Page: 254 Scramble Range: ALL
111.   When people move up int the stratification system because of an increase in higher status jobs, sociologists call it _____ mobility.
A)   structural
B)   exchange
C)   downward

112. Compared to 1940, there are many fewer blue collar and laboring jobs in today's society. A much larger proportion of jobs are white collar. This illustrates
    A) differential socialization.
    B) changes in the phenotype.
    C) the increasing elimination of racial and ethnic discrimination.
    D) structural mobility.
    E) informal social control.

113. If a society has 20 percent high-status positions, 30 percent middle-status positions, and 50 percent low-status positions in 1987, and ten years later, in 1997, has the same distribution of positions (20 percent, 30 percent, 50 percent) BUT with some people from high-status positions now in low-status positions, this would be an example of
    A) democratic mobility.
    B) structural mobility.
    C) exchange mobility.
    D) reciprocal mobility.
    E) reactionary mobility.

114. Tom, a young citizen of the small socialist nation called Setats Detinu, has been a lower-middle-class person for some time. All of a sudden, most of the jobs on the bottom third of the occupational structure are eliminated. At the same time, a bunch of high-tech, well-paying jobs open up and the government is anxious to fill them with people who are willing to learn. Tom is willing to learn and soon successfully occupies one of these new high-tech, well-paying upper-middle-class jobs. What is the sociological concept that applies?
    A) Structural mobility
    B) Horizontal mobility
    C) Fortuitous mobility
    D) Instrumental mobility
    E) Occupational cathexis

115. Structural mobility occurs
    A) in times of political unrest.
    B) during periods of change in government leadership.
    C) regardless of the rules governing status.
    D) in direct correlation with exchange mobility.
    E) only in the absence of exchange mobility.

116. A _____ plans for an ideal society. A(n) _____ plans to eliminate society.
    A) utopian; anarchist
    B) fascist; Marxist
    C) Marxist; fascist
    D) Marxist; Trotskyite
    E) communist; socialist

117.   If you think about what the ideal society would be like, then you are constructing
A)   a topia.
B)   a utopia.
C)   a dystopia.
D)   a neotopia.
E)   an introtopia.

118.   Which of the following statements about utopian societies is FALSE?
A)   The first ones originated during the Industrial Revolution
B)   None has ever been successful
C)   Some have been based on a religious set of ideas
D)   Some have been operated in a socialistic fashion
E)   They reflect a deep discontent with the quality of life in the larger society

119.   If it's your view that society is unnecessary and should be gotten rid of, leaving people to naturally and automatically do what needs to be done in order for individuals, society, and groups to survive, then you
A)   have thrown in your lot with the Civil Libertarians.
B)   have aligned yourself with those taking the Jeffersonian view of government.
C)   are a "vulgar" Trotskyite.
D)   are a "refined" Trotskyite.
E)   are an anarchist.

120.   According to Ralf Dahrendorf, Marx was only partly right. Dahrendorf argued that the state or government could never be completely eliminated. People would always have to differ greatly in terms of their
A)   native or natural ability.
B)   ownership of the means of production.
C)   control over the means of production.
D)   right of access to the necessities of life.
E)   ability to interact successfully or productively with others.

121.   Dahrendorf's critique of Marx's idea of a classless society amounted to saying that
A)   it is impossible to eliminate the private ownership of the means of production.
B)   it is not functional to eliminate the private ownership of the means of production.
C)   eliminating private ownership of the means of production would amount to anarchy.
D)   eliminating the private ownership of the means of production would ultimately increase the disparity between classes.
E)   ownership of the means of production is not the only factor leading to inequality.

Correct: B   Page: 258 Scramble Range: ALL
122. Dahrendorf, a conflict theorist, criticized Marx's idea of a classless society. He argued that stratification is inevitable because of
A) the fact that some people have more innate ability than others.
B) the need to have unequal power differences to coordinate activities.
C) the need or drive that some people have to distinguish themselves from the masses.
D) the threat that other countries have for national security, forcing an almost militaristic stratification system into existence.
E) hereditary wealth.

Correct: B   Page: 258 Scramble Range: ALL
123. According to Gaetano Mosca, human societies cannot exist without political organization. Moreover, said Mosca, whenever there is political organization, there must also be
A) a formal organization.
B) power inequalities.
C) some political ideology.
D) utopian goals.
E) some type of additional surplus produced by the political structure.

Correct: A   Page: 258 Scramble Range: ALL
124. In his book THE RULING CLASS (1896), Gaetano Mosca argued that societies must be stratified. A main part of his theory was that wherever there is _____, there must be inequalities of _____.
A) political organization; power
B) human society; reward
C) reward; human society
D) human nature; reward
E) instinct; prestige

Correct: D   Page: 258 Scramble Range: ALL
125. Mosca (THE RULING CLASS) assumed that it is human nature for people to
A) seek to protect those like themselves.
B) be willing to die for a cause.
C) be more willing to die for things than for causes.
D) be selfish and seek to further their own personal advantage.
E) seek to serve others, even at great personal cost.

Correct: A   Page: 258 Scramble Range: ALL
126. In THE RULING CLASS, Gaetano Mosca argued that when people come to occupy positions of great power, it is only natural for them to
A) use it to increase their personal wealth and power.
B) seek "decentralist" administrative and political policies.
C) begin to take a broader, overall view of reality in order to govern well.
D) try to expand the territorial boundaries of the society they find themselves in.
E) try to apologize for the fortuitous position in which they find themselves.

Correct: C   Page: 259 Scramble Range: ALL

127.   A vice-president in charge of personnel explains to the president of the company that the company has to pay accountants more money than it pays experienced secretaries. The vice-president explains that there are relatively few experienced accountants looking for employment but that there are relatively more experienced secretaries available for the available jobs in that line of work. The company must offer accountants more money than it offers secretaries because only in that way can the company hire accountants. Secretaries can be hired for less money because they are willing to settle for less money in order to get a job. According to your text, this kind of reasoning is an illustration of
A)   occupational strata theory of mobility.
B)   the main idea in Mosca's THE RULING CLASS.
C)   the functionalist theory of stratification.
D)   the evolutionary theory of stratification.
E)   the symbolic interactionist theory of stratification.

Correct: A   Page: 259 Scramble Range: ALL

128.   The proposition that greater rewards must be offered to people who fill very important positions in a society is basic to
A)   functionalist theory.
B)   conflict theory.
C)   evolutionary theory.
D)   all modern-day theories of stratification.
E)   anarchist thought.

Correct: E   Page: 259 Scramble Range: ALL

129.   One theory of social stratification is Davis and Moore's functionalist theory of stratification. According to this theory, a position is of high functional importance to a society depending on
A)   the amount of education and training required to fill it.
B)   the amount of risk a person takes in training for it and/or occupying it.
C)   whether or not it performs any useful function in society.
D)   whether or not it has any dysfunctions for the society at large.
E)   how hard it is to replace either the position or the person occupying it.

Correct: A   Page: 259 Scramble Range: A-D

130.   When one agrees that "no one would be expected to study for years to become a doctor or lawyer unless the person expected to earn a lot more than ordinary workers," one is
A)   accepting the essential principle of functionalist theory.
B)   accepting that occupation is an ascribed status.
C)   accepting the essential principle of conflict theory.
D)   pointing to differences in the extent to which workers control their own occupations.
E)   all of these

131. What sociological concept explains the difference in payment when a university pays the corporate finance professor more than the chaplain because it is necessary to do so to get a finance professor to come to the school (there are so many jobs for them in business), while many ministers without a church position would welcome the chance to be a chaplain?
    A) Functional equivalence
    B) Caste orientation
    C) Educational dysfunctions
    D) Replaceability
    E) Social role

132. Perhaps the key point in Davis and Moore's functionalist theory of stratification is that _____ is the dominant basis of functional importance.
    A) traditional recognition
    B) future orientation
    C) popularity among the general public
    D) status ascription vs. status achieved
    E) position replaceability

133. In terms of the functionalist theory, who is the LEAST replaceable within a hospital?
    A) Orderly
    B) Custodian
    C) Doctor
    D) Nurse
    E) Receptionist

134. Looking at the United States, we find that some occupations rank higher on income and others rank lower. In other words, we see inequality in economic rewards among occupations in our society.
    A) This inequality depends on the individual characteristics of those people in those occupations.
    B) To understand this inequality, functionalists would ask about how much the occupation controls itself.
    C) This inequality is also called status inconsistency.
    D) To understand this inequality, functionalists would ask about the education and training period for the occupations.
    E) All of these
    F) None of these

135. All profit in an exchange in excess of the minimum amount needed to cause an exchange to occur is
    A) cheating.
    B) unionized.
    C) good business.
    D) interest.
    E) exploitation.

Correct: C   Page: 263   Scramble Range: ALL
136.   According to the text, _____ first attempt to establish their positions as irreplaceable and then make their members irreplaceable in the position.
A)   high castes
B)   military personnel
C)   professionals
D)   international corporations
E)   Second World nations

Correct: E   Page: 263   Scramble Range: A-D
137.   The occupation of medical doctor in the United States is economically well rewarded and very prestigious. The occupation of nurse, in contrast, is comparatively poorly rewarded and much less prestigious.
A)   Functionalists would point to the longer education of doctors to explain this.
B)   Davis and Moore would argue that doctors are more important for the society than nurses.
C)   Conflict theorists would point out that doctors control their own occupation while nurses don't.
D)   Conflict theorists would point out that the difference between doctors and nurses is greater than the functionalists would predict.
E)   All of these
F)   None of these

Correct: B   Page: 264   Scramble Range: ALL
138.   Your text's analysis of unions argues that a main goal of unions is to
A)   exert pressure to make management increase jobs filled by ascription.
B)   use power to decrease replaceability.
C)   exchange their bourgeoisie status for the desired proletarian status.
D)   even out their status inconsistency.
E)   turn their occupations into skilled trades with no organization as such.

Correct: E   Page: 263   Scramble Range: A-D
139.   Replaceability of a position depends on
A)   the size of the labor market.
B)   educational preparation.
C)   the amount of specialized skills or training required.
D)   the power of members of an occupation to control the occupation.
E)   all of these
F)   none of these

Chapter 10: Comparing Systems of Stratification

True/False

Correct: F   Page: 265
1. Most simple societies eventually evolved into agrarian societies.

Correct: F   Page: 266
2. Hunting and gathering societies could survive because their members were extremely good hunters.

Correct: T   Page: 266
3. Hunting and gathering societies frequently couldn't survive and disappeared or died out.

Correct: T   Page: 267
4. Hunting and gathering societies were much less stratified than are the more complex societies.

Correct: F   Page: 267
5. Hunting and gathering societies were much more stratified than were agrarian societies.

Correct: T   Page: 267
6. Hunting and gathering societies were stratified primarily on the basis of age and sex.

Correct: T   Page: 267
7. Hunting and gathering societies had considerable material equality because of their universal poverty.

Correct: T   Page: 267
8. Hunting and gathering societies seemed to be universally poor, at least in the material sense.

Correct: T   Page: 267
9. Nomadic societies are not very stratified.

Correct: T   Page: 268
10. Agrarian societies were the first societies able to support cities.

Correct: F   Page: 268
11. Agrarian societies produced enough surplus so that work did not have to be as specialized as in earlier times.

Correct: T   Page: 268
12. Agrarian societies were probably the first societies in which there were full-time priests.

Correct: T   Page: 268
13. No societies lacking agriculture have a high degree of stratification.

Correct: T   Page: 268
14. Agrarian societies did not support employment of more than 10 percent of the population in nonfarming occupations.

Correct: F   Page: 269
15. Agrarian societies were less warlike than hunting and gathering societies.

Correct: T   Page: 269
16. Agrarian societies were the first in which there was substantial private property.

Correct: F   Page: 270
17. Agrarian societies were the first societies to eliminate slavery.

Correct: T   Page: 270
18. Constant warfare is among the causes of the amount of stratification in agrarian societies.

Correct: T   Page: 271
19. Agrarian societies probably were the most stratified societies in human history.

Correct: F   Page: 271
20. Agrarian societies were still sufficiently poor to prevent extreme stratification.

Correct: F   Page: 271
21. Because they produce little surplus food, agrarian societies tend to experience almost no warfare.

Correct: T   Page: 271
22. Agrarian societies often were ruled by an elite of different ethnic origins than the rest of the society's members.

Correct: T   Page: 271
23. Agrarian societies provided only the barest subsistence diets for most farming families.

Correct: F   Page: 271
24. Upward mobility was easier in agrarian societies than in complex industrial societies.

Correct: F   Page: 273
25. The more stratified the society, the lower the portion of income that goes to the elite.

Correct: T   Page: 273
26. Agrarian societies seemed to justify the conclusion that the more productive societies become, the more stratified they become.

Correct: F   Page: 274
27. The Industrial Revolution increased the degree of stratification found in societies.

Correct: F   Page: 275
28. Industrialization decreased the educational requirements needed by the average worker.

Correct: T   Page: 275
29. Occupational changes accompanying industrialization have made the average worker less--not more--replaceable.

Correct: F   Page: 275
30. Industrialization decreased the power of the average worker.

Correct: T   Page: 278
31. In their study of comparative mobility, Lipset and Bendix used data on fathers and sons only.

Correct: F   Page: 278
32. In their study of comparative mobility, Lipset and Bendix found that the United States had much more mobility than other industrialized nations.

Correct: T   Page: 278
33. In their study of comparative mobility, Lipset and Bendix found high rates of mobility for all industrialized nations.

Correct: T   Page: 278
34. In their study of comparative mobility, Lipset and Bendix primarily found high levels of structural mobility.

Correct: T   Page: 278
35. In their study of comparative mobility, Lipset and Bendix argued that high levels of mobility are a requirement of high-technology societies.

Correct: T   Page: 279
36. International comparisons of mobility show that high rates of mobility are characteristic of industrialized nations in general, not just the United States.

Correct: F   Page: 279
37. Blau and Duncan discovered that the United States has unusually low rates of long-distance mobility.

Correct: F   Page: 280
38. Long-distance mobility is more common in Sweden than in the United States.

Correct: F   Page: 280
39. Blau and Duncan found that family background (father's occupation) is wholly unrelated to status attainment.

Correct: T   Page: 280
40. Education is highly related to both family background and status attainment.

Correct: F   Page: 280
41. Sociologists have found that children from upper status households hold very little real advantage in status attainment.

Correct: F   Page: 281
42.   Family background has relatively little impact on status attainment.

Correct: T   Page: 282
43.   The age of your father has a significant effect on your status attainment.

Correct: T   Page: 285
44.   Hout found that increased access to college education has decreased the effects of family background on status attainment.

Reference Key: STORY10.1
For the United States, your text reports a correlation of .40 between the occupational prestige of the father and the occupational prestige of the son.

Correct: F   Page: Ch3   Refer to: STORY10.1
45.   The dependent variable here is father's prestige.
                                    NOTE: Cumulative question.

Correct: F   Page: Ch3   Refer to: STORY10.1
46.   This is an experiment.
                                    NOTE: Cumulative question.

Correct: F   Page: Ch4   Refer to: STORY10.1
47.   This shows that there is no relationship between father's and son's prestige.
                                    NOTE: Cumulative question.

Correct: T   Page: ResProc   Refer to: STORY10.1
48.   In this research, prestige is a concept.
                                    NOTE: Cumulative question.

Correct: F   Page: Ch9   Refer to: STORY10.1
49.   What we are trying to explain here is status inconsistency.
                                    NOTE: Cumulative question.

Correct: T   Page: 280   Refer to: STORY10.1
50.   What we are trying to explain here is status attainment.

Correct: T   Page: 280   Refer to: STORY10.1
51.   What we are trying to explain here is social mobility.

Correct: T   Page: 280   Refer to: STORY10.1
52.   This research will help us to understand the relationship between family background and other factors affecting mobility.

Correct: T   Page: Ch9   Refer to: STORY10.1
53.   In a society primarily based on ascription, we would expect this correlation to be higher.
                                    NOTE: Cumulative question.

Correct: F   Page: Ch9   Refer to: STORY10.1
54.   In a society based solely on achievement, we would expect this correlation to be higher.
                                    NOTE: Cumulative question.

Correct: T   Page: 271   Refer to: STORY10.1

55.   In an agricultural society we would expect this correlation to be higher.

Correct: T   Page: 282   Refer to: STORY10.1

56.   For children of older fathers we would expect this correlation to be lower.

Correct: F   Page: 283   Refer to: STORY10.1

57.   In Canada, this correlation is much higher.

Correct: F   Page: 284   Refer to: STORY10.1

58.   For daughters, this correlation is higher.

Correct: F   Page: 285   Refer to: STORY10.1

59.   According to Hout, this correlation has substantially increased due to a decline in structural mobility.

Reference Key: STORY10.2
A sociologist combined the General Social Surveys for 1989 and 1990 and examined the relationship between the respondents' highest educational degree and their fathers' highest degree. He confined his study to respondents aged 25 to 40. This is what he found:

Respondent's Highest Degree	Father's Highest Degree		
	Less than High School	High School	College or More
Less than High School	22%	4%	0%
High School	65%	68%	44%
College or More	13%	28%	56%
	-----	-----	-----
	100%	100%	100%

Correct: T   Page: Ch3   Refer to: STORY10.2

60.   The independent variable in this research is father's degree.
NOTE: Cumulative question.

Correct: T   Page: Ch3   Refer to: STORY10.2

61.   The dependent variable is respondent's degree.
NOTE: Cumulative question.

Correct: F   Page: Ch4   Refer to: STORY10.2

62.   This shows that there is no relationship between a father's education and his son's.
NOTE: Cumulative question.

Correct: T   Page: Ch4   Refer to: STORY10.2

63.   The 22% figure means that of those whose fathers did not complete high school, 22 out of 100 of the respondents also did not complete high school.
NOTE: Cumulative question.

Correct: F   Page: Ch4   Refer to: STORY10.2

64.   The 4% figure means that four out of 100 of the respondents who did not complete high school have fathers who completed high school.
NOTE: Cumulative question.

Correct: F Page: Ch4 Refer to: STORY10.2
65. This suggests that the higher your parents' education the lower yours is likely to be.

NOTE: Cumulative question.

Correct: F Page: 271 Refer to: STORY10.2
66. We would expect to find less of a relationship in an agrarian society.

Correct: T Page: 282 Refer to: STORY10.2
67. This suggests that education is, in part at least, an ascriptive status.

Correct: F Page: 282 Refer to: STORY10.2
68. In a society in which status was primarily ascriptive, we would expect less of a relationship than this.

Correct: T Page: Ch6 Refer to: STORY10.2
69. Kohn's research on differential socialization might help us to understand this relationship.

NOTE: Cumulative question.

Correct: T Page: 282 Refer to: STORY10.2
70. This illustrates one of the primary ways in which status attainment is related to family background.

Multiple Choice

Correct: C Page: 263 Scramble Range: ALL
71. Chapter 10 on the topic of stratification reminds us that virtually every important question asked by sociologists
   A) requires statistical analysis.
   B) requires tests of significance.
   C) requires comparisons.
   D) involves the use of computers in analyzing the data.
   E) involves control groups.

Correct: B Page: 257 Scramble Range: ALL   63
72. Suppose we ask, "How stratified is this campus?" The first sociological reply must be
   A) "At what time?"
   B) "Compared to what?"
   C) "In whose opinion?"
   D) "Why do you ask?"
   E) "Aren't you aware that the data are confidential?"

Correct: A Page: 265 Scramble Range: ALL
73. The majority of simple societies
   A) were hunting and gathering societies.
   B) were agrarian societies.
   C) consisted of several hundred members.
   D) were industrial.
   E) were highly stratified within age and sex.

Correct: D   Page: 267 Scramble Range: ALL
74. Your text states that the major fact of life in hunting and gathering societies was
A) that before acid rain and such, the land yielded sufficient abundance.
B) how to manage the movements of a group of 500-800 people.
C) the short workday and the length of the "unproductive" night
D) the threat of death.
E) food storage.

Correct: E   Page: 267 Scramble Range: ALL
75. The world's population was not able to grow until
A) war was reduced to a point that permitted some periods of peace.
B) the earth's climate permitted crops to be grown.
C) ancient superstitions demanding either human or animal sacrifice gave way to more modern religious beliefs.
D) humans developed language and could pass on this knowledge to the next generation.
E) there was an increase in food production.

Correct: E   Page: 267 Scramble Range: ALL
76. Ten thousand years ago the human population was still growing so slowly that it would have taken _____ years to double in size. Today it doubles in _____.
A) 200; 80 years
B) 500; 40 years
C) 1200; 40 years
D) 15,000; 37 years
E) 60,000; 37 years

Correct: A   Page: 267 Scramble Range: ALL
77. According to your text, all hunting and gathering societies are very small, but environmental conditions caused _____ to be tiny.
A) Eskimo societies
B) the land range covered by each
C) the Far East
D) societies in the Middle East
E) Andean society

Correct: B   Page: 267 Scramble Range: ALL
78. According to the text, when societies _____, many of them develop medium and high levels of stratification.
A) contain ethnic rather than racial minorities
B) are not nomadic but instead have a permanent location
C) focus on internal rather than on external problems
D) have insufficient economic surplus
E) fail to advance, evolve, or change

79. According to your text, _____ societies have very few possessions because of _____.
    A) Eskimo; the corrosive action of permafrost
    B) peaceful; greed's tendency to breed warfare against such societies
    C) nomadic; the constant need to move on
    D) agrarian; productive inefficiencies
    E) horticultural; productive inefficiencies

80. Since the beginning of time, the primary bases for stratification have been
    A) age and sex.
    B) sex and skill.
    C) sex and knowledge.
    D) skill and knowledge.
    E) accidents of birth.

81. Hunting and gathering societies were stratified to a significant degree. Usually the primary bases for stratification were
    A) hunting skill and fishing ability.
    B) reproductive ability and survival ability.
    C) contribution to daily life and being a repository for tribal lore.
    D) age and sex.
    E) religious caste membership and food productivity.

82. In hunting and gathering societies, there were two main bases for stratification. However, WITHIN each of those two
    A) there were from 3 to 12 further subdivisions.
    B) the members were largely free to determine their own further subdivisions.
    C) there were multiple systems for distributing goods unequally.
    D) one's political placement was important.
    E) there was not much further stratification.

83. The rule seems to be that the _____ a human society is, the less it is _____.

    A) more geographically mobile; vulnerable to attack
    B) smaller, poorer, and less secure; stratified
    C) more productive; internally differentiated
    D) less productive; vulnerable to "leisureitis"
    E) closer to the equator; subject to unrelenting hunger

84. Gideon Sjoberg estimates that no agrarian society had fewer than ____ of its members engaged in farming and usually MORE were needed at that task.
    A) 20 percent
    B) 40 percent
    C) 50 percent
    D) 75 percent
    E) 90 percent

85. Cities developed as a result of
    A) trade routes.
    B) surplus agricultural production.
    C) industrialization.
    D) the need for protection against invaders.
    E) an increase in culture.

86. When _____ occurred, two new social phenomena became possible: _____
    and _____.
    A) the invention of gunpowder; expansionism; government control
    B) the invention of the wheel; creation of a food surplus; storage
    C) surplus food production; specialization; cities
    D) surplus food production; leisure; socialization
    E) urbanization; occupational choice; divorce

87. The highest degree of inequality exists in
    A) hunting and gathering societies.
    B) herding societies.
    C) agrarian societies.
    D) societies in the process of industrializing.
    E) industrialized societies.

88. Agrarian societies lived in
    A) a chronic state of warfare.
    B) intermediate size cities rather than large ones or small ones.
    C) mobile tents rather than fixed dwelling places.
    D) hilly areas rather than flat plains, because of periodic floods and the need
         to use the plains for agriculture.
    E) more democratic circumstances than can be found in most industrialized
         nations today.

89. Frequency of external wars was much more likely to be "constant" when the
    level of agricultural development was
    A) high.
    B) medium.
    C) low.
    D) either high or low.
    E) nonexistent.

90. Societies did not use slaves until
    A) warfare was begun.
    B) a religious interpretation could be found to justify it.
    C) somewhat more advanced weapons for fighting had been invented.
    D) one's labor could produce a surplus.
    E) changes in moral reasoning suggested that enemies should not be killed if
         an alternative could be found.

91. According to your text, the ability to produce a surplus raises the possibility of humans becoming
     A) property.
     B) "political" animals.
     C) less stratified.
     D) arteriosclerotic.
     E) more intensely familistic.

92. In agrarian societies, the elite held power by
     A) harboring slaves.
     B) producing many crops.
     C) holding political office.
     D) dominating the military force.
     E) no means. There were no classes in agrarian societies.

93. In agrarian societies, _____ held power by _____.
     A) the intelligentsia; controlling the knowledge supply
     B) the landowners; controlling the water supply
     C) the warlords; threatening the elite
     D) the priesthood; dominating the average person
     E) the elite; dominating the military forces

94. The chronic warfare that characterized agrarian societies might best be explained by
     A) the need for more land per person because of the ability to use technology to farm more land.
     B) the need for vast lands for seasonal herding of animals.
     C) the prestige accompanying successful military exploits.
     D) the need to plunder neighboring peoples in order to have enough wealth to continue to equip one's own army.
     E) the mood of the times, which gave the highest prestige to men who performed well in combat.

95. In agrarian societies, ruling elites could live
     A) on a political rather than on an economic basis.
     B) an intellectual life on a higher plane than is possible today.
     C) in enormous splendor.
     D) very well politically, but not too well economically.
     E) at levels made possible only by a machine-based economy.

96. Which of the following characteristics of the elite was LEAST likely to be offered as proof that the elite belonged to a superior human species?
     A) Larger size
     B) Use of superior speech
     C) Use of proper etiquette
     D) Longer life expectancy
     E) Greater number of male offspring

Correct: B   Page: 274 Scramble Range: ALL
97.   Industrialized societies are
      A)   poorer than agrarian societies.
      B)   less stratified than agrarian societies.
      C)   more stratified than agrarian societies.
      D)   no different from agrarian societies.
      E)   less complex than hunting and gathering societies.

Correct: E   Page: 274 Scramble Range: ALL
98.   If previous trends had continued, the productivity made possible by
      industrialization would have produced _____, but it didn't turn out that way. In
      fact, things started to go in reverse.
      A)   greater urbanization
      B)   more suburbanization
      C)   greater racial and ethnic equality
      D)   a decrease in occupational specialization
      E)   an increase in stratification

Correct: C   Page: 275 Scramble Range: ALL
99.   Industrialization
      A)   serves no purpose in society.
      B)   wastes work time.
      C)   uses technology to make work more efficient.
      D)   was resisted for several hundred years.
      E)   changed work techniques but not skills needed to do the work.

Correct: A   Page: 274 Scramble Range: ALL
100. Industrialization
      A)   decreased the replaceability of the average worker.
      B)   decreased unemployment.
      C)   increased stratification and inequality.
      D)   increased the length of the workday.
      E)   increased the value of work in relation to other values.

Correct: A   Page: 275 Scramble Range: ALL
101. The term "industrialization" means
      A)   using technology to make work much more productive.
      B)   a greater percent of the population engaged in production.
      C)   getting more people to work harder or more productively.
      D)   a change in the motivations by which people work.
      E)   basing society more and more around the economic institutions of life.

Correct: B   Page: 275 Scramble Range: ALL
102. According to the functionalist theory of stratification, as positions
      _____, their relative rewards increase.
      A)   produce more and more goods
      B)   become less replaceable
      C)   are more directly related to government
      D)   have less inheritability
      E)   are newer and less institutionalized

103.   In modern industrial societies there has been a rapid trend toward more complex and skilled jobs, while unskilled jobs have been disappearing. The result has been to make the average worker _____ and therefore to _____.
A)   less replaceable; decrease wage differences between jobs
B)   more replaceable; increase unemployment by job displacement
C)   more replaceable; actually decrease skill levels required for jobs
D)   more stressed; have more occupational injuries
E)   work harder; increase the balance of payments deficit

104.   Industrialization changed the nature of work. One of the consequences of industrialization has been for the average worker to
A)   become much more alienated from work and from his/her co-workers.
B)   be more powerful and more able to resist coercion.
C)   be less powerful and less able to resist coercion.
D)   want to postpone retirement.
E)   have a continuous, rather than an interrupted, work career.

105.   It follows from the functionalist theory of stratification that as positions become _____, their relative rewards _____.
A)   more interesting; are more gratifying
B)   more replaceable; increase
C)   less replaceable; increase
D)   more entrenched; decrease
E)   more politicized; change cyclically

106.   Moving from the bottom of the stratification system to the top in one generation is called
A)   short-distance mobility.
B)   upward mobility.
C)   horizontal mobility.
D)   impossible.
E)   long-distance mobility.

107.   According to your text, which of the nationalities listed below has the highest amounts of DOWNWARD mobility?
A)   West Germans
B)   Swiss
C)   New Zealanders
D)   Canadians
E)   Australians

Correct: D Page: 279 Scramble Range: ALL

108. It is not the presence or absence of social mobility as such that distinguishes America's citizens from the Europeans. What does distinguish America's citizens in this regard is the Americans' greater likelihood of
A) experiencing mobility as a consequence of marriage across class boundaries.
B) status crystallization.
C) individual rather than structural mobility.
D) long-distance mobility.
E) finding mobility through high-tech industries.

Correct: E Page: 279 Scramble Range: ALL

109. Figure 10-1, International Comparisons of Mobility, shows that _____ has a higher percentage of upward mobility than the other nations in the figure.
A) West Germany
B) France
C) United States
D) Japan
E) Switzerland

Correct: B Page: 279 Scramble Range: ALL

110. Long-distance mobility is exemplified by the
A) son of a ditch digger becoming a store clerk.
B) son of a garbage collector becoming a physician.
C) great-grandson of a ditch digger becoming a store clerk.
D) great-grandson of a garbage collector becoming a physician.
E) son of an attorney becoming a truck driver.

Correct: B Page: 280 Scramble Range: ALL

111. Blau and Duncan found that the higher a man's status, the more
A) likely his work career was to have been geographically stable.
B) years of education his son is likely to receive.
C) alienated and unhappy he is in his vocation, job, or career.
D) his family life is marked by instability and unhappiness.
E) likely he is to become a substance abuser.

Correct: A Page: 281 Scramble Range: ALL

112. In talking about "status attainment," your text says that people's odds of rising are greater _____ and their odds of falling are greater _____.
A) the lower their origins; the higher they start
B) in the Great Lakes states; in the south central states
C) if they are unmarried; if they are married
D) if they are religious; if they are not religious
E) if they have vocational training; if they attend college

Correct: C   Page: 281 Scramble Range: ALL
113. Your text (citing Blau and Duncan) states that the lower the level from which a person starts, the greater
A) the odds are that the person will be static and experience no mobility.
B) the odds are that intermarriage will be a mobility mechanism.
C) the probability that the person will be upwardly mobile.
D) the probability that the person will experience horizontal mobility only.
E) the likelihood that individual mobility will prove to be more important to him/her than will structural mobility.

Correct: D   Page: 281 Scramble Range: ALL
114. Jencks found that economic equality
A) existed among brothers.
B) existed between father and son.
C) existed between mother and daughter.
D) does not necessarily exist among brothers.
E) does not necessarily exist between father and son.

Correct: C   Page: 281 Scramble Range: ALL
115. Christopher Jencks found that a man's occupational level is most strongly correlated with
A) his father's occupational level.
B) his brother's occupational level.
C) his educational level.
D) the presence of a full-time, nonemployed mother in his childhood home.
E) the degree of similarity between the occupational levels of his parents.

Correct: B   Page: 281 Scramble Range: ALL
116. In Cohen and Tyree's study of upward social mobility, the data confirmed _____ among people coming from poor families.
A) almost no mobility
B) a lot of mobility
C) low mobility for males but almost none for females
D) low mobility for females but almost none for males
E) declining rates of mobility

Correct: A   Page: 281 Scramble Range: ALL
117. In Cohen and Tyree's research about social mobility, the data indicated that _____ has greater importance for status attainment for people from poor homes than for other people.
A) education
B) having an extended family
C) getting first-hand experience with a variety of occupations
D) having strong interpersonal skills
E) entering the work world early in life

Correct: C   Page: 281 Scramble Range: ALL
118. Cohen and Tyree's research indicates that the main determinant of the family income of persons from all backgrounds is
A) ethnic background.
B) racial background.
C) marital status.
D) having or not having children.
E) traditionalism.

Correct: E   Page: 281 Scramble Range: ALL
119. Cohen and Tyree's research shows that "the probability of escape from poverty for _____ men and women, especially the latter, is considerably less than for _____ men and women."
A) ethnicity-centered; ethnicity-liberated
B) more intelligent; less intelligent
C) bilingual; single language
D) dogmatic; flexible
E) single; married

Correct: C   Page: 281 Scramble Range: ALL
120. According to your text, with _____ controlled, the influence of family background (father's occupation) on sons' status attainment is very modest.
A) race
B) intelligence
C) education
D) motivational levels
E) geographic residence

Correct: B   Page: 282 Scramble Range: A-D
121. Children from upper status families
A) are more likely to have long-distance mobility.
B) enjoy a substantial educational advantage.
C) enjoy an advantage in status attainment if their fathers are older.
D) are more likely to benefit from exchange mobility.
E) all of these

Correct: A   Page: 282 Scramble Range: A-E
122. Mare and Tzeng found that the older a son's father
A) the more education the child tends to complete.
B) the less education the child tends to complete.
C) the greater the chance of status inconsistency.
D) the lower the status of the father.
E) the more important the status of the mother.
F) none of these

123. Porter studied the Canadian stratification system and used the concept
      "vertical mosaic." What does "vertical mosaic" mean?
      A) A stratification system that is "diseased" in the sense that the Dutch
          stratification system is "diseased"
      B) A very large number of strata
      C) A stratification system with many horizontal occupational categories
      D) A stratification system consisting of distinct strata based on ethnicity
      E) A stratification system with indistinct strata, the result of Canada's
          relatively new occupational structure

124. John Porter and his colleagues studied status attainment in Canada. The
      Canadian study, which included women and which collected data from a
      sample of Canadians over the age of 17, found evidence to support the idea
      that Canadian society
      A) is more highly stratified along ethnic lines than is the United States.
      B) is more highly stratified against immigrants than is the United States.
      C) has a rate of social mobility almost identical to that of the United States.
      D) has more racial discrimination in an occupational sense than does the
          United States.
      E) has an occupational structure that has been "sliding" since about 1970.

125. Peter Pineo compared the correlations between fathers' occupational
      prestige and sons' occupational prestige for the United States and for
      Canada. He found that the correlation was 0.40 for Canada and _____ for
      the United States.
      A) 0.40.
      B) 0.32.
      C) 0.18.
      D) 0.55.
      E) 0.76.

126. Pineo compared the correlations between an individual's education and
      occupational prestige in Canada and the United States. The results were a
      correlation of 0.61 for Canada, and _____ for the United States.
      A) 0.23
      B) 0.43
      C) 0.60
      D) 0.71
      E) 0.81

127. When the Canadian status attainment data were examined, it was found that
      which of the following does NOT significantly affect the father-to-son
      transmission of status (Table 10-5)?
      A) Ethnicity
      B) Level of education
      C) Religiosity
      D) Length of residence as Canadian citizen
      E) Occupational sector of employment

Correct: B   Page: 284 Scramble Range: ALL
128. When the Canadian data were examined in terms of females' status attainment, it was found that Canadian women with full time jobs
   A) are more dependent on their husbands for status attainment than are women in the United States.
   B) come from higher-status backgrounds, have more education, and a higher-status occupation than do women in the United States.
   C) place less importance on women working outside the home than do women in the United States and feel that working outside the home is more inappropriate.
   D) exhibit a significantly lower correlation between education and occupation than do women in the United States.
   E) exhibit a significantly lower correlation between family background and status attainment than do women in the United States.

Correct: C   Page: 285 Scramble Range: A-D
129. The major source of high upward mobility in industrial societies has been
   A) changes in the phenotype.
   B) increased agricultural production.
   C) fewer unskilled and laboring jobs.
   D) the internal strains of status inconsistency.
   E) none of these

Correct: B   Page: 285 Scramble Range: A-D
130. Hout found that there has been an increase in exchange mobility in the recent past in the United States. He attributed this to
   A) inbreeding among the upper classes.
   B) an increase in the proportion of people with college degrees.
   C) the decrease in productivity in industry.
   D) changes in the family structure and two-earner households.
   E) all of these

Correct: D   Page: 285 Scramble Range: ALL
131. In the recent past, there has been a decrease in _____ in the United States, and an increase in _____.
   A) exchange mobility; structural mobility
   B) overall mobility; educational attainment
   C) status inconsistency; prestige
   D) structural mobility; exchange mobility
   E) vertical attainment; horizontal mobility

Topic 2: Inequality

True/False

Correct: T   Page: 289
1. People in the United States are less satisfied with their household's financial situation than those in Mexico and Canada.

Correct: F   Page: 289
2. People in Mexico are less satisfied with their household's financial situation than those in Mexico and the United States.

Correct: T   Page: 289
3. People in Mexico are less satisfied with their lives than those in the United States and Canada.

Correct: F   Page: 289
4. Income level greatly influences how satisfied people are with their lives in Mexico, Canada, and the United States.

Correct: T   Page: 289
5. Mexicans are more likely to be "quite satisfied" with their current family income than are people in the United States.

Correct: T   Page: 289
6. People in the United States are less likely than people in Mexico or Canada to be satisfied with their current income.

Correct: F   Page: 290
7. Upper-income people are more likely to be satisfied with their jobs than middle-income people in Mexico, Canada, and the United States.

Correct: F   Page: 290
8. Upper-income people in Canada, Mexico, and the United States are more likely to look forward to going back to work on Mondays than are lower and middle-income people.

Correct: F   Page: 290
9. A majority of people in the United States are very satisfied with their jobs.

Correct: T   Page: 290
10. Mexicans in all income brackets are more satisfied with their jobs than their counterparts in the United States and Canada.

Correct: T   Page: 290
11. Upper-income people are more likely than middle- and lower-income people to be interested in politics.

Correct: F   Page: 290
12. In Canada, Mexico and the United States, lower-income people are more likely to have participated in a legal demonstration.

Correct: T Page: 290
13. In Canada, the United States and Mexico, upper-income people are more likely to have participated in a legal demonstration.

Correct: T Page: 290
14. In the United States and Canada, upper-income people are more tolerant of people cheating on their income taxes.

Correct: F Page: 290
15. In the United States and Canada, lower-income people are more likely to be tolerant of people cheating on their income taxes.

Correct: T Page: 291
16. People with higher incomes are more likely to drink.

Correct: F Page: 291
17. People with lower incomes are more likely to drink.

Correct: T Page: 291
18. Americans watch more television than Canadians.

Correct: T Page: 291
19. A majority of lower-income people in Canada and the United States read a newspaper every day.

Correct: F Page: 292
20. The primary differences between lower- and higher-income people in Canada, the United States, and Mexico are in attitudes toward life and work.

Reference Key: TOP2-1
Pedro lives and works in Mexico. Peter lives and works in the United States. Pierre lives and works in Canada.

Correct: T Page: 289 Refer to: TOP2-1
21. Pedro is most likely to be satisfied with the financial situation of his family.

Correct: F Page: 289 Refer to: TOP2-1
22. Peter is most likely to be satisfied with the financial situation of his family.

Correct: F   Page: 289 Refer to: TOP2-1
23. Peter is the most likely to be satisfied with his income.

Correct: F Page: 290 Refer to: TOP2-1
24. Pierre is most likely to be satisfied with this job.

Correct: F Page: 290 Refer to: TOP2-1
25. Pierre is mostly likely to look forward to going to work on Mondays.

Correct: T Page: 290 Refer to: TOP2-1
26. Pedro is mostly likely to look forward to going to work on Mondays.

Correct: T Page: 290 Refer to: TOP2-1
27. Peter is most likely to take pride in his work.

Correct: T   Page: 290   Refer to: TOP2-1
28. Pierre is most likely to be interested in politics.

Correct: T   Page: 290   Refer to: TOP2-1
29. Pedro is least likely to be interested in politics.

Correct: F   Page: 290   Refer to: TOP2-1
30. Pedro is most likely to have participated in a legal demonstration.

Correct: T   Page: 291   Refer to: TOP2-1
31. Pierre is most likely to drink.

Correct: F   Page: 291   Refer to: TOP2-1
32. Pedro is most likely to drink.

Correct: F   Page: 291   Refer to: TOP2-1
33. Pedro is most likely to think of himself as a religious person.

Correct: T   Page: 291   Refer to: TOP2-1
34. Peter is most likely to think of himself as a religious person.

Multiple Choice

Correct: A   Scramble Range: A-D   Page: 290
35. When people in Mexico, the United States and Canada were asked how satisfied they are with their family income
    A) Mexicans were most likely to say they are quite satisfied.
    B) people from the United States were more likly than Canadians to say they are quite satisfied.
    C) Mexicans with higher incomes were less satisfied than those with higher incomes in the United States.
    D) Mexicans with low incomes were less satisfied than those with low incomes in the United States.
    E) all of these
    F) none of these

Correct: B   Page: 290   Scramble Range: A-C
36. In which of these countries are people least satisfied with their incomes?
    A) Canada
    B) United States
    C) Mexico

Correct: E   Page: 290-92   Scramble Range: A-D
37. Which of the following did the text's examination of Mexico, Canada and the United States find.
    A) Higher-income people are more likely to drink.
    B) Mexicans are more satisfied with their income than people in the United States.
    C) Higher-income people are more likely than lower income people to have participated in a legal demonstration.
    D) Income level seems to have little to do with overall satisfaction with life.
    E) All of these
    F) None of these

Chapter 11: Intergroup Conflict

True/False

Correct: F   Page: 300
1. According to the text, prejudice is the basic cause of intergroup conflict.

Correct: F   Page: 300
2. According to the text, prejudice is caused by the oversocialization of children, which creates rigid personalities.

Correct: T   Page: 301
3. According to the text, prejudice is more common among less educated Americans.

Correct: T   Page: 302
4. According to the text, prejudice will not disappear until the economic basis of conflict has been overcome.

Correct: F   Page: 302
5. According to the text, prejudice is most rapidly eliminated by bringing conflicting groups into close contact.

Correct: F   Page: 302
6. Allport's theory of contact is unable to help the social scientist to partially understand the history of race relations in the South.

Correct: T   Page: 302
7. Allport's theory of contact predicts that contact will increase prejudice if the groups are unequal in their status.

Correct: F   Page: 302
8. Allport's theory of contact supports the conclusion that the success of the Notre Dame football team against schools like Harvard and Yale at the turn of the century did much to reduce anti-Catholic feelings at these Protestant schools.

Correct: F   Page: 302
9. Allport's theory of contact predicts that contact will improve relations between two groups if one group is careful to SEEM submissive and acknowledges the "superiority" of the other group.

Correct: T   Page: 302
10. Allport's theory of contact predicts that contact will worsen relations between groups unless they are of equal status and are not competing with each other.

Correct: F   Page: 302
11. Allport's theory of contact predicts that relations between two groups will improve if they have the opportunity to compete freely.

Correct: F   Page: 302
12. Allport's theory of contact predicts that contact will improve relations only to the extent that the contact is close and frequent.

Correct: T   Page: 302
13. Allport's theory of contact predicts that prejudice will never disappear until the groups involved are status equals.

Correct: F   Page: 303
14. The Sherif studies of summer camps found that boys could be made prejudiced only against other boys of noticeably different racial or cultural backgrounds.

Correct: T   Page: 303
15. The Sherif studies of summer camps showed that intergroup competition rapidly produced prejudice.

Correct: T   Page: 303
16. The Sherif studies of summer camps strongly supported Allport's theory of contact.

Correct: F   Page: 303
17. The Sherif studies of summer camps led sociologists to see that Allport's theory of contact was and is incorrect.

Correct: T   Page: 303
18. The Sherif studies of summer camps showed that prejudice could disappear as rapidly as it came into being.

Correct: T   Page: 307
19. Sociologists now think that slavery caused many extreme racist beliefs and practices.

Correct: F   Page: 307
20. Racist attitudes cause slavery.

Correct: T   Page: 307
21. Slavery led to racist ideas to justify it.

Correct: T   Page: 307
22. The idea that African-Americans were more like livestock than human beings was a consequence of slavery.

Correct: T   Page: 307
23. Sociologists now believe that real economic conflicts underlie the bitter prejudice found in intergroup conflicts.

Correct: F   Page: 307
24. Groups that are the target of prejudice and discrimination are prevented from holding any but the lowest-status jobs in a society.

Correct: T   Page: 312
25. Some subordinate groups have been relatively well-to-do compared to the majority.

Correct: F   Page: 316

26. The image of Japanese-Americans as gardeners has no basis in historical reality.

Correct: T   Page: 316

27. By 1940, the average native-born Japanese-American male in the United States was much better educated than the average native-born white male in the United States

Correct: F   Page: 316

28. Japanese-Americans seldom marry someone of another ethnic or racial background.

Correct: F   Page: 319

29. The experience of Japanese-Americans refutes the notion that prejudice will disappear only after status equality has been achieved.

Correct: T   Page: 318

30. Asian-Americans as a group are much more likely than other Americans to have college degrees that offer direct entry to the highest-paying occupations.

Correct: T   Page: 318

31. Most immigrant groups have specialized in certain occupations.

Correct: T   Page: 321

32. Inability to speak English has sometimes given subordinate groups in the United States an advantage.

Correct: T   Page: 323

33. An enclave economy promotes more rapid initial economic progress for recently arrived ethnic and racial minorities.

Correct: T   Page: 323

34. In an enclave economy, business owners tend to give their workers a better deal than would employers outside the enclave.

Correct: F   Page: 323

35. In enclave economies, members of the minority group find that minority discrimination tends to bar them from promotion to supervisory positions.

Correct: F   Page: 323

36. The long-term upward mobility of minorities is best served by enclave economies when they remain in the enclave as long as possible.

Correct: F   Page: 324

37. Hispanic-Americans are an ethnic group.

Correct: F   Page: 324

38. The term "Hispanic" is used to refer to a distinct racial group with Mexican origins.

Correct: F   Page: 327
39. Cuban-Americans are more likely to be on welfare and have low education than other Hispanic-Americans.

Correct: F   Page: 327
40. Mexican-Americans are more likely to be on welfare and have low education than other Hispanic-Americans.

Correct: T   Page: 327
41. Native born Mexican-Americans have about the same median level of education as non-Hispanic whites have.

Correct: F   Page: 331
42. Mexican-Americans are more resistant to learning English than other immigrant groups have been.

Correct: F   Page: 330
43. Economic enclaves are very rare in Hispanic communities.

Correct: F   Page: 332
44. The material on immigration in your text doesn't apply to African-Americans because they have been in this country for many generations.

Correct: T   Page: 335
45. Lieberson, Sowell, and your text argue that moving from the South to the North has been similar to immigrating from a foreign country.

Correct: F   Page: 335
46. Southern poverty is more important in understanding the situation of Southern African-Americans than Northern African-Americans.

Correct: T   Page: 335
47. The general poverty and isolation of the South played a major role in slowing down African-Americans' progress.

Correct: F   Page: 336
48. Poverty is the major cause of the proportion of female headed households in the African-American community.

Correct: T   Page: 336
49. African-American women greatly outnumber African-American men in the United States.

Correct: T   Page: 336
50. In recent years the proportion of female-headed families has grown much more rapidly among African-Americans than among whites.

Correct: T   Page: 338
51. More than a third of white Americans have African-American neighbors.

Correct: T   Page: 338
52. Southern whites are more likely than most other Americans to live on the same block as African-Americans.

Correct: T   Page: 339
53. Firebaugh and Davis found that prejudice against African-Americans in the United States has declined in the past twenty years.

Correct: F   Page: 339
54. Decline in prejudice against African-Americans has generally been confined to the northern parts of the country.

Correct: F   Page: 339
55. Decline in prejudice against African-Americans in the past twenty years has caused a decline in discrimination.

Correct: T   Page: 339
56. A major legacy of slavery was to leave African-Americans without a sense of common cultural identity.

Correct: T   Page: 340
57. Members of ethnic immigrant groups often change their names to lower their visibility.

Reference Key: STORY11.1
As a result of a treaty signed with India, 100,000 inhabitants of the Island of Bluedonia are going to be brought to the United States as refugees from a religious civil war in their island nation. The native Bluedonians have been a hated minority in their own land since being greatly outnumbered by immigrants from India. The Indian majority is Hindu, but the native Bluedonians worship the goddess Isis--a faith brought to them from Egypt more than 2,000 years ago. The native Bluedonians also constitute a unique racial group: they have light blue skins and hair. International concerns that the Bluedonians would be completely wiped out by Hindu mobs led to the decision to bring them to the United States. You have been asked by the United States State Department for advice on how to protect the Bluedonians from hatred and prejudice and how to speed their rise to economic parity with other Americans. On the basis of Chapter 11, you can predict that the Bluedonians will have an easier time gaining economic and social equality if

Correct: F   Page: 323   Refer to: STORY11.1
58. they are careful to spread out around the country and not cluster in only a few places.

Correct: F   Page: 323   Refer to: STORY11.1
59. they are especially careful not to cluster in the same neighborhood.

Correct: F   Page: 323   Refer to: STORY11.1
60. they avoid being associated with a few occupations.

Correct: T   Page: 316   Refer to: STORY11.1
61. they make sacrifices to get their kids to college.

Correct: F   Page: 330   Refer to: STORY11.1
62. they avoid bilingualism.

Correct: F   Page: 307   Refer to: STORY11.1
63. they send out many missionaries to teach their Christian neighbors about Isis.

Correct: T   Page: 323   Refer to: STORY11.1
64.   they limit their contacts with non-Bluedonians during their first few years in the country.

Correct: F   Page: 307   Refer to: STORY11.1
65.   they take every opportunity to let other Americans get to know them and their unusual cultural traditions.

Correct: F   Page: 307   Refer to: STORY11.1
66.   they launch militant demonstrations demanding that they be given jobs currently held by others.

Correct: F   Page: 323   Refer to: STORY11.1
67.   they are careful to shop in stores other than those owned by other Bluedonians.

Correct: T   Page: 323   Refer to: STORY11.1
68.   they set up their own somewhat independent economy.

Correct: F   Page: 307   Refer to: STORY11.1
69.   the government designates a weekend each month when each Bluedonians family is a guest in the home of native-born Americans.

Reference Key: STORY11.2
A sociologist wanted to know if employers were biased in favor of men for management training programs. So he prepared a phony resume for a fictitious student who was about to graduate with a master's in business administration. He then created two forms of the resume. The forms were identical except on one of them the student was named Joan Andrews and the other carried the name John Andrews. The sociologist then sent the resumes to each of 500 companies running ads for management trainees. Half the companies got Joan's resume; the other half got John's. Which company got which was determined by flipping a coin. Eventually, John was offered an interview by 32 companies; Joan was offered an interview by 17 companies. The odds against this difference occurring by chance were more than 20 to 1.

Correct: T   Page: Ch3   Refer to: STORY11.2
70.   This study is an example of an experiment.
NOTE: Cumulative question.

Correct: T   Page: Ch3   Refer to: STORY11.2
71.   The independent variable in this study is gender.
NOTE: Cumulative question.

Correct: F   Page: Ch3   Refer to: STORY11.2
72.   The independent variable in this study is getting an interview.
NOTE: Cumulative question.

Correct: F   Page: 302   Refer to: STORY11.2
73.   This is an example of prejudice.

Correct: T   Page: 302   Refer to: STORY11.2
74.   This is an example of discrimination.

Correct: T   Page: Ch3   Refer to: STORY11.2
75.   There is little reason to suspect that this finding is spurious.
NOTE: Cumulative question.

Correct: F   Page: Ch3   Refer to: STORY11.2
76.   We would have greater confidence in this finding if this sociologist had based his study on personal observation of personnel officers as they evaluated applicants.
NOTE: Cumulative question.

Correct: F   Page: 314   Refer to: STORY11.2
77.   This is an example of middleman minorities.

Correct: T   Page: 302   Refer to: STORY11.2
78.   Allport's theory of contact could help us understand these findings.

Correct: T   Page: 314   Refer to: STORY11.2
79.   The idea of "cultural division of labor" could help us understand this finding.

Correct: T   Page: 314   Refer to: STORY11.2
80.   This could be used as an example of a caste system.

Correct: T   Page: 314   Refer to: STORY11.2
81.   Joan could increase her chances of getting interviewed by lowering her visibility by changing her name to Jan or Frank.

Multiple Choice

Correct: E   Page: 295   Scramble Range: A-E
82.   In the opening story in the chapter, it was pointed out that to the Australian aborigine the word "stranger" meant the same as
A)   curiosity.
B)   gift giver.
C)   one-who-is-sick.
D)   fool.
E)   enemy.
F)   none of these

Correct: B   Page: 295   Scramble Range: ALL
83.   At the start of the chapter on racial and ethnic inequality, the story is told about two groups of Australian natives who by chance meet in the bush or outback. In this instance, they spent a lot of time talking to one another as they
A)   each quietly looked about for potential weapons.
B)   tried to discover some kinship tie between the two groups.
C)   prayed fervently, knowing that fatal combat was unavoidable.
D)   considered the apparent socioeconomic condition of each other's group.
E)   tried to establish which of the groups was the darker, because if they were equally dark, serious conflict would break out.

Correct: D   Page: 296   Scramble Range: A-E
84. The chapter on intergroup conflict argues that inequalities in _____ among different racial and ethnic groups in a society are the basis of intergroup conflict.
    A) physical attractiveness and whose definition of beauty will prevail
    B) intelligence
    C) skilled training vs. innate ability
    D) property, power, and prestige
    E) ability to communicate differences and agreements
    F) all of the above.

Correct: B   Page: 297   Scramble Range: ALL
85. The chapter on racial, religious, and other types of conflicts is organized around which of the following global or general concepts?
    A) Racial conflict
    B) Intergroup conflict
    C) Styles of accommodation
    D) Prejudice as a cause of intergroup conflict
    E) Prejudice as a cause of discrimination

Correct: B   Page: 297   Scramble Range: ALL
86. When people think of themselves as sharing special bonds of history, culture, and kinship with others of the same ancestry, then they
    A) have the potential to become an ethnic aggregate.
    B) are an ethnic group.
    C) constitute a race.
    D) constitute a pan-racial group.
    E) have the potential to become a race if there is sufficient inbreeding to make the similarities persistent over time.

Correct: A   Page: 297   Scramble Range: ALL
87. Racial differences need not always produce intergroup conflict. Biological differences may be unchangeable, but what matters most is
    A) what we believe about these differences.
    B) how visible these differences are.
    C) the degree of race-mixing that has already happened and is irreversible.
    D) the degree to which further race-mixing has already happened and is irreversible.
    E) the extent to which the biologically more "fit" races can cooperate with those that are less "fit."

Correct: E   Page: 297   Scramble Range: A-E
88. Race is important to sociologists because of
    A) differences in skin color.
    B) differences in body build, particularly height.
    C) differences in intelligence.
    D) differences in culture.
    E) what people believe about these differences.
    F) all of these

Correct: B Page: 297 Scramble Range: ALL
89. "Ethnic group" usually refers to a
A) different cultural group outside the country.
B) different cultural group within the country.
C) different racial group outside the country.
D) different racial group within the country.
E) religious minority.

Correct: A Page: 298 Scramble Range: A-D
90. According to the 1990 census, the European nation most often identified by Americans as their primary ancestry was
A) Germany.
B) Italy.
C) Mexico.
D) Poland.

Correct: E Page: 298 Scramble Range: ALL
91. When a previously distinctive group does not hold on to its distinctive cultural features and disappears into the dominant or main culture in an area, sociologists say that it has
A) been socialized and in time will be completely acculturated.
B) high social solidarity but very low cultural solidarity.
C) become alienated from its original culture.
D) no sense of identity and has become anomic.
E) been assimilated.

Correct: C Page: 298 Scramble Range: ALL
92. Students in a college class considered it unimportant to know the religious affiliation of the students who would work with them on term projects. What is this an example of?
A) Accommodation
B) Assimilation
C) Cultural pluralism
D) Segregation
E) Discrimination

Correct: F Page: 300 Scramble Range: A-E
93. Which of the following is NOT a common outcome of intergroup conflict?
A) Assimilation
B) Segregation
C) Expulsion
D) Extermination
E) Accommodation
F) None of these

Correct: D Page: 300 Scramble Range: ALL
94. In the early history of the United States, many Americans felt that the appropriate treatment of the Indians should be
A) to move them to the area acquired by the 1833 land acquisition treaty.
B) assimilation.
C) to replace them on their original lands and to relocate the whites
D) extermination.
E) the suggestions set forth by William Jordan.

95. The act whereby a group is inhibited from having contact with others is called
   A) desegregation.
   B) assimilation.
   C) segregation.
   D) constitutional.
   E) accommodation.

96. When intergroup conflict disappears but the groups involved are able to keep their own cultures and related differences, then sociologists use which of the following concepts to refer to such a situation?
   A) Amalgamation
   B) Assimilation
   C) Accommodation
   D) Democratization
   E) Diffusion

97. Which of the following concepts identifies when intergroup conflict ends and diverse cultures exist within the same society?
   A) Amalgamation
   B) Diffusion
   C) Democracy or representative interaction
   D) Ethnic or cultural pluralism
   E) Conflict intoleration
   F) None of these

98. Prejudice has been found to be negatively correlated with
   A) church attendance.
   B) education.
   C) religious beliefs.
   D) race.
   E) intergroup conflict.
   F) all of these

99. One of the basic ideas of the chapter about intergroup conflict is that
   A) discrimination and prejudice are unrelated phenomena.
   B) status inequalities and role inequalities are the same thing in terms of the final result.
   C) prejudice can lead to status inequalities.
   D) status inequalities lead to prejudice and discrimination.
   E) prejudice is a behavior and discrimination is a state of mind.

Correct: E   Page: 301 Scramble Range: ALL
100. According to your text, until sociological studies of intergroup relations gave cause to believe otherwise, most theories of why people are prejudiced
A) looked to "instinctual causation" for an explanation.
B) felt that minority groups were themselves to blame for their plight.
C) felt that lack of education was to blame for the conflict situation.
D) were of the opinion that prejudice and discrimination were the same thing.
E) looked to the psychology of the individual for an explanation.

Correct: A   Page: 301 Scramble Range: ALL
101. According to your text, which of the following HAS been used as an explanation for the occurrence or absence of prejudice?
A) The authoritarian personality
B) Wish-fulfillment among the lower classes
C) A logical offshoot from the bio-sociological perspective
D) The use of today's state-of-the-art intelligence tests
E) The occurrence in subpopulations of perfect pitch

Correct: D   Page: 302 Scramble Range: ALL
102. According to your text, the view that curing prejudice will reduce conflicts between groups
A) is to impose causation on two variables that are not meaningfully correlated.
B) is rooted in the eighteenth-century idea of biological causation.
C) is to confuse hypothesis-making with hypothesis-testing.
D) is to confuse cause with effect.
E) is to propose a theory that can never be tested.

Correct: B   Page: 302 Scramble Range: ALL
103. For many years, many people and programs were oriented to simply _____, so that prejudice and discrimination would be eliminated. When they did it, prejudice and discrimination often increased instead.
A) outlaw discrimination
B) bring people together
C) practice "cerebral hygiene"
D) practice social-psychological "self-control"
E) improve the level of mental health of the general population

Correct: A   Page: 302 Scramble Range: ALL
104. Allport pointed out that prejudice will
A) intensify if the groups are engaged in competition.
B) intensify if the groups are not in competition.
C) intensify if the groups pursue common goals.
D) increase if two groups with equal status have contact with each other.
E) exist regardless of contact or status.

Correct: D   Page: 302 Scramble Range: ALL
105.   According to Allport's theory of contact, the situation in which prejudice
would be most likely to DECREASE would be
A)   a African-American school playing against a white school in football.
B)   a African-American team defeating a white team in an academic college
bowl.
C)   African-Americans and whites playing each other in tennis.
D)   integrated basketball teams .
E)   children from segregated elementary schools attending junior high
school together.

Correct: E   Page: 302 Scramble Range: ALL
106.   According to Gordon Allport's theory of contact, prejudice will INCREASE or
remain high if two groups have contact under conditions of _____.
A)   psychological uncertainty
B)   sociological uncertainty
C)   the majority group's own choosing
D)   embarrassment to the minority group
E)   status inequality

Correct: A   Page: 302 Scramble Range: ALL
107.   According to your text, contact overcomes prejudice only when people
A)   meet on equal terms to cooperate in pursuing common goals.
B)   are educated so that they can realistically evaluate social situations.
C)   are brought together so that they can come to know one another as
persons.
D)   have a chance to compete against one another in some activity such as
international soccer tournaments, world fairs, the United Nations, and so
on.
E)   come together under a common religious "umbrella" supported by a
political structure.

Correct: B   Page: 302 Scramble Range: ALL
108.   The Sherif studies of young boys at summer camp
A)   showed that friendships across group boundaries serve to reduce
prejudice.
B)   showed that cooperative tasks reduce intergroup conflict.
C)   were not reliable because they failed to use a control group.
D)   were examples of survey research.
E)   were examples of comparing four separate research groups.

Correct: D   Page: 303 Scramble Range: ALL
109.   In a summer camp experiment, the Sherifs were able to show that hostilities
can be produced in a few days
A)   when campers have it pointed out to them that they are from different
social classes.
B)   when it is pointed out to them that they are of different religions
C)   when there is an economic incentive for success as a group.
D)   among young boys of similar background and with long-standing
friendships.
E)   among campers who have above-average levels of status anxiety.

Correct: C   Page: 306 Scramble Range: A-E
110. The American dilemma that Gunnar Myrdal wrote about was
A) how to end slavery when it was believed essential to the American economy.
B) the contradiction between our racist practices and the teachings of the church.
C) the contradiction between our racist practices and democratic ideals.
D) the contradictory actions of a leading statesman who owned slaves while he was trying to have slavery abolished in his own state.
E) the economic inadvisability of slavery in an industrializing nation.
F) none of these

Correct: B   Page: 305 Scramble Range: ALL
111. By 1825 the United States had by far the _____ slave population in the Western Hemisphere, because slaves in the United States had _____.
A) smallest; a high birth rate but a higher death rate
B) largest; a high birth rate and a low death rate
C) smallest; a very high rate of slaves who escaped to Canada
D) largest; hybrid vigor due to interbreeding with native Americans
E) smallest; often been sold abroad to raise capital to fight the Civil War

Correct: A   Page: 304 Scramble Range: ALL
112. In Figure 11-1, your text gives you the opportunity to examine the destinations of the slavers during the period 1500 to 1870. One thing that is clear is that
A) only a small proportion were taken to North America.
B) the majority of the purchasers were whites and the majority of the sellers were Portuguese.
C) only about one-half of the slaves went to private farm owners, with the other half going to corporate business enterprises.
D) most of the slaves (76 percent) were shipped to northern states.
E) the majority of slaves shipped from Africa were eventually eligible for freedom, because they were technically "pay-out" slaves.

Correct: E   Page: 304 Scramble Range: ALL
113. According to Figure 11-1, Patterns of the slave trade, 1500-1870, which of the following areas received the most African-American slaves?
A) British North America
B) Spanish America
C) British Caribbean
D) French Caribbean
E) Brazil

Correct: E   Page: 304 Scramble Range: A-E
114. Compared with slaves in the Caribbean and South America, slaves in the United States had
A) fertility that was low and that could not be explained at the time.
B) a patriarchal and patrilocal family system.
C) relatively little economic value on an individual-to-individual basis.
D) no family structure and no coherent lifestyle.
E) lower death rates and higher birth rates.
F) all of these

115. Which of the following had the lowest percent of population who were slaves in 1790, according to your text?
A) Canada
B) Massachusetts and Maine
C) South Carolina and Virginia
D) North Carolina and Georgia
E) Delaware and Maryland

116. Stark's solution to intergroup conflict would seem to be to
A) educate people to reduce intergroup conflict.
B) increase contact among groups to reduce conflict.
C) help minority groups to adopt the speech and etiquette of the dominant group so they will be accepted by the dominant group.
D) help the minority groups to become equal in status to the dominant group so they will be accepted.
E) ignore the situation because time will reduce the conflict.

117. According to your text, a low standard of living, a lack of information, and a lack of political power all contribute to ethnic or racial minorities' inability to
A) obtain higher wages.
B) take action to secure the vote for themselves.
C) lower their mortality rate.
D) have what are considered normal marriages.
E) keep family members locally available.

118. Stanley Lieberson says that both real and imagined _____ differences between African-Americans and whites enter into the rhetoric of interracial conflict in the United States, but he also says that they are not the cause of the interracial conflict.
A) intellectual
B) emotional
C) physical
D) creativity
E) fecundity

119. Which of the following was NOT one of the factors identified by Edna Bonacich as a reason for members of subordinate groups working for substandard wages?
A) Economic motives
B) Family ties
C) Lack of information
D) Lack of political power
E) Low standard of living
F) None of these

Correct: C   Page: 308 Scramble Range: A-C
120.   A cultural or racial characteristic of a group which becomes a focus of symbol of group differences is refered to as a
A)   enclave.
B)   status indicator.
C)   marker.
D)   all of these
E)   none of these

Correct: C   Page: 309 Scramble Range: A-E
121.   What usually prompts efforts toward exclusion of minority groups?
A)   Criminal elements
B)   Disease
C)   Economic competition
D)   Inappropriate religious beliefs
E)   Welfare case increases
F)   All of these

Correct: C   Page: 314 Scramble Range: A-D
122.   Associating certain occupations with certain groups, such as secretarial occupations with women, can be seen as a type of
A)   accommodation.
B)   assimilative mechanism.
C)   caste system.
D)   functional equivalent of replaceability.
E)   None of these

Correct: E   Page: 314 Scramble Range: ALL
123.   Often minorities have been used as _____ in societies, according to the text.
A)   information processors
B)   governmental "anchors" to control other minorities
C)   authority figures
D)   religious leaders
E)   middlemen

Correct: B   Page: 314 Scramble Range: A-E
124.   Middleman minorities
A)   are groups whose immigrant status is in doubt.
B)   often become the scapegoats for social conflicts.
C)   are almost always identified on the basis of religion.
D)   help us to understand how differential socialization works.
E)   tend to become quickly assimilated into the upper classes.
F)   All of these

Correct: A   Page: 315 Scramble Range: ALL
125.   In 1907, their peak year of entry into the United States, the Japanese immigrants made up _____ of all immigrants arriving that year.
A)   3 percent
B)   12 percent
C)   19 percent
D)   26 percent
E)   68 percent

126.   According to the text, the first generation of Japanese-Americans worked hard to establish themselves economically. But the first generation did something else equally important. What was it?
A)   They saved their profit and reinvested it rather than spending it.
B)   They ingratiated themselves to the dominant white group, taking a nonthreatening role in society.
C)   They sent their children to school and emphasized educational success.
D)   They maintained social-psychological ties with Japan, using Hawaii as an almost literal stepping-stone.
E)   They ensured that only the best Japanese came to the United States so that the group as a whole would have a good reputation.

127.   An occupation in which Japanese-Americans were overrepresented was
A)   jewelry-crafting.
B)   scientific breeding of livestock.
C)   insurance underwriting.
D)   migratory labor.
E)   gardening.
F)   none of these

128.   The fact that in 1969 the average income of Japanese-Americans was 32 percent higher than that of white Americans can probably best be explained by
A)   Americanization during the internment experience.
B)   vocational training during internment.
C)   selective immigration (only those with marketable skills allowed to immigrate).
D)   a collective American conscience that has tried to right the wrong of internment during World War II.
E)   higher educational attainment.
F)   all of these

129.   Japanese-Americans had--and still have--which of the following?
A)   Higher levels of formal education than the general population
B)   Higher rates of return to their homeland than most other American minorities
C)   Higher fertility rates than the general population
D)   A lower sense of future-orientation
E)   Lower rates of deferred gratification

130. In the United States at the end of World War II, Japanese-Americans were much more likely than were other racial and ethnic groups to
A) find themselves without socioeconomic resources to meet the problems of everyday life.
B) have college degrees.
C) have a strong degree of self-hatred.
D) have material goods that could be sold in exchange for cash, such as jewelry, antiques, and the like.
E) marry only within their own group.

131. Asian-Americans as a group are much more likely than other Americans to have
A) paid employment at an early age.
B) pro-natalist norms.
C) interrupted work histories.
D) a preference for active rather than passive leisure activities.
E) college degrees.

132. In the 1920s, about _____ of Japanese-American marriages involved a non-Japanese spouse. Today, that figure is about _____.
A) 30 percent; 50 percent
B) 2 percent; 50 percent
C) 15 percent; 30 percent
D) 25 percent; 40 percent
E) 40 percent; 65 percent

133. Asian-Americans who receive college degrees tend to receive them in which of the following majors or academic areas?
A) Science, medicine, law, engineering
B) Large-scale agriculture, agronomy
C) Foreign languages, business communications, political science
D) Education, speech, journalism
E) Physical education, art, music, large-scale agriculture

134. According to Table 11-2, Comparative Earnings Ratios, in Constant Dollars (based on employed males), the earnings of Japanese-Americans in 1976 were approximately what percent of whites' earnings?
A) 67 percent
B) 72 percent
C) 87 percent
D) 93 percent
E) 112 percent

Correct: D   Page: 321 Scramble Range: ALL
135. When an American minority group is concentrated in a few locations
   A) it actually declines in visibility because of its ordinariness.
   B) the positive aspects of its culture become clearer.
   C) the positive and negative aspects of its culture balance each other out.
   D) its economic and political power is maximized.
   E) its ordinariness is translated into more equal opportunity.

Correct: D   Page: 321 Scramble Range: ALL
136. Americans who want to segregate minority groups geographically are most
   likely to overlook the fact that
   A) those minorities will learn American ways more slowly if they are
      segregated
   B) non English-speaking minorities will learn English more slowly if they are
      segregated.
   C) the minorities will feel a sense of security and comradeship when they
      go home to their neighborhoods.
   D) this will maximize the political power of the minority group.
   E) this practice is contrary to the ideals of the United States Constitution.

Correct: B   Page: 321 Scramble Range: ALL
137. Which of the following does your text discuss as almost a society in and of
   itself?
   A) The Hispanics in Texas
   B) The French in Canada
   C) The Mexican-Americans in California

Correct: C   Page: 323 Scramble Range: ALL
138. Which of these is NOT true regarding enclave economies?
   A) They tend to hasten the economic progress of minority groups in them.
   B) They occupy a distinct spatial location.
   C) Most enclave businesses in enclave economies are not minority-owned.
   D) They consist of a variety of businesses.
   E) In them, nonminority owners usually employ minority employees.

Correct: D   Page: 323 Scramble Range: ALL
139. Minority group members of enclave economies can eventually earn higher
   salaries when they are employed outside the enclave, if they have achieved
   sufficient levels of cultural assimilation to compete effectively. And in this
   assimilation effort, _____ is of primary importance.
   A) membership in a total institution
   B) accumulation of substantial savings
   C) becoming immune from claims by one's kin
   D) mastery of language
   E) finding employment in "old-country" occupations

Correct: C   Page: 324 Scramble Range: A-D

140.   Hispanic-Americans
A)   are primarily from Puerto Rico and Cuba, not Mexico.
B)   tend to lack fluency in English.
C)   prefer to be called Mexican-Americans, Puerto Rican-Americans and Cuban-Americans.
D)   rarely (less than 10%) experience discrimination.
E)   all of these
F)   none of these

Correct: D   Page: 328 Scramble Range: A-D

141.   Mexican-Americans
A)   are an ethnic group.
B)   are Americans who have immigrated from Mexico.
C)   are a racial group.
D)   are as likely to complete high school as whites in the United States
E)   All of these
F)   None of these

Correct: A   Page: 335 Scramble Range: ALL

142.   One of the biggest remaining handicaps to African-Americans as compared to whites in the United States today is
A)   the percent of female-headed families.
B)   lack of education.
C)   income of male-headed families.
D)   income of younger families where both husband and wife work.
E)   lack of a homeland.

Correct: D   Page: 335 Scramble Range: ALL

143.   According to your text, a substantially higher proportion of African-American than white families are poor because
A)   of the extreme occupational alienation felt by adult African-Americans.
B)   African-Americans continue to have an overly pessimistic view of the "African-American experience"
C)   the cost of living is higher for African-Americans than it is for whites.
D)   of the dramatic increase in female-headed African-American families.
E)   of the extraordinary decline in the percent of African-American professionals.

Correct: E   Page: 336 Scramble Range: A-E

144.   The primary cause of affluence is
A)   continued rather than interrupted work history.
B)   employment in high-tech growth industries.
C)   residence in the southeastern or midwestern states.
D)   networking.
E)   membership in a two-earner family.
F)   none of these

Correct: C   Page: 336 Scramble Range: ALL
145. As your text points out, a high proportion of African-American households are female-headed and do not have an adult male present. This presents a problem because
A) it reinforces the moral decay of the society.
B) it reinforces the lack of a homeland.
C) it virtually assures continuing poverty due to the disadvantage that African-American women have in the labor market.
D) it ensures that the children of these households will become criminals because of their damaged genotype.
E) it encourages a high birthrate.

Correct: D   Page: 336 Scramble Range: ALL
146. Inability to participate in which of the following makes it difficult or impossible for many African-American women to enjoy economic affluence?
A) Labor unions
B) After-work social occasions with co-workers
C) Alternate linguistic systems
D) Two-earner families
E) Reciprocal helping behavior

Correct: C   Page: 338 Scramble Range: ALL
147. Approximately ____ percent of white Americans live in neighborhoods without African-American residents.
A) 18
B) 30
C) 50
D) 70
E) 82

Correct: C   Page: 338 Scramble Range: ALL
148. The pattern of residential segregation by race is strongest in the big cities of the _____ United States.
A) midwestern
B) western
C) eastern
D) southwestern
E) northeastern

Correct: A   Page: 339 Scramble Range: A-D
149. Prejudice against African-Americans in the United States
A) has generally declined in the past twenty years.
B) has generally increased in the South while declining in the North.
C) can be attributed to lack of education in the population as a whole.
D) can be understood as a reaction to the special genotype of African-Americans.
E) all of these
F) none of these

150.   Which of the following has been a major barrier to African-American progress in the United States?
A) Harsh prejudice and discrimination as a result of slavery
B) Lack of a specific nation or culture of origin
C) Racial visibility
D) African-Americans greatly outnumber other racial and ethnic groups
E) all of these
F) none of these

True/False

Correct: F   Page: 343
1. The fact that the majority of players in the National Basketball Association are African-American supports the bio-sociological view that there are important racial differences.

Correct: T   Page: 343
2. At the beginning of this century, the number of Jews who excelled in their sports exceeded their percentage in the general population.

Correct: T   Page: 343
3. The text takes the position that minority groups can overcome discrimination most easily in occupations where the quality of individual performance is most easily and accurately assessed.

Correct: F   Page: 345
4. According to the text, when employers do not have to compete intensely for talented people, they will be much less likely to discriminate against minority groups.

Correct: T   Page: 345
5. Discrimination should cease in sports long before it does in most other high status occupations.

Correct: F   Page: 345
6. Discrimination in sports should cease long after it has ceased in other high status occupations.

Correct: F   Page: 347
7. Schollaert and Smith found that the racial composition of teams significantly influences attendance at games.

Correct: T   Page: 347
8. Schollaert and Smith found that the racial composition of teams did not influence attendance at games.

Correct: T   Page: 347
9. Schollaert and Smith found that the major determinant of sports attendance in a given year is how many games the team is winning.

Correct: F   Page: 347
10. Schollaert and Smith found that the major determinant of sports attendance in a given year is the racial composition of a team.

Correct: F   Page: 347
11. Schollaert and Smith found that the median income of an area and ticket prices had strong effects on sports attendance.

Correct: F   Page: 347
12. The text proves false the notion that minority groups are especially attracted to sports as an avenue to upward mobility.

Correct: F   Page: 347
13. The text concludes that American minorities--at various times, the African-Americans, the Irish, and the Jews--have NOT used sports as a vehicle for upward mobility. The notion that they have is itself a racist point of view.

Multiple Choice

Correct: E   Page: 343 Scramble Range: ALL
14. The text states that the Irish and the African-Americans have both dominated boxing in the United States. The text goes on to make the argument that the reason this is so is that
   A) coaching skills are focused on different minorities at various times.
   B) the Irish and the African-Americans share a distant but important genetic link.
   C) both the Irish and the African-Americans lack faith in the economic system.
   D) both the Irish and the African-Americans have high levels of motivation but relatively low levels of intellectual ability.
   E) both the Irish and the African-Americans were drawn to boxing as a way of being upwardly mobile when other methods of mobility appeared blocked to them.

Correct: C   Page: 343 Scramble Range: ALL
15. According to the text's discussion of minority groups, which of the following should be an area with the most rapid means of upward mobility for a talented minority group person?
   A) Author of fiction; short story writer
   B) Interior decorator; clothing designer
   C) Mathematician; computer programmer
   D) Corporate public relations; librarian
   E) Secretary; dog breeder

Correct: A   Page: 345 Scramble Range: ALL
16. When a minority group's overrepresentation in sports starts to decline, this signals that the group's overall status in society
   A) is improving, that the minority group is getting ahead in society.
   B) is declining, that the minority group no longer holds public interest.
   C) is beginning a cyclical ebb and flow in terms of public interest.
   D) is declining, as the minority group becomes owners rather than performers.
   E) is neither improving nor declining, but is maturing into a new phase of upward social mobility.

17.   Schollaert and Smith found that which of the following statements is FALSE?
  A)   Minority group athletes tend to be either above or below average performance in a sport, but they are rarely average.
  B)   Minority group athletes actually tend to have lower than average performance in sports, even though popular opinion believes otherwise.
  C)   Minority group dominance of specific sports is not associated with lower attendance.
  D)   Ownership of sports tends to be dominated by the same minority group that is overrepresented in specific sports.
  E)   Racism dominates men's athletics but is almost completely absent in women's athletics.

Chapter 12: Gender and Inequality

True/False

Correct: F   Page: 350
1.   In more than half of premodern societies, women are as likely as men to be political leaders.

Correct: T   Page: 350
2.   Wife beating is common and accepted in most premodern societies.

Correct: T   Page: 350
3.   The percentage of college students who are women is a good indicator of gender inequality.

Correct: F   Page: 350
4.   The United States has about as much gender inequality as China.

Correct: F   Page: 355
5.   Historically, sex roles and relationships have been influenced only a little by the ratio of males to females.

Correct: T   Page: 355
6.   Sex ratios are social structures, not traits of individuals.

Correct: T   Page: 355
7.   Women are more subject to the limits of traditional sex roles in societies where there is an excess of men.

Correct: T   Page: 355
8.   According to Table 12-5 in the text, women's status tends to be low in nations where men outnumber women.

Correct: T   Page: 355
9.   Where men outnumber women, women are less likely to be employed outside the home.

Correct: T   Page: 359
10.   The major cause of imbalanced sex ratios is female infanticide.

Correct: F   Page: 359
11.   Research indicates that female infanticide has been limited to non-Western societies.

Correct: T   Page: 359
12.   Female fetuses tend to be more robust and to have a higher rate of survival in the womb.

Correct: T   Page: 360
13.   In most societies today women tend to outlive men.

Correct: F   Page: 362
14.   One of the characteristics of Spartan society was the visible presence of many women characterized as "disreputable."

Correct: F   Page: 362
15.   Male homosexuality is not connected with societies having an excess of males.

Correct: F   Page: 362
16.   Sparta practiced female infanticide, thus producing an excess of males in the general population.

Correct: T   Page: 362
17.   In Sparta, females were offered as much education as were boys.

Correct: T   Page: 363
18.   Societies with an excess of women tend to be sexually permissive for both men and women.

Correct: F   Page: 363
19.   Sexual permissiveness for women but not for men tends to characterize societies with an excess of women.

Correct: T   Page: 363
20.   According to Guttentag and Secord's theory, all relationships between opposite-sexed persons--regardless of the context--are potentially affected when there is an excess of one of the sexes.

Correct: T   Page: 363
21.   An unfavorable sex ratio causes power dependencies in dyadic relationships for members of the sex in excess supply.

Correct: T   Page: 365
22.   Because we can never prove a theory, scientists assess theories by trying to disprove them.

Correct: T   Page: 367
23.   African-Americans in the United States have a greater excess of women as compared to men than do whites.

Correct: F   Page: 370
24.   The "woman movement" began and achieved its greatest prominence in the Western states, primarily because of the dyadic power imbalances in those states.

Correct: T   Page: 372
25.   When men are in short supply, women increasingly find they need to become self-supporting.

Correct: T   Page: 373
26.   In the United States today, women are still concentrated in the relatively low-paying occupations such as secretary and typist and are very underrepresented in highly unionized, skilled, high-paying occupations.

Correct: F   Page: 374

27. When people are asked to name traits they would prefer in a manager they would like to have working for them, they tend to favor more feminine traits.

Correct: T   Page: 379

28. African-American slave families took a very protective attitude toward the chastity of their daughters.

Correct: T   Page: 379

29. The shortage of men is clearly a major cause of female-headed households among African-Americans.

Correct: T   Page: 379

30. A major cause of female-headed households among African-Americans is a high infant mortality rate among African-Americans.

Correct: F   Page: 379

31. The prevalence of fatherless households among African-Americans is a consequence of a tradition of matriarchy in African-American culture.

Correct: T   Page: 381

32. Married African-American men are much more likely to rate their marriage as "very happy" than are African-American women.

Correct: F   Page: 382

33. Mexican-Americans have the same prevalence of female-headed households as African-Americans.

Correct: T   Page: 382

34. Among Mexican-Americans there is a severe shortage of women.

Reference Key: STORY12.1
The society of Eniam has few resources, inadequate nutrition and is at almost constant war with its neighbors. The sex ratio is .85.

Correct: T   Page: 355   Refer to: STORY12.1

35. Eniam has more women than men.

Correct: F   Page: 359   Refer to: STORY12.1

36. Eniam is very unlikely to practice female infanticide.

Correct: F   Page: 362   Refer to: STORY12.1

37. Eniam is likely to emphasize chastity among women.

Correct: F   Page: 362   Refer to: STORY12.1

38. Eniam is more like ancient Athens than Sparta.

Correct: F   Page: 362   Refer to: STORY12.1

39. Eniam norms are likely to require men to be chaste.

Correct: T   Page: 362   Refer to: STORY12.1

40. Eniam women are likely to be able to own property.

Correct: T   Page: 363   Refer to: STORY12.1
41.   Eniam men are likely to be undependable as spouses and lovers.

Correct: T   Page: 364   Refer to: STORY12.1
42.   We can expect Eniam women to get together to try to exercise structural power.

Reference Key: STORY12.2
In a situation, such as currently in the United States, where there are more women than men and men hold structural power,

Correct: T   Page: 363   Refer to: STORY12.2
43.   men also hold dyadic power.

Correct: F   Page: 364   Refer to: STORY12.2
44.   women are unlikely to support feminist organizations.

Correct: T   Page: 377   Refer to: STORY12.2
45.   we expect to find an increase in divorce rates.

Correct: T   Page: 377   Refer to: STORY12.2
46.   we expect an increasing number of female headed households. .

Correct: F   Page: 375   Refer to: STORY12.2
47.   we expect that the proportion of illegitimate births will decline.

Correct: F   Page: 375   Refer to: STORY12.2
48.   we expect to find men increasingly supporting norms of virginity and chastity for women.

Correct: T   Page: 373   Refer to: STORY12.2
49.   we expect for women to be increasingly in the workforce but relatively little change in their primary responsibility for domestic chores.

Correct: T   Page: 361   Refer to: STORY12.2
50.   we expect a decline in prostitution.

Reference Key: STORY12.3
Imagine a university, USH, with mostly "traditional aged" (18-22), residential students. The gender ratio of students at this school is .82. Imagine another school, UMO, which is similar in many ways but has a gender ratio of 1.22.

Correct: T   Page: 355   Refer to: STORY12.3
51.   There are more women than men at USH.

Correct: T   Page: 363   Refer to: STORY12.3
52.   Guttentag and Secord would predict that when couples disagree about what movie to watch, the woman's choice is more likely to prevail at UMO than at USH.

Correct: T   Page: 364   Refer to: STORY12.3
53.   Guttentag and Secord would predict that USH women are more likely than UMO women to support feminist organizations.

Correct: F   Page: 364   Refer to: STORY12.3
54.   We would expect that USH has a stronger engineering program than UMO.

Correct: F   Page: 363   Refer to: STORY12.3
55.   USH men are more likely to be dependable as boyfriends than UMO men.

Correct: T   Page: 361   Refer to: STORY12.3
56.   We expect that USH women are less likely to be virgins than UMO women.

Correct: T   Page: 361   Refer to: STORY12.3
57.   We expect more prostitution at UMO than at USH.

Reference Key: SHOW12.2
In class we examined the relationship between sex ratios and a variety of other factors in the 50 most populous countries of the world.

Correct: T   Page: Ch3   Refer to: SHOW12.2
58.   The independent variable in these examinations was sex ratios.
NOTE: Cumulative question.

Correct: F   Page: Show12.2   Refer to: SHOW12.2
59.   We found that the higher the proportion of men, the higher the status of women--for instance, the higher the literacy rates among women.
NOTE: ShowCase question.

Correct: F   Page: Show12.2   Refer to: SHOW12.2
60.   We found that the lower the proportion of men, the lower the fertility rate.
NOTE: ShowCase question.

Correct: F   Page: Show12.2   Refer to: SHOW12.2
61.   We found that the higher the proportion of men the higher the divorce rate.
NOTE: ShowCase question.

Multiple Choice

Correct: A   Page: 350 Scramble Range: ALL
62.   In premodern societies which of the following is most common?
A)   Rape
B)   Equal chances for women and men to gain positions of leadership
C)   Female-headed kin groups
D)   Equality within households even though there is not equality in the political realm.

Correct: B   Page: 350 Scramble Range: A-C
63.   Why is it important to look at the ratio of men and women who go to school and the ratio of men and women who are illiterate?
A)   This tells us about the quality of the educational insitutions in the society.
B)   This tells us the degree to which women are disadvantaged in economic and political institutions.
C)   This tells us about the religious practices of the society.
D)   none of these

Correct: A   Page: 354 Scramble Range: ALL
64. A male who wants to maximize statistically his chances of encountering a female and to minimize statistically his chances of having male competition should go to which of the following states?
A) New York
B) Ohio
C) Iowa
D) California
E) Michigan

Correct: B   Page: 354 Scramble Range: ALL
65. A female who wants to maximize statistically her chances of finding a male and to minimize statistically her chances of having female competition should go to which of the following states?
A) New York
B) Nevada
C) Maine
D) Ohio
E) Iowa

Correct: D   Page: 355 Scramble Range: ALL
66. Sex ratios are not traits of individuals; they are _____.
A) social norms
B) cultural norms
C) attitudes about sexual behavior
D) social structures
E) constants

Correct: E   Page: 355 Scramble Range: ALL
67. In nations where men outnumber women,
A) male infanticide is sometimes the custom.
B) women have high status because of their lower availability.
C) male status tends to be low because of the excess of males.
D) androgyny tends to be the norm.
E) female status tends to be low.

Correct: D   Page: 358 Scramble Range: ALL
68. In most human populations, for every 100 female births there are
A) 80-82 male births.
B) 97-98 male births.
C) 100 male births.
D) 105-106 male births.
E) 110-112 male births.

Correct: A   Page: 358 Scramble Range: ALL
69. The text discusses which of these as sometimes producing a shortage of men?
A) Geographic mobility
B) Educational opportunities
C) Economic fluctuations
D) Political trends
E) Genetic drift

Correct: B Page: 359 Scramble Range: ALL
70. The major cause of unbalanced sex ratios is
    A) unequal recruitment into remarriages.
    B) female infanticide.
    C) political changes.
    D) geographic mobility.
    E) absence of an available partner.

Correct: C Page: 358 Scramble Range: A-E
71. Males
    A) metabolize meat protein more efficiently than do females.
    B) are likelier to remain single than are females.
    C) have a lower rate of survival in the womb than do females.
    D) have less survival instinct than do females.
    E) have lower rates of effective coping behavior than do females.
    F) all of these

Correct: D Page: 360 Scramble Range: ALL
72. An excess of male infants is produced by which of the following sexual
    practices?
    A) Wide age difference between sexual partners
    B) Infrequent sexual intercourse
    C) Frequent sexual intercourse
    D) Postponing sexual intercourse until just before ovulation
    E) Intercourse with multiple male sexual partners during the fertile period

Correct: D Page: 361 Scramble Range: ALL
73. Which of the following is among the causes of unbalanced sex ratios?
    A) High rates of psychologically abnormal sexual behavior
    B) The fact that one sex tends to prefer sexual intercourse more often than
       does the other sex
    C) Long-term, low-level effects of pollution
    D) Warfare
    E) Occupational pressures

Correct: E Page: 360 Scramble Range: ALL
74. Athens in its classic period had a great excess of males. During most of this
    period, the main cause for the excess of males was
    A) Greek women migrating because of marriage to non-Greek men.
    B) non-Greek males migrating to Greece for economic opportunities.
    C) greater susceptibility of Greek women to heatstroke and malnutrition.
    D) abduction of Greek women by foreign invaders.
    E) female infanticide.

Correct: C Page: 361 Scramble Range: A-D
75. A society constantly at war and without adequate nutrition
    A) is likely to experience genetic drift.
    B) is likely to have more men than women.
    C) is likely to exhibit some of the same characteristics as Sparta.
    D) is likely to have a high proportion of African-Americans and Hispanics.
    E) all of these
    F) none of these

76.   Which of these sexual patterns was found in premodern Athens and is typical of societies with too few women?
   A)   "Disreputable" women were highly visible.
   B)   There were relatively few female prostitutes.
   C)   Celibacy for the unmarried was stressed.
   D)   Religion reaffirmed its intense interest in controlling sexual expression.
   E)   Sexual expression was contained within formal marriage.

77.   Which of these is FALSE regarding premodern Athens?
   A)   Women were classified as children, regardless of age.
   B)   "Respectable" women were isolated by extremely protective sexual norms.
   C)   Athenian women were throughout life the legal property of some man.
   D)   Because there were so few women, it was rare to find "disreputable" ones.
   E)   Women were denied all participation in politics.

78.   Where women are in excess supply
   A)   children tend to be more highly valued.
   B)   the infant mortality rate tends to be higher than usual.
   C)   the maternal mortality rate tends to be higher than usual.
   D)   men are often expected to practice sororal polygyny.
   E)   men are inclined to be less dependable as spouses and lovers.

79.   Where women are in excess supply there is
   A)   an excess of female infants and a high infant male mortality rate.
   B)   a high maternal mortality rate.
   C)   a high infant mortality rate.
   D)   greater likelihood of arranged marriage as a pattern of mate selection.
   E)   much less gender inequality.

80.   Where women are scarce they are treated as
   A)   rare commodities, and are able to demand rights of their own.
   B)   a degraded minority group, and are ordinarily powerless.
   C)   rare commodities, and exercise great political power.
   D)   a demographic minority, but are power-brokers and skilled at bargaining.
   E)   precious property, but without rights of their own.

81.   Which of the following is FALSE regarding premodern Sparta?
   A)   The Spartans practiced infanticide, but without sexual preference.
   B)   The Spartans had an excess of females.
   C)   Spartans offered girls as much education as boys.
   D)   From age 7 through 30, Spartan males had much contact with women.
   E)   Spartan women were not known for being shy or submissive.

Correct: A   Page: 362 Scramble Range: ALL
82.   Which of these is FALSE regarding the Spartans?
    A)   The Spartans had heavy penalties for rape and for adultery.
    B)   Spartan culture was sexually permissive for both sexes.
    C)   Spartan culture emphasized childbearing.
    D)   Spartan women usually did not marry until they were 20 or older.
    E)   Lesbianism was practiced openly by some Spartans.

Correct: A   Page: 363 Scramble Range: ALL
83.   Which of these is an example of dyadic power?
    A)   Monty always bosses Karen; Karen never bosses Monty.
    B)   The three Andrews boys play well together and rarely argue or fight.
    C)   The owner of a travel agency tires of her complaining employees and
          dismisses all six of them.
    D)   The students in a psychology class "train" their professor to lecture from
          the left side of her lecture desk.
    E)   The chairman of a board of directors didn't like the way the board
          members voted, so he vetoes their decision.

Correct: B   Page: 363 Scramble Range: ALL
84.   Within a dyad, the member with inferior power can be termed the _____
       member.
    A)   inferior
    B)   dependent
    C)   intransitive
    D)   flawed
    E)   nondemocratic

Correct: C   Page: 363 Scramble Range: A-E
85.   A social circumstance that can greatly influence dyadic power is the
    A)   climate within which the dyad is located.
    B)   extent to which power is defined as authority or as influence.
    C)   sex ratio within which the dyad is located.
    D)   ease with which scapegoats can be located.
    E)   extent to which the exercise of power is conscious or unconscious
    F)   none of these

Correct: D   Page: 364 Scramble Range: ALL
86.   Historically, men have usually lacked dyadic power, so they offset women's
       usually greater dyadic power by
    A)   giving women more opportunities outside the dyadic relationship.
    B)   distracting women with child care and housework.
    C)   preventing the internalization of social norms.
    D)   shaping law, education, occupations, and so on to serve male interests.
    E)   developing greater skills at micromanipulation.

Correct: A   Page: 364 Scramble Range: A-D
87. According to Guttentag and Secord, if an imbalance between the sexes continues for a substantial period, an appreciable number of the gender in excess supply may do which of the following?
A) Organize various types of activities to correct the situation.
B) Become demoralized, depressed, and develop higher illness rates.
C) Voluntarily become single parents by reproducing outside marriage.
D) Begin to manifest a higher suicide rate.
E) None of these

Correct: E   Page: 364 Scramble Range: ALL
88. If excess supply of one gender persists for a substantial period, that gender may institute organized activities to improve their situation, something that might improve their _____ power.
A) latent
B) intrusive
C) innovative
D) direct
E) structural

Correct: A   Page: 364 Scramble Range: ALL
89. According to Guttentag and Secord, when the sex ratio is unequal the gender in excess supply may
A) withdraw from dyadic relationships.
B) attempt to make the sex ratio more equal.
C) engage in psycho-sexual rationalization.
D) endorse polygamy as a marriage alternative.
E) have a higher mortality rate due to stress-related disease.

Correct: D   Page: 364 Scramble Range: ALL
90. When both structural and dyadic power favor men, the male response is to
A) share voluntarily some of their power with females.
B) divest themselves of some power by using power-brokers.
C) concentrate on structural power and ignore dyadic power.
D) exploit their advantages to the fullest.
E) leave much of their power unused.

Correct: E   Page: 364 Scramble Range: ALL
91. Many women deeply believe in and actively support norms upholding male privilege, illustrating the effects of
A) desensitization.
B) circumvention.
C) rationalization.
D) legalization.
E) internalization.

Correct: D   Page: 366 Scramble Range: ALL

92. The text discusses the recent shift in _____ from an excess of males to a slight excess of females.
    A) Indonesia
    B) Mauritania
    C) Japan
    D) Canada
    E) France

Correct: A   Page: 366 Scramble Range: ALL

93. According to the text, _____ in the United States today have a significant shortage of males.
    A) African-Americans
    B) Mexican-Americans
    C) Japanese-Americans
    D) Chinese-Americans
    E) none of the above

Correct: A   Page: 370 Scramble Range: ALL

94. Which of these is the correct historical sequence?
    A) "Woman movement" ---> suffragette movement ---> feminist movement
    B) Suffragette movement ---> "woman movement" ---> feminist movement
    C) Suffragette movement ---> feminist movement ---> "woman movement"
    D) "Woman movement" ---> feminist movement ---> suffragette movement
    E) Feminist movement ---> suffragette movement ---> "woman movement"

Correct: D   Page: 372 Scramble Range: ALL

95. Nancy Cott defines feminism as "a(n) _____ having three essential features: (1) opposition to all forms of stratification based on gender, (2) belief that biology does not consign females to inferior status, and (3) a sense of common experience and purpose among women to direct their efforts to bring about change."
    A) political party
    B) religion
    C) organization
    D) ideology
    E) syndrome

Correct: B   Page: 372 Scramble Range: ALL

96. Nancy Cott defines _____ as "an ideology having three essential features: (1) opposition to all forms of stratification based on gender, (2) belief that biology does not consign females to inferior status, and (3) a sense of common experience and purpose among women to direct their efforts to bring about change."
    A) the woman movement
    B) feminism
    C) the suffragette movement
    D) gynocracy
    E) sexual politics

97. The term "spinster" is related to which of these?
    A) The economic need to be self-supporting
    B) Enhancement of mate-selection chances by setting a "love-trap"
    C) Serving as an emotional rudder for an extended family
    D) Experiencing rapid personal change resulting in confusion of the self-concept
    E) Fabricating not-quite-true tales to enhance prospects in the marriage market

98. The text connects economic need to which of the following?
    A) Redundant labeling
    B) Span-shift
    C) Ex post facto lobbying
    D) The empty nest syndrome
    E) Spinsters

99. About _____ percent of women who are mothers of young children go off to work every day.
    A) 8
    B) 14
    C) 23
    D) 34
    E) 60

100. Occupations have become _____ than historically they have been.
    A) more static, career-wise
    B) more volatile, career-wise
    C) less stressful
    D) more demanding of employees' allegiance to the employer
    E) less gender-segregated

101. The majority of women now work outside the home, and they
    A) work at the insistence of their husbands or partners.
    B) work mainly because they want to, not because they have an economic need to work.
    C) usually work in a place and manner that allow them to return home during the lunch hour or soon after school hours are concluded.
    D) tend to work in jobs that are relatively lower-paying, compared to jobs occupied by men.
    E) tend to have relatively continuous--not interrupted--work careers.

Correct: B   Page: 373 Scramble Range: ALL

102. Which of the following is mentioned by the text as a factor that helps to explain the difference between men's and women's full-time employment pay differences?
A) Working by choice or working out of necessity
B) Turnover, or frequency with which women's work is interrupted for some reason
C) Sexual differences in distribution of talent and ability
D) Sexual differences in amount of formal education completed
E) The tendency of women to choose job security over riskier chances for advancement

Correct: E   Page: 373 Scramble Range: ALL

103. One of the reasons women tend to be paid less than men is that women still tend to shun some of the activities that lead to higher incomes. Women are less likely to enroll in majors leading to highpaying jobs and are more likely to enroll in majors leading to lower-paying jobs. The concept that helps to explain this fact is
A) gender resocialization.
B) transubstantiation.
C) bifurcation of interest.
D) gender indemnification.
E) sex-role socialization.

Correct: F   Page: 377 Scramble Range: A-D

104. The treatment of women as sex objects, especially in the mass media,
A) is typical of a situation where men outnumber women.
B) is explained by Kohn's research on differential socialization.
C) reflects structural mobility in the society.
D) is closely related to increases in public prostitution.
E) all of the above.
F) none of the above.

Correct: D   Page: 377 Scramble Range: A-D

105. According to your text, one of the major reasons for the preponderance of female headed households in the African-American community is
A) a tradition of matriarchy extending back to the days of slavery.
B) a moral decline in the society, especially in urban areas.
C) the structure of welfare payments.
D) a very high rate of infant mortality.
E) all of these
F) none of these

Correct: D   Page: 377 Scramble Range: A-D

106. One of the major reasons for the preponderance of female headed households in the African-American community is
A) a tradition of matriarchy extending back to the days of slavery.
B) a culture of promiscuity extending back to the days of slavery.
C) the structure of welfare payments.
D) a shortage of men.
E) all of these
F) none of these

Correct: D   Page: 378 Scramble Range: ALL
107. African-American men are at least twice as likely as African-American women to
A)   have an uninterrupted work history.
B)   seek and obtain a decree of divorce.
C)   marry someone older than themselves.
D)   marry someone of another race.
E)   marry someone who has been upwardly mobile.

Correct: C   Page: 378 Scramble Range: ALL
108. As _____ grow up, the proportion of males continues to drop because of higher mortality rates, especially due to accidents, drugs, and violence.
A)   the children of alcoholics
B)   the children of remarriages
C)   African-American children
D)   the children of Asian-Americans
E)   children in southeastern states

Correct: B   Page: 378 Scramble Range: A-D
109. Your text has a picture of one of the first bathing beauty contests. This took place within weeks of the ratification of the nineteenth amendment, giving women the right to vote.
A)   This inconsistency is not well explained by Guttentag and Secord's theory.
B)   Both of these reflect the consequences of a declining sex ratio in the United States.
C)   Only one of these, parading in scanty costumes, is related to the shortage of men.
D)   This illustrates the problem of structural mobility.
E)   All of these
F)   None of these

Correct: C   Page: 379 Scramble Range: ALL
110. The illegitimacy ratio is
A)   the percent of petitions for recognition of common law marriages denied by the courts.
B)   the percent of all children and adolescents participating in the underground economy.
C)   the proportion of all births that occur out of wedlock.
D)   the proportion of all children and adolescents citing disapproved ideologies to explain their disadvantaged situation.
E)   the percent of traditionally male jobs currently being occupied by females and resulting in male underemployment.

111.   Mexican-Americans
   A)   have more traditional ideas about gender roles than Americans who are not Hispanic.
   B)   have a severe shortage of men.
   C)   emphasize the importance of marriage and fidelity less than other Hispanics.
   D)   live in families which are as likely to be female headed as African-American families are.
   E)   all of these
   F)   none of these

Chapter 13: Family

True/False

Correct: F   Page: 389
1. Sociologists recently have discovered that societies exist in which there is no family.

Correct: F   Page: 390
2. Reproduction is an essential function of the family.

Correct: F   Page: 390
3. Primary bonds in the family are sexual.

Correct: F   Page: 391
4. "Kinship-structured" is a fancy way of saying "biological ties."

Correct: T   Page: 391
5. "Kinship" is a socially, rather than biologically, defined connection among people.

Correct: F   Page: 391
6. Sociologists define families primarily on the basis of kinship.

Correct: F   Page: 392
7. Most premodern societies practice monogamy.

Correct: F   Page: 392
8. In more than four-fifths of premodern societies, males do no domestic chores.

Correct: T   Page: 392
9. In most premodern societies, male dominance is the norm.

Correct: F   Page: 392
10. The nuclear family is the most common family form in premodern societies.

Correct: T   Page: 392
11. Most premodern societies have extended families.

Correct: T   Page: 398
12. In preindustrial Europe, most French children went out on their own and became independent by age 10.

Correct: T   Page: 398
13. In preindustrial Europe, parents were much less interested in their children than are parents today.

Correct: F   Page: 398
14. In preindustrial Europe there were fewer female-headed families than there are in the United States now.

Correct: T   Page: 398

15. In preindustrial Europe, the average household was not much larger than today.

Correct: T   Page: 398

16. In preindustrial Europe, most families lived in one room.

Correct: F   Page: 400

17. In contrast to today, preindustrial families were very rarely neglectful of their children.

Correct: F   Page: 402

18. In preindustrial Europe only the wealthy hired wet nurses to breast-feed and watch over their infants.

Correct: T   Page: 402

19. The average marriage today is probably happier than the average marriage 100 years ago.

Correct: F   Page: 404

20. In preindustrial Europe couples were more dependent on one another for companionship than are couples today.

Correct: T   Page: 404

21. In preindustrial Europe, primary emotional attachments were generally to people outside the family.

Correct: T   Page: 404

22. In preindustrial Europe, people's main emotional and social bonds were to people who were one's own sex and age peers.

Correct: F   Page: 404

23. In preindustrial Europe because most people were poor, people were free to marry for love, not for property.

Correct: F   Page: 407

24. Research about people's views of their family relationships reveals a picture of weak family ties.

Correct: F   Page: 407

25. A high divorce rate indicates that the marital relationship has become much less important than it used to be.

Correct: F   Page: 407

26. The rising divorce rate indicates that marriage has become less important to people than it used to be.

Correct: F   Page: 408

27. While the divorce rate in most nations of the world has been falling, it has been rising in the United States.

Correct: T   Page: 408
28.   The divorce rate has been rising in most nations of the world, just as it has been in the United States.

Correct: F   Page: 408
29.   In the United States today about 60 percent of people who marry get divorced.

Correct: T   Page: 409
30.   Most people who get married never get divorced.

Correct: F   Page: 409
31.   Most people who get married get divorced.

Correct: F   Page: 410
32.   More than 4 out of 10 married men report having sex with someone other than their spouse in the past year.

Correct: T   Page: 411
33.   Where men outnumber women, divorce rates will be low.

Correct: F   Page: 411
34.   The more Catholics, the less divorce.

Correct: F   Page: 411
35.   Living together before marriage lowers the probability of divorce.

Correct: T   Page: 412
36.   One thing in short supply in one-parent families is time.

Correct: T   Page: 412
37.   A primary consequence of female-headed families is poverty.

Correct: F   Page: 413
38.   "Broken" or single parent"homes are a primary cause of deviant behavior among children.

Correct: T   Page: 413
39.   Research finds that poor parenting, regardless of the structure of the family, is a primary cause of deviant behavior among children.

Correct: T   Page: 413
40.   It's not how many parents a child has in his or her home that matters, it's how effective they are at being parents that is of primary importance in how a child turns out.

Correct: F   Page: 413
41.   No matter how effective a parent is at being a parent, it is having both parents living at home that is of primary importance in discouraging children from deviant behavior.

Correct: F   Page: 413
42.   Gerald Patterson's research on problem kids found that undesirable behavior will cease if it is not rewarded.

Correct: T   Page: 413
43. Patterson's research on problem children found that parents of problem kids often refuse to recognize that their child's behavior is creating negative consequences and that the child's behavior probably ought to be changed.

Correct: T   Page: 413
44. Patterson's research on problem children found that children will continue antisocial behavior unless their parents use punishment to teach them not to do it.

Correct: T   Page: 413
45. Gerald Patterson's research on problem children found that problem kids tend to act in antisocial ways usually seen in 2- and 3-year-olds but that are inappropriate for older children in our culture.

Correct: T   Page: 413
46. Some parents who are inadequate in child-rearing activities can be retrained to become adequate parents in this regard.

Correct: T   Page: 415
47. First marriages tend to involve men and women of quite similar social status.

Correct: F   Page: 416
48. More financially successful men tend to remarry women with young children.

Correct: F   Page: 416
49. Couples who remarry have higher divorce rates even if there are no stepchildren in the home.

Correct: T   Page: 416
50. Most parents experience increased marital happiness and life satisfaction when the last child moves out of the house.

Reference Key: STORY13.1
A recent study, discussed in your text, found that women who had lived with their spouse prior to being married were 80 percent more likely to get divorced than women who had not.

Correct: F   Page: 411&Ch3   Refer to: STORY13.1
51. This means that living together before marriage causes divorce.

Correct: F   Page: 411&Ch3   Refer to: STORY13.1
52. This means that if you want to avoid divorce, avoid living together before marriage.

Correct: T   Page: Ch3   Refer to: STORY13.1
53. This correlation has problems of spuriousness.
NOTE: Cumulative question.

Correct: F   Page: Ch11   Refer to: STORY13.1
54. This finding is inconsistent with Guttentag and Secord's theory.
NOTE: Cumulative question.

Correct: F   Page: Ch3   Refer to: STORY13.1
55.   This research was an experiment.
NOTE: Cumulative question.

Correct: T   Page: 411   Refer to: STORY13.1
56.   This might be explained by the increased tendency of those least committed to marriage and reluctant to make commitments being more likely both to live together and to get divorced.

Correct: F   Page: 411   Refer to: STORY13.1
57.   This might be explained by the tendency of couples to live together only a short time before getting married.

Correct: F   Page: Ch11   Refer to: STORY13.1
58.   This finding would seem more likely in a society with more men than women.
NOTE: Cumulative question.

Multiple Choice

Correct: C   Page: 391 Scramble Range: A-D
59.   Kinship
A)   is much less important today than it was a hundred years ago.
B)   refers to a biological tie among individuals.
C)   is a socially defined connection among people.
D)   is primarily a feature of premodern economies.
E)   all of these
F)   none of these

Correct: B   Page: 391 Scramble Range: A-D
60.   The family, as defined in your text,
A)   includes both sexes, at least two of whom maintain a socially approved sexual relationship.
B)   is a kinship structured group.
C)   is a group that maintains a common residence.
D)   includes economic cooperation and reproduction.
E)   all of these

Correct: E   Page: 392 Scramble Range: A-D
61.   Most premodern societies
A)   are monogamous.
B)   are patrilocal.
C)   designate women as having final authority over care of infants.
D)   do not allow women to hold leadership roles.
E)   all of these
F)   none of these

62. In trying to define what "family" is, American sociologists today are tending to emphasize
A) other people's and organizations' response to the family.
B) blood kinship, regardless of whether or not there has been a formal ceremony.
C) the presence of some kind of ceremony, regardless of whether or not it is a religious ceremony.
D) what the family does, rather than who does or doesn't belong to the family.
E) legal definitions of the family rather than people's view of the family.

63. Most premodern societies
A) emphasize the nuclear family as the preferred family form.
B) keep track of kinship no further than aunts and uncles.
C) are matriarchal.
D) are matrilocal.
E) are patrilocal.

64. Most premodern societies are
A) not monogamous.
B) polyandrous.
C) polygynous.
D) bilateral.
E) promiscuous.

65. Extended families
A) include only one adult couple.
B) are smaller than nuclear families.
C) include at least two adult couples.
D) are more prevalent than 25-50 years ago.
E) no longer exist.

66. An adult couple and its children are termed a(n) _____ family.
A) nuclear
B) extended
C) stem
D) blended
E) isolated

67. An extended family is
A) smaller than a nuclear family.
B) composed of more than one nuclear family.
C) composed of an adult couple and its children.
D) one that gives attention to all of its members.
E) one that has reached the limit of its economic resources.

Correct: D   Page: 392 Scramble Range: A-D
68. Extended families in premodern societies most often included
     A) boarders and their children in the household.
     B) grandparents.
     C) sisters and their husbands and children.
     D) brothers and their wives and children.
     E) all of these

Correct: F   Page: 392-95 Scramble Range: A-D
69. The family is universal--all societies have families--and
     A) the functions of the family are consistent from society to society.
     B) sexual gratification is universally seen as an important function of the family.
     C) it is the primary economic unit in all societies.
     D) the family is "stronger" in more traditional, less modern societies.
     E) all of the these.
     F) none of these

Correct: C   Page: 393 Scramble Range: A-D
70. The incest taboo
     A) prohibits pre-marital sex.
     B) almost universally prohibits extra-marital sex.
     C) prohibits sexual intercourse between certain members of the same family.
     D) restricts sexual intercourse to married partners.
     E) all of these
     F) none of these

Correct: D   Page: 393 Scramble Range: ALL
71. What country has the lowest proportion of people who believe that their spouse shares the same sexual attitudes as they hold?
     A) Ireland
     B) United States
     C) France
     D) Japan
     E) Sweden

Correct: F   Page: 393 Scramble Range: A-D
72. Your text examines attitudes--such as whether spouses share sexual attitudes--about families in various modern societies. This examination shows
     A) that there is almost complete agreement about family values in modern societies.
     B) that the functions of the family are similar in modern societies.
     C) that a strong majority (over 70%) in most countries share sexual attitudes with their spouses.
     D) that less modern, more traditional societies have stronger families in the sense of their importance and their ties of intimacy.
     E) all of these
     F) none of these

73. According to your text, when did the offspring of traditional European couples ordinarily leave the parental household?
A)   Between age 10-15
B)   Between age 15-20
C)   Between age 18-25
D)   When both parents were dead
E)   When the male parent died

74. The majority of traditional European families
A)   lived in large mansions.
B)   were very large families.
C)   shared one-room.
D)   had excellent family relations.
E)   passed down carefully crafted furniture from generation to generation.

75. According to Table 13-7 in your text, what was the average household size in preindustrial societies (Italy, France, England, Japan, etc.)?
A)   4.5-5.8 persons
B)   5.8-9.2 persons
C)   7.0-10 persons
D)   8.0-14 persons
E)   10-14 persons

76. Edward Shorter, in his study of traditional European peasant families, found that the family usually contained
A)   a number of elderly members who were no longer capable of significant economic contribution.
B)   very few children over age eight.
C)   households that averaged ten to twelve people.
D)   no people who were not related by either blood or marriage.
E)   fewer people if it was wealthy.

77. Your text notes that the average married couple in the traditional European family had
A)   about six to eight children living in the household at any given time.
B)   about 10 years together before one of them died.
C)   approximately three in-laws living in the household.
D)   total control over the daily behavior of their offspring.
E)   a more companionate life style than the average married couple of today in the United States.

Correct: A   Page: 398 Scramble Range: ALL
78. According to Table 13-7 in your text, the average Italian household in the preindustrial era had about how many people in it?
A) 4.5
B) 8.2
C) 9.1
D) 12.0
E) 16.3

Correct: C   Page: 399 Scramble Range: ALL
79. Shorter discovered that the traditional European family
A) typically included a nuclear family living in a single household.
B) was somewhat larger than had been assumed.
C) often contained temporary members such as lodgers.
D) was emotionally very much like the middle-class American family of today.
E) lived in more or less constant fear of the local nobility.

Correct: E   Page: 402 Scramble Range: ALL
80. As compared with traditional European families, the families of today are
A) less likely to be prudish about sex.
B) more likely to let the children witness arguments between the parents.
C) less likely to consider the importance of naming a child after a relative.
D) more likely to ignore a crying child.
E) less likely to expose their children to dangers.

Correct: E   Page: 402 Scramble Range: A-D
81. In preindustrial Europe,
A) infants were often abandoned.
B) infants were often sent away to wet nurses.
C) children were most likely to die during harvest season.
D) parents often expressed relief over the death of a child.
E) all of these
F) none of these

Correct: A   Page: 404 Scramble Range: ALL
82. In traditional European families, couples were LEAST likely to marry for
A) love.
B) money.
C) land.
D) labor.
E) a large dowry.

Correct: D   Page: 404 Scramble Range: ALL
83. Which of the following is more common today than it was in the traditional peasant families of Europe?
A) Wife beating
B) Husband beating
C) Resentment and anger
D) Emotional attachments
E) More concern for property than for a spouse

Correct: D   Page: 404 Scramble Range: A-D
84. In preindustrial Europe, couples were
     A) generally the primary emotional support for each other.
     B) both involved in childcare in addition to farm chores.
     C) inclined to have mothers nurse their own children.
     D) less important to each other than strong peer attachments.
     E) all of these
     F) none of these

Correct: A   Page: 404 Scramble Range: ALL
85. When Shorter studied traditional European families, he found that a spouse
     was most likely to develop strong emotional ties with
     A) others who were the same age and sex rather than with his/her spouse.
     B) the children of the family rather than with his/her spouse.
     C) the local religious official.
     D) essential farm animals that were important for economic productivity.
     E) the local nobility, with the relationship approximating kinship.

Correct: A   Page: 404 Scramble Range: A-D
86. Industrialization made a lot of differences in the family in what way?
     A) It freed individuals from depending on inheritance for their livelihood.
     B) It made the family less important as a source of emotional attachments.
     C) It eliminated the importance of kinship networks.
     D) It made the family less affluent and, thus, less important to people.
     E) All of these
     F) None of these

Correct: F   Page: 404 Scramble Range: NONE
87. The industrial age
     A) made romantic love possible.
     B) created more choice about marriage partners.
     C) freed people from a dependence on inheritance.
     D) increased the affluence of the modern family.
     E) A and D only.
     F) All of these

Correct: E   Page: 405 Scramble Range: ALL
88. According to your text, "good parenting" is an invention of
     A) being a secure person, socially and psychologically.
     B) the action of human instincts on normal personality.
     C) the activities of Dr. Spock and other child-rearing experts.
     D) institutional social change of a positive type.
     E) modernization.

Correct: D   Page: 407 Scramble Range: ALL
89. Of American adults with a living parent, about _____ see their parents only
     once or twice a year, probably because they live a long distance away.
     A) one-twentieth
     B) one-fifteenth
     C) one-tenth
     D) one-third
     E) one-half

90. Which of the following is true about kinship bonds in modern America?
    A) They are usually kept within kin who are locally available.
    B) The bonds are less likely to be two-way bonds than in the past.
    C) There are likely to be fewer kinship bonds than in the past.
    D) The bonds are likely to be more shallow than in the past.
    E) Such bonds seldom result in economic exchanges.

91. A _____ probably indicates that the marital relationship is much more important to the couple than it used to be.
    A) low marital homicide rate
    B) high spousal violence rate
    C) low spousal violence rate
    D) high divorce rate
    E) higher birth rate

92. One of the reasons it is difficult to say precisely how much increase or decrease in divorce has taken place is that
    A) some nations do not make divorce records available to researchers.
    B) some respondents lie about whether or not they are divorced.
    C) it is very difficult to measure divorce rates in an accurate and valid way.
    D) the divorce rate is frequently balanced by the remarriage rate.
    E) many people do not want to listen to what sociologists have discovered about divorce rates.

93. According to the text, calculating the divorce rate is a complex matter. When time and trouble have been taken to calculate it appropriately, the divorce rate shows
    A) no change, other things taken into account.
    B) an increase in the number of divorces, but not in the percent of divorces.
    C) a mild increase.
    D) a dramatic increase.
    E) a slight decrease, when calculated according to the complex computation discussed in your text.

94. For weddings held in 1975, the projection is that 50 percent will result in divorce. Projections for more recent years suggest a _____ in divorce.
    A) slight increase
    B) moderate increase
    C) dramatic increase
    D) dramatic decrease
    E) slight decrease

Correct: E   Page: 409 Scramble Range: ALL
95. Maybe half of all MARRIAGES break up, but the vast majority of people never get divorced. The reason for this is that
A) most people these days do not get divorced; they obtain "dissolutions."
B) more marriages are ended by desertion or abandonment than by divorce.
C) many whose marriage breaks up never follow through and obtain a divorce.
D) a large minority of people get annulments, not divorces.
E) some people marry and divorce repeatedly.

Correct: A   Page: 409 Scramble Range: ALL
96. The argument about whether it is marriages or people who are the proper basis for computations about divorces basically revolves around the fact that
A) some people marry and divorce several times.
B) it is misleading to draw generalizations about people from data gathered from large geographic areas.
C) many people who are married wish they were divorced.
D) often only one member of a couple wants a divorce; the other wants to stay married.
E) statistics about deeply personal matters are always distortive.

Correct: C   Page: 410 Scramble Range: A-D
97. Extramarital sex in the United States
A) is widespread and growing.
B) illustrates the decline of the importance of the family.
C) is engaged in by less than one in twenty married people.
D) is engaged in by more than half of married people.
E) none of these

Correct: C   Page: 411 Scramble Range: A-C
98. According to Trent and South's international study, divorce rates
A) are higher when there is a lower proportion of women employed outside the home.
B) are lower when there is a larger proportion of Catholics in the country.
C) are highest in the most industrialized societies.
D) all of these
E) none of these

Correct: F   Page: 411 Scramble Range: A-D
99. The greater the proportion of women in the labor force
A) the lower the divorce rate.
B) the lower the level of technological productivity.
C) the higher the proportion of Catholics in the society.
D) the greater the impact of premarital sex.
E) all of these
F) none of these

Correct: C   Page: 411 Scramble Range: ALL
100. Compared to couples who don't, couples who DO live together before they get married
   A) are less likely to get divorced.
   B) are less likely to get divorced if they have lived together for three years or more.
   C) are more likely to get divorced.
   D) are just as likely to get divorced.

Correct: A   Page: 411 Scramble Range: A-D
101. Julia Ann and her boyfriend live together for a few years before they get married. Compared to other couples who didn't live together, they are
   A) more likely to get divorced.
   B) less likely to get divorced if they have children in the first three years of marriage.
   C) more likely to get divorced if they both work.
   D) less likely to get divorced.
   E) none of these

Correct: E   Page: 411 Scramble Range: ALL
102. _____ has contributed to the increase in female-headed families.
   A) Religious intolerance
   B) Increased affluence
   C) The lure of more welfare income
   D) Adequate day care for their children
   E) A shortage of eligible men

Correct: D   Page: 412 Scramble Range: A-D
103. The primary consequence of female-headed families is
   A) high levels of affection in those families.
   B) affluence because of higher welfare payments to such households.
   C) a broad-based social movement to increase the level of living in these households.
   D) poverty.
   E) none of these

Correct: C   Page: 412 Scramble Range: ALL
104. The major source of high family incomes is
   A) wives giving adequate backup at home so their husbands won't have to worry while working.
   B) protective tariffs to maintain high employment.
   C) two-earner couples.
   D) home equity loans.
   E) luck.

Correct: B   Page: 412 Scramble Range: ALL
105.   Your text discusses the illegitimacy ratio. In the United States today, approximately what percent of all newborns are born to women who are unwed?
A)   12 percent
B)   20 percent
C)   35 percent
D)   44 percent
E)   53 percent

Correct: F   Page: 413 Scramble Range: A-D
106.   Female headed families
A)   are strongly related to childhood delinquency.
B)   are increasingly rare among whites in the United States.
C)   are primarily a consequence of illegitimate births.
D)   generally give lower quality parenting to their children.
E)   all of these
F)   none of these

Correct: C   Page: 413 Scramble Range: A-D
107.   Delinquent behavior in children is strongly related to
A)   differences in genotype.
B)   differences in household composition.
C)   differences in quality of parenting.
D)   differences in severity of punishment.
E)   all of these

Correct: B   Page: 413 Scramble Range: ALL
108.   Gerald Patterson found that
A)   the way to get rid of undesirable behavior is not to reward it.
B)   children will not cease to misbehave unless they are forced to.
C)   children will cease to misbehave if their behavior is ignored.
D)   undesirable behavior will go away if you reward desirable behavior.
E)   parents' involvement has no effect on a child's behavior.

Correct: E   Page: 414 Scramble Range: ALL
109.   Among Canadians and Americans who divorce, about what percent remarry?
A)   20 percent
B)   35 percent
C)   48 percent
D)   65 percent
E)   80 percent

Correct: E   Page: 415 Scramble Range: ALL
110. Jacobs and Furstenberg studied the "conjugal careers" of a national sample of American women over a ten-year period. A major question was whether the women married men of a higher, lower, or similar economic position than that of their first husbands. When the data were analyzed, it was found that, on the average, the women married men who
A) had track records promising continued economic stability.
B) had working- or lower middle-class origins and who had been upwardly mobile to a greater extent than their first husbands.
C) were more downwardly mobile than their first husbands were.
D) were currently less successful than their first husbands, but had the probability of greater success in the future.
E) were no more, and no less, successful than their first husbands.

Correct: D   Page: 415 Scramble Range: ALL
111. When Jacobs and Furstenberg studied a national sample of remarried women in a ten-year period, it was found that they tended to marry men whose economic success was similar to that of their first husbands when the women
A) stayed in the same geographic area rather than relocate.
B) remained under parental influence after the first marriage ended.
C) remained in the work force rather than leave it after the first marriage ended.
D) remarried sooner rather than later following the first marriage.
E) took positive steps to increase their own employment opportunities.

Correct: B   Page: 416 Scramble Range: A-D
112. Couples remarrying
A) have a lower divorce rate.
B) have a higher rate of divorce if there are children.
C) have a lower rate of divorce if there are children.
D) are much less likely to enjoys sports.
E) none of these

Correct: C   Page: 416 Scramble Range: ALL
113. White and Booth studied a national sample to find out how stepchildren influenced relationships between a couple following remarriage. One thing they found was that remarriages with stepchildren tend to
A) spend more time on family togetherness activities.
B) be no more or less happy than marriages with their own biological children.
C) have a higher divorce rate.
D) have a lower rate of child abuse.
E) have higher than average church attendance.

Correct: D   Page: 416 Scramble Range: A-D
114. After their last child has left the "nest," parents
A) are more likely to get divorced.
B) are likely to be depressed and, in the case of mothers, even suicidal.
C) are more likely to have extramarital affairs.
D) tend to be happier and more satisfied.
E) none of these

115.   Sociologists today claim that the family is
A)   universal.
B)   losing its functional significance.
C)   only one of several structures that could be used to accomplish the same functions equally effectively.
D)   still in existence today primarily because of its ties to Judeo-Christianity.
E)   not likely to survive until the year 2030

116.   The decline of the family
A)   has been supported by recent research.
B)   argues that the functions of the family are best met by the modern family.
C)   is obvious when the contemporary family is compared with the traditional family.
D)   is a main theme of the family chapter in your text.
E)   none of these

Topic 4: Older Family

True/False

Correct: F   Page: 419
1. The proportion of Americans over age 65 has nearly doubled in the past ninety years.

Correct: T   Page: 419
2. African-Americans in the United States today have a shorter life expectancy than do whites.

Correct: F   Page: 419
3. Greater income equality and more equal health care have eliminated the previous gap between African-Americans' and white Americans' life expectancy.

Correct: F   Page: 419
4. Polls show that younger people think that the United States government spends too much on Social Security.

Correct: T   Page: 419
5. Polls show that it is younger people, not those over age 65, who think that the government spends too little on Social Security.

Correct: T   Page: 419
6. Older Americans are the happiest Americans.

Correct: F   Page: 420
7. Changes in the American age structure have produced more older individuals but it has not produced more older families.

Correct: T   Page: 422
8. Older people (those aged 65+) are likelier to watch more television than are people who are under age 65.

Correct: F   Page: 422
9. People aged 65 and over are less likely than people under age 65 to say that they find life to be exciting.

Correct: T   Page: 424
10. The older American family has high levels of contentment and satisfaction.

Multiple Choice

Correct: C   Page: 419 Scramble Range: ALL
11. The average life expectancy of Americans today is approximately _____ years.
    A) 55
    B) 62
    C) 75
    D) 87
    E) 92

Correct: E   Page: 419 Scramble Range: ALL
12. Research shows that _____ Americans are the happiest Americans.
    A) pre-teenage
    B) young adult (age 20-29)
    C) age 30
    D) early middle-age
    E) old (age 65+)

Correct: E   Page: 420 Scramble Range: ALL
13. One of the reasons men over 65 are likelier than women over 65 to say that they are very happy is that men over 65 are likelier to be
    A) healthy.
    B) involved in satisfying leisure.
    C) in contact with kin.
    D) involved with grandchildren.
    E) married.

Correct: D   Page: 420 Scramble Range: ALL
14. The text points out that which one of the following is among the reasons men over 65 are more likely than women over 65 to say they are very happy?
    A) Time for involvement in local politics
    B) Presence of grandchildren
    C) Greater health
    D) Income adequacy
    E) More interests outside the home

Correct: B   Page: 424 Scramble Range: ALL
15. Which of the following is cited by the text as a threat to the contentment and satisfaction levels of older Americans' households?
    A) Incomes that have declined more rapidly than those of any other age group
    B) High probability of their household becoming a one-person household
    C) Loss of meaningful contact with their adult offspring who become busy with their own families
    D) Remaining married when a divorce would be a more appropriate course of action
    E) Loss of interest in physical touching and sexual expression

16.   When discussions of poverty among older Americans arise, they are primarily discussions of the poverty of:

A)   widows
B)   widowers
C)   never-married elderly
D)   elderly who are estranged from their adult offspring
E)   elderly who never had children

Chapter 14: Religion

True/False

Correct: T   Page: 429
1. As defined in the text, religion must include some conception of a god or gods.

Correct: F   Page: 429
2. In defining religion, sociologists see questions of "ultimate meaning" as concerned primarily with economic survival.

Correct: T   Page: 429
3. As defined in the text, religion always includes answers to questions of ultimate meaning.

Correct: F   Page: 429
4. As defined in the text, religion need not assume the existence of the supernatural.

Correct: T   Page: 429
5. As defined in the text, religion always involves practices as well as beliefs.

Correct: T   Page: 429
6. As defined in the text, religion possesses the capacity to fulfill some desires that can be satisfied in no other way.

Correct: F   Page: 430
7. Recent research has found that earlier sociologists were incorrect in believing that religion can serve to legitimize social norms.

Correct: T   Page: 430
8. Religions justify norms.

Correct: F   Page: Ch4
9. Religions justify values.
NOTE: Cumulative question.

Correct: T   Page: 430
10. Legitimacy is the belief that a rule is right and proper.

Correct: T   Page: 430
11. Religions give legitimacy to social norms.

Correct: F   Page: 433
12. "Religious pluralism" means that one religion comes close to having a full religious monopoly.

Correct: T   Page: 433
13. Religious pluralism requires choice among religions.

Correct: F   Page: 433
14. The idea of religious economy assumes that religion is essentially an ascribed status.

Correct: T   Page: 434
15. According to church-sect theory, sects develop out of and away from churches.

Correct: T   Page: 434
16. According to church-sect theory, the higher people's socioeconomic position, the likelier they are to prefer that their religion be in low tension with the surrounding culture.

Correct: T   Page: 434
17. According to church-sect theory, successful sects tend to move to lower tension with their environment as time goes by.

Correct: T   Page: 434
18. According to church-sect theory, most churches previously were sects.

Correct: T   Page: 434
19. According to church-sect theory, sects arise in large part to satisfy needs that churches are not satisfying.

Correct: T   Page: 434
20. According to church-sect theory, as sects become churches, pressure grows for the formation of a new sect.

Correct: T   Page: 437
21. The text claims that secularization is self-limiting and will not lead to societies without religion.

Correct: F   Page: 436
22. "Secularization" is another term for religious pluralism.

Correct: F   Page: 439
23. Sociologists use the term "cult" to mean groups that follow a false faith and use mind control.

Correct: T   Page: 439
24. Christianity once was a cult movement.

Correct: T   Page: 439
25. A cult in one society could be called a sect in another.

Correct: T   Page: 439
26. An important consequence of secularization is cult formation.

Correct: T   Page: 439
27. Cult movements do best where the conventional religious organizations are weakest.

Correct: T   Page: 439
28. In the United States the Jehovah's Witnesses would be considered a sect while in other countries they would be considered a cult.

Correct: T   Page: 439
29. In the United States Roman Catholicism would be considered a church while in other countries it would be considered a sect.

Correct: T   Page: 439
30. Methodists would be considered cult members in some societies.

Correct: F   Page: 440
31. These days members of most Christian denominations essentially agree in their beliefs.

Correct: F   Page: 440
32. Modern sociologists use the term "charisma" to describe the magical powers of some cult leaders.

Correct: F   Page: 440
33. Charisma and attachments are almost completely unrelated approaches to religious growth.

Correct: T   Page: 440
34. Cults begin and grow through a network of attachments.

Correct: T   Page: 441
35. The American denomination with the largest membership is the Roman Catholic Church, enrolling 23.5 percent of the population.

Correct: T   Page: 441
36. The Roman Catholic Church enrolls more Americans than any other denomination, and the second largest membership is in the Southern Baptist Convention.

Correct: T   Page: 441
37. As religious bodies deemphasize the supernatural, they seem less able to satisfy religious needs, at least as indicated by membership decline.

Correct: T   Page: 441
38. As the memberships of some denominations are eroded by secularization, the emergence and growth of sects is facilitated.

Correct: T   Page: 443
39. Sect membership in the United States is highest where the overall rate of church membership and attendance is highest.

Correct: F   Page: 443
40. Church membership in the United States is lowest in the densely urban Northeastern region.

Correct: F   Page: 443
41. Areas of lower church membership also have lower rates of religious belief.

Correct: F   Page: 443
42.   Church membership is a good indicator of religious beliefs.

Correct: F   Page: 443
43.   Cult membership in the United States is highest where overall church membership is highest.

Correct: F   Page: 443
44.   Cults have the most members and the most social effect in the Middle Atlantic region of the United States.

Correct: F   Page: 443
45.   Belief in God is much lower in the Far West than elsewhere in the United States.

Correct: F   Page: 443
46.   Church attendance is much higher in the Deep South than in the Midwest.

Correct: T   Page: 443
47.   Church membership is much lower along the Pacific coast than elsewhere in the nation.

Correct: T   Page: 443
48.   Cult movements are strongest where both churches and sects are weakest.

Correct: F   Page: 445
49.   People raised in fundamentalist Christian homes are the ones most likely to join cult movements.

Correct: T   Page: 445
50.   People who claim to have "no religion" are much more likely than other Americans to express belief in astrology, reincarnation, psychic phenomena, and the like.

Correct: F   Page: 446
51.   The typical recruit to cults in the United States is somewhat maladjusted and from an intensely religious family.

Correct: T   Page: 447
52.   There is less diversity of churches and sects in Canada than in the United States.

Correct: F   Page: 448
53.   Cult movements are generally quite large and tend to attract a majority of those who drift away from conventional religion.

Correct: T   Page: 448
54.   There is a correlation between secularization and cult movements in both the United States and Canada.

Correct: F   Page: 450
55.   Currently, cults are more successful in the United States than in European nations.

Correct: F   Page: 450
56. Nations such as Sweden, Denmark, and Great Britain are much less secularized than is the United States.

Correct: T   Page: 450
57. Religious movements imported from India and Asia have been more successful in Northern Europe than in the United States or Canada.

Correct: F   Page: 451
58. Evangelical Protestant sects have found little interest and following in the predominantly Catholic countries of Latin America.

Correct: T   Page: 451
59. Majority religions tend to be less energetic and active.

Correct: T   Page: 453
60. College students in the United States are more likely to be attracted to cults such as Hare Krishna than to sects such as the Church of God in Christ.

Reference Key: STORY14.1
Vihandu lives in India, in a region dominated by various forms of Hinduism. Vihandu becomes part of the congregation at the mission of the Church of the Nazarene and converts to Christianity. Based on what is presented in the chapter on Religion:

Correct: F   Page: 439   Refer to: STORY14.1
61. Vihandu is joining a sect.

Correct: T   Page: 439   Refer to: STORY14.1
62. Vihandu is joining a cult.

Correct: F   Page: 453   Refer to: STORY14.1
63. We would guess that Vihandu is poor and uneducated.

Correct: T   Page: 453   Refer to: STORY14.1
64. We would guess that Vihandu is fairly successful and well educated.

Correct: F   Page: 446   Refer to: STORY14.1
65. We would guess that Vihandu had been an active Hindu before his conversion.

Correct: T   Page: 433   Refer to: STORY14.1
66. Vihandu lives in a society where there is religious pluralism.

Correct: T   Page: 440   Refer to: STORY14.1
67. We would guess that Vihandu had acquaintances in this congregation before he joined it.

Correct: F   Page: 446   Refer to: STORY14.1
68. We would guess that Vihandu was brought up in a strict Hindu family and is rebelling against that religious tradition.

Reference Key: STORY14.2
In June 1991, the Presbyterian Church hotly debated a proposal calling for less rigid rules concerning sexuality for unmarried men and women.

Correct: T   Page: 434   Refer to: STORY14.2
69. This illustrates the movement from sect to church.

Correct: F   Page: 439   Refer to: STORY14.2
70. This illustrates the movement from cult to sect.

Correct: F   Page: 436   Refer to: STORY14.2
71. This proposal, if accepted, would have increased the denomination's tension with its environment.

Correct: F   Page: 435   Refer to: STORY14.2
72. If this proposal were accepted, we would expect the denomination to successfully attract increased numbers of poor and minority people.

Correct: T   Page: 435   Refer to: STORY14.2
73. If this proposal were accepted, we would expect the denomination to be more successful in attracting better educated, middle-class people.

Correct: T   Page: 435   Refer to: STORY14.2
74. If this proposal were accepted. we would expect the average contribution to the Presbyterian Church to increase.

Correct: T   Page: 435   Refer to: STORY14.2
75. This proposal, and the serious debate of it, can be seen as part of the process of secularization.

Correct: T   Page: 433   Refer to: STORY14.2
76. Discussion of how this proposal would affect recruitment to the church can be seen as an excellent example of how a religious economy works.

Correct: F   Page: 434   Refer to: STORY14.2
77. This development seems contrary to what Niebuhr would expect.

Multiple Choice

Correct: A   Page: 427 Scramble Range: ALL
78. According to your text, which of these is the earliest date from which we have physical evidence of the faith and religion of our ancestors?
A) 100,000 years ago
B) 50,000 years ago
C) 25,000 years ago
D) 10,000 years ago
E) 2,500 years ago

Correct: A   Page: 427 Scramble Range: ALL
79. The term "religious economy" refers to
A) the marketplace of competing faiths in a society.
B) the tendency of religions to become more secular and more like businesses.
C) the market in artifacts, charms, and icons that has historically accompanied relgious revivals.
D) none of these

Correct: B   Page: 429 Scramble Range: ALL
80. The text states that two elements seem to be common to religions (as sociologists understand the meaning of religion). Those two elements are
A) an idea of life after death and a concept of the sacred.
B) answers to questions about ultimate meaning and some concept of the supernatural.
C) a concept of God and idea(s) about the concepts of right and wrong.
D) praise for the God(s) and an idea of some type of heaven/hell dualism.
E) life after death and some mechanism for the achievement of heaven or the equivalent.

Correct: B   Page: 429 Scramble Range: A-D
81. Religion always
A) includes prayer.
B) involves questions such as "what is the meaning of life?"
C) includes a belief in life after death.
D) involves mobility.
E) all of these

Correct: B   Page: 429 Scramble Range: ALL
82. Systems of thought that reject the supernatural
A) have to rely on science as the basis for those systems of thought.
B) cannot satisfy the concerns of most people.
C) are likelier than is religion to be logically consistent.
D) are likelier to find a market in the religious economy.
E) seem to be more enduring than those that are based on the supernatural.

83. The percent of the population of the United States who say that they are a relgious person varies by region, but the percent of people in the United States population who say this is in the range of
   A)   19 percent and lower.
   B)   20-30 percent.
   C)   40-50 percent.
   D)   70-80 percent.
   E)   90 percent and higher.

Correct: D   Page: 431 Scramble Range: A-D
84. Comparing religious self-conceptions among countries
   A)   shows that belief in God is lower in economically developed countries.
   B)   demonstrates the validity of the secularization thesis.
   C)   confirms that economically strong countries such as Japan have a very high proportion of people who consider themselves religious.
   D)   shows that the United States has a higher percentage of people who say they are religious than most other countries.
   E)   all of these
   F)   none of these

Correct: C   Page: 430 Scramble Range: ALL
85. Religion _____ social norms.
   A)   contradicts
   B)   values
   C)   legitimates
   D)   secularizes
   E)   ascribes

Correct: A   Page: 429 Scramble Range: A-D
86. Religion involves
   A)   practices as well as beliefs.
   B)   prayer.
   C)   belief in an afterlife.
   D)   charismatic manifestations.
   E)   all of these
   F)   none of these

Correct: A   Page: 430 Scramble Range: ALL
87. For a long time, sociologists have recognized the fact that religion does which of the following things?
   A)   Legitimizes important social norms
   B)   Reduces the need for social cohesion and solidarity
   C)   Decreases the power of political rulers
   D)   Increases the rate of deviance by making rules overly strict
   E)   Contributes to a decline in the quality of culture into which people are socialized

Correct: D   Page: 430 Scramble Range: ALL
88.   Which is the best example of legitimacy?
A)   Ben prays for his ailing grandmother because he wishes she would get well.
B)   Rashad obeys his parents because he knows they will ground him otherwise.
C)   Angel always stops at stop signs because she already has three tickets.
D)   Randall is a vegetarian because he believes in the commandment "Thou shalt not kill."
E)   Jasmine tells the truth because she is afraid that she will go to hell if she sins.

Correct: E   Page: 433 Scramble Range: A-E
89.   According to your text, a key issue in the study of religious economies is
A)   whether the religions involved are monotheistic or polytheistic.
B)   whether the monetary value generated by them is high, medium, or low.
C)   the physical means by which the message reaches the masses.
D)   the literal vs. the figurative "mix" in the religious economy.
E)   the extent to which the religious economy is regulated by the state.
F)   all of these

Correct: E   Page: 433 Scramble Range: A-E
90.   A situation in which many religions exist because they appeal to different kinds or types or categories of people in any one society is called
A)   religious democracy.
B)   supply-side religion.
C)   individualist orientation.
D)   collectivist orientation.
E)   religious pluralism.
F)   none of these

Correct: B   Page: 433 Scramble Range: A-D
91.   In a situation of religious pluralism, religion is
A)   less important.
B)   an achieved status.
C)   more secularized.
D)   less churchlike and more sectlike.
E)   all of these
F)   none of these

Correct: D   Page: 433 Scramble Range: ALL
92.   In the United States and some other nations, the individual is often in a position to compare religions and to decide which (if any) is "right" for him or her. Such a situation is described by your text as a(n)
A)   altruistic system.
B)   individualistic ethos.
C)   situation of religious anarchy.
D)   religious economy.
E)   sect-dominated religious system.

93. In THE SOCIAL SOURCES OF DENOMINATIONALISM, H. Richard Niebuhr said that ____ underlies the religious differences that split Christianity into many different denominations.
    A) different psychological needs
    B) the multifaceted nature of religion
    C) religion's natural tendency to become more complex
    D) lack of communication
    E) class conflict

94. Religion, according to Richard Niebuhr, has the unique ability to
    A) provide an orientation toward the historical past.
    B) give a solid foundation for human interaction in various institutions.
    C) lull people into a false sense of security in dangerous circumstances.
    D) make life seem bearable, even for those in misery.
    E) connect various social institutions that would otherwise be separate and distinct.

95. Religious groups with formal, quiet, traditional services are usually classified as _____ by sociologists.
    A) churches
    B) quasi-religions
    C) sects
    D) euphoric-charismatic
    E) apocalyptic

96. Niebuhr, in THE SOCIAL SOURCES OF DENOMINATIONALISM, argued that sects provide for the religious needs of
    A) people with higher levels of education.
    B) those who are converting from one religion to another.
    C) those who are low in the stratification system.
    D) those whose religious preferences tend toward intellectualism and formalism.
    E) people who are integrated into the mainstream of society.

97. The higher the _____ between a religious group and its environment, the more _____ it is.
    A) consistency; ecologically sound
    B) similarity; Adventist
    C) dissimilarity; denominational
    D) cooperation; symbiotic
    E) tension; sectlike

Correct: C Page: 435 Scramble Range: ALL
98. Consider the following prayer: "I feel your hand on my shoulder, Lord! I can hear you talking in my ear! I can even smell your Holy Presence!! So please help me through this sickness and get me well quick." Such a prayer illustrates aspects of a(n)
A) low-level religious economy.
B) high-level religious economy.
C) sect.
D) egoistic religion.
E) anomic religion.

Correct: A Page: 435 Scramble Range: ALL
99. A key to Niebuhr's theory about churches and sects is the idea that successful religious organizations always
A) shift their emphasis toward this world and away from the next.
B) have an original beginning rather than splitting off from a parent religion.
C) emphasize emotion, contact, and "otherworldliness" in daily life.
D) disapprove of emotion-changing drugs, alcohol, and similar substances.
E) see themselves as among the elect of the kingdom to come.

Correct: A Page: 435 Scramble Range: ALL
100. The higher the tension between a religious group and its environment, the
A) more sectlike it is.
B) likelier it is to disappear in a short period of time.
C) likelier it is to meet people's social needs.
D) more conformist it is.
E) more religious it is.

Correct: C Page: 435 Scramble Range: ALL
101. Which of the following are extreme opposites of one another, according to the text?
A) Church and state
B) Church and denomination
C) Church and sect
D) Meaningfulness and ritual
E) Cult and sect

Correct: A Page: 435 Scramble Range: ALL
102. Which sequence is correct as an indicator of church/sect theory?
A) Church-->sect-->church-->sect-->church
B) Synagogue-->church-->sect
C) Sect-->church-->church-->sect-->sect
D) Church-->synagogue-->denomination
E) Church-->denomination-->church

Correct: E   Page: 436 Scramble Range: ALL
103.   For a long time, many social scientists and some others have thought that
        the _____ process would lead to the disappearance of religion. There is
        now reason to think that religion may not disappear after all, for reasons
        explained by your text.
        A)   alienation
        B)   humanization
        C)   sacralization
        D)   scientification
        E)   secularization

Correct: D   Page: 437 Scramble Range: A-E
104.   According to your text, which of the following is a self-limiting process?
        A)   Alienation
        B)   Religious justification
        C)   Proselytization
        D)   Secularization
        E)   Mystification
        F)   None of these

Correct: B   Page: 437 Scramble Range: A-E
105.   Sarah comes from a very conservative family with strong religious faith and
        traditional religious practices. Sarah goes away to college and begins to rely
        on studying rather than on prayer, begins to see the Bible as symbolic rather
        than to be taken literally, and begins to go to church only at Christmas and
        Easter. Which concept applies?
        A)   Religious innovation
        B)   Secularization
        C)   Revival, as used in the chapter on religion
        D)   Atavism
        E)   Agnosticism
        F)   None of these

Correct: A   Page: 437 Scramble Range: ALL
106.   Which of the following is a process that leads eventually not to the END of
        religion but instead to a shift in the SOURCES of religion?
        A)   Secularization
        B)   Alienation
        C)   Affiliativeness
        D)   Transformationism
        E)   Religious ferality

Correct: D   Page: 437 Scramble Range: ALL
107.   The term used to refer to turning away from religious beliefs and activities
        toward beliefs and activities of the everyday, ordinary world is
        A)   "anomie."
        B)   "institutionalization."
        C)   "demystification."
        D)   "secularization."
        E)   "cultic innovation."

Correct: D   Page: 437 Scramble Range: ALL
108.   What the text calls "revivalism" is associated with which of the following?
A)   A larger percent of the population attending some church
B)   A larger percent of the population feeling uplifted by religious faith
C)   Many clergy taking jobs in the everyday occupational world, as a way of influencing the average person during the week
D)   The appearance of many sects
E)   A rising standard of living for those who are religious clergy, officials, and/or administrators

Correct: D   Page: 439 Scramble Range: A-D
109.   Islam and Christianity both
A)   began as churches.
B)   developed as secularization movements.
C)   began as attempts to find new values for an emerging middle class.
D)   began as cults.
E)   none of these

Correct: C   Page: 439 Scramble Range: A-D
110.   All religions begin as
A)   mobility statuses.
B)   sects.
C)   cults.
D)   revivals.
E)   all of these
F)   none of these

Correct: D   Page: 439 Scramble Range: ALL
111.   The difference between sects and cults is that
A)   cults revive the conventional religious tradition while sects reflect new or unconventional traditions.
B)   sects emphasize the spirituality of living a good life in this world while cults emphasize the next world.
C)   cults emphasize the spirituality of living a good life in this world while sects emphasize the next world.
D)   sects revive the conventional religious tradition while cults reflect new or unconventional traditions.

Correct: A   Page: 439 Scramble Range: A-D
112.   The difference between sects and cults
A)   can depend on the social or religious context.
B)   lies in the radicalness of their theology.
C)   determines the extent to which members are coerced.
D)   illustrates the difference between Eastern and Western religions.
E)   all of these
F)   none of these

Correct: A   Page: 439 Scramble Range: ALL
113. According to your text, all religions
A) begin as cult movements.
B) start out as churches and become denominations.
C) must necessarily enter a state of entropy.
D) are fated to disappear when people turn to science as a guide and as an answer to problems.
E) are parasitic on the religious economy.

Correct: C   Page: 439 Scramble Range: ALL
114. New religions _____ in all societies and nearly all of them _____.
A) overcome old ones; are an improvement
B) are seen as deviant; displace the previous ones
C) appear constantly; fail
D) occasionally lag behind; catch up
E) create innovations; are not an improvement

Correct: A   Page: 440 Scramble Range: A-E
115. The Rev. Sun Myung Moon, founder of the Unification Church (or, the "Moonies") is for the Moonies an example of which of these?
A) Charismatic authority
B) Legal authority
C) Bureaucratic authority
D) Neo-bureaucratic authority
E) Neo-traditional authority
F) All of these

Correct: C   Page: 440 Scramble Range: ALL
116. The term that sociologists use to refer to the special ability of religious founders to form attachments with those who will eventually become converts is
A) "koinonia"
B) "sizzle."
C) "charisma."
D) "legal-bureaucratic authority."
E) "secularism."

Correct: C   Page: 440 Scramble Range: A-E
117. Juan is extremely drawn to Myriam's way of seeing the world and impressed with her warmth and insight. He is soon enlisted to help with her cause. Myriam has
A) class.
B) sex.
C) charisma.
D) ascription.
E) revival.
F) none of these

118. About _____ percent of the United States population report enrollment in the Jewish religion.
   A)   2
   B)   7
   C)   15
   D)   11
   E)   21

119. Church membership in the United States is lowest in
   A)   the West.
   B)   the Northeast.
   C)   Texas.
   D)   cities.
   E)   the Great Lakes region.

120. Changes in membership among American denominations
   A)   shows a clear pattern of decline among most denominations.
   B)   tends to support the secularization thesis.
   C)   shows that churches are increasing in membership and sects are decreasing.
   D)   follows the general pattern of decline of religion in the United States.
   E)   all of these
   F)   none of these

121. Changes in membership among American denominations
   A)   shows a general growth in sects and decline in churches.
   B)   tends to support secularization theory.
   C)   shows a general growth in churches and decline in sects.
   D)   suggests that science is "triumphing" over religion in the United States.
   E)   all of these
   F)   none of these

122. Which of the following religions has the most members in the United States?
   A)   Roman Catholic.
   B)   Protestant.
   C)   Jewish.
   D)   Various cults.

123. Which of these is FALSE?
   A)   Religious institutions can be a major force in holding societies together.
   B)   Religion can be seen as giving divine sanction to other social institutions.
   C)   Religion can create "moral communities."
   D)   The northeastern coast of the United States is the most "unchurched."
   E)   Cities with high church membership rates have considerably lower rates of crime, suicide, venereal disease, and alcoholism than cities with low church membership rates.

Correct: A   Page: 444 Scramble Range: ALL
124. According to your text, the number of cult members per million residents in the United States is highest in
A) the Pacific states.
B) the Mountain states.
C) the "Deep South" states.
D) the Middle Atlantic states.
E) the New England states.

Correct: E   Page: 444 Scramble Range: ALL
125. The text cites the research of Welch (1983), who found that a major cause of low church membership on the West coast is
A) recent scandals involving misuse of church organization money.
B) the involvement of religion in political and social affairs.
C) the presence in the population of a high percent of people with positive self-concepts.
D) the absence of significant political, social, and personal problems.
E) a higher rather than lower rate of population movement.

Correct: E   Page: 444 Scramble Range: A-D
126. Which of the following situations are likely to be associated with high cult membership?
A) War
B) Lack of conventional church membership
C) Hurricanes
D) High rates of immigration
E) All of these
F) None of these

Correct: E   Page: 446 Scramble Range: ALL
127. When Stark and Bainbridge examined the social characteristics of Moonies, Scientologists, Krishnas, and so on, they found a strong overrepresentation of people who
A) were an only child in their family.
B) came from family backgrounds that were basically working-class.
C) had learned skills that are not in demand in the job world.
D) had a "me first, you next if at all" way of looking at the world.
E) had parents who claimed no religious affiliation.

Correct: C   Page: 446 Scramble Range: A-D
128. Who is the likeliest candidate for cult membership?
A) Rashinka grew up in a strictly religious family. He dropped out of high school and is employed at Burger King.
B) Mose went to Catholic schools, including college, and is now a management trainee with a large corporation.
C) Marie's family didn't go to church. She has a master's degree in business administration and a good job at a local insurance company.
D) Frank's family didn't attend church much. He is currently unemployed although he picks up occasional work in construction.
E) None of these

Correct: B   Page: 446 Scramble Range: A-D
129.   Cult movements
    A)   tend to attract a majority of those who drift away from conventional religions.
    B)   are generally quite small.
    C)   attract people who are psychologically on the "fringe."
    D)   serve as an outlet for people who are poor and disconnected from the rest of the society.
    E)   all of these

Correct: C   Page: 446 Scramble Range: A-C
130.   The secularization thesis predicts
    A)   that religion will fade away and become irrelevant in technological societies.
    B)   that science will become a religious movement.
    C)   that active efforts to start new faiths will increase as societies become more secular.
    D)   all of these
    E)   none of these

Correct: D   Page: 450 Scramble Range: A-E
131.   According to your text, cults are much more plentiful and successful
    A)   where there is a higher percent of the population over age 60.
    B)   where there is an abundance of people in the 25-45 age group.
    C)   where the high-tech industries are plentiful in the economy.
    D)   in northern Europe and Great Britain than in the United States.
    E)   in the rural areas than in the suburbs and in the suburbs more than in urban areas.
    F)   all of these

Correct: D   Page: 450 Scramble Range: ALL
132.   Which of the following has the largest number of cult movements per million population?
    A)   France, Austria, Netherlands, Germany
    B)   Belgium, Italy, Spain
    C)   Greenland, Iceland
    D)   Switzerland, Iceland and the United Kingdom
    E)   Yugoslavia, Bulgaria, Romania

Correct: F   Page: 450 Scramble Range: A-D
133.   Gordon Melton has investigated cult movements in the United States and Europe.
    A)   He has found that cult movements are much less common in Europe than in the United States.
    B)   His findings have supported the idea that cults flourish where general religious involvement is high.
    C)   He has found that cult movements are much less common in the United States than in Europe.
    D)   His findings suggest that cults and sects arise out the of the same conditions in the religious economy.
    E)   All of these
    F)   None of these

Correct: D   Page: 450   Scramble Range: A-D
134.   Iceland and Sweden have low rates of church attendance (4% and 6%). In these countries,
   A)   religious innovations have predominantly taken the form of sects.
   B)   secularization has led to little sect formation and few cults.
   C)   lack of attachments has created extremely high rates of deviance.
   D)   there is a high rate of cult movements.
   E)   all of these
   F)   none of these

Correct: C   Page: 450   Scramble Range: A-D
135.   Cults abound when
   A)   there is little religious pluralism.
   B)   poverty and unemployment are high.
   C)   the conventional religious tradition is weak.
   D)   there is less secularization in a society.
   E)   all of these

Correct: F   Page: 451   Scramble Range: A-D
136.   The development of Protestant sects in Latin America
   A)   is a very recent development--only in the last ten years or so.
   B)   has been almost nonexistent due to the monopoly of the Catholic church.
   C)   has been similar to the development of innovative religions in Northern Europe.
   D)   resembles cult formation in countries such as Canada and England.
   E)   all of these
   F)   none of these

Correct: B   Page: 453   Scramble Range: ALL
137.   The average cult convert these days is usually
   A)   a female, white, from a working-class background.
   B)   a well-educated person with excellent career potential.
   C)   a person who has experienced downward mobility, is Protestant and white.
   D)   a male, unmarried, stable in terms of mobility, and of rural origins.
   E)   a minority group male, age 15-25, with few kinship ties and of above-average intelligence.

Correct: C   Page: 453   Scramble Range: A-E
138.   Those who are poorer, less educated and generally marginal in a society tend to join
   A)   unions.
   B)   cults.
   C)   sects.
   D)   churches.
   E)   feminist organizations.
   F)   none of these

Correct: C   Page: 453 Scramble Range: A-C
139. The secularization thesis
    A) accurately predicts the decline in cult movements in Europe.
    B) suggests that as Latin American countries secularize they will become
        more politically stable.
    C) can be tested by examining the growth or decline of atheism in Russia
        after the breakup of the Soviet Union.
    D) all of these
    E) none of these

Chapter 15: Politics and the State

True/False

Correct: F   Page: 457
1. The "freedom of the commons" in medieval England was the right to grow crops on common land.

Correct: T   Page: 459
2. The story of the medieval English commons illustrates that the state tends to serve the elite.

Correct: F   Page: 459
3. The "tragedy of the commons" illustrates that what is best for the community is generally gained by allowing unrestrained individual freedom.

Correct: T   Page: 459
4. The "tragedy of the commons" illustrates the tension between individual and community.

Correct: T   Page: 459
5. What's best for any one specific individual often is bad for society as a whole.

Correct: T   Page: 460
6. The "commons experiment" showed that individuals, when unrestrained, tended to maximize individual gain.

Correct: F   Page: 460
7. The "commons experiment" showed that leaders tended to give all the players, including themselves, equal shares.

Correct: F   Page: 462
8. Mancur Olsen argued that the best way to ensure public goods is to avoid even the hint of force.

Correct: F   Page: 462
9. Public goods are goods and services distributed by governments.

Correct: T   Page: 462
10. Public goods are things which take a collective effort to create, produce, or maintain.

Correct: F   Page: 463
11. The state is a political subdivision in society.

Correct: T   Page: 464
12. According to your text, the primary function of the state is to make life predictable and secure.

Correct: T   Page: 463
13. Sociologists define the state as the institution in society that claims a monopoly on the legitimate use of force or coercion.

Correct: T   Page: 464

14. Thomas Hobbes argued that without the state life would be "solitary, poor, nasty, brutish and short."

Correct: F   Page: 464

15. Thomas Hobbes suggests that the political power of the state makes life "solitary, poor, nasty, brutish and short."

Correct: F   Page: 466

16. Agricultural societies tend to have a very low degree of stratification.

Correct: T   Page: 466

17. Generally speaking, the state arises with the development of agriculture.

Correct: T   Page: 466

18. Social scientists know of no agrarian state with a low degree of stratification.

Correct: F   Page: 466

19. In most societies when military specialists exist, they tend to have little to do and to have long periods of peace interrupted by sporadic conflict.

Correct: F   Page: 466

20. The coercive power of the state ensures the equitable distribution of goods and services.

Correct: F   Page: 466

21. Historically, the major difficulty with the state (or "nation") has been preventing it from becoming too weak.

Correct: T   Page: 466

22. Plato believed the state could be controlled by training a special set of leaders.

Correct: F   Page: 467

23. Democracy in England arose from the principle that when a few people own too much property, the state should redistribute the wealth.

Correct: T   Page: 467

24. Pluralism helps tame the state by depending on competing interest groups to restrain one another.

Correct: F   Page: 467

25. Pluralism helps tame the state because it encourages election of unselfish leaders.

Correct: T   Page: 469

26. Pluralism helps tame the state by relying on shifting coalitions of many minorities.

Correct: T   Page: 469

27. A pluralist society is marked by competing elites.

Correct: F   Page: 469
28.   Pluralism means that power is distributed among the people in the society.

Correct: F   Page: 472
29.   In Western democracies, "the people" make most of the decisions.

Correct: F   Page: 472
30.   Representative democracy, such as we have in the United States, is a direct democracy.

Correct: T   Page: 472
31.   "Government of the people, by the people and for the people" contradicts the idea of representative government.

Correct: T   Page: 476
32.   The Gallup Poll was started by George Gallup.

Correct: T   Page: 476
33.   It is usually easy to gauge public opinion without resorting to polling.

Correct: T   Page: 479
34.   One reason for the low proportion of women in political office is that most of the incumbents are men.

Correct: T   Page: 479
35.   Women are underrepresented in national elected office in both Canada and the United States.

Correct: T   Page: 480
36.   Today more than 80 percent of the United States population say they would vote for a qualified woman for president.

Correct: T   Page: 480
37.   Losing parties are more likely to nominate women than winning parties.

Correct: T   Page: 480
38.   A candidate's sex does not affect his or her chances of winning and election.

Correct: T   Page: 480
39.   Political incumbents enjoy a large advantage in elections.

Correct: T   Page: 482
40.   A political ideology is a theory of how societies ought to be run in terms of their political arrangements.

Correct: F   Page: 482
41.   People tend to hold a fairly consistent set of ideas, values and positions which can be called their world view or meaning system.

Correct: F   Page: 482
42.   Most people seem to base their political positions, and voting, on a fairly consistent political ideology.

Correct: T   Page: 485
43.   Elites tend to have fairly consistent sets of ideas, values and positions.

Correct: T   Page: 485
44.   Elites are more likely than nonelites to vote on the basis of principle or a consistent political view.

Correct: T   Page: 485
45.   A substantial portion of the population has no political opinions.

Correct: F   Page: 485
46.   People tend to be consistent over time in their views on particular issues.

Correct: T   Page: 485
47.   "Issue publics" refers to the group of people taking an interest in an issue of significance to them.

Correct: F   Page: 485
48.   People who participate in discussion of one issue tend to participate in discussion of others.

Correct: T   Page: 486
49.   Only elites can create and preserve ideologies.

Correct: T   Page: 487
50.   Representation in the United States and Canada is less representative of the range of political views in the society than in countries such as Germany and France.

Multiple Choice

Correct: B   Page: 458 Scramble Range: A-E
51.   Your text discussed the "tragedy of the commons." This tragedy occurred because the individual herd owner
   A)   could not cooperate to rid the commons of the grouse tick.
   B)   increased the number in the herd, for much gain and little cost.
   C)   found the head tax paid to the local noble to be more than the herd could yield at market.
   D)   failed to grasp the basic principle of capitalism: surplus value theory of labor.
   E)   could not be motivated to take an interest in the herds, but simply let them roam, frequently away from the unfenced commons.
   F)   none of these

Correct: B   Page: 458 Scramble Range: A-D
52.   The medieval English commons was owned by
   A)   all the peasants, in common.
   B)   the nobility.
   C)   those who grazed their herds on it.
   D)   the King.
   E)   all of these
   F)   none of these

Correct: D   Page: 459 Scramble Range: ALL
53.   The economic productivity of the commons was restored by
A)   the loss of many herd owners through economic competition in the market.
B)   eventual crisis-level cooperation to rid the commons of the grouse tick.
C)   placing import quotas on lamb being brought into Great Britain from New Zealand.
D)   using external constraints to control individual self-interest.
E)   using political game theory to turn commons farming into a zero-sum game.

Correct: A   Page: 459 Scramble Range: A-D
54.   Enclosure of the commons solved the problem of the overgrazing of the commons
A)   but left the common people no place to graze their herds.
B)   and created a more equitable distribution of wealth.
C)   and resulted in a more democratic situation.
D)   but also resulted in the nobility losing some of their property.
E)   all of these
F)   none of these

Correct: B   Page: 459 Scramble Range: A-E
55.   A dominant theme of the chapter on politics and the state is
A)   how to define a social problem versus a political problem.
B)   the conflict between individual liberty and social necessity.
C)   the dilemma of military preparedness and social welfare.
D)   how to turn a political area into a political state.
E)   how to be expansionist without overextending administrative resources.
F)   all of these

Correct: C   Page: 459 Scramble Range: A-E
56.   The problem of the freedom of the commons and its economic productivity was solved at the expense of
A)   the heirs of those who eventually received grazing rights.
B)   the political power of the commoners.
C)   individual freedom.
D)   territorial integrity.
E)   expanding markets.
F)   none of these

Correct: A   Page: 459 Scramble Range: ALL
57.   Your text suggests that the main reason for having government is
A)   practical necessity.
B)   the fact that governments have been inherited from previous generations.
C)   the fact that most people have an instinctive need to be governed.
D)   the desire and ability by some to enforce their will on others.
E)   the process of diffusion, or governments, once created, spreading to other nations.

Correct: C   Page: 460 Scramble Range: A-E
58. In the laboratory-based harvesting experiment, it was found that research participants tended to increase their harvests more in which of these conditions?
   A) In the democratic condition
   B) In the socialist condition
   C) In the overuse condition
   D) In the racial competition condition
   E) In the individual decision condition
   F) None of these

Correct: E   Page: 460 Scramble Range: A-D
59. According to the "harvesting experiment," people
   A) tend to increase their harvests over time.
   B) tend to increase their harvests when they have a sense of inequality.
   C) tend to maximize individual gain more and more.
   D) tend to use power for their own advantage.
   E) all of these
   F) none of these

Correct: D   Page: 460 Scramble Range: A-E
60. In the laboratory-based harvesting experiment, subjects in all groups tended to
   A) elect leaders on a rotating basis.
   B) use more fertilizer than was good for the land.
   C) engage in price fixing with another group.
   D) increase their harvests over time.
   E) pollute the environment in order to do business as usual.
   F) all of these

Correct: C   Page: 460 Scramble Range: A-E
61. In the laboratory-based harvesting experiment, which of the following did individuals do when they became leaders?
   A) Tried to perpetuate themselves as leaders, contrary to policy
   B) Gave more to some and less to others, and took less for themselves
   C) Gave themselves larger shares than they gave others
   D) Tried to involve others in decision making about distribution methods
   E) Tried to share power with their friends
   F) None of these

Correct: A   Page: 460 Scramble Range: ALL
62. In the laboratory-based harvesting experiment, the overwhelming majority of the participants voted to _____ under the condition of _____.
   A) have government regulations; overuse
   B) have private property; capitalism
   C) go to war; threatened markets
   D) suspend trade; falling prices
   E) halt the experiment; declining morale

Correct: B   Page: 461 Scramble Range: ALL
63. Mancur Olsen has argued that governments are unavoidable features of human societies. His conclusion rests on the simple fact that
    A) in order to create employment, some coordination is necessary.
    B) to provide for the best interests of the group, coercion is necessary.
    C) deviant behavior is an instinctive part of the human personality.
    D) communication of community needs has to be made known to all, and this requires some administrative structure.
    E) government tends to spread by cultural diffusion from one society to another.

Correct: A   Page: 462 Scramble Range: ALL
64. Your text concludes that the creation of public goods requires that the state
    A) use force or be ready to use force if necessary.
    B) give careful consideration to the definition of what is meant by "goods."
    C) distribute public goods with absolute equality if the state is to continue to exist over a long period of time.
    D) use as much for the public as for the administration of the state's necessary functions.
    E) effectively communicate its needs so that all citizens will be aware of what is required of them.

Correct: C   Page: 462 Scramble Range: ALL
65. Mancur Olsen (1965) concluded that in order to provide for _____, the use of coercion (force) is necessary.
    A) fair exchanges
    B) economic attachments
    C) public goods
    D) macro assessments
    E) charismatic authority

Correct: C   Page: 461 Scramble Range: A-D
66. Public goods are
    A) foods, such as cheese and milk distributed to women and children.
    B) materials confiscated by the government.
    C) things that take collective effort to create, produce or maintain.
    D) common world views among members of a particular society.
    E) all of these

Correct: E   Page: 461 Scramble Range: ALL
67. "We the People of the United States, in Order to form a more perfect Union, establish Justice, insure domestic Tranquility, provide for the common defense, promote the general Welfare, and secure the Blessings of Liberty" is an example of what your text means when it speaks about the concept of which of the following?
    A) Plutocracy
    B) The division of labor in government
    C) Autocracy
    D) Fascism
    E) Collective goods

Correct: D   Page: 463 Scramble Range: A-D
68. The state has
   A) the power of taxation.
   B) ownership of all property.
   C) a division of power reserved to itself.
   D) the exclusive right to use force.
   E) all of these
   F) none of these

Correct: C   Page: 463 Scramble Range: A-D
69. The state has a monopoly on
   A) the distribution of goods.
   B) the definition of the collective good.
   C) the legitimate use of force.
   D) the level of agricultural development.
   E) all of the these.

Correct: F   Page: 464 Scramble Range: A-D
70. Thomas Hobbes suggests that life is "solitary, poor, nasty, brutish and short"
   A) when the state is repressive.
   B) in an elitist state.
   C) in a pluralist state.
   D) without a commons.
   E) all of these
   F) none of these

Correct: B   Page: 464 Scramble Range: A-D
71. The development of the state requires
   A) changes in morality that allow one person to rule over another.
   B) the capacity to produce a surplus.
   C) explicit rules so as to keep power in check.
   D) public goods to be distributed.
   E) none of the above.

Correct: A   Page: 465 Scramble Range: ALL
72. According to Table 15-2, The State and Warfare, the scope of political
   organization was likeliest to be at the "state" level (rather than "local only" or
   "semistate") when the level of warfare was
   A) constant.
   B) common.
   C) occasional.
   D) infrequent.
   E) rare.

Correct: D   Page: 465 Scramble Range: A-E
73. Where there is relatively well-developed _____, only 22.8 percent of such
   societies have political structures that are solely local.
   A) militarism
   B) infrastructure
   C) education
   D) agriculture
   E) familism
   F) none of these

Correct: E   Page: 466 Scramble Range: A-D
74. The coercive power of the state
  A) ensures public goods.
  B) often exploits and represses citizens.
  C) develops with the capacity to produce a surplus.
  D) provides for security.
  E) all of these
  F) none of these

Correct: A   Page: 466 Scramble Range: ALL
75. The author of your text observes that one of the oldest dilemmas of political philosophy is how to have a state and
  A) keep it tame.
  B) maintain an aesthetic equilibrium.
  C) make it retrograde.
  D) give it away, too.
  E) still be able to draw its borders.

Correct: C   Page: 467 Scramble Range: A-D
76. Pluralists believe that the lesson of the "tragedy of the commons" is the need to protect private property. Marxists suggest that
  A) the lesson is the need for a division of powers.
  B) the tragedy was due to the interference of the wealthy industrialists.
  C) the tragedy was due to the ownership of the commons by the nobility.
  D) the lesson is the need for increased structural mobility.
  E) all of these
  F) none of these

Correct: A   Page: 467 Scramble Range: ALL
77. Rodney Stark, the author of your text, points out how _____ evolved from a single principle: the right to private property.
  A) English democracy
  B) the principle of one man, one vote
  C) concentration of power
  D) the principle of election by popular vote
  E) might makes right and, conversely, right makes might

Correct: C   Page: 467 Scramble Range: A-E
78. English democracy evolved from a single principle:
  A) the right to bear arms.
  B) the superiority of the average citizen.
  C) the right to private property.
  D) the right for privacy in habitation.
  E) a wish to be free from French rule.
  F) all of these

Correct: A   Page: 467 Scramble Range: A-D
79.   The principle of private property as a curb on state power in England came down, in practice, to the issue of
A)   taxation.
B)   grazing areas.
C)   naval warfare.
D)   harvesting.
E)   all of these
F)   none of these

Correct: D   Page: 467 Scramble Range: ALL
80.   Which of the following choices characterizes English democracy?
A)   Democracy had to survive in England or it would survive nowhere
B)   An institution mainly in the service of the interests of nobility
C)   Dependence on the subjugation of other peoples, nations, and races
D)   A process to produce compromise out of groups with competing interests
E)   A structure by which the nobility supervised the politics of the elected government

Correct: D   Page: 468 Scramble Range: A-D
81.   The suppression of unpopular speech or unpopular actions in a democracy is an example of
A)   the elitist state.
B)   the dominance of a minority.
C)   quotas.
D)   the tyranny of the majority.
E)   all of these
F)   none of these

Correct: E   Page: 468 Scramble Range: A-E
82.   James Madison spoke about the "tyranny of the minority," by which he meant that
A)   the majority was in a position to rule over the minority.
B)   the rich should APPEAR to be less wealthy and powerful than they are.
C)   the majority SHOULD govern over the minority in a democratic system.
D)   tyranny is not necessarily bad or undesirable if the party in power has been elected properly.
E)   a privileged few might gain power and use coercion to repress and exploit the majority.
F)   none of these

Correct: A   Page: 468 Scramble Range: ALL
83.   Your text cites James Madison's belief that democracy always faces two threats. These are
A)   the tyranny of the minority and the tyranny of the majority.
B)   the threat from home and the threat from abroad.
C)   the threat of the illiterate and the threat of the bureaucrat.
D)   the threat of an uninformed electorate and the threat of the mass media.
E)   the tyranny of the press and the tyranny of silence.

84. The concept of a government in which a single group remains in control is
a(n) "_____ state."
A) elitist
B) plutocratic
C) pluralist
D) despotic
E) authoritarian

85. Pluralism is a situation where
A) power is in the hands of a single minority elite.
B) power is exercised through democratic elections.
C) power is exercised by the majority.
D) power is shared among several minority elites.
E) all of these
F) none of these

86. The type of political state that exists when there are several (or many)
powerful elites and shifting coalitions is _____.
A) autocracy
B) political diversity
C) pluralism
D) parliamentarianism
E) multiple aristocracy
F) none of these

87. The difference between a pluralist state and an elitist state is
A) the number of minorities with power.
B) the level of taxation of ordinary citizens.
C) the extent to which "common people" are involved.
D) the extent to which the majority rules.
E) all of these
F) none of these

88. The idea that those in the highest positions of three major social institutions
tend to have similar backgrounds and social ties and without intentionally
doing so, seem to run the country as they see fit is the main idea in
A) THE COMMUNIST MANIFESTO.
B) what your text calls "Jeffersonian thinking."
C) Keller's STRATEGIC ELITES.
D) Mills's THE POWER ELITE.
E) what your text calls "rotten democracy."
F) none of these

Correct: B Page: 472 Scramble Range: ALL
89. The more widely accepted social scientific view about the political process in Western democracies is that
A) three major institutional elites largely determine what is to happen.
B) no single elite dominates, but neither do "the People" make most of the decisions.
C) when elections are closely supervised and fairly carried out, the "Will of the People" determines decision making.
D) having electoral process and written constitutions puts decisionmaking power in the hands of "the People."
E) the greatest amount of political stability is associated with rapidly educating the masses in preindustrial countries.

Correct: C Page: 472 Scramble Range: A-D
90. When people are asked whether they are interested in politics, a considerable number (20% in the United States) say they are not interested at all.
A) Your text suggests that this is one of the major reasons for opinion polling.
B) This percent in the United States is much higher than in countries such as Belgium and Mexico.
C) Your text suggests that this is one of the major reasons for representative democracy.
D) Your text suggests that this is a result of the "tragedy of the commons."
E) All of these
F) None of these

Correct: A Page: 472 Scramble Range: A-D
91. Representative government exists for two reasons:
A) practicality and indifference.
B) elitism and mobility.
C) pluralism and charisma.
D) the majority and the minority.
E) none of these

Correct: E Page: 476 Scramble Range: A-E
92. According to your text, which of these is the most influential source of information on populations' views about political and social issues?
A) The letters to the editor in public newspapers and magazines
B) The "Op-Ed" section of public newspapers
C) Nationally broadcast coverage of televised presidential news conferences
D) "Mail-back" questionnaires in magazines and newspapers
E) The Gallup Polls
F) None of these

Correct: D Page: 479 Scramble Range: ALL
93. _____ parties are most likely to nominate women.
A) Liberal
B) Majority
C) Winning
D) Losing
E) Conservative
F) Christian

Correct: E   Page: 480 Scramble Range: ALL
94.   Studies of political life in Canada, the United States, and Australia reveal that
       A)   women with the greatest ability prefer to marry (and manipulate) a male
             politician and thus gain power.
       B)   traditional political parties tend to discriminate against women politicians,
             while the more liberal parties tend not to do so.
       C)   women have interrupted, sporadic political lives because of the realities of
             the lives of women in these cultures.
       D)   women are more fit for supportive roles in politics due to the fact that they
             tend to lack the organizing skills so necessary for political success.
       E)   voters do not discriminate against women, but the political parties do.

Correct: C   Page: 480 Scramble Range: A-E
95.   In studying the Canadian election process, Hunter and Denton found that _____
       are responsible for the small number of women who win political office.
       A)   women candidates themselves
       B)   the attitudes of Canadian voters, many of whom cherish ethnic values
       C)   the elites of the women's own political parties
       D)   the realities of women's domestic life and economic necessity
       E)   the voter challenge procedures in individual voting precincts
       F)   all of these

Correct: E   Page: 480 Scramble Range: ALL
96.   When Hunter and Denton studied the election process of Canadian members
       of Parliament, they found that the main reason few women are elected was
       THAT
       A)   women typically campaign less aggressively than do men.
       B)   women in political parties tend to lack the "killer instinct" in politics.
       C)   women have domestic responsibilities that make it difficult for them to
             campaign effectively.
       D)   Canadian voters of both sexes tend to reject female candidates for
             attitudinal reasons.
       E)   women are less likely than men to get nominated by their party.

Correct: A   Page: 480 Scramble Range: A-C
97.   Women are less likely than men to win elections to political office because
       A)   most incumbents are men.
       B)   voters prefer male candidates.
       C)   women are perceived as too emotional for politics.
       D)   all of these
       E)   none of these

Correct: C   Page: 481 Scramble Range: A-C
98.   When women run for "open seats" for state legislatures or the U.S. House of
       Representatives, they
       A)   are successful less than 25 percent of the time.
       B)   are successful more than 75 percent of the time.
       C)   are successful about 50 percent of the time.
       D)   none of these

Correct: E   Page: 482 Scramble Range: ALL
99. Rodney Stark, author of your text, has done considerable research and examination of people's world views. He concludes that _____ do not have a logically consistent set of beliefs.
   A) the undereducated
   B) people who do not share our basic cultural orientation
   C) the oriental, Samoan, and Micronesian cultures
   D) more women than men
   E) most people

Correct: E   Page: 482 Scramble Range: A-E
100. Social scientists use the term _____ when referring to a set of strongly held beliefs based on a few abstract ideas used to guide a person's reactions to events.
   A) philosophy
   B) logical net
   C) mental envelope
   D) sociaxiom
   E) ideology
   F) none of these

Correct: A   Page: 484 Scramble Range: ALL
101. According to your text, abolitionist (antislavery) ideas spread and resulted in the Emancipation Proclamation and mass support for Lincoln because of
   A) the efforts of a small elite committed to abolition of slavery.
   B) technological changes that made this reasonable for most white farmers.
   C) most northern whites' basic sense of justice, fairness, and progress.
   D) northern education, which provided a broad base of understanding the rationale of antislavery ideas.
   E) the invention of the telegraph.

Correct: C   Page: 485 Scramble Range: ALL
102. According to the text, an occupation that ought to have many people with ideologies that are highly internally consistent is
   A) housewife.
   B) air traffic controller.
   C) politician.
   D) prostitute.
   E) male stripper.

Correct: C   Page: 485 Scramble Range: ALL
103. Your text specifically mentions that some people are likelier than others to have internally consistent ideologies because of
   A) being socialized in the dominant culture or subcultures.
   B) a deep-seated psychological need to have a consistent world view.
   C) the special positions they occupy and the roles they play.
   D) the specific brand of politics that appeals to them.
   E) being socialized by their parents and sent to a private school system.

Correct: D Page: 485 Scramble Range: ALL

104. The most severe shock to social science conceptions of public opinion occurred when
A) surprisingly, Richard M. Nixon was elected President.
B) not surprisingly, most people supported President Johnson in his plans for the Vietnam war.
C) it was possible to experiment with public opinion using specific issues.
D) panel studies began to be used.
E) double-blind research designs made it possible to investigate spurious correlations

Correct: B Page: 485 Scramble Range: A-D

105. Which of the following best illustrates the concept of "issue publics?"
A) The governor issues a press release about the problem of homelessness.
B) Marion and Dorothy carefully read the various candidates' white papers on community mental health.
C) Ramona spends a great deal of time handing out leaflets for the Republican nominee for a Senate seat.
D) The local school system develops a plan to allow the schools to be used as shelters for the homeless.
E) None of these

Correct: E Page: 485 Scramble Range: ALL

106. The concept "issue publics" refers to which of these?
A) A news bulletin or press conference by a political candidate for office
B) An abandoned infant that welfare regulations require be given over to the local office in charge of such child welfare
C) A matter that must be voted on by the people in a local, state, or national election
D) The public announcement of something that had heretofore been kept secret because of its potential for disrupting the political process
E) A topic about which some people in the general population take a special political interest

Correct: E Page: 487 Scramble Range: A-D

107. Comparing the United States and European countries in terms of political organizations, we find that
A) European parties tend to be more ideological.
B) European labor unions are a more significant cource of political ideologies than are unions in the United States.
C) there are fewer sources of political ideology in the United States than in European countries.
D) most people do not have political ideologies in Europe and in the United States.
E) all of these
F) none of these

Correct: D   Page: 487 Scramble Range: ALL
108. Because of _____ in both Canada and the United States (in contrast to the situation in France and Germany), political parties must try to appeal to the broad middle spectrum of voters rather than appeal to a narrow interest group within an electorate.
A) the role of the judiciary
B) the value justifications
C) the manipulation of the mass media
D) the geographic basis of representation used
E) the low level of voter motivation

Correct: B   Page: 487 Scramble Range: ALL
109. In the United States, one reason for citizens' and political parties' approach to political ideology is
A) the fact that the United States class system is shaped almost exactly like a pyramid.
B) geographic rather than proportional representation in the election process.
C) most people's preference for a strong ideological self-definition.
D) the fact that a total of about 80 percent identify with either the liberal or conservative political perspective (Gallup, 1970).
E) that the level of education in the United States does not lend itself to an ideological approach to serious public problems.

Chapter 16: Education and Occupation

True/False

Correct: F   Page: 492
1. "Occupational prestige" is a fancy term for "how much money they make."

Correct: F   Page: 492
2. Studies of occupational prestige found that there are big differences from one country to another in how jobs are ranked.

Correct: T   Page: 494
3. If we know a person's education and occupation, we can often guess many other things about her/him.

Correct: T   Page: 494
4. Most of the highest-prestige occupations require more than college degrees.

Correct: T   Page: 494
5. Studies of occupational prestige found that people rank jobs on the basis of the average education and income of people holding them.

Correct: T   Page: 494
6. Occupational prestige generally reflects education and income.

Correct: T   Page: 494
7. A person's occupational prestige often reflects a process begun when they were very young.

Correct: T   Page: 494
8. Differential socialization has a great deal to do with occupational prestige.

Correct: F   Page: 494
9. Modern workers are more productive than their grandparents because they work harder.

Correct: T   Page: 494
10. Modern workers are more productive than their grandparents.

Correct: T   Page: 495
11. In his time and motion research, Frederick Taylor found that, in effect, "easy does it."

Correct: T   Page: 495
12. In his time and motion research, Taylor concentrated on unskilled manual work.

Correct: T   Page: 495
13. In his time and motion research, Taylor discovered that frequent short breaks were more efficient than long breaks taken less often.

Correct: T   Page: 496
14. In North America, there are more white-collar than blue-collar jobs.

Correct: F   Page: 496
15. There has been little structural mobility in the past century.

Correct: F   Page: 496
16. Compared to 100 years ago, a lower proportion of people are in the labor force.

Correct: F   Page: 498
17. By now, women are almost as likely to be doctors as men.

Correct: T   Page: 498
18. Where women marry younger and have more children their labor force participation is lower.

Correct: T   Page: 499
19. Whites are almost twice as likely to hold professional and managerial jobs compared to African-Americans.

Correct: T   Page: 499
20. African-Americans are more likely than whites to be police officers.

Correct: T   Page: 499
21. Unemployment sometimes rises when the number of available jobs increases.

Correct: F   Page: 503
22. In 1920 only about 70 percent of all Americans age 16 or 17 were enrolled in school.

Correct: T   Page: 503
23. A century ago only an elite few finished high school.

Correct: F   Page: 503
24. Although many more people attend school these days, the proportion of Americans with college degrees is similar to forty years ago.

Correct: T   Page: 508
25. James Coleman's huge study of the impact of schools in the United States on student performance found that class size didn't matter.

Correct: F   Page: 508
26. James Coleman's huge study of the impact of schools in the United States on student performance found that African-Americans went to much poorer schools than did whites.

Correct: F   Page: 508
27. James Coleman's huge study of the impact of schools in the United States on student performance found that quality of labs and equipment influenced student achievement scores in science.

Correct: F   Page: 508
28. James Coleman's huge study of the impact of schools in the United States on student performance found that the more books in the school library, the better the students did.

Correct: T   Page: 510
29. Barbara Heyns's study of the effects of schooling found that schools were more important for kids from disadvantaged homes.

Correct: F   Page: 510
30. Barbara Heyns's study of the effects of schooling showed that young African-American students from poor homes learned less during the school year than did young, middle-class white students.

Correct: T   Page: 510
31. Barbara Heyns's study of the effects of schooling showed that the schools do more for poor students than for students from wealthy homes.

Correct: T   Page: 510
32. Barbara Heyns's study of the effects of schooling found that middle-class kids got ahead because they continued to learn during summer vacations.

Correct: T   Page: 510
33. Barbara Heyns's study of the effects of schooling found that reading books accounted for the summer learning advantage of middle-class students.

Correct: T   Page: 510
34. Barbara Heyns's study of the effects of schooling found that kids read more the closer they lived to a library.

Correct: F   Page: 511
35. The "High School and Beyond" data show that time spent on homework is not very strongly related to grades.

Correct: T   Page: 511
36. Students that don't study are more likely to drop out of school.

Correct: T   Page: 511
37. Only about one in four high school sophomores do an hour of homework daily.

Correct: F   Page: 511
38. There is surprisingly little difference between public schools and elite private schools in the amount of homework and in the dropout rate.

Correct: F   Page: 514
39. The poorer the country, the more family background influences school performance.

Correct: F   Page: 514
40. Children in industrialized countries are more dependent on schools for education than are children in poorer and less industrialized countries.

Correct: T   Page: 516
41. People today need more education than their parents in order to have the same relative amount of education as their parents.

Correct: T   Page: 516
42. College degrees are worth less than they used to be.

Correct: F   Page: 516
43. Colleges don't prepare students for careers as well as they used to.

Correct: F   Page: 516
44. About 25 percent of college graduates have family incomes under $20,000.

Correct: F   Page: 516
45. The education level of African-Americans and Hispanics is rapidly approaching the level of white non-Hispanics.

Correct: T   Page: 516
46. For most people, in order to stay at the same occupational level as your parents you need to have more education than your parents.

Correct: F   Page: 517
47. Randall Collins' view of America as a "credential society" implies that colleges teach specific job skills more effectively than can be done with on-the-job training at the workplace.

Correct: T   Page: 517
48. "Credentials," in the sense that Collins discusses them, are used to control access to occupations.

Correct: T   Page: 517
49. Emphasis on credentials serves to increase the power of an occupation.

Correct: T   Page: 519
50. John Meyer's theory of educational functions argues that being a college graduate is a status in the same way that being a plumber or father are statuses.

Correct: T   Page: 519
51. John Meyer's theory of educational functions claims that a major influence of education is to teach people how to play the roles appropriate to their educational statuses.

Correct: T   Page: 519
52. John Meyer's theory of educational functions would be falsified if cab drivers, for example, have similar lifestyles regardless of their educational differences.

Correct: F   Page: 519
53. John Meyer's theory of educational functions cannot explain why graduates of famous colleges and little-known colleges have similar tastes and lifestyles.

Correct: T   Page: 519
54. According to Meyer's theory of educational functions, levels of education--in and of themselves--are social statuses.

Correct: T   Page: 519
55. John Meyer's theory of educational functions is consistent with the phrase, "Once a high school grad, always a high school grad."

Correct: T   Page: 519
56. John Meyer's theory of educational functions claims that the educational system can create and confer status on new occupations.

Reference Key: STORY16.1
Manuel and Ralph grew up in the same town and went to school together. They have about the same IQ. Manuel's father is a local attorney. Ralph's father is a custodian who didn't finish high school. Ralph dropped out of high school and Manuel went on to complete college.

Correct: F   Page: 516   Refer to: STORY16.1
57. Ralph has about the same level of educational advantage as his father.

Correct: F   Page: 494   Refer to: STORY16.1
58. The two boys' fathers have about the same occupational prestige.

Correct: T   Page: 516   Refer to: STORY16.1
59. Ralph will be unlikely to hold the same level job as his father.

Correct: T   Page: 494&Ch6   Refer to: STORY16.1
60. Kohn's research on differential socialization can help us understand this story.
NOTE: Cumulative question.

Correct: T   Page: 510   Refer to: STORY16.1
61. Barbara Heyns's research on learning can help us understand this story.

Correct: T   Page: 516   Refer to: STORY16.1
62. Ralph is unlikely to earn as much money as Manuel.

Correct: F   Page: 510   Refer to: STORY16.1
63. We can guess that Ralph read more books outside of school than Manuel.

Correct: F   Page: 510   Refer to: STORY16.1
64. School was ineffective for Ralph.

Correct: F   Page: 519   Refer to: STORY16.1
65. This story suggests that "educational status" is wholly an achieved status.

Correct: F   Page: 494   Refer to: STORY16.1
66. This story demonstrates the change from a manual laboring to a knowledge economy.

Reference Key: STORY16.2

A sociologist used the General Social Survey for 1993 to examine the relationship between the respondents' (child's) highest educational degree and their fathers' highest degree. He confined his study to respondents aged 25 to 40. This is what he found:

Child's Highest Degree	Father's Highest Degree		
	Less than High School	High School	College or More
Less than High School	27%	6%	4%
High School	60%	67%	38%
College or More	12%	27%	58%
	-----	-----	-----
	100%	100%	100%

Correct: T   Page: Ch3   Refer to: STORY16.2
67. The dependent variable is respondent's degree.
     NOTE: Cumulative question.

Correct: F   Page: Ch3   Refer to: STORY16.2
68. This research was an experiment.
     NOTE: Cumulative question.

Correct: F   Page: ResProc   Refer to: STORY16.2
69. In this research, "father" is not a concept since it refers to a particular person.
     NOTE: Cumulative question.

Correct: T   Page: Ch1   Refer to: STORY16.2
70. The unit of analysis in this research is individual.
     NOTE: Cumulative question.

Correct: F   Page: Ch4   Refer to: STORY16.2
71. This shows that there is no relationship between a father's education and his son's.
     NOTE: Cumulative question.

Correct: F   Page: Ch4   Refer to: STORY16.2
72. The 27% means that 27 out of 100 people who did not complete high school had fathers who also did not complete high school.
     NOTE: Cumulative question.

Correct: T   Page: 494   Refer to: STORY16.2
73. This suggests that education is, in part at least, an ascriptive status.

Correct: F   Page: Ch10   Refer to: STORY16.2
74. In a society in which status was primarily ascriptive, we would expect less of a relationship than this.
     NOTE: Cumulative question.

Correct: T   Page: Ch10   Refer to: STORY16.2
75. This illustrates one of the primary ways in which status attainment is related to family background.
     NOTE: Cumulative question.

Correct: F   Page: 510   Refer to: STORY16.2
76. This finding seems inconsistent with what Barbara Heyns found in her research on schooling and achievement.

Correct: T   Page: 510   Refer to: STORY16.2
77. Heyns's research on the effects of summer learning could help us understand this finding.

Correct: T   Page: 494   Refer to: STORY16.2
78. This finding suggests that we would find a relationship between father's and son's occupational prestige.

Correct: T   Page: Ch11   Refer to: STORY16.2
79. This research illustrates the long-term effects of discrimination.
NOTE: Cumulative question.

Correct: F   Page: Ch10   Refer to: STORY16.2
80. Assuming that educational status is a good indicator of class postion, this table suggests that the gap between the rich and the poor is narrowing in the United States.
NOTE: Cumulative question.

Correct: T   Page: Ch2   Refer to: STORY16.2
81. This table supports social, rather than cultural, theories of assimilation and mobility.
NOTE: Cumulative question.

Multiple Choice

Correct: F   Page: 494 Scramble Range: A-D
82. "Occupational prestige" is
A) how well the job pays.
B) how much education it takes to hold the job.
C) the geographic mobility of the occupation.
D) the training it takes to do the job.
E) all of these
F) none of these

Correct: B   Page: 494 Scramble Range: A-D
83. "Occupational prestige" can be understood as
A) the income from a job type.
B) how good or bad people perceive the job to be.
C) the degree of skill or training required for an occupation.
D) the extent to which people are differentially socialized into various occupational positions.
E) all of these
F) none of these

84. When the 1947 Hatt and North study of occupational prestige was repeated in 1962, there was a correlation between the 1947 set of results and the 1962 set of results. The correlation was _____ .
    A) +.45
    B) -.21
    C) +.56
    D) +.17
    E) +.99

85. When researchers asked Canadians to rank occupational titles--including two nonexistent occupations called "biologer" and "archaeopotrist"--they found that
    A) most people gave the two nonexistent occupations an above-average rank.
    B) most people were unwilling to rank jobs about which they knew nothing.
    C) the French Canadians placed greater value on "artistic" occupations than did the English-speaking Canadians.
    D) a comparison with United States rankings produced a correlation of approximately +.36.
    E) the researchers found significant differences between the French- and English-speaking Canadians' rankings of occupations.

86. Research results support the idea that _____ appear to agree about the prestige rankings of various occupations.
    A) older people more so than younger people
    B) younger people more so than older people
    C) people from Western nations more so than non-Western nations
    D) urban dwellers more so than rural dwellers
    E) people from all over the world

87. Sociologists have conducted studies of the rating of occupational prestige in various countries of the world. The main finding that has emerged is that
    A) the USSR and its allies rate military jobs higher than other nations do.
    B) African nations tend to rate laboring occupations higher than do northern European nations, the United States, and Australia.
    C) there are some times when the expected findings fall apart and it becomes difficult to make predictions about job prestige.
    D) the ratings of specific occupations are about the same in the industrialized and in the less industrialized nations.
    E) prestige is a poor indicator of the regard in which people hold any particular job or occupation.
    F) none of these

Correct: C   Page: 494 Scramble Range: A-E
88. What generalization is justified about such nations as Germany, Great Britain, Japan, New Zealand, Ghana, Guam, India, Indonesia, the Ivory Coast, and the Philippines?
A) Their native stratification systems have been displaced by systems from the outside.
B) Only some of these nations have active educational institutions of a formal, effective type; the others have dormant educational institutions.
C) All of them seem to be in agreement about the prestige of various occupations.
D) All of them are nations in which there is a low to moderate correlation between educational achievement and social mobility.
E) Most of them are debtor nations and are postponing educational efforts while they repay debts to the World Bank.
F) none of these

Correct: B   Page: 492-93 Scramble Range: ALL
89. Your text includes Table 16-1, Occupational Prestige Scores. According to this table, the top two occupations (ranked highest) were _____ and the bottom two (ranked lowest) were _____ .
A) United States Supreme Court justice and dentist; clerk in a store and bartender
B) United States Supreme Court justice and physician; street sweeper and shoe shiner
C) banker and physician; mechanic and funeral director
D) United States congressman and diplomat; coal miner and cafe cook
E) mayor of a large city and physician; bartender and garbage collector

Correct: C   Page: 494 Scramble Range: A-D
90. Occupational prestige rankings reflect
A) the type of clothing needed for an occupation.
B) the amount of mobility needed to attain the occupation.
C) both the training needed for a job and its pay.
D) different values and priorities in different countries.
E) all of these

Correct: F   Page: 494 Scramble Range: A-E
91. Which of the following help us to understand why some people attain higher occupational prestige than others?
A) Kohn's research on differential socialization
B) The occupational prestige of their parents
C) A person's education
D) Barbara Heyns's research on summer learning
E) Discrimination
F) All of these
NOTE: Somewhat cumulative.

92. Having examined the kinds of jobs that are declining in number and the kinds of jobs that are on the increase, Peter Drucker concluded that we are changing from
   A) a service economy to a leisure economy.
   B) an industrial economy to a knowledge economy.
   C) a physical labor economy to a machine power economy.
   D) an economy of consumption to an economy of productivity.
   E) an introverted economy to a cross-national economy.

93. The proportion of adults working in the labor force has _____ over the past 100 years.
   A) increased
   B) stabilized
   C) declined
   D) declined except for Hispanics
   E) remained fairly constant

94. Industrialization effects women's labor force participation because it
   A) creates opportunities.
   B) is accompanied by later marriage and fewer children.
   C) promotes secularization.
   D) all of these
   E) none of these

95. According to your text, which of the following are specifically mentioned as factors affecting the percentage of women in the labor force of European nations?
   A) Ethnic identity and level of industrialization
   B) Level of industrialization and fertility rates
   C) Fertility rates and racial membership
   D) Formal identification with a religion and racial membership
   E) Gross national product derived from tourism and percent of population who migrate for employment

96. The rapid expansion of the female labor force participation in the United States first occurred on the _____ where it was precipitated by _____.
   A) West Coast; an excess of males
   B) Gulf Coast; the erosion of traditional norms after the 1870s
   C) Atlantic Coast; World War II, producing a shortage of males
   D) East Coast; an unfavorable sex ratio
   E) shores of the Great Lakes; an excess of male immigrants

Correct: C   Page: 497 Scramble Range: A-D
97. Women are just about as likely as men to be employed in professional and managerial occupations
A) due to increased exchange mobility in society.
B) and especially in the higher prestige occupations such as welfare worker.
C) but not the highest paid ones.
D) and this is why the average pay of men and women is approaching equality.
E) all of these
F) none of these

Correct: F   Page: 499 Scramble Range: NONE
98. Table 16-3 in the text presents the percentage of men, women, African-Americans and Hispanics in various occupations. It shows
A) that African-Americans are the group mostly likely to be police officers.
B) that the proportion of Hispanics who are farm workers is almost four times the proportion of African-Americans or whites.
C) that women are almost as likely as men to be in managerial and professional occupations.
D) the African-Americans and Hispanics are almost as likely as whites to be announcers.
E) both B and D.
F) all of these

Correct: C   Page: 499 Scramble Range: ALL
99. The term "unemployed" applies to those who are of legal working age and
A) without jobs.
B) without jobs due to no fault of their own.
C) without jobs and on the records as seeking work.
D) without jobs for a period of more than six weeks.
E) without paid employment.

Correct: B   Page: 499 Scramble Range: A-D
100. Unemployment statistics are difficult to interpret because
A) they include people in school.
B) they don't include everyone who is out of work.
C) so many people just don't want to work.
D) they reflect hiring quotas.
E) all of these
F) none of these

Correct: A   Page: 501 Scramble Range: ALL
101. Which of the following states has the highest dropout rate?
A) Florida.
B) Wyoming.
C) Ohio.
D) Wisconsin.
E) Minnesota.

Correct: B   Page: 499 Scramble Range: A-D
102.   High school drop outs are often unemployed because
       A)   they aren't very intelligent.
       B)   there are fewer and fewer unskilled jobs.
       C)   they are mostly African-American.
       D)   English is often their second language.
       E)   all of these

Correct: A   Page: 501 Scramble Range: ALL
103.   According to Figure 16-2, Percent Who Dropped Out of School, the dropout
       rates were lowest in the
       A)   upper Midwest.
       B)   eastern states.
       C)   northwestern states.
       D)   southern states.
       E)   southwestern states.

Correct: D   Page: 501 Scramble Range: ALL
104.   High school dropout rates are highest in which of the following states?
       A)   Minnesota and North Dakota
       B)   Colorado and New Mexico
       C)   West Virginia and Missouri
       D)   Louisiana and South Carolina
       E)   Oklahoma and Oregon

Correct: A   Page: 503 Scramble Range: ALL
105.   As we examine social change in nations around the world, it is evident that
       industrialization has led to_____ in nations where industrialization
       has occurred.
       A)   mass education
       B)   a great emphasis on higher education such as found in the United States
            and Canada
       C)   greater population stability and less internal migration
       D)   greater tensions between racial or ethnic minorities
       E)   privatization of occupational training

Correct: B   Page: 503 Scramble Range: A-D
106.   The transformation of the economy discussed in your text was
       A)   from one based on knowledge to one based on industrial labor.
       B)   based on mass higher education.
       C)   prompted by the threat of modern war.
       D)   preceded by a shift to more women in the labor force.
       E)   all of these

Correct: A   Page: 503 Scramble Range: ALL
107.   Today, about _____ of Americans earn college degrees.
       A)   one-third
       B)   one-tenth
       C)   half
       D)   two-thirds
       E)   three-fourths

Correct: C   Page: 503 Scramble Range: A-C
108. The average American today
A) is likely to have completed college.
B) is not as well educated as fifty years ago.
C) has at least completed high school.
D) all of these
E) none of these

Correct: A   Page: 505 Scramble Range: A-D
109. Compared to other selected countries, the math scores of 13-year-olds in the United States was
A) near the bottom.
B) about average.
C) close to the top.
D) higher than scores from France.

Correct: C   Page: 505 Scramble Range: A-C
110. When ETS studied literacy in the United States for Congress, they defined "literacy" as
A) being able to clearly communicate using written and oral speech.
B) the ability to read short essays.
C) being able to use written and printed information to function in the society.

Correct: D   Page: 507 Scramble Range: A-D
111. ETS studied literacy in the United States for Congress. They found that _____ percent of the adult population in the United States could function at the highest level of quantitative literacy.
A) 73
B) 57
C) 14
D) 4

Correct: A   Page: 508 Scramble Range: ALL
112. James Coleman and his associates investigated the factors that were related to how students did in school. One such factor was
A) the scores on a vocabulary test taken by the students' teachers.
B) the amount of drive for success the individual student had.
C) the quality of academic resources (labs, library, teachers' educational degrees).
D) whether or not the parents supported students' educational goals.
E) the number of hours spent by the PTA in supporting educational efforts of the school.

Correct: G   Page: 508 Scramble Range: A-E
113. Coleman found that student achievement is directly related to
A) school expenditures.
B) teacher training.
C) class size.
D) age and quality of buildings.
E) racial composition.
F) all of these
G) none of these

Correct: D   Page: 510 Scramble Range: ALL
114. When Barbara Heyns studied what is most strongly and consistently related to summer learning, she found it to be
A) participation in group activities stressing social skills, for example, scout camp.
B) the amount of time parents spend with their children in interactive behaviors.
C) sports activities.
D) reading.
E) educational travel on family vacation.

Correct: D   Page: 510 Scramble Range: A-D
115. Barbara Heyns, in her research on student achievement, found that
A) schools tend to ratify the differences children bring to school.
B) schools are least effective for minorities.
C) schools only educate those lucky enough to attend elite schools.
D) schools matter.
E) all of these
F) none of these

Correct: C   Page: 510 Scramble Range: A-D
116. Barbara Heyns found that schools are most effective for disadvantaged children
A) because their families go on fewer vacations.
B) and are effective for preventing delinquency.
C) but that these children are less likely to continue their schooling.
D) while affluent children would be better off without schools.
E) all of these
F) none of these

Correct: A   Page: 510 Scramble Range: ALL
117. Heyns's study stimulated other researchers to find other ways to assess the impact of schooling. Among these were Alexander, Natriello, and Pallas, who compared the cognitive development of those who remained in school with those who dropped out. Having studied 30,000 sophomores from 1,000 high schools at two points in time, these researchers concluded that
A) the dropouts had a much smaller increase in cognitive development than those who remained in school.
B) the dropouts had the same amount of cognitive development as did the students who remained in school.
C) cognitive development is unrelated to enrollment/nonenrollment in school.
D) cognitive development is more related to students' instincts for learning than to students' enrollment status.
E) dropouts actually had MORE cognitive development than did those students remaining enrolled in the school system.

118.   When Alexander, Natriello, and Pallas studied the effect of dropping out of school on students' cognitive development, they found that dropping out had the most severe negative effects on students in which of the following categories?
A)   Students who are older than average
B)   Single-parent students
C)   Students who work part-time while in school
D)   Students from the most disadvantaged backgrounds
E)   Students who were sexually active
F)   All of these

119.   A majority of _____ sophomores in the United States study more than an hour a day.
A)   white
B)   Hispanic-American
C)   African-American
D)   Asian-American
E)   all of these
F)   none of these

120.   More than 10 percent of _____ sophomores in the United States drop out before their senior year.
A)   white
B)   Hispanic
C)   African-American
D)   native American
E)   all of these
F)   none of these

121.   Students in Catholic schools are less likely to drop out because
A)   these schools have more elite students.
B)   these schools are better funded.
C)   these schools have fewer African-Americans.
D)   these schools have fewer Hispanics.
E)   all of these
F)   none of these

122.   When Heyneman and Loxley, sociologists on the staff of the World Bank, analyzed data on school effects in 29 nations, they found that _____, the less students' backgrounds influence their school performances.
A)   the more preindustrial a nation was
B)   the less socialist a nation was
C)   the more capitalist a nation was
D)   the more democratic a nation was
E)   the poorer a nation was

Correct: A   Page: 514 Scramble Range: ALL
123. Heyneman and Loxley found that, worldwide, the _____ the nation, the greater the economic returns for getting an education.
A) poorer
B) wealthier
C) more socialistic
D) more capitalistic
E) less illiterate

Correct: D   Page: 514 Scramble Range: ALL
124. The _____ the nation, the _____ the economic returns for getting an education.
A) more Western; more stable
B) wealthier; less stable
C) wealthier; greater
D) poorer; greater
E) poorer; lower

Correct: B   Page: 514 Scramble Range: A-E
125. When Heyneman and Loxley studied 29 nations to analyze data on school effects, one of the things they found was that which of the following had comparatively greater effects in the poorer nations?
A) The dominant religion(s)
B) School and teacher quality
C) Aspects of climate, especially temperature and average rainfall
D) Personality characteristics of students
E) Method of funding educational efforts
F) None of these

Correct: B   Page: 514 Scramble Range: A-E
126. Heyneman and Loxley's research found that the effects of school and teacher quality worldwide are comparatively greater
A) when educational systems are locally rather than nationally coordinated.
B) in the poorer nations.
C) in capitalist nations than in socialist nations.
D) in the Northern Hemisphere.
E) when the nation, although poor now, had a previous Golden Age of culture.
F) none of these

Correct: E   Page: 515 Scramble Range: A-E
127. According to Figure 16-4, Average Number of Students in Primary Classes in Europe, which of the following had the fewest pupils per teacher?
A) France
B) Germany
C) Albania
D) United Kingdom
E) Denmark

Correct: A   Page: 516 Scramble Range: A-E
128. Obtaining a college degree is not worth as much as it used to be, according to your text, because
A) more people are obtaining college degrees.
B) more employers are themselves training the new employees in required job skills.
C) industry has less need of highly educated workers.
D) oversupply of education has increased the value of a two-year degree at a junior college.
E) empty degrees are eroding employers' confidence in the value of education.
F) all of these

Correct: B   Page: 516 Scramble Range: ALL
129. The decline in the value of a college education is the result of
A) colleges ceasing to prepare people for careers.
B) colleges preparing so many people for careers.
C) an excess of extracurricular or leisure activities at colleges/universities.
D) high schools failing to prepare students adequately for college/university.
E) empty degrees, or failure to communicate knowledge but still allowing these people to graduate

Correct: A   Page: 516 Scramble Range: ALL
130. In providing access to the highest-prestige occupations, education
A) may not guarantee success, but it tends to be necessary.
B) is not correlated with success unless it is in a practical subject.
C) of one's parents is the critical variable, more important than one's own educational efforts.
D) actually closes many doors if the employer/supervisor has a low level of education.
E) is relatively unrelated to such access for minority group persons.

Correct: E   Page: 516 Scramble Range: A-E
131. Today, if people want to have the same educational advantage that their parents had, then these people have to
A) attend at least the same quality of school as did their parents.
B) concentrate more on the occupational training areas and less on the so-called humanities.
C) begin their planning as early as the tenth grade in high school.
D) make sure that they avoid the public colleges and universities.
E) stay in school longer than their parents did.
F) avoid sociology courses.

Correct: D   Page: 516 Scramble Range: ALL
132. According to the French sociologist Raymond Boudon, who has created mathematical models of educational "deflation,"
A) males suffer from this process more than do females.
B) students' parents are in the best position to stop the deflation process.
C) deflation necessarily accompanies the urbanization process.
D) the deflation occurs at all educational levels.
E) linear models are less predictive than are nonlinear models of the deflation process.

Correct: D   Page: 517 Scramble Range: ALL
133. The gains in educational attainment made by African-Americans and
Hispanics have unfortunately been partly offset by
A) these groups' fertility rates.
B) currently declining enrollments in these populations.
C) the empty degrees offered by the schools they attend.
D) the inflation of academic credentials.
E) these groups' low rates of labor-force participation.

Correct: E   Page: 517 Scramble Range: ALL
134. _____ theories of education claim that educational requirements and
credentials are meant to screen out those lacking the opportunity to attend
college or who rebel against the prevailing rules by which statuses are
assigned.
A) Watchdog
B) Cooptive
C) Presumptive
D) Informal
E) Allocation

Correct: E   Page: 517 Scramble Range: ALL
135. Many Marxist sociologists argue that the primary function of schools in the
United States is to
A) reduce class inequalities by giving students skills they will find useful.
B) increase students' class-consciousness.
C) separate the competent students from the incompetent ones.
D) neutralize tensions resulting from class conflict.
E) re-create the class structure in each generation.

Correct: C   Page: 517 Scramble Range: A-E
136. Randall Collins believes that the point of requiring teaching certificates or
credentials is to
A) provide work for local and state government employees.
B) give prospective teachers skills that will make them effective at their
jobs.
C) control entry to the teaching profession.
D) give parents confidence in the school system.
E) give teachers a tangible basis for self-confidence.
F) all of these

Correct: A   Page: 517 Scramble Range: A-D
137. A "credential society"
A) makes positions less replaceable than they really are.
B) means that job skills are more important than general knowledge.
C) makes it less difficult for people to find apprenticeships.
D) increases the likelihood of exchange mobility.
E) all of these
F) none of these

Correct: D   Page: 517 Scramble Range: A-D
138. Functionalists argue that rewards are based on replaceability. A credential society
A) decreases rewards by increasing access to positions.
B) tends to falsify this functionalist argument.
C) means that rewards are based on need rather than occupational replaceability.
D) makes positions less replaceable than they really are.
E) all of these
F) none of these

Correct: C   Page: 517 Scramble Range: A-D
139. When Randall Collins referred to America as a "credential society," he meant that
A) performance of many jobs in modern America requires training that takes place at high school or college.
B) job productivity requires more people with high school and college degrees.
C) many jobs require diplomas or certificates of education that are not pertinent to job requirements.
D) too many people rely on degrees and certificates as the basis for their sense of personal worth.
E) none of these

Correct: A   Page: 517 Scramble Range: ALL
140. _____ theories argue that the primary function of schools is to assign status and to place students in the stratification system, rather than train them.
A) Allocation
B) Bifurcation
C) Segmentation
D) Interactional
E) S.E.S.

Correct: D   Page: 519 Scramble Range: ALL
141. If John Meyer's theory of educational functions is correct, then we should expect to find that people who have completed only the eighth grade of school
A) press for less money to be spent on education in the community.
B) belong to different social classes, depending on parental background.
C) have less worth as human beings than do those with higher levels of education.
D) have similar life styles and play similar social roles.
E) are strong supporters of adult education programs.

Correct: C   Page: 519 Scramble Range: A-E

142. The chapter on education and occupation ends with a discussion of John Meyer's theory of educational functions. According to Meyer, completed levels of education
   A) are most useful during periods of economic stability.
   B) reflect the status of students' parents but do not predict mobility very well.
   C) are social statuses, and these influence behavior during a person's life.
   D) are directly related to job skills, in an almost one-to-one ratio, so that the more education one attains, the higher the job skills one receives.
   E) reflect family social status but little more.
   F) all of these

Correct: C   Page: 519 Scramble Range: ALL

143. According to Meyer's theory of educational functions, levels of education in and of themselves are which of the following?
   A) Holistic experiences
   B) Dysfunctional for society as a whole
   C) Social statuses
   D) In need of being eliminated from the educational institution
   E) In need of being reinforced as part of the educational institution

Correct: B   Page: 520 Scramble Range: ALL

144. Your text states that industrialized nations increasingly have become
   A) vocational education specialists.
   B) knowledge economies.
   C) inappropriately partial to education in the humanities.
   D) "bottom-heavy" in terms of levels of education completed.
   E) more dependent on technology and less dependent on information.

Chapter 17: Modernization

True/False

Correct: F   Page: 526
1. Modernization is the process of becoming technological.

Correct: F   Page: 527
2. In and of itself, new technology is social change.

Correct: T   Page: 527
3. New technology sometimes does not cause social change.

Correct: F   Page: 527
4. The lack of an idea of progress may have slowed social change in Europe during the nineteenth century.

Correct: F   Page: 529
5. Changes in roles are caused by social change, not the cause of it.

Correct: F   Page: 530
6. Cultural lag refers to a period when changes are not taking place.

Correct: F   Page: 530
7. Cultural lag refers to a period when one society has less technological sophistication than another.

Correct: F   Page: 530
8. Cultural lag is the remainder when you subtract the rate of innovations from the rate of population growth.

Correct: F   Page: 531
9. Diffusion is an example of an internal source of change.

Correct: T   Page: 531
10. The process of diffusion describes the spread of innovations from one society to others.

Correct: F   Page: 531
11. The process of diffusion causes the rate of social change to decline.

Correct: T   Page: 531
12. The process of diffusion helps explain why isolated societies have relatively low levels of technology.

Correct: F   Page: 532
13. The Spaniards learned about horses from the Native Americans.

Correct: T   Page: 532
14. The Italians learned about tomatoes from the Native Americans.

Correct: F   Page: 534
15. Conflict with other societies generally suppresses social change.

Correct: F   Page: 535
16. External, rather than internal, forces lead to social change.

Correct: F   Page: 536
17. Karl Marx's explanation of the rise of the West claimed that the Industrial Revolution took place before the rise of capitalism.

Correct: T   Page: 536
18. Karl Marx's explanation of the rise of the West claimed that the Industrial Revolution was caused by the rise of capitalism.

Correct: T   Page: 536
19. Karl Marx's explanation of the rise of the West said that the Industrial Revolution occurred because people began to work harder and smarter.

Correct: T   Page: 536
20. Karl Marx's explanation of the rise of the West claimed that the factors that caused the rise of capitalism would also lead to increased human suffering.

Correct: T   Page: 537
21. In capitalist economies prices and wages are set by supply and demand.

Correct: F   Page: 537
22. In capitalist economies only the very wealthy are motivated to become more productive.

Correct: T   Page: 537
23. In capitalist economies people are rewarded for saving and reinvesting their earnings.

Correct: T   Page: 538
24. Max Weber tried to explain why capitalism developed where and when it did.

Correct: F   Page: 539
25. Max Weber argued that the command structure of Catholicism produced the move toward capitalism in the West.

Correct: T   Page: 539
26. Max Weber argued that capitalism is an ideology.

Correct: F   Page: 539
27. According to Max Weber, a good way to measure the extent of the "spirit of capitalism" would be to measure the extent of membership in Protestant denominations.

Correct: T   Page: 539
28. For a time, some Protestant theologians taught that to become rich in this life was a sign that one was chosen by God to enter heaven.

Correct: T   Page: 540
29. State theorists of modernization argue that capitalism will develop whenever private property is secure against expropriation by the state.

Correct: T   Page: 540
30. State theorists of modernization claim that the profit motive caused the Industrial Revolution.

Correct: T   Page: 540
31. State theorists of modernization agree with Karl Marx that capitalism caused modernization.

Correct: F   Page: 541
32. State theorists agree with Max Weber that the Protestant Ethic helped lead to capitalism.

Correct: T   Page: 541
33. World system or dependency theory argues that the causes of modernization are not to be found within nations, but only in their relations with one another.

Correct: T   Page: 541
34. World system or dependency theory claims that the developed nations achieved their high standards of living by draining off wealth from less-developed nations.

Correct: F   Page: 542
35. World system or dependency theory argues that core nations are exploited by peripheral nations.

Correct: F   Page: 543
36. World system or dependency theory claims that today's less developed nations can make progress only if they can increase their trade with the developed nations.

Correct: T   Page: 543
37. World system or dependency theory claims that foreign firms control the internal policies of less-developed nations.

Correct: F   Page: 543
38. World system or dependency theory argues that reliance on exporting unprocessed raw materials will speed up modernization.

Correct: F   Page: 546
39. Jacques Delacroix's test of dependency theory provided it with strong support.

Correct: F   Page: 547
40. Jacques Delacroix's test of dependency theory found that specializing in the export of raw materials did reduce enrollments in secondary education.

Correct: T   Page: 547
41. Delacroix's research about GNP and secondary school enrollment suggests that modernization is influenced primarily by internal processes rather than by external processes of the world system.

Reference Key: STORY17.1
Albania and Romania have a large proportion of the labor force employed in agriculture (61% and 48%). Countries such as the United Kingdom, Belgium, and the United States have proportions of less than 5% in agriculture. The proportion in agriculture, in turn, correlates highly with agricultural productivity (the higher the proportion in agriculture the lower the productivity) and other measures of modernization.

Correct: T   Page: 526   Refer to: STORY17.1
42. We would expect that the higher the proportion in agriculture, the lower the extent of urbanization and industrialization.

Correct: F   Page: 531   Refer to: STORY17.1
43. Countries such as Romania and Albania would also be high on the number of televison sets per 1,000 population.

Correct: F   Page: 530   Refer to: STORY17.1
44. These differences among countries are an example of cultural lag.

Correct: T   Page: 536   Refer to: STORY17.1
45. Karl Marx would suggest that the failure to develop capitalist economies can explain the situation of Albania and Romania.

Correct: F   Page: 536   Refer to: STORY17.1
46. Karl Marx would explain these differences among countries on the basis of cultural diffusion, especially of religious ideology.

Correct: T   Page: 536   Refer to: STORY17.1
47. Max Weber would ask about the beliefs and ideologies of the Romanians and Albanians.

Correct: F   Page: 541   Refer to: STORY17.1
48. In trying to understand these differences among countries, world system theorists would ask about the extent of success of the Protestant Reformation in these countries.

Correct: T   Page: 540   Refer to: STORY17.1
49. State theorists would hypothesize that countries such as Albania and Romania had command economies.

Correct: T   Page: 518   Refer to: STORY17.1
50. World system theorists would hypothesize that private property is more secure in the more modernized states.

Correct: T   Page: 543   Refer to: STORY17.1
51. World system theorists would ask questions about the extent and range of exports from Albania and Romania.

Correct: F   Page: 543   Refer to: STORY17.1
52. State theorists would ask about the national dependency of Albania and Romania.

Correct: F   Page: 519   Refer to: STORY17.1
53. World system theorists would consider Albania a core nation.

Correct: T   Page: 546   Refer to: STORY17.1
54. Dependency theorists would expect to find a link between proportion employed in agriculture and the expansion of education.

Correct: F   Page: 523   Refer to: STORY17.1
55. Delacroix's study of dependency leads us to expect to find less specialization in exporting raw materials among the nations with a lower proportion in agriculture.

Multiple Choice

Correct: A   Page: 526 Scramble Range: ALL
56. The term _____ is used to refer to the process by which agrarian societies are transformed into industrial societies.
   A) modernization
   B) urbanization
   C) transference
   D) metamorphosis
   E) mechanization

Correct: B   Page: 526 Scramble Range: A-D
57. Modernization is the process of becoming
   A) technological.
   B) industrialized.
   C) more Western.
   D) more agricultural.
   E) none of these

Correct: C   Page: 526 Scramble Range: ALL
58. Conflicts, innovations, and population growth are all discussed by your text as being
   A) the results of cultural lag.
   B) corrosive of governmental authority over the masses.
   C) internal causes of social change in a society.
   D) causes for the lowering of revenues to the government.
   E) strongly and positively correlated with each other.

Correct: B   Page: 528 Scramble Range: ALL
59. According to your text's Table 17-1, Belief in Technological and Scientific Progress,
   A) people in the United States are much more likely than the Japanese to see scientific advances as harmful.
   B) People in Northern Europe tend to see technological development as a bad thing.
   C) the Japanese overwhelmingly view scientific advances as helping mankind.
   D) people in poorer countries such as Hungary and Mexico tend to see technological development as harmful.
   E) all of these
   F) none of these

Correct: A   Page: 527 Scramble Range: A-D
60. A major internal source of change is
A) technology.
B) genetic shift.
C) war.
D) climatic change.
E) all of these
F) none of these

Correct: E   Page: 527 Scramble Range: A-D
61. A major internal source of social change is
A) change in technology.
B) change in beliefs and values.
C) conflict.
D) change in population.
E) all of these
F) none of these

Correct: F   Page: 527 Scramble Range: A-D
62. The invention of the steam engine is an example of
A) cultural lag.
B) dependency syndrome.
C) world system theory.
D) conflict as a source of social change.
E) all of these
F) none of these

Correct: C   Page: 530 Scramble Range: ALL
63. Cultural lag is defined as
A) the relative distances between cultures in terms of evolutionary development.
B) the extent to which a culture is not fulfilling its own growth potential.
C) the situation that exists when one part of a culture changes faster than the other parts.
D) occurring when a culture temporarily rests or pauses in its historical evolution.
E) the relative failure of some nations to develop sufficiently in terms of human endeavors such as ballet, opera, and the other arts.

Correct: D   Page: 530 Scramble Range: ALL
64. _____ exists when parts of a society have not adjusted to changes elsewhere in the society.
A) Functionalism
B) Interactionism
C) Negative interaction
D) Cultural lag
E) Social asynchronicity

Correct: C Page: 530 Scramble Range: A-D
65. The idea of cultural lag
   A) is central to dependency theory.
   B) is illustrated by Weber's work in the Protestant Ethic.
   C) presupposes that society is a system.
   D) illustrates Marx's idea of capitalism as a source of social change.
   E) all of these
   F) none of these

Correct: D Page: 531 Scramble Range: A-E
66. Your text classifies the various sources of social change into two types
   A) classical and modern.
   B) progressive and retrogressive.
   C) change evocative and change suppressive.
   D) internal and external.
   E) cross-national and cross-cultural.
   F) none of these

Correct: C Page: 531 Scramble Range: A-E
67. Farmers in Tanzania are growing coffee as a cash crop. Coffee is not native to Tanzania, but was introduced there from other countries. What does this illustrate?
   A) A command economy
   B) The Delacroix hypothesis
   C) Diffusion
   D) The spirit of capitalism
   E) The Dorian effect in an agricultural setting
   F) None of these

Correct: D Page: 531 Scramble Range: ALL
68. Ralph Linton, quoted in your text, said, "The number of successful inventions originating within any one society is always small." Linton goes on to suggest that if every society had access solely to its own inventions, then
   A) there would have been and would now be less international conflict.
   B) international conflict would be less important as a cause of social change.
   C) cultures would have more internal integrity--would be more themselves.
   D) it is doubtful that any society would have advanced beyond the Stone Age.
   E) a more competitive situation would exist, and mankind would reap the often-observed benefits of competition.

Correct: C Page: 534 Scramble Range: A-E
69. Conflict with other societies
   A) tends to suppress social change.
   B) diverts energy from innovation.
   C) tends to stimulate innovation and social change.
   D) creates population growth and change.
   E) is central to Weber's understanding of the development of capitalism.
   F) none of these

Correct: E   Page: 534 Scramble Range: A-E
70. Your text used the Viking expansions of about A.D. 900 and the relative success of these various efforts to illustrate
    A) coordination as a facilitator of social change.
    B) cultural fit or complementarity as a facilitator of social change
    C) assimilation.
    D) diffusion as a source of social change.
    E) ecological sources of change.
    F) all of these

Correct: B   Page: 534 Scramble Range: A-D
71. People around the world who watch the most television
    A) are in the countries with the most TV sets per 1000 population.
    B) speak English.
    C) are generally watching it with technological innovations developed in their own country.
    D) are limited to watching only a few channels.

Correct: D   Page: 535 Scramble Range: ALL
72. Which of the following is FALSE?
    A) Change seems to be inherent in (or built into) all societies.
    B) Both internal and external forces can produce social change.
    C) Both internal and external forces can cause societies to break down.
    D) Social change necessarily means progress.
    E) Threats from other societies can be a source of social change.

Correct: C   Page: 534 Scramble Range: A-D
73. Your text discusses change in the number of television sets in various countries as an example of
    A) ecological sources of change.
    B) conflict.
    C) diffusion.
    D) internal sources of change.
    E) new culture.
    F) none of these

Correct: D   Page: 536 Scramble Range: A-D
74. The four major theories of modernization presented in your text are all trying to explain
    A) how modernization develops without capitalism.
    B) the sorts of cultural changes necessary for industrial takeoff.
    C) the causes or origins of capitalism in the West.
    D) why the West produced the industrial revolution.
    E) none of these

75. The idea that capitalism is the source of rapid modernization in Western societies is central to
    A) the state theory of modernization.
    B) the Marxian theory of modernization.
    C) the world system theory of modernization.
    D) the Weberian theory of modernization.
    E) all of these
    F) none of these

Correct: A   Page: 536 Scramble Range: ALL
76. Karl Marx praised capitalism because he felt that it
    A) stimulated the modernization and industrialization of Europe.
    B) exposed the corruption and weaknesses lying dormant in European nations.
    C) allowed workers to express themselves in labor or employment
    D) effectively purged the population of unfit people by exposing them to highly stressful work situations, thus leaving a Europe that was much healthier.
    E) neutralized the power of the monarchies and the upper classes.

Correct: D   Page: 536 Scramble Range: ALL
77. Marx felt that capitalism was a new mode of economic arrangements that
    A) allowed and even encouraged willing cooperation between the main social classes.
    B) neutralized the power of the bourgeoisie and heightened the power of the proletariat.
    C) freed the individual creativity of the average laborer, who could finally express his/her personality on the job through his/her work.
    D) unleashed the full productive potential of the population.
    E) was less efficient and less productive than feudalism, the mode of economic arrangement that preceded capitalism.

Correct: A   Page: 536 Scramble Range: ALL
78. Marx believed that Europe's great leap forward occurred because people suddenly began to work harder and smarter as a result of the
    A) inducements of capitalism.
    B) sudden decline in the available pool of laborers.
    C) sudden increase of laborers competing with one another for jobs
    D) return of Catholicism.
    E) reduction in class consciousness.

Correct: D   Page: 537 Scramble Range: ALL
79. The text states that capitalism stripped away the traditional bases of relationships between people and left only one basis for human relationships:
    A) administrative kinship.
    B) a command ecology.
    C) altruism.
    D) naked self-interest.
    E) a sense of membership in an urban industrial community.

Correct: B   Page: 537 Scramble Range: ALL
80.   Marx eventually wanted to make which of the following changes?
   A)   Introduce mass production techniques for items being labored on "by hand"
   B)   Keep modernization and get rid of capitalism
   C)   Inject into the forces of production ideas from India, China, and Japan
   D)   Find a way to make work a thing of the past, leaving only leisure for those who had for so long been exploited laborers
   E)   Bring about peaceful change, using the legal system already in place

Correct: E   Page: 537 Scramble Range: ALL
81.   Your text states that the secret of capitalism is
   A)   to pay the most money to those who try the hardest.
   B)   to coordinate large-scale activities using bureaucratic strategies.
   C)   to pay attention to workers' attitudes, feelings, and personal wishes.
   D)   to pay at least as much attention to the political area as to the economic area of business life.
   E)   to reward surplus production.

Correct: C   Page: 537 Scramble Range: A-E
82.   The lord of a medieval estate decided which fields were to be plowed, when to plant and what to plant, and then ordered his peasants to do it. This is an excellent example of
   A)   the satrap system.
   B)   an authoritarian personality, according to Rokeach.
   C)   a command economy.
   D)   an early incentive for efficient, high-level, quick productivity.
   E)   affiliational management.
   F)   none of these

Correct: E   Page: 537 Scramble Range: ALL
83.   The weakness of _____ is that those doing the work have nothing to gain by doing it well.
   A)   agribusiness
   B)   Japanese modes of industrial organization
   C)   plural coordination
   D)   Keynesian economics
   E)   command economies

Correct: A   Page: 539 Scramble Range: ALL
84.   Which of these views was set forth by John Calvin and came to have important economic consequences for the development of capitalism?
   A)   Predestination
   B)   Transubstantiation
   C)   Transmigration of good and evil, praise and blame
   D)   Encapsulation of religious authority
   E)   The system of indirect donation

85. According to the text, how did the Calvinist Protestants feel you could have a high degree of confidence that you were one of God's chosen, in good favor with God?
    A) By engaging in conspicuous consumption for a prolonged time
    B) By engaging in the conspicuous consumption of leisure rather than of material things
    C) By having visible, continuing economic success in business
    D) By giving to the church 20 percent or more of what you earned
    E) By having a sudden, almost unearned bonanza, which could only have come because you stood in God's favor

86. Max Weber, who wrote some of his works in response to Karl Marx, argued that the _____ ideas produced by _____ had motivated people both to limit their consumption and to pursue maximum wealth.
    A) political; Ludwig Feuerbach
    B) philosophical; Rousseau
    C) philosophical; Locke
    D) religious; Protestantism
    E) religio-political; Roman Catholicism

87. Which of the following was an important part of the development of industrial capitalism?
    A) A shift in how people regarded wealth
    B) The spread of the concept of "religious incorporation"
    C) Concentrating on the life in the world to come rather than on life in this world
    D) A decline in nationalism among important economic figures
    E) A complete substitution of capitalism for nationalism

88. Which theory of modernization believed that capitalism could develop fully only when the political environment was not repressive?
    A) Marxist theory of modernization
    B) Weberian theory of modernization
    C) State theory of modernization
    D) World system theory of modernization
    E) Liberal theory of modernization

89. According to the state theory of modernization
    A) Marx was correct in saying that capitalism led to rapid modernization of Europe.
    B) capitalism could only develop when the state was tamed.
    C) security of private property led to the development of capitalism.
    D) the state is a threat to the development of capitalism.
    E) B and D only.
    F) all of these
    G) none of these

90. Daniel Chirot has pointed out that the _____ always stifles economic development because it can't keep from overtaxing.
    A) New Democracy
    B) Democratic party
    C) inexperienced political party
    D) leadership in Third World nations
    E) untamed state

91. According to Daniel Chirot and the state theory of modernization, elites always _____ and therefore need to _____.
    A) overspend; become imperialistic
    B) underestimate resistance; use military or police force
    C) overreproduce themselves; increase taxes
    D) become lazy; increase their activity level
    E) share power with administrators; work at recovering their power

92. According to Chirot and the state theory of modernization, which of the following is a necessity if economic actors (or investors) are to take actions that maximize the economic productivity of their investments?
    A) Potential availability of foreign markets
    B) The use of formal contractual documents and a written legal system
    C) Predictability of the outcome of various business actions
    D) Awareness of the average person's attitudinal response to business actions
    E) Awareness of the relative value of various social goals as compared to other social goals

93. The disagreement between state theorists and Max Weber on the causes of capitalism can be summarized as an issue of
    A) spuriousness.
    B) causal order.
    C) lack of correlation.
    D) cultural relativism.
    E) all of these
    F) none of these

94. State theorists of modernization
    A) argue that Protestantism is an expression of capitalism, not one of its causes.
    B) agree with Weber that Protestantism helped lead to capitalism.
    C) disagree with Marx about the importance of the "spirit of capitalism."
    D) agree with world system theorists about the importance of dependency.
    E) none of these

Correct: C   Page: 541 Scramble Range: ALL
95. Imperialism as a type of economic and political behavior is central to which of
    the following theories of modernization?
    A) State theory of modernization
    B) Weberian theory of modernization
    C) World system theory of modernization
    D) Centripetal theory of modernization
    E) Ecological theory of modernization

Correct: B   Page: 541 Scramble Range: ALL
96. Immanuel Wallerstein wrote THE MODERN WORLD SYSTEM, in which he
    argued that there exists an international economy that
    A) is not politically united but that has the potential to become so.
    B) allows some nations to extract wealth from other nations without paying
       the huge costs of running an empire.
    C) encourages the major nations to extend credit to minor nations through
       the World Bank, with no strings attached.
    D) enables members of this club of nations to help nations that are not
       members of the club, thus encouraging internal development of Third
       World nations.
    E) engages in democracy-like decision-making activities.

Correct: B   Page: 542 Scramble Range: ALL
97. Wallerstein, in THE MODERN WORLD SYSTEM, insists that there is a
    stratification system among nations, with the equivalent of upper-class,
    middle-class, and lower-class nations. Which of these is Wallerstein's term for
    an upper-class nation?
    A) Centralist nation
    B) Core nation
    C) U.N.-member nation
    D) Security Council nation
    E) Prime nation

Correct: D   Page: 542 Scramble Range: ALL
98. According to Immanuel Wallerstein's MODERN WORLD SYSTEM theory of
    modernization, the _____ nations specialize in exporting raw materials to the
    _____ nations' very diversified economies.
    A) rural industrial; urban industrial
    B) nonunited; united
    C) peasant-dominated; administratively dominated
    D) peripheral; core
    E) Second World; Third World

Correct: A   Page: 542 Scramble Range: ALL
99. According to Wallerstein's view of dominance and dependency among nations,
    _____ nations may display features of both core and peripheral nations.
    A) semiperipheral
    B) parasitic
    C) middleman
    D) secondary
    E) dualistic

Correct: C   Page: 543 Scramble Range: ALL
100.   According to Wallerstein and others, the fundamental mechanism by which some nations exploit others is that the less-developed nations are dominated by
A)   time-honored traditions that make it almost impossible for revolt to occur.
B)   developed nations' implied threat of military action if revolt occurs.
C)   foreign firms and investors that control their economies.
D)   their own elites, who want to maintain the old traditions, one of which is playing a subordinate role to allegedly superior cultures.
E)   the United Nations, which is in reality nothing more than a pawn of such nations as France and the United States.

Correct: A   Page: 543 Scramble Range: A-E
101.   According to world system theory, who or what plans and controls the economic activities taking place in underdeveloped nations?
A)   Foreign firms and investors
B)   The United Nations
C)   The poor of those nations, because they are so numerous and because of their latent power
D)   The middle-class managerial elite of those nations
E)   The European universities that trained the elites of the underdeveloped nations
F)   All of these

Correct: D   Page: 543 Scramble Range: A-D
102.   According to world system theory, core nations
A)   have weak or unstable governments.
B)   have command economies.
C)   have a low standard of living for workers.
D)   have highly diversified economies.
E)   B and D.
F)   none of these

Correct: E   Page: 543 Scramble Range: ALL
103.   The dependency portion of world system theory states that _____ prevents modernization.
A)   locating powerful nations' military bases in less developed nations
B)   refusal to loan large sums of money to less developed nations
C)   IMF refusal to give dependency status to less developed nations
D)   conflict between the World Bank and the IMF
E)   specialization in the export of raw materials

Correct: C   Page: 545 Scramble Range: ALL
104.   According to Table 17-3, Per Capita GNP for Selected Nations, the nation with the highest per capita gross national product in dollars for 1994 was
A)   the Soviet Union
B)   Hong Kong
C)   Switzerland
D)   the United States
E)   Great Britain

Correct: D   Page: 545 Scramble Range: A-D
105. Delacroix tested what proposition from world system theory?
A) Changes in belief structures generate the preconditions for modernization.
B) Control by foreign firms and investors leads to less manufacturing capacity.
C) Internal sources of change are as critical as external sources.
D) Specialization in exporting raw materials prevents modernization.
E) All of these
F) None of these

Correct: B   Page: 547 Scramble Range: ALL
106. Jacques Delacroix conducted an empirical test of the dependency theory. He found that modernization is influenced primarily by
A) the education of ruling elites by foreign universities.
B) a country's internal processes rather than by external processes of the world system.
C) the health and viability of world markets more than by the world system.
D) implied military threat by the world's dominant nations.
E) the activities of such programs as the Rockefeller Foundation, the Fulbright Scholarships, Greenpeace, Feed the World, and the like.

Correct: C   Page: 548 Scramble Range: A-D
107. The most recent research on dependency theory discussed in your text (Firebaugh and Beck, 1994), examined 62 nations over a 23 year period. This research found
A) that economic development in the third world only benefits the rich.
B) strong support for dependency theory.
C) that investments in secondary education greatly speed development.
D) all of these
E) none of these

Topic 5: Stirrups

True/False

Correct: F   Page: 550
1. According to the text, the stirrup was invented in northwestern Europe, sometime in the sixth century.

Correct: T   Page: 550
2. Your text states that the use of the stirrup increased mounted soldiers' ability to fight effectively.

Correct: F   Page: 550
3. "The Frankish host," discussed in your text's Special Topic 5, was a small, round, whitish, highly nutritious bread, and the energy surges it produced gave soldiers great bursts of short-term energy.

Correct: F   Page: 550
4. The stirrup was invented by the Roman cavalry during the time of ancient Rome's conquest of Germany, France, and England.

Correct: T   Page: 550
5. According to the text, armored knights were less vulnerable to some types of attack during battle. Armored horses used by them were also less vulnerable to the same types of attack.

Correct: T   Page: 551
6. According to Special Topic 5 in your text, each knight was given a tract of land and the authority to tax all who lived on it in return for his service as a knight when called upon in time of need. This is the political system known as feudalism.

Correct: T   Page: 551
7. In feudal societies, land ownership is based on military obligations.

Multiple Choice

Correct: A   Page: 550 Scramble Range: ALL
8. According to the text, which of the following inventions increased greatly the effectiveness of military cavalry during the seventh and eighth centuries?
   A) Stirrups
   B) Bridles
   C) Saddle blankets
   D) Braided ribbons
   E) Durable ropes

Correct: C   Page: 550 Scramble Range: ALL
9. According to the text, _____ could not be very effective until _____ were used.
   A) cannon; durable pellets or balls
   B) frontal assaults; shields
   C) cavalry; stirrups
   D) infantry; leather soles
   E) battering rams; wheels

Correct: D   Page: 550 Scramble Range: ALL
10. During the seventh century, the _____ became more effective soldiers because they went to battle mounted on horses and wearing armor.
   A) Kurts
   B) Byzantines
   C) Aleuts
   D) Franks
   E) Vikings

Correct: E   Page: 550 Scramble Range: ALL
11. "The Frankish host" refers to
   A) the religious innovation of using a wafer to symbolize something important.
   B) an economic maneuver that intentionally creates dramatic currency fluctuations.
   C) any homeowner who is completely blunt and tactless with his or her guests.
   D) a religious leader whose charisma enables him or her to persuade many people to join a "jihad" or holy war.
   E) a mass of lightly armed infantry.

Correct: A   Page: 551 Scramble Range: ALL
12. In _____ societies, land ownership is based on military obligations.
   A) feudal
   B) primitive tribal
   C) Asiatic
   D) secular
   E) Western

Correct: C   Page: 551 Scramble Range: ALL
13.   In feudal societies, _____ is based on military obligations.
   A)   religious affiliation
   B)   lifespan
   C)   land ownership
   D)   homogamy
   E)   family density

Correct: B   Page: 551 Scramble Range: ALL
14.   In feudal societies, rulers grant title to large areas of land in return for
   A)   agreement to cultivate the land productively.
   B)   remaining ready to fulfill a military quota or obligation.
   C)   an exorbitant economic surcharge on purchase of the property.
   D)   continued religious piety.
   E)   water rights.

Chapter 18: Population Changes

True/False

Correct: F   Page: 555
1.   The first census was conducted in England by William the Conqueror.

Correct: F   Page: 557
2.   A population growth rate of less than 100 percent means that the population is shrinking.

Correct: F   Page: 557
3.   The population growth rate is gain or loss in population.

Correct: T   Page: 557
4.   We wouldn't need to use rates if we didn't want to compare.

Correct: T   Page: 557
5.   "Percent" is a type of rate.

Correct: T   Page: 557
6.   The crude death rate is the total number of deaths for a year divided by the total population.

Correct: T   Page: 557
7.   In demography, crude rates are based on the total population.

Correct: F   Page: 557
8.   The crude birth rate is the total number of births divided by the total number of women aged 15 to 44.

Correct: F   Page: 557
9.   "Fertility rate" is the rate of population growth.

Correct: F   Page: 559
10.   A birth cohort is made up of all women who bear children during a given year.

Correct: F   Page: 559
11.   The Germans gained an advantage over the French because they were the first to discover how to increase the size of birth cohorts retroactively.

Correct: F   Page: 561
12.   When a population is growing, the largest age cohorts are always those in their childbearing years.

Correct: T   Page: 561
13.   When a population is getting smaller, the younger cohorts will be the smaller cohorts.

Correct: T   Page: 562
14.   The first great shift in human population trends was caused by the invention of agriculture.

Correct: F   Page: 562

15. Population growth in agrarian societies tends to be slow but very stable.

Correct: T   Page: 563

16. Epidemics such as the Black Plague and smallpox periodically killed a third of the population or more.

Correct: T   Page: 567

17. Malthus's theory of population blamed rapid population declines on positive checks, such as famine and disease.

Correct: T   Page: 567

18. Malthus's theory of population used changes in mortality as the fundamental variable determining population size.

Correct: T   Page: 567

19. Malthus's theory of population assumed that fertility would always be high.

Correct: F   Page: 567

20. Malthus's theory of population assumed that mortality would always be high.

Correct: F   Page: 567

21. Malthus's theory of population predicted that population growth would always follow an upward curve.

Correct: T   Page: 567

22. Malthus's theory of population appeared to explain the past patterns of population change in early agrarian societies quite well.

Correct: T   Page: 567

23. The population explosion in less-developed nations was made possible by a rapid increase in the food supply.

Correct: F   Page: 568

24. The initial impact of the Industrial Revolution was to halt runaway population growth.

Correct: F   Page: 569

25. The demographic transition was predicted by Malthus's theory.

Correct: T   Page: 569

26. The demographic transition refers to a shift from high fertility and high mortality to low fertility and low mortality.

Correct: T   Page: 570

27. Even primitive human societies often have been able to limit their fertility. Malthus's theory of population ignored this fact.

Correct: T   Page: 570

28. Anthropologists have learned that people in primitive societies know effective methods for limiting fertility.

Correct: T   Page: 570
29. The latest version of demographic transition theory holds that fertility will decline when more than half of the labor force does not farm.

Correct: F   Page: 570
30. The latest version of demographic transition theory holds that fertility will decline wherever contraceptives are cheap and easy to obtain.

Correct: T   Page: 570
31. The latest version of demographic transition theory holds that fertility is reduced when women marry at an older age.

Correct: F   Page: 570
32. Telephones per 1,000 is one of the demographic transition thresholds; however, TVs per 1,000 is not.

Correct: T   Page: 572
33. Less-developed nations' sudden decline in mortality resulted from a few elements of modern technology imported from developed nations.

Correct: T   Page: 572
34. The population explosion in less-developed nations was produced by a decline in mortality.

Correct: T   Page: 572
35. The population explosion in less-developed nations is an example of cultural lag.

Correct: F   Page: 572
36. Modernization of agriculture contributed toward overall modernization, but it was largely unrelated to the second population explosion.

Correct: T   Page: 573
37. Recently, the fertility rate has begun to fall in many less industrialized nations.

Correct: F   Page: 574
38. The demographic transition has not yet begun in Asia or Latin America.

Correct: F   Page: 574
39. The latest version of demographic transition theory holds that there is little hope that fertility will decline soon in Latin America or Asia.

Correct: F   Page: 574
40. As life expectancy in a society increases, so does the fertility rate.

Correct: T   Page: 579
41. The fertility rates for most industrialized nations is now below replacement level.

Correct: T   Page: 580
42. The sixth great transformation in population trends leads to the largest birth cohorts being the oldest.

Correct: F   Page: 582
43.   The major cause of recent famines in the world has been population pressure.

Reference Key: STORY18.1
Albania and Romania have a large proportion of the labor force employed in agriculture (61% and 48%). Countries such as the United Kingdom, Belgium and the United States have proportions of less than 5 percent in agriculture. The proportion in agriculture, in turn, correlates highly with agricultural productivity (the higher the proportion in agriculture the lower the productivity) and other measures of modernization.

Correct: F   Page: 557   Refer to: STORY18.1
44.   The "61%" means that 61 out of every thousand people in the labor force are employed in agriculture.

Correct: T   Page: 560,567   Refer to: STORY18.1
45.   We would expect that Albania has a fertility rate above replacement level.

Correct: T   Page: 560,567   Refer to: STORY18.1
46.   We expect that Albania has an expansive population structure.

Correct: F   Page: 560,567   Refer to: STORY18.1
47.   We would predict that Albania has a constrictive population structure.

Correct: F   Page: 570   Refer to: STORY18.1
48.   We expect that Albania's high school enrollment is fairly high.

Correct: T   Page: 572   Refer to: STORY18.1
49.   Albania's infant mortality rate is likely to be fairly high.

Correct: F   Page: 569   Refer to: STORY18.1
50.   Albania is probably in the midst of the third great shift in human population trends.

Correct: T   Page: 556
51.   The Albanian fertility rate is probably higher than the Albanian's ideal birth rate.

Correct: F   Page: 556
52.   People in Albania are probably having fewer children than they want.

Multiple Choice

Correct: C   Page: 555 Scramble Range: ALL
53. William the Conqueror instigated the production of what is now known as the DOMESDAY BOOK because he
    A) was concerned about the possible end of the world or the apocalypse as promised in the Book of Revelations.
    B) worried about having enough people to undertake the tearing down of Hadrian's Wall, which stretched completely across the country.
    C) suspected that he was not getting all of the taxes due him from his subjects.
    D) was the only one of the major European nobility who had not published a book.
    E) had heard of the prophecies of Dafyd, a Welsh mystic and holy man, who foresaw economic chaos for the entire country.

Correct: E   Page: 555 Scramble Range: NONE
54. The major reason for a country to conduct a census is to
    A) estimate tax revenue.
    B) estimate military power.
    C) estimate demographic transition.
    D) develop agricultural policies.
    E) A and B
    F) all of these

Correct: C   Page: 555 Scramble Range: ALL
55. A population count, often broken down into useful categories such as sex, age, occupation, marital status, and the like, is a
    A) stratified sample.
    B) survey group.
    C) census.
    D) selective interview group.
    E) social stratum.

Correct: D   Page: 555 Scramble Range: ALL
56. Which of the following is a term referring to the description of a population (or to population studies)?
    A) Apocrophy
    B) Cryptography
    C) Cartography
    D) Demography
    E) Censography

Correct: C   Page: 555 Scramble Range: A-D
57. Demography is
    A) the science of mapping populations.
    B) the study of fertility rates.
    C) a specialization within sociology.
    D) closely related to micro-sociological theories.
    E) all of these
    F) none of these

Correct: B   Page: 555 Scramble Range: A-D
58.   ·A sociologist who examines changes in the household composition of families
      in the United States is
      A)   engaged in micro sociology.
      B)   doing demography.
      C)   examining demographic transition.
      D)   applying Malthusian theory.
      E)   all of these
      F)   none of these

Correct: D   Page: 557 Scramble Range: ALL
59.   Which of the following is a demographic computation that is ordinarily
      preferred because it gives more useful information for appropriate questions?
      A)   The crude birth rate
      B)   The age-specific growth rate
      C)   The neonatal impact rate
      D)   The fertility rate
      E)   The gross reproduction rate

Correct: B   Page: 557 Scramble Range: ALL
60.   The net population gain (or loss) divided by the size of the population is the
      A)   uncontrolled birth rate.
      B)   growth rate.
      C)   controlled increase rate.
      D)   reproduction/replacement rate.
      E)   balance equation.

Correct: C   Page: 557 Scramble Range: ALL
61.   For any given year, the net population gain (or loss) depends on only three
      factors or variables. Which of the following four alternatives is NOT one of
      them?
      A)   The increase (or decrease) due to migration
      B)   The increase (or decrease) in births
      C)   The increase (or decrease) due to febrility
      D)   The increase (or decrease) in deaths

Correct: C   Page: 557 Scramble Range: A-D
62.   If we were comparing the number of A's in two classes, one with 100 students
      and the other with 15 students, we should use
      A)   age-specific demographics.
      B)   attrition measures.
      C)   rates.
      D)   controls for causal order.
      E)   all of these
      F)   none of these are appropriate.

Correct: E   Page: 557 Scramble Range: ALL
63.   The _____ is computed by dividing the total number of births for a year by the total population for that year.
   A)   fecundity rate
   B)   refined reproduction rate
   C)   national birth rate
   D)   fertility rate
   E)   crude birth rate

Correct: A   Page: 557 Scramble Range: A-E
64.   Dividing the total number of deaths for a year by the total population for the year produces the _____ rate.
   A)   crude death
   B)   morbidity
   C)   refined morbidity
   D)   fertility
   E)   underreproduction
   F)   none of these

Correct: D   Page: 557 Scramble Range: ALL
65.   The number of births divided by the total number of women within a certain age span (usually 15 through 44) is called which of the following?
   A)   The expansion rate
   B)   The specific growth rate
   C)   The viable reproduction rate
   D)   The fertility rate
   E)   The potential reproduction rate
   F)   None of these

Correct: D   Page: 557 Scramble Range: NONE
66.   We generally use fertility rates rather than crude birth rates
   A)   to correct for variation in the size of the populations.
   B)   because the number of children women have during their lives varies from place to place and person to person.
   C)   to adjust for the variations in cultural norms regarding sexuality.
   D)   because the proportion of women who are of child-bearing age varies from place to place.
   E)   A and D.
   F)   none of these

Correct: D   Page: 558 Scramble Range: ALL
67.   The "age-specific death rate" is calculated by
   A)   determining the number of deaths in specific job categories, for each age category.
   B)   subtracting the number of deaths from the total number of persons in each job category.
   C)   dividing the number of deaths in the population by the number in the total population, by specific cause(s) of death.
   D)   separating the population into age categories and then computing the number of deaths per 1,000 of each age group.
   E)   calculating the death rate as ordinarily computed, but breaking it down by age, sex, occupation, income, and education.

68. According to Table 18-1, Contrasting Canada's Crude Birth Rate and Fertility Rate, which of the following is strongly but negatively correlated with the fertility rate in Canada?
    A)   Telephones per 1,000 population
    B)   Number of pets per 1,000 population
    C)   The total amount of water softener sold per province
    D)   The percent of the population using unbottled water
    E)   The approximate number of trees per square mile

Correct: A   Page: 559 Scramble Range: A-E
69. A birth cohort is defined as
    A)   all of the people born in a given time period, usually one year.
    B)   a calculation or computation to determine the subgroups in a population grouping.
    C)   a group of females who have had children in a given time period, usually one year.
    D)   a group of parents, married or unmarried, who have had children in a given time period, usually one year.
    E)   a group of parents who have had children by birth or by adoption, in a given time period, usually one year.
    F)   none of these

Correct: D   Page: 559 Scramble Range: ALL
70. Which of the following is TRUE about a birth cohort?
    A)   Other cohorts can affect it, but not as much as it can affect itself.
    B)   Its members split off into different age categories as time goes by.
    C)   It is affected to an extreme degree by sterility in the parental generation.
    D)   It can get smaller over time, but it cannot get any larger.
    E)   It can recruit members at a later date if necessary.

Correct: C   Page: 559 Scramble Range: ALL
71. According to your text, one main reason that France was nearly defeated in 1918 by the Germans was that
    A)   the French had been using too many young soldiers (age 18-25) and not enough experienced ones (age 25-35).
    B)   the French population pyramid was top-heavy.
    C)   Frenchmen killed in previous military efforts caused the French fertility rate to drop.
    D)   French troops had killed too many German women and not enough German men, with the result that the German troops were 10 percent greater in number than the French troops.
    E)   the French were significantly lagging behind the Germans in terms of going through the Demographic Transition.

Correct: A   Page: 561 Scramble Range: A-E
72. "Expansive," "stationary," and "constrictive" are types of
    A)   population structures.
    B)   birth control strategies.
    C)   mortality policies.
    D)   family policies.
    E)   demographic utopias.
    F)   none of these

Correct: F   Page: 561 Scramble Range: A-D
73. The term "stationary population structure"
     A) refers to fixed locations, such as hospitals, for childbirth.
     B) occurs when agricultural change allows expansion.
     C) develops when fertility falls below replacement level.
     D) has more younger than older people.
     E) all of these
     F) none of these

Correct: D   Page: 561 Scramble Range: ALL
74. Suppose this example reflects the situation in a population: Twelve
     grandparents have a total of ten children who become parents; those ten in
     the parental generation go on to have a total of five children in all. This would
     illustrate which of the three types of population structures discussed in your
     text?
     A) An altruistic structure
     B) A hyperfertility structure
     C) A retentive structure
     D) A constrictive structure
     E) An introverted structure

Correct: A   Page: 562 Scramble Range: ALL
75. The current population of the world is estimated to be approximately
     A) 5 billion.
     B) 16.5 billion.
     C) 950 million.
     D) 10 billion.
     E) 80 million.

Correct: A   Page: 562 Scramble Range: ALL
76. According to the text, the FIRST great shift in human population trends began
     about _____ years ago due to the _____.
     A) 10,000; development of agriculture
     B) 10,000; development of contraception
     C) 2,000; development of cities
     D) 1,500; development of mechanized warfare
     E) 1,000; emergence of Europe from the Dark Ages

Correct: C   Page: 562 Scramble Range: A-E
77. According to your text, the first population explosion occurred in Europe and
     North America as a result of
     A) more effective contraception.
     B) increased death rates.
     C) modernization.
     D) lower moribundity.
     E) prolonged national warfare.
     F) none of these

Correct: D   Page: 562 Scramble Range: ALL

78. According to your text, it is safe to say that the most deaths due to famine occurred in which of the following broad time periods?
    A) 1845-1895
    B) 1895-1920
    C) 1910-1930
    D) 1930-1965
    E) 1965-1985

Correct: D   Page: 563 Scramble Range: ALL

79. When the Black Death struck, about what percent of the population of Europe and Asia died as a direct result of it?
    A) 5 percent
    B) 10 percent
    C) 23 percent
    D) 40 percent
    E) 60 percent

Correct: A   Page: 563 Scramble Range: ALL

80. According to your text, shortly after the first Spanish expedition reached the New World, smallpox and measles epidemics wiped out about what percent of the inhabitants of Mexico and the West Indies?
    A) 75 percent
    B) 50 percent
    C) 40 percent
    D) 20 percent
    E) 15 percent

Correct: D   Page: 567 Scramble Range: ALL

81. While there was a high loss of life in the Thirty Years War in Northern Europe, the Taiping Rebellion in China (1851-64) had an even higher loss of life, with approximately how many killed?
    A) 4 million
    B) 5-6.5 million
    C) 8-10 million
    D) 20-30 million
    E) 55-60 million

Correct: E   Page: 567 Scramble Range: ALL

82. Thomas Malthus set forth his ideas on population in his book ESSAY ON POPULATION. In it, and in elaborations and refinements later, Malthus gave his explanation of why there is a tendency for the food supply to increase _____ while population increases _____.
    A) locally; regionally
    B) reasonably; unreasonably
    C) agronomically; naturally
    D) agronomically; geometrically
    E) arithmetically; exponentially

83. According to Adam Smith, writing in AN INQUIRY INTO THE NATURE AND CAUSES OF THE WEALTH OF NATIONS, human populations tend to grow or decline according to the
   A) availability of the necessities of life, especially food.
   B) financial well-being of the political body governing the population.
   C) extent to which mining, forestry, and other extractive industries have been constructed in an efficient manner.
   D) religious folkways of the people.
   E) amount of fit between religious and political folkways.

84. Malthus referred to war, divorce and famine as
   A) demographic drifts.
   B) fertility modifiers.
   C) positive checks.
   D) transition phenomena.
   E) all of these
   F) none of these

85. Malthus felt that available food supply served to limit expansion of human population unless the population controlled its own rate of increase. If the population did not exercise control over its own rate of increase, then
   A) preventive controls would begin to appear.
   B) positive checks would control the rate of increase.
   C) rate of emigration would necessarily have to expand.
   D) fecundity rate per capita would necessarily have to decrease.
   E) fecundity rate per capita would necessarily have to increase.

86. The Malthusian theory of population predicts populations will
   A) occur in recurring cycles of growth and decline.
   B) follow a long-range, unbroken upward trend.
   C) follow a long-range, unbroken downward trend.
   D) follow no particular discernable pattern or trend.
   E) eventually stabilize and exhibit a no-growth pattern.

87. Malthusian theory regards _____ as the fundamental variable that determines population size.
   A) individual motivation
   B) warfare
   C) religious and/or philosophical beliefs
   D) governmental planning of economic realities
   E) mortality

Correct: B   Page: 573 Scramble Range: A-E
88. The second population explosion can be understood as
A) the result of the lack of education.
B) an instance of cultural lag.
C) due to lack of access to contraceptives.
D) resulting from industrialization.
E) a consequence of infant mortality.
F) none of these

Correct: F   Page: 573 Scramble Range: NONE
89. The second great shift in population trends
A) was caused by the modernization of agriculture.
B) greatly increased population growth.
C) developed out of the Industrial Revolution.
D) was inconsistent with Malthusian theory.
E) A and C.
F) all of these
G) none of these

Correct: A   Page: 568 Scramble Range: A-D
90. The Industrial Revolution
A) first affected agriculture.
B) led to declining population growth.
C) produced the population changes predicted by Malthus.
D) marked the end of disease as a factor in population growth.
E) all of these

Correct: E   Page: 569 Scramble Range: ALL
91. The term _____ describes when the number of births each year equals the
number of deaths.
A) falling replication level
B) latent population decimation
C) manifest population decimation
D) zero-sum maintenance
E) replacement-level fertility

Correct: B   Page: 569 Scramble Range: ALL
92. _____ is achieved when each woman has slightly more than two children
and when the age structure adjusts accordingly.
A) Demographic equilibrium
B) Zero population growth
C) Population equilibrium
D) Growth/no-growth stabilization
E) Population mini-max

Correct: D   Page: 569 Scramble Range: ALL
93.   The third great shift in population was seen when
A)   the baby boom occurred in Canada, the United States, and other
industrialized nations.
B)   a "boomlet," or mini-boom, occurred in Europe and the United States after
the Vietnam War.
C)   the Third World nations began to exhibit lower fertility rates.
D)   fertility started to decline in the more modernized nations that went
through the Industrial Revolution.
E)   the lower fertility rates of the more modernized nations spread to the less
modernized nations.

Correct: B   Page: 569 Scramble Range: ALL
94.   According to your text, a major factor in people deciding to have large
families, even in Europe today, is
A)   the need to have many people working to bring income into the family.
B)   to have many children in case infant and childhood mortality removes
some.
C)   attempting to influence the political process by overreproducing voters of
one's own political preference.
D)   ignorance about the existence and availability of contraception.
E)   fear about the long-term consequences of contraception.

Correct: E   Page: 569 Scramble Range: A-E
95.   According to the text, a major factor motivating people to have large families
is
A)   the high value placed on emotional relationships within families.
B)   the desire to create many political alliances between families.
C)   secularism.
D)   antinatal norms.
E)   fear that some children will die before reaching adulthood.
F)   none of these

Correct: A   Page: 569 Scramble Range: ALL
96.   According to Kingsley Davis's "demographic transition theory," a main reason
that modernization naturally leads to lower fertility is that
A)   children cease to be an economic asset and become an economic burden.
B)   women's option to be employed brings satisfactions other than family life.
C)   men feel less obligated to marry their sexual partners, and birth control
makes marriages consensual rather than obligatory.
D)   couples more strongly prefer companionate relationships.
E)   modern life is so filled with insecurities that many couples defer child-
bearing until later in life.

Correct: C   Page: 570 Scramble Range: ALL
97. Anthropologists have found that techniques for limiting fertility
A) have historically been used by men, but their use by women is a relatively recent phenomenon.
B) have historically been urged by religious officials, and only recently has this been reversed.
C) have been known and often practiced in even very primitive societies.
D) in primitive societies produced such heightened mortality that only in the recent past have fertility-limiting practices or devices been used.
E) are responsible for vastly increasing the maternal mortality rate when they are used in an unsupervised way in Africa and Asia.

Correct: E   Page: 570 Scramble Range: ALL
98. Demographers have suggested a number of thresholds of modernization that must be crossed before fertility is substantially reduced. Which of the following is NOT one of those thresholds?
A) At least 70 percent of adults can read.
B) Infant mortality falls to 65 deaths per 1,000 infants.
C) More than half of the persons from age 5 to 19 are enrolled in school.
D) The average life expectancy reaches 60 years.
E) Per capita gross national product reaches $5,500.

Correct: D   Page: 570 Scramble Range: A-D
99. Demographic transition occurred because of
A) changes in contraceptive technology.
B) increased fecundity among Western women.
C) changes in agricultural technology.
D) the increased real cost of children.
E) all of these
F) none of these

Correct: E   Page: 570 Scramble Range: A-D
100. When we find a low fertility rate in a country, we expect to find
A) a lower proportion of the population working in agriculture.
B) a lower child mortality rate.
C) a higher life expectancy.
D) a higher literacy rate.
E) all of these
F) none of these

Correct: C   Page: 570 Scramble Range: A-D
101. When we find a low fertility rate in a country, we expect to find
A) a predominantly agrarian economy.
B) a high child mortality rate.
C) a high life expectancy.
D) that the wanted fertility is lower than the actual fertility rate.
E) all of these
F) none of these

Correct: A   Page: 573 Scramble Range: ALL
102. The most rapid decline in fertility rate for a large population occurred in
   A) rural China in the 1970s.
   B) rural Canada in the 1850s.
   C) the western United States in the 1950s.
   D) the Soviet Union in the 1790s.
   E) urban Japan in the 1600s.

Correct: F   Page: 574 Scramble Range: A-D
103. India's fertility rate
   A) has continued to increase.
   B) is now below replacement level.
   C) is the primary cause of recent famines.
   D) has dropped because of coercive government policies that make a third child illegal.
   E) all of these
   F) none of these

Correct: A   Page: 575 Scramble Range: A-D
104. Table 18-4, Fertility in Selected Nations: 1965-1991, shows that
   A) fertility has dramatically declined in most countries in Asia and Latin America.
   B) fertility has declined most in the countries of sub-Sahara Africa.
   C) fertility has increased dramatically in North African countries.
   D) the largest countries have the lowest declines in fertility.
   E) all of these

Correct: A   Page: 576 Scramble Range: A-D
105. Your text points to what major factor to account for China's rapid decline in fertility?
   A) Dramatic growth in the Gross National Product.
   B) Reduction of the percent employed in agriculture to about 30%.
   C) Foreign aid from the United States.
   D) The high percentage (80%) of those aged 5-19 who are in school.
   E) All of these
   F) None of these

Correct: A   Page: 577 Scramble Range: A-D
106. The fertility rate increases when
   A) the percent not employed in agriculture declines.
   B) the percent of high school graduates increases.
   C) the percent of farms with telephones increases.
   D) the GNP increases.
   E) all of these
   F) none of these

Correct: C   Page: 577 Scramble Range: A-D
107.   The term "numeracy about children" refers to
A)   demographic predictions about the size of the school age population.
B)   the fertility threshold necessary to reduce infant mortality rates.
C)   people having a clear notion of what size family they would like to have.
D)   the process of calculating the economic costs of decreased infant mortality.
E)   none of these

Correct: C   Page: 577 Scramble Range: A-C
108.   When people can answer questions about how many children they would like to have, they have
A)   demographic transition.
B)   fertility.
C)   numeracy about children.
D)   all of these
E)   none of these

Correct: A   Page: 578 Scramble Range: A-D
109.   What has led population experts to say the "Contraception is the best form of contraception"?
A)   The difference between wanted fertility and actual fertility.
B)   The failure of demographic transition theory to predict fertility increases in sub-Saharan Africa.
C)   The continuing increase in population in industrialized countries.
D)   The success of coercive birth control policies in China and India.
E)   All of these
F)   None of these

Correct: D   Page: 578 Scramble Range: A-D
110.   Wanted fertility refers to
A)   planned pregnancies.
B)   goals to increase the productivity of crop land.
C)   the problem of people in poor nations wanting to have more children than they can afford.
D)   the number of children a couple wishes to have.
E)   All of these
F)   None of these

Correct: B   Page: 579 Scramble Range: A-D
111.   A major reason why the fertility rates have not declined in sub-Saharan African nations is that
A)   wanted fertility is high.
B)   contraceptives are difficult to obtain.
C)   economic development has been slow.
D)   there is a high proportion of people engaged in agriculture.
E)   all of these
F)   none of these

Correct: D   Page: 580 Scramble Range: ALL
112. The key to understanding population lies in the most basic premise of micro sociology:
   A) family relationships are society's most important primary group.
   B) conflict is inherent in human behavior.
   C) small groups are more harmonious than are large groups.
   D) human behavior is based on choice.
   E) small-group behavior has consequences for society.

Correct: C   Page: 577 Scramble Range: ALL
113. According to your text, which of the following has a strong, negative correlation with the fertility rate in China?
   A) Having 5 or more rooms in dwelling units
   B) Reserving 1-2 days per week for the purpose of family leisure
   C) Percentage of farms with TVs
   D) Amount of national budget spent on military defense
   E) Number of light bulbs in use in the average household

Correct: C   Page: 579 Scramble Range: A-D
114. A society in which the largest birth cohorts are the oldest
   A) is experiencing population growth.
   B) have zero or stable population growth.
   C) has a fertility rate below replacement level.
   D) all of these

Correct: D   Page: 582 Scramble Range: ALL
115. Your text ends the chapter on population and demography with which of the following general conclusions about the future of population growth in the world?
   A) Further population reductions are unlikely in Second World nations.
   B) In Third World nations, fertility reductions seem unwise unless mortality rates also can be reduced.
   C) It seems unlikely that nations such as Bangladesh will ever be able to increase agricultural production significantly.
   D) It is probable that predictions of worldwide famine have been overly pessimistic; fertility will probably continue to decline and food supplies increase.
   E) The world is headed for a famine of global proportions, possibly accompanied by wars fought for food rather than for economic gain.

Topic 6: Baby Boom

True/False

Correct: F   Page: 584
1. The baby boom discussed in your text refers to a sudden decline in the birth rate of the United States.

Correct: T   Page: 584
2. The baby boom discussed in Special Topic 6 refers to a relatively sudden increase in the birth rate.

Correct: F   Page: 584
3. The baby boom discussed in your text's Special Topic 6 was interesting in part because it occurred in the United States but did not occur in Canada.

Correct: T   Page: 584
4. The baby boom discussed in your text's Special Topic 6 occurred in Canada as well as in the United States.

Correct: F   Page: 584
5. The baby boom discussed in your text's Special Topic 6 turned out to be brief and unimportant, an excellent example of change that is expected to be dramatic but ends by having little effect: an anticlimax change.

Correct: T   Page: 586
6. The baby boomers tended to have lower--not higher--SAT scores than previous generations.

Correct: T   Page: 586
7. The dramatic effects of the baby boom continued as the babies moved through the life cycle.

Correct: F   Page: 586
8. According to the text, the Levi Strauss company laid off 3,200 workers because of excess production capacity. The baby boomers were too tall and too slim for the jeans the company made.

Multiple Choice

Correct: D   Page: 584 Scramble Range: A-E
9. The baby boom resulted in an increased birth rate that
    A) was concentrated in the working class and in the managerial class.
    B) overwhelmingly involved Roman Catholics and Baptists.
    C) was able to fill the previously underpopulated school systems.
    D) remained high for almost twenty years.
    E) has now almost disappeared in regard to its effects on society.
    F) all of these

Correct: B   Page: 584 Scramble Range: A-E
10. The baby boom discussed in Special Topic 6 in your text occurred
    A) at and during the Great Depression.
    B) following World War II.
    C) during the Kennedy presidency.
    D) during the Vietnam War.
    E) just before the Carter presidency.
    F) none of these

Correct: A   Page: 586 Scramble Range: ALL
11. According to the text, which of the following was lower for the baby boomers than for previous generations?
    A) SAT scores
    B) Interest in self-improvement
    C) Overall life-satisfaction
    D) Car ownership
    E) Available health care

Correct: D   Page: 586 Scramble Range: A-E
12. Which of the following has characterized the baby boomers?
    A) They have a higher fertility rate than their parents' generation.
    B) They have a lower suicide rate than persons lower in the class system.
    C) They have lower levels of education than their parents have.
    D) They achieved lower Scholastic Aptitude Test (SAT) scores than previous generations.
    E) They showed a preference for college majors in the humanities.
    F) None of these

Correct: A   Page: 564 Scramble Range: ALL
13. According to your text, the baby boomers are less likely than either those younger or older to
    A) consider themselves Republicans.
    B) listen to records and play video games.
    C) have an interest in high-paying jobs.
    D) have an interest in politics.
    E) be concerned about nuclear disarmament.
    F) none of these

Correct: F   Page: 564 Scramble Range: A-D
14. Compared to those who are younger, American baby boomers
    A) smoke less.
    B) favor capital punishment less.
    C) want larger families.
    D) attend church more.
    E) all of these
    F) none of these

Correct: C   Page: 588 Scramble Range: ALL
15. The text ends its discussion of the baby boomers by pointing out that they
    A) have had more social mobility than other people have had.
    B) have initiated more liberal social reforms than generations before them.
    C) have been a source of stress for their society.
    D) are so overeducated that it is difficult to find jobs for them.
    E) are more alienated than generations before them.

Chapter 19: Urbanization

True/False

Correct: F   Page: 591
1. Ancient Rome was the first urban society.

Correct: T   Page: 591
2. Modernization of farming makes urbanization possible.

Correct: T   Page: 593
3. Historically, city size has been limited by transportation.

Correct: F   Page: 593
4. Preindustrial cities had considerably less of a problem with pollution than cities do today.

Correct: T   Page: 593
5. Preindustrial cities were piled high with garbage and filth.

Correct: T   Page: 595
6. In seventeenth century cities, more than half of the children died before age 6.

Correct: F   Page: 597
7. Preindustrial cities were safer to walk in at night than most major American cities today.

Correct: T   Page: 597
8. Preindustrial cities existed largely because of their economic functions.

Correct: T   Page: 598
9. Preindustrial cities had even higher proportions of strangers and newcomers than do most modern cities.

Correct: F   Page: 598
10. In 1900 a majority of the United States population still lived on farms.

Correct: F   Page: 599
11. Modern farming methods require less labor, but they do not get as much production from a given amount of land as can be gained by use of "old-fashioned" methods.

Correct: T   Page: 599
12. The modern farmer can feed almost fifty people.

Correct: F   Page: 599
13. One major reason for the increase in farm productivity in the last century has been the willingness of farmers to work longer hours.

Correct: F   Page: 600
14. In 1980 it took only half as much labor as it did in 1900 to produce a bushel of wheat.

Correct: T   Page: 600
15. In 1900 it took more than thirty times as much labor to produce a bushel of wheat as it did in 1980.

Correct: F   Page: 603
16. According to demographers, a "metropolis" is a city with more than 50,000 people.

Correct: T   Page: 604
17. The fixed-rail metropolis is highly centralized.

Correct: F   Page: 604
18. The fixed-rail metropolis tends to grow outward, evenly in all directions.

Correct: F   Page: 605
19. The freeway metropolis tends to resemble a huge spider or octopus.

Correct: T   Page: 605
20. The fixed-rail metropolis tends to have a very dense commercial center.

Correct: F   Page: 605
21. The fixed-rail metropolis is found primarily in the western United States.

Correct: T   Page: 606
22. The freeway metropolis tends to grow outward, evenly in all directions.

Correct: F   Page: 606
23. The freeway metropolis tends to be highly centralized.

Correct: F   Page: 606
24. The fixed-rail metropolis is the style of city most Americans say they prefer to live in.

Correct: T   Page: 606
25. The freeway metropolis is less dense than the fixed-rail metropolis.

Correct: T   Page: 607
26. The freeway metropolis is especially suited to the development of shopping centers.

Correct: F   Page: 607
27. The freeway metropolis is becoming outmoded.

Correct: T   Page: 607
28. The freeway metropolis is the style of city most Americans seem to prefer.

Correct: T   Page: 608
29. The theory of ethnic succession argues that integration will occur between groups with the same average status.

Correct: F   Page: 608
30. The theory of ethnic succession predicts that once a neighborhood has become associated with a subordinate racial group, it will stay that way.

Correct: F   Page: 608
31.   The theory of ethnic succession cannot account for recent changes in the degree to which African-Americans live in segregated neighborhoods.

Correct: F   Page: 610
32.   There has been no significant decline in the degree to which African-Americans live in segregated neighborhoods.

Correct: T   Page: 609
33.   The theory of ethnic succession recognizes that cities are as much process as structure.

Correct: T   Page: 614
34.   "Gemeinschaft" is a term used to describe small cohesive communities.

Correct: F   Page: 614
35.   In the gemeinschaft community people tend to be strangers to one another.

Correct: T   Page: 614
36.   In URBANISM AS A WAY OF LIFE, Wirth argued that city life forces the individual to be impersonal and withdrawn from others.

Correct: F   Page: 617
37.   Research shows that urbanism leads to a lack of close attachments and, hence, to high rates of deviant behavior.

Correct: F   Page: 617
38.   People who live in dense neighborhoods are more prone to alcoholism and mental illness.

Correct: F   Page: 617
39.   Studies of crowding found that dense neighborhoods produce many pathological effects, including alcoholism and mental illness.

Correct: F   Page: 619
40.   Studies of crowding found that people in crowded homes formed more intimate relations with one another.

Correct: F   Page: 619
41.   Studies of crowding lead us to expect that current trends in housing probably will lead to more people having poorer mental health and more negligent child care.

Correct: T   Page: 619
42.   Studies of crowding found substantial micro effects of crowding.

Correct: F   Page: 592
43.   People in small towns and rural areas are more apt than people in cities to participate in religion.

Correct: T   Page: 592
44.   People in cities are more apt than people in small towns and rural areas to participate in religion.

Reference Key: STORY19.1
A sociologist found that there was a strong positive correlation between the extent of residential crowding (more than one person per room in households) and various forms of deviance--especially interpersonal violence such as assault and homicide.

Correct: F   Page: 619   Refer to: STORY19.1
45. This finding is consistent with mass society theory.

Correct: T   Page: ResProc   Refer to: STORY19.1
46. "Violence," in this research, is a concept.
NOTE: Cumulative question.

Correct: F   Page: Ch3   Refer to: STORY19.1
47. The dependent variable here is crowding.
NOTE: Cumulative question.

Correct: F   Page: 618   Refer to: STORY19.1
48. This suggests a strong positive relationship between modernization and violence.

Correct: F   Page: Ch7   Refer to: STORY19.1
49. This finding might be used to support the strain theory of deviance.
NOTE: Cumulative question.

Correct: T   Page: Ch7   Refer to: STORY19.1
50. This research might be used to support the control theory of deviance.
NOTE: Somewhat cumulative question.

Correct: F   Page: 619   Refer to: STORY19.1
51. This finding helps us to understand the concentration of violence in urban centers in the United States

Correct: F   Page: 619   Refer to: STORY19.1
52. This finding suggests that we will see an increase in interpersonal violence as cities continue to grow.

Multiple Choice

Correct: D   Page: 691 Scramble Range: ALL
53.   About what percent of people in the United States are urban residents today?
   A)   16 percent
   B)   38 percent
   C)   55 percent
   D)   77 percent
   E)   88 percent

Correct: B   Page: 593 Scramble Range: ALL
54.   Which of the following is characteristic of preindustrial cities?
   A)   Quiet, populated by long-time residents, and oriented to commerce
   B)   Small, filthy, packed with people, disorderly, dangerous
   C)   Ruled by religion, of small to moderate size, very quiet, stable
   D)   Not very commercial, of moderate size, Gemeinschaft-dominated, with many animals
   E)   Oriented toward defense of the city, of moderate size, business-dominated, and containing few minority groups

Correct: C   Page: 593 Scramble Range: ALL
55.   According to the text, the population of ancient Rome grew as large as
   A)   75,000.
   B)   100,000.
   C)   500,000.
   D)   800,000.
   E)   1,300,000.

Correct: E   Page: 593 Scramble Range: ALL
56.   Your text provides Table 19-1, Population of Major Cities in Preindustrial Europe, which shows that between the fourteenth and sixteenth centuries, the largest cities listed in the table--London, Paris, and Rome--had populations in which of the following ranges?
   A)   1.2-1.5 million
   B)   700,000-1 million
   C)   500,000-700,000
   D)   80,000-100,000
   E)   35,000-59,000

Correct: E   Page: 593 Scramble Range: A-E
57.   A major reason why preindustrial cities remained small was
   A)   relatively continuous raids by hostile forces.
   B)   the low fertility rate of urban areas.
   C)   there were too many cities for the population, so each city was smaller.
   D)   the in-migration tended to equal the out-migration.
   E)   poor transportation for food supply.
   F)   all of these

Correct: F   Page: 593 Scramble Range: NONE
58. Preindustrial cities were limited in size by
    A) disease.
    B) poor transportation.
    C) low agricultural productivity.
    D) reliance on nearby farms.
    E) A and C.
    F) all of these

Correct: D   Page: 593 Scramble Range: ALL
59. In preindustrial cities, garbage came to be a problem. It was hailed as a major step forward when cities began to
    A) give stiff fines for those littering the public areas with garbage.
    B) hire crews of the poorest people to clear the garbage away at night.
    C) create the occupational category of garbage collector, which was a new status at the time.
    D) keep a herd of pigs that ate the garbage in the streets during the night.
    E) invent the equivalent of sewers at the side of streets and to sweep the garbage into those openings.

Correct: C   Page: 594 Scramble Range: A-E
60. Which of the following was specifically mentioned by your text as a major reason for the high population density of preindustrial cities?
    A) The population of cities' surrounding areas tended to be small.
    B) Most preindustrial cities tended to have multistoried dwelling units.
    C) The cities were surrounded by massive walls for defense.
    D) The populations of the cities felt that there was safety in numbers.
    E) Occupational efficiency was so low that only a large population was able to provide the work needed to maintain a society.
    F) All of these

Correct: D   Page: 595 Scramble Range: ALL
61. In seventeenth century London _____ of the infants and children died before age 6.
    A) almost a third
    B) fewer than 10 percent
    C) over three-quarters
    D) more than half
    E) close to 80 percent

Correct: E   Page: 597 Scramble Range: ALL
62. There were several reasons why people were attracted to preindustrial cities, in spite of the drawbacks of living in such cities. Which of the following is NOT one of those reasons mentioned in the text?
    A) The pursuit of vice
    B) Adventure
    C) Economic attractions
    D) The pursuit of new ideas and innovations
    E) Relative safety of the city, compared with the countryside

63.   About what percent of the population of the United States lived on a farm in
      1961 (Table 19-2)?
      A)   8 percent
      B)   27 percent
      C)   36 percent
      D)   48 percent
      E)   58 percent

64.   Which of the following categories of people constantly replenished city
      populations in preindustrial cities?
      A)   Adventuresome, single, young adults
      B)   The offspring of the poor and working classes of the city
      C)   Slaves, imported by free immigrants, who were later abandoned and
           became free citizens
      D)   Refugees from warfare in surrounding areas and/or nations
      E)   Intact family units seeking an opportunity for a stable life style

65.   _____ made it necessary for people to live in cities.
      A)   Lack of food and shelter
      B)   The problem of inheritance
      C)   The enclosure movement
      D)   Industrialization
      E)   Demographic transition
      F)   None of these

66.   Your text states that _____ is the result of _____ and therefore is
      happening around the world.
      A)   suburbanization; urbanization
      B)   industrialization; urbanization
      C)   urbanization; industrialization
      D)   urbanization; cross-cultural contact
      E)   cross-cultural contact; urbanization

67.   According to your text, _____ requires _____ because it depends upon the
      coordinated activities of large numbers of specialized workers who must
      perform their tasks in a few central locations.
      A)   decentralization; specialization
      B)   urban mobility; mechanized transportation
      C)   industrialization; urbanization
      D)   urban education; mass media
      E)   urban education; similarity of backgrounds

68. The agricultural revolution in the United States came about from the application of science and engineering to farming. The MAJOR effect, according to the text, was
   A)   the swelling of the farm-dwelling population, because that is where the work was.
   B)   a huge reduction in the labor required for increased productivity.
   C)   a serious assault on the ecostructure that, though widely recognized, was ignored.
   D)   an increase in the fertility rate of rural-dwelling persons.
   E)   a decrease in the available foodstuffs in urban markets.
   F)   all of these

69. The agricultural revolution
   A)   allowed cities to grow.
   B)   was based in the willingness of farmers to work longer hours.
   C)   increased the numbers engaged in agriculture.
   D)   reflected increased fertility rate prior to demographic transition.
   E)   all of these
   F)   none of these

70. Your text discusses commercial production of eggs in the United States and Canada to illustrate which of these issues?
   A)   Increased efficiency in egg production
   B)   Vulnerability of farming to diseases of grain and livestock
   C)   Vulnerability of farming to periodic fluctuations in climate
   D)   Sensitivity of egg production to fluctuations in nations' abilities to compete on a small but nevertheless international market
   E)   Governmental intrusion into private commercial markets
   F)   All of these

71. Which of the following is most important for the existence of cities?
   A)   Social disorganization
   B)   Railroads
   C)   Tractors
   D)   Structural steel
   E)   All of these
   F)   None of these

72. Compared to 1980, it took approximately _____ labor to produce a bushel of wheat in 1900.
   A)   twice as much
   B)   half as much
   C)   five times as much
   D)   thirty times as much
   E)   the same amount of

Correct: C   Page: 600 Scramble Range: A-D
73. Industrialization required urbanization because
    A) new markets were necessary to support expansion of the economy.
    B) increased fertility required increased housing.
    C) of the need for specialization.
    D) the shortage of labor required a demographic transition.
    E) all of these
    F) none of these

Correct: A   Page: 600 Scramble Range: A-D
74. A division of labor to simplify production is called
    A) specialization.
    B) structural mobility.
    C) demographic crowding.
    D) urbanization.
    E) none of these

Correct: E   Page: 602 Scramble Range: A-E
75. American demographers classify a locale as which of the following if it has a population of more than 2,500?
    A) Metropolitan area
    B) Suburb
    C) Town
    D) Quasi-metropolis
    E) Urban place
    F) None of these

Correct: B   Page: 603 Scramble Range: NONE
76. According to the census bureau, a locale with more that 50,000 residents is called
    A) an SMSA.
    B) a city.
    C) a metropolis.
    D) a community.
    E) either A or C.

Correct: D   Page: 603 Scramble Range: A-C
77. Ennock is a community of 4,000 residents, most of whom work in a nearby community of nearly 85,000. Ennock is
    A) a metropolitan area.
    B) a central city.
    C) an SMSA.
    D) an urban place.
    E) part of a fixed rail metropolis.
    F) both D and E.

Correct: E   Page: 603 Scramble Range: ALL
78. In 1950 the concept of the _____ was created.
    A) CMCA
    B) DRGE
    C) URCT
    D) WREU
    E) SMSA

79. Your text discusses two types of metropolis. What is the basis for the distinction between the two?
    A)   The type of occupations dominant in each
    B)   The amount of land use given over to industry and to residential use
    C)   The philosophy underlying the founding of the city at its time of origin
    D)   The type of transportation system in the city as it began to grow
    E)   Whether or not the local geography imposed restrictions on the city's growth

Correct: B   Page: 605 Scramble Range: ALL
80. When the earliest large American cities began their expansion, they had a strong tendency to
    A)   expand rather evenly in all directions, so that they looked like spider webs.
    B)   expand unevenly along the rail lines, so that they looked like spiders.
    C)   expand into different urban regions that were more planned than today's cities are.
    D)   take into account the artistic or aesthetic aspects of architecture more than is the case in modern society.
    E)   live in peaceful coexistence with the surrounding rural environment because the city depended more on the rural activities..

Correct: C   Page: 605 Scramble Range: ALL
81. In the earliest large American cities with heavy reliance on rail lines, the focal point of the city was
    A)   political activity.
    B)   what people at the time called "Millionaire's Row."
    C)   the center of the city.
    D)   where the city was encroaching into the rural area.
    E)   the artistic, musical, and other aesthetic activities of the city.

Correct: D   Page: 606 Scramble Range: ALL
82. Which of the following helped to create cities that were spread outward more evenly and were more decentralized?
    A)   The advent of inter-regional government
    B)   The invention of the telephone
    C)   The need to expand westward when land ran out, so that the Great Frontier began to become a productive part of American culture/society
    D)   Cars, trucks, freeways
    E)   Taxation by geographic representation

Correct: C   Page: 606 Scramble Range: ALL
83. Although decentralization has caused substantial changes and/or upheaval in the earliest large American cities, it has NOT caused such change and/or upheaval in many _____ cities because they tend to _____.
    A)   European; have a stronger tradition
    B)   Great Lakes area; be shaped by geography
    C)   western United States; be newer cities
    D)   southern United States; be more relaxed
    E)   Canadian; have more space for growth

84.   Over the years, there has been a demonstrable trend for the metropolis to
      become
      A)   more violent.
      B)   a place of more intense land use.
      C)   more vibrant in its central core area.
      D)   more decentralized.
      E)   less precarious in terms of its tax base.
      F)   none of these

85.   According to your text, Los Angeles, California, has
      A)   the largest central city core of any city in the United States.
      B)   the second largest central city core, outranked only by New York, New
           York.
      C)   no one downtown area; it has at least eight downtowns.
      D)   what demographers call "vertical distribution" of its dense population.
      E)   a downtown area shaped more by waterfront and original rail lines than by
           other physical features.

86.   Ahamo (population 110,000) doesn't really have a city center--it has four or five
      commercial areas scattered around the city. Ahamo
      A)   is more likely to be in the Western rather than the Eastern United States.
      B)   is a freeway metropolis.
      C)   is probably a relatively new city.
      D)   is likely to have industries concentrated in its suburban areas.
      E)   all of these
      F)   none of these

87.   In 1972 the Gallup Poll asked Americans: "If you could live anywhere you
      wanted to, would you prefer a city, a suburban area, a small town, or a farm?"
      What percent preferred to live in a city?
      A)   4 percent
      B)   13 percent
      C)   34 percent
      D)   52 percent
      E)   76 percent

88.   When the 1972 Gallup Poll asked Americans who wanted to live on a farm or
      in a small town how far from a major urban area they would like to be, three
      out of four said that they would like to live
      A)   just outside the metropolis city limits.
      B)   as far away as possible, but would like to be on a main freeway or
           highway leading to the city.
      C)   within one hour commuting distance from the city, but would not want to
           be near a main traffic road because of crime commuting out from the city.
      D)   within a ten-minute drive from the city.
      E)   no more than thirty miles from the city.

Correct: D   Page: 608 Scramble Range: ALL
89.   Park and Burgess proposed the "theory of ethnic succession," in which they
      argued that when a particular ethnic group _____, at that point their
      ethnicity will not be a barrier in choosing where to live.
      A)   achieves at least the midpoint of educational achievement
      B)   becomes genetically invisible in a genotype sense
      C)   becomes politically dominant over those ethnic groups remaining in the
           pariah groups
      D)   becomes economically equal to the majority group
      E)   becomes known as a cultural elite (music, art, science, literature)

Correct: B   Page: 608 Scramble Range: A-E
90.   Park and Burgess proposed that racial and ethnic segregation is primarily
      based on
      A)   religious differences.
      B)   economic and status differences.
      C)   the old neighborhoods of the fixed rail metropolis.
      D)   patterns of sex ratios among various groups.
      E)   cultural lag.
      F)   all of these

Correct: A   Page: 609 Scramble Range: ALL
91.   In their attempt to refine Park and Burgess's theory of ethnic succession,
      Guest and Weed were able to demonstrate that as _____ disappear, so do
      racial and ethnic neighborhoods.
      A)   economic status inequalities
      B)   visible skin color differences
      C)   occupational specializations
      D)   inexpensive methods of transportation to and from ethnic neighborhoods
      E)   urban newspapers published in foreign languages

Correct: E   Page: 609 Scramble Range: ALL
92.   In comparing 1960 and 1970 data, Guest and Weed found that all
      neighborhoods had generally become more integrated, but that which of the
      following had made the greatest gains in terms of being integrated into urban
      American neighborhoods?
      A)   Filipinos
      B)   Hispanics
      C)   Mexican-Americans only
      D)   Northeastern Europeans
      E)   Asians

Correct: D   Page: 609 Scramble Range: A-D
93.   In their examination of racial and ethnic neighborhoods, Guest and Weed
      A)   found that neighborhoods disintegrated as individual families became
           more affluent and moved away.
      B)   found that neighborhoods tend to shift quickly in fixed rail cities.
      C)   found that cities are very similar in the extent of racial and ethnic
           segregation.
      D)   found that the economic status of the group was more important than the
           economic status of individuals.
      E)   all of these
      F)   none of these

94.   According to the text, _____ is the most racially segregated of major American cities.
A)   Seattle
B)   Houston
C)   St. Louis
D)   New Orleans
E)   Chicago

95.   Guest and Weed suggest that one reason western cities tend to be more integrated no matter which ethnic or racial group is examined is that western cities
A)   have a cowboy mentality, which encourages upward mobility.
B)   are more affluent.
C)   are newer.
D)   are more urban.
E)   are dominated by frontier psychology, which stresses self-reliance.

96.   Karl Taeuber studied growth and decline in American urban areas using the index of dissimilarity. According to Taeuber, integration is occurring primarily as a result of
A)   both majority and minority groups moving into totally new areas.
B)   African-Americans moving into suburbs or neighborhoods populated mainly by whites.
C)   whites moving once again into predominantly African-American central city areas.
D)   whites moving from the predominantly African-American northern cities into southern cities.
E)   changing methods of calculating levels or degrees of integration.
F)   all of these

97.   Which of the following would be a very good example of what Ferdinand Tonnies meant by the concept "Gesellschaft"?
A)   A group of very close sorority members who have known one another since they have been in school
B)   A type of economic production characteristic of a preindustrial society
C)   A large urban post office with many workers, each of whom stays for a while and then leaves to take another job elsewhere
D)   The people in a Texas county who gather together for the annual family reunion, to exchange memories and take photographs of one another
E)   The type of political system that characterizes rapidly industrializing nation-states such as Uganda and the Cameroons

Correct: C Page: 614 Scramble Range: ALL
98. "Gemeinschaft" and "Gesellschaft" are concepts suggested by Ferdinand Tonnies. In Tonnies' view of Gesellschaft and Gemeinschaft, "Gemeinschaft" refers to which of the following?
    A) A style of urban government in which the outlying areas are in control of the central urban core areas
    B) There is political cooperation based on ethnic/racial communication
    C) Small groups with common values and agreement, as in the case of farming villages
    D) The extent to which occupations are a part of the self-concept, as in the case of coal miners
    E) The level of aggregate formation in human populations

Correct: B Page: 614 Scramble Range: ALL
99. The French sociologist Durkheim believed that conformity to the norms is caused by _____: thus _____, by destroying _____, destroys _____.
    A) folkways; mores; attachments; family
    B) attachments; urbanization; attachments; norms
    C) folkways; attachments; mores; norms
    D) community; gentrification; agreements; laws
    E) motivation; gentrification; communities; society

Correct: E Page: 614 Scramble Range: ALL
100. According to Wirth's URBANISM AS A WAY OF LIFE, urban interaction is impersonal because of
    A) frequent residential relocation.
    B) the naturally selfish orientation of urbanites.
    C) urban economies' capitalist orientation.
    D) urbanites' diminished need for any personal relationships.
    E) frequent interaction with complete strangers.

Correct: D Page: 616 Scramble Range: ALL
101. The view that many of the mentally ill eventually find themselves in the poorest areas of cities after they become ill because of their inability to get and hold jobs is known as the _____ explanation for this phenomenon.
    A) urban conductivity
    B) deferred mobility loss
    C) interclass
    D) social drift
    E) status loss

Correct: D Page: 616 Scramble Range: A-D
102. The problem with anomie or mass society theories is
    A) time order.
    B) spuriousness.
    C) the link between attachments and deviance.
    D) the link between attachments and urbanization.
    E) all of these
    F) none of these

Correct: D   Page: 618 Scramble Range: ALL
103.   In discussing anomie theories of urban life, your text describes the effects of crowding and concludes that population density has no effect on people at the _____ but does have an effect at the _____.
A)   marketplace; polling place
B)   job; residence
C)   structural level; functional level
D)   macro level; micro level
E)   point of personal equilibrium; social equilibrium level

Correct: A   Page: 619 Scramble Range: ALL
104.   When Gove, Hughes, and Galle tested anomie theory in the urban environment, what they found suggests that crowding can have negative effects on which of the following?
A)   The individual family unit
B)   Leisure activities in public places (beaches, parks, toboggan runs, and the like)
C)   The polling places where people vote
D)   The productivity of the occupational or work environment
E)   The content of the mass media, such as television, radio, and so on

Chapter 20: The Organizational Age

True/False

Correct: T   Page: 623
1. The need for formal organizations stemmed mainly from an increase in the size of organizations.

Correct: T   Page: 624
2. Formal organizations are often called "rational organizations."

Correct: F   Page: 624
3. The first formal organizations were created during the seventeenth century.

Correct: T   Page: 625
4. The Prussian army trained officers to take similar actions in similar situations.

Correct: F   Page: 625
5. The Prussian army left details of organization--such as what equipment to issue--to unit commanders.

Correct: T   Page: 627
6. Functional divisions are created by dividing an organization so as to separate major tasks into their own units.

Correct: F   Page: 627
7. Vertical integration means to promote senior managers up through the ranks from humble beginnings.

Correct: F   Page: 630
8. Swift and Co. replaced the spoils system of meat distribution.

Correct: F   Page: 630
9. Agrarian societies require more control than modern societies do.

Correct: T   Page: 630
10. Growth of government was a part of modernization.

Correct: F   Page: 531
11. Civil service systems are similar to spoils systems of government service.

Correct: T   Page: 631
12. In a spoils system, government employees are prevented from making a career of government service.

Correct: T   Page: 631
13. According to Weber, bureaucracies have written rules and records.

Correct: T   Page: 632
14. According to Weber, bureaucracies have appointment and promotion based on merit.

Correct: F   Page: 632
15. According to Weber, bureaucracies have geographic divisions.

Correct: F   Page: 632
16. According to Weber, bureaucracies have informal rather than formal systems of authority.

Correct: F   Page: 632
17. According to Weber, "bureaucracy" means by definition "inefficient procedures."

Correct: F   Page: 632
18. According to Weber's definition of the term, "bureaucracy" must be typified by a contempt for the public.

Correct: F   Page: 632
19. According to Weber, bureaucracies have government regulation.

Correct: T   Page: 632
20. According to Weber, bureaucracies have functional divisions.

Correct: F   Page: 633
21. Attempts to improve an organization by changing its organizational blueprint would reflect the natural system approach to organizational analysis.

Correct: T   Page: 633
22. According to the natural system approach, the overriding goal of organizations is to survive.

Correct: F   Page: 634
23. Goal displacement is the process of setting realistic management objectives.

Correct: T   Page: 634
24. Differences in interests, such as among managers, owners, and workers, can be understood as goal conflicts.

Correct: T   Page: 634
25. Management and workers rarely share the same goals.

Correct: F   Page: 636
26. When people design organizations they need to choose between the rational system model and the natural system model.

Correct: T   Page: 638
27. Developments at the Du Pont Company showed that functional divisions work well when a company pursues a limited range of activities.

Correct: T   Page: 638
28. Developments at the Du Pont Company showed that functional divisions break down when firms become highly diversified.

Correct: T   Page: 638
29. Developments at the Du Pont Company showed that diversity could be overcome by autonomous divisions.

Correct: F   Page: 638
30. Developments at the Du Pont Company showed that centralized authority could make organizations more effective.

Correct: T   Page: 639
31. Blau's theory of administrative growth predicts that the more units in an organization, the larger the administrative component.

Correct: F   Page: 639
32. Blau's theory of administrative growth concludes that the larger the organization, the more efficient it can be.

Correct: T   Page: 640
33. Blau's theory of administrative growth helps explain the decentralization of modern organizations.

Correct: F   Page: 640
34. The main principle of current management is consolidation and centralization of authority.

Correct: F   Page: 641
35. According to Thompson, the less important a decision, the less willing people in an organization will be to use discretion.

Correct: T   Page: 641
36. Discretion is the freedom to make choices and decisions.

Correct: F   Page: 641
37. Thompson argues that the formal systems in organizations are more centralized than the natural systems.

Correct: T   Page: 642
38. Lack of clear goals and objectives is one of the weaknesses of government organizations.

Reference Key: STORY20.1
General Motors is a large corporation engaged in a variety of business and manufacturing enterprises. Chevrolet, one of GM's divisions, is fairly autonomous. The head of Chevrolet has a variety of divisions reporting to him: production, sales, accounting, finance, and so on.

Correct: F   Page: 633 Refer to: STORY20.1
39. This describes, in part, GM's natural system.

Correct: T   Page: 633 Refer to: STORY20.1
40. This describes, in part, GM's formal system.

Correct: T   Page: 610   Refer to: STORY20.1
41. GM is an example of a diversified organization.

Correct: F   Page: 631   Refer to: STORY20.1
42.   GM is not an example of a rational bureaucracy.

Correct: T   Page: 625   Refer to: STORY20.1
43.   GM is employing a strategy similar to that employed by Helmuth von Moltke of the Prussian Army.

Correct: F   Page: 627   Refer to: STORY20.1
44.   This is an example of vertical integration.

Correct: F   Page: 627   Refer to: STORY20.1
45.   GM is employing the same strategy as McCullum's railroad.

Correct: F   Page: 631   Refer to: STORY20.1
46.   GM is an example of a spoils system.

Correct: T   Page: 638   Refer to: STORY20.1
47.   GM is employing a strategy similar to that employed by Du Pont shortly after World War I.

Correct: F   Page: 634   Refer to: STORY20.1
48.   Competition between Chevrolet and Pontiac (another GM division) is a good example of goal conflict.

Correct: F   Page: 627   Refer to: STORY20.1
49.   Chevrolet's organization is an example of geographic division.

Correct: T   Page: 627   Refer to: STORY20.1
50.   Chevrolet's organization is an example of functional division.

Correct: T   Page: 630   Refer to: STORY20.1
51.   Chevrolet is pursuing a strategy similar to that of Gustavus Swift, the meat packer.

Correct: F   Page: 634   Refer to: STORY20.1
52.   Chevrolet is an example of goal displacement.

Correct: F   Page: 640   Refer to: STORY20.1
53.   Blau would predict that, because of economies of scale, as Chevrolet grows its administrative costs will decline.

Correct: T   Page: 640   Refer to: STORY20.1
54.   Drucker would probably suggest that Chevrolet be broken into even smaller operating units.

Correct: F   Page: 640   Refer to: STORY20.1
55.   Management by objectives would be more appropriate for Chevrolet managers than for GM managers.

Correct: F   Page: 641   Refer to: STORY20.1
56.   Thompson, a natural system theorist, would predict that competition between Chevrolet and other GM divisions will increase over time.

Correct: F Page: 641 Refer to: STORY20.1

57. Thompson, a natural system theorist, would predict that divisions such as Chevrolet will be the main source of innovation and change in the organization.

Reference Key: STORY20.2

Roselie opened a fruit stand with her husband in 1960. It grew and prospered and by 1965 she had 10 employees. In 1967, she opened another store in a different part of town and a third store in a neighboring town. In 1970, she purchased several orchards. By 1980, there were 11 stores and Roselie also owned a fruit packing plant in Florida. In 1988, Roselie Fruit became Roselie Enterprises when she began manufacturing toy trains and bottling sparkling water. In 1991, Roselie retired and the firm was renamed Roselie and Daughters Enterprises.

Correct: F Page: 627 Refer to: STORY20.2

58. In 1960, the most appropriate organization would have been functional divisions.

Correct: T Page: 624 Refer to: STORY20.2

59. In 1960, an informal organization would have been most appropriate.

Correct: F Page: 627 Refer to: STORY20.2

60. In 1960, this is a good example of vertical integration.

Correct: F Page: 627 Refer to: STORY20.2

61. In 1967, functional divisions would have been most appropriate.

Correct: T Page: 627 Refer to: STORY20.2

62. In 1967, geographic divisions would have been most appropriate.

Correct: F Page: 634 Refer to: STORY20.2

63. In 1967, Roselie Fruit would have been a good example of goal displacement.

Correct: T Page: 627 Refer to: STORY20.2

64. By 1980, Roselie Fruit would be a good example of vertical integration.

Correct: T Page: 637 Refer to: STORY20.2

65. In 1980, both functional and geographic divisions probably would be appropriate.

Correct: T Page: 638 Refer to: STORY20.2

66. In 1988, autonomous divisions would be most appropriate.

Multiple Choice

Correct: C   Page: 624 Scramble Range: ALL
67. An organization based on the application of logical rules is called
    A) a diverse organization.
    B) a government organization.
    C) a rational organization.
    D) an irrational bureaucracy.
    E) a university.
    F) none of these

Correct: E   Page: 624 Scramble Range: ALL
68. The first large formal organizations were created during which of the following historical periods?
    A) 3000-5000 B.C.
    B) A.D. 800-1000
    C) the 1600s
    D) A.D. 1750-1880
    E) the 1800s

Correct: C   Page: 624 Scramble Range: ALL
69. The first large formal organizations were created in three different sectors of society. These were
    A) government, economy, and the arts.
    B) government, military, and the economy.
    C) government, business, and the military.
    D) business, the military, and education.
    E) education, business, and politics.

Correct: E   Page: 625 Scramble Range: A-E
70. Helmuth von Moltke, who took command of the Prussian army in 1857, dealt with the almost overwhelming scope and scale of modern warfare by
    A) concentrating on what he called the "connective tissues" of warfare.
    B) concentrating on increasing the destructive power of weapons.
    C) training his personnel so that their levels of individual motivation approached fanaticism.
    D) taking into the military only the highest levels of physical, psychological and intellectual functioning, regardless of recruits' social class origins.
    E) training corps of subordinate managers he could count on.
    F) all of these

Correct: A   Page: 625 Scramble Range: ALL
71. Your text seems to imply that a major reason why Napoleon's army lost the Napoleonic Wars was that
    A) it was too large to be managed in traditional ways.
    B) economic and political administration should never be vested in one office and/or one person.
    C) the average soldier's attachments were to home and family, not to relatively distant military offices.
    D) the average officer had little motivation to fight a war in which he had little to gain personally.
    E) nationalism was on the decline in Europe at this particular time, and it continued to decline.

72. When Helmuth von Moltke took command of the Prussian army in 1857, he rapidly built up a new army system based on
    A) soldiers' loyalty to persons rather than to principles.
    B) limited geographic scope of operation for each subunit of the army.
    C) a period of intense resocialization that came to be called military basic training.
    D) using troops with high levels of specialization in military technology.
    E) using highly trained and interchangeable staff officers.

73. When Helmuth von Moltke created an army organized on the basis of type of armament and function--cavalry, infantry, and artillery as separate branches of service with separate commanders--this marked the appearance in Europe of
    A) military bureaucracy.
    B) vertical integration.
    C) overlapping organization.
    D) the divisional system.
    E) none of these

74. The concept of "geographic divisions" as a type of business organizational structure to solve the problem of "the overloaded manager" was illustrated in your text by which of the following?
    A) The steamship lines
    B) The railroads
    C) The land-grant college system
    D) The interstate highway system
    E) Proportional representation
    F) None of these

75. According to your text, the then-new industrial firms of the 1870s and 1880s created functional divisions that controlled each step in production through a process called
    A) production subdivision.
    B) parallel operation.
    C) vertical integration.
    D) cybernetics.
    E) mechanization.

76. In the example of Swift and Co., originally a meat-packing firm, we see an instance of
    A) territoriality carried to a dysfunctional degree.
    B) the positive consequences of antitrust legislation.
    C) management based on availability of local managerial talent.
    D) divisions based on different functions rather than geographic location.
    E) business coordination based on economics rather than on ideology.

Correct: A   Page: 630 Scramble Range: A-D
77. Sierra is the chief executive officer (CEO) of a corporation. Reporting to her are the directors of sales, production, finance and human resources. This is an example of
A) functional divisions.
B) vertical integration.
C) a spoils system.
D) autonomous divisions.
E) none of these

Correct: E   Page: 631 Scramble Range: ALL
78. Your text illustrated the spoils system by using which of the following as an example?
A) The oil and gas industry
B) The meat-packing industry
C) The railroad industry
D) The relationship between education and business
E) The civil service area of government

Correct: B   Page: 631 Scramble Range: A-D
79. When Martha was appointed to be the executive director of the agency she replaced all the managers with people of her own choosing. This is an example of
A) a civil service system.
B) a spoils system.
C) decentralization.
D) vertical integration.
E) none of these

Correct: A   Page: 631 Scramble Range: ALL
80. The spoils system as discussed in your text refers to which of these?
A) The supporters of winning politicians are given favors or benefits.
B) The military is forced to draw its recruits mainly from the lowest segments of the socioeconomic system.
C) The children entering the educational bureaucracy have been so pampered that the schools are hard-pressed to find methods to teach them.
D) The best meat is distributed to stores serving the elite, while the poorer meat goes to those lower in the socioeconomic system.
E) Higher-level bureaucrats enjoy high-level fringe benefits, while lower-level bureaucrats enjoy fewer and less desirable benefits.

Correct: A   Page: 631 Scramble Range: ALL
81. A major problem with the spoils system is that
A) people are prevented from making a career of government service.
B) lower-level organization employees become disenchanted and depressed.
C) there are periodic outbreaks of illness of varying levels of severity among those who get contaminated food.
D) the various social institutions begin to become uncoordinated and are at risk of getting out of control altogether.
E) the school system becomes less effective when it is forced to fit itself to the abilities of the weakest students.

82.   The civil service system was intended to replace the spoils system with
A)   a system of horizontal functioning.
B)   a refrigeration system.
C)   a system that could be analyzed in terms of the methods of modern managerial accounting.
D)   a system of merit.
E)   a structure in which people are given precedence over principles.

83.   Which of the following is NOT part of bureaucracy, according to Weber and as the term is explained by your text?
A)   Organization based on specific organizational goals
B)   Functional specialization
C)   The use of detailed records and written rules
D)   Expert training of managers
E)   None of these

84.   "A clear statement of goals, a formal organization with suitable operating principles and procedures, appropriate selection and training of leaders in terms of these principles and procedures, and clear lines of authority and communication" are all characteristics of what your text calls
A)   formal organization.
B)   natural systems.
C)   dysfunctional bureaucracy.
D)   bifurcation of interest.
E)   management by delegation of authority.

85.   According to Weber, and as explained by your text, which of the following pairs of concepts are inseparable from one another?
A)   Hierarchy and management
B)   Progress and management
C)   Progress and bureaucracy
D)   Bureaucracy and rationality
E)   Rationality and goal-setting

86.   Which one of the following is a feature of a truly bureaucratic organization, in the purest sense of that term?
A)   Emphasis on the natural organization
B)   Occurrence of favoritism based on friendship, kinship, or ethnic ties
C)   Hierarchy or levels of authority
D)   Much inefficiency and red tape
E)   Communication among workers so that rules are unnecessary
F)   None of these

Correct: B   Page: 633 Scramble Range: ALL
87.   Which of the following does your text discuss as an alternative to the bureaucratic view of large-scale organizations?
A)   Rational system approach
B)   Natural system approach
C)   Functional system approach
D)   Management by objectives approach
E)   Infrastructural approach

Correct: D   Page: 633 Scramble Range: A-D
88.   Managers and analysts who emphasize the informal and unintended characteristics of organizations
A)   are employing a rational systems approach.
B)   bring a Marxist view of power to the organization.
C)   focus on the lines of authority in the hierarchy.
D)   follow a natural systems approach.
E)   all of these
F)   none of these

Correct: A   Page: 634 Scramble Range: A-D
89.   When organizations change their goals in order to survive, as in the TVA example and the March of Dimes example, some sociologists follow Philip Selznick's idea and refer to it as
A)   goal displacement.
B)   creative targeting by corporate boards of directors.
C)   goal transmutation.
D)   corporate deviance.
E)   none of these

Correct: C   Page: 634 Scramble Range: ALL
90.   Which of the following would be an excellent example of what your text calls "goal conflict"?
A)   A neighborhood peer group at play gets into a fight over whether or not a point has been scored in a sandlot soccer game.
B)   A university seeks to give its students freedom while the city's other citizens want the students to be more controlled.
C)   A football coach is expected to win football games and also to give the less skilled players a chance to play in the games.
D)   A professor wants the audio-visual department to videotape her class; the audio-visual department has other things to do.
E)   Two referees at a tennis match cannot agree on an "out" ball.

Correct: E   Page: 636 Scramble Range: ALL
91.   While the _____ approach overemphasizes the organization blueprint, the _____ approach tends to forget that there is one.
A)   functional system; dysfunctional system
B)   functional system; administrative system
C)   bureaucratic system; administrative system
D)   administrative system; rational system
E)   rational system; natural system

Correct: C   Page: 636 Scramble Range: A-D
92. The Widget corporation manufactures toy airplanes. It expands to manufacture bicycles, washing machines, and pipe fittings. This is
A) a natural progression of vertical integration.
B) consolidation into functional integration.
C) diversification.
D) autonomous division.
E) A and C.
F) none of these

Correct: F   Page: 638 Scramble Range: A-E
93. Du Pont, discussed in your text, illustrated
A) the problem of span of control
B) the limits of functional divisions.
C) the need for decentralization.
D) an autonomous division approach.
E) the cost of success.
F) all of these

Correct: D   Page: 638 Scramble Range: A-D
94. Du Pont, discussed in your text,
A) illustrates the limits of geographic divisions.
B) became wealthy manufacturing plastics in the First World War.
C) illustrates the benefits of vertical integration.
D) illustrates the limits of functional division.
E) all of these
F) none of these

Correct: D   Page: 638 Scramble Range: ALL
95. The organizational principle of functional divisions, a very successful arrangement for organizations under some circumstances, turns out to be a disastrous arrangement for organizations that are
A) vertically distributed.
B) rationally coordinated.
C) involved in mutually beneficial activities with the government.
D) engaged in a broad range of activities.
E) organized under the distant management of a board of directors.

Correct: A   Page: 638 Scramble Range: ALL
96. Considerable research has demonstrated that there are limits on the number of people a given person can supervise effectively. This number is called the "span of control." Research suggests that no executive should have more than _____ subordinates who report directly to him or her.
A) seven
B) fifteen
C) twenty-five
D) forty to fifty
E) sixty

Correct: B   Page: 638 Scramble Range: A-D
97. A workable system for a diversified organization such as Nestle Corporation that manufactures and distributes many different kinds of goods and services is
A) the elliptical system.
B) autonomous divisions.
C) the elimination of administrative coordination.
D) a pyramidal organizational structure.
E) none of these

Correct: B   Page: 639 Scramble Range: A-E
98. According to Blau's administrative theory, the greater the number of units, the
A) greater the potential productivity.
B) greater the effort required to coordinate them.
C) less the potential productivity.
D) more bimodal is the productivity of the organization.
E) less satisfying individual employees find their work.
F) all of these

Correct: B   Page: 640 Scramble Range: ALL
99. The reason for creating larger organizations has always been to achieve savings. However, at some point such savings must be weighed against the
A) increased pressure occurring because of more organizational visibility.
B) costs of greater resources needed to manage the larger organization.
C) increasing levels of taxation of profits as organizational size increases.
D) exponential increase of expenditures for advertising the efforts of such large firms.
E) public resentment that emerges as such firms become increasingly visible.

Correct: C   Page: 640 Scramble Range: ALL
100. According to the doctrine often called "management by objectives," if business performance falls, what should top-level management do?
A) Try to gain more control
B) Change organizational objectives
C) Appoint new people
D) Conduct a marketing survey
E) Attempt to change the habits or preferences of consumers

Correct: D   Page: 640 Scramble Range: ALL
101. "Management by objectives" requires which of the following by upper-level managers?
A) Coordination of corporate goals with upper-level managers of other corporations
B) Almost automatic firing of previous employees when there is a corporate takeover
C) Consultation and retraining of middle-level managers when they fail to achieve business objectives
D) Giving middle-level managers authority for decisions and responsibility for the results of those decisions
E) Consultation with lower-level employees about how to improve the organization and its business performance

Correct: B   Page: 640   Scramble Range: A-D
102.   Management by objectives is an alternative to
A)   vertical integration.
B)   centralization of control.
C)   functional integration.
D)   rational systems approaches.
E)   all of these
F)   none of these

Correct: E   Page: 641   Scramble Range: A-E
103.   James D. Thompson developed a number of theoretical propositions about
decentralization in organizations. For example, Thompson suggests that the
more a particular position in an organization depends on other positions in
the organization, the less willing people in that position will be to
A)   accept their span of control as defined by management.
B)   function under vertical integration.
C)   function as members of a divisional system.
D)   engage in transubstantiation.
E)   exercise discretion.
F)   none of these

Correct: A   Page: 641   Scramble Range: ALL
104.   Thompson, in his theoretical propositions about decentralized organizations,
says that the MORE serious the potential consequences of making an error
are perceived to be, the less willing people will be to
A)   make decisions and carry them out.
B)   allow others to make decisions for the organization.
C)   engage in group decision-making.
D)   absent themselves from the workplace.
E)   allow any overlap between the business sphere and the personal
sphere.

Correct: D   Page: 641   Scramble Range: ALL
105.   According to your text, organizational efforts at decentralization are ordinarily
followed by
A)   middle-level managers.
B)   lower middle-level managers.
C)   a quantum increase in organizational productivity.
D)   organizational movement toward recentralization.
E)   decentralization in competing business organizations.

Correct: A   Page: 641   Scramble Range: ALL
106.   According to Thompson's propositions about organizations, the greater the
external threat to decisions made in an organization, the likelier the persons
making those decisions will be to
A)   form coalitions or similar agreements with the sources of those threats.
B)   take total control over the responsibility for making those decisions.
C)   try to expedite the actions stemming from those decisions.
D)   engage in activities that the espionage subculture refers to as "mole
behavior."
E)   gain maximum visibility at the local level; resorting to the use of mass
media if necessary.

107. Business bureaucracies in North America have a very clear standard by which to judge their performance level (in a way that government bureaucracies do not). That standard is
   A) ability to attract competent new employees.
   B) whether or not corporate records are detailed and accurate.
   C) whether or not the state renews the bureaucracy's charter.
   D) the percent of income tax levied on the bureaucracy..
   E) profit and loss.

Chapter 21: Social Change and Social Movements

True/False

Correct: T   Page: 647
1. Rosa Parks was arrested for refusing to give her seat on a bus to a white man.

Correct: F   Page: 647
2. Racial segregation in the South was a product of custom, not of law.

Correct: T   Page: 647
3. It was a crime for Rosa Parks to refuse to give up her seat to a white man.

Correct: F   Page: 648
4. A small group of men in Rosa Parks' church called for the first bus boycott.

Correct: F   Page: 649
5. A social movement is a group seeking to create or cause social change.

Correct: F   Page: 649
6. Social movements always aim to cause social change.

Correct: F   Page: 649
7. Social movements don't need to be organized.

Correct: T   Page: 649
8. The collective behavior approach to social movements emphasizes the role of ideology.

Correct: T   Page: 649
9. The resource mobilization approach to social movements emphasizes ideology.

Correct: T   Page: 650
10. For a social movement to occur, people involved must have hope.

Correct: T   Page: 650
11. African-Americans in the South were controlled through economic domination.

Correct: F   Page: 652
12. Forty years ago it was illegal to discriminate against African-Americans.

Correct: T   Page: 652
13. Forty years ago African-Americans in the South who registered to vote were often shot.

Correct: F   Page: 652
14. Although public facilities in the South were separate for whites and African-Americans they were generally equal and even identical.

Correct: F   Page: 654
15. When people have rising expectations we can expect a social crisis.

Correct: F   Page: 654
16. The precipitating event of the Civil Rights Movement was Rosa Parks refusing to give up her seat.

Correct: F   Page: 654
17. Rosa Parks was an unknown seamstress before the Montgomery bus boycott.

Correct: T   Page: 655
18. The Civil Rights Movement developed out of the political action committee of a single church.

Correct: F   Page: 655
19. The MIA was a Mississippi organization committed to voter registration.

Correct: T   Page: 659
20. In order to stop the Montgomery bus boycott, the police began to arrest African-American carpool drivers for imaginary violations.

Correct: F   Page: 663
21. In the Freedom Summer Project, more than 1,000 African-American college students registered voters in rural Mississippi.

Correct: T   Page: 664
22. Most of the students in Freedom Summer were fairly well-to-do.

Correct: T   Page: 665
23. Recruits to social movements such as the Civil Rights Movement are fairly similar to recruits to cults such as the Unification Church.

Correct: F   Page: 665
24. Those who lack a sense of personal efficacy often join social movements to increase their self-esteem.

Reference Key: STORY21.1
In 1990 there were several well-publicized cases of ROTC cadets being dismissed from ROTC because they were gay or lesbian. At one state university, several concerned students visited a sympathetic professor they knew. Among them, they submitted resolutions to both the Faculty Senate and the Student Senate calling for ROTC to be expelled from their campus because it violated the university policies about discrimination on the basis of sexual preference. The group then called on their friends and colleagues, and talked to several groups they knew, and succeeded in circulating and presenting large petitions to the Senates. As a consequence, ROTC was banned from the university.

Correct: T   Page: 649   Refer to: STORY21.1
25. This was a social movement.

Correct: F   Page: 654   Refer to: STORY21.1
26. The precipitating event here was the visit to the faculty member's office.

Correct: T   Page: 649   Refer to: STORY21.1
27. Collective behavior theorists would emphasize the commitment on the part of these people in understanding their success.

Correct: T   Page: 656   Refer to: STORY21.1

28. A major factor in success here was soliciting the resources of faculty.

Correct: T   Page: 665   Refer to: STORY21.1

29. It is most likely that these students were relatively well-to-do.

Correct: F   Page: 665   Refer to: STORY21.1

30. It is relatively likely that these students came from a working-class background.

Correct: T   Page: 650   Refer to: STORY21.1

31. This story illustrates all of the four propositions Stark develops to explain how social movements OCCUR.

Correct: F   Page: 650   Refer to: STORY21.1

32. People were recruited to this cause very differently than to the Civil Rights Movement.

Correct: F   Page: 659   Refer to: STORY21.1

33. If current ROTC students had organized to oppose this effort, we would call them an "oppositional movement."

Multiple Choice

Correct: D   Page: 647 Scramble Range: ALL

34. Rosa Parks refused to leave the Montgomery bus in
    A) 1938
    B) 1982
    C) 1962
    D) 1955
    E) 1948

Correct: E   Page: 648 Scramble Range: A-D

35. The people who first started the Montgomery bus boycott after Rosa Parks was arrested were
    A) local college professors.
    B) women.
    C) members of Mrs. Parks' church.
    D) acquaintances of Mrs. Parks.
    E) all of these
    F) none of these

Correct: D   Page: 648 Scramble Range: A-D

36. The people who called the first bus boycott in Montgomery, after Rosa Parks was arrested, were
    A) African-American organizers from northern states.
    B) college students.
    C) members of SNCC.
    D) members of Mrs. Parks' church.
    E) all of these
    F) none of these

Correct: B   Page: 649 Scramble Range: A-D
37.   When people organize to cause or prevent social change we call them
      A)   a conspiracy.
      B)   a social movement.
      C)   an expression of structural mobility.
      D)   defenders of the status quo.
      E)   none of these

Correct: A   Page: 649 Scramble Range: A-D
38.   The collective behavior approach to social movements emphasizes
      A)   the role of ideology.
      B)   resource mobilization.
      C)   networks of attachments.
      D)   leadership.
      E)   all of these
      F)   none of these

Correct: C   Page: 649 Scramble Range: A-D
39.   The approach to understanding social movements that emphasizes deeply felt
      grievances as the cause of these movements
      A)   has been discredited by sociologists.
      B)   is the resource mobilization approach.
      C)   can be described as the collective behavior approach.
      D)   tends to emphasize the importance of ideological leadership.
      E)   all of these
      F)   none of these

Correct: A   Page: 649 Scramble Range: NONE
40.   When a sociologist asks "Why do these people want change so badly?",
      A)   She is taking a collective behavior approach to understanding social
           movements.
      B)   The next question is likely to be about the sincerity of the leaders.
      C)   She is taking a resource mobilization approach to understanding social
           movements.
      D)   She is taking a natural systems approach to the analysis of social
           movements.
      E)   B and C.
      F)   All of these

Correct: F   Page: 649 Scramble Range: A-D
41.   McCarthy and Zald's analysis of social movements
      A)   stresses the role of deeply felt grievances.
      B)   emphasizes the ideological commitment of leadership.
      C)   tends to ignore the role of resources in making social movements
           successful.
      D)   tends to be limited to movements attempting to create social change.
      E)   all of these
      F)   none of these

Correct: B Page: 649 Scramble Range: A-D
42. The resource mobilization approach to social movements
   A) has been discredited by sociologists.
   B) emphasizes the role of leadership and organization.
   C) emphasizes the role of ideology and deeply felt grievances.
   D) has been strongly challenged by Zald and McCarthy.
   E) none of these

Correct: A Page: 649 Scramble Range: ALL
43. The major proponent(s) of resource mobilization theory is(are)
   A) Zald and McCarthy.
   B) Killian.
   C) M. L. King.
   D) Max Weber.
   E) McAdam and Jucer.

Correct: D Page: 649 Scramble Range: A-D
44. A recent analysis of the "war on drugs" emphasizes the gains made by
   political leaders who have actively manipulated public opinion about cocaine.
   A) This is a good example of collective behavior analysis.
   B) This is a good example of rational systems analysis.
   C) This is a good example of strain theory.
   D) This is a good example of resource mobilization theory.
   E) none of these

Correct: B Page: 649 Scramble Range: A-D
45. The author of your text criticizes the collective behavior approach for
   A) being too cynical.
   B) focusing too exclusively on the grievances voiced by social movements.
   C) overemphasizing the problems of publicity and resources.
   D) paying too much attention to organizational realities.
   E) all of these
   F) none of these

Correct: C Page: 650 Scramble Range: A-E
46. Your text lists four propositions about how social movements OCCUR. Which
   of the following does NOT belong on the list?
   A) A grievance
   B) Hope
   C) Countermovements
   D) Precipitating event
   E) A network of attachments
   F) They all belong

Correct: B Page: 650 Scramble Range: A-D
47. According to your text, in order for a social movement to succeed it must have
   A) a precipitating event.
   B) effective mobilization of people and resources.
   C) national publicity.
   D) a commitment to changing society.
   E) all of these
   F) none of these

Correct: A   Page: 650 Scramble Range: A-D
48.   A social movement organized to oppose the changes proposed by another
      social movement is called
      A)   a countermovement.
      B)   an oppositional movement.
      C)   a reactionary group.
      D)   a negative movement.
      E)   none of these

Correct: D   Page: 650 Scramble Range: A-D
49.   People are recruited to social movements
      A)   primarily because of their shared grievances.
      B)   somewhat randomly.
      C)   primarily from the lower classes.
      D)   through networks of attachments.
      E)   all of these

Correct: B   Page: 650 Scramble Range: ALL
50.   Your text distinguishes between elements important for the social movement
      to _____ and those elements important for a social movement to
      _____.
      A)   originate, win
      B)   occur, succeed
      C)   decline, flourish
      D)   ratify, change

Correct: C   Page: 650 Scramble Range: NONE
51.   Forty years ago, African-American women in the South
      A)   were less likely than white women to be employed.
      B)   primarily worked as secretaries and store clerks.
      C)   were more likely to be employed than white women.
      D)   were more able to work at traditional "men's jobs" than were white
           women.
      E)   A and B.
      F)   none of these

Correct: B   Page: 650 Scramble Range: A-D
52.   Your text refers to control of African-Americans through discrimination in
      hiring and promotion as
      A)   negative exchange mobility.
      B)   economic domination.
      C)   political control.
      D)   personal domination.
      E)   none of these

Correct: A   Page: 652 Scramble Range: A-D
53.   African-Americans who registered to vote in the South forty years ago
      A)   were often shot and killed.
      B)   tended to be more educated and from the North.
      C)   were recruited by SNCC.
      D)   were rare because so few African-Americans were literate.
      E)   all of these
      F)   none of these

54.   Which of the following is NOT an example of the political domination of
       southern African-Americans?
       A)   Literacy tests
       B)   Shooting African-Americans who registered to vote
       C)   White control of the courts and police
       D)   Discrimination in hiring
       E)   Lack of African-American officials

55.   In the South forty years ago, the slightest familiarity from an African-American
       man to a white woman was likely to result in
       A)   arrest.
       B)   death.
       C)   public humiliation.
       D)   getting fired.
       E)   none of these

56.   When people begin to believe that things can be made better rapidly it is
       called
       A)   a breeding ground for revolution.
       B)   developmental expectations.
       C)   a revolution of rising expectations.
       D)   a lowering of personal domination.
       E)   none of these

57.   Rising expectations tend to lead to social crises
       A)   when the expectations continue to rise.
       B)   when the gap between expectation and reality widens.
       C)   when precipitating incidents occur.
       D)   when there are deep felt grievances.
       E)   none of these

58.   The J-curve of social crises was formulated by
       A)   James Davies.
       B)   Jacob Zald.
       C)   Max Weber.
       D)   Alvin Gouldner.
       E)   Carol Mosher.

59.   The precipitating event for the Civil Rights Movement was
       A)   Mrs. Parks refusing to give up her seat.
       B)   the mass meeting at the courthouse.
       C)   the death of the white civil rights workers.
       D)   Mrs. Parks' arrest.
       E)   none of these

Correct: A   Page: 654 Scramble Range: A-D
60. An event that communicates to people with a shared grievance and increasing hopes that now is the time for action is called
A) a precipitating event.
B) an originating event.
C) a resource utilization precipitator.
D) an attachment focus.
E) all of these
F) none of these

Correct: C   Page: 654 Scramble Range: A-D
61. Mrs. Parks arrest for refusing to give up her seat to a white man was
A) an originating cause.
B) a resource utilization precipitator.
C) a precipitating event.
D) an attachment focus.
E) all of these
F) none of these

Correct: F   Page: 655 Scramble Range: NONE
62. Mrs. Parks' arrest
A) reflected increased concern and sense of threat in the white community.
B) was probably an isolated incident.
C) reflected changes in the mood of the African-American community.
D) reflected rising expectations among African-Americans.
E) C and D.
F) all of these

Correct: C   Page: 655 Scramble Range: A-D
63. A gay student is kicked out of ROTC. Students and faculty organize to abolish ROTC for violating the university's discrimination policy. Kicking the student out of ROTC, in the case, is called
A) an attachment focus.
B) an originating event.
C) a precipitating event.
D) a resource mobilization precipitation.
E) none of these

Correct: E   Page: 655 Scramble Range: A-D
64. A major reason why Mrs. Parks' arrest led to the development of a social movement was
A) the shared sense of injustice in the African-American community.
B) that she was a prominent member of the African-American community.
C) the importance of church groups in the African-American community.
D) a shared belief that the time for resistance had come.
E) all of these
F) none of these

Correct: B   Page: 655 Scramble Range: A-D
65. The major internal factor that turned the initial Montgomery boycott into a major social movement was
A) the support of northern whites.
B) the African-American churches.
C) good publicity.
D) independent actions on the part of many African-Americans.
E) all of these

Correct: F   Page: 655 Scramble Range: A-E
66. The African-American churches were important in the development of the Civil Rights Movement because
A) they formed the basis for a network of attachments.
B) they were the only institutions controlled by African-Americans.
C) African-American ministers were skilled and experienced organizers.
D) African-American ministers did not depend on whites for their incomes.
E) they provided physical facilities for meetings.
F) all of these

Correct: A   Page: 656 Scramble Range: A-E
67. African-American ministers were naturals to lead the Civil Rights Movement because
A) they didn't depend on whites for their incomes.
B) they were educated.
C) they were articulate.
D) they were men.
E) they could raise money.
F) none of these

Correct: F   Page: 656 Scramble Range: A-D
68. The MIA was
A) the Mississippi Improvement Agency.
B) an organization of college students.
C) led by Jo Ann Robinson--the woman who organized the original boycott.
D) primarily active in voting registration in Mississippi.
E) all of these
F) none of these

Correct: B   Page: 656 Scramble Range: A-D
69. The MIA was
A) an organization of college students.
B) the Montgomery Improvement Association.
C) led by Jo Ann Robinson--the woman who organized the original boycott.
D) primarily active in voting registration in Mississippi.
E) all of these
F) none of these

Correct: B   Page: 659 Scramble Range: NONE

70.   The White Citizens' Councils
A)   were especially prominent in northern cities.
B)   were a social movement.
C)   organized in support of integration.
D)   showed that African-Americans were not alone in hoping for change.
E)   C and D.
F)   all of these

Correct: D   Page: 659 Scramble Range: A-D

71.   Most of the original recruits to the white countermovement were
A)   prominent political figures.
B)   professional-status whites.
C)   middle-status whites.
D)   low-status whites.
E)   none of these

Correct: F   Page: 659 Scramble Range: A-E

72.   Which of the following was NOT a tactic used by the white community to strike
back at the Montgomery bus boycott?
A)   Ticketing carpool drivers for imaginary violations.
B)   Firing African-Americans who refused to ride the buses.
C)   Arresting carpool riders for loitering.
D)   Bombing houses.
E)   Indicting (bringing criminal charges against) African-American leaders.
F)   all of these tactics were used.

Correct: B   Page: 633 Scramble Range: A-D

73.   The Southern Christian Leadership Conference, founded in 1957, was formed
by
A)   white liberals.
B)   African-American ministers from southern communities.
C)   northern whites who came south to help in the movement.
D)   college students at African-American colleges.
E)   none of these

Correct: F   Page: 660 Scramble Range: A-D

74.   The Civil Rights Movement was
A)   founded by African-American ministers in 1957.
B)   a formal coalition of groups which first met as an organization in 1962.
C)   another name for SNCC.
D)   primarily an organization of college students.
E)   all of these
F)   none of these

Correct: E   Page: 661 Scramble Range: NONE
75. SNCC was
   A) primarily an organization of college students.
   B) a African-American power group committed to returning violence for
       violence.
   C) developed by African-American ministers from across the South.
   D) the sponsor of the Freedom Summer Project in 1964.
   E) A and D.
   F) all of these
   G) none of these

Correct: D   Page: 661 Scramble Range: A-D
76. The sponsor of the 1964 Freedom Summer was
   A) the ACLU.
   B) the Southern Christian Leadership Conference.
   C) CORE.
   D) SNCC.
   E) none of these

Correct: B   Page: 662 Scramble Range: ALL
77. During 1964, North Pike County, Mississippi, spent more than $30 on each
   white student and _____ on each African-American student.
   A) $1.30
   B) $.76
   C) $3.08
   D) $6.10
   E) $10.20

Correct: B   Page: 663 Scramble Range: A-D
78. The key to the success of the Freedom Summer Project
   A) was the registering of a majority of African-Americans in five Mississippi
       counties.
   B) was the violence directed at the white middle- and upper-class students.
   C) was the support of Martin Luther King and other clergy.
   D) was the idealism of these college students.
   E) all of these

Correct: A   Page: 664 Scramble Range: A-D
79. In his examination of Freedom Summer Volunteers, McAdam found that
   volunteers were
   A) biographically available.
   B) primarily from state colleges and universities.
   C) generally working- or lower-middle-class.
   D) generally in conflict with their parents.
   E) all of these
   F) none of these

Correct: C   Page: 664 Scramble Range: A-D
80. By "biographically available," McAdam meant people
    A) whose family and friends support their beliefs.
    B) whose personal background lead them to believe in the movement.
    C) who have few other responsibilities.
    D) who have a sense of personal power or potency.
    E) all of these

Correct: E   Page: 665 Scramble Range: A-D
81. People who join social movements tend to
    A) have a sense of personal power.
    B) be optimistic.
    C) be unmarried.
    D) be self-assured.
    E) all of these
    F) none of these

Correct: D   Page: 665 Scramble Range: A-D
82. The reason that young students play a conspicuous role in social movements
    is
    A) their idealism.
    B) their energy.
    C) their intellectual sophistication.
    D) their freedom from responsibilities.
    E) all of these
    F) none of these

Correct: F   Page: 665 Scramble Range: A-D
83. Those who don't believe that they can change the world
    A) are less likely to try and, thus, less likely to succeed.
    B) are less likely to come from privileged backgrounds.
    C) have little sense of personal power or potency.
    D) are less likely to become active in social movements.
    E) A and D.
    F) all of these
    G) none of these

Correct: D   Page: 667 Scramble Range: ALL
84. The text's chapter on collective behavior and social movements is limited to
    the analysis of behaviors that are
    A) in some way associated with the mass media.
    B) peer group related actions or behaviors.
    C) in no way connected to reference groups.
    D) in some way related to social change.
    E) not brought about as a response to physical environmental change.